Criminal Procedure:
The Constitution and the Police

Ninth Edition

Robert M. Bloom
Professor of Law
Boston College Law School

Mark S. Brodin
Professor of Law and Michael and Helen Lee
Distinguished Scholar
Boston College Law School

Published by Wolters Kluwer Law & Business in New York.

No part of this publication may be reproduced or transmitted in any form or by any means, electronic or mechanical, including photocopy, recording, or utilized by any information storage or retrieval system, without written permission from the publisher. For information about permissions or to request permissions online, visit us at www.wolterskluwerlb.com, or a written request may be faxed to our permissions department at 212-771-0803.

To contact Customer Service, e-mail customer.service@wolterskluwer.com, call 1-800-234-1660, fax 1-800-901-9075, or mail correspondence to:

Wolters Kluwer Law & Business
Attn: Order Department
PO Box 990
Frederick, MD 21705

Printed in the United States of America.

2 3 4 5 6 7 8 9 0

ISBN 978-1-4548-9136-9

Library of Congress Cataloging-in-Publication Data

Names: Bloom, Robert M., 1946- author. | Brodin, Mark S., 1947- author.
Title: Criminal procedure : the constitution and the police / Robert M. Bloom, Professor of Law, Boston College Law School; Mark S. Brodin, Professor of Law, Boston College Law School.
Description: Ninth edition. | New York : Wolters Kluwer, [2019] | Includes bibliographical references and index.
Identifiers: LCCN 2019020051 | ISBN 9781454891369
Subjects: LCSH: Searches and seizures—United States. | Police questioning—United States. | Right to counsel—United States. | Evidence, Criminal—United States. | United States. Constitution. 4th Amendment. | United States. Constitution. 6th Amendment.
Classification: LCC KF9630 .B578 2019 | DDC 345.73/05—dc23
LC record available at https://lccn.loc.gov/2019020051

Criminal Procedure:

The Constitution and the Police

About Wolters Kluwer Legal & Regulatory U.S.

Wolters Kluwer Legal & Regulatory U.S. delivers expert content and solutions in the areas of law, corporate compliance, health compliance, reimbursement, and legal education. Its practical solutions help customers successfully navigate the demands of a changing environment to drive their daily activities, enhance decision quality and inspire confident outcomes.

Serving customers worldwide, its legal and regulatory portfolio includes products under the Aspen Publishers, CCH Incorporated, Kluwer Law International, ftwilliam.com and MediRegs names. They are regarded as exceptional and trusted resources for general legal and practice-specific knowledge, compliance and risk management, dynamic workflow solutions, and expert commentary.

To my wife, Tina, my children, Martha, David, and Ritza, my grandchildren, Liam and Matthew, and to the memory of my parents, Henry and Martha, and to the memory of my good friend and colleague Peter (Pedro) Donovan

—R.M.B.

To the memory of Shirley and Hy, who taught me the meaning of justice.

—M.S.B.

As the late Robert F. Drinan, S. J. often quoted, "The first duty of government is to protect the powerless from the powerful." Code of Hammurabi, 1772 B.C.

The authors wish to dedicate this edition to all those in the criminal courts throughout the land — prosecutors, defense counsel, and judges — who strive to assure fair and just results consistent with the fundamental protections against governmental overreaching afforded by our Bill of Rights.

Summary of Contents

Contents | xi
Table of Figures | xv
Preface | xvii
Acknowledgments | xix

Chapter 1 Overview of Constitutional Criminal Procedure | 1

PART I. SEARCH AND SEIZURE — THE FRAMEWORK OF THE FOURTH AMENDMENT

Chapter 2 Introduction to the Fourth Amendment | 11
Chapter 3 When Does the Fourth Amendment Apply? | 17
Chapter 4 What Does the Fourth Amendment Require?—The Doctrine of Justification | 45
Chapter 5 Search and Arrest Warrants | 121
Chapter 6 Warrantless Searches and Seizures | 143
Chapter 7 The Exclusionary Rule: Rationale, Operation, and Limitations | 195

PART II. INTERROGATION AND CONFESSIONS

Chapter 8 The Voluntariness Standard | 249
Chapter 9 The *Miranda* Approach | 261
Chapter 10 The Sixth Amendment "Right to Counsel" Approach | 329

PART III. OTHER INVESTIGATIVE PROCEDURES

Chapter 11   Other Investigative Procedures — Eyewitness
Identification, Bodily Intrusions, Examination of
Physical Attributes, Entrapment, and "High-Tech"
and Computer Searches   341

Chapter 12   September 11, 2001, and Its Aftermath   367

Checklist and Review Problems   **377**

Table of Cases   *389*
Index   *401*

Contents

Table of Figures   *xv*
Preface   *xvii*
Acknowledgments   *xix*

Chapter 1   **Overview of Constitutional Criminal Procedure**   **1**

PART I. SEARCH AND SEIZURE — THE FRAMEWORK OF THE FOURTH AMENDMENT

Chapter 2   **Introduction to the Fourth Amendment**   **11**

Chapter 3   **When Does the Fourth Amendment Apply?**   **17**

    §3.1   Governmental Action — Public Versus Private Search   17
    §3.2   Reasonable Expectation of Privacy   22

Chapter 4   **What Does the Fourth Amendment Require? — The Doctrine of Justification**   **45**

    §4.1   Probable Cause — The Standard for Search and Arrest   46
    §4.2   Reasonable Suspicion — The Standard for Stop and Frisk   70
    §4.3   What Constitutes a Stop?   74
    §4.4   The Expansion of *Terry*: Demand for Identification, Vehicle Stops, Detention of Effects, Protective Sweeps, and Plain Feel   78
    §4.5   Administrative Searches   103

Chapter 5   **Search and Arrest Warrants**   **121**

    §5.1   Note on the Warrant Requirement   121
    §5.2   The Components of a Valid Search Warrant   122
       §5.2.1   Neutral and Detached Magistrate   122

	§5.2.2	The Probable Cause Showing	123
	§5.2.3	The Particularity Requirement and the Plain View Doctrine	125
§5.3		Execution of a Search Warrant	135
§5.4		Administrative Search Warrants	137
§5.5		Anticipatory Search Warrants	137
§5.6		The Arrest Warrant Requirement	138
§5.7		The Components of a Valid Arrest Warrant	139

Chapter 6   Warrantless Searches and Seizures   143

§6.1	Introduction	143
§6.2	Exceptions That Require Probable Cause: The Emergency Exception (Exigent Circumstances)	144
§6.3	Exceptions That Require Probable Cause: Search Incident to Arrest	154
§6.4	Exceptions That Require Probable Cause: Automobile Search and the Container Doctrine	164
§6.5	Exceptions That Require Reasonable Suspicion: Stop-and-Frisk and Investigative Detentions	170
§6.6	Administrative and Inventory Searches	170
§6.7	Warrantless Intrusion Requiring No Justification: Consent	172
§6.8	The Plain View Doctrine	184
§6.9	The Problem of Pretext	191

Chapter 7   The Exclusionary Rule: Rationale, Operation, and Limitations   195

§7.1		The Rationale of the Exclusionary Rule	195
§7.2		The Derivative Evidence (Fruit-of-the-Poisonous-Tree) Doctrine	199
§7.3		Limitations on the Exclusionary Rule	215
	§7.3.1	Standing	216
	§7.3.2	Limitation to Criminal Trial Versus Other Proceedings	227
	§7.3.3	The Good Faith Exception	231
	§7.3.4	The Impeachment Exception	243
	§7.3.5	Harmless Error	244

PART II. INTERROGATION AND CONFESSIONS

Chapter 8   The Voluntariness Standard   **249**

Chapter 9   The *Miranda* Approach   **261**

§9.1   The *Miranda* Decision   261
§9.2   The Components of *Miranda*   264
        §9.2.1 Custody   264
        §9.2.2 Interrogation   274
        §9.2.3 The Substance and Adequacy of the
                Warnings   286
        §9.2.4 Waiver of *Miranda* Rights   291
        §9.2.5 Waiver After Invocation of the Right to
                Silence or to Counsel   303
§9.3   Limitations on the Scope of the *Miranda* Exclusionary
        Rule   316
        §9.3.1 Use of the Statement for Impeachment   317
        §9.3.2 The Public Safety Exception   319
        §9.3.3 Suppression of the Fruits of a Statement
                Obtained in Violation of *Miranda*   326
§9.4   Summary—What's Left of *Miranda*?   328

**Chapter 10   The Sixth Amendment "Right to Counsel"
               Approach**   **329**

§10.1   The *Massiah* Doctrine   329
§10.2   The "Deliberately Elicit" Standard   330
§10.3   At What Point Does the *Massiah* Doctrine
        Apply?—The Initiation of Judicial Proceedings   332
§10.4   Waiver and Exceptions to the *Massiah* Doctrine   333
§10.5   Overview of Interrogation and Confessions   338

PART III. OTHER INVESTIGATIVE PROCEDURES

**Chapter 11   Other Investigative Procedures—
               Eyewitness Identification, Bodily
               Intrusions, Examination of Physical
               Attributes, Entrapment, and "High-Tech"
               and Computer Searches**   **341**

§11.1   Eyewitness Identification   341

§11.2   Bodily Intrusions and Examination of Suspect's Physical Attributes   348

§11.3   Entrapment   354

     §11.3.1   The Common Law Defense   355

     §11.3.2   Due Process   356

§11.4   "High-Tech" Searches   361

     §11.4.1   Electronic Surveillance and Wiretapping   361

     §11.4.2   Searches of Computers   362

Chapter 12   September 11, 2001, and Its Aftermath   367

§12.1   Introduction   367

§12.2   Terrorism and the Fourth Amendment   374

Checklist and Review Problems   377

Table of Cases   *389*

Index   *401*

Table of Figures

3.1	Zones of Privacy Expectation	27
4.1	Standards of Justification — Summary	46
4.2	Arrest/Stop and Frisk — Justification	78
4.3	Administrative Search Balancing Analysis	107
6.1	Automobile Search	167
7.1	Derivative Evidence Doctrine — Exceptions	204
10.1	Approaches to Interrogation and Confession	338

Preface

No area of the law evokes more passionate debate about the tension between the prerogatives of government and the liberty of the individual than constitutional criminal procedure. The social and political history of the United States in the past six decades has been written in significant part by the opinions of the Supreme Court, adjusting and readjusting this balance.

As the Court under Chief Justice Earl Warren gave definition to the 1960s with landmark civil liberties decisions like *Mapp* and *Miranda*, so the Burger, Rehnquist, and Roberts Courts reflect the conservative shift of the political landscape in their decisions since the 1980s, lifting many constraints on the police in their "wars" on crime, drugs, and terrorism. Particularly noteworthy are those cases that have put the viability of the exclusionary rule, the remedy for unconstitutional police action, in question. With the curtailment of protections by the U.S. Supreme Court, state courts in recent years have turned to their own constitutions to reassert safeguards against the excesses of law enforcement, what some have dubbed the "new federalism."

While there is undeniably an ideological dimension to the cases in the criminal procedure area, there is also a wealth of legal doctrine and concepts that must be assimilated by both student and practitioner. It is the purpose of this book to facilitate this mastery, while at the same time keeping the reader focused on the overarching policy issues raised in the cases.

The book's functional organization is designed to assist in the critical task of problem solving. This is accomplished by breaking down the constitutional analysis of police conduct into component issues. The "search and seizure" chapters of the book are organized to pose first the threshold issue of whether the Fourth Amendment applies, and then deal with the discrete questions of justification and the requirement for a warrant. The chapters on interrogation and confessions sequentially follow the questions that must be resolved to determine the admissibility of a statement obtained by the police from the suspect.

The format is a combination of text, examples, and explanations. Each chapter begins with an accessible summary of the controlling law, followed by a set of examples of increasing difficulty that explore the basic concepts and then challenge the reader to apply them in situations (frequently derived from reported cases) in the ever-present gray areas. The explanations permit students to check their own understanding of the material and provide additional insights not developed in the text. The goal is to convey the richness of the evolving case law, while at the same time helping to demystify this highly complex domain of law. We aim, in short, to simulate the Socratic classroom at its best.

Mark Brodin
Robert Bloom
Newton, Massachusetts

Acknowledgments

Mark Brodin wishes to gratefully acknowledge three mentors who kindled his interest in, and shaped his thoughts about, criminal law and procedure: the Honorable Joseph L. Tauro and attorneys Moe Tandler and Reuben Goodman.

Robert Bloom wishes to recognize three departed colleagues and mentors: Dean Richard G. Huber and Professors James Houghteling and Sanford J. Fox.

Both authors wish to thank Dean Vincent Rougeau for his support and encouragement, and gratefully acknowledge the generosity of the R. Robert Popeo and the Michael and Helen Lee Distinguished Scholar Funds. In addition, we recognize the late Robert F. Drinan, S. J., former dean of Boston College Law School, who devoted his entire life to fighting injustice.

We benefited for this latest edition from the research assistance of law students Dana Borelli and Sarah Murphy.

Criminal Procedure:

The Constitution and the Police

Overview of Constitutional Criminal Procedure

Consider the following scenario. Two police officers patrolling in a marked cruiser observe an SUV pull up to a street corner. A man emerges and begins talking with an individual whom the officers recognize as Michael Chestnut, previously identified by an informant as the top narcotics dealer in that neighborhood. The first man hands Chestnut a large leather pouch and promptly departs. Chestnut, now noticing the police cruiser, begins running in the opposite direction. The officers pursue and overtake him. They inform Chestnut that he is under arrest, handcuff him, and take the pouch, which they open to find several plastic bags filled with white powder. Chestnut is brought to the station house and booked for unlawful possession of narcotics. In an interrogation room some time later, he is questioned by a detective and makes several incriminating statements. The substance seized from Chestnut is sent to the police lab and is determined to be cocaine. Chestnut is charged accordingly under state law.

Before the 1960s, Chestnut's encounter with the police would represent the first step in a criminal justice process that focused almost exclusively on the question of guilt or innocence. The way in which the police conducted the arrest, search, and interrogation of Chestnut would not be pertinent to the proceedings, unless made so by local law. Given the circumstances described above, either a guilty plea or a verdict of guilt after trial would be the likely conclusion of the process.

The criminal justice system underwent a transformation in the 1960s, a revolution from above initiated by the Supreme Court. By the end of a decade of ground-breaking precedent, the matter of an accused's guilt or innocence came to share the judicial spotlight with questions concerning the legality of police conduct. Were the arrest of Chestnut and the seizure of his pouch lawful? Was the interrogation properly conducted? These questions were to be answered not under local law, but according to the U.S. Constitution as interpreted by the Supreme Court. And the answers would determine whether the prosecutor could use the evidence seized and the statements obtained against Chestnut at trial, or whether they would be kept from the jury by operation of an exclusionary rule. Criminal procedure had been constitutionalized and federalized.

How did this dramatic makeover come about?

The Constitution approved in Philadelphia in 1787 delicately divided sovereign power between the states on the one hand and the newly formed federal government on the other. Each had the power to prosecute offenders of its criminal laws in its own courts. Those prosecuted in the federal system were beneficiaries of the considerable procedural protections established by the Bill of Rights (the first ten amendments to the Constitution), most notably the rights to be free from unreasonable search and seizure and from compelled self-incrimination. Those prosecuted in state court (which group has always constituted the large majority of criminal defendants) were afforded only those protections provided by state constitution or other local law, usually significantly less than their federal counterparts.

The seeds of change were sown with the adoption after the Civil War of the Fourteenth Amendment, which provides that the states may not deprive any person of life, liberty, or property without "due process of law." This constraint on state power raised the possibility that defendants in state prosecutions might be able to claim procedural rights resembling those afforded federal defendants. The "incorporation" of such rights against the states, however, was a long time coming. At first, the Supreme Court applied the Due Process Clause to state trials by employing an amorphous standard of "fundamental fairness" rather than the specific safeguards of the Bill of Rights. In the few cases in which the Clause was successfully invoked to reverse state criminal convictions, such as *Rochin v. California*, 342 U.S. 165 (1952),[1] the Court refused to define the mandate of due process more precisely than prohibiting law enforcement officers from engaging in conduct that "shocks the conscience," a high standard rarely met.

The disparity in treatment between criminal defendants in the federal and state systems was magnified when, in 1914, the federal courts adopted an exclusionary remedy requiring suppression of evidence obtained in

---

1. Los Angeles deputy sheriffs entered Rochin's home without a warrant to search for narcotics. When they forced open the door to his bedroom, he shoved two capsules into his mouth. The deputies seized Rochin and attempted to recover the capsules, but he swallowed them. They then took him to a doctor who pumped his stomach with a chemical solution, and he vomited the capsules. The Court ruled that the prosecution could not use the capsules as evidence at trial. See §11.2.

violation of the Fourth Amendment. See *Weeks v. United States*, 232 U.S. 383 (1914). A search that would be deemed illegal under federal standards and consequently result in exclusion of the evidence (and oftentimes dismissal or acquittal) in federal court might nonetheless be considered lawful in a state prosecution, under the less stringent due process measure, permitting introduction of the evidence (and probable conviction). Even after the Supreme Court imposed the same federal constitutional standards on searches conducted by state and local police in 1949, the exclusionary remedy was not mandated in state prosecutions.[2] As a result, dramatically inconsistent outcomes could follow, depending upon which court system the accused happened to be prosecuted in.

In the early 1960s, the Court, under the leadership of Chief Justice Earl Warren, set out on a new path of uniform application of *both* constitutional standards *and* remedies. Specific provisions of the Bill of Rights were incorporated through the Due Process Clause and applied to the conduct of state and local police. In the seminal case of *Mapp v. Ohio*, 367 U.S. 643 (1961),[3] the Court held that the violation of a state defendant's right against unreasonable search required the same remedy as was mandated in federal prosecutions, namely suppression of the evidence obtained from the search. Five years later, in *Miranda v. Arizona*, 384 U.S. 436 (1966), the Court imposed on both state and federal authorities a comprehensive set of rules (and corresponding exclusionary remedy) designed to protect the accused's Fifth Amendment right against compelled self-incrimination.

Before the decade was out, the Sixth Amendment rights to counsel[4] and to jury trial,[5] as well as the Eighth Amendment protection against cruel and unusual punishment,[6] were also applied to the states. No longer would an accused's fate in the criminal justice process depend so fortuitously upon whether he was prosecuted by state or federal authorities. A uniform body of constitutional principles now applied to both sovereigns. The Warren Court also expanded the scope of habeas corpus, thus providing state prisoners with more ready access to federal court to enforce their newly found rights. See *Fay v. Noia*, 372 U.S. 391 (1963).

Not surprisingly, these developments generated considerable controversy in both legal and political arenas. Critics argued that the balance

---

2. See *Wolf v. Colorado*, 338 U.S. 25 (1949). It should be noted that by 1961, several of the states had adopted the exclusionary rule through their own legislature or courts.

3. Cleveland police officers forced their way into Mrs. Mapp's house, without a warrant, to seek information regarding a person wanted in connection with a recent bombing. They handcuffed Mapp after a struggle and then conducted an intensive search, during which they seized allegedly obscene materials. The Court ruled that the prosecution could not use the materials as evidence at trial.

4. *Gideon v. Wainwright*, 372 U.S. 335 (1963).

5. *Duncan v. Louisiana*, 391 U.S. 145 (1968).

6. *Robinson v. California*, 370 U.S. 660 (1962).

between state and federal responsibility in the administration of criminal justice had been upset by the imposition of one-size-fits-all nationwide standards, and that the fundamental concepts of federalism and "state's rights" had been trampled upon. See, e.g., *Mapp v. Ohio*, supra, 367 U.S. at 680 (Harlan, J., dissenting). Others complained that the Warren Court decisions would tie the hands of law enforcement officers and make the world safe for criminal offenders.[7] Harsh criticism was leveled at the use of the criminal trial as a vehicle for enforcing norms of police conduct, rather than simply a means for determining the guilt or innocence of the accused.

The lightning rod of the controversy was (and remains) the exclusionary rule itself. As Benjamin Cardozo posed the question: Should the criminal go free because the constable has blundered? *People v. Defore*, 150 N.E. 585 (N.Y. 1926). Justice Tom Clark justified an affirmative answer in *Mapp* by noting that other remedies, such as civil actions for money damages and criminal prosecutions against the offending officers, had proven worthless, leaving suppression as the only effective means to enforce the Fourth Amendment. Police officers and prosecutors would abide by constitutional constraints, it was asserted, if they knew that evidence obtained unlawfully could not be used in court. Beyond this deterrence rationale, the *Mapp* Court added "the imperative of judicial integrity:" "The criminal goes free, if he must, but it is the law that sets him free. Nothing can destroy a government more quickly than its failure to observe its own law, or worse, its disregard of the charter of its own existence." 367 U.S. at 659.

Yet discontent with the exclusionary remedy has persisted. Chief Justice Warren Burger, in one of his early dissents on the Court, bitterly criticized the doctrine that hides probative evidence from the fact finder. See *Bivens v. Six Unknown Named Agents of the Federal Bureau of Narcotics*, 403 U.S. 388 (1971) (Burger, C.J., dissenting). Heralding a change in the Court's thinking that would come some years later, the Chief Justice disputed both the efficacy and necessity of the exclusionary rule, and argued for the substitution of other means (such as civil actions) to enforce constitutional dictates. Characterizing the deterrence rationale as nothing more than a wistful dream with no empirical support, Burger deplored the "high price" that exclusion extracts from society — "the release of countless guilty criminals."[8]

---

7. Beginning with Richard Nixon's successful presidential campaign in 1968, "law and order" has become a major theme in American politics, and being "tough on crime" a virtual prerequisite for success at the polls.

8. 403 U.S. at 416. The actual number of persons released by operation of the exclusionary rule has been a source of much disagreement. See, e.g., Oaks, *Studying the Exclusionary Rule in Search and Seizure*, 37 U. Chi. L. Rev. 665 (1970); Spiotto, *Search and Seizure: An Empirical Study of the Exclusionary Rule and Its Alternatives*, 2 J. Legal Stud. 243 (1973); *Impact of the Exclusionary Rule on Federal Criminal Prosecutions*, U.S. Gen. Acctg. Office (GGD-79-45) (1979).

In explaining what he saw as the failure of the suppression remedy to deter unlawful police conduct, Burger observed that the rule provides no direct sanction against the offending officer; that the prosecutor who may lose the case because of the suppression generally has no official authority over the offending officer; that the time lapse between the police misconduct and the final ruling excluding the evidence is often so long that whatever educational effect it might have had is long lost; and that in any event, much police action is not directed at ultimate prosecution of the subject and therefore is not conducted in anticipation of a trial requiring proof. Moreover, the exclusionary remedy is inflexible and allows for no proportionality—regardless of the magnitude of the police wrongdoing or the nature of the crime involved, the remedy is always the same. 403 U.S. at 416-418.

Since the 1970s the Court, influenced by this critique, has significantly chipped away at the scope and applicability of the exclusionary rule. Limitations have been imposed on those deemed to have standing to raise Fourth Amendment objections, as well as on the types of proceedings in which the suppression remedy applies (it has been held inapplicable, for example, in grand jury proceedings). A "good faith" exception now largely removes from the reach of the remedy police action that, although unlawful in retrospect, was committed in the reasonable belief that the action did not violate the Fourth Amendment. Concerned with the societal costs of the exclusionary rule, the Court has also modified substantive constitutional doctrine (such as diluting the standard for probable cause) in a manner that maximizes deference to police discretion. Without completely abandoning *Mapp* or *Miranda* (as we will see in Chapter 9), the Court has nonetheless been able to curtail their impact dramatically.

The Court's most recent encounters with the exclusionary rule raise serious questions about its continued viability. In determining that a violation of the "knock-and-announce" rule (see §5.3) does not require suppression of evidence discovered in the search, Justice Scalia (writing for the five-justice majority in *Hudson v. Michigan*, 547 U.S. 586 (2006)) elevated the "social costs" of suppression, particularly "the risk of releasing dangerous criminals into society," to the center of an analysis now on a collision course with the suppression remedy itself.[9] The exclusionary rule, he asserted, has "always been our last resort." Like Burger before him, Scalia questioned the effectiveness of the remedy in deterring police misconduct and identified civil actions against the police, as well as departmental disciplinary procedures, as preferable alternatives.[10]

---

9. Justice Kennedy, whose concurring opinion made up the fifth vote for the majority, read Scalia's opinion narrowly and saw no threat "to the continued operation of the exclusionary rule."

10. See also *Herring v. United States* and *Davis v. North Carolina*, sec. 7.3, infra.

In response to federal cutbacks, some states have expanded their own enforceable rights for persons accused of crimes. Ironically, given the beginning of our story, state law now often provides defendants with greater protections than their federal counterparts have. See Friedman, *The Constitutional Value of Dialogue and the New Judicial Federalism*, 28 Hastings Const. L.Q. 93 (2002); Cauthen, *Expanding Rights Under State Constitutions: A Quantitative Appraisal*, 63 Albany L. Rev. 1183 (2000); Utter, *State Constitutional Law, the United States Supreme Court, and Democratic Accountability*, 64 Wash. L. Rev. 19, 27 (1989). This emergence of state constitutional protections, a development urged by Justice William Brennan (a frequent dissenter in the Burger and Rehnquist Court's decisions) in an influential law review article published in 1977,[11] has raised a number of thorny issues regarding the relationship between the federal and state sovereigns.

Although it is the ultimate authority on matters of federal law, see *Martin v. Hunter's Lessee*, 14 U.S. (1 Wheat.) 304 (1816), it has long been held that the Supreme Court has no power to review a state court decision that is based on independent and adequate state law grounds. *Abie State Bank v. Weaver*, 282 U.S. 765, 773 (1931); *Herb v. Pitcairn*, 324 U.S. 117, 125-126 (1945). The Court's jurisdiction over state judgments is limited to correcting errors of federal law. In 1983, however, in a decision purporting to reaffirm this principle, the Court actually expanded its authority to review state court judgments when it insisted there must be a "clear" indication that the state court was relying on independent and adequate state grounds. *Michigan v. Long*, 463 U.S. 1032, 1040-1041 (1983) (overturning a decision of the Michigan Supreme Court that suppressed marijuana evidence taken from defendant's trunk). Justice Stevens characterized the Court's approach as a reversal of the traditional presumption against Supreme Court review. 463 U.S. at 1066-1067 (Stevens, J., dissenting). Some commentators have suggested that this new willingness to overturn state court decisions was in reaction to the expansion of state constitutional rights.[12]

In any event, state courts remain free to interpret their own law so as to provide greater protection for individual rights than that mandated by the federal Constitution—what has been called the new federalism.[13] "The federal constitution sets the floor for individual rights; state constitutions establish the ceiling." *LeCroy v. Hanlon*, 713 S.W.2d 335, 338 (Tex. 1986). The

---

11. William J. Brennan, Jr., *State Constitutions and the Protection of Individual Rights*, 90 Harv. L. Rev. 489, 491 (1977): "State courts cannot rest when they have afforded their citizens the full protections of the federal constitution. State constitutions, too, are a font of individual liberties, their protections often extending beyond those required by the Supreme Court's interpretation of federal law. The legal revolution which has brought federal law to the fore must not be allowed to inhibit the independent protective force of state law—for without it, the full realization of our liberties cannot be guaranteed."

12. See, e.g., Eric B. Schnurer, *The Inadequate and Dependent "Adequate and Independent State Grounds" Doctrine*, 18 Hastings Const. L.Q. 371 (1991).

13. See Shirley S. Abrahamson, "*State Constitutional Law, New Judicial Federalism, and the Rehnquist Court*," 51 Clev. St. L. Rev. 339 (2004).

Supreme Court of New Mexico has held, for example, that the state version of the Fourth Amendment provides more protection to motorists stopped at the border. *State v. Cardenas-Alvarez*, 25 P.3d 225 (N.M. 2001) (reasonable suspicion of criminal activity required to justify prolonged stop). New Jersey has imposed stricter standards on police for automobile searches, see *State v. Cooke*, 751 A.2d 92 (N.J. 2000) (state constitution requires finding of exigent circumstances), and to access cell phone location information. *State v. Earls*, 214 N.J. 564 (2013). Montana has more protective standards for custodial interrogations. *State v. Spang*, 48 P.3d 727 (Mont. 2002) (suspect sufficiently invoked his right to counsel under state law).

Some states have read their constitutional provisions more expansively than the Supreme Court even when the wording of the state provision is identical to the federal Constitution.[14] Others, however, have explicitly chosen to link their law to that of the federal Constitution.[15]

Example

Assume that a warrant is obtained to search Michael Chestnut's home. The search is conducted and a large quantity of cocaine is found. It turns out, however, that the police affidavit submitted in support of the warrant and reviewed by the issuing magistrate failed to demonstrate probable cause, thus rendering the search unlawful under the Fourth Amendment (as discussed in Chapter 4). Chestnut is charged with unlawful possession of cocaine in state court. Would the cocaine seized be admissible at Chestnut's trial:

a. Before the decision in *Mapp v. Ohio*?

b. Immediately after the decision in *Mapp v. Ohio*?

c. Today?

Explanation

a. Because the exclusionary remedy had not yet been imposed on the states through the Fourth Amendment, the answer would depend on whether the particular state had adopted such a rule of its own. If Chestnut were prosecuted in a state that had not done so, the illegality of the search would not be a factor in his prosecution.

---

14. See Utter, *State Constitutional Law*, supra, 64 Wash. L. Rev. at 46.

15. The Florida constitution, for example, was amended by general election in 1982 so that the provision relating to search and seizure would be construed in conformity with the Fourth Amendment of the U.S. Constitution as interpreted by the U.S. Supreme Court. Similarly, by an initiative petition, California requires that all relevant evidence be admissible in its courts, thus limiting the exclusionary remedy only to that mandated by federal law.

b. *Mapp* mandated an exclusionary remedy, applicable in all state (as well as federal) prosecutions, for violation of the Fourth Amendment. Given the lack of probable cause, the cocaine would not be admissible in evidence and Chestnut would likely go free.

c. One of the major cutbacks in the exclusionary remedy in recent years has been the Supreme Court's adoption of a "good faith exception." See §7.3.3. By obtaining a warrant, the officers have ensured against suppression of the cocaine under the Fourth Amendment so long as their reliance upon the warrant is deemed in retrospect to have been reasonable. If Chestnut is prosecuted in a state whose own law rejects the good faith exception, he will be able to keep the evidence from the jury. Chestnut's fate, in short, is once again dependent on the locus of his prosecution.

PART I

Search and Seizure — The Framework of the Fourth Amendment

Introduction to the Fourth Amendment

The right of the people to be secure in their persons, houses, papers, and effects, against unreasonable searches and seizures, shall not be violated, and no Warrants shall issue, but upon probable cause, supported by Oath or affirmation, and particularly describing the place to be searched, and the persons or things to be seized.

U.S. Const., amend. IV

The Fourth Amendment reflects one of the fundamental grievances that the American colonists had against the English Crown. Designed to reduce the smuggling activity taking place in the colonies, the hated writs of assistance were open-ended licenses to search, issued with minimal judicial supervision and without demonstration of specific justification. Royal customs officers armed with such writs had virtually unconstrained discretion to search whenever, wherever, and whomever they chose.[1]

In adopting the Fourth Amendment as a central component of the Bill of Rights, the Framers sought to avoid such abuses by providing for security against "unreasonable" searches and seizures, insisting that there be verified demonstration of "probable cause" before a warrant could issue, and requiring that the warrant "particularly" describe (and thus limit) the scope of the permissible search.

---

1. The writs authorized officials to "go into any House, Shop, Cellar, Warehouse or Room . . . and in case of resistance, to break open Doors, Chests, Trunks and other Packages, there to seize and from thence to bring any Kind of Goods or Merchandise whatsoever, prohibited and uncustomed." Navigation Act of 1662, 13 14 Car. II, Ch. 11, 5 (1662).

2. Introduction to the Fourth Amendment

A basic question regarding interpretation of the Amendment has been the relationship between its two clauses—one proscribing "unreasonable search and seizure" and the other setting forth the requirements for issuance of a warrant—which are ambiguously joined by the conjunction "and." One reading is that the warrant clause gives meaning to the prohibition in the first clause, so that a search is presumptively "unreasonable" when conducted without a warrant. A unanimous Court decreed in *Mincey v. Arizona*, 437 U.S. 385, 390 (1978), that "[t]he Fourth Amendment proscribes all unreasonable searches and seizures and it is a cardinal principle that searches conducted outside the judicial process, without prior approval by judge or magistrate, are *per se* unreasonable under the Fourth Amendment, subject to a few specifically established and well delineated exceptions."

For those advocating this "warrant preference" school of interpretation, the prophylactic interposition of a neutral magistrate between the police officer and the citizen *prior to* the search is the main protection afforded by the Fourth Amendment. See *Chimel v. California*, 395 U.S. 752, 766 n.12 (1969) (the Fourth Amendment is "designed to prevent, not simply redress" unlawful police action by way of the warrant process). This view still has considerable influence when police seek to search one's home. See *Kyllo v. United States*, 533 U.S. 27 (2001) (discussed in §3.2).

But recent years have witnessed the ascendancy of a contrary interpretation, where the clauses are read separately and thus the reasonableness of a search does not turn on whether a warrant was obtained (or whether there was a recognized excuse for not seeking one), but rather on the contextual circumstances justifying the search and the manner in which it was conducted.[2] The main protection afforded by the Amendment in this view lies not in prior judicial screening, but in after-the-fact review of police conduct to ensure that it was "reasonable," given what was known by the officers at the time.

Reflecting the "reasonableness" school of interpretation, Justice Scalia asserted in 1991 that the "Fourth Amendment does not by its terms require a prior warrant for searches and seizures," noting that the warrant requirement has become so riddled with exceptions that it is basically meaningless.[3] More recently he observed:

> The Fourth Amendment provides, in relevant part, that "[t]he right of the people to be secure in their persons, houses, papers, and effects, against unreasonable

---

2. An early articulation can be found in *United States v. Rabinowitz*, 339 U.S. 56, 65-66 (1950): "A rule of thumb requiring that a search warrant always be procured whenever practicable may be appealing from the vantage point of easy administration. But we cannot agree that this requirement should be crystallized into a *sine qua non* to the reasonableness of a search. . . . The relevant test is not whether it is reasonable to procure a warrant, but whether the search is reasonable."

3. *California v. Acevedo*, 500 U.S. 565, 581-585 (1991) (concurring).

searches and seizures, shall not be violated, and no Warrants shall issue, but upon probable cause." Grammatically, the two clauses of the Amendment seem to be independent—and directed at entirely different actors. The former tells the executive what it must do when it conducts a search, and the latter tells the judiciary what it must do when it issues a search warrant. But in an effort to guide courts in applying the Search-and-Seizure Clause's indeterminate reasonableness standard, and to maintain coherence in our case law, we have used the Warrant Clause as a guidepost for assessing the reasonableness of a search, and have erected a framework of presumptions applicable to broad categories of searches conducted by executive officials. Our case law has repeatedly recognized, however, that these are mere presumptions, and the only constitutional requirement is that a search be reasonable.[4]

Justice Stevens agreed that while the Court has not expressly disavowed the preference for warrants, its decisions suggest that "the exceptions have all but swallowed the general rule."[5]

This focus on "reasonableness" now dominates the Court's Fourth Amendment jurisprudence. The approach balances liberty against security interests, as illustrated in *United States v. Knights*, 534 U.S. 112 (2001), upholding a search of defendant's apartment despite the failure to obtain a warrant and the absence of probable cause. "The touchstone of the Fourth Amendment is reasonableness, and the reasonableness of a search is determined by assessing, on the one hand, the degree to which it intrudes upon an individual's privacy and, on the other, the degree to which it is needed for the promotion of legitimate governmental interests." 534 U.S. at 118-119. As a condition of Knights' probation for a drug offense, he had agreed to submit to searches at any time. Without deciding that this constituted a waiver of his Fourth Amendment rights, the Court instead ruled the search (for items connected to arson of a power transformer) reasonable by weighing the governmental interest in combating crime against the probationer's diminished expectation of privacy.

The basic Fourth Amendment concepts to be explored in the chapters that follow are:

1) **Prior justification for police action**—The police must possess information sufficient to constitute probable cause (or an alternative standard of justification) in order to conduct a lawful search or seizure (Chapter 4).

2) **Limited scope of police action**—Even when justified by probable cause or otherwise, searches and seizures are confined by limitations of space and time. The scope of the permissible search is generally

---

4. *City of Los Angeles v. Patel*, 135 S. Ct. 2443, 2458 (2015).
5. *Florida v. White*, 526 U.S. 559, 569 (1999) (dissenting).

defined by the original justification that permitted it (Chapters 5 and 6).

3) **The use of warrants**—The warrant process, by which law enforcement officers seek prior authorization to search or arrest from a neutral magistrate, is mandatory in certain situations, but discretionary in others. Chapter 5 will consider the evolving line drawn between the two, as well as the requirements for a valid warrant.

4) **Reasonableness analysis**—As noted above, the Court has increasingly relied on a concept of "reasonableness" to define the requirements of the Fourth Amendment. The strict standard of probable cause articulated in earlier cases has been diluted, and in some areas replaced by a balancing test that weighs the governmental necessity for the search against the magnitude of the privacy intrusion. Illustrative are the "administrative search" cases discussed in Chapter 4, which substitute the societal interest in conducting the search for the traditional requirement that there be specific justification.

5) **The remedy for violations**—How is the Fourth Amendment enforced? Chapter 7 will take up the operation of the exclusionary rule and the continuing controversy surrounding it.

But before looking at these issues, we must first explore a threshold question: *In what situations is the Fourth Amendment applicable?* It is to this question that we turn our attention in the next chapter.

Example

Pamela Principal at Oakdale Public High School received an anonymous telephone call informing her that Steve Student was selling illegal drugs and storing his inventory in his girlfriend Sally Snook's locker. Principal checked Steve's file and discovered that he had been absent on numerous occasions during the school year and had frequently been disruptive in the classroom. Principal obtained the master key from the janitor and proceeded to open both Steve's and Sally's lockers. In Steve's, Principal found a notebook listing the names of several students with dates, quantities, and moneys received. In Sally's locker, she found a large quantity of marijuana. Principal turned over both the notebook and the marijuana to the local police. A school disciplinary hearing is scheduled to determine whether Steve and Sally should be expelled; and Steve has been charged in juvenile court with possession of marijuana with intent to distribute.

How would you frame the legal issues raised regarding the searches and seizures described here?

Explanation

At the outset, we need to determine whether the Fourth Amendment is applicable in these circumstances. This question, as we will see in Chapter 3, involves two subquestions: First, is Pamela Principal a *government official* whose conduct is limited by constitutional constraints, or is she acting in a purely private capacity? Second, do the students have a *reasonable expectation of privacy* in their school lockers?

If we determine that the Fourth Amendment is implicated because a governmental actor has intruded into a protected area, then we need to address the *justification* issue: Did Pamela Principal possess sufficient information to justify search of the lockers? Was her reliance on an anonymous informant proper? Should she (or someone on her behalf) have sought prior authorization (*a warrant*) from a judicial officer before opening the lockers?

If we conclude that there was not sufficient justification or that a warrant was required, then there has been a violation of the Fourth Amendment, and our attention turns to *remedy*. Will Steve be able to exclude the evidence seized by Principal at the school disciplinary hearing? At the juvenile court hearing? Does Steve have the right to exclude the evidence taken from Sally's locker—does he, in other words, have "*standing*" to complain about a search of someone else's things?

These questions will be addressed in the chapters that follow.

CHAPTER 3

When Does the Fourth Amendment Apply?

There are two threshold requirements that must be met before the Fourth Amendment will be applicable in a particular situation. The first, which applies to all provisions of the Bill of Rights, is that the conduct in question must be governmental, not private. Second, the conduct must constitute a "search," defined with reference to privacy concepts. Thus, the Fourth Amendment is implicated only when a public actor intrudes into an area deemed one in which the citizen may reasonably expect privacy.

§3.1 GOVERNMENTAL ACTION — PUBLIC VERSUS PRIVATE SEARCH

The Fourth Amendment applies only to governmental, not private, conduct. As the Court observed in 1921, the origin and history of the Amendment clearly show that it was intended as a restraint upon the activities of sovereign authority only. *Burdeau v. McDowell*, 256 U.S. 465, 475 (1921).[1] Where the actor is an agent of federal, state, or local government, this requirement

---

1. Private persons illegally entered and searched McDowell's office, seized certain papers, and turned them over to a government prosecutor, who intended to use them in a criminal case against McDowell. He unsuccessfully sought a court order for return of the papers, on the theory that their seizure violated the Fourth Amendment. The Court held that because the government had played no role in the search, the Amendment did not apply, and the papers could be used in evidence against McDowell at trial.

is met.[2] Where, however, a private party acting on his own acquires evidence that the government later seeks to introduce in a criminal case, neither the Fourth Amendment nor its exclusionary remedy is implicated.

When a private individual acts *at the direction* of a government agent or pursuant to an official policy, the search implicates the Amendment. Thus, where a police officer directs an airline or hotel employee to open a traveler's suitcase, the Fourth Amendment is triggered. Similarly, railroads complying with federal regulations mandating drug screening of employees act under the constraints of the Fourth Amendment. See *Skinner v. Railway Labor Executives Association*, 489 U.S. 602 (1989).

Where there is no direct governmental command or policy, but merely acquiescence in the private actor's search, the issue becomes more difficult. Suppose, for example, that police officers stand by while private persons conduct an illegal search. Is the Fourth Amendment applicable? Several courts have concluded that it is.[3]

Two factors considered in determining whether the private party is acting as an "instrument of the state" are: 1) the degree of government encouragement, knowledge, and or acquiescence with regard to the private actor's conduct; and 2) the purpose underlying the private party's action — was he pursuing a governmental interest (such as the discovery of criminal activity or evidence thereof), or did he act to promote his own personal or business objectives (such as protecting against accidents, false claims, or potential liability), which makes the action private in nature. See *United States v. Feffer*, 831 F.2d 734 (7th Cir. 1987); *United States v. Walther*, 652 F.2d 788 (9th Cir. 1981). Thus, when an airline employee opened a suspicious package and turned the white powder found inside over to Drug Enforcement Agency (DEA) agents, the search was not deemed purely private because: 1) the employee had previously reported information and turned over packages to the DEA on 11 occasions, sometimes receiving a small payment, and thus acted with the government's acquiescence; and 2) he testified that he opened the package in order to discover evidence of crime, with the expectation of a reward

---

2. The Fourth Amendment has been applied to the actions of civil authorities as well as law enforcement personnel. See, e.g., *O'Connor v. Ortega*, 480 U.S. 709 (1987) (state hospital supervisor), *New Jersey v. TLO*, 469 U.S. 325 (1985) (public school principal), and *Safford Unified Sch. Dist. No. 1 v. Redding*, 557 U.S. 364 (2009) (public school principal).

3. See, e.g., *United States v. Newton*, F.2d 1149 (7th Cir. 1975) (search of luggage by airline employee in presence of federal agents, summoned when employee became suspicious about appearance of luggage, constituted "search" within scope of Amendment); *Stapleton v. Superior Court*, 447 F.2d 967 (Cal. 1968) ("police need not have requested or directed search in order to be guilty of 'standing idly by'; knowledge of illegal search coupled with failure to protect petitioner's rights suffices"). But compare *Pleasant v. Lovell*, 654 F. Supp. 1082 (D. Colo. 1987) (mere acceptance by federal agents of information from unpaid informant was insufficient to make search public);

Gundlach v. Janing, 401 F. Supp. 1089 (D. Neb. 1975), aff'd 536 F.2d 754 (8th Cir. 1976) (mere knowledge by police that private person might conduct illegal search was insufficient to transform search into governmental act).

from the DEA, and not for any purpose of his employer. *Walther*, supra, 652 F.2d at 792. The Fourth Amendment was therefore triggered.

An otherwise private search may be transformed into one subject to constitutional constraints if the law enforcement recipient of the items subjects them to additional examination. In *Walter v. United States*, 447 U.S. 649 (1980), sealed film canisters were mistakenly delivered to a company whose employees, noting the highly suggestive labels, opened them and tried unsuccessfully to observe the images on the films. Suspecting that they were pornographic, the employees turned the films over to FBI agents, who viewed them on a projector. Because the agents went a step beyond what the private actors had done, the Fourth Amendment came into play.

The further examination by a government agent must be substantial in order to trigger constitutional protection. In *United States v. Jacobsen*, 466 U.S. 109 (1984) (discussed in §3.2), Federal Express employees opened a damaged package and found several plastic bags containing a suspicious white powder. They repacked the parcel and summoned federal drug agents, who reopened it and subjected the powder to a field test for cocaine. The powder tested positive. Although the agents went a step beyond the initial examination conducted by the FedEx people, the Court considered it *de minimis* (the test could simply detect the presence of cocaine), thus not triggering the Fourth Amendment.

Examples

1. Upon leaving the Friendly Department Store, Alva Alpha was stopped by a store security guard who suspected her of shoplifting. The guard seized Alpha's shopping bag, opened it, and discovered several items of clothing that had been taken but not paid for. The incident was immediately reported to the police and the items turned over to them. May Alva Alpha mount a Fourth Amendment challenge to use of the clothing as evidence at her shoplifting trial?

2. Curious Jack, an employee of Consolidated Utility Company, was in Sam Clay's basement to read the gas meter. Spotting a large parcel enclosed in brown paper, Jack proceeded to unwrap what turned out to be a painting. An amateur art expert, he recognized it as a priceless work that had been stolen a month before from the Metropolitan Gallery. Jack took the painting and turned it over to the local police. May Clay invoke the Fourth Amendment to seek suppression of the painting at trial?

3. Claude von Wealthy stands accused of murdering his wife by injecting her with a lethal dose of insulin. The prosecution intends to introduce into evidence a black bag containing a hypodermic needle, which von Wealthy's stepson found while he and a private investigator were looking for incriminating evidence in the defendant's bedroom closet.

Upon discovery, the bag was turned over to the police, who subjected the hypodermic needle to a chemical analysis at the police laboratory, revealing traces of insulin. Von Wealthy moves to suppress the evidence. Does the Fourth Amendment apply?

4. An anonymous computer hacker happened upon evidence of sexual exploitation of children on a local computer and reported to police, including the user's IP address and street address, and attached several graphic images of one child's abuse. A warrant was obtained based on this information. Does the hacker's conduct implicate the Fourth Amendment? What if the police ask him to retrieve images of other children from the computer as well?

Explanations

1. Security guards are generally not subject to Fourth Amendment constraints so long as they act independent of police direction. See, e.g., *United States v. Shahid*, 117 F.3d 322 (7th Cir. 1997) (shopping mall security officers). Some courts have held that security personnel should be treated as governmental actors when they go beyond the protection of their employer's interests and take on a quasi-law enforcement function. See, e.g., *People v. Zelinski*, 155 Cal. Rptr. 575, 594 P.2d 1000 (1979) (store detectives become public actors subject to Fourth Amendment when they hold customer for police and turn over evidence for criminal trial). Where the privately employed guard also happens to be a police officer (as on a private detail), some courts have imposed Fourth Amendment limitations. See *Commonwealth v. Leone*, 386 Mass. 329 (1982) (special police officer privately employed as plant security guard). But compare *United States v. Cintron*, 482 Fed. Appx. 353 (10th Cir. 2012) (reserve police officer was acting in his private capacity as security guard at bar when he searched and detained defendant). "Determining when an individual is acting as a private citizen or a government agent can be difficult, including when the individual is an off-duty police officer working as a security guard." *United States v. Cintron*, supra, 482 Fed. Appx. at 356 (a private security officer who is state licensed and possesses arrest powers is likely to be deemed a state actor). See *Romanski v. Detroit Entertainment, LLC*, 428 F.3d 629 (6th Cir. 2005). Compare *Lindsey v. Detroit Entertainment, LLC*, 484 F.3d 824 (6th Cir. 2007) (unlicensed security personnel not state actors); *Johnson v. LaRabida Children's Hospital*, 372 F.3d 894 (7th Cir. 2004) (hospital security guard was not state actor even though a special policeman, because he was not authorized to carry a firearm or carry out police functions).

The actions of private security personnel could, of course, give rise to civil liability under tort theories of recovery even if the Fourth Amendment is not applicable.

2. The resolution of this question turns in large part on whether the meter reader is a public or private employee. If Consolidated is a private entity, Jack's actions are probably not proscribed by constitutional limitations. If, however, Consolidated is a publicly owned and operated utility, the Fourth Amendment would likely apply even though Jack is not a law enforcement officer. Compare *United States v. Goldstein*, 532 F.2d 1305 (9th Cir. 1976) (evidence that Goldstein was using an illegal blue box to avoid being billed for calls, acquired through investigation by a special agent of the private telephone company, was beyond the reach of the Fourth Amendment: "Although communications carriers may sometimes give the appearance of governmental agencies, they in fact are private companies which possess none of the criteria which might make them responsible under the Fourth Amendment as government bodies.") with *Vega-Rodriguez v. Puerto Rico Telephone Co.*, 110 F.3d 174 (1st Cir. 1997) (quasi-public telephone company was government actor subject to Fourth Amendment when engaged in video surveillance of its employees).

Significant involvement by law enforcement personnel in an otherwise private search converts it into one subject to constitutional constraints. Thus, where DEA officers targeted a suspicious package at a UPS facility, encouraged the UPS employee to open it, and even assisted her in doing so, the Fourth Amendment was triggered. *United States v. Souza*, 223 F.3d 1197 (10th Cir. 2000). See also *United States v. Booker*, 728 F.3d 535 (6th Cir. 2013) (physician's conduct in performing rectal exam to remove cocaine from defendant was attributable to the police, who had brought him to hospital for that purpose). But compare *United States v. Crowley*, 285 F.3d 553 (7th Cir. 2002) (package deliverer was not acting as agent of the police when she opened defendant's package and found drugs).

Some courts have refused to apply the Fourth Amendment to public employees not acting in a law enforcement capacity. See, e.g., *United States v. Soderstrand*, 412 F.3d 1146 (10th Cir. 2005) (co-worker of defendant at state university was not a state actor when she conducted a search of defendant's safe, because even though a state employee, she acted solely in a private capacity); *State v. Schofner*, 800 A.2d 1072 (Vt. 2002) (town tax assessors discovered marijuana while assessing defendant's property).

3. Because the bag and its contents were obtained by way of a private search with no government involvement, the Fourth Amendment would not apply to the discovery. This is the case even if the intention of the stepson and private investigator was to acquire evidence to be used at

trial. When the law enforcement officials subsequently had the contents chemically tested at a laboratory, however, they exceeded the scope of the private intrusion and that constituted a public search implicating the Amendment. See *State v.Von Bulow*, 475 A.2d 995, 1012 (R.I. 1984) ("No matter how egregious actions may appear in a society whose fundamental values have historically included individual freedom and privacy, the exclusionary rule cannot be invoked by defendant to bar the introduction of evidence that was procured by [persons] while acting as private citizens. . . . Similar principles do not, however, govern our review of the evidence-gathering techniques employed by the state [the subsequent chemical testing of the fruits of the private search]. When the government significantly expands a prior private search, the independent governmental search is subject to the proscriptions of the Fourth Amendment.").

The chemical analysis performed in this example appears more intrusive than the field test in *United States v. Jacobsen*, 466 U.S. 109 (1984) (discussed above) because it was conducted in the laboratory, not on the scene, and the tests were designed to disclose more than simply the presence of contraband. See also *United States v. Runyan*, 275 F.3d 449 (5th Cir. 2001) (police exceeded scope of private search when they examined more computer disks containing child pornography than were viewed by the private searchers).

4. The initial hacking was purely private, and thus the warrant obtained based on it is not subject to challenge on the grounds that the underlying information was obtained in violation of the Fourth Amendment. But any evidence subsequently turned over by Hacker in response to the police request becomes governmental and triggers the Amendment. See *United States v. Steiger*, 318 F.3d 1039 (11th Cir. 2003). See also *United States v. Grimes*, 244 F.3d 375 (5th Cir. 2001) (computer repairperson who discovered images of child pornography and reported them to police acted privately and without government encouragement or acquiescence).

§3.2 REASONABLE EXPECTATION OF PRIVACY

a) What Constitutes a "Search"?

The definition of what constitutes a "search" within the meaning of the Fourth Amendment was, until 1967, closely tied to property law concepts. Police action would be deemed a search if it constituted a common law trespass. As methods of surveillance and eavesdropping became more technologically sophisticated and could be accomplished without the necessity for physical intrusion, this definition became outdated and underinclusive.

Katz v. United States, 389 U.S. 347 (1967), brought the Fourth Amendment into the modern era. Federal agents, suspecting him of bookmaking, placed a listening device against the wall of a public phone booth that was being used by Charles Katz. Because there was no penetration of the booth, and thus no trespass, the lower court ruled that the agents did not conduct a "search" when they listened in on Katz's incriminating conversation. Disagreeing, the Supreme Court held that the Amendment "protects people, not places," and its reach cannot turn solely upon whether a physical intrusion occurred. Rather, applicability derives from the concept of privacy: "The Government's activities in electronically listening to and recording words violated the privacy upon which Katz justifiably relied while using the telephone booth and thus constituted a search and seizure within the meaning of the Fourth Amendment." (For more on electronic surveillance, see §11.4.1.)

While *Katz* seemed at first to represent an expansion of the constitutional protection against unreasonable search, decisions in recent years have construed the test narrowly. The Fourth Amendment applies only where: 1) the citizen has manifested a *subjective* expectation of privacy; and 2) that expectation is one that society (through the Court) accepts as *objectively reasonable*. *California v. Greenwood*, 486 U.S. 35, 39 (1988). It is not enough, in other words, for the target to *believe* that he is acting in private; that belief must be deemed *reasonable*. Supreme Court decisions have tended to take a restrictive view of what society considers a justifiable privacy expectation.

In an otherwise unanimous decision ruling that police violated the Fourth Amendment rights of a suspect when they placed a global positioning system (GPS) tracking device on his Jeep Grand Cherokee and monitored his movements for a month, the majority (in an opinion by Justice Scalia) returned to property law concepts, concluding that the installation of the device by *trespass* on his property triggered the Amendment's protections. *United States v. Jones*, 565 U.S. 400 (2012). Justice Alito's concurring opinion (joined by three others) would have reached the same conclusion by applying "reasonable expectation of privacy" analysis. Justice Sotomayor wrote a separate opinion expressing the view that *Katz* did not displace the common-law trespass test, but merely "augmented" it.

Responding to the next ramp-up of sophisticated surveillance techniques, a 5-4 majority in *Carpenter v. United States*, 138 S. Ct. 2206 (2018), ruled that the "sweeping model" of tracking through cell-site location records implicates the Fourth Amendment warrant requirement, as it maps a subject's precise movements both in the present and the past.

b) Public Exposure and Assumption of Risk

One important limitation on the definition of search derives from the observation in *Katz* that "what a person knowingly exposes to the public, even in his own home or office, is not subject to Fourth Amendment protection." Protection is afforded only for "what he seeks to preserve as private." The police cannot be expected to avert their eyes from evidence of criminal activity that could be observed by any member of the public.

The Court significantly broadened this "public exposure" analysis when it ruled that one who conveys information to a third party, even in an apparently private communication, cannot reasonably rely on that person maintaining his confidentiality. When Teamsters president Jimmy Hoffa and drug dealer James White made incriminating statements to associates who, unbeknownst to them, were government informants, they assumed the risk of betrayal and disclosure. *Hoffa v. United States*, 385 U.S. 293 (1966) (informant later reported conversation to government agents); *United States v. White*, 401 U.S. 745 (1971) (government agents listened in on conversation transmitted by radio device worn by the informant).

Misplaced reliance on the loyalty of others is not, the Court held, entitled to constitutional protection. When one party to the conversation "invites" the government in, Fourth Amendment constraints do not apply. (In contrast, the government intruded on Mr. Katz as the *uninvited ear* into his telephone conversation.) See also *United States v. Davis*, 326 F.3d 361 (2d Cir. 2003) (once defendant invited confidential informant into his residence, he forfeited his privacy interest, and informant's secret videotaping of drug deal did not implicate Fourth Amendment); *United States v. Longoria*, 177 F.3d 1179 (10th Cir. 1999) (defendant's expectation that confidential informant would not disclose conversation was not one society would consider reasonable, even though he spoke in Spanish and believed that informant did not understand Spanish).

Assumption-of-risk analysis has been extended to institutional third parties. An individual who imparts financial information to a bank in the usual course of business,[4] or who automatically conveys the numbers he dials to the telephone company for billing purposes (by means of a pen register),[5] has no reasonable expectation of privacy in such information. She runs the risk that the recipient may divulge the information to the government, and

---

4. *United States v. Miller*, 425 U.S. 435 (1976).

5. *Smith v. Maryland*, 442 U.S. 735 (1979). See also *Commonwealth v. Cote*, 407 Mass. 827 (Sup. Jud. Ct. 1990) (defendant who used telephone message service whereby both defendant and caller were aware that third party was taking messages has no reasonable expectation of privacy in message records, and thus no search occurred when prosecution subpoenaed them).

has forfeited Fourth Amendment protection. After the events of 9/11/2001, the Bush Administration invoked this analysis to gain widespread access to phone and financial records.

In her concurrence in *United States v. Jones*, Justice Sotomayor expressed concern about applying the third-party disclosure rational in this digital age, where so much of our personal data is necessarily conveyed to third parties like cell phone or internet providers. (See also *Riley v. California*, Chapter 6, involving search of data on a cell phone.)

The Court in *Carpenter v. United States*, 138 S. Ct. 2206 (2018), shared Justice Sotomayor's concern in holding that an individual maintains a legitimate expectation of privacy regarding his physical movements as revealed by cell-site location information (in that case over the course of 127 days, placing him in the vicinity of four charged robberies), even though this information is conveyed to the third-party wireless carrier. Given the unique nature of cell-site records — providing the government near perfect surveillance and even allowing it to travel back in time to retrace a person's whereabouts — the Court declined to extend the third-party discourse doctrine to cover them: "There is a world of difference between the limited types of personal information addressed in *Smith* and *Miller* and the exhaustive chronicle of location information casually collected by wireless carriers today."

The search thus required a warrant supported by probable cause. The decision, Chief Justice Roberts emphasized, is a narrow one, not disturbing application of third-party disclosure doctrine in other contexts such as more conventional surveillance, nor foreclosing case-specific exigent circumstances like bomb threats, active shootings, and child abductions.

By third-party disclosure logic, a trash collector may turn one's garbage over to the police at their request, and evidence of crime found inside is not subject to Fourth Amendment challenge. *California v. Greenwood*, 486 U.S. 35 (1988) reasoned:

> Respondents exposed their garbage to the public sufficiently to defeat their claim to Fourth Amendment protection. It is common knowledge that plastic garbage bags left on or at the side of a public street are readily accessible to animals, children, scavengers, snoops, and other members of the public. Moreover, respondents placed their refuse at the curb for the express purpose of conveying it to a third party, the trash collector, who might himself have sorted through respondents' trash or permitted others, such as the police, to do so. Accordingly, having deposited their garbage in an area particularly suited for public inspection and, in a manner of speaking, public consumption, for the express purpose of having strangers take it, respondents could have no reasonable expectation of privacy in the inculpatory items they discarded.

486 U.S. at 40-41. Several state courts have, however, rejected this logic, and interpreted their own constitutional provisions more broadly.[6]

With the disclosure by Edward Snowden of the global surveillance of telecommunication records (metadata) by the National Security Administration (NSA), Congress amended the USA Patriot Act in 2015 by providing that the collection be performed by private phone companies, and subsequent access by the government would need to be approved by the FISA Court. See Chapter 12.

A person's external physical characteristics that are exposed to the public are deemed outside the scope of Fourth Amendment protection. "No person can have a reasonable expectation that others will not know the sound of his voice, any more than he can reasonably expect that his face will be a mystery to the world." United States v. Dionisio, 410 U.S. 1, 13 (1973). The government can thus require persons to submit exemplars of their voice,[7] handwriting,[8] or fingerprints[9] without infringing any interest protected by the Fourth Amendment. Physical attributes not on public display and whose examination requires bodily intrusion, such as blood type, do however fall within the Amendment's purview.[10]

c) Physical Setting, Vantage Point, and Enhancement Devices

Turning to searches of particular places, the physical setting is of great importance in determining whether the Fourth Amendment is implicated. An individual enjoys the highest expectation of privacy in her home, and only somewhat less in the "curtilage" immediately surrounding and in close proximity to it. Consequently, these locales are entitled to Fourth Amendment protection. Unoccupied and undeveloped areas (even if fenced

---

6. The Supreme Judicial Court of Massachusetts concluded that society would believe it "objectively reasonable to expect that conversational interchange in a private home will not be invaded surreptitiously by warrantless electronic transmission." Commonwealth v. Blood, 400 Mass. 61, 70, 507 N.E.2d 1029, 1034 (1987). See also Burrows v. Superior Court, 13 Cal. 3d 238 (1974) (rejecting the reasoning later adopted in United States v. Miller, supra, regarding the disclosure of bank records); Washington v. Boland, 115 Wash. 2d 571, 800 F.2d 112 (Wash. Sup. Ct. 1990) and State v. Morris, 680 A.2d 90 (Vt. 1996) (rejecting the Greenwood analysis and holding that seizure and inspection of trash left at curbside intrudes on privacy expectations and thus constitutes a search within the state constitution); State v. Crane, 254 P.3d 117 (N.M. App. 2011) (using state constitution to find an expectation of privacy in motel guest when sealed garbage bags placed in dumpster were opened).

7. United States v. Dionisio, supra.

8. United States v. Mara, 410 U.S. 19 (1973).

9. Davis v. Mississippi, 394 U.S. 721 (1969).

10. See Skinner v. Railway Labor Executives Association, 489 U.S. 602 (1989) (blood, urine, and breath analysis all constitute "searches"); Schmerber v. California, 384 U.S. 757 (1966) (extraction of blood sample from arrestee by physician at police direction implicated Fourth Amendment); Winston v. Lee, 470 U.S. 753 (1985) (proposed surgery on defendant to remove bullet that police believed would link him to crime was subject to Fourth Amendment); Cupp v. Murphy, 412 U.S. 291 (1973) (applying Fourth Amendment to scraping of defendant's fingernails to obtain blood samples linking defendant to murder). See also §11.2.

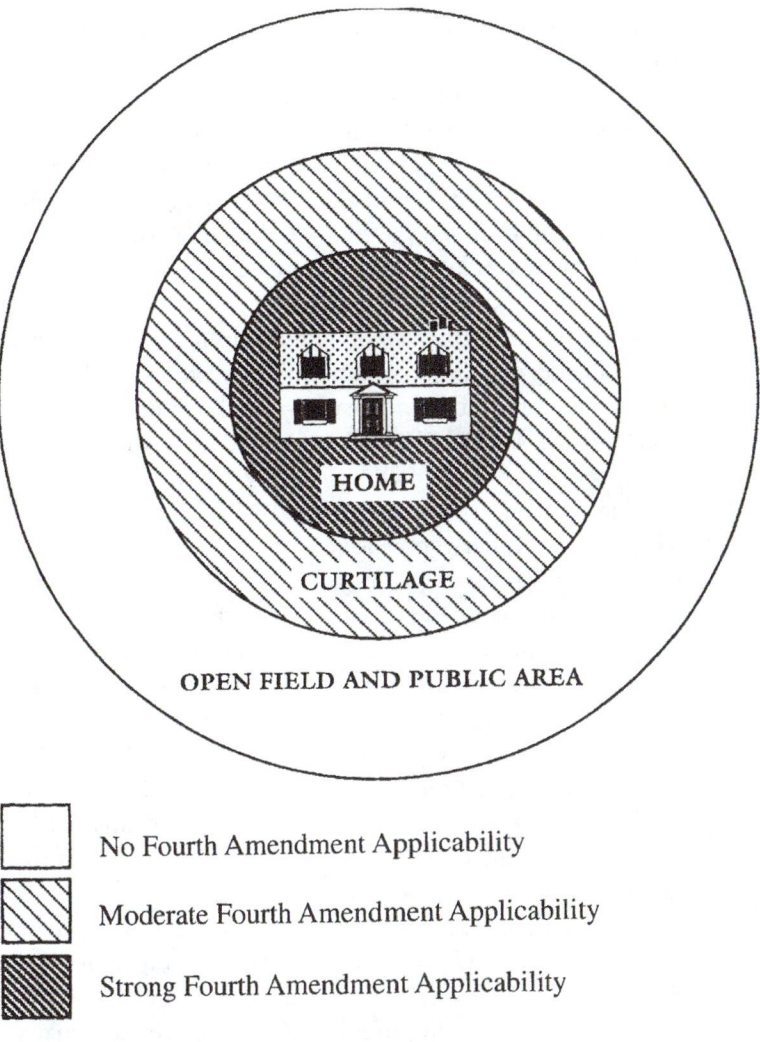

No Fourth Amendment Applicability

Moderate Fourth Amendment Applicability

Strong Fourth Amendment Applicability

Figure 3-1. Zones of Privacy Expectation

in and posted with "No trespassing" signs) generally fall outside the Fourth Amendment. As the Court explained in *Oliver v. United States*, 466 U.S. 170 (1984), "open fields do not provide the setting for those intimate activities that the amendment is intended to shelter from government interference or surveillance." 466 U.S. at 179.[11] See Figure 3-1.

---

11. *United States v. Dunn*, 480 U.S. 294 (1987) addressed the distinction between "curtilage" and "open fields," looking to the following factors in determining whether an area is curtilage (and thus within the home's umbrella of protection): 1) proximity to the home; 2) whether the area is within an enclosure surrounding the home; 3) the nature of the uses to which the area is put; and 4) the steps taken to protect the area from observation. One federal judge has referred to curtilage as an "imaginary boundary line between privacy and accessibility to the public." See *United States v. Redmon*, 138 F.3d 1109, 1112 (7th Cir. 1998).

Even if an area is within a traditionally protected setting, Fourth Amendment protection may be lost by application of the privacy expectation concept, as illustrated by the aerial surveillance cases. *California v. Ciraolo*, 476 U.S. 207 (1986) held that naked-eye observation of a fenced-in backyard deemed within the home's curtilage from an aircraft at 1,000 feet did not constitute a "search" because in "an age where private and commercial flight in the public airways is routine, it is unreasonable for respondent to expect that his marijuana plants were constitutionally protected from such observation."

Nor was the Fourth Amendment implicated when police flew by helicopter 400 feet over defendant's partially covered greenhouse, located next to his mobile home, and made naked-eye observations of marijuana plants inside. *Florida v. Riley*, 488 U.S. 445 (1989). Despite the fact that the contents of the greenhouse could not be observed from ground level, the Court concluded that no search had occurred because a member of the public could have similarly positioned himself in an aircraft and made the same observations through the uncovered sections of the roof. Although Riley "no doubt intended and expected that his greenhouse would not be open to public inspection, and the precautions he took protected against ground-level observation," the routine nature of air travel rendered his expectation unjustified. The plurality qualified its decision by emphasizing that the flight had been within legal parameters (including Federal Aviation Administration regulations), did not interfere with the normal use of the greenhouse by way of undue noise, wind, dust, or threat of injury, and did not reveal any intimate details connected with the use of the defendant's home.[12]

The overflight cases demonstrate expectation of privacy analysis includes the factor of vantage point as well as setting. Where police observations are made from a location to which the public has lawful access (from air or ground), the viewing of otherwise protected areas may not implicate the Fourth Amendment. Where, however, police must physically enter the area to make their observations, as an intrusion into a fenced backyard, a "search" has likely taken place.

---

12. One state appellate court, distinguishing *Ciraolo* and *Riley*, ruled that a search occurred when a sheriff piloted a helicopter 200 feet over the defendant's property and observed marijuana plants. The court found determinative the low altitude of the flight compared to *Ciraolo* (1,000 feet) and *Riley* (400 feet) and the excessive noise created by the flight, which witnesses testified disrupted the neighborhood. See *Colorado v. Pollock*, 796 P.2d 63 (Colo. Ct. App. 1990).

A further issue arises when police employ devices that enhance the usual sensory abilities. What effect does this have on the privacy analysis? Take a police officer standing on a public street who can observe marijuana plants growing in a bay window of Joe's home. Having placed the plants in public view, Joe can have no reasonable expectation of privacy with regard to them, and the officer's observations do not constitute a search.[13] But if the plants are in a location in the home that *cannot* be seen with the naked eye and the officer discovers them only by use of binoculars or telescope, has a search occurred?

Where the device merely *enhances sensory perception* and facilitates surveillance that otherwise would be possible without the enhancement, the Fourth Amendment is not implicated. Such devices include a flashlight,[14] an aerial camera,[15] photographic or video recording,[16] a drug-detection dog,[17] and field tests for narcotics.[18] Where the use of the device prolongs the search beyond what is required to complete its purpose, as where a routine traffic stop is delayed to allow a sniffer dog to arrive and circle the vehicle, the Fourth Amendment may be violated. See *Rodriguez v. United States*, 135 S. Ct. 1609 (2015).

Thus, when police attached an electronic tracking device to an automobile and monitored it on public roads, no Fourth Amendment right was infringed because the movements of the car could have been observed by the naked eye. *United States v. Knotts*, 460 U.S. 276 (1983). When, however, the police continued to monitor a beeper installed in a container *after* it was taken into a home, the constraints of the Amendment applied because the device revealed information that could not have been obtained through unaided surveillance. *United States v. Karo*, 468 U.S. 705 (1984). And, as noted above, *United States v. Jones*, 132 S. Ct. 945 (2012), found the Fourth Amendment

---

13. Those observations can therefore be used in an affidavit to establish probable cause to obtain a warrant to search the home and seize the plants. It must be emphasized, however, that the officer cannot enter the home without a warrant. See §§5.1, 5.2.2.

14. *Texas v. Brown*, 460 U.S. 730 (1983); *United States v. Dunn*, 480 U.S. 294 (1987).

15. *Dow Chemical Co. v. United States*, 476 U.S. 207 (1986).

16. *United States v. McIver*, 186 F.3d 1119 (9th Cir. 1999).

17. *United States v. Place*, 462 U.S. 696 (1983) (detection dog at airport). But see *Commonwealth v. Johnston*, 515 Pa. 454 (1987) (use of drug-sniffing dog does constitute a search within state constitution because "a free society will not remain free if police may use this, or any other crime detection device, at random and without reason").

18. *United States v. Jacobsen*, 466 U.S. 109 (1984). The Court also premised its decision on the limited nature of the intrusion represented by a litmus test that can detect only the presence or absence of cocaine. Similar reasoning led the Court in *Illinois v. Caballes*, 543 U.S. 405 (2005) to rule that use of a narcotics-detection dog around the exterior of an automobile did not violate the motorist's privacy rights and thus did not implicate the Fourth Amendment. Concerned that the detection abilities of these trained canines are far more fallible than originally believed and that the decision threatened to legalize suspicionless sweeps of cars and pedestrians, dissenting Justice Souter would have found a "search" implicating the Fourth Amendment.

violated when police installed a GPS tracking device and monitored Antoine Jones's automobile travels for nearly a month, and *Carpenter v. United States*, 138 S. Ct. 2206 (2018) when the subject's whereabouts were tracked by cell-site records.

The physical setting in which an enhancement device is used plays a significant role in determining whether the subject's reasonable expectation of privacy has been violated. Surveillance into the home (where it has been consistently recognized the individual has a heightened privacy interest) is most likely to trigger the Fourth Amendment's protections. Thus, while use of a drug-detection dog to sniff luggage at a public airport does not implicate the Fourth Amendment (*United States v. Place*, infra), placing the dog immediately adjacent to the defendant's apartment to determine the presence of narcotics within has been held to bring the Amendment into play. See *United States v. Thomas*, 757 F.2d 1359 (2d Cir. 1985). Similarly, Justice Scalia, writing for the Court in *Florida v. Jardines*, 133 S. Ct. 1409 (2013), concluded that use of a drug-sniffing dog on a porch of a home to investigate a tip that marijuana was being grown inside constituted a search. Compare *United States v. Colyer*, 878 F.2d 469 (D.C. Cir. 1989) (dog sniff of defendant's sleeper unit on train not subject to Fourth Amendment); *United States v. Lingenfelter*, 997 F.2d 632 (9th Cir. 1993) (use of dogs to detect drugs by sniffing around outside of warehouse did not constitute search).

As Justice Harlan observed in his concurrence in *Katz*, Fourth Amendment analysis always requires reference to "place." 389 U.S. at 361.

The central importance of setting was confirmed in a case involving high-tech snooping into the home. Thermal-imaging devices detect levels of heat, permitting police to "see through" walls. Suspecting that marijuana was being cultivated inside, federal agents pointed their imager at Danny Kyllo's home; the scan revealed levels of heat consistent with the use of grow lights. That information led to the issuance of a search warrant and the discovery of a large indoor growing operation. Emphasizing the sanctity of the home and drawing a "firm line at the entrance to the house," the Court in an opinion by Justice Scalia held that when the government employs a "device that is not in general public use, to explore details of the home that would previously have been unknowable without physical intrusion, the surveillance is a 'search' and presumptively unreasonable without a warrant." *Kyllo v. United States*, 533 U.S. 27, 40 (2001). (Oddly, the widespread use of GPS devices did not seem to factor into the Court's reasoning in *Jones*, discussed above.)

Justice Stevens, writing for the four *Kyllo* dissenters, questioned the workability of the majority's "firm" rule, particularly given the difficulty of determining in our technological age whether a sense-enhancing device had come into "general public use." "In any event," Stevens mused, "putting aside its lack of clarity, this criterion is somewhat perverse because it seems likely that the threat to privacy will grow, rather than recede, as the use of intrusive equipment becomes more readily available." 533 U.S. at 47.

While clearly at the core of Fourth Amendment protection, we have seen that the home is not the only area sheltered. Charles Katz, you recall, was in a public telephone booth when his conversation was unlawfully "searched." Antoine Jones was in his Jeep Cherokee. An administrator at a state hospital was held to have a reasonable expectation of privacy in his office, even though "it is the nature of government offices that others such as fellow employees, supervisors, visitors, and the general public may have frequent access." *O'Connor v. Ortega*, 480 U.S. 709, 717 (1987). A public school student has a reasonable expectation that her purse will not be searched by an administrator. *New Jersey v. TLO*, 469 U.S. 325 (1985) (discussed in §4.5).

Not surprisingly, however, a prisoner has no justifiable expectation that his cell will be free from intrusion prompted by security concerns. *Hudson v. Palmer*, 468 U.S. 517 (1984).[19] In sum, whether a "search" implicating the Fourth Amendment has occurred depends on justifiable privacy expectations, which in turn are a function of both 1) the setting observed, and 2) the vantage point from which the observation is made. The definition of search is clearly not a semantic question but a value judgment as to what police conduct should be subject to constitutional scrutiny. The Court's narrow definition in decisions such as the overflight cases discussed above led Justice Brennan to invoke the frightening image of the Orwellian Big Brother watching us. See *Florida v. Riley*, 488 U.S. 445, 466 (1989) (dissenting). The more recent decision in *Kyllo* suggests that a majority of the Court may now share his concern.

Recall that this chapter has dealt solely with the threshold question of Fourth Amendment applicability. In the following chapters, we turn to its requirements and mandates.

Examples

1. John is growing marijuana plants in a backyard garden immediately adjacent to his home. The small yard is surrounded by an eight-foot-high stockade fence. A hot tub is located next to the garden. Has a "search" occurred in any of the following situations?
   a. Police officer climbs over the stockade fence into the yard, enters the garden, and observes the plants.
   b. Police officer climbs a stepladder that she placed on the public sidewalk, peers over the fence, and observes the plants.

---

19. Where, however, the search is motivated by a prosecutor's desire to seize evidence, Fourth Amendment protections have been held to apply. See *United States v. Cohen*, 796 F.2d 20 (2d Cir. 1986).

    c. Police officer obtains the consent of John's neighbor and observes the plants from the neighbor's second-story bedroom window.

    d. Assume instead that John's marijuana plants are located 75 feet from his house in a wooded area of his unfenced property, surrounded by a dense circle of pine trees. Police officer enters the property and observes the plants through the trees.

    e. Assume instead that John's marijuana plants are located 75 feet from his home inside a wooden shed. Police officer enters the property and looks into the shed through an open window, observing the plants.

    f. Assume the same facts as in example 1e, except that the officer enters the shed in order to make her observations.

    g. Now assume that John is conducting an indoor growing operation. The marijuana plants are in his den, and the windows are covered by thick shades. Detectives park their van across the street and aim a high-tech listening device toward the house, picking up incriminating conversations that John is having with customers within.

2. Police officer, with the permission of the landlord, entered a crawl space under Paul Parrott's first-floor apartment. The crawl space is used only when repairing pipes and wiring, but neither the tenants nor the public has regular access to it. Officer spent two hours in the space and heard Parrott engage in what appeared to be numerous sales of narcotics. Did Officer obtain the information through a "search"?

3a. Drug enforcement agents stationed themselves (with the permission of the landlord) in a third-floor apartment across the street from Bad Thad's first-floor apartment. With the aid of a telescope, the agents were able to observe through the open curtains of the kitchen window Thad weighing and packaging a white powder, and to read the label on a jar used by Thad that indicated that it contained a solution known to be a diluent for cocaine. Does the agents' conduct constitute a "search"?

3b. Assume that instead of viewing the inside of Thad's apartment, the agents trained their telescope on a small plot of land located behind the apartment. The land is enclosed by a fence and not open to view from the ground. Through the telescope, the agents observed marijuana plants. Does the agents' conduct constitute a "search"?

4. Acting on a hunch that narcotics activity was being conducted at 987 Fisher Road, Oakdale, police decided to collect the occupants' garbage and search it for evidence. In Oakdale, trash is not collected at curbside but rather by municipal workers who come to the back of homes to pick up trash bags placed outside by residents. Disguised as a trash collector, Officer Daly walked to the back of 987 Fisher Road and found four plastic trash bags tied at the top and leaning against the wall of the home.

Daly removed the bags and took them to the police station, where she opened them. Inside she found a spiral notebook, which had been ripped into quarters. Daly pieced together the shredded papers, which turned out to document hundreds of narcotics sales. Has a "search" taken place?

5. FBI agents arrested James Lyons on drug trafficking charges and discovered in his possession a padlock key and an Ace Storage Company rental agreement for unit 792. The agents went to the storage company, inserted the key into the lock on unit 792, and confirmed that the key turned the tumbler. They relocked the unit without opening it and reported the fact that Lyons's key opened the lock. Based on that connection, a search warrant was issued for unit 792. Defendant moves to suppress the evidence found on the grounds that the previous insertion of the key into the lock was itself a "search" not in conformity with Fourth Amendment requirements. How should the court rule?

6. While walking through JFK Airport, Donald was subjected to a sniff from a drug-detection dog being used by federal agents. The dog had been trained to detect cocaine, which he indicated was present on Donald's person. Donald was arrested and searched, and cocaine was found in his jacket pocket. Prior to trial, he moved to suppress the cocaine on the grounds that the dog sniff constituted a "search" that was not conducted in conformity with Fourth Amendment requirements. How should the court rule?

7. David Copper was suspected of involvement in a bank fraud scheme. As part of their investigation, the police requested and received from the Friendly Bank the application that he had filed for a large commercial loan. The document confirmed their suspicions, and David was indicted. Prior to trial, he moved to suppress the application on the ground that it was obtained in violation of the Fourth Amendment. Has a "search" occurred?

8. Suspecting Carol Smooth of failure to report taxable income, IRS agents placed a "mail cover" on her. This permitted the agents to observe and record all information (name and return address of sender, place and date of postmark, etc.) located on the outside of envelopes in her incoming mail. The agents were able to gather evidence indicating that Carol maintained secret Swiss bank accounts. Carol seeks suppression of the evidence, claiming that the mail cover was an illegal search under the Fourth Amendment. Has a "search" occurred?

9. Believing Matt Mailer is involved in a massive Ecstasy drug production ring, federal agents installed a "mirror port" on Mailer's Internet account at his service provider's facility. The port allowed the government to learn the to/from addresses of Mailer's e-mail messages, the IP addresses of the Web sites that he visited, and the total volume of information sent to

or from his account. Mailer seeks suppression of this evidence, claiming the government's surveillance of his e-mail and Internet activity violated the Fourth Amendment. Has a "search" occurred?

10. John Sherman, director of security operations for Atlantic Bell Telephone Company, received a number of complaints from women alleging that Simon Sleaze (a former boyfriend of each) was making frequent obscene telephone calls to them. To verify these complaints, Sherman installed a pen register on Sleaze's landline residential telephone line. While such devices are routinely used to identify long distance calls for billing purposes, the device placed on Sleaze's line was set to record local numbers dialed as well. The pen register confirmed that he was in fact placing calls to the complainants, and pursuant to company policy, this information was turned over to the district attorney's office. Criminal charges have been brought against Sleaze, and he seeks to suppress the pen register evidence on Fourth Amendment grounds. Has a "search" occurred?

11. Melvin Skinner is prosecuted for drug smuggling based on a large amount of marijuana discovered in his motor home. Cell tower location data tracking his phone was used as the basis for the warrant to search the home. Skinner moves to suppress the evidence seized. What are his best arguments?

Explanations

1a. A search has occurred here because the officer physically entered the protected curtilage of the home in order to make her observations. Under the factors set forth in *United States v. Dunn*, 480 U.S. 294 (1987), the garden is in close proximity to the home, is within an enclosure surrounding the home (the fence), is used for intimate activities (the hot tub), and John has taken steps to protect the privacy of the area (erecting the stockade fence). The garden is an area so intimately tied to the home that it should be placed under its umbrella of protection as curtilage. See *United States v. Swepston*, 987 F.2d 1510 (10th Cir. 1993) (chicken shed in close proximity to house and enclosed by barbed wire fence). But see *Reeves v. Churchich*, 484 F.3d 1244 (10th Cir. 2007) (shared and unshielded area outside duplex was not curtilage). Moreover, as the trespass test has re-emerged in *United States v. Jones*, had the officer instead made her observations from a walkway or driveway that was a regular approach to the house and used by visitors, there would have been no reasonable expectation of privacy, and thus no search. See *United States v. French*, 291 F.3d 945 (7th Cir. 2002); *United States v. Beene*, 818 F.3d 157 (5th Cir. 2016) (defendant's driveway was not part of curtilage, and thus police were permitted to bring sniffer dog there to sniff his vehicle).

1b. No search has taken place here. While the setting remains the same as in example 1a, the vantage point from which the officer made her observations is now one to which the public has lawful (although not usual) access. On the reasoning of the aerial surveillance cases, *California v. Ciraolo* and *Florida v. Riley*, although John has protected against observations from the ground level, his property may be subjected to an aboveground view from a publicly accessible location without implicating the Fourth Amendment. A stepladder would not be regarded as an extraordinary enhancement device triggering the Amendment.

Thus, the observations made by the officer could be lawfully used to establish probable cause for the issuance of a search warrant to enter the premises and seize the plants. See Chapter 5. It must be emphasized, however, that the observation of contraband itself *does not* permit warrantless police entry into the curtilage. "Incontrovertible testimony of the senses that an incriminating object is on the premises belonging to a criminal suspect may establish the fullest possible measure of probable cause. But even where the object is contraband, this Court has repeatedly stated and enforced the basic rule that *the police may not enter and make a warrantless seizure.*" *Coolidge v. New Hampshire*, 403 U.S. 443, 468 (1971) (emphasis added). See also *United States v. Whaley*, 781 F.2d 417 (5th Cir. 1986) (holding unlawful sheriff's warrantless entry into curtilage and seizure of marijuana plants following his observation of plants from road); *State v. Nance*, 562 S.E.2d 557 (Ct. App. N.C. 2002) (officer's initial observation of emaciated horses from adjacent property and roadway was permissible, but entry onto defendant's land and seizure of horses violated Fourth Amendment). There is, in short, a material difference between *observing* contraband in the home or curtilage from a lawful vantage point (an act that is not a search) and *entering* those areas to seize the item after observing it.

1c. The officer's vantage point, although lawful, is one to which the public does not have general access. Does John have a reasonable expectation that his marijuana plants will be free from police observation when his neighbor can view them from a bedroom window? While the Supreme Court does not appear to have ruled directly on this question, its "assumption of risk" decisions would seem to place the officer's observations outside the scope of Fourth Amendment coverage. See, e.g., *United States v. Taborda*, 635 F.2d 131 (2d Cir. 1980) (unenhanced visual observations made by police from apartment across street from defendant's apartment was not a search); *People v. Saurini*, 607 N.Y.S.2d 518 (App. Div. N.Y. 1994) (observations from neighbor's yard with latter's consent); *Gates v. State*, 495 S.E.2d 113 (1997) (same). John has, in other words, assumed the risk that his neighbor would permit such an observation.

Even where officers trespass on the neighbor's property to make their observations of defendant's property, courts have concluded that no search has occurred. In *Sarantopoulos v. State*, 629 So. 2d 121 (Fla. 1993), despite the fact that the trespassing officers used a stepladder to peer into defendant's yard, the court reasoned that since the neighbor could have observed the plants from a stepladder or roof, this was a risk the defendant took. The trespass did not make the search illegal. A similar result was reached in *United States v. Fields*, 113 F.3d 313 (2d Cir. 1997), where officers stood in the side yard of a three-family apartment house and peered into a window whose shade was partially raised. No search was deemed to have occurred despite the trespass because the officers were in a location where other tenants were free to come and go. See also *People v. Claeys*, 118 Cal. Rptr. 2d 139 (Ct. App. Cal. 2002) (officer's observation of marijuana plants in defendant's backyard from neighbor's yard did not violate Fourth Amendment, even though officers did not obtain neighbor's permission to enter yard).

1d. No search has occurred because this wooded area would almost certainly be deemed beyond the protected curtilage of the home. See, e.g., *State v. Martwick*, 604 N.W.2d 552 (Wis. 2000) (marijuana plants located 75 feet from house in dense woods). *Oliver v. United States*, 466 U.S. 170 (1984) teaches that open fields are not entitled to Fourth Amendment protection, even when efforts at concealment are made. This is true even where the officer's conduct constitutes a common law trespass onto the property. See, e.g., *United States v. McKeever*, 5 F.3d 863 (5th Cir. 1993) (marijuana plants located in underbrush beyond cleared area behind building were not within curtilage and thus could be viewed by trespassing officers). Even where police used a backhoe to dig up large areas of the defendant's farm and found the body of a murder victim, the Supreme Court of Wisconsin held that the Fourth Amendment was not implicated. *Conrad v. State*, 218 N.W.2d 252 (Wis. 1974).

1e. The police may enter the open fields surrounding John's home and make observations without triggering the Fourth Amendment. Only if they intrude upon the curtilage of the home will the constitutional protections come into play. Given the distance between the home and the shed and the fact that the shed was not within an enclosure that surrounded the home, it is unlikely that it would be considered within the protected area. See *United States v. Dunn*, 480 U.S. 294 (1987) (officers permitted to make observations into barn not within curtilage of home). See also *United States v. Pennington*, 287 F.3d 739 (8th Cir. 2002) (plain-view observation into underground bunker located in open field); *United States v. Van Damme*, 48 F.3d 461 (9th Cir. 1995) (observations through doors of greenhouse located 200 feet from home); *United States v. Domitrovich*, 852 F. Supp. 1460 (E.D. Wash. 1994) (thermal imaging scan of lean-to located 50 feet from residence); *People v. Channing*, 97 Cal. Rptr. 2d 405 (Ct. App. Cal. 2000) (observation of marijuana under green tarp near defendant's trailer).

1f. Yes, a search has occurred. The critical distinction is between making observations from a lawful vantage (as in the open fields of the previous example) and entering the structure. *United States v. Dunn*, supra, assumed (without having to decide) that a barn located in an open field and used by the property owner for business purposes was entitled to Fourth Amendment protection against warrantless entry. Subsequent cases have so held. See *United States v. Pennington*, 287 F.3d 739 (8th Cir. 2002). John's shed, even if in an open field, could not be entered without triggering the Fourth Amendment. *United States v. Santa Maria*, 15 F.3d 879 (9th Cir. 1994) (entry into locked trailer outside curtilage).

1g. Because the listening device provided police with conversations that they would not otherwise have had access to, and the device is not in general public use, this would constitute a search as defined by *Kyllo v. United States*, 533 U.S. 27 (2001).

2. It must be determined whether Parrott had a constitutionally protected expectation that conversations within his apartment (a setting entitled to the highest degree of privacy protection) would be beyond the reach of the government's ear. His subjective expectation, standing alone, is not sufficient to invoke the protections of the Fourth Amendment. That expectation must be *reasonable*; i.e., one that society is willing to enforce. Among the considerations that courts have looked to in such situations is whether the person conducting the surveillance had a lawful right to be where he was. Thus, it has generally been held that an individual has no reasonable expectation of privacy in conversations that can be heard by the unaided ear of an eavesdropper who is lawfully in an adjoining apartment or hotel room. See, e.g., *United States v. Hessling*, 845 F.2d 617, 619 (6th Cir. 1988); *United States v. Agapito*, 620 F.2d 324, 330-332 (2d Cir. 1980); *United States v. Jackson*, 588 F.2d 1046, 1051-1052 (5th Cir. 1979); *United States v. Marlar*, 828 F. Supp. 415 (N.D. Miss. 1993) (canine sniff outside door of defendant's motel room). On this reasoning, Parrott has not been subjected to a search because the officer was lawfully in the crawl space by permission of the landlord.

   It can be argued, however, that there is a meaningful distinction between running the risk that someone may be listening at the wall of an occupied contiguous apartment and risking that someone would be listening from a crawl space closed to both public and tenants. The Supreme Judicial Court of Massachusetts relied on this distinction in ruling that *a search had occurred* under these circumstances within the meaning of the state constitution. *Commonwealth v. Panetti*, 406 Mass. 230, 547 N.E.2d 46 (1989). The court relied on a noted treatise that asserted that

"resort to the extraordinary step of positioning themselves where neither neighbors nor the general public would ordinarily be expected to
be" implicated the Fourth Amendment. 1 W. LaFave, Search and Seizure
2.3(1) at 392 (2d ed. 1987).

Another issue raised by this problem is the authority of the landlord
to agree to a search of the tenant's property. Third-party consent is discussed in §6.7.

3a. The place observed here is the interior of a residence, a setting embody-
ing the highest degree of privacy security. If, however, Thad (who failed
to close his curtains) conducted his activities in a manner that could be
seen by the unaided viewing of persons lawfully placed outside (including from the building across the street), then he is entitled to no Fourth
Amendment protection. But because the agents had to resort to enhancement by way of the telescope in order to observe intimate details of
Thad's conduct within his home, the Amendment is arguably implicated.
The Second Circuit held in a case on these facts that any enhanced viewing of the interior of a home impairs a legitimate expectation of privacy,
and that citizens need not protect against such enhanced surveillance
(e.g., by closing all curtains) in order to preserve that expectation. *United
States v. Taborda*, 635 F.2d 131 (2d Cir. 1980).

Query: Would the proscription against intrusions into the home
embodied in *Kyllo v. United States*, 533 U.S. 27 (2001), which is limited to
devices "not in general public use," exclude use of a telescope? Given
that Court's emphasis on the sanctity of the home, the answer is probably
negative.

3b. The setting for the observation has now changed from the interior of
the home to curtilage, an area afforded somewhat less protection against
intrusion. Although *Riley* and *Ciraolo* permitted naked-eye observation
of curtilage areas (even if enclosed) from lawful aerial vantage points,
the agents here used an enhancement device to obtain their view. Thad
would thus argue the Fourth Amendment should be applicable.

Where a surveillance camera was used to observe the open areas
of an industrial complex, however, the Court concluded that no search
had occurred. See *Dow Chemical v. United States*, 476 U.S. 227 (1986). Thad
would attempt to distinguish *Dow Chemical* on the ground that the setting there was considered an open field, an area not entitled to any
Fourth Amendment protection. Given that the matter observed by the
agents in our example—the growing of contraband—is not the kind
of intimate activity usually associated with the home, *Riley* suggests that
Thad may meet with little success. *Kitzmiller v. State*, 548 A.2d 140 (Md.
Ct. Spec. App. 1988), concluded that no search had occurred where an
officer, with the aid of binoculars, observed marijuana plants within the

curtilage of the defendant's home from a vantage point in a tree 40 feet above the ground. See also *Rook v. State*, 679 N.E.2d 997 (Ind. 1997).

The increasing use of footage from body cameras worn by police should not change the analysis in these cases as long as the officer is in a lawful vantage point. See discussion of the Plain View Doctrine, §6.8.

4. The Fourth Amendment does not protect against the seizure and examination of the contents of trash bags left at the curb. This is so because 1) public exposure of the trash forfeits any reasonable expectation of privacy in the bags; and 2) once the trash is conveyed to third-party collectors, the homeowner assumes the risk that they will turn the bags over to police. See *California v. Greenwood*, 486 U.S. 35 (1988).

In our example, however, the closed bags were left within the curtilage of the home, an area afforded greater protection than the curbside. Several courts have found this distinction to be determinative. See *Commonwealth v. Ousley*, 393 S.W.3d 15 (Ky. 2013); *State v. Rhodes*, 565 S.E.2d 266 (N.C. 2002). But compare *United States v. Redmon*, 138 F.3d 1109, 1112 (7th Cir. 1998) (no expectation of privacy with regard to trash left in curtilage where it is publicly accessible and left for collection); *United States v. Long*, 993 F. Supp. 816 (D. Kan. 1997) (no expectation of privacy with regard to trash left on trailer next to garage).

Another distinction between this example and *Greenwood* is that the police here reconstructed documents that had been ripped up by the homeowner. U.S. District Judge Joseph Tauro concluded that use of a shredding machine manifests an expectation of privacy, which overrides the presumption in *Greenwood* and was violated by the police action. See *United States v. Alan N. Scott*, 776 F. Supp. 629 (D. Mass. 1991):

> Here, defendant had taken steps to protect his privacy rights by shredding his trash. In *Greenwood* the Court stated that it was common knowledge that trash left on the curb is accessible to snoops and scavengers. But, it is not common knowledge that snoops and scavengers may retrieve shredded materials and then painstakingly reconstruct them to learn the contents. Society would accept as reasonable, therefore, defendant's belief that once he shredded his documents, they would be shielded from public examination.

On appeal, the First Circuit disagreed, holding that the defendant assumed the risk that through human ingenuity, the papers could be put back together. 975 F.2d 927 (1st Cir. 1992). See also *United States v. Hall*, 47 F.3d 1091 (11th Cir. 1995) (no reasonable expectation of privacy in shredded documents placed in garbage bag in closed dumpster).

5. Lyons clearly had a reasonable expectation of privacy in the contents of the locked locker. The question raised here is whether that expectation extends to the lock itself. Several courts have concluded that the insertion

of a key into a lock for the limited purpose of identifying its owner does not constitute a search. See *United States v. Salgado*, 250 F.3d 438 (6th Cir. 2001); *United States v. $109,179 in U.S. Currency*, 228 F.3d 1080 (9th Cir. 2002); *United States v. Lyons*, 898 F.2d 210, 213 (1st Cir. 1990) ("the insertion of a key into a lock, followed by the turning of its tumbler in order to determine the fit, is so minimally intrusive that it does not implicate a reasonable expectation of privacy").

U.S. District Judge Woodlock, in a dissenting opinion in *United States v. Lyons*, analogized the key insertion to *Arizona v. Hicks*, 480 U.S. 321 (1987) (discussed in §6.8), which held that a search occurred when officers lifted stereo components to reveal the serial numbers imprinted on the bottom. He concluded that the insertion of the key, like the lifting of the equipment, exposed enough information about the object to trigger the protections of the Fourth Amendment.

6. *United States v. Place*, 462 U.S. 696 (1983), held that the use of a drug-detection dog at a public airport to determine the presence of a contraband substance did not trigger the protections of the Fourth Amendment. *Place*, however, involved a sniff of the defendant's luggage. The dog in this example was used on the defendant's own person, in which case the nature of the intrusion was greater. In the case upon which this example is based, the Ninth Circuit Court of Appeals found this distinction determinative and concluded that a search occurred when the detection dog sniffed the defendant himself. See *B.C. v. Plumas Unified School District*, 192 F.3d 1260, 1266 (9th Cir. 1999); *United States v. Beale*, 736 F.2d 1289 (9th Cir. 1984). See also *United States v. Kelly*, 128 F. Supp. 2d 1021 (S.D. Tex. 2001). Compare *Illinois v. Caballes*, 543 U.S. 405 (2005) (no search where dog sniffed odors emanating from defendant's stopped vehicle); *United States v. Brock*, 417 F.3d 692 (7th Cir. 2005) (no search where dog sniffed the outside locked door of a residence bedroom because police had obtained consent from the suspect's housemate to enter common areas, and sniff could only detect presence of contraband without providing any information about lawful activity within the bedroom, which would entail a reasonable expectation of privacy).

Florida v. Jardines, 133 S. Ct. 1409 (2013), held that use of a drug-sniffing dog on the front porch to investigate a tip that marijuana was being grown inside the home was a trespassory intrusion of the curtilage that constituted a "search" triggering the Fourth Amendment. See also *United States v. Whitaker*, 820 F.3d 849 (7th Cir. 2016) (use of drug-sniffing dog to search hallway outside defendant's apartment invaded his reasonable expectation of privacy). Since *Jardines* is premised on a trespass rationale, the decision does not inhibit use of sniffer dogs during a traffic stop. *United States v. Winters*, 782 F.3d 289 (6th Cir. 2015).

7. Did David have an expectation of privacy that society (through the courts) recognizes as reasonable with regard to his loan application? Because he had voluntarily submitted it to the bank, the case appears to fall within the assumption of risk doctrine. In *United States v. Miller*, 425 U.S. 435 (1976), an account depositor was held to have incurred the risk that information concerning his financial transactions would be revealed by his bank to the government. David in effect forfeited his expectation of privacy in the application when he submitted it to the bank and thus has no Fourth Amendment protection. See *United States v. Grubb*, 469 F. Supp. 991 (E.D. Pa. 1979).

   Recognizing the central role that banks play in our society and the reality that a customer's disclosure of information to a bank is not entirely volitional, several state courts have found a legitimate expectation of privacy in bank records under their own constitutions. See *A.G. Edwards, Inc. v. Secretary of State*, 772 N.E.2d 362 (Ill. 2002); *Charnes v. DiGiacomo*, 612 P.2d 1117 (Colo. 1980); *Commonwealth v. Dejohn*, 403 A.2d 1283 (Pa. 1979) (*Miller* "opens the door to a vast and unlimited range of very real abuses of police power"); *Burrows v. Superior Court*, 118 Cal. Rptr. 166, 169, 529 P.2d 590, 593 (1974) ("the customer of a bank expects that the documents, such as checks, which he transmits to the bank in the course of his business operations, will remain private," and such expectation is reasonable). See also *People v. Blair*, 159 Cal. Rptr. 818, 825, 602 P.2d 738, 745 (Cal. Sup. Ct. 1979) (credit card company's disclosure of defendant's account statement to prosecutor constituted a search under California law: "A person who uses a credit card may reveal his habits, his opinions, his tastes, and political views, as well as his movements and financial affairs. No less than a bank statement, the charges made on a credit card may provide a virtual current biography of an individual.").

   Several federal and state statutes protect financial records in certain contexts. See, e.g., Right to Financial Privacy Act, 12 U.S.C. §3402 (adopted in response to *United States v. Miller*).

8. Because the information placed on the outside of envelopes is voluntarily exposed by the sender to postal workers (and others) in the ordinary course of business, the investigative mail cover has been placed in the "assumption of risk" category and held not to constitute a search for Fourth Amendment purposes. See *United States v. Hinton*, 222 F.3d 664 (9th Cir. 2000); *United States v. Choate*, 576 F.2d 165 (9th Cir. 1978); *United States v. Leonard*, 524 F.2d 1076 (2d Cir. 1975). Like the pen register in *Smith v. Maryland*, 442 U.S. 735 (1979), the mail cover records information disclosed to the carrier and thus invades no reasonable expectation of privacy.

   Interception of the *contents* of mail or telephone conversations, of course, would be beyond the scope of the public exposure doctrine and thus constitute a search. If, however, a participant in the conversation discloses it to the government, under the "misplaced reliance" cases (*Hoffa v. United States* and *United States v. White*), the Fourth Amendment is not implicated.

Similarly, license plate numbers that are exposed to the public are not protected under the Fourth Amendment because there is no subjective expectation of privacy in license plates, and even if there is, it is not one that society is prepared to recognize as reasonable. See *United States. v. Diaz-Castaneda*, 494 F.3d 1146 (9th Cir. 2007).

9. The constitutionality of computer searches that reveal the to/from addresses of e-mail messages and the IP addresses of Web sites visited has not been determined by the Supreme Court. However, in *United States v. Forrester*, 512 F.3d 500 (9th Cir. 2008), the Ninth Circuit held that a "mirror port" similar to the one described in this example did not constitute a "search" under the Fourth Amendment and thus was not unconstitutional. Making the comparison to the pen register in *Smith v. Maryland*, the court reasoned that e-mail and Internet users have no expectation of privacy in the addresses of their messages or the IP addresses of the Web sites that they visit because they should know that this information is provided to and used by Internet service providers for the specific purpose of routing of information. Furthermore, also like *Smith v. Maryland*, the court held that e-mail to/from addresses and IP addresses do not reveal any more about the contents of communication than do phone numbers. IP addresses, like certain phone numbers, may indicate the underlying contents of communications, but the court in *Smith* and *Katz* drew a line between "unprotected addressing information and protected content information."

The court in *Forrester* also compared the surveillance of e-mail messages to government surveillance of physical mail. The Supreme Court has ruled that the government cannot search sealed mail, but they can observe whatever information is on the outside of the mail because that information is voluntarily transferred to third parties. See *United States v. Jacobsen*, 466 U.S. 109 (1984). The to/from content of the e-mail addresses is an outside, visible address and is, therefore, not protected by the Fourth Amendment.

10. This problem raises both issues regarding Fourth Amendment applicability: Has a search occurred? If so, was it governmental or private in nature?

Regarding the latter, if Sherman is employed by a private utility company and acted without any request or encouragement from a governmental actor, then the placement of the pen register is outside the scope of the Fourth Amendment. If, on the other hand, the district attorney had requested that the dialing information be gathered by the company, either in this particular case or generally whenever a complaint is made, that would constitute sufficient governmental involvement to trigger the Fourth Amendment. Something in between, such as the district attorney's longstanding policy of accepting pen register information from the phone company, may constitute acquiescence in the private search and thus convert it to governmental conduct. In this latter situation, the court would look to the company's motivation in collecting the information.

If it were determined that the phone company had been motivated primarily by a desire to investigate criminal law violations in aid of the police, and not by an independent business purpose (such as protecting harassed customers), that would point to a conclusion that the conduct implicated the Fourth Amendment. Compare *United States v. Cleaveland*, 38 F.3d 1092 (9th Cir. 1994) (electric company examined defendant's meter to recover its financial loss for stolen power) and *United States v. Pervaz*, 118 F.3d 1 (1st Cir. 1997) (Cellular One employees tracked cloned cell phone primarily to protect its customers) with *United States v. Walther*, 652 F.2d 788 (9th Cir. 1981) (action of airline employee in opening "Speed Pak" was that of a government agent because only reason he opened case was his suspicion that it contained illegal drugs, and employee, who at one time had been a listed informant, expected a reward from Drug Enforcement Administration). See also *United States v. Feffer*, 831 F.2d 734 (7th Cir. 1987); *United States v. Koenig*, 856 F.2d 843 (7th Cir. 1988).

Assuming that there is state action, the second question is whether a "search" has occurred, which translates into whether Sleaze had a reasonable expectation of privacy in the numbers dialed from his residential telephone. Because using the telephone automatically discloses to the phone company the numbers dialed (for billing purposes), *Smith v. Maryland* placed the pen register outside the scope of Fourth Amendment protection. The Court has consistently held that the Amendment does not apply to information conveyed by A to B when B reveals it to the government, even if is conveyed by A on the assumption that it will remain private. A assumes the risk that B will spill the beans. More recently, Justice Sotomayor (in her concurrence in *United States v. Jones*), has warned that this third-party disclosure rational threatens the privacy of so much intimate information in the digital age.

A number of state courts have disagreed with *Smith v. Maryland* and held that use of the pen register in the manner set out in this example does constitute a search within their own constitutions. The New Jersey Supreme Court reasoned that the telephone user's disclosure to the company of numbers dialed is necessitated by the nature of the instrumentality, and the disclosure is made for a limited business purpose. *State v. Hunt*, 450 A.2d 952, 956 (N.J. 1982). See also *People v. Mason*,

989 P.2d 757 (Colo. 1999); *Richardson v. State*, 865 S.W. 2d 944 (Tex. 1993); *Commonwealth v. Melilli*, 555 A.2d 1254 (Pa. 1989). If Sleaze is prosecuted in one of these states, he has a basis to seek suppression of the evidence. Moreover, 18 U.S.C. §3121 prohibits installation of a pen register without a court order except in certain situations involving the protection of the user or provider, or in connection with a foreign intelligence investigation (see Chapter 12).

It must be remembered that applicability of the Fourth Amendment is just the threshold stage of legal analysis of any search and seizure problem. The fact that a search has occurred means that the Fourth Amendment applies. Whether the Amendment's provisions have been violated is the question to which we turn our attention in the chapters that follow.

11. This case raises expectation of privacy issues regarding both third-party disclosure, as in *Smith v. Maryland*, as well as public exposure as in *Knotts* and *Jones*. In the case upon which this problem is loosely based, *U.S. v. Skinner*, 690 F.3d 772 (6th Cir. 2010), the court utilized both analyses to conclude: 1) that Skinner had forfeited his expectation of privacy in his location by voluntarily conveying signals to the third-party provider; and 2) because the cell-site data merely provided police with information they could have visually observed on a public highway. *Jones* was distinguished because there was no secretive placing of a tracking device, and thus no trespass, and because there was no long-term tracking of his whereabouts. This result is overturned by *Carpenter v. United States*, 138 S. Ct. 2206 (2018), holding such surveillance implicates the Fourth Amendment warrant requirement.

What Does the Fourth Amendment Require? — The Doctrine of Justification

Once it is determined that the Fourth Amendment applies in a particular situation (see Chapter 3), the question arises as to what it requires. The fundamental premise underlying the Fourth Amendment is that the police must have justification (or cause) *before* they conduct a search or seizure. The fact that they find contraband or evidence of crime is not sufficient to justify a search *after* the fact. Determination of the requisite level of cause necessary to justify a search or seizure represents an effort to balance the interest of effective law enforcement, on the one hand, and individual liberty on the other. The nature of the constraint placed on the police by the Amendment will depend in large part on how much (or how little) information they are required to possess about the suspect before they engage in intrusive action.

Although probable cause is the only standard of justification explicitly mentioned in the Fourth Amendment,[1] the courts have invoked the reasonableness clause to craft modifications to fit different types of police action. As we will see, the requisite justification has generally been tied to the scope and degree of intrusion: the greater the invasion of privacy, the more cause that must be demonstrated. On the sliding scale, "probable cause" and "reasonable suspicion" represent the two descending benchmarks. Another form of justification has evolved in the so-called administrative search area,

---

1. While the only textual reference to "probable cause" appears in the warrant clause of the Amendment, that same standard has been held to apply to warrantless searches and seizures as well. The Supreme Court has recognized that setting a lower standard for warrantless searches would create an incentive for police to avoid the warrant process, a result the Court has generally sought to avoid. See *Wong Sun v. United States*, 371 U.S. 471, 479-480 (1963).

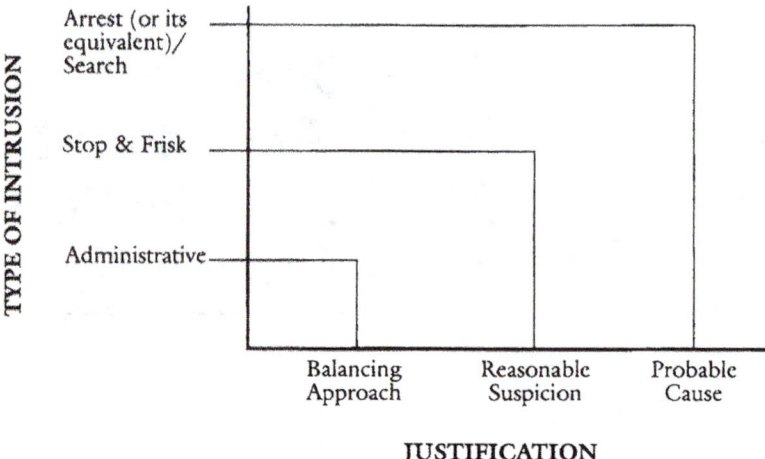

Figure 4-1. Standards of Justification—Summary

where a balancing test is used to weigh the importance of the societal interest served against the interference with individual privacy to determine the appropriate level of justification. (See Figure 4-1.)

§4.1 PROBABLE CAUSE—THE STANDARD FOR SEARCH AND ARREST

Probable cause is the measure of justification that applies to full-scale intrusions—searches, seizures, and arrests. When the police act by way of a warrant, the determination of whether probable cause exists is made by a magistrate prior to the proposed action (see Chapter 5). When the police act without a warrant (as they are permitted to do in certain situations, see Chapter 6), they themselves make the initial evaluation of probable cause; but that determination is reviewable in court after the search on a motion to suppress the evidence discovered.

Probable cause is defined as that quantity of facts and circumstances within the police officer's knowledge that would warrant a reasonable person to conclude that the individual in question has committed a crime (in the case of an arrest) or that specific items related to criminal activity will be found at the particular place (in the case of a search). The information may include reasonably trustworthy hearsay, as well as the officer's own personal observations. An adequate showing of probable cause requires specific and concrete facts, not merely conclusory speculations. On a scale of probability, probable cause is something more than just hunch or suspicion, but considerably less than proof beyond a reasonable doubt. As Justice Hugo Black once put it: "Of course it would strengthen the probable-cause presentation if eyewitnesses could testify that they saw the defendant commit the crime but nothing in our Constitution requires that the facts be established with that degree of certainty." *Spinelli v. United States*, 393 U.S. 410, 429 (1969) (Black, J., dissenting).

The Court has emphasized that probable cause is "a fluid concept" that is "not readily, or even usefully, reduced to a neat set of legal rules." It "requires only a probability or substantial chance of criminal activity, not an actual showing of such activity." Probable cause "is not a high bar." *District of Columbia v. Wesby*, 138 S. Ct. 577, 586 (2018).

As noted above, somewhat different showings are required for arrest and search situations. The implications of this difference can be seen in the so-called staleness problem with regard to search warrants. Because items relating to crime are often readily transportable, probable cause to search must include a likelihood that the items sought are *presently* at the place to be searched. Timeliness of the information relied upon by police is more important there than in the context of an arrest, where probable cause (to believe the suspect committed a crime) generally does not dissipate with time.

The Supreme Court has emphasized that "the central teaching of our decisions bearing on the probable cause standard is that it is a practical, nontechnical conception. In dealing with probable cause, as the very name implies, we deal with probabilities. These are not technical; they are the factual and practical considerations of everyday life on which reasonable and prudent men, not legal technicians, act." *Illinois v. Gates*, 462 U.S. 213, 231 (1983). As a "fluid concept — turning on the assessment of probabilities in particular factual contexts — [probable cause is] not readily, or even usefully, reduced to a neat set of legal rules." *Id.* The concept of probable cause is designed to protect citizens from "rash and unreasonable interferences with privacy and from unfounded charges of crime, while giving fair leeway for enforcing the law in the community's protection." *Maryland v. Pringle*, 540 U.S. 366, 370 (2003).

The "fair probability" and non-technical nature of probable cause is illustrated by *Florida v. Harris*, 133 S. Ct. 1050 (2013). The Florida Supreme Court ruled in favor of the motorist who had moved to suppress evidence resulting from a narcotics dog's alert, insisting that the dog's field performance records and other specific checklist documentation of reliability be produced to establish probable cause. The Supreme Court reversed, characterizing the Florida court's strict evidentiary requirements inconsistent with the "flexible common-sense standard" of *Gates*. Evidence of the dog's satisfactory performance in a certification or training program can itself suffice.

How specifically must the information point to the subject of the search or arrest? In *Pringle*, the police officer searched a car and found $763 in rolled-up cash in the glove compartment and five glassine bags of cocaine between the back-seat armrest and the back seat. All three occupants denied ownership of the items and were arrested. Pringle, the passenger in the front seat, argued there was insufficient cause to connect him with the contraband, and the state court of appeals agreed. The U.S. Supreme Court reversed, concluding that there *was* probable cause to arrest all three because a reasonable inference could be made that *any or all* had knowledge of and control over the cocaine. Probable cause is not "undercut or avoided by simply pointing to the fact that coincidentally there exists probable cause to search or seize another." 540 U.S. at 373.

When weighing the adequacy of probable cause in a given case, courts focus on the source of the information in the possession of the police, as well as the conclusions that may be reasonably drawn from it. If the information is based on the officer's own observations, credibility is usually presumed. If, however, the officer has obtained information from a third party, the reliability of that source must be weighed together with the accuracy of the inferences drawn. While courts tend to credit information conveyed by named victims or witnesses, the credibility of unnamed informants (a frequent source of probable cause) cannot be presumed, but must instead be demonstrated.

In *Aguilar v. Texas*, 378 U.S. 108 (1964) and *Spinelli v. United States*, 393 U.S. 410 (1969), the Supreme Court established a structure for evaluating probable cause based on information supplied by confidential informants. The two-pronged test focuses separately on the credibility of the informant (Why should the police believe this person?) and the basis of her knowledge (How does the informant know what she claims to know?). The information supporting each prong must be sufficiently specific so that the conclusions reached can be meaningfully evaluated by a court. A mere conclusory assertion by the officer that "the informant is credible" will not suffice; rather, the basis for that conclusion must be set out—e.g., "This informant has provided reliable information on previous occasions, which led to the arrest and conviction of John Doe and Richard Roe." Similarly, the statement that the "informant has advised me that narcotics are being sold at this address" will not satisfy the knowledge prong. The facts underlying the informant's assertion must be articulated—e.g., "The informant states that she purchased narcotics at this address earlier today." Where the informant speaks from her own personal knowledge, courts have generally credited the information. See *United States v. Nordby*, 156 F.3d 1240 (9th Cir. 1998).

Case law has developed a variety of alternative methods to fulfill the *Aguilar/Spinelli* test. The knowledge prong may be satisfied by setting out detailed information supplied by the informant from which it may reasonably be inferred that she is speaking from personal knowledge and not mere rumor or conjecture. See *Draper v. United States*, 358 U.S. 307 (1959). The credibility prong may be demonstrated where the informant implicates herself in criminal activity, on the premise that such admission against self-interest carries some assurance of reliability.[2] Independent corroboration by police of specific facts asserted by the informant can be a factor in satisfying either prong (although verification of innocent details is obviously less significant than facts involving criminal activity). See *Draper*, supra. The corroboration must be sufficient to "permit the suspicions engendered by the informer's tip to ripen into a judgment that a crime was probably being committed." *Spinelli*, supra, 393 U.S. at 418.

The traditional two-pronged analysis of probable cause based on informant information was modified by the Supreme Court in *Illinois v. Gates*, 462 U.S. 213 (1983). While reaffirming the importance of evaluating both the informant's credibility and basis of knowledge, the Court abandoned the insistence that the prongs be considered as completely distinct elements. It substituted a "totality-of-the-circumstances" approach that looks at the overall reliability of a tip, and in which a deficiency in one of the prongs may be compensated for by a strong showing on the other, or by some other indicia of reliability. Where, for example, "a particular informant is known for the unusual reliability of his predictions of certain types of criminal activities in a locality, his failure, in a particular case, to thoroughly set forth the basis of his knowledge surely should not serve as an absolute bar to a finding of probable cause based on his tip." 462 U.S. at 233. A tip from an informant whose past reliability could not be determined might similarly be deemed adequate if the information was sufficiently detailed to justify the inference that she was speaking from personal knowledge of the circumstances.

Gates thus replaced an approach to probable cause that it considered "an excessively technical dissection of informants' tips" with an analysis that "permits a balanced assessment of the relative weights of all the various indicia of reliability (and unreliability) attending an informant's tip." 462 U.S. at 234. The revised standard asks whether there is a "fair probability that contraband or evidence of a crime will be found in a particular place." 462 U.S. at 238. This change was prompted in part by the Court's concern that rigorous application of the *Aguilar/Spinelli* approach would prevent the police from relying on anonymous tips. "Such tips, particularly when supplemented by independent police investigation, frequently contribute to the solution of otherwise perfect crimes." 462 U.S. at 237-238.

---

2. *United States v. Harris*, 403 U.S. 573, 583 (1971) ("Common sense in the important daily affairs of life would induce a prudent and disinterested observer to credit these statements. People do not lightly admit a crime and place critical evidence in the hands of the police in the form of their own admissions. Admissions of crime carry their own indicia of credibility."). See, e.g., *United States v. Black*, 8 Fed. Appx. 408 (6th Cir. 2001). Where it appears, however, that the informer is implicating herself to curry favor with the police to work out a deal, courts have discounted the weight of self-implication. See *State v. Ward*, 580 N.W.2d 67 (Minn. App. 1998).

Despite *Gates*, the *Aguilar/Spinelli* test retains some importance. First, it delineates the two fundamental factors — reliability and basis of knowledge — to be considered in weighing informant information under the new totality-of-circumstances analysis. Second, several states have adhered to the traditional two-pronged test in interpreting their own constitutional provisions regarding search and seizure. See, e.g., *Commonwealth v. Pinto*, 476 Mass. 361, 67 N.E.3d 713 (2017) (reasonable suspicion); *Hart v. State*, 397 P.3d 342 (Alaska Ct. App. 2017); *State v. Atchley*, 142 Wash. App. 147, 173 P.3d 323 (Wash. Ct. App. 2007) (probable cause to search). See generally Shirley S. Abrahamson, *State Constitutional Law, New Judicial Federalism, and the Rehnquist Court*, 51 Clev. St. L. Rev. 339, 343 (2004).

It should be noted that where an officer has probable cause justifying a particular intrusion, the fact that the officer may have acted for ulterior reasons is irrelevant. Where, for example, a narcotics detective stops a car for a traffic violation, but his *actual motivation* is to search for drugs, the legality of the search is determined solely by the existence of probable cause for the stop. See *Whren v. United States*, 517 U.S. 806 (1996) and *Arkansas v. Sullivan*, 532 U.S. 769 (2001), discussed in §6.9.

Examples

The Basics

1. Officer Peters has concluded, based on intuition developed over 30 years of experience, that cocaine is being sold out of Apt. 3 at 10 Main Street. Does he have probable cause to search?

2. Officer Peters, while acting undercover, observed a white powdery substance on the kitchen table in Apt. 3 at 10 Main Street. He further observed several persons sniffing this powder and appearing to get high. They paid large amounts of cash to the tenant in return for plastic bags of the powder. Based on his firsthand observations, as well as his long experience with narcotics, Officer Peters has concluded that the substance is cocaine. Does he have probable cause to arrest the participants and seize the powder?

3. The police assert that they have received reliable information from a credible person and believe that narcotics are being stored at Apt. 7 at 4 Central Street. Do they have probable cause to search?

4. An informant reported to the police that one Fred Fraper, traveling from Chicago, would arrive at the Denver train station on either September 8 or 9 carrying a tan zipper bag that would contain heroin. The informant, who had previously provided accurate and reliable information to the police regarding narcotics, presented a detailed physical description of Fraper and the clothing that he would be wearing and reported that he

would be walking very fast. Police officers staked out the train station, and on September 9, they observed a man precisely fitting that description disembark a Chicago train and proceed to walk quickly toward an exit. Is there probable cause to arrest?

5. FBI agents have observed one Pete Pinelli, who is "known to" law enforcement officers as a bookmaker, entering and leaving a particular apartment over the course of five days. A "reliable" informant told the agents that Pinelli is operating a bookmaking business at the apartment by use of two telephones inside. A check with the telephone company revealed that the apartment does have two telephones installed. Do the police have probable cause to search the apartment?

6. The Chicago Police Department received an anonymous handwritten letter stating that Sue and Lance Bates, who live in the Greenway condominiums, were making their living selling narcotics. The letter detailed the usual manner in which the operation was carried out. Lance would typically fly to Miami, where he would purchase the drugs. Sue would drive their Volvo down and meet him. Lance would then drive the car home with the narcotics in the trunk, and Sue would return home by plane. The letter asserted that Sue would be driving to Miami again on May 3, that Lance would fly down some days later, and that he would promptly return by car with over $100,000 worth of drugs. The writer also stated that there were drugs worth a similar amount in the Bates' basement.

   Subsequent police investigation confirmed the Bates' address and revealed that Lance Bates had a reservation to fly to Miami on May 5. Arrangements were made for surveillance, and he was observed boarding the flight, arriving in Florida, proceeding to a hotel, and departing the following morning in the Volvo traveling north.

   Do the police have probable cause to search the Bates' car? Their condominium? Do the police have probable cause to arrest Lance?

The Plot Thickens

7. Officers of the Yarmouth Police Department executed a search warrant for a motel room occupied by one Kevin Karp and discovered several items belonging to persons whose homes had recently been burglarized. Later that day, one of the officers received a call from an anonymous female who told him there was a motor home full of stolen goods parked in front of George Grape's house. The caller described items that she had seen that matched some of those taken in the prior burglaries. She added that Grape was about to move the motor home because he said the police were getting much too close, and that he referred to the raid on Karp's motel room, indicating that Karp was his "supplier."

The informant refused to identify herself because she said she feared Grape would kill her, but she finally acknowledged that she was Grape's former girlfriend, Lynn Lotus. She told the officer that they had recently broken up and that she wanted to "burn him real bad."

The officer, after verifying that a motor home was parked at the address stated by the caller, applied for a warrant to search it for stolen goods. Is there probable cause to search the motor home?

8. Police received a tip from a confidential source who had provided information in the past that resulted in several indictments. The informant stated that Raymond Frank and a person named Mike were importing narcotics using a furniture company as a cover. The source indicated that Mike lived in Concord, California. Using telephone toll records, the police determined that Frank spoke frequently with a Michael Best, who resided in a town near Concord. A second, unrelated snitch was asked what she knew about Michael Best. She advised police that Best and a partner were dealing narcotics "in a big way." She further stated that the narcotics were coming through the port of San Francisco. Checking cargo records, police discovered that two shipments of furniture from Colombia had arrived at the port within the past six weeks, and that Raymond Frank had signed for them and trucked them away.

Police learned that another shipment of furniture from Colombia was due on June 1. Surveillance was established at the docks. When the shipment arrived, it passed through a routine customs inspection. Raymond Frank was later observed loading the shipment into his truck and departing. Frank drove to a warehouse in Concord, where he met with two other persons unknown to the police.

Do the police have probable cause to search the truck for narcotics?

The Ingredients in the Probable Cause Recipe

9. Detective Casey received an anonymous telephone call asserting that Sammy Shay was dealing narcotics to students at the local high school. Casey made several observations of Shay on school grounds, but was unable to confirm that he was involved in illegal activity. The detective decided to check whether Shay had any prior criminal record and learned that he had four convictions for narcotics offenses (one on school premises) within the past eight years. Does Casey now have probable cause to arrest Shay when she observes him at the school?

10. While on routine patrol, two plainclothes officers observed several men standing on a street corner. On a hunch that a narcotics transaction was taking place, the officers approached the men and yelled at them to freeze. They immediately fled, and the officers gave chase. Is there probable cause to arrest?

11. Janice Dow was standing on a street corner in Manhattan known to police as "cocaine alley." Officers observed her from their cruiser at 12:30 A.M. In the next 50 minutes, they observed her conversing separately with six persons in very short conversations. Based on their long experience in the narcotics bureau and their knowledge of this area of the city, the officers concluded that Dow was dealing drugs. Does their conclusion constitute probable cause to arrest?

12. A clerk at a convenience store telephoned police and reported that a man with a small handgun protruding from his rear pocket had just left the store and departed in a gray pickup truck with license plate 32HTN. The clerk did not indicate that the man had engaged in any criminal or suspicious conduct. Officers have spotted the vehicle. Do they have probable cause to arrest for illegal possession of a handgun or to search the vehicle for the weapon?

13. A 12-year police veteran was driving an unmarked police vehicle and pulled behind a car with two occupants. He immediately observed a man, with money in his hand, approach the driver's window. After a brief conversation, the man handed the money to the driver and the driver appeared to place an unidentified "small object" in the man's hand. Based on his experience, the officer believed he had witnessed a drug transaction and followed the car. Is there probable cause to arrest the driver and to search the vehicle incident to arrest?

14. Officer Jones lawfully stopped Bobby Boot for speeding. As Jones approached the car, he noticed that there was an open beer can in the cup holder and that Boot was shaking and breathing rapidly. When Jones asked Boot if he could search the car and Boot refused, the officer deployed Pepper, his trusted police dog. Pepper conducted a sniff of the vehicle and alerted the officer to drugs in the trunk. Jones opened the trunk and found 200 pseudoephedrine pills in a gym bag. Was there probable cause to search the trunk?

Here Today, Gone Tomorrow/Here Tomorrow, but Not Today

15. On June 13, Detective Holmes received information from a source (who had provided reliable information on three prior occasions) that Alfred Red had just hijacked a shipment of cell phones. The informant indicated that he had observed the loot being stored in Red's Plymouth Voyager van, awaiting transfer to a "fence." Holmes confirmed that such a hijacking had taken place and learned further that Red had been suspected in several other hijackings. The police proceeded to Red's residence but were unable to find him or his Voyager. Two weeks later, Red's Voyager is observed parked outside his home. Do the police have probable cause to search the van?

16. Federal agents received reliable information that Richard Shale was engaged in the sale of child pornography. They were further told that a shipment of obscene photographs had been mailed to Shale's residence from a distributor in Canada. Postal authorities confirmed that a package from Canada addressed to Shale was en route and would be delivered in the normal course in two days. The agents, fearful that if they waited until delivery of the package to seek a warrant, the materials would be moved by the time they obtained one, have applied now for a warrant to search Shale's home in two days. May such a warrant be issued?

Explanations

The Basics

1. The answer, of course, is no. The most basic rule regarding probable cause is that there must be concrete facts and circumstances known to the officer that can be articulated (either to a magistrate in an application for a warrant prior to search or arrest, as discussed in Chapter 5, or to a judge reviewing the search or arrest after it occurs) and measured against an objective standard: Would a reasonable person knowing those facts reach the same conclusion? Unless the specific facts are there, probable cause is absent.

Police action grounded on hunch or suspicion is precisely what the Fourth Amendment forbids. As Chief Justice Warren put it: "The demand for specificity in the information upon which police action is predicated is the central teaching of this Court's Fourth Amendment jurisprudence." *Terry v. Ohio*, 392 U.S. 1, 21 n.18 (1968). More recently, Justice Breyer (joined by Justices Stevens, O'Connor, and Souter) criticized a "fill-in-the-blanks" request for a warrant because "nowhere does it indicate how Detective Woodson knows, or why he believes, that Overton committed the crime." *Overton v. Ohio*, 534 U.S. 982 (2001) (statement respecting denial of petition for writ of certiorari).

2. Unlike example 1, the facts and circumstances leading to the officer's conclusion are set out and thus subject to meaningful review. Moreover, because the source of information is the officer himself, no problem of credibility is raised (as there is whenever an unnamed informant is used). Additionally, in the assessment of probable cause, the courts grant some deference to the police officer's experience and expertise. As Chief Justice Burger wrote: "A trained officer draws inferences and makes deductions—inferences and deductions that might well elude an untrained person. Thus when used by trained law enforcement officers, objective facts, meaningless to the untrained, can be combined with permissible deductions from such facts to form a legitimate basis for

suspicion of a particular person and for action on that suspicion." *United States v. Cortez*, 449 U.S. 411, 412 (1981).

In all probability, a court would find that Officer Peters's conclusion was reasonable and that he has demonstrated probable cause.

3. Unlike example 2, the source of the information here is not a police officer, but an unnamed third party. While probable cause may properly be based on such hearsay information, the showing here falls short on two counts. There are no facts set out to support the assertion that the informant is reliable and credible. Similarly absent are underlying facts or circumstances to support the conclusion that narcotics are on the premises. We are given no information concerning the source of the informant's knowledge, and thus we do not know whether she has seen the narcotics or is merely repeating rumors or other secondhand information. Thus, there is no concrete basis upon which a reasonable person would conclude that narcotics were on the premises to be searched. See *Aguilar v. Texas*, 378 U.S. 108 (1964); *Spinelli v. United States*, 393 U.S. 410 (1969).

    An informant's face-to-face tip to officers may be viewed as more reliable than a telephone tip, as the officer has the better opportunity to assess the in-person informant's credibility and demeanor. And a tip about a neighbor or someone close to the informant may also enhance its credibility, as there is the risk of retaliation. See *United States v. Valentine*, 232 F.3d 350, 354 (3d Cir. 2000).

4. Probable cause to arrest exists where the facts and circumstances within the officer's knowledge and of which she has fairly trustworthy information are sufficient to warrant a person of reasonable caution to believe that an offense has been or is being committed. The problem in this example is that while there is a basis (although somewhat conclusory) set out for believing in the reliability of the informant (his previous accurate information), there is no factual basis for evaluating the accuracy of his conclusion that Fraper would be carrying heroin.

    Nonetheless, the Supreme Court ruled on similar facts in *Draper v. United States*, 358 U.S. 307 (1959), that probable cause to arrest existed because the deficiencies in the information known to the police were overcome by the detailed nature of the informant's report, as well as the verification of those details by police observations at the train station. The Court reasoned that "with every other bit of information being thus personally verified, [the police] had reasonable grounds to believe that the remaining, unverified bit of information—that Draper would have heroin with him—was likewise true." The *Draper* view that independent police verification of facts supplied by the informant can salvage an otherwise inadequate showing of cause has become an important component of contemporary probable cause analysis. As we will see, however, where the corroboration is of innocent or nonsuspicious details, courts are less likely to credit the informant's conclusions.

In *State v. Kant*, 382 Mont. 239, 367 P.3d 726 (2016), the search warrant for defendant's home (where marijuana plants and drug paraphernalia were found) was reviewed favorably under the *Illinois v. Gates* standard. Although no information pointed to the previous reliability of the informant, he was "known to law enforcement," and the detective independently corroborated the phone numbers, addresses, and vehicle registrations the informant provided. The court found further support in the fact that the informant had made admissions against his own interest. See also *Commonwealth v. Tapia*, 463 Mass. 721, 978 N.E.2d 534 (2012) (sufficient nexus between defendant's drug-selling activities and her apartment was established by previously reliable informant's tip that he had overheard defendant say she needed to procure drugs for sale at her apartment, and police observations tracking her from controlled buys back to her apartment).

5. The bald conclusory assertion that Pinelli is "known as" a bookmaker is entitled to only little weight without facts to support it. While the reputation of the subject among law enforcement persons may be weighed in the probable cause determination, specific facts must be set out to support it. See *United States v. Harris*, 403 U.S. 573, 581-582 (1971). Moreover, the fact that Pinelli has been observed by police frequenting a particular apartment that contains two telephones is as consistent with innocent behavior as it is with criminal behavior and is insufficient to justify a reasonable person concluding that evidence of a crime will be found on the premises.

If probable cause exists here, it must therefore be premised on the informant's tip. Measured against the two-pronged test, the tip is insufficient. First, there is no underlying factual support for the assertion that the informant is reliable. Second, there is no indication of how the informant knew that Pinelli was running a bookmaking operation. Did the informant herself place a bet with Pinelli (as in *Harris*, where the informant purchased liquor from the defendant), or is she relying on third-party sources? Nor does the tip describe the subject's activities in sufficient detail so that it may reasonably be inferred that the informant is speaking from firsthand knowledge, as was the case in *Draper*.

Finally, while the police investigation corroborated the informant's tip regarding Pinelli's connection to the apartment, as well as the presence of two telephones there, verification of those innocent facts falls short of the considerable detail confirmed by police in *Draper*. The Court so held in *Spinelli v. United States*, 393 U.S. 410 (1969), the case on which this example is based.

In *Elliott v. State*, 417 Md. 413, 10 A.3d 761 (Ct. App. Md. 2010), probable cause for arrest was found lacking despite the previously reliable informant's detailed tip that a man named Winston would be arriving at a shopping center with a large quantity of marijuana. Some of the details were found to be inaccurate, and the officers failed to corroborate others.

6. Application of the traditional two-pronged test to measure probable cause based on the tip would probably require a negative answer to each question. Under that analysis, we start with the tip itself; if deficiencies are found, we then look to whether the results of the police investigation "would permit the suspicions engendered by the informant's report to ripen into a judgment that a crime was probably being committed." *Spinelli*, supra, 393 U.S. at 418. The letter here fails to establish that: 1) there is a factual basis for believing the informer is credible and reliable; and 2) there is a factual basis for crediting the informant's conclusion that the subjects were dealing narcotics. It can be argued that the detailed nature of the tip, together with the police corroboration of those details, satisfy the second prong. The problem is that, given the anonymous nature of the letter, there remains no basis for satisfying the credibility prong. There is simply no indication (such as the provision of accurate information on prior occasions, as in *Draper*) as to why the police should believe the informant.

With the abandonment of strict adherence to the two-pronged analysis and substitution of a totality-of-circumstances approach, a different result may be reached. *Illinois v. Gates*, 462 U.S. 213 (1983) reasoned on facts similar to those in this example that the detailed nature of the letter to the Bloomingdale police, together with independent verification of much of the information, constituted probable cause to search the Gates' home and car:

> In *Gates* the anonymous letter contained a range of details relating not just to easily obtained facts and conditions existing at the time of the tip, but to future actions of third parties ordinarily not easily predicted. The letter writer's accurate information as to the travel plans of each of the Gates was of a character likely obtained only from the Gates themselves, or from someone familiar with their not entirely ordinary travel plans. If the informant has access to accurate information of this type, a magistrate could properly conclude that it was not unlikely that he also had access to reliable information of the Gates' alleged illegal activities.

462 U.S. at 245. As Justice White noted in his concurrence, while it is possible that a vindictive travel agent could have provided the detailed information on the Gates' activities, probable cause is a matter of probabilities and not certainties.[3]

---

3. 462 U.S. at 271. Justice White, concurring in the majority's conclusion that the police did have probable cause, reached that conclusion through the *Aguilar-Spinelli* framework. He reasoned that the police corroboration of the predictions set out in the anonymous letter gave rise to the inference that the informant was credible and that he had obtained his information in a reliable manner, thus satisfying both prongs of the traditional analysis. 462 U.S. at 267-272.

It is important to note that the *Gates* approach (unlike *Aguilar-Spinetti*) permits reliance on anonymous tips by allowing a strong showing that the informant's conclusions are accurate (the knowledge prong) to remedy a weak or nonexistent showing as to her credibility. Given the overlap in possession cases between probable cause to arrest and to search, there would seem to be sufficient cause in our example 6 both to arrest Lance for possession of unlawful drugs and to search the car and the condominium.

One caveat: While *Gates* clearly permits police corroboration to redeem an anonymous tipster's unknown reliability or to make up for a weak showing on the basis for her knowledge, some courts have read *Gates* to require that the corroboration be more than merely innocent details. In *United States v. Solomon*, 728 F. Supp. 1544 (S.D. Fla. 1990), for example, the sheriff received an anonymous message on the telephone tip line asserting that one George Solomon, of a stated description and address, was transporting cocaine from Fort Lauderdale, Florida, to North Carolina. The message relayed that on the following day, Solomon would leave his residence at approximately 6:00 A.M. and travel north on Interstate 95 in his maroon Chevrolet Camino with a white female of a particular description. The caller stated that Solomon would have cocaine in his car. Police staked out Solomon's home the next day and corroborated all that the caller had said with regard to the subject's description and his early morning departure with the described female. The officers stopped Solomon, placed him under arrest, and searched his car.

The U.S. District Court granted Solomon's motion to suppress the evidence seized on the ground that the police acted without probable cause. The court ruled that corroboration of the innocent and nonsuspicious details of the tip, such as the description of the suspect and his companion, as well as the time and route of their travels, could not suffice to establish a fair probability that contraband would be found on Solomon. The court distinguished *Gates* as a case where the corroborated details were suspicious — the police tracked the subjects from Illinois to Florida, a known source of drugs, and Lance spent a very short period of time there before returning north. In contrast, Solomon lived in Florida and was apprehended near his home merely because the police corroborated that he was taking a trip north on the interstate. Whether this reading of *Gates* is persuasive for other courts remains to be seen. Compare *People v. Rollins*, 382 Ill. App. 3d 833, 892 N.E.2d 21 (2008) (anonymous tip was sufficient to provide reasonable suspicion for vehicle stop where it was alleged a black male from Chicago in a car of a specific description was selling drugs from the trunk, and police observations corroborated the details).

The Plot Thickens

7. The weakness in the probable cause showing here, as in *Gates*, is the anonymous nature of the tip. If the police do not know who is providing

the information, they obviously cannot check the informant's prior track record for accuracy or evaluate the basis of her knowledge. Unlike *Gates*, however, this informant finally acknowledged her identity. If she truly was the suspect's former girlfriend, then she had a close vantage point from which to observe his activities. Moreover, she asserted that she had personally seen the stolen goods on the premises and was able to give a description of them, which was consistent with the description of the items taken in the prior burglaries. She also knew of the search that had just been conducted in the motel room. In short, the informant seems to have had a solid basis of knowledge concerning the defendant's activities.

Although there is no indication that the caller had previously supplied accurate information, the officers were able to corroborate the presence of the motor home in the location that she had stated. At this point, they had more than a mere hunch that seizable items were present in the trailer. Under the *Gates* totality-of-the-circumstances standard, they had established probable cause for the issuance of a warrant to search. See *Massachusetts v. Upton*, 466 U.S. 727, 731 (1984) ("The informant's story and the surrounding facts possessed an internal coherence that gave weight to the whole.").

Crucial to the determination in *Upton* that probable cause had been established was the identification of the caller as someone in a position to know about the suspect's activities. The Massachusetts Supreme Judicial Court, whose decision holding the warrant had been issued without adequate cause was reversed by the Supreme Court, viewed the question of the caller's identity with considerably more skepticism. Noting that the caller may have adopted a convenient cover for her true identity, the Massachusetts court treated her as an anonymous informant, and thus the basis for crediting her statements (her close relationship to the suspect) disappeared. *Commonwealth v. Upton*, 390 Mass. 562, 570, 458 N.E.2d 717, 722 (1983). The U.S. Supreme Court concluded, however, that the inference that the caller was Upton's girlfriend was a reasonable one for the officer and the magistrate to have drawn. Thus, while "no single piece of evidence by itself was conclusive, the pieces fit neatly together and, so viewed, support the magistrate's determination that there was a 'fair probability that contraband or evidence of crime' would be found in Upton's motor home."[4]

---

4. Upon remand, the Massachusetts Supreme Judicial Court again concluded that probable cause to search the motor home was lacking. See *Commonwealth v. Upton*, 394 Mass. 363, 476 N.E.2d 548 (1985). Describing the *Gates* totality-of-the-circumstances standard as unacceptably shapeless and permissive, the Supreme Judicial Court chose to apply state constitutional provisions regarding search and seizure and continued to apply the *Aguilar-Spinelli* analysis through its own constitution.

An interesting issue in our example is raised by the informant's statement that she wanted to "burn" Grape. Should a court assessing probable cause discount a source's information because of a possible motivation to falsely accuse the suspect? The few courts that have explicitly dealt with such situations have not been moved by that factor. In *United States v. Copeland*, 538 F.2d 639, 642 (5th Cir. 1976), the source, who was the father-in-law of the suspect, admitted that he had "an axe to grind" with him. The court dismissed this with the observation that this antagonism "may explain Westmoreland's motivation in providing the government with the tip, but it does not necessarily lessen his credibility." See also *United States v. Bishop*, 264 F.3d 919 (9th Cir. 2001) (fact that informant's actions may have been motivated by "spite" is not enough to undermine credibility of his statements to police); *United States v. Elliott*, 893 F.2d 220 (9th Cir. 1990) (informant's ill will toward defendant did not undercut her credibility); *United States v. Hunley*, 567 F.2d 822 (8th Cir. 1977) (fact that source of probable cause information had been promised a break if he cooperated with the police does not necessarily lessen his credibility). But compare *Hale v. Fish*, 899 F.2d 390 (5th Cir. 1990) (where informant had "ample motive to lie," government needed to demonstrate a "strong basis of knowledge" in order to render his information reliable for probable cause); *State v. Williams*, 193 S.W.3d 502 (Tenn. 2006) (defendant's girlfriend, in midst of domestic disturbance with defendant, may have provided information against him out of revenge and thus could not be considered presumptively reliable, but police corroboration and her strong basis in knowledge about drugs in his residence established probable cause).

8. We must determine whether the facts and circumstances within the knowledge of the police and of which they had reasonably trustworthy information were sufficient to warrant a person of reasonable caution to believe that contraband would be found in the truck. The primary indication of criminal activity here comes from the two informants. The observations made by the officers themselves, as well as the information they discovered, were innocuous and would not constitute adequate cause to believe criminal activity was occurring. The police investigation is important, however, insofar as it tended to corroborate certain aspects of the informant's reports.

Using the traditional *Aguilar-Spinelli* analysis, the credibility prong of the analysis seems to be satisfied for one of the informants by the assertion of past reliability. When we turn to the other prong and focus on the basis for the informant's conclusions—how did they obtain their information?—the picture becomes more problematic. There is no indication that the tips were based on their own personal knowledge, as opposed to information obtained from others, rumor, or speculation. Further, there are no alternative indicia of reliability, such as the self-implication of the informant in the criminal activity, the indication of a close relationship to the subject, or the supplying of great detail as to the subject's activities (leading to the inference of a close relationship). There is an absence, therefore, of a solid basis for crediting the informants' conclusions.

The question then becomes whether the corroboration of certain innocent details by the police, or the mutual corroboration of the two tips, can make up for the deficiencies regarding the conclusion prong. Police investigation and surveillance confirmed that Raymond Frank spoke frequently to Michael Best on the telephone, but the conclusion that he is the "Mike" referred to by the first informant was speculative. The police further confirmed that Raymond Frank had picked up two shipments of furniture from a country that is a major source of narcotics, and that he picked up the shipment now in question. The confirmation here appears to fall far short of that in *Draper*, where numerous parts of the informant's report were confirmed. The police have not confirmed a relationship between Frank and Best beyond telephone calls. Moreover, the fact that the cargo passed a routine customs inspection, while certainly not conclusive (we would want more information about how thorough an inspection it was), is certainly cause for some skepticism regarding the presence of narcotics. It is doubtful therefore whether the police investigation provided sufficient corroboration to bring the informant's assertions up to the standard of probable cause. But see *Richardson v. Quitman County, Georgia*, 912 F. Supp. 2d 1354 (M.D. Ga. 2012) ("Because the identified informant in this case had reliably provided drug information in the past and because some details predicting future travel were verified almost immediately by [deputy's] investigation, the Court finds that the information was sufficiently reliable under the totality of the circumstances even if [the deputy] did not ask if the informant based certain information on personal knowledge or hearsay."); *United States v. Talley*, 108 F.3d 277 (11th Cir. 1997) (police corroboration of informant's description of suspect's car and residence was sufficient to establish probable cause to search car).

In this example, we have the additional fact that the tips from independent informants appear to corroborate each other. Courts have been impressed with this kind of mutual reinforcement. See, e.g., *United States v. Laws*, 808 F.2d 92, 103 (D.C. Cir. 1986) ("[T]he mutually-supporting nature of the two tips is an important ingredient in the probable-cause mix. There is no indication that the informants were acting cooperatively. The fact that two apparently unassociated persons make the same assertion increases the probability that it is true."); *United States v. Vanness*, 85 F.3d 661 (D.C. Cir. 1996) (where three independent informants had reported defendant's drug-dealing activities, the tips were found to be "mutually reinforcing," and therefore contributed to a valid warrant). In this example, however, the tips are only partially supportive of one another. Informant 1 fingered Raymond Frank and Mike, while Informant 2 fingered Michael Best and an unidentified partner. On close examination, the information is not completely congruent.

Whether the information constitutes probable cause under the relaxed standard of *Illinois v. Gates* is a close question. The tips lack the level of detail found so compelling in *Gates*, and the corroboration by way of police investigation is not as strong as it was in that case. On similar facts, the Ninth Circuit concluded that probable cause was lacking. See *United States v. Freitas*, 716 F.2d 1216 (9th Cir. 1983).

The Ingredients in the Probable Cause Recipe

9. The anonymous tip, even when supplemented by the officer's confirmation that Shay hangs around the school, is insufficient to establish probable cause as there is no basis to credit the information and no corroboration of illegal conduct. May the police officer consider the suspect's past criminal record in the probable cause determination? There are obvious concerns about the use of such information to establish cause, given the prospect that anyone with a criminal record would presumably be subject to arrest and or search at any time.

Certainly the mere existence of a criminal record could not, of itself, constitute probable cause to believe the person is presently involved in criminal activity. The Supreme Court has held, however, that knowledge of the suspect's prior criminal activity may be used as confirmation of an informant's tip, so long as the officer is acting on hard information and not just rumor. See *United States v. Harris*, 403 U.S. 573 (1971). As the Court put it in *Jones v. United States*, 362 U.S. 257, 271 (1960), "that [the suspect] was a known user of narcotics made [the informant's] charge against him much less subject to skepticism than would be such a charge against one without such a history and reduced the chances of a reckless or prevaricating tale." One court has described the element of prior convictions as bearing "weightily on the issue of probable cause." See *United States v. Laws*, 808 F.2d 92, 103 (D.C. Cir. 1986). See also *United States v. Strother*, 318 F.3d 64 (1st Cir. 2003) (prior convictions can certainly be considered, along with other information in the determination of probable cause); *State v. Maddox*, 152 Wash. 2d 499, 98 P.3d 1199 (2004) (prior convictions of a suspect may be used in determining probable cause, particularly when a prior conviction is for a crime of the same general nature). Prior convictions, particularly if dated, cannot alone corroborate an informant's account. *United States v. Olson*, 408 F.3d 366 (7th Cir. 2005).

Is the additional knowledge of Shay's prior convictions in our example enough to push the showing up to the probable cause threshold? In light of the anonymous nature of the tip and the officer's inability to confirm any illegal activity in the school yard, it would appear unlikely that the sum total adds up to probable cause.

10. Plainly, a mere hunch is inadequate to establish probable cause. There must be specific facts to support a reasonable conclusion that a crime has been committed, and that the defendant committed it. May the officers base their action on the fact that the suspects fled when they were approached?

    The courts have long held that flight from a law officer can be counted as a factor in the establishment of reasonable suspicion or probable cause. *Sibron v. New York*, 392 U.S. 40, 66-67 (1968), noted that furtive actions and flight at the approach of law officers are "strong indicia of *mens rea*, and when coupled with specific knowledge on the part of the officer relating the suspect to the evidence of crime, they are proper factors to be considered in the decision to make an arrest." Thus "if a police officer identifies himself while approaching a suspect and the suspect flees, the suspect's conduct suggests that he knowingly seeks to evade questioning or capture. Such conduct ordinarily supplies another element to the [probable cause] calculus." *United States v. Amuny*, 767 F.2d 1113, 1124 (5th Cir. 1985).

    Flight alone is generally not itself sufficient to establish justification; the officer must be able to point to other specific information. Unprovoked flight from police in an area known for heavy narcotics trafficking, however, may be sufficient to establish reasonable suspicion (discussed in §4.2) for a stop. See *Illinois v. Wardlow*, 528 U.S. 119 (2000).

    Police, of course, should not be able to transform a hunch into reasonable suspicion or probable cause by reason of conduct such as flight that they themselves have provoked. "That," the Supreme Court has warned, "would have the same essential vice as a proposition we have consistently rejected that a search unlawful at its inception may be validated by what it turns up." *Wong Sun v. United States*, 371 U.S. 471, 484 (1963). See also *United States v. Fisher*, 229 F.3d 1154 (6th Cir. 2001) (in analyzing totality of circumstances, factors such as attempts to flee upon confrontation with police are useful). Even walking away from police at a fast pace (particularly in a high crime area) may give rise to reasonable suspicion. See *United States v. Bumpers*, 705 F.3d 168 (4th Cir. 2013).

    The Massachusetts Supreme Judicial Court has discounted flight from police as a basis for reasonable suspicion in the case of black males in locales where they have been disproportionately targeted for stops. "[W]here the suspect is a black male stopped by the police on the streets of Boston, the analysis of flight as a factor in the reasonable suspicion calculus cannot be divorced from the findings in a recent Boston Police Department (department) report documenting a pattern of racial profiling of black males in the city of Boston." *Commonwealth v. Warren*, 475 Mass. 530 (2016) (Geraldine Hines, J.) "Such an individual, when approached by the police, might just as easily be motivated by the desire to avoid the recurring indignity of being racially profiled as by the desire to hide criminal activity. Given this reality for black males in the city of Boston, a judge should, in appropriate cases, consider the report's findings in weighing flight as a factor in the reasonable suspicion calculus." As a dissenting judge noted in *United States v. Franklin*, 323 F.3d 1298, 1305 (11th Cir. 2003), "[w]here an individual's flight is provoked, it cannot support reasonable suspicion. The police may not frighten an individual into fleeing, and then assert his flight as a justification for pursuing and stopping him." (police approached Franklin in full SRT gear, including military fatigues, body armor, boots and sidearms).

In our example, there would probably not be adequate cause to arrest the men because all the officers had was a hunch, together with the subjects' flight. Moreover, because the officers were in plain clothes, it is unclear what significance the flight had in any event. *Wong Sun*, supra, 371 U.S. at 482 (flight from an officer who fails to identify himself as such must be regarded as ambiguous conduct). Compare *United States v. Jones*, 619 F.2d 494, 498 (5th Cir. 1980) ("evasive actions and flight from two strange men riding in an unmarked car and exhibiting no indicia of lawful authority were only natural reactions to the circumstance") *Marshall v. Teske*, 284 F.3d 765 (7th Cir. 2002) ("because the officers were not identifiable as police, a reasonable officer in their position would not have assumed that Marshall was *knowingly* running away from police officers"), and *United States v. Amuny*, supra, 767 F.2d at 1125 (six unmarked cars surrounded a plane and the officers failed to identify themselves) with *Manners v. Cannella*, 891 F.3d 959 (11th Cir. 2018) (Manners willfully failed to stop when directed to do so by an officer following with cruiser flashing lights and siren, and continued for three blocks); *United States v. Dawdy*, 46 F.3d 1427 (8th Cir. 1995) (arrestee's response to invalid arrest or stop may provide independent probable cause where arrestee resisted police officer's attempt to handcuff him), *United States v. Holloway*, 962 F.2d 451, 461 (5th Cir. 1992) (suspect's attempt to escape from police after their show of authority by reversing his automobile and ramming another police unit created sufficient probable cause to arrest him), *United States v. Gentry*, 839 F.2d 1065, 1070 (5th Cir. 1988) (fact that subject sought to flee in his vehicle from scene of a large drug transaction, combined with information that more purchasers would be arriving at the scene, gave troopers probable cause to arrest), and *United States v. Martinez-Gonzalez*, 686 F.2d 93, 99-100 (2d Cir. 1982) (where subject looked frightened and ran back into his apartment in response to agents walking toward him at a normal pace, displaying their badges, and identifying themselves as police officers, their reasonable suspicion grew into probable cause to arrest).

11. To what extent may Dow's presence in a high-crime area count toward probable cause? Like past criminal record and flight, such presence can be used as a factor but may not, of itself, justify arrest or search. As the Supreme Court ruled in Brown v. Texas, 443 U.S. 47, 52 (1979), "the fact that appellant was in a neighborhood frequented by drug dealers, standing alone, is not a basis for concluding that appellant himself was engaged in criminal conduct." Weighing presence in a high-crime area too heavily in the probable cause equation would obviously subject all residents and passersby to unjustified search on sight. Nonetheless, the courts have generally concluded that location in a high-crime area is a relevant factor in determining probable cause. When an officer observes suspicious conduct, it may take on a special meaning if it happens in a locale where criminal activity is extensive. See Adams v. Williams, 407 U.S. 143, 147-148 (1972) (fact that subject was in a high-crime area contributed to the reasonableness of the search for weapons under the Terry standard, discussed in §4.2).

    As one court put it: "Although no presumption of guilt arises from the activities of inhabitants of an area in which the police know that narcotics offenses frequently occur, the syndrome of criminality in those areas cannot realistically go unnoticed by the judiciary. It too is a valid consideration when coupled with other reliable indicia or suspicious circumstances. We make this statement warily, for it is all too clear that few live in these areas by choice." United States v. Davis, 458 F.2d 819, 822 (D.C. Cir. 1972). See also United States v. Valentine, 232 F.3d 350, 356 (3d Cir. 2000) ("The constellation of likely criminal acts in a high-crime area at 1:00 a.m. goes well beyond simply carrying a gun without registration or with altered serial numbers. Indeed, given the large number of potential crimes and the danger posed by an armed criminal, we think that if the police officers had done nothing and continued on their way after receiving the informant's tip, the officers would have been remiss. People who live in communities torn by gunfire and violence are entitled to be free from fear of victimization and have police investigate before shootings occur."); United States v. Lenoir, 318 F.3d 725, 729 (7th Cir. 2003) ("a person's flight upon seeing the police approach in a high crime area establishes reasonable suspicion to justify a Terry stop").

    In our example, there was not much more than the character of the area for the police to go on. They merely observed conversations occurring, not furtive conduct or objects changing hands. Compare United States v. Perkins, 363 F.3d 317 (4th Cir. 2004) (investigative stop was warranted where officers, in response to tip that men in a car were displaying rifles, recognized passenger in vehicle as known drug dealer, and car was parked in front of known drug house in drug-ridden neighborhood), United States v. Green, 670 F.2d 1148 (D.C. Cir. 1981) (probable cause existed where officer with aid of binoculars observed currency and objects being exchanged in neighborhood notorious for narcotics trafficking). There would appear to be insufficient cause to arrest Dow.

This example also raises the troublesome question of how much deference courts should grant to police expertise. The whole point of having a legal standard of probable cause requiring specific information and not mere hunch, and of placing ultimate review in the courts, is to subject police conduct to independent judicial scrutiny. Yet the courts have properly recognized that police officers do develop expertise that is extremely useful in ferreting out crime. Thus, while probable cause was originally defined from the vantage point of the reasonably prudent *person*, it has often come to be viewed from the perspective of a reasonable *police officer* in light of her training and experience. See, e.g., *District of Columbia v. Wesby*, 138 S. Ct. 577, 586 (2018) (probable cause is viewed from the standpoint of an objectively reasonable police officer).

"This process allows officers to draw on their own experience and specialized training to make inferences from and deductions about the cumulative information available to them that might well elude an untrained person." *United States v. Arvizu*, 534 U.S. 266 (2002). The officer may be in the best position "to know the routines and patterns of the geographic area, and whether it is more prone to crime." *United States v. Bonner*, 363 F.3d 213, 219 (3d Cir. 2004). The information "must be seen and weighed not in terms of analysis by scholars, but as understood by those versed in the field of law enforcement." *Illinois v. Gates*, 462 U.S. 213, 232 (1983). For the view that *both* perspectives — reasonable person and reasonable police officer — should factor into the evaluation of probable cause, see *United States v. Prandy-Binnett*, 995 F.2d 1069, 1071 (D.C. Cir. 1993).

Deference to police experience does not mean deference to a hunch. The officer must still be able to articulate specific and concrete information upon which the expert conclusion was based. There remains the risk, nonetheless, that deference becomes delegation, and that courts abdicate their independent role in the probable cause review. Illustration of the problem may be found in those cases where the officer's past success rate seems to substitute for hard information. See, e.g., *United States v. White*, 655 F.2d 1302, 1304 (D.C. Cir. 1981) ("The two officers who had observed the sale had previously demonstrated their ability to recognize narcotics transactions; ninety-five to ninety-six percent of their prior, similar observations had led to the arrest of persons possessing drugs.").

12. Probable cause exists only if there are specific facts pointing toward criminal activity on the part of the subject. If possession of a handgun is a violation of law in the jurisdiction, the information in our

example (reported by a named source through his firsthand observations) would seem to constitute such cause. If, however, possession is a crime only in the absence of a permit to carry the weapon and, further, if the officer has no knowledge whether the subject lacks a permit, then the information known to the officer would appear insufficient to constitute probable cause. In *Commonwealth v. Couture*, 407 Mass. 178 (1990), the Supreme Judicial Court reasoned: "The police only knew that a man had been seen in public with a handgun. This unadorned fact, without any additional information suggesting criminal activity, does not give rise to probable cause. The police in this case had no reason to believe, before conducting the search of the vehicle, that the defendant lacked a license to carry the firearm. A police officer's knowledge that an individual is carrying a handgun, in and of itself, does not furnish probable cause to believe that the individual is illegally carrying that gun." 407 Mass. at 181.

One might ask how the police are to investigate possible illegal possession in this situation. The obvious answer would be that they may effect a brief investigative stop (see §4.2) and ask the subject to produce a permit. The Massachusetts court, however, foreclosed that option as well by holding that there was no reasonable suspicion of criminal activity that would justify such a detention. Given these rulings, enforcement of the gun law in Massachusetts appears problematic.

13. "The exchange of small objects for currency is an important and sometimes decisive factor in determining the existence of probable cause." *Shelton v. United States*, 929 A.2d 420, 423 (D.C. Ct. App. 2007). The probable cause test is based on a reasonableness analysis. In *Shelton*, upon which this example is loosely based, the court held that the officer's suspicions may have justified a *Terry* stop, but that probable cause was lacking. This case involves a two-way transaction that has a number of innocent explanations. The officer did not recognize either of the suspects as having a criminal record, he did not see the driver retrieve the "small object" from a suspicious container or location, and there was no attempt to flee or conceal the contraband. Compare *Pennsylvania v. Dunlap*, 941 A.2d 671 (Pa. 2007), *cert. denied* 129 S. Ct. 448 (2008) (probable cause did not exist after police observed the exchange of money for a small object when the suspect did not flee and the police did not actually see any drugs) with *Commonwealth v. Thompson*, 604 Pa. 198, 212, 985 A.2d 928, 936 (Sup. Ct. Pa. 2009) (in analyzing a hand-to-hand exchange, police officer's experience is a relevant factor in determining probable cause).

There likely would have been sufficient evidence for probable cause if the exchange had taken place in an area where drug activity was common or if there had been other evidence pointing to a drug transaction.

In *United States v. Orozco*, 982 F.2d 152 (5th Cir. 1993), probable cause was established when an officer witnessed a suspect in a high-crime area make three apparent sales of heroin after concealing the heroin in a balloon in his mouth, which was easily recognizable as a sign of narcotics trafficking. See also *Prince v. United States*, 825 A.2d 928 (D.C. Ct. App. 2003) (probable cause was based on officer's observation of an exchange of money for a small object and the subject approaching other cars in a suspicious manner in a high narcotics area). "A two-way exchange of apparent drugs for money is not a precondition to a finding of probable cause to make an arrest; rather, the real key in these cases is how the observed transaction fits into the totality of the circumstances, and if there are sufficient other factors present, one need not always have a completed two-way transaction to create probable cause." *Jefferson v. United States*, 906 A.2d 885, 888 (D.C. Ct. App. 2006).

14. If there is indeed probable cause, then the search of the trunk, including the athletic bag inside, would be allowed (see §6.4). It must be noted that the initial sniffing by the police dog would not be deemed a search under the Fourth Amendment, as there is no expectation of privacy (see §3.2c) so long as it did not significantly expand the duration of the stop. The crucial question thus becomes whether the information provided by Pepper is reliable, given that the signs of the motorist's nervousness do not themselves indicate criminal activity but are relatively common for someone stopped by police. To answer this question, we must consider the training that the dog had received, the tests that he had been put through, and whether he had ever given false alerts before. See *Florida v. Harris*, 133 S. Ct. 1050 (2013).

Here Today, Gone Tomorrow/Here Tomorrow, but Not Today

15. Probable cause to search a location is defined with reference to a particular point in time. The information known to the police must permit the reasonable conclusion that items related to crime are *presently* at the place to be searched. Probable cause to search does not last indefinitely — like bread, it gets stale over time.

In our example, it would not be reasonable to believe that the hijacked cell phones will remain in Red's van for an extended period of time. Given the nature of this type of crime, the likelihood is that Red will transfer the loot as quickly as possible, and most probably before the end of two weeks. By the time the police found Red's van, probable cause had likely dissipated.

Probable cause may become stale when too much time has elapsed between the suspected occurrence and the issuance of a search warrant. The staleness issue varies with the particular situation and the nature of the crime. Where the criminal activity is of a continuing nature or the items to be seized are unlikely to be moved, a time gap between receipt of the information and the proposed search may not be fatal. Thus, a search of a residence based on reliable information that the homeowner was in the business of selling narcotics was upheld despite the delay of 23 months between the last of 12 controlled buys and the issuance of the warrant. See *United States v. Greene*, 250 F.3d 471 (6th Cir. 2001). The court explained: "A staleness determination should be flexible, resting on numerous factors, such as: [T]he character of the crime (chance encounter in the night or regenerating conspiracy?), the criminal (nomadic or entrenched?), the thing to be seized (perishable and easily transferable or of enduring utility to its holder?), the place to be searched (mere criminal forum of convenience or secure operational base?). . . . Evidence of ongoing criminal activity will generally defeat a claim of staleness." See also *Andresen v. Maryland*, 427 U.S. 463, 478 n.9 (1976) (no staleness despite three-month delay because documents sought were ordinary business records) and *United States v. Madiedo*, 972 F.2d 1345 (9th Cir. 1992) (probable cause to search for business records related to drug smuggling scheme existed, despite a yearlong delay between information being obtained and the warrant's execution, because the records are of the type "typically maintained over a long period of time"); *United States v. Urban*, 404 F.3d 754, 775 (3d Cir. 2005) (no staleness where warrant affidavit contained evidence "that the plumbing inspectors' misconduct was an established, routine practice that had spanned numerous years and had continued at least up until just months prior to the District Court's initial authorization of the video surveillance in February of 2000. We therefore conclude that the evidence of the plumbing inspectors' continuous misconduct leading up to the time of the first affidavit's issuance was not stale, and therefore provided probable cause for the video surveillance."). Compare *United States v. Grant*, 108 F. Supp. 2d 1172 (D. Kan. 2000) (probable cause was too stale where affidavit did not allege that defendant was involved in an ongoing conspiracy or continuous illegal drug activity over a substantial period of time).

Current information may be used to revive stale information. In *United States v. Viegas*, 639 F.2d 42 (1st Cir. 1981), police sought to justify their search of the defendant's luggage by relying on an informant's tip received a year before asserting that the defendant was dealing cocaine. While recognizing that the stale information could not by itself establish probable cause, the court nevertheless ruled that it served to corroborate the suspicions of the officers based on current observations of the defendant at Logan Airport, and thus probable cause was established. See also *United States v. Pene-Rodriguez*, 110 F.3d 1120, 1130, 1131 (5th Cir. 1997) (contemporary observations corroborated stale informant's tip).

In contrast to probable cause to search, information establishing probable cause to arrest generally does not become stale over time. If there is reason to believe that Alfred Red has committed larceny, that information will keep indefinitely (or at least until contradictory information is discovered indicating that he is not the culprit). Probable cause to arrest is not time-specific because it does not depend on the presence of specified items at a particular location.

16. The Court in *United States v. Grubbs*, 126 S. Ct. 1494 (2006), placed its imprimatur on the use of "anticipatory warrants," which are conditioned upon an event such as delivery of a package at a particular location. Observing that "because the probable cause requirement looks to whether evidence will be found *when the search is conducted*, all warrants are, in a sense, anticipatory." The Court articulated two requirements for conditional warrants: It must be shown not only that if the triggering condition occurs, there is a fair probability that contraband or evidence of a crime will be found in a particular place, but it must also be shown that there *is probable cause to believe the triggering condition will occur.* 126 S. Ct. at 1500.

For examples of anticipatory warrants, see *United States v. Golson*, 743 F.3d 44 (3d Cir. 2014) (upheld warrant anticipating the controlled delivery of a package intercepted by a postal inspector and fitted with a GPS device indicating the parcel had been opened); *United States v. Whited*, 539 F.3d 693 (7th Cir. 2008) (upholding anticipatory warrant for controlled buy of child pornography, as triggering event of defendant taking package into his home was proven). Compare *United States v. Rowland*, 145 F.3d 1194 (10th Cir. 1998) (affidavit did not provide probable cause for anticipatory search warrant because it failed to establish sufficient nexus between pornographic videotapes and defendant's residence).

Generally, failure to comply with the triggering event voids the warrant. See, e.g., *United States v. Perkins*, 887 F.3d 272 (6th Cir. 2018) (triggering event was not satisfied because package was delivered to defendant's fiance rather than defendant).

For more on the use of anticipatory warrants, see §5.5 of Chapter 5.

§4.2 REASONABLE SUSPICION — THE STANDARD FOR STOP AND FRISK

As we have seen, the amount of justification required for search or arrest is probable cause. Much police activity, however, does not reach the level of these full-scale intrusions. Police routinely stop citizens on the street or pull them over in their automobiles in order to question them briefly or to enforce traffic laws. If probable cause were required in these situations, such investigative stops would be impermissible in most cases.

Recognizing the importance of the "stop and frisk" in the scheme of effective law enforcement, the Supreme Court in *Terry v. Ohio*, 392 U.S. 1 (1968), set a new level of justification — "reasonable suspicion" — falling below probable cause. Officer McFadden's attention was drawn to two men on a Cleveland street corner who appeared to the experienced officer to be "casing" a store for a robbery. Acting on his suspicions, McFadden approached the men and asked them to identify themselves. When they mumbled something in response, McFadden patted the men down, felt a pistol on each, and removed the guns. The men were placed under arrest for possession of a concealed weapon. Prior to trial, they moved unsuccessfully to suppress the guns.

The Supreme Court rejected Ohio's argument that the stop-and-frisk practice does not implicate the Fourth Amendment at all because it falls short of a full-blown search or arrest, but it also rejected the defendant's position that police must possess probable cause. In appropriate circumstances and in an appropriate manner, officers may briefly detain a person to investigate possible criminal activity.

Observing that street encounters between citizens and police officers are "incredibly rich in diversity," ranging from exchanges of information to hostile confrontations, the Court invoked the *Fourth Amendment's reasonableness clause* to fashion a flexible standard for measuring the lawfulness of such encounters. With an approach that has set the tone for subsequent Fourth Amendment jurisprudence, the Court weighed the governmental interest in conducting stops and frisks against the interference with individual liberty and concluded that the officer must be prepared to articulate the specific facts giving rise to "reasonable suspicion" that criminal activity may have been afoot. Because the additional step of patting down or frisking constitutes a further intrusion, it requires additional justification: reasonable suspicion that the suspect may be armed and dangerous.[5] The scope of this protective search is limited by the exigencies that justify its initiation,[6] and is therefore restricted to that which is necessary to discover weapons — usually an initial pat-down of the suspect's clothing to determine whether he is carrying a weapon, followed by a reach into pockets or other hidden areas if (and only if) the pat-down reveals the likely presence of a weapon.

Measured against these standards, the Court ruled that Officer McFadden had lawfully stopped and frisked Terry and his companions to investigate a

---

5. The *Terry* Court rejected Justice Harlan's view (set out in his concurrence) that the right to frisk follows automatically from the right to stop. Courts have not, however, always been rigorous in enforcing this requirement for separate justification. Where there is reasonable suspicion to believe the subject is involved in a serious crime (particularly one of violence), a frisk is generally deemed reasonable without more justification.

6. The Court observed: "The Fourth Amendment proceeds as much by limitations upon the scope of governmental action as by imposing preconditions upon its initiation." 392 U.S. at 28-29.

possible crime, and the evidence seized could be admitted at trial. As *Terry* illustrates, an officer conducting an investigative stop and frisk need not (as with probable cause to arrest) have reason to believe that a crime *has been* committed; it will suffice if the officer has reason to believe a crime is *about to be* committed.

Like probable cause, the definition of reasonable suspicion is of necessity a flexible one:

> Courts have used a variety of terms to capture the elusive concept of what cause is sufficient to authorize police to stop a person. Terms like "articulable reasons" and "founded suspicion" are not self-defining; they fall short of providing clear guidance dispositive of the myriad factual situations that arise. But the essence of all that has been written is that the totality of the circumstances—the whole picture—must be taken into account. Based upon that whole picture, the detaining officers must have a particularized and objective basis for suspecting the particular person stopped of criminal activity.

United States v. Cortez, 449 U.S. 411, 417 (1981).

Reasonable suspicion is considerably *less* than proof by a preponderance of the evidence, but considerably *more* than an inchoate and unparticularized suspicion or hunch. *United States v. Sokolow*, 490 U.S. 1 (1989). In making the determination, due regard is granted to the officer's unique experience and training. *United States v. Arvizu*, 534 U.S. 266 (2002). Reasonable suspicion may be based upon information received from an informant, but need not carry all of the indicia of reliability required in probable cause analysis. *Adams v. Williams*, 407 U.S. 143 (1972). Reasonable suspicion may even be based upon an anonymous telephone tip so long as the police are able to corroborate certain of its details.

In *Alabama v. White*, 496 U.S. 325 (1990), police received an anonymous tip that one Vanessa White would be leaving a particular apartment at a particular time in a particular vehicle, that she would be going to a particular motel, and that she would be in possession of cocaine. They proceeded to the apartment building, observed a woman leave the building and enter the car described, and followed her along the route toward the motel. Having thus corroborated some of the predictions of the caller, the Court held the police were justified in stopping and detaining White just short of the motel. Adopting a totality-of-the-circumstances approach reminiscent of *Illinois v. Gates* (see §4.1), the Court concluded that while the tip itself was inadequate to justify police action (because there was no basis for crediting either the caller's veracity or the accuracy of his predictions), police corroboration established sufficient indicia of reliability to constitute reasonable suspicion and thus permit an investigative stop. When an informant is shown to be right about some things, so the reasoning goes, that increases the probability that she is right about the other facts asserted. In addition, the caller was able to predict White's future actions, demonstrating "inside information—a special familiarity with respondent's affairs." 496 U.S. at 330.[7] But absent some indication of credibility, an anonymous tip will not support a Terry stop. *Florida v. J. L.*, 529 U.S. 266 (2000) (tip provided no predictive information and therefore left police without means to test informant's knowledge or credibility).

An anonymous caller's 911 report that a pickup truck had run her off the road was deemed sufficient to provide reasonable suspicion for the stop of the truck in *Navarette v. California*, 134 S. Ct. 1683 (2014). Observing that an anonymous tip alone seldom demonstrates the informant's basis of knowledge or veracity, here the caller described the model of the truck and its license plate number, and the police confirmed its location soon after the call. In addition, 911 callers can usually be identified, providing a safeguard against false reports.

Alabama v. White summed up the relation between the two standards of justification: "Reasonable suspicion is a less demanding standard than probable cause not only in the sense that reasonable suspicion can be established with information that is different in quantity or content than that required to establish probable cause, but also in the sense that reasonable suspicion can arise from information that is less reliable than that required to show probable cause." 496 U.S. at 330.

Many of the cases interpreting the reasonable suspicion standard have arisen in the context of stops in airport terminals of persons suspected of involvement in narcotics trafficking. The following are among the red flags of the so-called "drug courier profile" relied upon by courts in determining whether the detention was justified. The subject 1) paid cash for the airline ticket, 2) traveled under an assumed name, 3) did not check luggage, 4) traveled to or from a narcotics source city, 5) stayed only a brief time in the destination city, and 6) appeared nervous. Although no one factor alone is itself sufficient, a combination may amount to reasonable suspicion that criminal activity is afoot. *United States v. Sokolow*, 490 U.S. 1 (1989).[8]

---

7. Emphasizing that the tipster had predicted White would be carrying a brown attache case containing the cocaine, but that the woman observed by the police was empty-handed, the dissenters were not impressed: "Millions of people leave their apartments at about the same time every day carrying an attache case and heading for a destination known to their neighbors. An anonymous neighbor's prediction about somebody's time of departure and probable destination is anything but a reliable basis for assuming that the commuter is in possession of an illegal substance—particularly when the person is not even carrying the attache case described by the tipster." 496 U.S. at 330 (Stevens, J., joined by Brennan and Marshall, JJ., dissenting).

8. The dissenters bemoaned the profile's "chameleon-like way of adapting to any particular set of observations." 490 U.S. at 13 (Marshall, J., dissenting). Justice Marshall cited cases in which contradictory characteristics were considered suspicious, including being the first passenger to deplane, the last to deplane, and deplaning in the middle of the crowd; holding a round-trip ticket and holding a one-way ticket; traveling nonstop and changing planes; carrying no luggage and carrying luggage; traveling alone and traveling with companions; acting too nervously and acting too calmly.

As we saw regarding probable cause, a frequently recurring question is the role of the suspect's flight in the determination of justification for police action. Unprovoked flight from police in a high-crime area has been held sufficient to establish reasonable suspicion for a stop. *Illinois v. Wardlow*, 528 U.S. 119 (2000).

§4.3 WHAT CONSTITUTES A STOP?

"Obviously," the Court observed in *Terry*, "not all personal intercourse between policemen and citizens involves seizures of persons." The Fourth Amendment is implicated only when the officer, "by means of physical force or show of authority, has in some way restrained the liberty" of the subject. *Terry v. Ohio*, 392 U.S. 1, 20 n.16 (1968). The demarcation between a stop and something less intrusive (as where, for example, the officer merely addresses questions to a citizen who is free to ignore them and leave) will separate those situations in which the officer can act only with "reasonable suspicion" from those in which no justification is required because the Fourth Amendment does not come into play.

In defining what constitutes a "stop," or seizure of the person, the Court has adopted an objective test:

> [A] person has been seized within the meaning of the Fourth Amendment only if, in view of all the circumstances surrounding the incident, a reasonable person would have believed that he was not free to leave. Examples of circumstances that might indicate a seizure, even where the person did not actually attempt to leave, would be the threatening presence of several officers, the display of a weapon by an officer, some physical touching of the person of the citizen, or the use of language or tone of voice indicating that compliance with the officer's request might be compelled.

United States v. Mendenhall, 446 U.S. 544, 554 (1980).

Take the familiar case of a person chased by police on foot. The Court has held that no seizure occurs where the police have not yet caught the subject or placed any physical restraint upon him. *California v. Hodari D.*, 499 U.S. 621 (1991) (rejecting Hodari's argument that he was "seized" at the time he tossed away a rock of cocaine because mere pursuit created a reasonable belief on his part that he was not free to leave). There must be actual application of force or submission to police authority for a seizure to occur.

In a similar vein, a bus passenger is not necessarily seized when confronted by officers conducting a drug interdiction sweep. In *Florida v. Bostick*, 501 U.S. 429 (1991), armed and uniformed officers approached passenger Bostick as he sat in the cramped confines of the bus. They asked to see his ticket and identification, advised him they were searching for narcotics, and requested to inspect his luggage. The Court refused to adopt the analysis of the state supreme court, which had held such encounters were *per se* seizures implicating the Fourth Amendment. Opting instead for *ad hoc* inquiry, the Court instructed: "In order to determine whether a particular encounter constitutes a seizure, a court must consider all the circumstances surrounding the encounter to determine whether the police conduct would have communicated to a reasonable person that the person was not free to decline the officer's requests or otherwise terminate the encounter." 501 U.S. at 439. Remanding for further development of the record, the Court noted that the officers did not remove their guns or point them at Bostick, and that he was advised he could refuse to consent to search of his luggage.

In a similar situation the Court found no seizure, even though the bus passenger was not advised of his right to refuse consent, because there were no threats, intimidation, or show of force, and no blocked exits. *United States v. Drayton*, 536 U.S. 194 (2002). The dissenters (Souter, joined by Stevens and Ginsburg) found it hard to imagine that Drayton, in the confined quarters of a bus, felt free to decline the police request.

The Court has cautioned that the reasonable person test is "necessarily imprecise, because it is designed to assess the coercive effect of police conduct." *Michigan v. Chesternut*, 486 U.S. 567, 573 (1988). What constitutes a "restraint on liberty prompting a person to conclude that he is not free to leave will vary, not only with the particular police conduct at issue, but also with the setting in which the conduct occurs." The standard has been defended on the grounds that the alternative—a subjective test—would peg applicability of the Fourth Amendment to the peculiar state of mind and eccentricities of the person confronted.

Since *Delaware v. Prouse*, 440 U.S. 648 (1979), stops of motorists on the road have been held to require at least reasonable suspicion to believe a traffic offense has occurred. *Prouse* rejected the notion that police could conduct "routine" stops *without any cause* to check the driver's license and registration. The usual questioning accompanying such stops, together with the request for license and registration (and a field computer check of driver and vehicle) are generally not deemed "investigatory" and thus require no further justification. See, e.g., *United States v. Galvan-Muro*, 141 F.3d 904 (8th Cir. 1998) (no investigatory "stop" occurred even though motorist was detained for 15 minutes). But compare *United States v. Ramos*, 42 F.3d 1160 (8th Cir. 1994) (separation of brothers stopped for not wearing seat belts, for purpose of further questioning, expanded the scope of detention and thus required reasonable suspicion of criminal activity).

Questions regarding immigration status seem to be fair game. *Muehler v. Mena*, 544 U.S. 93 (2005) concluded that because the suspect's initial detention in her residence was lawful and the detention was not prolonged by the questioning, no additional seizure occurred when she was questioned about her immigration status. *Arizona v. United States*, 132 S. Ct. 2492 (2012) also deemed immigration status questions part of a lawful stop.

The threatening presence of several officers, display of a weapon, physical touching of the motorist, or use of intimidating language or tone may convert a traffic stop into a detention requiring further justification. *United States v. White*, 81 F.3d 775, 779 (8th Cir. 1996). See also *United States v. Hammond*, 890 F.3d 901 (10th Cir. 2018) (officer's encounter with vehicle occupant became *Terry* "stop" when he stopped him for a broken brake light, then learned the passenger and the vehicle had previously been involved in weapons possession and instructed him to exit the vehicle to search for weapons); *United States v. Lewis*, 674 F.3d 1298 (2012) (consensual encounter in parking lot evolved into an investigatory detention after two of the men admitted they were carrying guns).

At the other end of the intrusion spectrum, the question arises as to when the duration of an investigative stop ripens into the equivalent of a full-scale arrest, requiring probable cause. If, for example, the subject of the stop is brought to the station house and detained for questioning, reasonable suspicion will no longer suffice; probable cause must be shown. *Dunaway v. NewYork*, 442 U.S. 200 (1979). See also *Kaupp v. Texas*, 123 S. Ct. 1843 (2003) (detention equivalent to arrest occurred when youth was taken shoeless in his underwear from neighbor's home to patrol car and transported to scene of crime, then to the police station).

Drawing the critical line between a stop and a more substantial intrusion was the subject of *Florida v. Royer*, 460 U.S. 491 (1983), which involved the detention at Miami International Airport of an individual believed to fit the drug courier profile. Royer was approached by two detectives and, at their request, turned over his airline ticket and driver's license and then accompanied them to an interrogation room. His luggage was brought in, and at the officers' request, Royer opened his suitcase, revealing marijuana. The entire sequence of events took approximately 15 minutes. In ruling that by the time the suitcase was opened the detention had become a more serious intrusion than an investigative stop (which is permitted on mere reasonable suspicion), the Court wrote:

> The predicate permitting seizures on suspicion short of probable cause is that law enforcement interests warrant a limited intrusion on the personal security of the suspect. The scope of the intrusion permitted will vary to some extent with the particular facts and circumstances of each case. This much, however, is clear: an investigative detention must be temporary and last no longer than is necessary to effectuate the purpose of the stop. Similarly, the investigative methods employed should be the least intrusive means reasonably available to verify or dispel the officer's suspicion in a short period of time.

460 U.S. at 500. The Court concluded that Royer had been subjected to the functional equivalent of an arrest, and absent probable cause, that was unlawful.

Together with duration, courts weigh the degree of intrusion and the amount of force used on the subject in determining whether a stop has crossed the boundary and become the equivalent of an arrest. There is no bright-line rule. *United States v. Sharpe*, 470 U.S. 675 (1985) rejected the 20-minute limit proposed by the Model Code of Pre-Arraignment Procedure, and (in an apparent retreat from *Royer*) warned against too much judicial second-guessing of whether the police acted in the least intrusive and most expeditious manner in conducting the investigative stop. "In evaluating whether an investigative detention is unreasonable," the Court cautioned, "common sense and ordinary human experience must govern over rigid criteria." 470 U.S. at 685.

In exceptional circumstances, detentions ranging from 40 minutes to 16 hours have been held permissible as *Terry* stops because that was the time necessary to effectuate the original purpose of the stop—to confirm or dispel the initial suspicion. In *Sharpe*, the officers were following two vehicles suspected of involvement in drug trafficking, but initially were able to stop only one. The first driver was detained for a period of 40 minutes, which was the time it took to overtake the second driver and return him to the location of the first vehicle. In *United States v. Montoya de Hernandez*, 473 U.S. 531 (1985), an air traveler from Colombia was detained incommunicado by customs officials for 16 hours because she was suspected of being a balloon swallower, a smuggler who hides narcotics in her alimentary canal. In both cases, the Court treated the detentions as stops, not arrests, because it concluded that their duration did not exceed the time necessary to complete the preliminary field investigation. In the case of the balloon swallower, 16 hours was the time necessary to await a bowel movement.[9]

In the more routine situation, the lawful duration of a border patrol stop will be the short time necessary to ask a few questions or request a document regarding immigration status. *United States v. Chacon*, 330 F.3d 323 (5th Cir. 2003). Use of a drug-sniffing dog will not extend this time, but must fit within it. *United States v. Garcia-Garcia*, 319 F.3d 726 (5th Cir. 2003).

To summarize, decisional law has established gradations of justification that correspond to the scope and degree of the particular intrusion. If police merely question an individual on the street without detaining her against her will, the Fourth Amendment is not implicated. At the point at which a reasonable person would believe she is no longer free to leave and is being detained, a stop has occurred and the Fourth Amendment is triggered, requiring that the officer have reasonable suspicion that criminal activity is afoot. To support the additional intrusion of a pat-down frisk, the officer must have reasonable suspicion that the subject is armed and dangerous. Finally, if the nature and duration of the detention rise to the level of a full-scale arrest or its equivalent, probable cause must be shown. Figure 4-2 demonstrates the connection between degree of intrusion and justification required.

---

9. The *Montoya de Hernandez* Court did emphasize that its decision was rendered in the unique context of a customs inspection.

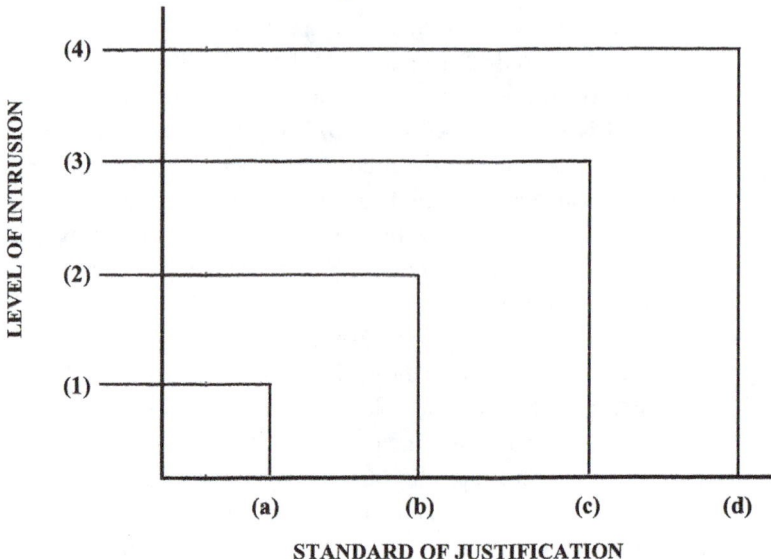

(1) Subject confronted but free to leave.
(2) Stop — subject confronted and not free to leave.
(3) Frisk — limited to pat-down search.
(4) Arrest or intrusion equivalent to arrest.

(a) No justification required.
(b) Reasonable suspicion that criminal activity is afoot. More than a hunch or unparticularized suspicion.
(c) In addition to (b), reasonable suspicion that suspect is armed and dangerous.
(d) Probable cause.

Figure 4-2. Arrest/Stop and Frisk—Justification

§4.4 THE EXPANSION OF *TERRY*: DEMAND FOR IDENTIFICATION, VEHICLE STOPS, DETENTION OF EFFECTS, PROTECTIVE SWEEPS, AND PLAIN FEEL

The authority of police officers to briefly detain subjects for investigative purposes on information amounting to reasonable suspicion has been expanded beyond the street-encounter context of *Terry*. A demand for identification from the subject is deemed proper, as a "request for identity has an immediate relation to the purpose, rationale, and practical demands of a *Terry* stop." *Hiibel v. Sixth Judicial District Court of Nevada*, 542 U.S. 177 (2004). If authorized by state law, police may arrest for failure to comply. *Arizona v. United States*, 132 S. Ct. 2492 (2012) allows the checking of immigration status so long as it does not extend the lawful stop.

An officer may stop a vehicle and briefly detain the motorist where the officer has "at least articulable and reasonable suspicion" that he is violating the law, including motor vehicle infractions. *Delaware v. Prouse*, 440 U.S. 648 (1979). The stop also encompasses the authority to order the driver and passengers out of the car (based on the Supreme Court's premise that such order is a minimal intrusion beyond the stop itself and is justified by safety concerns). *Pennsylvania v. Mimms*, 434 U.S. 106 (1977); *Maryland v. Wilson*, 519 U.S. 408 (1997).[10] And a dog sniff of the exterior of the car is permitted so long as getting the dog to the scene does not prolong the otherwise justifiable stop. *Illinois v. Caballes*, 543 U.S. 405 (2005). Where the use of the dog extends the time of the stop beyond what is required to complete its purpose, such as the issuance of a warning ticket, it will be deemed unlawful. See *Rodriguez v. United States*, 135 S. Ct. 1609 (2015). The motorist's immigration status may also be checked so long as the stop is not prolonged. *Arizona v. United States*, supra.

If the officer has reason to believe that the driver or occupant is armed and dangerous, then the officer may frisk and also conduct a limited search of the interior of the car immediately within the subject's control. Such a search is permissible even where the suspect is being held by police *outside* the car because of the possibility that he may break away or have access to weapons in the car after he is released. In *Michigan v. Long*, 463 U.S. 1032 (1983), police officers saw a car swerve into a ditch and, stopping to investigate, made observations that the driver was intoxicated and that there was a large hunting knife on the floorboard. The Court held that the officers were justified in searching the passenger compartment as well as frisking the driver because they were aware of specific facts that would "warrant reasonable officers in believing that the suspect is dangerous and the suspect may gain immediate control of weapons."

In *Arizona v. Johnson*, 129 S. Ct. 781 (2009), the Court reiterated the requirements of *Terry* with regard to automobile stops. First, the detention must be lawful, and second, the officer must reasonably suspect that the person stopped is armed and dangerous. In *Johnson*, the officer acted reasonably in questioning the occupants and then ordering them out of the vehicle pursuant to *Maryland v. Wilson*. The unanimous Court held that the scope of the vehicle stop extends until such time as the officer no longer needs to control the scene and informs the driver that he is free to leave. Discussions about matters not related to the reason for the stop do not convert the encounter into something different from a stop.

Reasonable suspicion that a package or piece of luggage contains contraband or evidence of a crime has been held to justify its temporary seizure.

---

10. Some states have rejected these decisions and have interpreted their own constitutions to require reasonable suspicion of criminal activity before persons may be ordered out of a stopped vehicle. See, e.g., *Commonwealth v. Gonsalves*, 429 Mass. 658, 711 N.E.2d 108 (1999).

United States v. Place, 462 U.S. 696 (1983); *United States v.Van Leeuwen*, 397 U.S. 249 (1970). Applying the *Terry* balancing test, the Supreme Court has concluded that where reasonable suspicion exists, the governmental interest in briefly detaining such personal effects outweighs the minimal intrusion to the owner. As with stops of the person, these seizures must be limited in both time and scope. Thus a suitcase may be temporarily held by law enforcement agents at an airport for the purpose of subjecting it to a narcotics-sniffing dog, but a detention of 90 minutes has been deemed excessive and unreasonable. *United States v. Place*.

The *Terry* rationale has even been applied to permit a protective sweep of a home in which an arrest is being made. Where the officers possess "a reasonable belief based on specific and articulable facts that an area to be swept harbors an individual posing a danger to those at the arrest scene," the officers may engage in a limited search for such an individual. *Maryland v. Buie*, 494 U.S. 325 (1990). See also §6.3. The sweep may extend only to a cursory inspection of those spaces where a person may hide, and may last only as long as is required to resolve the suspicion. This expansion of the stop and frisk doctrine led Justice Brennan to observe in dissent:

> *Terry* and its early progeny permitted only brief investigative stops and extremely limited searches based on reasonable suspicion but this Court more recently has applied the rationale underlying *Terry* to a wide variety of more intrusive searches and seizures prompting my continued criticism of the emerging tendency on the part of the Court to convert the *Terry* decision from a narrow exception into one that swallows the general rule that searches are reasonable only if based on probable cause.

494 U.S. at 339.

Terry was invoked in *Illinois v. McArthur*, 531 U.S. 326 (2001), to justify officers in preventing McArthur from entering his home while they sought and obtained a search warrant. His wife had informed police that her husband had hidden marijuana under the couch. When he refused to consent to a search, one officer left for a warrant while the other remained with McArthur, restricting his access to the home unless accompanied by the officer. The Court found the temporary restriction imposed upon him to be reasonable because there was probable cause to search the home, the restriction was limited to two hours, and the police had good reason to believe he would destroy the marijuana before they returned with a warrant.

As previously noted, when an officer believes the subject of a stop is armed and dangerous, the officer may conduct a pat-down search. Originally, the scope of this intrusion was limited to a pat-down for weapons. But it has since been expanded to allow an officer, who feels an object that is immediately recognized as contraband, to seize the object (the so-called plain feel doctrine). See *Minnesota v. Dickerson*, 508 U.S. 366 (1993).

Examples

What Constitutes a Stop?

1. Two federal drug agents in plain clothes approached Mindy as she proceeded through an airport terminal. They identified themselves and requested to see her identification and ticket, which she produced. They then posed several questions about her travel plans and returned her papers. At the agents' request, Mindy accompanied them to a nearby office. Was Mindy subjected to a stop during the initial encounter (before she proceeded to the office)? After she followed the agents to the office? Does it matter whether the agents *intended to* detain her? Does it matter whether Mindy *actually believed* she was not free to leave?

2. Officers on routine patrol passed a pedestrian, who changed direction and ran when he saw the cruiser. The officers followed alongside, and the man picked up speed and turned the corner. When the officers saw the man pull a plastic bag from his pocket and throw it to the ground, they retrieved it and found a suspicious white powder. The man was then stopped and placed under arrest. He was later charged with narcotics possession. Defense counsel has moved to suppress the evidence on the ground that it was the fruit of an illegal seizure—i.e., the initial pursuit of the defendant *before* they had reasonable suspicion. How should the court rule?

3. In the course of its work, U.S. Immigration and Customs Enforcement (ICE) conducts factory surveys to determine whether illegal aliens are present at a worksite. Uniformed and armed officers disperse themselves throughout the building and systematically approach each employee. After identifying themselves and displaying their badges, the officers ask questions relating to the employee's citizenship. During the survey, employees are free to continue their work. Does this conduct amount to a stop implicating the Fourth Amendment requirement for justification?

4. The City of Fantasy has experienced a violent crime wave. Mayor Hack responds by instructing the police patrolling in high-crime areas to be "aggressive," specifically to stop citizens and demand identification from them. As legal counsel to the mayor, how would you advise her regarding the legality of this practice?

5. An officer in a high-crime area observed a couple in a car and suspected an act of prostitution. When asked what they were doing, they replied, "Waiting for Bill" and pointed to a man who was approaching. The officer asked, "Are you Bill?" The man's response could not be understood because he had something in his mouth. When the officer ordered him to spit it out, the man spat out vials of what appeared to be crack cocaine. Was this a stop?

Reasonable Suspicion to Stop and Frisk

6. Two experienced officers on cruiser patrol at 4:00 A.M. observed a late-model Cadillac traveling along Main Street with a youthful driver and passenger, both appearing to be in their early twenties. Although the Cadillac did not commit any traffic violation, the officers' attention was drawn to it. As the cruiser approached the car from the adjoining lane, the driver raised his hand to his face, thereby obscuring his features from the officers' view. Their suspicions aroused, the officers stopped the vehicle. Was this stop justified?

7. Officer Mann, while on routine foot patrol in an area of New York City known for its brisk narcotics traffic, made observations of Sam Slam over a period of several hours. During that period, he saw Sam converse with several persons known to the officer as narcotics users. Mann did not over-hear any of the conversations, nor did he see anything pass between Sam and those he spoke with. The officer finally confronted Sam at a restaurant and ordered him to step outside, which he did. While questioning Sam on the street, Officer Mann reached into Sam's pocket and pulled out several packets that contained heroin. Was this seizure justified?

8. Officer Jones observed Felix, whom she recognized as an enforcer for a local drug gang, emerge from a notorious crack house that has been the scene of many violent encounters. When Felix spotted Jones, he turned and ran in the opposite direction. Jones ordered Felix to stop and then administered a pat-down search. The search revealed no weapons, but Jones felt a lump in Felix's pocket, which she examined further with her fingers. She felt cellophane, commonly used to package crack cocaine. Jones seized the cellophane bag, which contained a small amount of crack cocaine. Was this seizure lawful?

9. An officer on patrol in a high-crime area at 2:15 A.M. was informed by a person known to him and who had provided information in the past that an individual in a nearby car was in possession of narcotics and had a gun at his waist. The officer approached the car, tapped on the window, and asked the occupant to open the door. Instead, the occupant rolled down the window, at which point the officer reached into the car and removed a revolver from the occupant's waistband. Was this seizure justified?

10. While on routine patrol a police officer observed a person who was suspected of having committed a robbery the week before. In the absence of information amounting to probable cause to arrest, may the officer nevertheless briefly detain the suspect to question her concerning the robbery?

11. An experienced police officer observed three men in flashy clothes conversing on a street corner. Acting on a hunch that a drug transaction was occurring, the officer approached the men and addressed a question to

them about their activities. They immediately turned away and began to quickly depart. May the officer stop and frisk them at this point?

12. Officer Smith pulls over the driver of a pickup truck for speeding. Upon approaching the vehicle, Smith observes a Confederate flag on the antenna and a bumper sticker stating MORE GUNS — LESS CRIME. In addition, the officer notices that the suspect is wearing a camouflage jacket and a pin on his lapel stating, KISS ME, I'M A MONTANA MILITIAMAN. Concerned that the suspect was carrying a firearm, Officer Smith searches the vehicle for weapons. Is he justified in doing so?

13. At 9:15 A.M., narcotics agents at the Dallas–Ft. Worth airport observed a young woman disembark a flight from Miami, Florida. She carried a small gym bag and walked quickly to a restroom. As she walked, she looked around as if she was expecting to meet someone. She left the restroom and went to a set of telephones, where she made a call lasting 30 minutes. She then proceeded to the baggage claim area, where she waited for several minutes but did not pick up any baggage. Their attention drawn to her, the agents approached the woman, displayed their identification, and asked if they could speak with her. She appeared extremely nervous and began to perspire; her voice cracked and her hands trembled. She agreed to speak with the agents and, at their request, gave them her airline ticket. When they asked for identification, she replied that she had lost her wallet. The agents asked how long she intended to stay in Dallas and she replied one week. At that point, the agent noticed that her ticket indicated that she was scheduled for a return flight to Miami that afternoon. Is there justification to further detain the woman?

The Proper Scope of the Investigative Detention — When Does a Stop Grow into an Arrest?

14. Two police officers were approached by a pedestrian (previously unknown to them) who stated that a person named Leon was in Joe's Grill on Oak Street and that Leon had several bags of heroin for sale. She provided a detailed description of this individual and his clothing. The officers proceeded to Joe's Grill but found no one of that description. Immediately upon leaving the bar, they observed an individual meeting Leon's description walking quickly away along the sidewalk. The officers approached this person, blocked his movement, and asked him to identify himself. He nervously responded that he was Leon Silver. At that point, one of the officers asked the subject to remove his shoes, which he did, and they continued to question him. What level of cause is required to justify this encounter, and did the police possess it?

Overview — Putting It All Together

15. On Tuesday at 2:30 P.M., Officer Harvey was on routine cruiser patrol in a suburban neighborhood that had been experiencing a spate of daytime burglaries. Harvey's attention was drawn to a car parked in a residential driveway. The car's trunk was open, exposing several large green plastic trash bags which appeared full and of the type reportedly used to remove the loot in the break-ins. The uniformed officer made a U-turn and pulled into the driveway behind the car. At that moment the driver had just closed the trunk and was beginning to back out, but the police car now blocked her exit. The driver got out of the car and, appearing quite upset, asked the officer to move the cruiser. The officer responded instead by asking the driver for identification, which she produced. The identification indicated an address on the other side of town. At that point, the officer frisked the driver, took the keys to her car from her coat pocket, opened the trunk, and then also opened the trash bags inside. Finding TVs, stereo components, jewelry, and cash, the officer placed the driver under arrest. It was later determined that the items had been stolen from a nearby residence. The driver (now defendant) moved to suppress the items. Were the officer's actions justified?

16. Deputy Sheriff Boyer was on cruiser patrol when he heard a report over the police radio that a bank had just been robbed and that the four male perpetrators, armed with guns, had escaped in a 1975 red Ford Maverick with no license plate. Ten minutes later, Boyer observed a vehicle of that description (but with a license plate) traveling in the direction away from the bank. He followed the car and signaled for it to stop, which it did. As Boyer approached the car, he observed two men and a woman inside, and they appeared startled. Boyer drew his revolver and ordered the occupants out. As they complied, the deputy observed a bulge in the pocket of the driver. Boyer patted the subject down, felt a hard object, and reached into the subject's pocket, removing a small-caliber pistol. What level of justification did the deputy need for each stage of this encounter, and did he have such justification?

Explanations

What Constitutes a Stop?

1. A person is considered to have been seized within the meaning of the Fourth Amendment if, in view of all the circumstances surrounding the incident, a reasonable person in such situation would believe that she was not free to leave. In *United States v. Mendenhall*, 446 U.S. 544 (1980), the case upon which example 1 is based, the Supreme Court splintered as to whether under this definition a seizure had taken place during the initial encounter. Emphasizing that the encounter

occurred in a public place, that the agents did not demand to see the subject's papers but rather merely requested them, and that there was no display of weapons or any other force, Justice Stewart (joined only by Justice Rehnquist) concluded that no stop had occurred because nothing in the record suggested that Mendenhall had any objective reason to believe that she was not free to end the conversation and proceed on her way. Three members of the Court assumed that the confrontation amounted to a seizure, but concluded that it was justified because there were sufficient facts to establish reasonable suspicion. 446 U.S. at 560 (Powell, J., concurring in part and concurring in the judgment). The four remaining Justices, while believing that a remand on the question was desirable, treated the encounter as a stop and concluded there was insufficient justification for it. 446 U.S. at 570-571 (White, J., dissenting).

The reasonable person standard obviously leaves considerable room for such differences of opinion, and the particular factual context of the encounter becomes of primary importance. In *Florida v. Royer*, 460 U.S. 491 (1983) (discussed in §4.3), the Court reviewed an airport encounter quite similar to that in *Mendenhall* but concluded that a stop had occurred, explaining:

> Asking for and examining Royer's ticket and his driver's license were no doubt permissible in themselves, but when the officers identified themselves as narcotics agents, told Royer that he was suspected of transporting narcotics, and asked him to accompany them to the police room, while retaining his ticket and driver's license and without indicating in any way that he was free to depart, Royer was effectively seized for the purposes of the Fourth Amendment. These circumstances surely amount to a show of official authority such that a reasonable person would have believed he was not free to leave.

460 U.S. at 501-502. The only obvious distinction between Royer's experience (deemed a seizure) and Mendenhall's (not a seizure) seems to be that the police returned Mendenhall's papers while they retained Royer's.

While the reasonable person standard is imprecise, some things are clear concerning its operation. One is that the *actual* belief of the subject that she is (or is not) being detained is not determinative. "The test is an objective one, concerned with whether a reasonable person would feel he could leave, [and] it does not matter whether a particular defendant feels intimidated or at ease." *United States v. Berryman*, 717 F.2d 651, 655 (1st Cir. 1983). What counts is whether a reasonable person in the subject's situation "would feel free to disregard the police and go about his business." *United States v. Grant*, 696 F.3d 780, 783 (8th Cir. 2012). The officer's conversational tone points towards a conclusion against detention.

See *United States v. Fields*, 823 F.3d 20, 28 (1st Cir. 2016) (even though backup officers had arrived).

Similarly, because the standard focuses on the state of mind of the subject, the *actual but unstated* intention of the officers to detain is irrelevant to the inquiry. See *United States v. Hensley*, 469 U.S. 221, 235 (1985). As the Supreme Court has noted in the *Miranda* context, "[by] limiting analysis to the objective circumstances of the interrogation, and asking how a reasonable person in the suspect's position would understand his freedom to terminate questioning and leave, the objective test avoids burdening police with the task of anticipating the idiosyncrasies of every individual suspect and divining how those particular traits affect each person's subjective state of mind." *J.D.B. v. North Carolina*, 564 U.S. 261, 271 (2011).

Thus, in our example, neither the agents' intent nor Mindy's subjective perceptions are determinative on the issue of whether a seizure occurred. As in tort law, the reasonable person reigns supreme here.

Factors considered by courts in applying the *Mendenhall* test include 1) the number and positioning of the officers involved, 2) the tone of voice used by the officers, 3) whether the encounter occurred in a public place, 4) whether the subject's path was blocked, 5) whether the subject was asked to accompany the police or step aside with them, and 6) whether the officers retained the subject's identification, ticket, or other possession for more than a minimal amount of time. See, e.g., *United States v. Gonzales*, 842 F.2d 748 (5th Cir. 1988), *overruled on other grounds*, *United States v. Hurtado*, 905 F.2d 74 (5th Cir. 1990).

The failure to notify the suspect that she is free to leave weighs (but not determinatively) in favor of the conclusion that the encounter amounted to a seizure. See *United States v. Berryman*, supra. Conversely, informing the subject he has the right to leave points towards a finding of no seizure. *United States v. Wilson*, 413 F.3d 382, 387 (3d Cir. 2005); *United States v. Ortega-Santana*, 869 F.2d 12 (1st Cir. 1989) (fact that subject was twice informed that he was free to leave required conclusion that his accompanying agents to their office was not a seizure). See also *United States v. Morgan*, 270 F.3d 625 (8th Cir. 2001) (at end of routine stop, officer engaged suspect in small talk regarding war on drugs and, although officer did not indicate suspect was free to go, court found that reasonable person would have felt free to go).

Also pointing toward a conclusion that a seizure has occurred is the statement to the subject that she is suspected of criminal activity. In *United States v. Rodriguez-Escalera*, 884 F.3d 661 (7th Cir. 2018), the officer, while telling the subject she was free to go, continued to interrogate her saying he suspected there was something illegal in her car. See also *United States v. White*, 890 F.2d 1413 (8th Cir. 1989) (reasonable person would not feel free to depart, despite agents' assurances, because in response to his question as to why they had stopped him, agents told subject that he exhibited characteristics of a drug trafficker); United States v. Berry, 670 F.2d 583, 597 (5th Cir. 1982) ("Statements which intimate that an investigation has focused on a specific individual easily could induce a reasonable person to believe that failure to cooperate would lead only to formal detention."). Although a particularized focus on the suspect is certainly a factor to be considered, it is not be a *per se* rule. See United States v. Glass, 128 F.3d 1398 (10th Cir. 1997).

In sum, where the officers merely approach the individual, display their badges, and ask questions, it is unlikely that a seizure will be found. See United States v. Hanson, 801 F.2d 757, 761 (5th Cir. 1986).

For other cases raising the issue of whether airport encounters constitute a seizure, see Reid v. Georgia, 448 U.S. 438 (1980) and Florida v. Rodriquez, 469 U.S. 1, 5 (1985) ("The initial contact between the officers and respondent, where they simply asked if he would step aside and talk with them, was clearly the sort of consensual encounter that implicates no Fourth Amendment interest.").

Remember that if we conclude the agents did not "stop" Mindy within the meaning of the Fourth Amendment, they need not demonstrate *any level* of cause to justify their action. Regardless of our conclusion as to the initial encounter, however, it would appear that a seizure did occur when Mindy was asked to accompany the agents to the office, and thus reasonable suspicion would be required at that point in the events.

2. As we have seen, there is no bright-line rule to determine what constitutes a seizure. Rather, the test is whether a reasonable person, viewing the particular conduct of the police and the surrounding circumstances, would have believed that her liberty was constrained and she was not free to leave. In certain limited circumstances a police chase may constitute a seizure, as in Brower v. County of Inyo, 489 U.S. 593 (1989), where the motorist had been chased for 20 miles and finally crashed into a roadblock set up by the police.

On the facts in this example, however, no seizure occurred during the initial pursuit. A unanimous Supreme Court held in Michigan v. Chesternut, 486 U.S. 567 (1988) that such brief pursuit by police, with nothing else, would not have communicated to a reasonable person that they sought to capture him or otherwise restrain his freedom. Because no stop occurred, the police were not required to have a particularized objective basis for suspecting the subject of criminal activity in order to so pursue him. Two members of the Chesternut Court, Justices Kennedy and Scalia, proposed a change from the Mendenhall test that would require the officers' pursuit to actually achieve a "restraining effect" before a seizure could be said to occur. 486 U.S. at 577 (Kennedy, J., concurring). The Court appears to have adopted this position in California v. Hodari D., 499 U.S. 621 (1991), which underscores the fact that the chase itself is not sufficient to constitute a seizure. Rather, there must be either an application of restraining force on the subject, or the latter must yield to the officers.

It should be noted that some states find a chase to be a seizure under their own laws. See, e.g., *Commonwealth v. Sykes*, 449 Mass. 308 (2007) (officers left vehicle and chased defendant after he collided with a tree, abandoned his bike, and ran from them). However, there must be something more than merely chasing on foot, or following in a cruiser—there must be some show of authority such as activating the cruiser's blue lights or blocking the car. See *Commonwealth v. Powell*, 459 Mass. 572, 577 (2011); *Commonwealth v. Perry*, 62 Mass. App. 500 (2004).

3. The Supreme Court answered this question in the negative in *INS v. Delgado*, 466 U.S. 210 (1984). "Interrogation relating to one's identity or a request for identification by the police does not, by itself, constitute a Fourth Amendment seizure. Unless the circumstances of the encounter are so intimidating as to demonstrate that a reasonable person would have believed he was not free to leave if he had not responded, one cannot say that the questioning resulted in a detention under the Fourth Amendment." 466 U.S. at 210. Again, however, the members of the Court sharply disagreed on the application of the *Mendenhall* test. The dissenters found it "plain beyond cavil that the manner in which the INS conducted these surveys demonstrated a show of authority of sufficient size and force to overbear the will of any reasonable person." *Id.* at 229.

In another factory seizure case, *Martinez v. Nygaard*, 831 F.2d 822 (9th Cir. 1987), the court held that a worker was not seized even when grabbed by the shoulder by an INS officer because the action was designed only to get the worker's attention, and he was released immediately. In addition, the worker later testified that he was not put in fear. The basis for this ruling would seem questionable given the objective, not subjective, focus of the *Mendenhall* standard. A co-worker was, however, held to have been seized when she was physically prevented from leaving her work area.

4. While this sort of brief detention may appear so minimal as to require no specific justification, the Supreme Court has held in several contexts that *any* detention (within the *Mendenhall* definition) triggers the Fourth Amendment and thus must be justified by a showing of reasonable suspicion. In *Brown v. Texas*, 443 U.S. 47 (1979), officers stopped an individual in a high-crime area of El Paso because he looked suspicious and they wanted to ascertain his identity. The Court ruled the stop unconstitutional, explaining:

> In the absence of any basis for suspecting appellant of misconduct, the balance between the public interest and appellant's right to security and privacy tilts in favor of freedom from police interference. . . . [E]ven assuming that [a strong social] purpose is served to some degree by stopping and

> demanding identification from an individual without any specific basis for believing he is involved in criminal activity, the guarantees of the Fourth Amendment do not allow it. When such a stop is not based on objective criteria, the risk of arbitrary and abusive police practices exceeds tolerable limits.

443 U.S. at 52. The Court observed that while "the record suggests an understandable desire to assert a police presence that purpose does not negate Fourth Amendment guarantees." Id. at 51.

The Court has ruled unlawful the common police practice of stopping motorists at random to check their driver's license and registration. See Delaware v. Prouse, 440 U.S. 648 (1979). Although such spot checks are minimal intrusions, they are nevertheless "constitutionally cognizable" and thus may be conducted only where there is "articulable and reasonable suspicion" that the motorist is unlicensed or unregistered or is otherwise in violation of law. 440 U.S. at 661.

The determinative issue in example 4 is whether the proposed "aggressive" encounters on the street amount to seizures triggering the Fourth Amendment. The case of Florida v. Bostick, 501 U.S. 429 (1991), holding that drug sweeps of buses do not necessarily constitute seizures, might indicate that the proposed street encounters are not within the purview of the Amendment and thus can occur without any specific justification. The question is how aggressive the police officers can be: Can they forcibly restrain the individual until she identifies herself? The Court indicated an affirmative answer in Hiibel v. Sixth Judicial District Court of Nevada, 542 U.S. 177 (2004), holding that if reasonable suspicion exists, police may demand identification.

5. The court ruled it was a stop in Commonwealth v. Houle, 622 N.E.2d 638 (Mass. App. Ct. 1993). A uniformed officer ordering a person in authoritarian language to spit out what was in his mouth is of such a nature that it would reasonably be regarded as offensive in ordinary social intercourse. Years later the court revisited this scenario in Commonwealth v. Evans, 34 N.E.3d 772 (Mass. App. Ct. 2015) and reached the same result.

In our example Bill could reasonably be expected to believe that he had to comply. The result of compliance was an intrusion on Bill's privacy. A stop requires reasonable suspicion that criminal activity is afoot, and the officer had no reasonable suspicion that Bill was involved in a criminal act. Presence in a high-crime area is inadequate to support such suspicion. The court reasoned that Bill could have been chewing gum or tobacco or could have had a speech impediment, and therefore the fact that there was something in his mouth was not enough to establish reasonable suspicion. But compare Commonwealth v. Thomas, 646 N.E.2d 428 (Mass. App. Ct. 1993) (seizure of cocaine packets in defendant's mouth was permissible because the white packets were plainly visible to the officer during casual conversation, giving rise to probable cause).

In *Clayton v. State*, 616 So. 2d 615 (Fla. Dist. Ct. App. 1993), seven officers in three vehicles wearing jackets reading "Sheriff's Office Drug Task Force" observed the defendant toss a waist pouch into the back of his truck in a convenience store parking lot. Two of the police vehicles pulled up and four officers jumped out. One ran up to the defendant and asked aggressively, "What was that you threw in the truck?" The defendant replied, "That was my gun." The court held it a stop and required a showing of reasonable suspicion of criminal activity. The threatening presence of several officers as well as their authoritarian tone made it reasonable for the defendant to believe the question was a command rather than a request. A similar result was reached in *State v. Jason*, 2 P.3d 856 (N.M. 2000), where officers in their cruiser followed two juveniles walking down the street, ordered them to approach, and asked if they were armed. See also *Commonwealth v. McClease*, 750 A.2d 320 (Pa. 2000) (request to motorist to stay in his vehicle constituted a stop). But compare *United States v. Waldon*, 206 F.3d 597 (6th Cir. 2000) (no stop occurred where officer simply approached suspect at a bus stop, mentioned that he was investigating a bank robbery, and asked him what he was doing in the area, because no indication that officer conducted himself in intimidating or coercive manner and, although officer asked for an ID, he did not take the wallet).

Reasonable Suspicion to Stop and Frisk

6. Given the totality of circumstances, did the officers have concrete facts that would establish a reasonable suspicion that the subjects were involved in criminal activity? The answer is probably no. The fact that the youths were in an expensive automobile late at night is not sufficient in itself to give the officers anything more than a hunch that something criminal was afoot. Even if the driver's gesture obscuring his face reasonably appeared to the officers as a deliberate attempt at concealment (as opposed to an off-hand movement), there is still very serious doubt whether justification for a *Terry* stop was present. The Massachusetts Supreme Judicial Court, while refusing to rule as a matter of law that such secretive conduct could never constitute reasonable suspicion in conjunction with other circumstances, held that the circumstances in our example did not justify a stop of the Cadillac. See *Commonwealth v. Bacon*, 381 Mass. 642 (1980).

Even if the stop was justified, the officers would be able to pat down the suspects only if they reasonably believed that they were armed and dangerous. Presence in a high-crime area where there has been violent shooting before is not enough to lead an officer to believe that a suspect is armed and dangerous. This was the situation in *Commonwealth v. Gomes*, 453 Mass. 506 (2009), where the court suppressed drugs found after officers searched a man in a high-crime area because his criminal history did not include any weapons-related offenses and there was no evidence that he made particular gestures or used any body language that would cause the officers to believe that he was carrying a weapon.

7. Sam was clearly subjected to a stop, and thus Officer Mann must be prepared to articulate the facts giving rise to a reasonable suspicion that Sam was involved in criminal activity. Given the limited information known to him, Mann will be unable to do so. As the Supreme Court observed in the companion case to *Terry*, upon which this example is based, the officer was completely ignorant regarding the content of the conversations between Sam and the narcotics users and could point to no concrete indication that criminal transactions were occurring: "So far as he knew, they might indeed have been talking about the World Series." *Sibron v. New York*, 392 U.S. 40, 47 (1968). "The inference that persons who talk to narcotics addicts are engaged in the criminal traffic of narcotics is simply not the sort of reasonable inference required to support an intrusion by the police upon an individual's personal security." 392 U.S. at 62. Moreover, as Justice Harlan observed in his concurrence, at the time the officer confronted Sibron in the restaurant there was no apparently imminent crime about to occur, as there was in *Terry* where Officer McFadden interrupted what he reasonably believed was an unfolding robbery.

Because the stop was unlawful, the evidence seized during the subsequent search must be suppressed under the exclusionary rule. (See Chapter 7.) Even if the stop had been justified, however, Officer Mann's reach into Sam's pocket was not. In order to justify a frisk, Officer Mann would have to be able to articulate facts from which it may be reasonably inferred that Sam was armed and dangerous. As the *Sibron* Court concluded, "the suspect's mere act of talking with a number of known narcotics addicts over an eight-hour period no more gives rise to reasonable fear of life or limb on the part of the police officer than it justifies [the initial stop]." *Id.* at 64.

In addition to the absence of adequate justification in the form of reasonable suspicion, the scope of the search conducted by Officer Mann exceeded permissible bounds:

> The search for weapons approved in *Terry* consisted solely of a limited patting of the outer clothing of the suspect for concealed objects which might be used as instruments of assault. Only when he discovered such objects did the officer in *Terry* place his hands in the pockets of the men he searched. In this case, with no attempt at an initial limited exploration for arms, [the officer] thrust his hand into Sibron's pocket and took from him envelopes of heroin. His testimony shows that he was looking for narcotics, and he found them. The search was not reasonably limited in scope to the

accomplishment of the only goal which might conceivably have justified its inception — the protection of the officer by disarming a potentially dangerous man.

Id. at 65.

8. Given the information regarding Felix's reputation, the stakeout, and the evasive action, there appears to be enough justification for both a stop and a frisk. This is especially true in light of *Illinois v. Wardlow*, 528 U.S. 119 (2000), which permits consideration of evasive action. See also *United States v. Franklin*, 323 F.3d 1298, 1302 (11th Cir. 2003) ("While flight is not proof of wrongdoing, it is indicative of such. Innocent persons might run from police officers; but flight creates an ambiguity; and the officers may stop the person to resolve the ambiguity. Franklin's flight was particularly suspicious because of its nature and its duration. He ran away at full speed as soon as he saw the officers. He did not turn and start to walk away. He did not act like he was going about his business. Instead he took off in 'headlong' flight. While any kind of flight, even walking away, might support a finding of reasonable suspicion, 'headlong flight' — wherever it occurs — is the consummate act of evasion.").

Officer Jones, however, goes beyond a lawful frisk in our example by fingering the lump in the pocket. Because this occurred after Jones apparently concluded there was no weapon, it is beyond the scope of a traditional frisk. Thus, the further invasion and resulting seizure are unlawful. If, however, as part of the frisk, she immediately recognized the package as cocaine, this would fall under the plain feel doctrine established by *Minnesota v. Dickerson*, 508 U.S. 366 (1993).

9. There are several problems regarding the police actions here. First, unlike Officer McFadden in *Terry*, the officer in this example acted on the basis of information supplied by a third party rather than on his own personal observations. Second, while the informant had previously supplied information, we do not know if it turned out to be accurate. Third, we do not know anything about the basis of the informant's conclusion that the subject was in possession of narcotics and a gun. Fourth, even if the officer had reasonable grounds to suspect that the subject was in violation of the law and was armed and dangerous, he did not limit his initial action to a pat-down of the clothing, but rather, immediately intruded into the driver's waistband and removed the gun.

Despite similar complications, the Court held in *Adams v. Williams*, 407 U.S. 143 (1972) that the officer's actions were lawful. Conceding that the informant's tip would not satisfy the requirements for justification of a full-scale search or arrest (requiring probable cause), the Court nevertheless ruled that the information carried enough indicia of reliability to justify a forcible stop. Further, "[w]hen Williams rolled down his window, rather than complying with the policeman's request to step out of the car so that his movements could more easily be seen, the revolver allegedly at Williams' waist became an even greater threat. Under these circumstances the policeman's action in reaching to the spot where the gun was thought to be hidden constituted a limited intrusion designed to insure his safety, and we conclude that it was reasonable." 407 U.S. at 148.

Adams v. Williams explicitly rejected the argument that reasonable suspicion can only be based on the officer's own personal observations. As with probable cause, the source may be a third party so long as the information carries sufficient indicia of reliability. Examples of such information would be the description of an assailant by the victim herself and the warning from a credible confidential informant that a specific crime is about to occur. *Alabama v. White*, 496 U.S. 325 (1990) added anonymous tips (with sufficient police corroboration) to the permissible sources of information leading to reasonable suspicion. But *Florida v. J. L.*, 529 U.S. 266 (2000) refused to allow a Terry stop based exclusively on an anonymous tip.

United States v. Johnson, 364 F.3d 1185 (10th Cir. 2004) applied the standards articulated in *White* and *J. L.* Police received an anonymous "suspicious person" call reporting that a black male adult was pushing a female juvenile. The man was described as thin, 35 years old, five feet nine inches tall with short curly hair and wearing a jacket with "USA" on it. The white female was also described in detail. They were walking in what was known as the "War Zone," a high-crime area. The officers approached the pair described, who denied the male was pushing and threatening the female, and there was no sign of any such activity. The defendant, however, acted fidgety and fingered the walkie-talkie button on his cell phone. After further conversation, the officer advised Johnson that he was going to pat him down. The suspect indicated that he had a gun; the officer patted him down and removed it, and then placed him under arrest.

The court ruled the Fourth Amendment had not been violated. The anonymous tip carried sufficient reliability, given the facts that the caller had provided the dispatcher with his cell phone number and in his eight-minute call offered a description of the pair that was quickly confirmed by the officer's observations. Combined with the defendant's nervousness, the totality of the circumstances was sufficient to justify the stop.

In upholding the police action in that case, *Adams v. Williams* explicitly referred to the fact that the stop occurred in a high-crime area. 407 U.S. at 144. See also *United States v. Brignoni-Ponce*, 422 U.S. 873, 884 (1975) ("Officers may consider the characteristics of the area in which they encounter a vehicle."); *United States v. Cortez*, 449 U.S. 411, 419 (1981) ("Of critical importance, the officers knew that the area was a crossing point for illegal aliens."). But compare *United States v. Guillen-Cazares*, 989 F.2d 380 (10th Cir. 1993) (even though area was near the border and the road was often used to circumvent the checkpoint, court held there was no reasonable suspicion to stop two heavily loaded cars driving close together because many cars on the road might possess these characteristics); *United States v. Hernandez-Lopez*, 761 F. Supp. 2d 1172 (D.N.M. 2010) (even though driver was near the border and began swerving when border patrol agent followed him, there was no reasonable suspicion to stop the vehicle because the driver's actions described a large category of travelers).

Courts have tended to weigh the location of a stop quite heavily. The "reputation of an area for criminal activity is an articulable fact upon which a police officer may legitimately rely." *United States v. Rickus*, 737 F.2d 360, 365 (3d Cir. 1984). See also *United States v. Goodrich*, 450 F.3d 552 (3d Cir. 2006) ("The lateness of the hour of the stop further supports the inference of criminal activity, especially when considered alongside the area's reputation for criminal activity."). Obviously, as with probable cause, location alone is insufficient in itself to justify a *Terry* stop; there must still be particular facts pointing to the suspect's involvement in criminal activity. See *United States v. Kimball*, 25 F.3d 1 (1st Cir. 1994).

The courts apply an objective rather than a subjective analysis to determine whether a frisk is justified. In *Commonwealth v. Johnson*, 602 N.E.2d 555 (Mass. 1992), the defendant's vehicle almost hit a police car. A chase ensued and another police car headed him off. The first officer saw the defendant place something in the waistband of his pants, so he drew his weapon while the other officers pulled the defendant out of the car. He was subjected to a pat-down search and the officer pulled out of his waistband a bag of white powder and three bullets in a pouch. At trial, the state failed to show that the officer *actually believed* the bulge to be a weapon. Was there adequate justification for a frisk? The court concluded that there was. The stop was reasonable because the defendant had committed a traffic violation. The chase and the observation of the defendant putting something in his waistband gave the officer reasonable suspicion that the defendant might be armed. Thus, the officer was justified in conducting a frisk. And even though the officer failed to testify that he believed that the defendant was armed, the court nonetheless found the scope of the search justified, reasoning that the subjective belief of the officer was not determinative.

Assume that a sobriety checkpoint has been set up (see §4.5) and the officer spots an approaching motorist turn instead down an unpaved road, apparently to avoid the checkpoint. Would this create reasonable suspicion to stop the motorist? In *State v. Griffin*, 366 N.C. 473, 749 S.E.2d 444 (2013), the court concluded that a three-point turn in front of a well-marked checkpoint, though legal, gave rise to reasonable suspicion that criminal activity was afoot, specifically driving under the influence. Several courts agree. See *State of New Mexico v. Anaya*, 217 P.3d 586 (N.M. 2009).

Other courts, however, have found avoidance of a roadblock insufficient, by itself, to create reasonable suspicion. See *United States v. Neff*, 681 F.3d 1134 (10th Cir. 2012) (no reasonable suspicion where driver exited the highway after seeing three signs advising of an upcoming drug checkpoint); *State v. Bryson*, 755 N.E.2d 964 (Ohio Ct. App. 2001) (no reasonable suspicion where driver turned around in a driveway to avoid roadblock because citizens may wish to avoid encounters with the police for any number of reasons other than fear of being caught for a crime).

10. The issue here is whether a stop is permissible where its purpose is not (as was Officer McFadden's) to investigate a crime that is about to occur, but rather to investigate a crime that has *already* occurred. While recognizing that *Terry* was premised on the societal interest in permitting police to intervene to prevent crime, the Court has nonetheless authorized the use of stop and frisk for the investigation of past felonies, finding that the interest in solving such crimes and removing perpetrators from the streets outweighs the individual liberty interest invaded. *United States v. Hensley*, 469 U.S. 221 (1985). It is, of course, still necessary that the justification be grounded in specific and articulable facts that the person was involved in a felony.

11. A mere hunch clearly is not adequate to detain an individual, however briefly. The issue raised in this example is whether the refusal of the men to respond to the officer's questions gave him the reasonable suspicion required to stop them. The answer is no. "A person approached by an officer need not answer any question put to him; indeed, he may decline to listen to the questions at all and may go on his way. He may not be detained even momentarily without reasonable, objective grounds for doing so; and his refusal to listen or to answer does not, without more, furnish those grounds." *Florida v. Royer*, 460 U.S. 491, 498 (1983).

Similarly, a subject's refusal to consent to a search of her baggage or other possessions cannot be used as the sole basis for reasonable suspicion. See *United States v. Machuca-Barrera*, 261 F.3d 425 (5th Cir. 2001). "To suggest otherwise would mean that all innocent persons must submit to searches to avoid arousing the suspicion of law enforcement officers, in disregard of the underlying premises of the Fourth Amendment." *United States v. Malachi*, 728 F. Supp. 777, 781 (D.D.C. 1989). "If refusal of consent were a basis for reasonable suspicion, nothing would be left of Fourth Amendment protections. A motorist who consented to a search could be searched; and a motorist who refused consent could be searched as well." *United States v. Santos*, 403 F.3d 1120 (10th Cir. 2005).

With the decision in *Illinois v. Wardlow*, 528 U.S. 119 (2000), however, unprovoked flight in a high-crime area might provide sufficient justification for a stop.

In our example, the officer had neither reasonable suspicion that criminal activity was afoot nor reasonable suspicion that the subjects were armed and dangerous. There can thus be no lawful stop or frisk.

12. This example presents an interesting intersection of First and Fourth Amendment issues. *Estep v. Dallas County*, 310 F.3d 353 (5th Cir. 2002) held that the display of a National Rifle Association (NRA) sticker on a suspect's car could not in and of itself satisfy reasonable suspicion. The court however did not foreclose the inclusion of such displays in a totality-of-the-circumstances analysis. If the subject in this example exhibited other threatening behavior, then the bumper sticker, pin, and flag could perhaps enter into a demonstration of reasonable suspicion.

    Another such intersection occurred where an individual was videotaping a police station from a public sidewalk across the street. Officers approached him, and when he refused to identify himself, handcuffed him and took the camera. The court in *Turner v. Driver*, 848 F.3d 678 (5th Cir. 2017), a federal civil rights action, found no clearly established First Amendment right to record police activity, and regarding the Fourth Amendment, concluded it was objectively reasonable to suspect Turner was casing the station or stalking officers, giving rise to reasonable suspicion to stop and question him, but not probable cause to handcuff and arrest.

13. Clearly, if there was reasonable suspicion to suspect this woman of criminal activity, it must be based on something more than her innocuous conduct prior to being approached by the agents. While she may have matched some of the factors in the drug courier profile — she traveled from a known source city for narcotics, was young, appeared unusually nervous, and carried little luggage — these characteristics are shared by so many travelers that to permit stops based on them would subject large numbers of innocent persons to intrusive police activity. See *Reid v. Georgia*, 448 U.S. 438, 441 (1980). Her inability to produce identification, together with the inconsistency between her stated travel plans and those reflected on her ticket, however, do raise particular suspicion about her. On similar facts, the Fifth Circuit Court of Appeals found the suspicion to be reasonable and thus sufficient to justify an investigative detention. *United States v. Gonzales*, 842 F.2d 748 (5th Cir. 1988).

    The *Gonzales* court observed that law enforcement officials "are entitled to evaluate the specific and articulable facts known to them in light of their experience in narcotics enforcement, and we are inclined to give due credit to the experience and expertise of these officers." 842 F.2d at 753. See also *United States v. Harvey*, 205 F. Supp. 2d 546 (2002) (reasonable suspicion is a commonsense proposition and courts may credit the practical experience of officers in their assessment of it). The Supreme Court has underscored the proposition that the officer's experience is entitled to deference: "Among the circumstances that can give rise to reasonable suspicion are the agent's knowledge of the methods used in recent criminal activity and the characteristics of persons engaged in such illegal practices." *United States v. Mendenhall*, 446 U.S. 544, 563 (1980). Because of their expertise, officers are able to "perceive and articulate meaning in given conduct which would be wholly innocent to the untrained observer." *Brown v. Texas*, 443 U.S. 47, 52 n.2 (1979). As with probable cause, however, deference must not become abdication of responsibility for detached judicial review of police conduct.

The Proper Scope of the Investigative Detention — When Does a Stop Grow into an Arrest?

14. In evaluating the legality of a Terry stop, it must be determined 1) whether there was justification (in the form of reasonable suspicion) for the stop; and 2) whether the degree of intrusion into the suspect's liberty was reasonably related in scope to the situation. The officers in this example probably had reasonable suspicion to believe the subject was involved in criminal activity based on the pedestrian's information and their location of a man of Leon's description near the bar. (Keep in mind, however, the pedestrian is regarded as an anonymous source and there was no accurate prediction of future action to enhance the reasonable suspicion. See *Florida v. J. L.* 529 U.S. 266 (2000).) This permitted a brief investigative detention for questioning and, if reasonable suspicion that he was armed and dangerous arose, a frisk for weapons. In addition, both a request for identification, *Hiibel v. Sixth Judicial District Court of Nevada*, 542 U.S. 177 (2004), as well as a check of immigration status, *Arizona v. United States*, 132 S. Ct. 2492 (2012), have been held within the proper scope of a Terry stop.

   The problem here is that the officers immediately took the additional step of having the subject remove his shoes, thus raising the issue as to whether they exceeded the permissible scope of a Terry stop. While there is no bright-line test for determining when a stop becomes the functional equivalent of an arrest (thereby requiring probable cause), the Supreme Court has looked to the duration of the detention, as well as the question of whether the police employed "the least intrusive means reasonably available to verify or dispel the officer's suspicion in a short period of time." See *Florida v. Royer*, 460 U.S. 491, 500 (1983); *United States v. Sharpe*, 470 U.S. 675 (1985). Even though the detention in our example did not approach the duration of the stop in *Royer* (nearly 15 minutes), the removal of Leon's shoes was an escalation of the intrusion that does not appear to have been the least restrictive investigative method. Mere questioning would have achieved the result sought—information from the subject to confirm or dispel the initial suspicion.

Moreover, neither the information from the original source nor the officers' own observations gave them any reason to suspect that Leon was armed and dangerous or would attempt to flee, and thus the action taken cannot be justified as protective. Compare *United States v. Lee*, 317 F.3d 26, 31 (1st Cir. 2002) ("The passage of time brought with it new knowledge (e.g., the discovery of the bogus cards in Lee's wallet and the sighting of the newly acquired merchandise) that escalated the level of suspicion. These emergent developments amply justified the continued detention.").

It appears, therefore, that the officers' conduct was not "reasonably related in scope to the circumstances which justified the interference in the first place," as required by *Terry v. Ohio*, 392 U.S. 1, 20 (1968). The Massachusetts Supreme Judicial Court so concluded in holding that the stop had become an arrest in the case upon which this example is based. See *Commonwealth v. Borges*, 395 Mass. 788, 482 N.E.2d 314 (1985).

Once the stop here is upgraded to the functional equivalent of an arrest, it is clear that it was without adequate justification because the requisite probable cause was lacking. Neither the knowledge nor the credibility prong of the traditional test is met with regard to the previously unknown pedestrian's information. All that the police corroborated themselves was Leon's description. Thus there was insufficient information from which the officers could reasonably conclude that Leon had committed a crime.

It should be noted that while they are certainly critical factors to weigh, neither handcuffing nor drawing a weapon will necessarily convert a *Terry* stop into an arrest (thus requiring probable cause). See *United States v. Moore*, 329 F.3d 399 (5th Cir. 2003) (handcuffing); *United States v. Hernandez*, 219 F. Supp. 2d 556 (S.D.N.Y. 2002) (weapon). Rather, in evaluating whether an investigative detention is unreasonable, "common sense and ordinary human experience must govern over rigid criteria." *United States v. Sharpe*, 470 U.S. 675, 695 (1985). Thus, where a single officer confronting three persons in a high-crime area had reasonable suspicion that the suspects were engaged in criminal activity and were armed and dangerous, the officer's demand that the driver turn off the ignition and surrender his car keys was deemed a reasonable protective measure that did not convert the stop into an arrest. See *Commonwealth v. Moses*, 408 Mass. 136 (1990) ("It is common knowledge that a person who wants to avoid police questioning, very often will recklessly drive away, resulting in serious injury to the police officer and bystanders. [Thus the officer's actions] were similar to and consistent with the protective measures that have been sanctioned in *Terry*."

408 Mass. at 140.). Compare *Farag v. United States* 587 F. Supp. 2d 436 (E.D. N.Y. 2008) (4 1/2-hour custodial detention of airline passengers at terminal by uniformed officers in SWAT gear with shotguns and police dogs constituted de facto arrest, rather than *Terry* stop).

Similarly, the fact that the officer drew his gun on the suspect did not convert the stop into an arrest where there was reasonable suspicion of narcotics dealing, a pattern of activity generally involving deadly weapons, and the confrontation occurred in a high-crime area. See *United States v. Hardnett*, 804 F.2d 353, 357 (6th Cir. 1986) ("We believe that the use of arms in the present case was reasonably necessary under the circumstances. The officers were acting in a situation which justified a fear for personal safety. The officers had been told by [the informant] that the occupants of the car in front of her home were armed. Therefore, when the officers approached the car, it was reasonable for them to display their weapons for their own protection. Under these circumstances, the use of arms did not convert the investigative stop into an arrest."). See also *United States v. Hood*, 774 F.3d 638 (10th Cir. 2014) (officers were fully justified in drawing their guns and ordering defendant to the ground to protect their own safety); *United States v. Jones*, 759 F.2d 635, 640-641 (8th Cir. 1985) ("We believe that, viewed through the eyes of a cautious and experienced police officer, [the limited actions of removing their guns] from their holsters to make their weapons more accessible were reasonable precautions as they initially approached and evaluated the situation. These activities did not constitute an 'arrest' of Jones."). Nonetheless the drawing of guns is one of the trappings of a formal arrest. *United States v. Ceballos*, 654 F.2d 177, 184 (2d Cir. 1981); *United States v. Rabbia*, 699 F.3d 85 (1st Cir. 2012). A seizure can also occur where the officer repeatedly asks the subject to take his hands out of his pocket, fearing a weapon. See *United States v. Black*, 525 F.3d 359 (4th Cir. 2008).

Should the calculus change for *Terry* stops in states where carrying a firearm in public is lawful? Not according to the Fourth Circuit: "The risk inherent in a forced stop of a person who is armed exists even when the firearm is legally possessed. The presumptive lawfulness of an individual's gun possession in a particular state does next to nothing to negate the reasonable concern an officer has for his own safety when forcing an encounter with an individual who is armed with a gun and whose propensities are unknown." *United States v. Robinson*, 846 F.3d 694 (4th Cir. 2017).

One area of controversy concerning judicial review of the reasonableness of police conduct is whether the focus should be solely on the specific events in question, or whether generalizations about the type of crime may be weighed. Judge Bownes criticized his colleagues' use of general characteristics of certain kinds of lawbreakers or high-crime neighborhoods in evaluating the reasonableness of a stop in *United States*

v. Trullo, 809 F.2d 108, 118 (1st Cir. 1987) (dissenting). See also *United States v. Ceballos*, supra, 654 F.2d at 182-184 ("The initial question before us is whether the blocking of appellant's car and the approach by the officers with guns drawn was so intrusive as to be tantamount to an arrest. This question must be resolved based on the particular facts of this case, and the degree of intrusion, the amount of force used, and the extent to which appellant's freedom of movement was curtailed. [Although we agree that narcotics traffickers are often armed and violent], that generalization, without more, is insufficient to justify the extensive intrusion which occurred in this case. If it were, any narcotics suspect, even if unknown to the agents and giving no indication that force is necessary, could be faced with a maximal intrusion based on mere reasonable suspicion.").

Some courts have applied the *Terry* rationale to justify seizures of individuals within their homes. In a case that could have been ripped from a TV crime show script, police officers in *United States v. Gori*, 230 F.3d 44 (2d Cir. 2000) arrested a subject in possession of a kilogram of cocaine who immediately agreed to cooperate and called his source. A buy was arranged, and the officers set up surveillance in the hallway of the designated apartment building. As they watched the door of the suspected stash house, a delivery person happened by with an order of food for the occupants. The officers accompanied her to the door, and when it was opened for her, they displayed their badges and guns and ordered the occupants out into the hall. The Second Circuit upheld the seizure by applying the *Terry* rationale — the police acted reasonably when they ordered the suspects out through the door that had been voluntarily opened, as they had reasonable suspicion that there were drugs inside.

In her dissent, then-Judge Sotomayor harshly criticized what she characterized as "the unprecedented step of holding that police officers do not violate the Fourth Amendment's protection of the home when they seize an individual standing inside his or her home without a warrant or applicable warrant exception [see Chapter 6] and based only on reasonable suspicion that a crime is being committed therein." 230 F.3d at 57. "Henceforth," she warned, "police officers with only reasonable suspicion and no warrant need only wait outside the door of a home until the door happens to open, and, once it does, they can order the occupants out of their home and conduct a search and investigation in order to get the probable cause necessary for an arrest of a suspect or seizure of evidence." Her approach was followed in *Hadley v. Williams* 368 F.3d 747 (7th Cir. 2004) ("We are mindful of cases in other circuits which hold that when the front door swings open in response to the knock of the police, the police can, by virtue of the 'plain view' doctrine, seize anything they see through the open doorway, since by opening the door the person who opened it consented to their presence on the threshold . . . Since few people will refuse to open the door to the police, the effect of [this] rule is to undermine, for no good reason that we can see, the principle that a warrant is required for entry into the home, in the absence of consent or compelling circumstances.")

Overview — Putting It All Together

15. The threshold task is to identify each gradation of intrusion, and then determine whether the requisite justification was present. The police officer was entitled to address questions to the driver without any justification at all, so long as the encounter remained voluntary. Once the officer blocked the individual's path with the cruiser and refused to move, however, a forcible stop occurred (a reasonable person in those circumstances would believe she was not free to leave), and the Fourth Amendment kicked in with the requirement that there be reasonable suspicion that the driver was engaged in criminal activity. See *United States v. Kerr*, 817 F.2d 1384 (9th Cir. 1987). See also *United States v. See*, 574 F.3d 309 (6th Cir. 2009) (blocking defendant's car constituted a seizure, requiring reasonable suspicion).

    What specific facts were known to the officer at that point? That the driver was parked in a neighborhood where break-ins were occurring, that she had green trash bags in the trunk, and that she appeared nervous in the face of the officer and cruiser blocking her path. The officer did not then know who lived in the residence or what automobiles they owned, and thus did not know whether the driver was leaving her own home or not. These facts are inadequate to constitute reasonable suspicion, and thus the initial stop of the driver was unlawful. See *United States v. Kerr*, supra. Moreover, the detention was already in progress by the time the officer saw the driver's identification and learned she was not a resident of the home, and this after-the-fact knowledge (even assuming it would raise the level of suspicion to reasonable, which is not altogether clear) cannot be weighed in measuring the legality of the initial stop. See *United States v. Nunley*, 873 F.2d 182, 185 (8th Cir. 1989) ("The government rightly relies only on the agents' observations before the investigative stop began. It does not argue that Nunley's reactions after the officer explained his mission (e.g., her shaking hands or quivering voice) helped establish a reasonable suspicion.").

    The subsequent frisk was also impermissible. The only additional information learned by the officer at that point — that the suspect did not reside at that address but rather on the other side of town — is not an adequate basis for suspecting that the driver was armed and dangerous, and thus there was no justification for a frisk. Such police action is premised on the need for an officer to protect herself against an attack.

Moreover, the scope of the frisk is limited to a pat-down. Only if the officer feels something that she reasonably believes may be a weapon can she enter the pockets or clothing of the subject. Officer Harvey, apparently without feeling anything like a weapon, reached into the subject's pocket and removed her keys. Compounding the illegality, the officer used the keys to open the trunk and then searched the bags. This latter action requires probable cause to believe that seizable items will be found (see §6.4), a standard that is clearly not met here. Lastly, there does not appear to be probable cause to arrest because the officer at that point had no basis for determining that the items were stolen.

16. When Deputy Boyer signaled the car to pull over, that clearly constituted a stop requiring reasonable suspicion that criminal activity was afoot. The only information that he had linking this car to the bank robbery was a report he heard over the police radio. Can reasonable suspicion be based on such a report? The Supreme Court has answered yes. Both *United States v. Hensley*, 469 U.S. 221 (1985) and *Whiteley v. Warden*, 401 U.S. 560 (1971) establish that an officer may rely on information received from the police radio or a police flyer, but that the information itself must meet the standard of probable cause. The issue is "whether the officers who issued the flyer possessed probable cause to make the arrest or reasonable suspicion to effect a stop. It does not turn on whether those relying on the flyer were themselves aware of the specific facts which led their colleagues to seek their assistance." *Hensley*, 469 U.S. at 231. The Court explained: "In an era when criminal suspects are increasingly mobile and increasingly likely to flee across jurisdictional boundaries, this rule is a matter of common sense: it minimizes the volume of information concerning suspects that must be transmitted to other jurisdictions and enables police in one jurisdiction to act promptly in reliance on information from another jurisdiction." *Id.*

The focus thus shifts to the basis the officers who issued the radio report had for the description of the perpetrators. If bank employees or eyewitnesses provided the police with the description of the red Maverick, that would constitute credible and reliable information on which either reasonable suspicion or probable cause could properly be based. If, on the other hand, the description was based solely on an anonymous tip, justification would be lacking. Therefore, it would be necessary to find out what information the police possessed prior to their issuance of the radio report.

Assuming that the report was based on reliable information, it would appear that Deputy Boyer had reasonable suspicion to stop the Maverick. The car met the description given except for the presence of a license plate. That variance, together with the conflict between the four male occupants reported and the two male and one female occupants observed by the officer several minutes later, is probably not significant enough to undercut the reasonableness of Boyer's stop (although it may defeat the existence of probable cause). Moreover, his own observations that the occupants appeared nervous contributed to the reasonableness of his suspicion.

Deputy Boyer clearly escalated the stop when he drew his gun, although this action does not automatically convert the stop into an arrest (which would require probable cause). Where an officer's action is justified by reasonable concerns for her safety, the courts have generally held that the drawing of guns or other protective action is within the scope of a permissible stop. The radio report indicated that the perpetrators were armed, and it would appear therefore that Boyer, who was alone and outnumbered, was justified in taking this action. Moreover, an officer is authorized to order the occupants out of a vehicle that she has lawfully stopped, *Pennsylvania v. Mimms*, 434 U.S. 106 (1977); *Maryland v. Wilson*, 519 U.S. 408 (1997). Thus Boyer's order to the occupants was also within proper bounds.

The deputy's observation of a bulge in the pocket of one of the occupants, together with the information he had received over the radio, provided him with reasonable suspicion to believe the subject was armed and dangerous. Boyer was thus justified in patting him down and, upon feeling an object that might be a weapon, reaching into the pocket and removing it.

In sum, Deputy Boyer conducted a lawful stop and frisk under these circumstances. See *United States v. Jacobs*, 715 F.2d 1343 (9th Cir. 1983).

§4.5 ADMINISTRATIVE SEARCHES

A third form of justification has arisen out of the distinction between searches related to criminal investigations and those conducted for another purpose, such as a housing code inspection. As we have seen, the former must be supported by specific information tying the subject to a crime that has been or is about to be committed (probable cause or reasonable suspicion). Searches not related to criminal investigations (at least in their inception), however, are judged against an open-ended test of reasonableness that has produced a form of justification not dependent on particularistic information. In recent years, the "administrative search" rationale has, in the eyes of some critics, served as the vehicle for diluting or even abandoning the requirement of prior justification

The concept of the administrative or regulatory search was first recognized in the 1967 decision of *Camara v. Municipal Court*, 387 U.S. 523, which involved a health code inspection of residential dwelling units. Holding that such inspections were subject to Fourth Amendment constraints, the Court nonetheless rejected the conclusion that the appropriate standard of justification was "traditional criminal law probable cause." Invoking the reasonableness clause, the Court balanced the public interest in enforcing safety codes against the "relatively limited invasion of the urban citizen's privacy" (given that the inspections are "neither personal in nature nor aimed at the discovery of evidence of crime") and concluded that such searches could be conducted so long as "reasonable legislative or administrative standards for conducting an area inspection are satisfied with respect to a particular dwelling." Such standards would focus on the type of building, the condition of the surrounding area, and the time that has passed since the last inspection, rather than specific knowledge of the particular dwelling to be viewed. Unlike the justification required for criminal searches, which is designed to ensure that there is a reasonable likelihood that the subject is involved in criminal activity, the justification envisioned in *Camara* is designed simply to ensure evenhandedness and avoid arbitrary or selective enforcement. (The issue of when a warrant is required in the context of administrative searches is discussed in §§5.4 and 6.6).

The Court has explained that the standard of probable cause is "peculiarly related to criminal investigations, not routine, noncriminal procedures. The probable-cause approach is unhelpful when analysis centers upon the reasonableness of routine administrative caretaking functions, particularly when no claim is made that the protective procedures are a subterfuge for criminal investigations." *Colorado v. Bertine*, 479 U.S. 367, 371 (1987). The constraints placed upon administrative searches operate not to ensure prior knowledge of probable wrongdoing, but to limit discretion and prevent arbitrary treatment of individuals. The courts have therefore imposed a requirement that such searches be conducted according to neutral standardized criteria and procedures that seek to prevent the administrative search from being used as a pretext for an investigative foray.

As Judge Richard Posner has put it, the difference between the traditional criminal search and those characterized as administrative is that the constitutionality of the former is assessed at the level of the individual search, while the latter are evaluated as to the entire program. *Edmond v. Goldsmith*, 183 F.3d 659 (7th Cir. 1999), *aff'd City of Indianapolis v. Edmond*, 531 U.S. 32 (2000) (discussed below).

A good example of the balancing approach used in the administrative search cases is *Vernonia School District 47J v. Acton*, 515 U.S. 646 (1995),[11] involving the validity of a policy requiring every student participating in athletics to submit to random urinalysis for drugs. In upholding the suspicionless drug testing, the Court balanced the intrusion on students' Fourth Amendment interests against the school's legitimate interest in detecting

---

11. *York v. Wahkiakum School Dist. No. 200*, 163 Wash. 2d 297 (2008) declined to follow *Vernonia* on state constitution grounds.

drug use. Athletes have a lesser privacy expectation because they routinely submit to medical examinations, such as scoliosis screening; dress together in locker rooms; and voluntarily participate in regulated sports. Further, the method by which urine was obtained was not intrusive and the test would determine only specific drugs, with the results reported only to those school personnel legitimately needing to know. *Vernonia* was expanded in *Board of Education v. Earls*, 536 U.S. 822 (2002),[12] upholding (on the same balancing approach) the "Student Activities Drug Testing Policy" requiring any middle or high school student participating in extracurricular activities to submit to random drug testing.

The administrative search rationale has been applied in a wide range of contexts to dispense with the prerequisite for individualized suspicion. These include inspections of licensed or highly regulated business establishments;[13] arson investigations of fire scenes;[14] fixed checkpoints near the border to stop vehicles and briefly question the occupants to detect illegal aliens;[15] fixed sobriety checkpoints to look for signs of intoxication in motorists passing through;[16] routine inventory searches of impounded automobiles and personal effects of arrestees;[17] preventing injury or violence in a home;[18] an invasive bodily search for weapon and contraband of individuals detained at a jail or other detention facility who were arrested for a minor offence;[19] and mandatory drug testing of security and safety

---

12. *Theodore v. Delaware Valley School Dist.*, 575 Pa. 321 (2003) declined to follow *Earls* on state constitution grounds.

13. *New York v. Burger*, 482 U.S. 691 (1987) (warrantless inspection of automobile junkyards); *Donovan v. Dewey*, 452 U.S. 594 (1981) (warrantless inspections of mines); *United States v. Biswell*, 406 U.S. 311 (1972) (warrantless searches of federally licensed gun dealers). The Court reasoned that persons choosing to engage in such highly regulated or licensed enterprises do so with knowledge that they will be subject to periodic inspections and thus have reduced expectations of privacy. Compare *Marshall v. Barlow's Inc.*, 436 U.S. 307 (1978) (holding unconstitutional the practice of warrantless inspections under the Occupational Safety and Health Act on the grounds that the industries covered have not traditionally been pervasively regulated).

14. *Michigan v. Clifford*, 464 U.S. 287 (1984); *Michigan v. Tyler*, 436 U.S. 499 (1978).

15. *United States v. Martinez-Fuerte*, 428 U.S. 543 (1976). Search of the vehicle, a far more serious intrusion, may only be conducted if there is probable cause to believe that it contains aliens. See *United States v. Ortiz*, 422 U.S. 891 (1975) (search at fixed checkpoint); *Almeida-Sanchez v. United States*, 413 U.S. 266 (1973) (search by roving patrol units). Vehicles may be stopped by roving patrols near the border and occupants briefly questioned about their immigration status only upon reasonable suspicion that the vehicle contains illegal aliens. *United States v. Brignoni-Ponce*, 422 U.S. 873 (1975).

16. *Michigan Dept. of State Police v. Sitz*, 496 U.S. 444 (1990).

17. *Colorado v. Bertine*, 479 U.S. 367 (1987) (inventory of contents of van impounded after owner was arrested for drunk driving); *Illinois v. Lafayette*, 462 U.S. 640 (1983) (inventory of arrestee's shoulder bag); *South Dakota v. Opperman*, 428 U.S. 364 (1976) (inventory of car impounded for multiple parking violations).

18. *Brigham City, Utah v. Stuart*, 126 S. Ct. 1943 (2006).

19. *Florence v. Board of Chosen Freeholders of County of Burlington*, 132 S. Ct. 1510 (2012).

workers.[20] It should be pointed out that since September 11, 2001, administrative border searches have become more extensive. The Court in *United States v. Flores-Montano*, 541 U.S. 149 (2004), for example, allowed a border inspection to include removal, disassembly, and reassembly of a vehicle.

Typical of the calculus employed in the administrative search cases (see Figure 4-3) are the following excerpts from decisions upholding employee drug screening:

> "Because the testing program adopted by the Customs Service is not designed to serve the ordinary needs of law enforcement [but instead to detect drug use among personnel involved in drug interdiction], we have balanced the public interest in the Service's testing program against the privacy concerns implicated by the tests, without reference to our usual presumption in favor of the procedures specified in the Warrant Clause, to assess whether the tests required by Customs are reasonable. We hold that the suspicionless testing of employees [involved in] the interdiction of illegal drugs is reasonable." *National Treasury Employees Union v. Von Raab*, 489 U.S. 656, 679 (1989).
>
> "In light of the limited discretion exercised by the railroad employers under the [drug-testing] regulations, the surpassing safety interests served by toxicological tests [of employees following accidents], and the diminished expectation of privacy that attaches to information pertaining to the fitness of covered employees, we believe it is reasonable to conduct such tests in the absence of a warrant or reasonable suspicion that any particular employee may be impaired." *Skinner v. Railway Labor Executives Assn.*, 489 U.S. 602, 634 (1989).

In contrast, a Georgia statute mandating drug screening for candidates for public office was invalidated because such positions did not involve high-risk, safety-sensitive tasks. *Chandler v. Miller*, 520 U.S. 305 (1997).

The premise that noncriminal searches should be measured by laxer standards than those seeking evidence for use in prosecution has been extended far beyond the realm of routine inspections and applied where "special needs, beyond the normal need for law enforcement, make the warrant and probable cause requirement impracticable." *New Jersey v. TLO*, 469 U.S. 325, 351 (1985). Some form of individualized suspicion, but not probable cause, must be demonstrated in these cases. *New Jersey v. TLO*, for example, involved the search of a student's purse by an assistant principal who suspected her of violating the public high school's rule against smoking. The search turned up evidence of marijuana use. Striking the balance between "the schoolchild's legitimate expectations of privacy and the school's equally legitimate need to maintain an environment in which learning can take place," the Court dispensed with both the requirement for

---

20. *National Treasury Employees Union v. Von Raab*, 489 U.S. 656 (1989) (urinalysis of Customs Service employees involved in drug interdiction); *Skinner v. Railway Labor Executives Assn.*, 489 U.S. 602 (1989) (blood and urine tests of railroad employees involved in serious accidents).

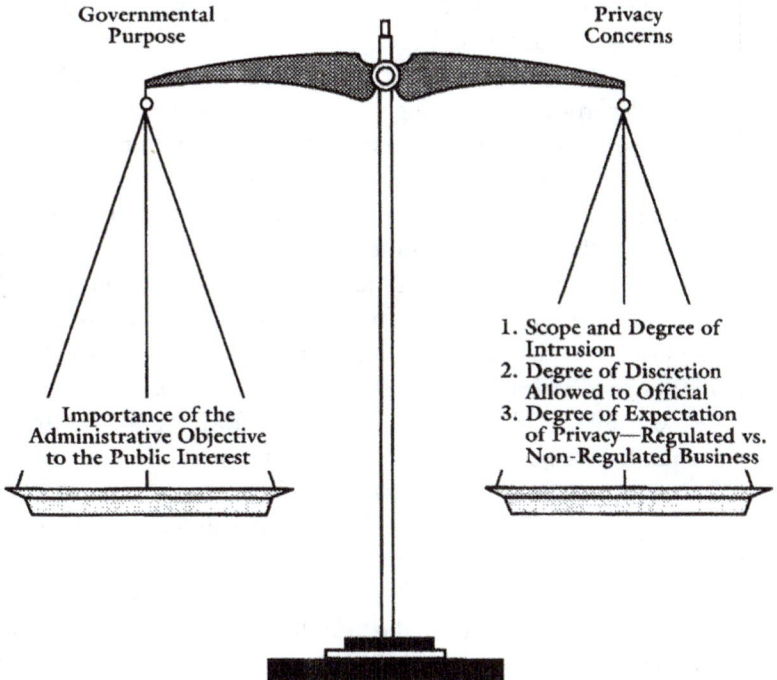

Figure 4-3. Administrative Search Balancing Analysis

a warrant and for probable cause. 469 U.S. at 340. It imposed instead the less onerous standard that there be reasonable grounds for suspecting that the search will turn up evidence that the student is in violation of either school rules or the law.

Revisiting the student search issue in *Safford Unified School District v. Redding*, 557 U.S. 364 (2009), the Court held that a significantly more intrusive strip search of the subject's underwear for over-the-counter drugs would require greater justification than that enunciated in TLO.

In *O'Connor v. Ortega*, 480 U.S. 709 (1987), where the search of a government employee's office was conducted by agency personnel as part of an investigation of work-related misconduct, and *Griffin v. Wisconsin*, 483 U.S. 868 (1987), where a probation officer searched the home of a probationer to determine whether he was complying with the terms of probation,[21] the appropriate standard of justification was held to be reasonable suspicion.

---

21. *Griffin* was expanded in *United States v. Knights*, 534 U.S. 112 (2001), upholding a search of probationer's home on reasonable suspicion rather than probable cause even though conducted for purposes of a criminal investigation, reasoning that the condition of probation consenting to such searches rendered it reasonable under the Fourth Amendment. *Knights* was further extended in *Samson v. California*, 126 S. Ct. 2193 (2006) to permit suspicionless searches of parolees by police officers where that is a mandatory condition of release and consented to by the parolee.

The primary purpose of these searches was not to gather evidence for a criminal prosecution, and the "special needs beyond normal law enforcement" (the need to maintain supervision and discipline) were found to justify departure from the higher standard of probable cause. The analysis in these cases was characterized critically by Justice Brennan as a "Rorschach-like" balancing test sanctioning full-scale searches on a relaxed standard of reasonableness. TLO, supra, 469 U.S. at 360 (Brennan, J., dissenting).

While the separate treatment afforded administrative searches is premised on the assumption that they are conducted for noncriminal purposes, the line between administrative and criminal searches is not always clear. The Court has placed in the administrative search category inspections that are designed at least in part to secure evidence of crime. New York v. Burger, 482 U.S. 691 (1987) upheld a statute authorizing police officers to make warrantless inspections of automobile junkyards despite the fact that this "administrative" scheme operated in close conjunction with the criminal justice process. (The New York Court of Appeals had struck down the statute as a mere pretext to permit searches for evidence of crime.)

Later decisions seemed to reflect the Court's desire to sharpen that line when the primary goal of the search is indeed law enforcement. Ferguson v. City of Charleston, 532 U.S. 67 (2001) struck down the state hospital's policy of testing pregnant women for cocaine use, concluding that the pervasive participation of the police in drafting and monitoring the program (and ultimately arresting and prosecuting users) precluded its characterization as an administrative "special needs" practice. Although the ultimate objective was to use the threat of criminal prosecution to get women into substance abuse treatment, the program had an immediate goal of generating evidence for law enforcement purposes. Similarly, a traffic checkpoint program designed to interdict illegal narcotics was held to violate the Fourth Amendment in City of Indianapolis v. Edmond, 531 U.S. 32 (2001) because its primary purpose was to detect evidence of criminal wrongdoing and thus was motivated by a "general interest in crime control."

Illinois v. Lidster, 124 S. Ct. 885 (2004), however, allowed police to set up a suspicionless highway checkpoint to obtain information from motorists about a crime committed the week before at the same location. The Court distinguished Edmond because the law enforcement purpose here was not to determine whether the motorists themselves were implicated in crime, but instead to seek their help in solving the earlier crime. Individualized suspicion "has little role to play" in this context. The Court also emphasized that the police stopped every vehicle, and that each stop lasted only 10 to 15 seconds and merely involved a question about whether the motorist had seen anything the previous weekend (and a flyer seeking assistance in identifying the vehicle involved in the crime).

Lidster for the first time permitted suspicionless stops for the investigation of past crimes. The wide license to law enforcement is discounted by the Court's observations that the police generally lack resources to conduct such checkpoints, and that public support for them may be lacking (as they create traffic jams and other problems).

The fact that Lidster himself was convicted of driving under the influence as a result of evidence obtained at the checkpoint demonstrates that even where the original purpose of a search is regarded as "administrative," contraband or incriminating evidence discovered *may be admitted in a criminal prosecution*. Courts have not required the actors (housing inspectors, school principals, police officers, etc.) to look the other way when such evidence is uncovered, and have generally rejected the view that because administrative searches are permitted without individualized cause, their fruits should be inadmissible in a criminal trial. *New York v. Burger*, supra, 482 U.S. at 716 ("The discovery of evidence of crimes in the course of an otherwise proper administrative inspection does not render that search illegal or the administrative scheme suspect.").

By way of another example, in *Maryland v. King*, 133 S. Ct. 1958 (2013) the defendant was subjected to a routine DNA cheek swab upon his arrest for assault. When the result implicated him in an unsolved rape, King moved to suppress the evidence. The 5-4 decision by Justice Kennedy found the minimal scope of the intrusion was outweighed by the government interest in ascertaining the identity of the arrestee. Submittal of the DNA sample to the Combined DNA Index System (CODIS) was not deemed a significant additional invasion of privacy. A skeptical Justice Scalia authored the dissent, emphasizing that the length of time it takes to actually get the DNA analyzed belies its usefulness for identifying an arrestee.

In sum, the characterization of a search as "administrative" places it outside the usual Fourth Amendment requirement for individualized justification, and into an area where relaxed standards of reasonableness apply. Therein lies the potential for dilution of Fourth Amendment protections. (See the discussion of the problem of pretext in § 6.9.)

Examples

1a. David Bly was ticketed on an international flight to London. As he approached the airport loading gate, he was subjected to a routine security check. Boarding passengers and their carry-on luggage must pass through a metal detector. The detector indicated the presence of a metal object in Bly's briefcase, and a security officer took the briefcase and opened it. Inside she found a large-caliber pistol. Both the gun and Bly were turned over to local police, and he was charged with unlawful possession of a firearm. Bly moves to suppress the gun on the grounds that the search violated the Fourth Amendment. What standards should the court use to measure the legality of this search?

1b. Suppose that Abdul Khan is scheduled on the same flight. While being processed at the ticket counter, a "selectee alert" (based on a "hijacker profile" developed by the Federal Aviation Administration/FAA) came over the computer. That designation requires the airline (pursuant to FAA regulations) to put all the passenger's checked baggage through an X-ray machine. The X-ray could not penetrate one bag, and a manual search was conducted, resulting in the discovery of narcotics. Khan, claiming he was singled out because of his Muslim name, seeks to suppress the drugs before trial. What result?

2. The state of Maine is considering institution of a "Stop Drunk Driving" program designed as an aggressive response to the problem. State police officers will be assigned to various checkpoints on the highways, where they will flag down motorists and briefly converse with them in an effort to detect signs of intoxication. If an officer believes a driver may be drunk, the driver will be referred to another officer, who will conduct a series of sobriety tests. As legal counsel to the state, what would you advise as to the constitutionality of this program?

3. Springfield State Hospital adopted a mandatory screening program for employees involved in direct patient care. The program, growing out of concern for patient safety as well as efficient operation of the hospital, is designed to detect both infection by the AIDS virus and use of narcotics. A notice was posted informing employees that random blood testing would be conducted. Elmer King, a nurse at the hospital, was tested pursuant to the program and narcotics were found in his blood. When King refused to resign his position, the test results were turned over to the district attorney. Does this procedure violate the Fourth Amendment?

4. Trooper Wyman stopped a motorist for speeding and, after determining he was under the influence of alcohol, arrested him. The driver had a brief-case next to him on the seat, which Wyman seized for safekeeping. After transporting the driver to the police station and delivering him to the booking officer, the trooper proceeded to inventory the contents of the briefcase. While doing so, she discovered several marijuana cigarettes in a paper bag. The driver was then charged with unlawful possession. Did the trooper violate the Fourth Amendment when she opened and searched the briefcase? Does it matter that the trooper admits that she was keeping an eye out for contraband at the same time she was conducting the inventory?

5. The Newtowne School Committee voted to institute a policy condi-tioning participation in certain student activities on the consent of the student (together with his or her parents) to random drug testing (by way of urinalysis conducted by a reputable testing service). The activities include athletics, student government, and theater productions. Is the policy vulnerable to a Fourth Amendment challenge?

6. A teacher at the Warwick Public High School noticed a commotion around a locker outside her classroom and informed Vice Principal Skull. Skull identified the locker as belonging to Bill Kits, who had been a constant behavior problem and was suspected of selling drugs at school. Skull used the master key to open the locker, but found only three dozen boxes of Girl Scout cookies. The vice principal took these and later, after learning there had been a theft of such cookies from the school cafeteria, turned the boxes over to the police. Kits now seeks to suppress the evidence before his trial in juvenile court. What result?

7. Billy Blood was convicted of bank robbery, served his sentence, and was released on parole. Pursuant to the federal DNA Act, 42 U.S.C. §14135a and 18 U.S.C. §3142, his parole officer requested that he submit a blood sample to be included in a massive database of DNA profiles used by law enforcement agencies. He refused, contending that the Act violates his Fourth Amendment rights. Will his challenge be successful?

Explanations

1a. If the search of Bly's briefcase were to be judged by traditional Fourth Amendment standards, it would clearly be unlawful. There was no probable cause or reasonable suspicion to justify subjecting the briefcase to a metal detector scan; even after the scan indicated the presence of a metal object, that is scant basis for concluding that Bly was involved in criminal conduct.

This search would not, however, be measured by traditional standards. The primary impetus for airport screening, which passengers now take for granted, is concern for the safety of passengers and crew, not criminal prosecution. The standards for evaluating the airport search program are found in the administrative search cases, which establish that searches conducted as part of a general regulatory scheme rather than pursuant to a criminal investigation do not require individualized cause directed at the particular person or place to be searched.

What constitutional standards apply? As a threshold matter, the inspection must not be a subterfuge for a search seeking evidence of crime. If a building code inspector is sent into Smith's apartment at the instigation of the police to search for stolen VCRs, that search could not be characterized as administrative and the traditional requirement for particularized cause would apply. See United States v. $124,570 U.S. Currency, 873 F.2d 1240 (9th Cir. 1989). In our example, there is no indication that the inspection of Bly was anything but routine. The basic test of an administrative search scheme is derived from the Fourth Amendment standard of reasonableness. As Camara teaches, it must appear on balance that the governmental need to search outweighs the intrusion, or as the

Court later put it, that "the privacy interests implicated by the search are minimal, and where an important governmental interest furthered by the intrusion would be placed in jeopardy by a requirement of individualized suspicion." *Skinner v. Railway Labor Executives Association*, supra, 489 U.S. 602, 624 (1989).

That seems clearly to be the case in our example, where the risk of air terrorism is measured against the relatively minor annoyance of the screening. Beyond that threshold, there must be an assurance of evenhandedness in the inspection process. That is, the decision as to who will be screened and the scope of the search cannot be left to the discretion of the officer. Rather, objective standardized criteria must control throughout the process. Assuming that all passengers are subjected to the airport screening, that the procedures are set out with sufficient detail and clarity so that the discretion of the officer is constrained, and that there is uniform application, the program would be considered reasonable and pass muster under the Fourth Amendment.

In one of the first decisions to review the nationwide airport safety program, the Ninth Circuit emphasized the additional factor of notice in its decision upholding the program. Would-be passengers were informed of the upcoming screening by conspicuous signs before they got into the boarding line, and they had the option to avoid the screening by electing not to board the aircraft. *United States v. Davis*, 482 F.2d 893 (9th Cir. 1973). In this sense, it could be said that they consented to the search. (See § 6.7.)

That same court later suppressed evidence not related to air safety that was discovered during an airport screening. In *United States v. $124,570 U.S. Currency*, 873 F.2d 1240 (9th Cir. 1989), airport security officers discovered a large sum of money in a traveler's briefcase. By prior agreement with the Customs Service to aid in the enforcement of currency and narcotics law, the officers seized the money and turned it over to government agents, who later linked it to narcotics trafficking. Because the security officers were not acting with the single-minded objective of air safety, but also with the purpose of discovering evidence of illegal narcotics activity, the Ninth Circuit held that the administrative search rationale did not apply. Warning of the danger that screening of passengers could be subverted into a general search for evidence of crime, the court emphasized the importance of preventing criminal investigatory motives from coloring administrative searches. 873 F.2d. at 1244.

Nonetheless, as a general rule, evidence *inadvertently* discovered during a bona fide administrative search may be admitted at a criminal trial. See, e.g., *United States v. McCarty*, 648 F.3d 820 (9th Cir. 2011) (pornographic materials discovered during a routine TSA search of defendant's bag). What prompted the suppression of evidence in *$124,570 U.S. Currency* was that the search was conducted from the outset for the dual purpose of finding evidence for prosecution as well as to protect air passengers.

1b. Abdul will probably not succeed in suppressing the narcotics. The anti-hijacking screening program is a quintessential administrative search, which on balance will be deemed reasonable given the grave potential risk to the public (especially since September 11, 2001; see Chapter 12) weighed against the minimal intrusion on Abdul. The absence of individualized suspicion is not fatal to these searches. The use of the profile will be countenanced as long as "reasonable" under the circumstances. (For more discussion of racial and ethnic profiling, see §6.9 and Chapter 12.) And if the initial intrusion is justifiable as part of a regulatory effort to prevent hijacking, the incidental discovery of contraband does not offend the Fourth Amendment. See *United States v. Hartwell*, 436 F.3d 174 (3d Cir. 2006).

2. As a general rule, motorists can be stopped only if there is specific justification in the form of reasonable suspicion or probable cause to believe the driver or occupants are in violation of the law. *Delaware v. Prouse*, 440 U.S. 648 (1979) held that suspicionless discretionary spot checks of motorists to inspect license and registration violated the Fourth Amendment. The Court emphasized, however, that it was not foreclosing other methods of spot checking in furtherance of an important governmental purpose as long as the decision as to whom to stop was not left to the unconstrained discretion of the officer. By way of example, the Court offered a roadblock in which *all* cars were stopped.

   Prouse anticipated the sobriety checkpoint program upheld in *Michigan Department of State Police v. Sitz*, 496 U.S. 444 (1990). All drivers were stopped and briefly (an average of 25 seconds) observed for signs of intoxication. If such signs were found, the driver would be detained for sobriety testing and, if the indication was that the driver was intoxicated, an arrest would be made. Rejecting a constitutional challenge to the program, the Court held that the initial seizures that occurred when cars were stopped were reasonable under the Fourth Amendment. Applying the balancing test that substitutes for the probable cause requirement, the Court weighed the magnitude of the governmental interest in eradicating the drunk driving problem against the slight intrusion to motorists stopped briefly at the fixed checkpoints. Evenhandedness was ensured because the locations of the checkpoints were chosen pursuant to written guidelines and the police were directed to stop every approaching vehicle—the officers themselves did not decide whom to stop. The fact that motorists were not notified of the upcoming checkpoints or given an opportunity to make a U-turn to avoid them was not regarded as fatal to the legality of the Michigan program.

   Measured by the *Camara* balancing test, we have in our example the same compelling public interest in highway safety that existed in Sitz. On the other side of the balance, however, we have a more serious intrusion into individual liberty than in that case. Unlike the fixed checkpoints in *Sitz*, the Maine program involves flagging down motorists on the road. The Court has traditionally treated roving patrol stops as significantly more intrusive than fixed checkpoint stops: "[Unlike roving patrols, at] traffic checkpoints the motorist can see that other vehicles are being stopped, he can see visible signs of the officers' authority, and he is much less likely to be frightened or annoyed by the intrusion." *United States v. Ortiz*, 422 U.S. 891, 894-895 (1975), quoted with approval in *Sitz*, 496 U.S. at 452-453. A court may therefore conclude that the surprise and unannounced nature of the intrusion in the Maine program outweighs the public interest supporting it.

Even if the program survives this initial stage of scrutiny, other problems remain. There would have to be specific guidelines determining who would be stopped and what procedures they would be subjected to. As far as we know, there are no constraints upon the officer's discretion regarding both matters. Such unbridled authority would likely result in the program being declared violative of the Fourth Amendment. See, e.g., *United States v. Ramos*, 733 F. Supp. 260 (S.D. Tex. 1989) (holding illegal a one-man roving checkpoint in which an officer stopped drivers to check for license and registration, where there was no plan or limitations controlling location, who would be stopped, and what procedures would be followed, because it permitted "unconstrained exercise of discretion"). Compare *People v. Rister*, 803 P.2d 483 (Colo. 1990) (upholding sobriety checkpoint program where the discretion of the officers was constrained by requirement that all cars be stopped).

Emphasizing that "adherence to a neutrally devised, preplanned blueprint in order to eliminate arbitrariness and discretion has been the principal prerequisite for abandoning the requirement of individualized suspicion in roadblock stops," the Massachusetts Supreme Judicial Court held that the stop of a motorist 15 minutes after the scheduled deadline for termination of a roadblock was unconstitutional. See *Commonwealth v. Anderson*, 406 Mass. 343, 349 (1989). Compare *State v. Duarte*, 149 P.3d 1027 (N.M. App. 2006) ("We neither fall on the side of a bright-line approach by which any deviation from a plan or script will render the roadblock unreasonable, nor on the side of incremental intrusion by deviating field officers.")

In *Covert v. State*, 612 N.E.2d 592 (Ind. Ct. App. 1993), a case involving auto safety checkpoints at which lights, brakes, tires, and mufflers were inspected, the court found that the public interest in auto safety was not as compelling as controlling drunk driving and did not justify the intrusion on motorists' liberties. See also *State v. Debooy*, 996 P.2d 546 (Utah Sup. Ct. 2000) (checkpoints where officers performed sweeping inspections for traffic violations was too broad and risked giving police authority to stop every car on the road).

It should be noted that drug interdiction checkpoints, unlike sobriety checkpoints, are primarily directed at searching for evidence of crime. Consequently, such programs do not to fit the administrative search rationale. See *City of Indianapolis v. Edmond*, 531 U.S. 32 (2001). See also *Commonwealth v. Rodriguez*, 430 Mass. 577 (2000) (drug interdiction checkpoints do not present the same public benefit as do sobriety checkpoints, namely the "special need" of removing drunk drivers from the road).

What about roadblocks designed to secure evidence of crime? *Illinois v. Lidster*, 124 S. Ct. 885 (2004) upheld a roadblock set up to obtain information and witnesses with regard to a past crime. Individualized suspicion, the Court concluded, "has little role to play" in this context. The police stopped every vehicle and for a very brief period. The Virginia Supreme Court in *Burns v. Commonwealth*, 261 Va. 307, 322 (2001) similarly upheld a roadblock designed to discover evidence of a brutal murder: "A roadblock is not an unconstitutional infringement on an individual's privacy if it is carried out pursuant to a plan or practice which is explicit, contains neutral criteria, and limits the conduct of the officers undertaking the roadblock."

3. The Supreme Court has upheld suspicionless mandatory drug and alcohol testing in two contexts. The U.S. Customs Service program requiring employees involved in drug interdiction or who carry firearms to provide urine samples for analysis was upheld in *National Treasury Employees Union v. Von Raab*, 489 U.S. 656 (1989). And federal regulations mandating blood and urine testing of railroad employees following major accidents were upheld in *Skinner v. Railway Labor Executives Association*, 489 U.S. 602, 634 (1989). Both decisions applied the *Camara* balancing test rather than the requirement for particularized suspicion. This was deemed appropriate because the programs were not designed to serve the ordinary needs of law enforcement (obtaining evidence of crime), but instead were adopted to protect the public interest by ensuring a safer workplace. The Customs Service regulations explicitly provided that the test results could not be turned over to any other agency or a prosecutor.

Under the *Camara* analysis, the public interest served by the program is balanced against the intrusion on individual privacy. Both *Skinner* and *Von Raab* recognized the compelling governmental interest in preventing substance abusers from performing safety-sensitive jobs and held this outweighed the privacy interests of persons in those positions. The intrusions were considered relatively minor. Moreover, the employees worked in jobs that historically had been highly regulated, and were specifically notified that they were subject to screening under the programs. (In *Von Raab*, they were notified five days in advance of the test date.) Consequently, the subjects had a reduced expectation of privacy with regard to the intrusions. Lastly, the screening procedures were set out in detail and allowed little or no discretion (in, for example, determining which employees would be tested or when) on the part of the officials conducting them.

Applying this analysis to example 3, the public interest in detecting narcotics users and those with the AIDS virus and preventing them from working in patient care is clear and weighty. This concern for the safety of patients and co-workers would probably be held to outweigh the limited intrusion into the bodily integrity and privacy of those subject to the program. Further, the hospital employees would have a diminished expectation of privacy, given the tight regulation of their workplace and the fact that they received notice of the screening program.

More information would be required, however, regarding the degree of discretion left to the officials implementing the screening program. Unless there are neutral written guidelines delineating the manner in which the program operates to ensure evenhandedness as to who is tested, when, and how, the program may be struck down as unreasonable.

Another potential problem is that the Springfield State Hospital program apparently permits officials to turn the test results over to criminal prosecutors, which they have done in King's case. The program upheld in *Von Raab* specifically precluded this, and neither that case nor *Skinner* explicitly confronted the question of use of the results in a criminal prosecution because both cases were declaratory judgment challenges to the implementation of the programs at their outset. While as a general rule, evidence discovered during a lawful administrative search is admissible in a subsequent criminal trial, it is conceivable that a court would not permit such use here, where the program's constitutionality is founded upon its noncriminal purpose.

For civil actions raising the issue of AIDS testing in a hospital context, compare *Leckelt v. Board of Commissioners of Hospital District No. 1*, 909 F.2d 820 (5th Cir. 1990) (upholding program) with *Glover v. Eastern Nebraska Community Office of Retardation*, 867 F.2d 461 (8th Cir. 1989) (holding program violated Fourth Amendment).

4. As we will see in Chapter 6, this search cannot be upheld as incident to the arrest because it was not contemporaneous with it. It does not fit the automobile exception because there was no probable cause to search the vehicle. The Supreme Court has held, however, that suspicionless inventory searches may be conducted of impounded automobiles or objects. See *Colorado v. Bertine*, 479 U.S. 367 (1987) (backpack in impounded vehicle); *Illinois v. Lafayette*, 462 U.S. 640 (1983) (personal effects of arrestee); *South Dakota v. Opperman*, 428 U.S. 364 (1976) (glove compartment of impounded vehicle). The justification for such a suspicionless search is that it is being conducted not for the purpose of investigating criminal

conduct, but for administrative reasons, i.e., protecting the police from danger (a bomb inside the briefcase); protecting the owner's property while he is in police custody; and protecting the police from claims of lost, stolen, or damaged property. The search can permissibly include the opening of packages found within the object to be inventoried.

The main prerequisite for a lawful inventory is that it is conducted according to standardized procedures or established protocol. The insistence on such procedures serves three purposes: 1) it ensures evenhanded treatment of all subjects, 2) it precludes (or at least discourages) use of the inventory as a pretext for an investigatory search, and 3) it ensures that the intrusion is limited in scope to the extent necessary to carry out the caretaking function. It has been held that the standard practice must be that of the department and not simply the routine followed by the individual officer. See *United States v. Kordosky*, 909 F.2d 219 (7th Cir. 1990); *United States v. Torres*, 828 F.3d 1113 (9th Cir. 2016) (officer's inventory search was reasonable because it was standard departmental practice to search the air filter while inspecting the engine of a vehicle).

In the absence of such procedures, the police may not conduct a lawful inventory. See *Florida v. Wells*, 495 U.S. 1, 4 (1990) ("The Florida Highway patrol had no policy whatever with respect to the opening of closed containers during an inventory search. We hold that absent such a policy, the instant search was not sufficiently regulated to satisfy the Fourth Amendment.").

Ideally, the procedures should be set out in writing, as in a state trooper manual, for example. See *United States v. Wanless*, 882 F.2d 1459, 1463 (9th Cir. 1989); *United States v. Le*, 402 F. Supp. 2d 1068 (D.N.D. 2005) (North Dakota Highway Patrol Policy Manual). They should explicitly control the scope and extent of the inventory and leave no discretion to the officer conducting it. The Court upheld an inventory conducted pursuant to criteria that allowed the officer to choose between impounding the vehicle or parking it locked in a public place (and thus not searching it), but it emphasized that such discretion must be constrained by "standard criteria and [be exercised] on the basis of something other than suspicion of criminal activity." *Colorado v. Bertine*, 479 U.S. at 375. The officer must not be allowed so much latitude that inventory searches are turned into "a purposeful and general means of discovering evidence of crime." See also *1975 Chevrolet v. Texas*, 801 S.W.2d 565 (Tex. 1990).

In example 4, we would have to determine whether the trooper was acting according to established inventory procedures and, if so, whether those procedures sufficiently constrained her discretion with regard to the conduct of the search. Assuming we find affirmative answers to both questions, and that we have no indication that she was engaged in a pretextual search, the inventory would be permitted by the Fourth Amendment.

The result is not changed by the trooper's admission that she kept an eye out for contraband while conducting the inventory. A legitimate nonpretextual inventory search is not made unlawful simply because the investigating officer remains vigilant for evidence during his inventory search. *United States v. Khoury*, 901 F.2d 948, 959 (11th Cir. 1990). If, however, Trooper Wyman exceeded the scope of the standardized procedures in her hunt for contraband, then the search would be unlawful. In *Khoury*, the officer flipped through the pages of an impounded notebook pursuant to procedures requiring him to determine whether there was anything of value hidden in the pages. But when he proceeded to read the pages and determined that the book contained incriminating entries, his additional inspection was held to violate the Fourth Amendment. See also *United States v. Flores*, 122 F. Supp. 2d 491 (S.D.N.Y. 2000) (DEA agent exceeded scope of inventory search by examining cell phone and calendar book found in defendant's car, because they were not considered "containers" under DEA policy).

5. This policy obviously goes significantly farther than that involved in *Vernonia School District 47J v. Acton*, 515 U.S. 646 (1995), which was limited to participation in athletics. Suspicionless searching of students who want to take part in student government or dramatic plays is much harder to justify because the need to screen for drugs is less compelling and the expectation of privacy greater than that of student athletes, whose activities are more regulated and who engage in group showering and dressing. These distinctions did not, however, impress the Supreme Court in *Board of Education v. Earls*, 536 U.S. 822 (2002), upholding such omnibus testing of students on the rationale of a lesser expectation of privacy for students participating in extracurricular activity, and the important government interest in deterring drug use in schools.

6. While applying the Fourth Amendment to searches conducted by school officials on school property, *New Jersey v. TLO*, 469 U.S. 325 (1985) did not mandate the traditional requirements for warrant or probable cause. Rather, the student's privacy interest was balanced against the need to maintain discipline in a reasonableness analysis. In order to be constitutionally valid, the search of Kits's locker must be justified at its inception and the scope of the search must be reasonably related to the circumstances that necessitated it.

With regard to the first issue, there is serious question in our example as to whether Vice Principal Skull had reasonable grounds for suspecting that the search would turn up evidence that Kits had violated the law or the rules of the school. All we have here is the commotion in front of the locker and the generalized suspicion that Kits may be dealing drugs. Compare *Singleton v. Board of Education*, 894 F. Supp. 386 (D. Kan. 1995) (prior to locker search, adult had identified student as person who had stolen $150 from her car) and *Greenleaf v. Cote*, 77 F. Supp. 2d 168 (D. Me. 1999) (previously reliable student-informant reported that she had heard girls discussing how they had been drinking beer in locker room). If sufficient justification is found, it would appear that the scope of the locker search was permissible because drugs could be found in the place searched. Finally, the fact that the search begins as an administrative search but then turns up evidence of crime does not preclude admission of the evidence at Kits's criminal trial. See also *State v. Jones*, 666 N.W.2d 142 (Iowa 2003) (upholding search of student's locker, turning up marijuana, when he did not report for the annual locker clean-out).

Does the existence of the master key reduce the already lowered expectation of privacy a student has in his or her locker at public school? At least one court has held that within the setting of a police station, an officer's locker carries a reasonable expectation of privacy even though the department retains a master key. See *United States v. Speights*, 557 F.2d 362 (3d Cir. 1977). See also *State v. Rodriguez*, 529 S.W.3d 81 (Tex. App. 2015) (college student had reasonable expectation of privacy in her dorm room even though resident assistant had a master key).

Faced with a dramatically more intrusive search into a female student's underwear for over-the-counter drugs, the Court ruled in an 8-1 decision that sufficient justification, in the form of specific cause to believe that the drugs were hidden in that sensitive location, was required. *Safford Unified School District v. Redding*, 557 U.S. 364 (2009).

The Second Circuit has approved suspicionless strip searches of females initially entering the custody of a juvenile detention center, but it requires reasonable suspicion that the subject possesses contraband for any subsequent searches. See *N.G. v. Connecticut*, 382 F.3d 225 (2d Cir. 2004). The former falls in the "special needs beyond law enforcement" category; the latter does not.

Judge Sotomayor disagreed on the first point and would have required individualized suspicion for *all* strip searches of juveniles in custody, given "the uniquely invasive and upsetting nature" of such procedures. 382 F.3d at 238 (concurring in part and dissenting in part). While there is a special need to prevent juvenile inmates from possessing contraband, the government did not, in her view, adequately demonstrate that the strip searches were substantially related to this goal and that there were no less intrusive alternatives. See also *Kelsey v. County of Schoharie*, 567 F.3d 54 (2009) (incidental observation of the body of an arrestee during a required clothing exchange is not an unreasonable search under the Fourth Amendment) (Sotomayor, J., dissenting); *Smith v. Taylor*, 217 Fed. Appx. 97 (2d Cir. 2007) (when a prison directive instructs that only two officers be present for a strip search, the presence of four officers could render that search unreasonable).

7. First, it is clear that the extraction of blood for DNA profiling constitutes a "search" within the meaning of the Fourth Amendment. See *Skinner v. Ry. Labor Executives' Ass'n*, 489 U.S. 602 (1989). Second, since the purpose of this intrusion is clearly law enforcement, it would not fit the category of "special needs" searches that can be justified without individualized suspicion. See *Ferguson v. City of Charleston*, 532 U.S. 67 (2001).

   However, the Court has modified the justification required for certain searches of probationers and parolees. In *United States v. Knights*, 534 U.S. 112 (2001) it upheld a search of Knights's home even though police lacked a warrant and had only reasonable suspicion that they would find evidence of arson, not probable cause. Without deciding that Knights had waived his Fourth Amendment protection by agreeing to the condition of probation that he submit to searches at any time, the Court found the search reasonable under a totality-of-the-circumstances test, balancing the degree of intrusion against the state's interest.

   The Ninth Circuit used this same analysis in upholding DNA profiling of convicted offenders without any individualized suspicion. In *United States v. Kincade*, 379 F.3d 813 (9th Cir. 2004) it ruled that blood tests are a minimal intrusion into a person's privacy and bodily integrity when weighed against the compelling governmental interests furthered by DNA testing of parolees. Therefore, Blood's Fourth Amendment challenge will probably fail.

   On a related matter, the Court ruled in a 5-4 decision in *Dist. Attorney's Office v. Osborne*, 129 S. Ct. 2308 (2009) that a convict has no constitutional right to obtain access to the state's evidence for DNA testing to prove his innocence.

Search and Arrest Warrants

A warrant is a judicial authorization for police action, either to search a particular place (a search warrant) or to arrest a particular person (an arrest warrant). In this chapter, we will explore the basic prerequisites for a valid warrant.

§5.1 NOTE ON THE WARRANT REQUIREMENT

By requiring authorization of a magistrate prior to a proposed search or arrest, the warrant process affords protection against unilateral action of overly zealous police officers. But demanding prior judicial authorization for *all* searches and arrests, regardless of the urgency of the particular circumstances, would impair effective law enforcement. Thus, while the Supreme Court has traditionally articulated a preference for warrants (see Chapter 2), it has carved out numerous categorical exceptions premised on either the impracticality of seeking a warrant in exigent circumstances or the diminished expectation of privacy in the area searched. These exceptions will be discussed in Chapter 6. In those cases that do not fall within the established exceptions, such as the search of one's home, the police are required to obtain a warrant before conducting a search.

§5.2 THE COMPONENTS OF A VALID SEARCH WARRANT

The basic purpose served by the warrant process is to interpose a disinterested magistrate between the police and the individual whom they seek to search or seize. "The point of the Fourth Amendment, which often is not grasped by zealous officers, is not that it denies law enforcement the support of the usual inferences which reasonable men draw from evidence. Its protection consists in requiring that those inferences be drawn by a neutral and detached magistrate instead of being judged by the officer engaged in the often competitive enterprise of ferreting out crime." *Johnson v. United States*, 333 U.S. 10, 13-14 (1948). Once issued, the warrant also serves the additional purpose of confining the scope of the intrusion to the areas and items specified. A warrant must meet the following requirements:

1. It must be issued by a **neutral and detached magistrate.**
2. There must be presented to the magistrate an adequate showing of **probable cause** (either to search or arrest) supported by oath or affirmation. This is usually in the form of an affidavit from a police officer.
3. The warrant must **describe with particularity** the place to be searched and the items or persons to be seized.

Because warrants are of necessity issued *ex parte* (if the subject of the search is tipped off to the application for the warrant, the evidence sought may be removed or destroyed), challenges to the issuance of a warrant will be heard after the search has occurred on the defendant's motion to suppress the evidence seized.

§5.2.1 Neutral and Detached Magistrate

While it is not constitutionally required that the person issuing the warrant be an attorney or judge, he or she must be 1) "neutral and detached," and 2) "capable of determining whether probable cause exists for the requested arrest or search." *Shadwick v. City of Tampa*, 407 U.S. 345, 350 (1972). The issuer must be part of the judicial apparatus, such as a court clerk or magistrate, and not be associated with the prosecutor's office or the police.[1] Where the

---

1. The state attorney general in charge of investigating and prosecuting a murder case, for example, was held not to be the neutral and detached magistrate required by the Constitution and thus could not lawfully issue a search warrant for the defendant's car. See *Coolidge v. New Hampshire*, 403 U.S. 443 (1971). But a magistrate who had formerly been an assistant U.S. Attorney and had worked on an unrelated case involving the same defendant was considered sufficiently detached to issue a warrant. See *United States v. DeLuna*, 763 F.2d 897, 908 (8th Cir. 1985); *United States v. Outler*, 659 F.2d 1306, 1312 (5th Cir. 1981), *overruled on other grounds, United States v. Steele*, 147 F.3d 1316 (11th Cir. 1998).

issuing magistrate accompanied the police as they executed a warrant for obscene materials and assisted them in determining what items to seize, this rendered him not sufficiently detached to satisfy the requirements of the Fourth Amendment, as he was "not acting as a judicial officer, but as an adjunct law enforcement officer." *Lo-Ji Sales v. New York*, 442 U.S. 319, 327 (1979). Nor can the magistrate have a financial interest in the issuance of the warrant. See *Connally v. Georgia*, 429 U.S. 245 (1977) (invalidating a scheme in which the justice of the peace was paid a fee only if he issued a warrant).

The issuer must also have the training and experience necessary to meaningfully assess the probable cause showing. A court clerk was held to have this capacity with regard to arrest warrants for minor municipal offenses. *Shadwick, supra.* More sophisticated determinations of probable cause require a judge.

§5.2.2 The Probable Cause Showing

The Fourth Amendment provides that a warrant may be issued only upon probable cause, supported by oath or affirmation. The concept of probable cause is discussed in Chapter 4. The actual demonstration of probable cause usually comes in the form of a sworn affidavit prepared by the investigating officers and presented to the magistrate. Some jurisdictions permit the issuance of warrants on sworn oral testimony, even communicated by telephone, where compelling circumstances justify dispensing with the written affidavit.[2]

A court subsequently reviewing the issuance of a warrant to determine whether probable cause existed will limit its focus to the information that was presented to the magistrate at the time.[3] Challenges take two forms. The first is an assertion that the probable cause showing was inadequate *on its face.* See §4.1 of Chapter 4. As we will learn in §7.3.3, the "good faith exception" to the exclusionary rule significantly affects such challenges. Evidence seized pursuant to a search warrant issued on an inadequate demonstration of probable cause will be suppressed only if the affidavit is "so lacking in indicia of probable cause as to render belief in its existence entirely unreasonable." *United States v. Leon*, 468 U.S. 897 (1984).

The second type of challenge goes *behind* the affidavit and disputes the truthfulness of the facts set out. In order to mount such a credibility challenge, the defendant must negotiate several difficult obstacles. See *Franks v. Delaware*, 438 U.S. 154 (1978).

---

2. See, e.g., Fed. R. Crim. P. 41(c). The magistrate is required to record the conversation by mechanical or stenographic means.

3. Permitting the record to be expanded with information known to the police but not disclosed to the issuing magistrate would "render the warrant requirements of the Fourth Amendment meaningless." *Whiteley v. Warden*, 401 U.S. 560, 565 n.8 (1971).

- First, defendant must make a substantial preliminary showing that the affidavit contains 1) a false statement, 2) made by the affiant police officer, 3) either knowingly and intentionally or with reckless disregard for the truth. Neither inadvertent nor negligent misstatements of the officer, nor false statements of informers or other sources, are sufficient to satisfy this threshold requirement.
- Second, it must be demonstrated that the false statement was necessary to the finding of probable cause. If there was sufficient information even without the false statement, the misrepresentation is treated as harmless error.

A defendant who succeeds at making this showing is then entitled to a full evidentiary hearing (with witnesses and documentary evidence) in which he must prove (by a preponderance of the evidence) that the affidavit contained a knowing or reckless falsehood. If defendant establishes this, the judge excises the false statements from the affidavit and determines whether the remainder makes out probable cause to search. If it does not, then the search conducted pursuant to the warrant was unlawful.

It must be emphasized that the false statement that triggers the *Franks* remedy must be that of the officer who filed the affidavit, not the sources relied on. Showing that an informant lied to the police will not result in suppression of the evidence. Where, however, the defendant can demonstrate that the officer created a fictional informant[4] or deliberately misrepresented what an informant reported,[5] the *Franks* remedy is available. Given that the identity of confidential informants is protected from disclosure by a generally recognized privilege,[6] making such a showing is difficult (if not impossible) for most defendants.

---

4. See, e.g., *Commonwealth v. Lewin*, 405 Mass. 566 (1989); *Commonwealth v. Ramirez*, 416 Mass. 41 (1993). But see *United States v. Pace*, 898 F.2d 1218 (7th Cir. 1990) (similarity of 29 affidavits filed by vice officers is not sufficient to make *Franks* showing); *Commonwealth v. Singer*, 29 Mass. App. 708, 564 N.E.2d 1037 (Mass. App. Ct. 1991) (fact that officers had filed numerous affidavits setting out similar stories from the same informant is not sufficient to prove that the informant was fictional).

5. In *Franks*, for example, the defendant submitted written statements from two sources who were named in the warrant as having described the defendant's typical attire to the police, but who now testified that they did not provide any such information. See also *State v. Schmitt*, 623 N.W.2d 409 (N.D. 2001) (unchallenged testimony of informants contradicting affidavit and sheer number of false statements therein supported inference of officer's reckless disregard for truth). The affiant's omissions may also trigger the *Franks* remedy. See, e.g., *State v. Hendricks*, 61 P.3d 722 (Kan. 2003) (officer's omissions raising questions about informant's credibility and motivation to lie undermined demonstration of probable cause).

6. See *McCray v. Illinois*, 386 U.S. 300 (1967) (holding that the Constitution does not compel disclosure of an informant's identity for purpose of challenging the probable cause showing, but only if the informant has material testimony on defendant's guilt or innocence, as where he was present at the crime scene). The court may conduct an *in camera* hearing on the veracity challenge, in which the judge questions the officer and the informant outside the presence of counsel to ascertain the facts without disclosing the identity of the informant. See, e.g., *United States v. Barone*, 787 F.2d 811 (2d Cir. 1986).

Franks recognizes that there is no constitutional mandate that "every fact recited in the warrant affidavit is necessarily correct, for probable cause may be founded upon hearsay and upon information within the affiant's own knowledge that sometimes may be garnered hastily." 438 U.S. at 165. All that is constitutionally required is that the officer filing the affidavit not *deliberately or recklessly* misrepresent the facts.

§5.2.3 The Particularity Requirement and the Plain View Doctrine

The Fourth Amendment requires that warrants "shall issue particularly describing the place to be searched and the person or things to be seized." This language was inserted to avoid the detested "writs of assistance" of the colonial period, which were open licenses to search whenever, wherever, and whomever the officers chose. A valid warrant not only ensures that there is sufficient justification for the search; it also functions to limit its permissible bounds.

The standard of particularity regarding *the place to be searched* requires that the description be sufficiently precise so that the officer executing the warrant can "with reasonable effort ascertain and identify the place intended." *Steele v. United States*, 267 U.S. 498, 503 (1925). Minor errors or inconsistencies will not generally invalidate the warrant, so long as they do not present a significant risk that some other premises may be mistakenly searched.[7]

The standard of particularity regarding *the items to be seized* requires that the description leave nothing to the discretion of the officers. See *Marron v. United States*, 275 U.S. 192, 196 (1927). Thus, where the description requires the executing officers to interpret a statute or legal concept to determine which items may be seized, the particularity requirement is violated.[8] Where, however, the items are readily identifiable as contraband, the courts have permitted generic descriptions. Thus, warrants authorizing the seizure of all items related to illegal gambling or narcotics manufacture have generally

---

7. In one case, for example, a typographical error in the address of the apartment to be searched did not invalidate the warrant because the executing officer checked with the magistrate by telephone and ascertained the correct address before searching. *United States v. Arenal*, 768 F.2d 263 (8th Cir. 1985). See also *United States v. Pelayo-Landero*, 285 F.3d 491 (6th Cir. 2002) (search warrant adequately described mobile home, even if postal address was incorrect, because the warrant included specific directions to the home, described the trailer, and included a photograph).

8. A warrant authorizing the seizure of "illegally obtained films" was invalidated because of the discretion that it allowed the officers in determining which films were illegal. See *United States v. Cook*, 657 F.2d 730 (5th Cir. 1981). A warrant for seizure of "all evidence of association" between the defendant and seven other persons was similarly struck down as overbroad. See *United States v. Washington*, 782 F.2d 807, 819 (9th Cir. 1986). Failure to limit broad descriptive terms by dates may render a warrant overbroad. See, e.g., *United States v. Ford*, 184 F.3d 566, 576 (6th Cir. 1999).

been upheld. See *United States v. DeLuna*, 763 F.2d 897, 908 (8th Cir. 1985); *United States v. Alexander*, 761 F.2d 1294 (9th Cir. 1985).[9] The particularity requirement is afforded its most scrupulous enforcement when the items to be seized implicate First Amendment rights, such as books or organizational membership lists. See *Zurcher v. Stanford Daily*, 436 U.S. 547, 565 (1978); *Stanford v. Texas*, 379 U.S. 476, 485 (1965).

Applying the particularity requirement to computer searches presents unique problems, as digital files can be disguised to hide their true contents. We will discuss this topic in §11.4.2.

These established standards have been significantly modified (and diluted) by the adoption of the "good faith exception" (see §7.3.3), which limits the exclusionary remedy to situations where the search warrant is "so facially deficient—i.e., in failing to particularize the place to be searched or the things to be seized—that the executing officer cannot reasonably presume it to be valid." *United States v. Leon*, 468 U.S. 897, 923 (1984).

In *Maryland v. Garrison*, 480 U.S. 79 (1987), for example, the warrant authorized a search of one Marty McWebb and his third-floor apartment. The officers believed at the time and represented to the magistrate that there was only one apartment on that floor. It turned out, however, that there were two separate apartments on the third floor, one occupied by McWebb and the other by Garrison. Without realizing this, the officers searched both apartments and discovered contraband in Garrison's.

The Court upheld the search despite the ambiguity in the warrant and the officers' mistake on the scene. With regard to the former, the Court held that the validity of the warrant must be measured based on the information known at the time that the warrant was issued, and the subsequent discovery that the third floor was divided does not retroactively invalidate the warrant. Further, the mistake made by the officers in executing the warrant was "objectively understandable and reasonable," and thus did not violate the particularity requirement of the Fourth Amendment. While observing that "the purposes justifying a police search strictly limit the permissible extent of the search," the Court nonetheless recognized the need to allow "some latitude for honest mistakes that are made by officers in the dangerous and difficult process of making arrests and executing search warrants." 480 U.S. at 86.

In another application of the good faith exception in the context of the particularity requirement, the Court in *Massachusetts v. Sheppard*, 468 U.S. 981 (1984) (also discussed in §7.3.3) similarly upheld a search even though the warrant mistakenly described the items to be seized as controlled substances

---

9. But warrants with catchall language like "material evidence of" or the "fruits and instrumentalities of" specified narcotics violations have been deemed not sufficiently particularized. See *United States v. Crozier*, 777 F.2d 1376, 1381 (9th Cir. 1985), and *United States v. Clark*, 31 F.3d 831 (9th Cir. 1994).

instead of evidence of a recent homicide, which was what the officers were actually looking for and seized. Because the issuing judge had assured the officers that he would correct the inaccuracy and the officers reasonably relied on that representation when they executed the warrant, the search and seizure of items not described in the warrant was upheld. There was, the Court ruled, an "objectively reasonable basis for the officers' mistaken belief" that the warrant authorized the search for evidence linking Sheppard to the murder. 468 U.S. at 988. See also *Messerschmidt v. Millender*, 132 S. Ct. 1235 (2012) (it was not entirely unreasonable for officers executing a warrant in residence of known gang member to believe that they had probable cause to search for all firearms, even though there was only probable cause for a shotgun).

But there was no such objectively reasonable mistake where the officers relied on and executed a warrant that utterly failed to describe the things to be seized, even though *the application* for the warrant did describe them, and even though the officers confined their search of the ranch to those items. See *Groh v. Ramirez*, 540 U.S. 551 (2004). In this civil action for damages, the Court explained that the particularity requirement serves not only the purpose of preventing general searches but also to assure that the subject of the search is notified of its specific limits. Executing a warrant that left blank the portion calling for a description of the items seized was, in the Court's view, tantamount to searching without any warrant at all.

In sum, the Fourth Amendment particularity requirement, read together with the good faith exception, mandates that either 1) the place searched and the items seized be specifically and accurately described in the warrant, or 2) if not correctly described, the mistake is deemed to have been objectively reasonable. A failure to particularize in the warrant itself, or an unreasonable mistake in its execution, will invalidate the search.

One additional gloss on the particularity requirement is the "plain view" doctrine (discussed more fully in §6.8), which recognizes that in the course of searching for the items described in the warrant, police may come upon contraband or other evidence of crime. Rather than being required to ignore the discovery or to seek another warrant specifically describing the new items, the police are permitted to seize them at that time, provided that two conditions are met. First, the items must be in plain view while the officers are within the confines of the originally authorized search. Thus, officers executing a warrant to search for rifles would be permitted to seize marijuana that they discover in a bedroom closet where rifles could be hidden. They would not, however, be permitted to seize marijuana in a small desk drawer because that location is obviously not within the proper scope of a search for rifles. Second, the items must be immediately apparent as contraband or evidence of crime and not require any further search or analysis. Thus, the officers could not seize a bottle of pills on the hunch that they might be a controlled substance and send them off for laboratory testing.

The plain view doctrine, in sum, permits *seizure* of an item that has already come into the officer's view during the course of a lawful search; it does not authorize any additional *search* beyond that described in the warrant.

Examples

1. Consider the following documents:

State of New York County
of Westchester } Circuit of Westchester County

Search Warrant

On this 5th day of May, 2011, Police Officer Harvey Lance has subscribed and sworn to before me an application for search warrant and accompanying affidavit. Upon examination of the affidavit, I find that it states facts sufficient to show probable cause.

I therefore authorize a search of the home of Lester Webster, located at apartment 6 in the building at 231 Longfellow Avenue, Scarsdale, New York, and I further authorize a seizure of all electronic appliances stolen in the burglary of Joe's Appliance Store, Main Street, Scarsdale, on April 24, 2011.

Issued May 5, 2011 ss/Judge Linda Black

State of New York County
of Westchester } Circuit of Westchester County

Application for Search Warrant and Affidavit in Support of Application

Police Officer Harvey Lance now appears before the undersigned judge of the Circuit Court of Westchester County and requests the issuance of a warrant to search the home of Lester Webster, located at apartment 6 in the building at 231 Longfellow Avenue, Scarsdale, New York, and to seize the following articles and things: all items taken in the burglary of Joe's Appliance Store, Main Street, Scarsdale, on April 24, 2011, which constitute evidence of that crime.

Applicant further states that he has probable cause to believe that the above listed things to be seized are evidence of the offense of burglary and are now located upon the premises indicated above. Probable cause is based upon the following:

An informant, who has provided accurate information to me on several occasions in the past (leading to the arrest of one Raymond Rowe and one Sally Stowe) and who wishes to remain unidentified, reported to me today that on May 2, 2011, she was in the apartment of Lester Webster at the above address and observed several electronic appliances, including a color TV and video camera, and that Webster stated to her that he had taken those and other items when he broke into Joe's Appliance Store on April 24. I confirmed with the store manager that a break-in did occur that day and that several items, including a color TV and video camera, were taken.

ss/Harvey Lance

Subscribed and sworn to before me on the 5th day of May, 2011.

ss/Judge Linda Black

Does this warrant comply with the requirements of the Fourth Amendment?

Some Twists and Turns

2. Assume that the warrant in example 1 was issued, and the search of Lester Webster's apartment was conducted. Police seized several items, including some that were later confirmed to have been taken from Joe's Appliance Store. Would the lawfulness of the search be undercut by any of the following additional facts?

   a. Subsequent to the search, Police Officer Harvey Lance was overheard telling a fellow officer in the courthouse men's room that he had concocted the entire story about an informant being in Webster's place and seeing the loot because Lance had a hunch Webster was the perpetrator, but had no hard information to go by.

   b. Assume instead that Lance is overheard telling a fellow officer that there actually was an informant who provided the information about Webster set out in the affidavit, but that the informant had been inaccurate on three of six previous occasions when she had given Lance tips.

   c. While the officers were searching Webster's apartment, they discovered an automatic assault weapon in his hall closet. As possession of this weapon is a crime, they seized it. The officers then found in the closet a small cigar box, which they opened to discover unlawful hollow-nosed bullets inside. The officers seized the bullets.

   d. When the officers appeared at Webster's apartment to conduct the search, they found him and three other persons inside. They frisked all four men and found an unlawful pistol on one of the visitors.

   e. Assume instead that when the officers appeared to conduct the search, Webster was leaving his apartment. After identifying themselves and showing him the warrant, the officers requested that he remain. When he refused, one officer detained Webster in the hallway while the others conducted the search.

Explanations

1. In order to satisfy constitutional requirements, the warrant must 1) be issued by a neutral and detached magistrate, 2) be based on a showing of probable cause supported by oath or affirmation, and 3) describe with particularity the place to be searched and the items to be seized.

   The first requirement appears to be met. The warrant is signed by a judge of the county court, a judicial officer who has (as far as we know) no association with the prosecutor or police and no personal or financial stake in the issuance.

   The probable cause showing is properly in the form of a sworn affidavit from the officer. Does the showing amount to probable cause to believe that seizable items are present at the place to be searched? As pointed out in Chapter 4, probable cause may be based on hearsay information provided by a third party. When the source is an unnamed informant, as is the case here, there must be information in the affidavit supporting the officer's reliance on both the informant's credibility and the accuracy of his conclusion that incriminating evidence will be found (although under the *Illinois v. Gates* totality-of-the-circumstances standard, a strong showing in one regard may compensate for a weak showing in the other). The informant's credibility is adequately supported in Officer Lance's affidavit by the assertion of past reliability. The informant's conclusion that the loot from the burglary is present at the apartment seems well supported by her own personal observations and Webster's incriminatory statement. Moreover, the police officer's own investigation corroborated that the burglary had occurred and that the items described by the informant had indeed been taken from Joe's Appliance.

   A question may be raised regarding the time lapse between the informant's observations and the application for the warrant. As noted in §4.1, probable cause to search must be based on information sufficiently fresh to make it likely that the items will still be at the location to be searched. The application here is filed three days after the informant asserts that she saw the stolen items. Although it could be argued that it was no longer reasonable to conclude that the items would still be there on the date that the warrant is actually executed, the time lapse is probably not great enough to support this contention.

   The Fourth Amendment has been interpreted to require that a search warrant be executed within a reasonable time of its issuance to ensure that probable cause still exists at the time of the search. "If the police were allowed to execute the warrant at leisure, the safeguard of judicial control over the search which the Fourth Amendment is intended to accomplish would be eviscerated." *United States v. Bedford*, 519 F.2d 650, 655 (3d Cir. 1975). Thus, Officer Lance must conduct the search promptly and without unreasonable delay.

Turning to the particularity requirement, it would appear that the place to be searched is specified sufficiently enough that the officer executing the warrant can ascertain the location with reasonable effort. There is, however, serious question as to the particularity of the items to be seized. Given the principle that the description should leave little or nothing to the discretion of the officer executing the warrant, the authorization to seize "all electronic appliances stolen in the burglary of Joe's Appliance Store" on the specified date is probably inadequate. Because a precise description of the items stolen (including serial numbers) could apparently have been obtained from the store manager at the time of issuance, such specificity should have been provided. See *United States v. Guidry*, 199 F.3d 1150, 1154-1155 (10th Cir. 1999). Unlike contraband such as narcotics, there is nothing about the characterization of "stolen" property that makes it readily identifiable. See *Commonwealth v. Rutkowski*, 406 Mass. 673, 676 (1990) ("To describe general items like guns and jewelry as 'stolen' adds nothing instructive to a description in a warrant."); *Namen v. Alaska*, 665 P.2d 557 (Alaska Ct. App. 1983) (search warrant for defendant's residence authorizing seizure of jewelry stolen from a certain home on a certain date did not satisfy particularity requirement because it did not provide meaningful guidance to the officers conducting search as to what items could be seized, especially because an inventory of items stolen was available at time of issuance). Compare *United States v. Strand*, 761 F.2d 449, 453 (8th Cir. 1985) (upheld warrant that authorized a search for "stolen mail" because generic description nevertheless permitted officers to readily identify items of mail not addressed to or from the person being searched). See also *United States v. Brown*, 984 F.2d 1074 (10th Cir. 1993) (portion of warrant authorizing search for "any other item which the Officers determine or have reasonable belief is stolen while executing this search warrant" was overbroad).

Certain crimes, such as those involving money laundering or fraud, often require so extensive a search of records that there is no feasible way to limit the search to evidence of crime. In such cases, the courts have admonished law enforcement officials to conduct themselves in a manner that minimizes unwarranted intrusions upon privacy. See *Andresen v. Maryland*, 427 U.S. 463, 482 (1976). As Circuit Judge Jon Newman has written: "It is true that a warrant authorizing seizure of records of criminal activity permits officers to examine many papers in a suspect's possession to determine if they are within the described category. But allowing some latitude in this regard simply recognizes the reality that few people keep documents of their criminal transactions in a folder marked 'drug records.'" *United States v. Riley*, 906 F.2d 841, 845 (2d Cir. 1990).

The problem of describing the items to be seized with sufficient particularity is especially challenging when the search is for documents on a computer. For more on computer searches, see Chapter 11.

The warrant in our example amounts to a license to seize any item that *conceivably* could have been taken from an appliance store. Moreover, the failure to particularize the actual items stolen (when such information was available) would probably not be excused as an objectively reasonable good faith error under *Maryland v. Garrison*, 480 U.S. 79 (1987) and *Massachusetts v. Sheppard*, 468 U.S. 981 (1984). As the Court noted in *United States v. Leon*, 468 U.S. 897, 923 (1984), the good faith exception does not apply if the warrant is "so facially deficient—i.e., in failing to particularize the place to be searched or the things to be seized—that the executing officers cannot reasonably presume it to be valid." See also *United States v. Stubbs*, 873 F.2d 210, 212 (9th Cir. 1989) (executing officers could not have reasonably presumed a facially overbroad warrant authorizing seizure of all of defendant's business records to be valid).

Some Twists and Turns

2a. The defendant could pursue a challenge to the veracity of the affidavit under the terms of *Franks v. Delaware*, 438 U.S. 154 (1978). The formidable preconditions may be summarized as follows: 1) the defendant must allege specifically which portions of the search warrant affidavit are claimed to be false; 2) the defendant must challenge the statements as deliberate or reckless falsehoods, not simply unknowing or negligent; 3) the false statements must be those of the officer filing the affidavit, not the informant or other sources; 4) a detailed offer of proof, including affidavits, must accompany the allegations; and 5) the challenged statements must be necessary to the establishment of probable cause.

Assuming that the witness who overheard Officer Lance is willing to file a sworn statement to that effect, Webster has a good chance of making a successful preliminary showing of deliberate perjury on matters that go to the very heart of the probable cause set forth in the affidavit. Setting aside the informant's assertions would leave this affidavit with no other information on which to base probable cause to search Webster's apartment.

The challenge would then proceed to an evidentiary hearing in which Webster would actually have to prove (by a preponderance of the evidence) that the police officer engaged in a deliberate or reckless falsehood. This would now require the testimony of the witness to Lance's admission. In all likelihood, the officer would deny under oath that he falsified the affidavit, and the ultimate fact question would have to be resolved by the judge. If it were determined that the officer did in fact concoct the story about the informant, then the warrant would be held unlawful as having been issued without probable cause, and the items seized ruled inadmissible in evidence.

2b. Unlike example 2a, the deliberate falsehood here less clearly undercuts the existence of probable cause in the affidavit. The omission of information concerning the informant's past unreliability on three of six occasions, even if shown to have been deliberate, may be considered harmless in the sense that the warrant would have been issued anyway had this been disclosed. Such omissions have not been the stuff of successful *Franks* challenges. See, e.g., *United States v. Graham*, 275 F.3d 490 (6th Cir. 2001) (even if juxtaposition of two paragraphs in affidavit were misleading regarding defendant's illegal possession of weapons, and affidavit omitted exculpatory evidence regarding defendant, there was still sufficient showing of probable cause); *United States v. Reeves*, 210 F.3d 1041 (9th Cir. 2000) (detective's failure to disclose informant's criminal history involving dishonesty did not warrant *Franks* hearing); *United States v. Hadfield*, 918 F.2d 987 (1st Cir. 1990) (officer failed to reveal that same request for warrant had earlier been submitted to and denied by another magistrate, and also that the source of information relied upon for the firearms seizure was uncertain about whether the particular weapon used by defendant was a lawful BB gun or an unlawful .22 caliber); *United States v. Parcels of Land*, 903 F.2d 36 (1st Cir. 1990) (omission of information showing that defendant had substantial sources of legitimate income and that several big-ticket purchases he made were financed through loans and not cash); *United States v. Rumney*, 867 F.2d 714 (1st Cir. 1989) (omission of facts that primary source of information had changed his story several times and had a criminal record); *United States v. DiCesare*, 765 F.2d 890 (9th Cir. 1985) (officer failed to reveal that a previous arrest of defendant referred to in the affidavit had not resulted in prosecution).

2c. While a primary purpose of the warrant is to limit the scope of the search to the particular items described, the police are permitted to seize other articles of contraband or evidence of crime that they come upon in the ordinary course of the original search. The rationale for this plain view doctrine is that once the lawful search uncovers the article, no additional invasion of privacy occurs when the officers view it. Seizure of the item, which clearly does amount to an incremental intrusion, is nevertheless justified on the grounds that it would make little sense to require the officer either to ignore the item or to seek a warrant for its seizure (for which he now clearly has probable cause).

    The two prerequisites for plain view seizure are that 1) the item in question was found while the officer confined his search to the original parameters authorized in the warrant; and 2) the item was immediately apparent as contraband or evidence of crime.[10] The first requirement

---

10. Circuit Judge Selya described the concept of "immediately apparent" as "akin to that underlying the incandescent light bulb. When an officer spots an object not described in the warrant, authority to seize depends upon knowledge—the extent to which bits and bytes of accumulated information then and there fall into place. The sum total of the searcher's knowledge must be sufficient to turn on the bulb; if the light does not shine during the currency of the search, there is no immediate awareness of the incriminating nature of the object." *United States v. Rutkowski*, supra, 877 F.2d 139, 142 (1st Cir. 1989).

ensures that the officer has lawfully arrived at the place from which the plain view is made and that the scope of the authorized search is not exceeded; the second limits the additional items that can be seized to those that (without need for further examination) are obviously incriminating. Both requirements operate to prevent the plain view doctrine from becoming a license for a general search.

In example 2c, the warrant authorized a search of the apartment for electronic appliances. The officers were therefore acting within lawful confines when they opened the bedroom closet, where such items could be hidden, and discovered the assault weapon. Moreover, the gun was immediately apparent to them as an unlawful weapon; they did not need to engage in further examination to determine that. See, e.g., *United States v. Perrotta*, 289 F.3d 155, 167 (1st Cir. 2002) (billy club and brass knuckles, found during search pursuant to loan-sharking conspiracy investigation, were immediately apparent as illegal weapons). Compare *Coolidge v. New Hampshire*, 403 U.S. 443 (1971) (the probative value of the automobile seized in plain view was not clear until its interior was subjected to vacuuming and microscopic analysis); *United States v. McLevain*, 310 F.3d 434, 441-442 (6th Cir. 2002) (incriminating nature of twist tie, cigarette filter, spoon with residue, and unlabeled prescription bottle was not immediately apparent to allow them to be identified as drug paraphernalia); *United States v. Rutkowski*, 877 F.2d 139, 143 (1st Cir. 1989) (seizure of metal strips could not be justified under plain view doctrine because it was not immediately apparent that they were incriminating: "Possession of platinum is not itself illegal. Furthermore, when he found the metal in the envelopes, he was not able to identify it as platinum — much less to identify it as stolen platinum."). The seizure of the weapon, which the officers could readily see was illegal, was therefore lawful, despite the fact that it was not specified in the warrant.

The seizure of the bullets is another story. The officers did not find the bullets in plain view during an appropriate search for electronic appliances. They clearly exceeded the proper scope of a search for televisions and VCRs when they opened a small cigar box. Compare *United States v. Rutkowski*, supra (officers executing a warrant to search for jewelry and coins had right to open coffee can and envelopes contained in it); *United States v. Hamie*, 165 F.3d 80 (1st Cir. 1999) (officers searching for evidence of credit card fraud were entitled to open briefcase and silver box found inside); *United States v. Weinbender*, 109 F.3d 1327 (8th Cir. 1997) (officer did not exceed scope of permissible search when he removed a piece of drywall from closet wall because there was reasonable probability he would find items described in warrant; the officers were informed specifically that the defendants used hiding spaces in that particular area of the house). Although the box itself in our example was found in plain view during the authorized search, it was not immediately apparent that it contained evidence of crime.

Because the bullets were not specified in the warrant, and the plain view doctrine is inapplicable, seizure of them was unlawful.

2d. Armed with a warrant to search Webster's apartment for specified items, may the officers frisk persons found inside at the time of the search? *Ybarra v. Illinois*, 444 U.S. 85 (1979) ruled unlawful the frisk of patrons who happened to be in a tavern at the time that it was searched for narcotics pursuant to a warrant. Neither the affidavit in support of the warrant nor the warrant itself made any reference to unlawful activity of customers at the tavern. A person's mere presence in a place suspected of criminal activity does not give rise to justification to search that person. In contrast, given the reduced expectation of privacy in a car, as well as the greater likelihood of complicity in the driver's criminal enterprise, presence in an automobile being lawfully searched permits examination of a passenger's belongings. See *Wyoming v. Houghton*, 526 U.S. 295 (1999), discussed in §6.4. See also *Maryland v. Pringle*, 540 U.S. 366 (2003), discussed in §4.1 above.

If any authority to frisk exists in example 2d, it must emanate from the officer's reasonable suspicion that the occupants of the apartment were armed and dangerous. See §4.2. The officers must be able to point to some threatening gesture or other aggressive action on the part of the occupants that provided a reasonable belief that danger was at hand. Otherwise, the frisk resulting in the seizure of the weapon was unlawful.

2e. Armed with a warrant to search Webster's apartment for specified items, may the officers detain him for the duration of the search? The Court has answered this affirmatively in *Michigan v. Summers*, 452 U.S. 692 (1981), in which the occupant of a home about to be searched was detained by the executing officers and later arrested when narcotics were found on the premises. The Court reasoned that the existence of probable cause to search the home provides an adequate basis for suspecting criminal activity on the part of its resident, and that justifies the detention. Moreover, detention during the search was viewed as only a slight increment above the intrusion of the search itself. And it serves the legitimate purposes of preventing flight in the event incriminating evidence is found and of facilitating the orderly completion of the search (by making the resident available, for example, to open locked doors or containers).

§5.3 EXECUTION OF A SEARCH WARRANT

Most jurisdictions have limitations on the period during which a search warrant can be executed. See, e.g., Fed. R. Crim. P. 41(c)(1) (10 days). Even without these rules, a long delay could result in the dissipation of probable cause. See §4.1. In addition, rules sometimes require that the warrants be executed during the daytime hours unless otherwise authorized. See Fed. R. Crim. P. 41(c)(1).

Another constraint on execution is the old common law requirement that police knock on a dwelling's door and announce their identity and purpose before attempting forcible entry. *Wilson v. Arkansas*, 514 U.S. 927 (1995) held that the Fourth Amendment incorporates this mandate. (18 U.S.C. §3109 requires federal law enforcement officers to give such warning.) Recognizing the need for flexibility in light of countervailing law enforcement concerns, however, a unanimous Court held that the requirement is governed by the reasonableness clause. *United States v. Banks*, 540 U.S. 31 (2003) concluded that an interval of 15 to 20 seconds from the officers' knock and announcement of a search warrant until their forced entry was reasonable, given the possibility of destruction of the narcotics evidence. "Reasonable wait time" is to be determined by how long it would take for the occupants to dispose of the evidence sought. Drugs that could easily be flushed down the toilet would necessitate a shorter wait time than stolen rifles.

Circumstances justifying a "no-knock" entry include a threat of physical violence or escape. See *United States v. Bates*, 84 F.3d 790 (6th Cir. 1996). The Court, however, has refused to create a blanket exception to the knock-and-announce rule when the object of the search is drugs, rejecting the argument that such searches invariably involve exigent circumstances. *Richards v. Wisconsin*, 520 U.S. 385 (1997). Rather, police must have reasonable suspicion that knocking and announcing their presence before entering would "be dangerous or futile, or inhibit the effective investigation of the crime."

The Fourth Amendment does not hold officers to any higher standard when a "no-knock" entry results in destruction of property at the scene. *United States v. Ramirez*, 523 U.S. 65 (1998). Several courts have ruled that an entry obtained by ruse (such as false assertion of an emergency) does not violate knock-and-announce requirements. See *Coleman v. United States*, 728 A.2d 1230 (D.C. Ct. App. 1999) (and citations).

The knock-and-announce requirement lost its bite when the Court ruled in *Hudson v. Michigan*, 126 S. Ct. 2159 (2006) that the exclusionary remedy would not be applied to evidence obtained by a search conducted in violation of the rule. For the four dissenters, "knock and announce" had been rendered a nullity because there was no longer any incentive for police to comply. See §7.3 for further discussion of *Hudson*.

In another matter related to the execution of a warrant, the Court has refused to permit media "ride-alongs" during searches of residences, concluding that the presence of reporters observing and photographing the event violates the privacy rights of the homeowner. See *Wilson v. Layne*, 526 U.S. 603 (1999). The Court distinguished the situation where the presence of a third party directly aids in the execution of the warrant, as in the case of an owner identifying stolen property.

§5.4 ADMINISTRATIVE SEARCH WARRANTS

As discussed in §4.5 of Chapter 4, warrants have been required for certain administrative and regulatory searches. Unlike traditional search and arrest warrants, *Camara*-type warrants are not issued on the basis of particularized probable cause. Rather, what is required is a showing that the location to be inspected was chosen according to a prescribed plan that relies on neutral criteria (as, for example, the date of last inspection). *See Marshall v. Barlow's Inc.*, 436 U.S. 307 (1978).

§5.5 ANTICIPATORY SEARCH WARRANTS

As discussed in §4.1, the Court in *United States v. Grubbs*, 547 U.S. 90 (2006) unanimously approved of the use of anticipatory warrants. These differ from traditional search warrants in that at the time of issuance, they are not supported by probable cause that the item related to the crime is *presently* at the place to be searched. Instead they are issued upon a showing that seizable items will be at the place to be searched at a specified time *in the very near future*. *Grubbs* reasoned that because the probable cause requirement looks to the future point in time when the search is actually conducted, all warrants are "anticipatory."

In addition to the usual requirement of probable cause that evidence of a crime will be at the place searched at the time of execution, an anticipatory warrant is conditioned on the occurrence of an event (e.g., delivery of a package) and can be issued only on a showing of probable cause that the triggering event will occur (by definition, the event has not occurred at the time of issuance).

While the actual occurrence of the triggering event is essential to the ultimate lawfulness of the search, some courts have accepted *equivalent* compliance with the conditions. In *Commonwealth v. Colondres*, 471 Mass 192 (2015), the Supreme Judicial Court denied defendant's motion to suppress, even though only two of the three triggering events had occurred. Defendant's nephew (the original subject of the investigation) was seen entering and then leaving Colondres' apartment, but was arrested outside before he could make the delivery of cocaine to the customer. The court nonetheless found that the discovery of cocaine on the nephew was an adequate substitute for the third event — the delivery — because it gave the police probable cause to believe that defendant was running a stash house.

§5.6 THE ARREST WARRANT REQUIREMENT

As indicated in §5.1, while a warrant is generally required to authorize the seizure of things (unless the circumstances fit within an established exception to the warrant requirement), this is not so with regard to seizures of the person, namely arrests. Warrantless arrest is the rule, and arrest by warrant the exception. Decisional law permits police to arrest without prior judicial authorization so long as the arrest occurs in a public place and there is probable cause (see §4.1) to believe the subject has committed a crime. Warrantless arrest is permitted even if there is sufficient time to seek an arrest warrant and no practical impediment to doing so. *United States v. Watson*, 423 U.S. 411 (1976).

The one context in which the Court has imposed a warrant requirement is where the arrest occurs in a home rather than a public place. Given the sanctity of that locale in Fourth Amendment jurisprudence, an arrest warrant is required to enter and effect a nonexigent arrest of the subject in his own home. *Payton v. New York*, 445 U.S. 573 (1980). The Fourth Amendment draws a firm line at the entrance to one's home, and absent exigent circumstances (discussed in Chapter 6) that line cannot be crossed without a warrant. The curtilage of the home is also off limits without an arrest warrant. *Sims v. Stanton*, 706 F.3d 954 (9th Cir. 2013).

A warrantless arrest may be made in the doorway of the subject's home, because that is considered a public place. *United States v. Santana*, 427 U.S. 38 (1976); *LaLonde v. County of Riverside*, 204 F.3d 947, 955 (9th Cir. 2000). See also *United States v. Watson*, 273 F.3d 599, 602-603 (5th Cir. 2001) (an arrest on a porch is not considered "inside" the home for the purpose of the warrant requirement).

A valid arrest warrant implicitly carries the authority to enter the suspect's own dwelling (when there is reason to believe that he is there) and to search for him anywhere in the house that he may be found. *Valdez v. McPheters*, 172 F.3d 1220, 1224 (10th Cir. 1999). There is no necessity to have a search warrant in addition to the arrest warrant; the latter is deemed sufficient to protect the interest of the arrestee in the privacy of his home. Where the police seek to arrest a suspect in the residence of a third party, however, they must (again absent exigent circumstances) obtain a search warrant to enter and search that home for the suspect. Such warrant is issued on a showing of probable cause to believe the suspect is on the premises, and is deemed necessary to protect the third party's privacy interest in his home. *Steagald v. United States*, 451 U.S. 204 (1981). Without this requirement an arrest warrant would be a license for police to enter and search any building where the suspect might be, including the homes of friends, relatives, and acquaintances.

In sum, while arrests on the street or in public buildings may be made without prior authorization from a magistrate, an arrest warrant is required for the arrest of a person in his own home, and a search warrant is required for his arrest in the home of another (to protect the interests of the third person).

As Justice Rehnquist observed in his dissent in *Steagald*, the issue will inevitably arise as to what constitutes the suspect's *own* home. At what point in the suspect's stay with another, for example, does the third party's home (which ordinarily can be entered only by way of a search warrant issued on the basis of probable cause to believe the suspect is present) become the *suspect's* residence, so that it may be entered with merely an arrest warrant (issued on the basis of probable cause to believe he committed the crime)? The answer lies in whether the suspect has an expectation of privacy in the dwelling, in which case an arrest warrant would be required.

In light of *Minnesota v. Olson*, 495 U.S. 91 (1990), discussed in §7.3, this could include an overnight guest. However, for purposes of *Steagald*, it is unclear whether such guest would be considered in his own home, perhaps negating the need for a search warrant to protect the third party. The importance of this distinction lies in the difference between the showings required for the two warrants, as discussed in § 4.1.

§5.7 THE COMPONENTS OF A VALID ARREST WARRANT

Like the search warrant, an arrest warrant must be issued by a neutral and detached magistrate. The probable cause required focuses on facts and circumstances that connect the suspect to specific criminal activity. See §4.1. The suspect must be particularly identified in the warrant either by name or with a sufficiently specific description so that the officers may locate him with reasonable effort.

Example

Jack, a suspect in a bank robbery, has been a fugitive for a number of months. The police have just received a tip that he has been staying at a house leased to his girlfriend, Jill.

a. With regard to Jack, what paperwork is required for police to enter the house and arrest him lawfully?

b. With regard to Jill, what paperwork is required for police to enter and arrest Jack lawfully?

Explanation

a. Although Jack may be lawfully arrested in a public place without a warrant so long as the police have probable cause to believe that he has committed a crime, a warrant is required if the arrest is to occur in a private home. When the police seek to cross the threshold of a residence, a magistrate must agree beforehand that the information known to the police amounts to probable cause. The type of warrant required depends on whether the home is the arrestee's or a third party's. An arrest warrant is all that the police need to enter and arrest Jack if the house is *his* residence. *Payton v. New York*, 445 U.S. 573 (1980) (an arrest warrant implicitly authorizes entry into the suspect's own dwelling when there is probable cause to believe he is present). In all likelihood, given *Minnesota v. Olson*, this would be deemed Jack's residence.

This is true even if he shares the house with Jill. See *United States v. Ramirez*, 770 F.2d 1458 (9th Cir. 1985). If the house is considered the sole residence of Jill, an arrest warrant is still all that is required to protect *Jack's* rights (although Jill is entitled to the protection of a search warrant). An arrestee cannot claim greater Fourth Amendment protection in the home of a third party than he can in his own house. See *United States v. Gorman*, 314 F.3d 1105, 1110-1111 (9th Cir. 2002); *United States v. Kaylor*, 877 F.2d 658 (8th Cir. 1989) (arrest warrant, together with the officer's reasonable belief that subject was inside, justified entry into a third party's home as far as the arrestee's rights are concerned).

Thus, for Jack, all that would be required to enter and effect his arrest would be an arrest warrant.

b. With regard to Jill, the question of whether the house is exclusively hers or is also the residence of Jack becomes more important. If it is solely her residence, then (absent her consent; see §6.7) a search warrant is required to protect her privacy interest in the home. See *Steagald v. United States*, 451 U.S. 204 (1981). Securing a search warrant would require that the police present the magistrate with probable cause to believe that Jack will be found at Jill's home. The magistrate, and not the police, would weigh the reliability of the tip as to Jack's whereabouts. If Jack shared the house with Jill, an arrest warrant would be sufficient to effect his arrest. The arrest warrant would issue on probable cause to believe Jack committed the crime. Jill could not claim the additional protection of a search warrant.

The question of how a court should decide this critical question of residence has received little attention in the case law. One court has warned against equating a temporary stay with residence: "We would impermissibly diminish the protection offered by *Steagald* were we to hold that, for purposes of the homeowner's Fourth Amendment rights, the dwelling is the 'home' of whoever happens to be staying there. The Fourth Amendment right to be secure against warrantless searches within the home is too vital to justify entry without a search warrant to execute an arrest warrant upon a guest in the home." *Perez v. Simmons*, 884 F.2d 1136, 1141-1142 (9th Cir. 1988).

6

Warrantless Searches and Seizures

§6.1 INTRODUCTION

Although the Supreme Court has traditionally espoused the view that searches conducted outside the warrant process are presumptively unlawful (see Chapter 2), it has nevertheless recognized that in many situations, it is impracticable (and indeed dangerous) to require police to delay action pending judicial authorization. The Court has carved out several categorical exceptions to the warrant requirement accordingly — classes of cases in which warrantless searches are deemed reasonable. Given the Court's focus on reasonableness (as discussed in Chapter 2), in reality, searches without a warrant are treated as presumptively lawful, unless they fall outside the recognized exceptions explored in this chapter.

We focus on three basic questions:

- What are the characteristics common to searches in each category that justify circumvention of the warrant process?
- What specific requirements must be met for the exception to apply?
- What is the permissible scope of a search within the exception?

As we shall see, the extent of police activity covered by these "few specifically established and well-delineated exceptions" (*Katz v. United States*, 389 U.S. 347, 357 (1967)) has grown considerably in recent years. Moreover, while the original rationale lay in the impracticality of securing a warrant, recent years have seen a movement toward justifying warrantless searches on other grounds, primarily reduced expectation of privacy. This trend has led Justice Stevens to accuse the Court majority of paying only "lip service" to the fundamental principle that searches conducted outside the judicial process are per se unreasonable under the Fourth Amendment. See *California v. Acevedo*, 500 U.S. 565, 585 (1991) (Stevens, J., dissenting).

In studying the exceptions to the warrant requirement, it is helpful to categorize them in terms of the justification required before the police may act. We have therefore divided them into three groups (with reference to the concepts discussed in Chapter 4): 1) exceptions that require *probable cause*, 2) exceptions that require *reasonable suspicion*, and 3) exceptions that require *administrative justification*. A fourth category of warrantless intrusion encompasses two doctrines, *consent* and *plain view*, which virtually circumvent the Fourth Amendment and require no specific justification.

§6.2 EXCEPTIONS THAT REQUIRE PROBABLE CAUSE: THE EMERGENCY EXCEPTION (EXIGENT CIRCUMSTANCES)

Perhaps the purest example of an exception premised on the impracticability of obtaining a warrant is the emergency exception. Where the exigencies of the situation compel police to act immediately or risk either imminent danger to themselves or others, destruction of evidence, or escape of a suspect, it would be unreasonable to require resort to the warrant process. This exception excuses the necessity for either a search or arrest warrant. See Chapter 5.

The prerequisites for a warrantless search or arrest under the emergency exception are that: 1) the circumstances presented the police with a sufficiently compelling *urgency*, making resort to the warrant process both impracticable and risky; and 2) the police had justification amounting to *probable cause* to believe that items relating to crime would be found (in the case of a search) or that the suspect had committed a crime (in the case of an arrest).

Most of the cases under this exception have involved "hot pursuit." When police are in immediate pursuit of a suspect fleeing the scene of a crime, they are permitted to chase him into a building or home without a warrant to effect an arrest. While inside, they may conduct a warrantless search for the suspect and any weapons to which he may have access.

In *Warden v. Hayden*, 387 U.S. 294 (1967), two cab drivers who had witnessed an armed robbery followed the perpetrator to a particular house and summoned police. Officers arrived within minutes, entered the house, and proceeded to search it for the robber. While looking for him, they discovered and seized evidence connected to the robbery, as well as two guns. Hayden was then found and arrested, and the items were later offered in evidence over his objection at trial. The Supreme Court ruled them admissible because the entry into the home, although warrantless, was reasonable under the exigent circumstances to prevent the escape of the fleeing suspect. Once inside, the officers could lawfully search for the suspect and seize evidence and weapons found in plain view (see §6.8), while searching those areas where the suspect or weapons might be hidden.

It must be emphasized that the exigencies of a hot pursuit are not, on their own, sufficient to fit a case within the emergency exception. The police must also have probable cause to believe the subject has just committed a crime *and* that he is in the particular dwelling. As *Warden v. Hayden* demonstrates, the police need not themselves have witnessed the crime or the perpetrator's flight; probable cause may be based on other reliable sources. The emphasis is on the heat of the chase — there must be "immediate and continuous pursuit" from the scene of the crime. *Welsh v. Wisconsin*, 466 U.S. 740, 741 (1984). Once the pursuit turns cold, the excuse for circumventing the warrant process evaporates.

Warrantless entry into a dwelling may not be permissible even under exigent circumstances where the suspect is sought for a minor crime. In *Welsh v. Wisconsin*, supra, police entered the suspect's home and arrested him for the noncriminal offense of drunk driving. The Court refused to sanction circumvention of the warrant process under those circumstances. While withholding decision on whether the Fourth Amendment imposes "an absolute ban on warrantless home arrests for certain minor offenses," the Court held that the gravity of the offense for which the suspect is sought is an important factor to consider in applying the emergency exception. "Home entry should rarely be sanctioned when there is probable cause to believe that only a minor offense has been committed." 466 U.S. at 750 n.11.

In addition to hot pursuit, the emergency exception is also applicable to other situations where the delay required to obtain a warrant would create an imminent risk of destruction of evidence, escape of the suspect, or danger to police or others. See *Minnesota v. Olson*, 495 U.S. 91 (1990). This requires a fact-specific analysis to determine whether resort to the warrant process (including a telephonic warrant, where applicable)[1] was truly impracticable.

In *Olson*, the prosecution sought to justify a warrantless entry and arrest of the suspect in a duplex unit that the police had surrounded. Although there was probable cause to believe that Olson had been the driver of a getaway car involved in a robbery and murder the day before, the Court held that failure to obtain a warrant could not be excused under the circumstances presented. The gravity of the crime and the likelihood that the suspect is armed must be considered as factors in assessing the urgency of the situation. Although a grave crime had been committed, Olson was suspected

---

1. See, e.g., Fed. R. Crim. P. 41(a)(2). See also *United States v. Alvarez*, 810 F.2d 879 (9th Cir. 1987).

only of being a driver, not the murderer. Further, the police had already recovered the murder weapon, and there was no suggestion of danger to anyone in the building. Finally, the police had the building surrounded and Olson could not have escaped. The Court concluded that these facts "do not add up to exigent circumstances."

Exigent circumstances justifying warrantless entry into a home exist where police reasonably believe an occupant is seriously injured or in imminent danger. In *Brigham City, Utah v. Stuart*, 126 S. Ct. 1943 (2006), officers responded to a loud-party call and observed through a screen door a physical altercation among four adults and a juvenile. The "ongoing violence" provided sufficient justification to make the entry reasonable. See also *U.S. v. Snipe*, 515 F.3d 947 (9th Cir. 2008) (finding exigent circumstances when a hysterical male phoned the police at 5:00 A.M. instructing the dispatcher to "[g]et the police over here now.").

Because the emergency exception has the obvious potential to swallow the Fourth Amendment's warrant provisions, it is not surprising that courts have been careful to contain its borders. The scope of the permissible search is strictly limited by the exigencies upon which it is based. Thus, the hot pursuit intrusion into a dwelling is limited to those areas where the suspect or weapons may be hidden. It is not a general search. *Mincey v. Arizona*, 437 U.S. 385 (1978), rejected the argument that the exception justified an extensive, four-day warrantless search of a homicide scene. Not questioning the right of police to make warrantless entries and searches when they reasonably believe a person inside is in need of immediate aid or when they come upon a homicide scene and promptly survey the immediate area for victims or the perpetrator, the Court concluded that the search far exceeded the necessities of the moment: "All the persons in Mincey's apartment had been located before the investigating homicide officers arrived there and began their search. And a four-day search that included opening dresser drawers and ripping up carpets can hardly be rationalized in terms of the legitimate concerns that justify an emergency search." 437 U.S. at 393.

Under the same principle that the scope of an emergency search must be limited by the nature of the emergency, a two-hour search of a residence that was the scene of a murder and suicide attempt was ruled unlawful because the victims had already been removed and the area secured. See *Thompson v. Louisiana*, 469 U.S. 17 (1984). Moreover, the search had widened to include opening drawers and examining items in a wastebasket. And while a warrantless entry into a burning dwelling for the purposes of determining the source of the fire and extinguishing it is permitted, once the origin of the fire is discovered and it is brought under control the authorities must obtain a warrant to conduct a further investigation of the premises. See *Michigan v. Clifford*, 464 U.S. 287 (1984); *Michigan v. Tyler*, 436 U.S. 499 (1978).

The standard for application of the emergency exception has been articulated as follows: The police must be faced with circumstances that would cause a reasonable person to believe that entry was necessary to prevent physical harm to the officers or other persons, the destruction of relevant evidence, the escape of the suspect, or some other consequence improperly frustrating legitimate law enforcement efforts. The exigencies must be viewed from the totality of facts known to the officers at the time of the intrusion. Moreover, because the phrase "exigent circumstances" necessarily implies insufficient time to obtain a warrant, the government has the burden of showing that a warrant could not have been secured in time. See *Bailey v. Newland*, 263 F.3d 1022, 1033 (9th Cir. 2001); *United States v. Davis*, 313 F.3d 1300 (11th Cir. 2002). Exigent circumstances will normally not exist where the suspects are unaware of the police surveillance or presence. See *United States v. Santa*, 236 F.3d 662 (11th Cir. 2000); *United States v. Hernandez*, 214 F. Supp. 2d 1344 (S.D. Fla. 2002); *United States v. Davis*, 170 F. Supp. 2d 1234 (M.D. Fla. 2001).

The case of *Kentucky v. King*, 131 S. Ct. 1849 (2011), raises the interesting issue of the applicability of the emergency exception when the necessity was created by the police. The police smelled marijuana coming from inside an apartment. Arguably, that gave them probable cause. Rather than get a warrant, however, the officers knocked loudly on the door, identifying themselves as police. When they heard people moving inside, and fearing that the drug evidence would be destroyed, they entered the home. The Court decided in an 8-1 decision that what the officers heard inside the apartment provided sufficient grounds to believe that the evidence would be destroyed. Recognizing that the police created the exigency by knocking, the majority nonetheless ruled that this was permissible, so long as the police were not "engaging or threatening to engage in conduct that violates the Fourth Amendment." Justice Ginsburg, dissenting, worried that this approach would dissipate the warrant requirement for drug cases. She would permit the exigency exception only where the exigency exists "when police come on the scene, not subsequent to their arrival, prompted by their own conduct." What options do police have when faced with a situation where they anticipate that incriminating evidence at a particular location may be destroyed or removed, but the compelling justification required for a warrantless emergency search is absent? First, they may secure the premises to prevent persons from entering while they await a warrant. See *Segura v. United States*, 468 U.S. 796 (1984); *Illinois v. McArthur*, 531 U.S. 326 (2001) (refusal to allow defendant to enter residence without a police officer until a search warrant was obtained was a "reasonable seizure" that did not violate Fourth Amendment), discussed in §4.4. Second, the officers may seek a telephonic warrant as authorized in some jurisdictions including the federal system. See n.1, supra.

Does the natural metabolization of alcohol in the bloodstream, resulting in the loss of evidence of intoxication, constitute the kind of exigency that justifies a *per se* exception to the warrant requirement? The Court answered "no" in *Missouri v. McNealy*, 133 S. Ct. 1552 (2013), opting instead for a case-by-case determination based on the totality of the circumstances. Such an approach in *Schmerber v. California*, 384 U.S. 757 (1966) concluded that the drawing of defendant's blood at the hospital was reasonable given the time it took to transport him from the accident scene and the diminishing blood-alcohol level over that period. The *McNealy* Court noted that in the years since *Schmerber*, advances had been made allowing the quicker processing of warrant applications, lessening the exigency where available.

Examples

1a. Walking by Josie's Convenience Store, Officer Jones heard the proprietor inside scream, "Stop, thief!" and observed a man in a ski mask running from the store with pistol in hand. Jones pursued him on foot as he entered a nearby house, followed the man in, and arrested him. Was this action lawful?

1b. Assume instead that the day after the robbery, police observed a man meeting the description of the perpetrator standing on the sidewalk. They attempt to arrest him, but he flees inside the house. May they pursue him inside and make a warrantless arrest?

2. Unlucky Larry was observed by Officer Bones as he robbed the Main Street Bank with a gun and then fled into the Chesterfield Hotel across the street. Bones pursued Larry into the 24-room hotel. Not seeing which room Larry entered, Bones played his lucky number and entered Room 333. He immediately observed a bundle of new, large-denomination bills on the floor and seized it. Bones then searched the room and discovered Larry hiding in the shower stall, where he was placed under arrest. Were the officer's actions lawful? Would the seizure of the bills be lawful if they had been found by Bones while searching the drawer of a night table prior to apprehending Larry?

3. Federal agents received reliable information that a Purple-throated Polynesian parrot (who not only repeats phrases but does simultaneous translation from English to French), an endangered species whose importation into the United States is a felony, had been delivered to the home of taxidermist Grant Greedy. Greedy had been under investigation for several months, and the agents had developed probable cause to believe he was operating an illegal enterprise out of his home in which animals that were near extinction were killed, stuffed, and sold to unscrupulous collectors.

   After receiving the information about the Polynesian parrot, several agents proceeded to Greedy's home to wait for their supervisor, who was seeking a warrant to search the premises. Before it could be issued, however, the agents observed Greedy leave the dwelling, bid farewell to his brother Lee, and depart in his car. Two agents followed Greedy, who appeared to realize they were pursuing him and began driving evasively at great speed. The agents finally overtook him and pulled him over at a gas station. Before being taken into custody, Greedy yelled to the attendant (whom he appeared to know), "Call Lee and tell him to get rid of the bird, quick!" Fearing destruction of the precious animal, the agents proceeded immediately back to Greedy's home and entered just as Lee was about to place the parrot into the trash compactor. They seized the bird and arrested Lee. Was this lawful?

4. Informant Z told drug investigators that Maxy Mum had sold her cocaine on numerous occasions. The agents asked Z to arrange another sale with Maxy, and it took place on the sidewalk outside Maxy's apartment. The agents witnessed the transaction from a remote location. After later confirming that the substance sold by Maxy was cocaine, the agents asked Informant Z to arrange another sale to occur inside Maxy's apartment. At the appointed time, Z went into the apartment. She came out 15 minutes later and informed the agents that the sale had occurred and that a large quantity of cocaine remained on the premises. Fearing that the contraband might be sold off to others, the agents moved in immediately and arrested Maxy and seized the cocaine. Was this lawful?

5. Police were summoned by UPS employees who had a suspicious package that had been returned by the driver as "addressee unknown." When opened, it was found to contain a substance believed to be cocaine. After conducting a field test confirming that, the police resealed the package and placed it in the "undelivered" section at UPS. They then waited for someone to pick it up, and a woman appeared some hours later to claim the package. The police followed her to a home known to them to be that of Sherman West, long suspected of being a major narcotics dealer but who had eluded prosecution by being particularly attentive to surveillance. Within minutes after the woman entered West's home with the package; the police entered, arrested both of them, and seized the cocaine. Was this lawful?

Explanations

1a. Yes, the warrantless entry and arrest were lawful. As discussed in §5.5 of Chapter 5, under ordinary circumstances a warrantless entry into a home to effect an arrest would violate the Fourth Amendment. An arrest warrant would normally be required to enter the suspect's own home, and a search warrant to enter a third party's residence. In this example, however, police were not engaged in a routine arrest, but rather were in hot pursuit of a suspect whom they had probable cause to believe had just committed an armed robbery and was presently in the dwelling. Because of these exigent circumstances the absence of prior judicial authorization to enter, search for, and arrest the suspect would be excused under the emergency exception. See *Warden v. Hayden*, 387 U.S. 294 (1967).

1b. Yes, the warrantless entry and arrest were lawful. Although there is no hot pursuit from the scene of the crime, the police may chase the suspect into his home without a warrant when they attempt to effect a lawful arrest in a public place, but are unsuccessful because the suspect retreats inside. (Remember that police may make a warrantless arrest in a public place so long as they have probable cause to believe the subject committed a felony; see §5.5.) See *United States v. Santana*, 427 U.S. 38 (1976) (suspect was observed in doorway of her home and retreated inside before police could apprehend her). "A suspect may not defeat an arrest which has been set in motion in a public place, and is therefore proper under *Watson*, by the expedient of escaping to a private place." 427 U.S. at 43.

2. In order to conduct a lawful hot pursuit arrest, Officer Bones needed probable cause to believe that Larry had just committed a crime, and that he had fled into Room 333. As an eyewitness to the robbery, Bones certainly meets the first prerequisite. Regarding the second, however, because the building contained 24 rooms and Bones did not have any information indicating which room Larry may have fled into, probable cause to search Room 333 (or any other particular room at the Chesterfield) was lacking. In a case involving similar facts, a divided Ninth Circuit Court of Appeals (sitting *en banc*) held that the hot pursuit exception did not apply. See *United States v. Winsor*, 846 F.2d 1569 (9th Cir. 1988). The dissenters, observing that the officer had pursued the fleeing felon without interruption from the scene of the crime to the hotel and that the safety of the officer and other occupants was threatened by the presence of the armed perpetrator, would have permitted warrantless intrusion into each of the 24 rooms.

Assuming that entry into the room to effectuate an arrest could be justified under the emergency exception, Officer Bones would be permitted to search anywhere the perpetrator might be hiding or weapons accessible to him might be found. *Warden v. Hayden*, 387 U.S. 294 (1967). Because the bundle of bills was in plain view upon entering, it could properly be seized. In our variation where the officer opened a night table drawer and discovered the money, that seizure would also be lawful if it were determined that Bones was searching for weapons and not engaged in a general search of the room. Regarding the separate question of whether Larry, given his tenuous connection to the hotel room, would have standing to pursue a motion to suppress, see §7.3.1 of Chapter 7.

3. Probable cause is a necessary, but not sufficient, condition to conduct a lawful search of a home. Thus, although the agents had probable cause to believe that criminal activity was occurring in the house and that evidence of such activity was present, the Fourth Amendment generally requires that a magistrate weigh the justification, authorize entry, and prescribe the contours of a permissible search. To circumvent the warrant process, the exigencies must be sufficiently compelling to fit within the emergency exception; namely, where "real immediate and serious consequences" will "certainly occur" if police action is postponed. *Thacker v. City of Columbus*, 328 F.3d 244 (6th Cir. 2003). Common situations include 1) hot pursuit of a fleeing felon, 2) imminent destruction of evidence, 3) the need to prevent a suspect's escape, and 4) a risk of danger to the police or others. In the context of example 3, the police needed facts from which they could reasonably conclude that the evidence would be destroyed or removed before they could secure a search warrant. Because it appears that such facts existed here, and because the police had probable cause to search, the emergency exception is likely to apply. See *United States v. Mikel*, 102 F.3d 470 (11th Cir. 1996) (officer seeing suspect talking on cellular phone while being pursued could have reasonably concluded that he was instructing his associate in the apartment to destroy evidence, thus presenting exigent circumstances).

In approaching the fact-specific determination of whether the emergency exception applies, courts have considered the following factors: 1) the degree of urgency, taking into account the amount of time necessary to obtain a warrant (the availability of telephonic warrants is also weighed in this context); 2) the reasonableness of the belief that the contraband was about to be destroyed or removed; 3) the possibility of danger to the police who are watching the location; 4) common behavioral characteristics of persons involved in the particular criminal activity (big-time narcotics dealers, for example, are generally known to be armed); 5) any indication that the suspects were aware the police are on their trail; and 6) whether the emergency arose from action of the police themselves. See *United States v. Howard*, 106 F.3d 70, 74 (5th Cir. 1997). The presence of drugs alone does not give rise to exigent circumstances justifying warrantless entry and search. *United States v. Santa*, 236 F.3d 662 (11th Cir. 2000) (occupants were unaware that they were under police investigation, so there was no reason to believe that evidence might be destroyed).

With regard to the last factor mentioned above, whether the police themselves created the urgency, the Supreme Court at one point took a skeptical view, refusing to hold that an arrest on the street can provide its own exigent circumstance justifying a warrantless search of the arrestee's house. See *Vale v. Louisiana*, 399 U.S. 30, 35 (1970) (rejecting the government's argument that arrest created a risk that persons inside would destroy the narcotics). As one circuit court observed, "an exception to the warrant requirement that allows police fearing the destruction of evidence to enter the home of an unknown suspect should be supported by clearly defined indicators of exigency that are not subject to police manipulation or abuse." *United States v. Aquino*, 836 F.2d 1268, 1272 (10th Cir. 1988).

Where, for example, police knocked on the door of a person whom they had cause to believe was an armed and dangerous narcotics dealer, then kicked his door down and entered when he retreated into another room, the Fifth Circuit ruled that

> the government could not justify a warrantless search on the basis of exigent circumstances of its own making. Agents Byant and Keefer knew when they knocked on the patio door that, once having made their presence known to Munoz-Guerra (and possibly to other occupants), it would be necessary to conduct a security search of the premises and to restrain the condominium's inhabitants. Warrantless entry was thus a foregone conclusion the instant the agents revealed themselves to Munoz-Guerra at the patio door.

United States v. Munoz-Guerra, 788 F.2d 295, 298 (5th Cir. 1986).

In *Kentucky v. King*, 131 S. Ct. 1849 (2011), however, the Court held that the exigency doctrine may apply even if the police action (knocking on the door and announcing their presence) foreseeably created the urgency, so long as "the police did not create the exigency by engaging or threatening to engage in conduct that violates the Fourth Amendment." In our example 3, the urgent concern about the possible destruction of the parrot arose because of the unanticipated departure of the suspect. It was not the inevitable result of action by the police themselves designed to circumvent the warrant requirement. The probability is good, therefore, that the warrantless search would be held lawful within the emergency exception.

The government has the burden of demonstrating that exigent circumstances existed, and it must present something more than an unsupported belief by law enforcement officers. See *United States v. Anderson*, 154 F.3d 1225, 1233 (10th Cir. 1998) (neither agent's belief that Anderson's child pornography collection was being stored inside office building, nor his concern about the presence of an incinerator, nor Anderson's failure to respond to the agent's knocking on the office doors, justified warrantless entry). Compare *United States v. Scroger*, 98 F.3d 1256 (10th Cir. 1996) (officers' warrantless entry into defendant's residence was justified by exigent circumstances where defendant answered door holding hotplate commonly used to manufacture methamphetamine; defendant's fingertips were stained rust-colored, a common result from methamphetamine production; residence had odor of methamphetamine production; and it was highly likely that evidence would have been destroyed if officers waited to seek a warrant).

4. The police in these circumstances would be hard-pressed to claim exigency. They had probable cause to arrest (and most likely to search the apartment as well) based upon the transaction that occurred the day before, together with the arrangement for the upcoming sale. There was more than sufficient time to apply for an arrest and search warrant before the upcoming transaction. See *United States v. Beltran*, 917 F.2d 641 (1st Cir. 1990). See also *United States v. Santa*, 236 F.3d 662 (11th Cir. 2000) (because occupants were unaware that they were under police investigation, there was no reason to believe that evidence might be destroyed while officers sought warrant); *Guite v. Write*, 147 F.3d 747 (8th Cir. 1998) (exigent circumstances may not have justified warrantless entry into defendant's home where officers knew he was inside and had enough personnel to cover the house and prevent his escape while warrant was obtained).

5. The facts that support application of the emergency exception here are that 1) the police were not aware of the destination of the package until it was actually delivered, 2) the destination was the abode of a suspected drug dealer likely to be suspicious of tampering with the package, and 3) the narcotics in the package could be destroyed quickly and easily. Together with the probable cause to believe narcotics were on the premises, the exigencies of this situation would appear to justify the warrantless entry, arrest, and seizure.

   If the police had information tying the package to a particular location *prior* to delivery, the excuse for circumventing the warrant process would no longer exist. See, e.g., *United States v. Johnson*, 12 F.3d 760 (8th Cir. 1993) (warrantless entry was illegal where package was addressed to a clearly identifiable address, and postal inspectors were able to obtain search warrant shortly after package was delivered). See also *United States v. Arias*, 992 F. Supp. 832 (S.D. W. Va. 1997) (police had sufficient time and information to apply for warrant where they suspected presence of drugs in defendants' motel room for days and where approximately three and a half hours lapsed between confirmation of presence of drugs in room and actual entry); *United States v. Romero*, 967 F. Supp. 1093 (N.D. Ind. 1997) (exigent circumstances did not exist for warrantless entry into defendant's home based on co-conspirators' drug-related arrests at another location, when law enforcement officers had time to secure telephonic warrant but did not do so).

   Caveat: Would example 5 be an appropriate case for an anticipatory search warrant? See § 5.5.

§6.3 EXCEPTIONS THAT REQUIRE PROBABLE CAUSE: SEARCH INCIDENT TO ARREST

Unlike the generic emergency exception just discussed, the other warrant exceptions are divided along specific categorical lines and are (or at least originally were) based on the exigencies presented by a particular type of confrontation between police officer and citizen. The two most frequently encountered are the search incident to an arrest (discussed in this section) and the search of a motor vehicle stopped on the road (discussed in § 6.4).

When a police officer places an individual under arrest, there is an obvious danger that the arrestee may violently resist and use any weapon on his person or within his reach. Recognizing this, as well as the risk that evidence within the arrestee's control may be destroyed, courts long ago carved out an exception to the warrant requirement that permits search of the person and the immediate surrounding area. The impracticality of obtaining a search warrant in the heat of an arrest obviously justifies this limited license.

The basic prerequisite for such a search is that the underlying arrest be lawful, i.e., based on probable cause to believe the subject has committed a crime (see Chapter 4) and, in the case of an arrest in a private building, that there be a valid arrest warrant (see §5.5). The general rule is that the arrest *must precede* the search, as it is the former that justifies the latter and not the reverse. The Court has on one occasion sanctioned a search incident to an arrest where the arrest followed the search, but only because the officer had probable cause to arrest prior to the search and merely delayed announcement of the formal arrest. See *Rawlings v. Kentucky*, 448 U.S. 98 (1980).

Based on the fundamental tenet that license to conduct a search without prior judicial approval should be strictly circumscribed by the necessities of the moment, the scope of the search incident to an arrest is limited to the person of the arrestee (including pockets) and the "grabable space" from which he could reach weapons or evidence. See *Chimel v. California*, 395 U.S. 752 (1969). The search must occur at the time of the arrest; once the subject is securely in custody and the immediate exigencies of the arrest disappear, so too does the excuse for circumventing the warrant process. Thus, a search is deemed incident to an arrest only if it is substantially contemporaneous with it and confined to the immediate vicinity of the arrest.[2]

---

2. Some cases have permitted delayed searches in unusual circumstances. In *United States v. Edwards*, 415 U.S. 800 (1974), the seizure and search of Edwards's clothing ten hours after his arrest and placement in a jail cell was held reasonable because the delay was necessitated by the lack of any substitute clothing. One court has read *Edwards* to authorize a delayed search of the suspect's clothing only — but *not* personal effects — on a theory of reduced expectation of privacy. See *United States v. Monclavo-Cruz*, 662 F.2d 1285, 1289-1290 (9th Cir. 1981) (warrantless search of suspect's purse at station house was not permissible under *Edwards*). Other courts have permitted late "searches incident" of wallets and purses without adequate explanation. See *United States v. Sonntag*, 684 F.2d 781 (11th Cir. 1982); *Curd v. City Court*

Since *Chimel*, the Court has broadened the scope of the exception in significant ways. First, it has increased the license to search the immediate area by authorizing seizure and opening of *containers*. *United States v. Robinson*, 414 U.S. 218 (1973), held that a cigarette pack found on the arrestee's person could be removed and opened by the officer at the time of the arrest, and established a categorical rule permitting the seizure and opening of personal objects found on the arrestee.

An important limitation on the authority to open containers is that this must occur *contemporaneously* with the arrest. Where agents seized a footlocker during an arrest but did not open it until an hour later back at their office, the search was unlawful—the exigent circumstances created by the arrest no longer existed, and thus a warrant was required to search the contents of the private receptacle. See *United States v. Chadwick*, 433 U.S. 1 (1977). This special protection for closed suitcases, bags, and packages, premised on the high expectation of privacy the owner has in them, came to be known as the "container doctrine." (We will discuss this further in § 6.4.)

In *Riley v. California*, 134 S. Ct. 2473 (2014), a unanimous Court refused to extend *Robinson* to modern cell phones. The rationales in 1973 for allowing physical objects to be opened—the possible risk to the officer by a weapon inside and the potential for destruction of evidence—do not apply in the context of the digital contents of cell phones. While such data can be wiped clean remotely, there are steps the police can take to prevent this, like disconnecting it from the network (by battery removal or turning the phone off) or placing the phone in a Faraday bag isolated from radio waves. Moreover, the amount of data potentially stored on a cell phone makes its search profoundly more intrusive than the search in *Robinson*. "There is an element of pervasiveness," Chief Justice Roberts wrote, "that characterizes cell phones but not physical records. Prior to the digital age, people did not typically carry a cache of sensitive personal information with them as they went about their day. Now it is the person who is not carrying a cell phone, with all that it contains, who is the exception." Thus, a warrant is required.

Riley represents the Supreme Court's official entry into the digital data age. (The implications of the National Security Administration's massive collection of phone data, as well as cell tower tracking by law enforcement, are discussed in Chapter 12).

A second extension of *Chimel* applies to arrests of persons stopped in automobiles. The Court designated the entire interior of the passenger compartment (as well as containers found there) as within the proper scope of a contemporaneous search incident to the arrest, even if the subjects have already been removed from the vehicle and cannot actually reach into it. *New York v. Belton*, 453 U.S. 454 (1981), permitted the pockets of a jacket found on the rear seat to be opened while the arrestees stood *outside* and away from the car. Reasoning that articles "within the relatively narrow compass of the passenger compartment of an automobile are in fact generally, even if not inevitably, within the area into which an arrestee might reach in order to grab a weapon or evidentiary item," the Court opted for a bright-line standard. "A single, familiar standard is essential to guide police officers, who have only limited time and expertise to reflect on and balance the social and individual interests involved in the specific circumstances they confront." 453 U.S. at 458.

Robinson and *Belton* represent an important (and some would say disturbing) trend in Fourth Amendment jurisprudence—the rejection of case-by-case review in favor of categorical rules. Arrested for operating a motor vehicle after his license had been revoked, Robinson argued that the opening of the cigarette pack could not be justified by either rationale of the search incident exception: It was highly unlikely that a weapon was hidden inside, and equally unlikely that evidence of the crime for which Robinson was arrested would be found in the package. (What was found were heroin capsules.)

The Supreme Court rejected the proposition that there must be litigated in each case the issue of whether the rationale supporting the search incident exception applied. 414 U.S. at 235. Recognizing that a police officer's determination as to how and where to search the arrestee is "necessarily a quick ad hoc judgment," the Court granted blanket authority to conduct the search, not dependent on whether in the particular case there actually was a need to secure weapons or evidence. So long as the arrest is lawful, no additional justification is required to conduct a search incident to it.[3] Some states have rejected this approach.[4]

Belton's bright-line rule was extended to arrests *outside* the vehicle as well. In *Thornton v. United States*, 541 U.S. 615 (2004), the officer did not make

---

of Judsonia, Arkansas, 141 F.3d 839 (8th Cir. 1998) (search of purse 15 minutes after arrest). See also *State v. Wade*, 573 N.W.2d 228 (Wis. Ct. App. 1997) (search of purse before giving it back to the defendant while she was still in custody at police station justified on safety grounds).

3. In *Gustafson v. Florida*, 414 U.S. 260 (1973), a companion case to *Robinson*, the Court upheld a search incident to an arrest for a minor traffic offense even though under state law, the officer was not mandated to arrest the suspect but could have instead issued him a summons. The Court has gone a step further and affirmed police authority to make arrests even for misdemeanors (such as failure to wear a seat belt) that are punishable only by a fine. *See Atwater v. City of Lago Vista*, 532 U.S. 318 (2001). This concept was again extended in *Virginia v. Moore*, 553 U.S. 164 (2008), which upheld an arrest not authorized by the state statute. The scope of the intrusion was further extended in *Florence v. Burlington*, 123 S. Ct. 1510 (2012), which allowed for strip searches once the arrestee was detained in a jail setting.

4. Massachusetts, for example, enacted the following statute after *Robinson*: "A search conducted incident to an arrest may be made only for the purposes of seizing fruits, instrumentalities, contraband, and other evidence of the crime for which the arrest has been made, in order to prevent its destruction or concealment; and removing any weapon the arrestee might use to resist arrest or effect his escape." Mass. Gen. L. ch. 276, 1. Thus, a defendant arrested on outstanding warrants for violation of a domestic protection order and a drug offense could not lawfully be subjected to a seizure and opening of his pill container, as it could not reasonably be thought to contain a weapon, contraband, or evidence of the crimes that precipitated the arrest. *Commonwealth v. White*, 469 Mass. 96 (2014).

contact with the arrestee until he had already left his vehicle. Nonetheless, search of the passenger compartment was deemed permissible under the *Belton* rule. For Justices O'Connor, Scalia, Stevens, and Souter, writing separately, *Belton* had been transformed from an exception justified by the twin rationales of *Chimel* into a "police entitlement."

Justice Scalia, in his concurrence in *Thornton*, suggested that the search there was justifiable because of the possibility of drugs being located in the vehicle, without resort to a categorical rule. The Court adopted this very approach in *Arizona v. Gant*, 129 S. Ct. 1710 (2009), where the defendant was arrested for driving with a suspended license, handcuffed, and placed in the back of the patrol car. Officers then searched the interior of Gant's car and discovered a bag of cocaine in the pocket of a jacket on the backseat.

The Court returned to the dual justifications of *Chimel* — to prevent the destruction of evidence and to protect the police. Drawing back from *Belton*, which allows search of the interior of a car *regardless* of whether the suspect was realistically within reaching distance of it, *Gant* held instead that a search incident to a lawful arrest can be effected only when either 1) the arrestee is unsecured and within reaching distance of the passenger compartment at the time of the search, or 2) it is "reasonable to believe [that] evidence relevant to the crime of arrest might be found in the vehicle." The latter would have provided a basis for the searches in both *Belton* and *Thornton*, the Court noted.

Although *Gant* only briefly mentioned *Robinson* and did not specifically overrule *Belton*, it does seem to raise questions about the continued viability of categorical analysis in the search incident to arrest context. The right to conduct such a search is premised on an arrest actually occurring. A unanimous Court, in an opinion authored by Chief Justice Rehnquist, held that an officer who opts to issue a traffic citation to a suspect in lieu of an arrest may not conduct such a search. *Knowles v. Iowa*, 525 U.S. 113 (1998). In the absence of an arrest, neither rationale of *Chimel* — protection of the officer or prevention of the destruction of evidence — applies.

Given the wide authority to make an arrest for even minor offenses (see *Atwater v. City of Lago Vista*, 532 U.S. 318 (2001), and *Virginia v. Moore* (2008), n.2, above), together with the refusal to second-guess the arresting officer's motivation (see *Whren v. United States*, 517 U.S. 806 (1996), discussed in §6.9), the search incident exception represents significant license for warrantless police action and thus potential for abuse, prompting Justice O'Connor to warn:

> Indeed, as the recent debate over racial profiling demonstrates all too clearly, a relatively minor traffic infraction may often serve as an excuse for stopping and harassing an individual. After today, the arsenal available to any officer extends to a full arrest and the searches permissible concomitant to that arrest.

Atwater v. City of Lago Vista, supra, 532 U.S. at 372 (dissenting).

157

The scope of a search incident to arrest was expanded yet again in *Maryland v. Buie*, 494 U.S. 325 (1990), to permit a "protective sweep" of the premises when police make an arrest in a home. The officers are authorized to search areas (including closets and other spaces) in the immediate vicinity of the arrest from which an attack could be launched against them. Where the police have reasonable suspicion to believe that they are in danger from accomplices lurking elsewhere, they may also make a cursory inspection of those other spaces, but the sweep may last no longer than is necessary to dispel the reasonable suspicion of danger (and in any event must end by the time the arrest is complete and the suspect is removed from the premises).

A motorist stopped and arrested for drunk driving may be subjected to a breath test as an incident of the arrest. *Birchfield v. North Dakota*, 136 S. Ct. 2160 (2016).

What if the officer discovers, after making an unlawful investigatory stop (i.e., without reasonable suspicion), a valid basis for an arrest (e.g., a pre-existing arrest warrant)? May a lawful search incident be conducted? See *Utah v. Strieff*, 136 S. Ct. 2056 (2016), discussed in § 7.2.

Examples

1. In which of the following circumstances has the officer conducted a lawful search incident to an arrest?

   a. Officer Keystone, with a hunch that Patty Pedestrian is carrying narcotics in her sports bag, stops her and searches the bag. The officer finds cocaine and places Patty under arrest.

   b. Officer Keystone, with probable cause to believe that Patty Pedestrian is carrying unlawful narcotics in her sports bag, stops her and searches the bag. The officer finds cocaine and places Patty under arrest.

   c. Officer Keystone, with probable cause to believe that Patty Pedestrian is carrying narcotics in her sports bag, stops her and places her under arrest. The officer seizes the bag and opens it 20 minutes later at the police station.

   d. Officer Keystone has probable cause to believe that Patty Pedestrian, whose hair is wet, has been trespassing in a private lake. He arrests her, seizes her small purse, and finds a ziplock bag of heroin inside.

2. Ned Numbers, an accountant, is suspected of masterminding a major tax fraud scheme. Armed with a warrant for his arrest, Internal Revenue Service (IRS) agents entered his 15-room home in Scarsdale, found Ned sitting at his desk in the study, and placed him under arrest. While one agent removed Ned from the chair, frisked him, and cuffed him, a second opened the drawers of his desk. A list of clients (many of whom were suspected of participation in the fraud scheme) was found in Ned's

coat pocket, and an illegally imported pistol was discovered in his desk drawer. Could the agents lawfully seize these items?

3. Speedy was observed driving above the speed limit by Officer Radar and was pulled over. Radar took Speedy's license and registration and went back to her cruiser to run a routine computer check, which revealed that there was an outstanding warrant for Speedy's arrest for burglary. Radar informed Speedy that he was under arrest, handcuffed him, and placed him in the backseat of the cruiser. The officer then returned to Speedy's vehicle and searched the entire passenger compartment. She found burglary tools in a closed brown paper bag in the back seat, opened the glove compartment and found a pistol, and then searched the trunk and discovered an assault rifle. Which, if any, of these items were lawfully seized? What if the assault rifle had been found in the car's hatchback instead of the trunk?

4. Two police officers arrived at Addison's home with a warrant for his arrest on charges of armed bank robbery. They were informed by the gardener that Addison was inside with two friends. The officers entered the home and encountered Addison as he was on his way upstairs from the basement. He was placed under arrest in the kitchen, and one of the officers went down to the basement, where he observed a pistol on a shelf near the furnace. May this weapon be lawfully seized? What if the gun had been discovered in the closed drawer of a tool cabinet?

Explanations

1a. "It is axiomatic that an incident search may not precede an arrest and serve as part of its justification." *Smith v. Ohio*, 494 U.S. 541, 543 (1990) (quoting *Sibron v. New York*, 392 U.S. 40, 63 (1968)). The purpose of the exception is to permit the officer to protect herself and prevent the destruction of evidence while effecting a lawful arrest, not to allow searches that then provide the cause to arrest. Probable cause to arrest must therefore exist prior to the inception of the search. See *United States v. Ho*, 94 F.3d 932, 935 (5th Cir. 1996). Keystone's action here violated the Fourth Amendment.

1b. Because the officer had sufficient justification to arrest prior to the search of the bag, and thus information obtained through the search is not being used to justify the arrest, the officer's action here would be lawful even though the search preceded the arrest. See *Rawlings v. Kentucky*, 448 U.S. 98 (1980). With probable cause to arrest already existing, the officer could have chosen to place Patty under formal arrest before he searched the bag, but he was not required to do so. The sequence here does not circumvent the requirement for proper justification prior to the arrest, and *Rawlings* gives the police discretion to delay formal arrest until the search is conducted.

With regard to opening the sports bag, the officer is permitted to contemporaneously seize and open a container found on the arrestee or within the immediate space around her. See *United States v. Robinson*, 414 U.S. 218 (1973).

1c. Because the exigency no longer existed at the station house, and there is a reasonable expectation of privacy in containers such as sports bags, a warrant must be obtained in order to open the bag. *United States v. Chadwick*, 433 U.S. 1 (1977). See also, e.g., *United States v. Monclavo-Cruz*, 662 F.2d 1285 (9th Cir. 1981) (warrantless search of arrestee's purse in agent's office one hour after arrest was not permissible); *People v. Julio*, 666 N.Y.S.2d 171 (N.Y. App. Div. 1997) (search of defendant's bag was not permissible where bag was not searched contemporaneously with arrest and was in police control the entire time of defendant's detainment). Compare *State v. Wade*, 573 N.W.2d 228 (Wis. Ct. App. 1997) (police officer could reasonably conduct warrantless search of defendant's purse before giving it to her while she was still in custody at the police station, where police had taken possession of purse at the arrest scene but had not examined its contents at that point; officer was justified in later examining contents of purse for police safety reasons because defendant was about to gain access to purse while still in custody).

1d. This presents an interesting problem in light of the recent case of *Arizona v. Gant*. Analyzed under the *Robinson* categorical approach, the arrest automatically gives rise to the right to search the purse, notwithstanding the absence of either of *Chimel*'s justifications—there is no evidence of trespassing to be found in the purse, and no indication that it contains a weapon that could be used against the officer. *Gant*, however, seems to draw back from this standardized approach and looks to the facts of the specific encounter. It should be noted, however, that *Gant* dealt with a search incident in the automobile context, where the Court has been more relaxed in its enforcement of the Fourth Amendment.

2. A case-by-case approach to the search incident doctrine would require a determination as to whether, in the context of the particular arrest, the police officer had reason to fear the arrestee was armed and dangerous, would reach for a weapon, or would seek to destroy evidence nearby. Such an approach was suggested by Justice Marshall in dissent in *United States v. Robinson*, 414 U.S. 218 (1973). The Court opted instead for a categorical rule permitting search of both the subject and the immediate space no matter who the subject is or what the underlying offense is. Thus, Ned could not successfully challenge the search on grounds that the agents had no reasonable basis to fear that he (a meek accountant) was armed or would seek to destroy evidence within his grasp. So long

as the arrest warrant was valid, then the entry into his home, the arrest, and the search were all lawful.

With regard to the pistol, if Ned were already cuffed at the time the desk was searched, he could argue that the authority to search the space around him had expired, as he could no longer reach out. Even if the cuffing had not been accomplished yet, Ned could argue that he was no longer within arm's reach of the desk. The courts have, however, been reluctant to second-guess officers as to the precise timing and contours of a search incident. Illustrative is the observation of the Eighth Circuit Court of Appeals: "A warrantless search incident to an arrest may be valid even though a court, operating with the benefit of hindsight in an environment well removed from the scene of the arrest, doubts that the defendant could have reached the items seized during the search." *United States v. Lucas*, 898 F.2d 606, 609 (8th Cir. 1990). See also *United States v. Abdul-Saboor*, 85 F.3d 664 (D.C. Cir. 1996), in which the defendant was taken into custody in the bedroom, then removed from the room and handcuffed in a chair several feet away, at which time the bedroom was searched. Upholding the search, the D.C. Circuit held that a search is conducted incident to an arrest so long as it is an integral part of a lawful custodial arrest process:

> Indeed, we specifically advised trial courts not to focus upon whether the suspect held the item in his grasp or could have reached for it at the moment of the arrest. The relevant distinction turns not upon the moment of the arrest versus the moment of the search but upon whether the arrest and search are so separated in time or by intervening events that the latter cannot fairly be said to have been incident to the former.

85 F.3d at 668. See also *In re Sealed Case*, 153 F.3d 759 (D.C. Cir. 1998).

In *United States v. Lucas*, supra, the subject was seated at the kitchen table with two other men as the officers entered to arrest him. He began to rise, and one officer attempted to apprehend him. By the time the officer reached Lucas, the latter's hand was within inches of a cabinet door. A struggle ensued on the floor, and Lucas was finally cuffed and moved into the living room. At the same time, another officer opened the cabinet that Lucas had been attempting to reach and found a pistol inside. Lucas argued that the gun had been unlawfully seized because he had already been handcuffed and removed from the kitchen at the time. Observing that the two other men in the kitchen were being monitored by another officer but had not been cuffed, the court held that the warrantless search was valid.

Courts have similarly upheld searches where the subject had already been handcuffed even if no confederates were present at the scene. See, e.g., *United States v. Abdul-Saboor*, supra, 85 F.3d 664 (D.C. Cir. 1996) (defendant handcuffed at chair four feet from bedroom being searched); *United*

States v. Hudson, 100 F.3d 1409, 1419 (9th Cir. 1996) (defendant hand-cuffed and removed from house); United States v. Mitchell, 64 F.3d 1105, 1110 (7th Cir. 1995) (defendant handcuffed during search of briefcase); United States v. Bennett, 908 F.2d 189 (7th Cir. 1990) (subjects handcuffed and held against wall). But compare United States v. Hardeman, 36 F. Supp. 2d 770 (E.D. Mich. 1999) (warrantless search of living room and bedroom nearly half hour after defendant had been arrested and removed from premises failed to qualify as search incident to arrest).

While Ned's contention (in our example) that the search of the desk exceeded the proper scope of a search incident may be persuasive given the original rationale of Chimel v. California, the courts seem quite willing to give police the benefit of the doubt in such situations. In light of the Belton rationale for a standardized approach, many courts follow a relaxed approach for searches incident to arrest which discounts the control aspect emphasized in Chimel. "If the search is limited to the area under the defendant's control at the time of his arrest, the fact that it is no longer under his control at the time of the search does not invalidate the search." United States v. Tejada 524 F.3d 809, 812 (7th Cir. 2008). United States v. Shakir, 616 F.3d 315 (3d Cir. 2010). The Third Circuit opined that in light of Gant, courts should return to the justification underlying Chimel and refocus attention on the suspect's ability or inability to access weapons or destroy evidence at the time that the search incident to arrest is conducted.

3. Because the suspect was handcuffed in a police vehicle, it might appear that the search could not be justified. New York v. Belton, 453 U.S. 454 (1981), however, resolved such doubts: Police may search the entire passenger compartment of the vehicle, as well as containers (like the closed paper bag in our example) found therein, contemporaneous with a lawful arrest of the occupant. This would seem to authorize seizure of the burglary tools, as well as the pistol, because both were found in the passenger compartment. The trunk is off-limits in a Belton search because of its inaccessibility. Thus, the rifle was not lawfully seized.

If there was reason to believe that evidence related to the crime would be found and the rifle had been found in the hatchback, its seizure would probably be deemed lawful. Courts have regarded the hatchback area as an extension of the passenger compartment because occupants can reach it without leaving the car. See, e.g., United States v. Mayo, 394 F.3d 1271 (9th Cir. 2005) (there is no distinction between covered and uncovered hatchback cargo areas and the hatchback area is much more easily viewed as part of the passenger compartment than as the equivalent of a conventional trunk); United States v. Olguin-Rivera, 168 F.3d 1203 (10th Cir. 1999) (officers could lawfully search rear cargo area of sport utility vehicle, even though it was covered by a built-in, retractable vinyl covering); United States v. Caldwell, 97 F.3d 1063 (8th Cir. 1996) (officer lawfully searched hatchback area).

The twist in our example is that the suspect was not only removed from the vehicle, as in *Belton*, but was handcuffed and secured in the back of the police cruiser. In the years before *Arizona v. Gant*, courts were inclined to uphold searches of the passenger compartment even after the suspect had been cuffed and removed from the immediate vicinity of the vehicle. See, e.g., *United States v. Mitchell*, 82 F.3d 146, 151 (7th Cir. 1996). As the Seventh Circuit explained in one case:

> [Defendant] seeks to distinguish *Belton* on the ground that the arrestees in that case appear to have been made less secure than he was cuffed and secured in the rear of the police car, and somewhat closer to their car. If those differences in degree are to control, the Court's preference for a straight-forward rule for guidance of police officers and avoidance of hindsight determinations in litigation would be frustrated. We think, under *Belton*, such a search is deemed reasonable, without determining whether the officer had rendered [Defendant] incapable of reaching into the van.

Even before *Arizona v. Gant*, a few courts were willing to take particular circumstances into account. *United States v. Vasey*, 834 F.2d 782, 786-787 (9th Cir. 1987), held unlawful a search of a defendant's car 30 minutes after he was arrested, handcuffed, and placed in the police vehicle. The court observed: "The *Belton* Court did not completely abandon Fourth Amendment privacy rights at the expense of establishing a bright line test for law enforcement personnel.... The *Belton* holding does have limits and those limits were exceeded here.... It was readily apparent to the officers and to this court that Vasey had virtually no opportunity to reach into the vehicle at the time the search occurred." See also *United States v. Green*, 324 F.3d 375 (5th Cir. 2003) (search of automobile not justified as incident to arrest where defendant had exited automobile and was 20-25 feet away); *United States v. Ramos-Oseguera*, 120 F.3d 1028 (9th Cir. 1997) (search invalid where it occurred after defendants were arrested and taken to the police station, but before police had the car towed away); *United States v. Mendez*, 139 F. Supp. 2d 273 (D. Conn. 2001) (search of vehicle not incident to defendant's arrest where defendant, upon seeing a police officer, ducked into vehicle, then exited and walked into a convenience store, where police officer arrested him); *United States v. Chapman*, 196 F. Supp. 2d 1279 (M.D. Ga. 2002) (warrantless search of vehicle not justified where defendant had been handcuffed prior to search and escorted into house).

Arizona v. Gant supports this individualized focus. In our example, Speedy had no access to the passenger compartment at the time of the search. However, under *Gant's* second justification, it might be found that an arrest for burglary would give reasonable cause to search the interior of the automobile for items related to that crime.

As we will see in the next section, if the initial search that produced the burglar's tools and pistol was justified, it might provide probable cause for the further search of the trunk.

4. *Maryland v. Buie*, 494 U.S. 325 (1990), permits the officers to take two precautionary steps when effecting a home arrest: 1) They may, without any additional justification, look in closets and other spaces immediately adjoining the place of the arrest in which persons might be hiding who might attack them; and 2) beyond that confined area, they may also make a limited protective sweep of other portions of the premises if and only if they have reasonable suspicion (articulable facts that, together with rational inferences from those facts, would warrant a reasonably prudent officer's believing) that persons posing a danger are present there. This sweep is limited in scope to a cursory inspection of those spaces where a person might be found and may last no longer than is necessary to dispel the suspicion.

In our example, the basement area is outside the confined space that the officers may inspect automatically adjacent to the arrest. It would therefore be necessary for them to have specific facts establishing reasonable suspicion that persons posing a danger were in the basement. The officers knew only that two friends were present with Addison in the home, and that fact would appear inadequate to justify a sweep of the basement. If the officers had information that accomplices from the robbery were present, that would probably suffice.

A determination that the officers did have reasonable suspicion that persons posing a danger were in the basement would justify a cursory sweep of the area for such persons. The weapon in plain view on the shelf would be fair game to seize. See §6.8. The officers would not, however, be permitted to open the drawers of a tool chest (where a person obviously could not hide). If the gun had been found there, its seizure would be unlawful.

It should be noted that even if an arrest occurs immediately *outside* the home, a number of circuits would permit a cursory sweep inside if the officers had reasonable suspicion that individuals posing a danger to the arrest scene were inside the home. See, e.g., *Sharrar v. Felsing*, 128 F.3d 810, 823-824 (3d Cir. 1997); *United States v. Colbert*, 76 F.3d 773 (6th Cir. 1996).

§6.4 EXCEPTIONS THAT REQUIRE PROBABLE CAUSE: AUTOMOBILE SEARCH AND THE CONTAINER DOCTRINE

Ever since Prohibition, motor vehicles have been closely associated with certain types of criminal activity—from transportation of bootleg liquor to importation of illegal aliens. It is not surprising that they have long been a major focus of law enforcement attention. Beginning in the 1920s, the courts have increasingly opened the automobile to warrantless search on the basis of several different rationales.

Recognizing the impracticality of obtaining a warrant to search a car stopped by police on the open road, *Carroll v. United States*, 267 U.S. 132 (1925), authorized warrantless search where the officers have probable cause to believe that there is contraband or other evidence of criminal activity in the vehicle. While *Carroll* was premised on the rationale that, given their mobility, cars are not likely to remain in place while police seek a warrant, subsequent decisions have dramatically expanded the automobile exception to encompass searches conducted under circumstances where the vehicle has been immobilized and secured. By 1999, the Court had explicitly abandoned reliance on exigency to justify the warrantless automobile search. See *Maryland v. Dyson*, 527 U.S. 465 (1999) (probable cause is only requirement).

The shift in rationale began in *Chambers v. Maroney*, 399 U.S. 42 (1970), which upheld the warrantless search of a car that had been stopped on the road but was searched *subsequently* at the police station after it had been seized and its occupants taken into custody. The Court reasoned that because the police had probable cause to believe the car contained evidence of a recent robbery, and thus could have lawfully searched it on the road (under *Carroll*), it was constitutionally permissible to conduct the delayed search as well:

> Arguably, because of the preference for a magistrate's judgment, only the immobilization of the car should be permitted until a search warrant is obtained; arguably, only the "lesser" intrusion is permissible until the magistrate authorizes the "greater." But which is the "greater" and which is the "lesser" intrusion is itself a debatable question and the answer may depend upon a variety of circumstances. For constitutional purposes, we see no difference between on the one hand seizing and holding a car before presenting the probable cause issue to a magistrate and on the other hand carrying out an immediate search without a warrant. Given probable cause to search, either course is reasonable under the Fourth Amendment. 399 U.S. at 5152. This dubious equation of the *seizure* of an automobile with the *search* of its contents (criticized by Justice Harlan in dissent) pointed the way to the contemporary rationale of the automobile search exception — reduced expectation of privacy in an automobile.

While *Carroll* and *Chambers* subjected cars to warrantless search (either on the scene or later) when they are stopped on the road and the police have probable cause to believe seizable items are present, *United States v. Ross*, 456 U.S. 798 (1982), and *California v. Acevedo*, 500 U.S. 565 (1991), defined the broad scope of that search. Premised on the assumption that citizens have considerably less privacy expectation in their automobiles than in their homes (because cars travel the open roads and are subject to government license and regulation), these cases permit warrantless search of the entire automobile, as well as containers found within it, limited only by the size and nature of the items for which there is probable cause to search.

In *Ross*, the police, with probable cause (based on an informant's tip) to believe that narcotics were hidden in the automobile, stopped and searched it. In the trunk, they found and opened a paper bag containing heroin. Police conducted a second and more thorough search of the car at the station, discovering a leather pouch in the trunk, which they opened to find a considerable amount of cash. Abandoning the doctrine that had afforded closed containers special protection under the Fourth Amendment, the Court ruled that if there is probable cause to search a stopped vehicle, that search may extend to any part of the car (trunk, glove compartment, interior of upholstered seats) and any packages, luggage, or other containers that might contain the object of the search. Probable cause to believe a van is transporting illegal aliens or stolen televisions, for example, would not justify a search of the glove compartment or a briefcase found on the front seat. But probable cause to believe the van is carrying narcotics subjects it (and any containers in it) to a probing examination.

Acevedo went a step further, holding that police are not required to obtain a warrant to open a container found in a car, even if their probable cause to search is limited to just that container and not the car itself. With probable cause to believe that a paper bag in Acevedo's car contained narcotics, but lacking cause to search the rest of the car, officers stopped the car, seized the bag, and opened it. The Court upheld the search and opted (as it has for searches incident to arrest, see §6.3) for a clear and unequivocal rule: Police may search an automobile and any containers within it when they have probable cause to believe that contraband or evidence of crime is present *anywhere* inside. The only remaining limit on the scope of the permissible search derives from the size and shape of the items sought—police may search only where such items may be hidden. Moreover, it does not matter that the container in question is known to the officer to be the property of a passenger not suspected of criminal activity. Given the reduced expectation of privacy with regard to property transported in cars (as the Court sees it), officers with probable cause to search a car may inspect a passenger's belongings so long as they are capable of concealing the object of the search. *Wyoming v. Houghton*, 526 U.S. 295 (1999).

Two final points regarding the automobile exception should be noted. First, it has been applied to other moving vehicles such as boats and airplanes because of their mobility and the diminished privacy expectation associated with them. Even a mobile home parked in a lot but not fixed to the ground is subject to search under the automobile exception. See *California v. Carney*, 471 U.S. 386 (1985). The Court has, however, refused to sanction the search of a motorcycle parked in the partially enclosed top portion of the driveway abutting a home (that defendant's girlfriend lived in, and which he stayed a few nights per week), as that area was deemed within the highly-protected curtilage. *Collins v. Virginia*, 138 S. Ct. 1663 (2018).

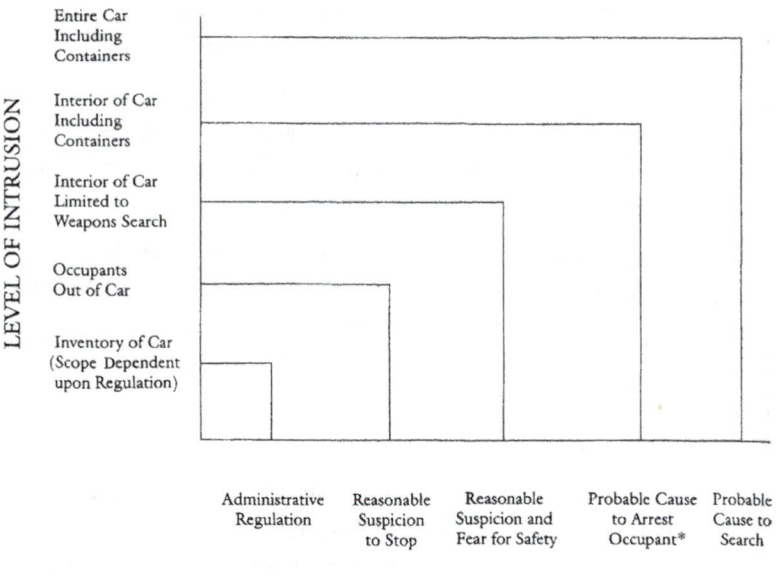

Figure 6-1. Automobile Search
*As a result of *Arizona v. Gant*, the occupant would need to be within reaching distance of the car, or there must be reason to believe that evidence relevant to the arrest might be found in the auto.

Second, the exception is not the exclusive means of conducting a warrantless search of a vehicle. Other exceptions, such as search incident to an arrest and the inventory search, may also be applicable.

Figure 6-1 summarizes the automobile search exception.

Examples

In which of the following circumstances has the officer conducted a lawful search under the automobile exception?

a. The police have probable cause to believe that Driver had supplied the weapons used by the perpetrators in a bank robbery two weeks before. The officers stop Driver's car, place him under arrest, and search the entire vehicle. In the trunk, they discover documentary evidence of the weapons deal.

b. Now assume that the police have probable cause to believe that Driver is on his way to a meeting with unknown persons for the purpose of selling illegal weapons. They stop his car, place him under arrest, and search the car. In the trunk, they find a large green duffel bag, which they open to discover assault rifles.

c. Would it matter in example b if, instead of searching the car at the scene, the officers had it towed to the police garage and searched it there later that day?

d. Would it matter in example b if, instead of probable cause to believe weapons were present *somewhere* in the vehicle, the information known to the police was specifically that the weapons were in the green duffel bag?

e. Would it matter in example b if, instead of probable cause to believe that Driver was on his way to sell rifles, the police had probable cause to believe he was in possession of a stolen large-screen projection television?

Explanations

a. The lawful arrest of Driver permits the officers to search the car's passenger compartment, but *not* the trunk, incident to the arrest. See §6.3. To fit within the automobile exception, which would permit search of *any* part of the car (and *any* containers) where the items sought might be found, the officers need probable cause to believe that contraband or evidence of crime will be found within. In our example, there is no indication that the police had any cause to believe such items were in the vehicle. The alleged crime had occurred two weeks before, and no information ties the car to current criminal activity. In the absence of probable cause to search, the automobile exception does not apply, and the search of the trunk would be unlawful.

b. The probable cause to arrest Driver for the impending transaction also provides a basis for concluding that the illegal weapons are present in the vehicle. This permits a search of the entire vehicle wherever the weapons may be hidden, including the trunk and the duffel bag found within the trunk. See *United States v. Ross*, 456 U.S. 798 (1982); *California v. Acevedo*, 500 U.S. 565 (1991).

c. While the original rationale for the automobile exception was the impracticality of obtaining a warrant to search a car stopped on the open road and thus capable of being driven off, subsequent decisions discussed above make clear that if there is probable cause to search the car, the police have the option of searching it on the scene or impounding it and searching it at a later time.

   The delayed-search option was made available by the Court even though there is no longer any practical impediment to obtaining a warrant because the rationale for the automobile exception is now rooted in the diminished expectation of privacy associated with a car as compared to a home.

Reference to the original rationale, mobility, can still occasionally be found in the case law. In *United States v. Williams*, 827 F. Supp. 641 (D. Or. 1993), the engine of the defendant's car had frozen, so he left the vehicle in a repair garage. The police knew the garage was locked and the defendant had no access to the car. Could the police conduct a warrantless search if they had probable cause that contraband or other evidence of criminal activity was in the car? The court answered no: "A primary justification for the vehicle exception, the inherent mobility of motor vehicles, is not present here. Without mobility or other exigent circumstances, the government may not invoke the vehicle exception to the warrant requirement." 827 F. Supp. at 645. Contrast *United States v. Hatley*, 999 F.2d 392 (9th Cir. 1993), where although the defendant's car was inoperable in his driveway, it *appeared* to be mobile. If it is reasonable for the officer to believe the car is operable, the court held, the vehicle exception applies.

Then-Judge Sotomayor penned the decision in *United States v. Howard*, 489 F.3d 484 (2d Cir. 2007), upholding the admission of narcotics discovered in two warrantless automobile searches even though the defendants had been taken away from the vehicle and transported to the police barracks. The district court had suppressed the evidence because the vehicle was unoccupied and immobilized, giving police ample time to procure a warrant. Overturning that order, the Second Circuit applied the automobile exception, emphasizing the rationale of diminished expectation of privacy in automobiles. There being probable cause to search, no warrant was required.

d. The distinction between probable cause to search the car and probable cause to search only a container within the car is no longer of significance. Rejecting the distinction that had been drawn in earlier decisions, *Acevedo* adopts a categorical rule that permits the search of the entire car, including containers, so long as there is probable cause to believe that items related to a crime will be found in the place searched. See, e.g., *United States v. Carter*, 300 F.3d 415 (4th Cir. 2002) (officer had probable cause to search interior of car, including suitcase located in the locked truck, upon smelling burned marijuana during traffic stop); *United States v. Alverez*, 235 F.3d 1086 (8th Cir. 2002) (police officers' observations gave them probable cause to believe there was contraband in defendant's spare tire, thus expanding scope of search under the automobile exception and permitting them to remove spare tire from trunk and examine it more closely); *United States v. Payne*, 119 F.3d 637 (8th Cir. 1997) (agents had probable cause to believe that suitcase in defendant's car contained contraband, and thus were entitled to stop car and search suitcase located in trunk). But compare *United States v. Edwards*, 242 F.3d 928 (10th Cir. 2001) (police did not have probable cause to believe that rental car contained contraband, so defendant could challenge search of luggage located in locked trunk).

Some states, interpreting their own constitutions, have continued to follow the "container doctrine" cases (*United States v. Chadwick*, 433 U.S. 1 (1977) and *Arkansas v. Sanders*, 442 U.S. 753 (1979)). *State v. Savva*, 616 A.2d 774 (Vt. 1991), for example, recognized a higher expectation of privacy for containers used to transport personal possessions within an automobile. Thus, police needed a warrant to search a brown paper bag found in the hatchback.

e. The only remaining Fourth Amendment limit on the scope of a search conducted pursuant to the automobile exception is defined by the size and nature of the items for which there is probable cause to search. Because a projection television could not be hidden in a duffel bag, opening the bag would not be lawful.

§6.5 EXCEPTIONS THAT REQUIRE REASONABLE SUSPICION: STOP-AND-FRISK AND INVESTIGATIVE DETENTIONS

As discussed in Chapter 4, police action, such as a stop and frisk, that is less intrusive than full-blown arrest or search may be conducted without a warrant on a showing that the officer had justification amounting to "reasonable suspicion." The impracticality of obtaining a warrant in such circumstances is obvious. The permissible scope of the intrusion, as well as related issues, are discussed in §§4.2-4.4.

§6.6 ADMINISTRATIVE AND INVENTORY SEARCHES

As discussed in Chapter 4, administrative searches are conducted for noncriminal purposes, such as safety code inspections. Having examined the nature of the nonspecific justification required for such searches under the Fourth Amendment (see §4.5), we will now consider the applicability of the warrant requirement.

In its early administrative search cases, the Court indicated a preference for warrants. *Camara v. Municipal Court*, 387 U.S. 523 (1967), and *See v. City of Seattle*, 387 U.S. 541 (1967), imposed a requirement for a warrant prior to health and safety inspections of dwellings and commercial premises. The Court observed that requiring a warrant would not frustrate the government purpose because code violations could not usually be corrected in the time needed to secure a warrant. Subsequent cases have recognized numerous exceptions to the warrant requirement where delay might jeopardize the efficacy of the enforcement scheme. *United States v. Biswell*, 406 U.S. 311 (1972), for example, authorized warrantless inspections of gun dealers because illegal weapons could be quickly removed.

Similar to the doctrinal evolution we have witnessed in the automobile search exception, the impracticability rationale underlying exceptions to the administrative warrant requirement has given way to reliance on diminished privacy. "Pervasively regulated" businesses, such as gun dealerships, engender lesser privacy expectations among their owners, who have implicitly consented to strict governmental monitoring. When a dealer chooses to engage in this pervasively regulated business and to accept a federal license, he does so with the knowledge that his business records, firearms, and ammunition will be subject to inspection. *United States v. Biswell*, supra, 406 U.S. at 316. The Court explained in dispensing with the requirement for a warrant prior to statutory inspection of automobile junkyards: "Because the owner or operator of commercial premises in a closely regulated industry has a reduced expectation of privacy, the warrant and probable cause requirements have lessened application in this context." *New York v. Burger*, 482 U.S. 691, 701 (1987). The liquor industry similarly fits within this category. See *Colonade Catering Corps. v. U.S.*, 397 U.S. 72 (1970).

In determining whether a particular industry is "pervasively regulated" and thus subject to warrantless searches under a statutory scheme, the Court looks to the history of regulation in the industry, as well as the hazardous nature of the enterprise. A warrant is required prior to Occupational Safety and Health Act (OSHA) inspections because of the absence of a long tradition of close government supervision in that area. See *Marshall v. Barlow's Inc.*, 436 U.S. 307 (1978). The mining industry, however, which has been subject to government regulation and involves hazardous work, could be subjected to warrantless inspections under a legislative safety program. See *Donovan v. Dewey*, 452 U.S. 594 (1981).

The Court has been expansive in classifying businesses as pervasively regulated, leading the dissenters in *New York v. Burger*, supra, to protest: "If New York City's administrative scheme renders the vehicle-dismantling business closely regulated, few businesses will escape such a finding. Under these circumstances, the warrant requirement is the exception not the rule."

More recently, in *City of Los Angeles v. Patel*,[5] the Court refused to classify hotel registration as "pervasively regulated," and therefore required a warrant for law enforcement to obtain the register. Justice Sotomayor, for a 5-4 majority, pointed out that over the past 45 years, the Court has identified only four industries regarded as "pervasively regulated": auto junkyards,

---

5. 135 S. Ct. 2443 (2015).

mining, firearms, and liquor. All these industries pose a considerable risk to public welfare. To include hotels in this list would unduly expand a narrow exception to the warrant requirement.

Exceptions to the warrant requirement have been carved out in the other noncriminal contexts, as discussed in §4.5. In the "special needs" cases, it has been held that there is no requirement for a warrant when a school principal searches a student's purse for drugs,[6] a supervisor searches a government employee's office for evidence of professional misconduct,[7] or a probation officer searches a probationer's home.[8] In holding that no warrant is necessary to conduct drug screening of employees in safety sensitive or narcotic interdiction jobs, the Court observed that a warrant requirement would frustrate the objective of the testing program because evidence of drugs and alcohol in the body dissipates rapidly. *Skinner v. Railway Labor Executives Association*, 489 U.S. 602 (1989); *National Treasury Employees Union v. Von Raab*, 489 U.S. 656 (1989).

The inventory search exception also permits warrantless examination of impounded automobiles and personal effects. *Colorado v. Bertine*, 479 U.S. 367 (1987); *Illinois v. Lafayette*, 462 U.S. 640 (1983). See § 6.4.

§6.7 WARRANTLESS INTRUSION REQUIRING NO JUSTIFICATION: CONSENT

An individual who is protected by a constitutional right may waive such protection. Just as she may relinquish her Sixth Amendment right to counsel, she may choose not to assert her Fourth Amendment right against unreasonable search and seizure. If there is a valid waiver, the police may proceed uninhibited by any of the requirements of that Amendment; they may search without a warrant or justification, and the scope of such search is proscribed only by whatever limits the consenting individual may delineate.

Consent must be *voluntary* to be valid—a coerced waiver is not an effective abandonment of any constitutional right. Unlike waivers of rights protected by the Fifth and Sixth Amendments, however, a Fourth Amendment waiver need not also be knowing and intelligent. We will see in Chapter 9 that a valid waiver of one's privilege against self-incrimination can occur only after the subject has been specifically informed of the right to remain silent and to counsel, and after she indicates an understanding of those rights. In contrast, a valid waiver of Fourth Amendment rights is not

6. *New Jersey v. TLO*, 469 U.S. 325 (1985).
7. *O'Connor v. Ortega*, 480 U.S. 709 (1987).
8. *Griffin v. Wisconsin*, 483 U.S. 868 (1987).

dependent on a showing that the consenter was informed of or understood that she had a right to refuse.

In Schneckloth v. Bustamonte, 412 U.S. 218 (1973), the occupants of an automobile stopped by police were asked by the officer if he could search the car, and one agreed. Rejecting the position that knowledge of the right to refuse is a prerequisite for an effective consent,[9] the Court instead adopted a voluntariness standard evaluated on the basis of the totality of the circumstances (a similar standard applies to confessions; see Chapter 8). Courts are to look to the tactics used by the police to secure consent, as well as the particular vulnerabilities of the subject (age, intelligence, level of education, emotional state, etc.) to determine whether the consent was coerced or voluntary. Knowledge of the right to refuse is a factor, but it is not by itself determinative.

The Court reaffirmed this approach in Ohio v. Robinette, 519 U.S. 33 (1996), in which a driver was stopped for speeding. After returning the motorist's license, the officer asked for and obtained consent to search the entire car, in the course of which drugs were found. Overturning the Supreme Court of Ohio, which had reversed the defendant's conviction because he had not been told he could refuse, the Court emphasized that consent is to be determined from a fact-specific review of the totality of circumstances.

While failure to inform the subject of the right to refuse is not itself fatal to the validity of her consent, the converse fact that the police did so inform the subject is a strong factor pointing toward the conclusion that the consent was voluntary. In Florida v. Bostick, 501 U.S. 429 (1991), the drug sweep case discussed below, the Court found it "particularly worth noting" that the police specifically advised Bostick that he had the right to refuse consent to search his luggage. See also United States v. Mendenhall, 446 U.S. 544 (1980) (Court considered it "highly relevant" that defendant had been told twice of her right to refuse before she gave her consent to a search).

Although the fact that the subject is in custody at the time of consent is relevant in determining voluntariness, custody by itself does not render consent invalid. See United States v. Watson, 423 U.S. 411 (1976) (defendant's post-arrest consent to search his car was effective).

Because it need not be demonstrated that the waiver was knowing and intelligent as well as voluntary, it is considerably easier for the government to secure a valid waiver of Fourth Amendment rights than other constitutional protections. The Court has explained this difference in part by emphasizing the practical importance of the consent search to law enforcement work: "In situations where the police have some evidence of illicit activity,

---

9. In his dissent, Justice Marshall complained that this rejection permitted the police "to capitalize on the ignorance of citizens so as to accomplish by subterfuge what they could not achieve by relying only on the knowing relinquishment of constitutional rights." 412 U.S. at 288.

but lack probable cause to arrest or search, a search authorized by valid consent may be the only means of obtaining important and reliable evidence." *Schneckloth v. Bustamonte*, supra, 412 U.S. at 227. The Court asserted that it would be "thoroughly impractical to impose on the normal consent search the detailed requirements of an effective warning," and "unrealistic to require police officers to always inform detainees that they are free to go before a consent to search may be deemed voluntary." *Ohio v. Robinette*, supra, 519 U.S. at 39.

The Court has also distinguished the rights protected by the Fourth Amendment from other constitutional rights. The rights to counsel, to a jury trial, and against compulsory self-incrimination, the Court has reasoned, affect the fundamental fairness of the criminal trial, thus making it appropriate to apply a strict standard of waiver to them. The protections against unreasonable search and seizure are of "a wholly different order, and have nothing whatever to do with promoting the fair ascertainment of truth at a criminal trial." *Schneckloth v. Bustamonte*, supra, 412 U.S. at 242. A more lenient standard of waiver is thus thought to be appropriate.

To be voluntary, consent to search must not be the product of threats, pressure, intimidation, or harassment. Mere submission to overpowering authority does not constitute consent. *Bumper v. North Carolina*, 391 U.S. 543 (1968), for example, invalidated a search predicated upon the consent of a 66-year-old black woman confronted by four white police officers who falsely represented to her that they had a warrant to search. More recently, in a case involving a 17-year-old boy awakened in his bedroom at 3:00 A.M. by police officers who told him "we need to go and talk," his response of "okay" was not regarded as consent but a "mere submission to authority." See *Kaupp v. Texas*, 123 S. Ct. 1843 (2003).

The Court has defined the appropriate inquiry in determining the voluntariness of a consent as whether a reasonable person in the subject's position would have felt free to decline the officer's request. See *Florida v. Bostick*, 501 U.S. 429 (1991). Bostick was a bus passenger confronted by armed officers dressed in green "raid" jackets who were "sweeping" the bus for drugs. When they displayed their badges and asked if they could search his luggage, he agreed. Rejecting the state supreme court's conclusion that such confrontations are *per se* coercive, the Court remanded for application of the reasonable person standard: "The Fourth Amendment proscribes unreasonable searches and seizures; it does not proscribe voluntary cooperation. The cramped confines of a bus are [but] one relevant factor that should be considered in evaluating whether a passenger's consent is voluntary." 501 U.S. at 434. Other factors pointing toward a conclusion that Bostick's consent was valid were that he had been advised by the officers that he could refuse their request, and that the officers did not draw their guns or threaten him. In another case, where plainclothes police officers conducted a drug and weapons sweep on a bus at a rest stop, the Court recently reaffirmed that valid consent to search (measured by the totality test) can occur even though the passenger is not informed of his right to refuse consent. *United States v. Drayton*, 536 U.S. 194 (2002) (discussed in §4.3 of Chapter 4).

Waiver of Fourth Amendment rights can be made by the person whose property is searched or by a third party who shares common authority over, and access to, the property. One of two cousins who shared use of a duffel bag, for example, could consent to its search and thus waive the rights of the other. See *Frazier v. Cupp*, 394 U.S. 731 (1969). Similarly, a girlfriend who shared a defendant's bedroom could consent to its search, thereby waiving his rights. See *United States v. Matlock*, 415 U.S. 164 (1974). Indeed, the Court has held that the third party need not have actual authority over the area—*apparent authority* will suffice. In *Illinois v. Rodriguez*, 497 U.S. 177 (1990), the defendant's former girlfriend, who told police that she shared the defendant's apartment, let them in with her key and permitted them to search. In fact, she had moved out one month earlier. Where the facts and surrounding circumstances known to the officer warrant a man of reasonable caution to conclude that the consenting party had authority over the premises, consent is valid even if *actual* authority is absent.

Common authority for purposes of a consent search rests not on property law concepts, but on "mutual use of the property by persons generally having joint access or control for most purposes, so that it is reasonable to recognize that any of the co-inhabitants has the right to permit the inspection in his own right and that the others have assumed the risk that one of their number might permit the common area to be searched." *Matlock*, supra, 415 U.S. at 172. Simply having legal authority to enter the premises is not sufficient. Thus, where a hotel clerk permitted inspection of a guest's room, this did not constitute a waiver of the defendant's Fourth Amendment rights because there was no mutual use of the premises. See *Stoner v. California*, 376 U.S. 483 (1964).

What if one co-occupant consents to a search while the other is present and refuses to consent? In *Georgia v. Randolph*, 126 S. Ct. 1515 (2006), the defendant's estranged wife gave police permission to search the marital residence for drugs after defendant unequivocally refused the police request. The Court ruled the search unreasonable and ordered the evidence suppressed. Justice Souter, writing for the 5-3 majority, analyzed the question of Fourth Amendment reasonableness in consent cases in light of customary social expectations, which prevents one from entering a home where a co-tenant objects. If an emergency situation exists such as domestic violence, Souter suggested, a warrantless entry might be allowed. He further noted that the information from the consenting co-tenant may provide enough information to establish probable cause to obtain a warrant.

To effectively refuse consent, a co-occupant must be physically present at the time. In *Fernandez v. California*, 134 S. Ct. 1126 (2014), the objecting co-occupant was taken into police custody on suspicion of assaulting his girlfriend, who later consented to a search of their apartment. Rejecting Fernandez's argument that his objection should remain effective even after his departure, especially given that the police themselves removed him, Justice Alito wrote for the Court: "An occupant who is absent due to a lawful detention or arrest [there was probable cause to believe that Fernandez had abused his girlfriend] stands in the same shoes as an occupant who is absent for any other reason." Thus "consent [may be] provided by an abused woman well after her male partner had been removed from the apartment they shared." Ginsburg noted for the three dissenters that "the police could readily have obtained a warrant to search the shared residence."

The scope of a consent search is determined by the permission granted. The subject, for instance, may agree to a search of a suitcase but explicitly exclude the opening of a folder found inside. In *Thompson v. Louisiana*, 469 U.S. 17 (1984), the Court held that a daughter's summoning of police to her mother's home to render medical assistance did not constitute an open-ended invitation for detectives to conduct a general exploratory search for evidence of a homicide committed on the scene. As we shall see in §6.8, however, any contraband or evidence observed by police in plain view while they confine themselves to the terms of the consent search may properly be seized.

Consent has played a critical role in upholding searches of parolees and probationers who must agree to submit to certain searches as a condition of their release. See, e.g., *Sampson v. California*, 547 U.S. 843 (2006); *U.S. v. Massey*, 461 F.3d 177 (2d Cir. 2006). And "implied consent" (for the privilege of operating a motor vehicle) has been held to justify imposition of penalties on motorists who refuse to submit to alcohol testing, but the Supreme Court has upheld such statutes involving breath tests, but not blood draws, as the latter are more intrusive searches implicating the Fourth Amendment. See *Birchfield v. North Dakota*, 136 S. Ct. 2160 (2016).

Examples

1. Larry Lane, a law student, rents an apartment on the third floor of a three-family private residence. The police suspect Lane of involvement in a criminal enterprise selling stolen copies of the upcoming state bar examination to law school graduates. Unfortunately for the investigators, there is not sufficient probable cause to seek a warrant to search the apartment or arrest Lane. Under which of the following circumstances could a valid consent search be conducted?

   a. Three officers visit Lane and ask his permission to search the apartment. After he becomes outwardly nervous and indecisive, one of the officers tells him that it "sure won't look good on your law school record if you refuse to let us look around your place." Lane finally agrees to a search, and the officers find and seize copies of the upcoming bar examination in his desk.

    b. Three officers visit Lane's apartment in his absence and speak to Kirk, a man Lane has hired to clean for him every other week. The officers explain to Kirk that they would like to look around, and he lets them in. The officers find and seize copies of the upcoming bar examination in Lane's desk.

    c. Janis Close, a former (now estranged) live-in girlfriend of Lane's, calls the police and tells them that she has proof of his criminal activities. At her suggestion, the officers meet her at Lane's apartment. She opens the door with her key (which she failed to return when she moved out two months prior) and leads the officers into the living room, where they observe several copies of the upcoming bar examination on a coffee table. Close then brings them to the adjoining study and opens the top drawer of Lane's desk, revealing an answer key to the bar examination. The officers seize all the incriminating documents.

    d. Officers visit Lane's apartment in his absence and speak to his landlord, who lives on the first floor. The officers ask if they could search Lane's car, which is parked in the driveway. The landlord, who has Lane's permission to move the car if it is blocking other vehicles, agrees and opens the locked doors with a key that Lane had provided him. The officers find incriminating evidence under the front seat.

    e. Officers visit Lane's apartment, inform him that they are investigating the unauthorized release of a state bar examination, and ask him if they can search his car parked in the driveway. Lane replies: "Sure, go ahead." The officers locate a briefcase in the trunk, which they open to discover copies of the upcoming bar examination. In addition, they came upon a small bottle of pills under the front seat, which they take and which, upon laboratory analysis, turn out to be a controlled substance.

2. Sally White was pulled over on Florida Route 12 when a trooper observed her weaving between the lanes. After White produced her license and registration, the trooper stated: "We've had a lot of trouble with people moving drugs and money along this road. Would you mind if I have a look in your trunk?" White agreed and opened the trunk for the trooper. The officer's attention was drawn to a spare tire, which appeared unusual — it was the wrong type and size for the vehicle, was extremely heavy when he lifted it, and had white powder residue on its rim. Based on his knowledge that narcotics were often smuggled in such tires, the trooper pulled out his knife and cut open the tire. Inside, he found an automatic weapon and several kilograms of cocaine. Was this search lawful?

    Would it matter if Sally had been seated in the police cruiser at the officer's request while he ran a routine computer check of her vehicle, and consented to the search while there?

3. A Greyhound bus on its way to Miami made a brief stop in Mobile, Alabama. Officer Wallace of that city's drug interdiction unit boarded the bus and announced: "With your cooperation, I'd like to check the gear on board for contraband. With your consent, please bring down your luggage from overhead and have it open so I can do a quick on-board inspection." Gus complied, and Wallace discovered cocaine in his carry-on. Arguing that he was never told he could refuse, Gus seeks to suppress. What result?

Explanations

1a. A waiver of Fourth Amendment rights need not be knowing and intelligent. Thus, even if Lane had flunked Criminal Procedure and can establish that he in fact did not know he had a right to refuse the officers' request, that in itself will not obviate his consent if it is determined to have been voluntary. *Schneckloth v. Bustamonte*, 412 U.S. 218 (1973); *United States v. Erwin*, 155 F.3d 818 (6th Cir. 1998); *United States v. Page*, 154 F. Supp. 2d 1320 (M.D. Tenn. 2001).

The key issue here is whether Lane's agreement to the search was voluntary or coerced. Voluntariness is determined on the basis of the totality of the circumstances. Given his age and level of education, Lane faces an uphill battle in persuading the court that his consent was compelled. He would point to his nervous state as an indication of his vulnerability as well as to the officer's statement about ruining his record as a sign that pressure was brought to bear on him. Making a case for coerced waiver usually requires much more, however. See, e.g., *United States v. Reinholz*, 245 F.3d 765 (8th Cir. 2001) (defendant's consent to search automobile not voluntary where defendant was illegally arrested, spread-eagled, patted down, handcuffed, and placed in unmarked police car and driven 25 minutes to junior high school parking lot); *United States v. Pena-Saiz*, 161 F.3d 1175 (8th Cir. 1998) (defendant did not voluntarily consent to search conducted in drug interdiction office at airport where defendant believed she was under arrest and that she had to submit to search, and the officers did nothing to allay her fears but, rather, told her, "This is what we do. We talk to people, we search people's bags, we pat-search people. This is what we do every day."); *United States v. Ramirez-Chilel*, 289 F.3d 744 (11th Cir. 2002) (consent prompted by show of official authority); *United States v. Replogle*, 176 F. Supp. 2d 960 (D. Neb. 2001) (defendant's consent to search was not voluntary where defendant allowed officers to enter and search property only in submission to probation order, especially given number of uniformed and armed law enforcement agents outside house at the time). Compare *United States v. Tompkins*, 130 F.3d 117 (5th Cir. 1997) (consent valid even though obtained only after officer told defendant that he would obtain a search warrant for the premises if defendant refused to permit a search).

1b. Assuming that there was no coercion of Kirk, the issue here is whether Kirk was in a position to waive Lane's privacy rights in the apartment. Fourth Amendment rights can be waived by third parties, but only if those persons have (or reasonably appear to have) common authority over and access to the premises. A person on the premises for the purpose of performing a service like cleaning would not have either actual or apparent authority to give consent. See *Kaspar v. City of Hobbs*, 90 F. Supp. 2d 1313 (D.N.M. 2000) (caretaker lacked control over house for most purposes, precluding claim that he could admit police and consent to search); *People v. Walter*, 890 P.2d 240 (Colo. Ct. App. 1994) (babysitter hired by defendant's wife on occasional basis did not have authority to consent to search of defendant's bedroom); *People v. Keith M.*, 625 N.E.2d 980 (Ill. App. Ct. 1993) (police officers did not have reasonable grounds to believe housekeeper could consent to search of defendant's house, where housekeeper was not resident). Compare *State v. Boyd*, 695 N.E.2d 843 (Ohio 1998) (adult babysitter had authority to consent to search of common areas of apartment, including bathroom, where sitter regularly watched defendant's children over period of years, made personal use of premises for herself and her own child, and had authority to determine whom to admit to apartment).

1c. Janis Close's consent to the search could operate to waive Lane's Fourth Amendment rights in either of two situations: 1) she shares actual common authority over the apartment with Lane, as in *United States v. Matlock*, 415 U.S. 164 (1974) (see, e.g., *United States v. Kim*, 105 F.3d 1579 (9th Cir. 1997), holding that by instructing his associate to rent storage units in his own name, defendant assumed risk that associate would allow search of units); or 2) she has *apparent* authority to grant permission to search, as in *Illinois v. Rodriguez*, 497 U.S. 177 (1990).

Because Close has not lived in the apartment for two months and thus no longer has joint access or control, she lacks actual authority to consent. Her consent may nonetheless operate effectively against Lane if the facts and surrounding circumstances known to the officers would warrant a reasonable person to conclude that she had authority over the premises. Based on this objective standard, the facts that Close has a key and ready access are important elements in establishing apparent authority, but probably are not sufficient in themselves. It would aid the government's cause if the police had been aware that Close had possessions of her own in the apartment. See *United States v. Gevedon*, 214 F.3d 807 (7th Cir. 2000) (defendant's estranged wife had authority to consent to search of defendant's home and detached garage/shop, though the wife no longer lived in the home, where defendant never told the wife that she could not go into the area and the wife had a divorce court order giving her sole possession of the home); *United States v. Shelton*, 181 F. Supp. 2d 649 (N.D. Miss. 2001) (although defendant's wife was separated from defendant and moved out of the house in which she had no ownership interest, she had authority to consent to a search because she retained the key and alarm access code and had personal belongings at the residence, and defendant made no attempt to exclude her).

Assuming that Close is held to have had apparent authority over the apartment and, further, that the living room was an area that she shared access to and control over, the documents found there in plain view were lawfully seized.

More troublesome is the fact that Close entered the study and opened Lane's desk to police examination. Because that room, and particularly the desk, were most likely the exclusive province of Lane, the search and seizure there would be unlawful. See, e.g., *United States v. Rodriguez*, 888 F.2d 519, 523 (7th Cir. 1989) (wife had no authority, apparent or actual, to consent to search of closed boxes in an area of house that she did not occupy); *United States v. Basinski*, 226 F.3d 829, 834 (7th Cir. 2000) ("For purposes of searches of closed containers, mere possession of the container by a third party does not necessarily give rise to a reasonable belief that the third party has authority to consent to a search of its contents"; friend to whom defendant gave locked briefcase for safekeeping did not have authority to consent to search of briefcase). Compare *United States v. Tucker*, 57 F. Supp. 2d 503 (W.D. Tenn. 1999) (defendant's girlfriend had actual authority to consent to officer's search of closed, clearly marked ammunitions box, where defendant did not lock box, did nothing to conceal markings on box, stored box in common area of apartment, and did nothing to restrict girlfriend's access to box); *United States v. Perez*, 948 F. Supp. 1191 (S.D.N.Y. 1996) (defendant's father had authority to consent to search of defendant's bedroom in apartment rented by father, though defendant had been the sole occupant and user of the bedroom for over four years, father did not use the bedroom for any purpose, and father had never gone into personal boxes and papers in the defendant's closet, as father's entry into the bedroom and removal of defendant's suitcase from the closet, in presence of officers, indicated he had permission to gain access to the room and containers therein).

Some courts have been particularly protective of containers found in shared space. See, e.g., *United States v. Welch*, 4 F.3d 761, 764 (9th Cir. 1993) (third party who consented to a search of car to which he had joint access did not have power to consent to a search of a purse found in the trunk); *United States v. Chang*, 838 F. Supp. 695 (D.P.R. 1993) (third party's consent to search anything in his motel room did not give the agents authority to search luggage belonging to his two companions); *Marganet v. State*, 927 So. 2d 52 (Fla. 2006) (girlfriend did not have actual or apparent authority to consent to the search of her boyfriend's shaving kit located inside a suitcase in their shared hotel room because the items did not belong to her, she was uncertain of the contents, and she had not been given permission to access the shaving kit).

What if Janis Close acted out of spite against Lane in opening his apartment to a search? A few courts have considered the antagonistic relationship between the third-party consenter and the subject of the search as a factor weighing against waiver and have held invalid warrantless searches where the cohabitating spouse acted out of anger, spite, or hostility in consenting to the search. See, e.g., *May v. State*, 780 S.W.2d 866 (Tex. Ct. App. 1989) (and cases cited). But most decisions conclude otherwise. See *People v. Bishop*, 51 Cal. Rptr. 2d 629, 640 (Cal. Ct. App. 1996) ("The existence of antagonism by one spouse against the other may reveal motives for consenting to a search, and it may bear on the weight of credibility of any testimony given by the antagonistic spouse, but it does not change that spouse's position with reference to the right to give such consent."); *Commonwealth v. Noonan*, 720 N.E.2d 828, 833 (Mass. App. Ct. 1999) ("Antagonism that may spring up between the occupants does not invalidate the consent, for the relevant analysis in…consent cases focuses on the relationship between the consenter and the property searched, not the relationship between the consenter and the defendant."). See also *United States v. McAlpine*, 919 F.2d 1461, 1464 (10th Cir. 1990) (rejecting the view that if the consent was given for the purpose of implicating the defendant in a crime, it invalidates the consent).

One type of consent case attracting attention is the child "dropping a dime" on his parents. In *Davis v. State*, 422 S.E.2d 546 (Ga. 1992), the Georgia Supreme Court held that a ten-year-old child did not have sufficient authority to consent to the search of his parents' home. This was the case even though the child had been left alone and had the run of the house. See also *Cooper v. State*, 706 So. 2d 369 (Fla. Dist. Ct. App. 1998) (detective's warrantless entry into motel room was not rendered valid by consent of a 15-year-old girl who answered the door, as detective could not have reasonably believed that she possessed common authority to grant him entry). See also *State v. Schwarz*, 332 Mont. 243 (2006) (a youth under the age of 16 does not have the capacity or the authority to relinquish her parents' privacy rights); and *State v. Ellis*, 351 Mont. 95 (2009) (a 13-year-old girl does not have the authority to consent to a search of her bedroom in defendant's residence.) But compare *Rainwater v. State*, 240 Ga. App. 370 (1999) (consent by 15-year-old valid). The Tenth Circuit has held that the minority of the third-party consenter does not *per se* bar a finding of authority to consent, but is merely a factor to be weighed. See *United States v. Gutierrez-Hermosillo*, 142 F.3d 1225 (10th Cir. 1998) (14-year-old had authority to consent to search of motel room she occupied with father).

Some types of searches may not be amenable to consent by third parties. The bugging of a hotel room with the consent of the defendant's companion, for example, was deemed beyond the scope of consent, as it was too intrusive and surveillance could occur even without the third party being present. *United States v. Shabazz*, 883 F. Supp. 422 (D. Minn. 1995).

If Lane were present at the scene and objected to the search, the police could not proceed. "A physically present co-occupant's stated refusal to permit entry prevails, rendering the warrantless search unreasonable." *Georgia v. Randolph*, 126 S. Ct. 1515, 1518-1519 (2006). See also *U.S. v. Johnson* 656 F.3d 375 (6th Cir. 2011).

1d. Does the landlord's consent operate to waive Lane's rights? Because the landlord's authority to enter Lane's car is limited to moving it around the driveway and does not constitute mutual use and access, he does not appear to have actual authority to consent to this search. See *United States v. Brown*, 961 F.2d 1039 (2d Cir. 1992) (landlady who was authorized to enter defendant's apartment when necessary to turn off electrical appliances or lights could not authorize search of premises); *United States v. Elliott*, 50 F.3d 180 (2d Cir. 1995) (landlords generally do not have common authority over apartment units leased to tenants as to be able to give consent to search). Whether the landlord has apparent authority would depend upon the particular facts and circumstances of his statements to, and actions in front of, the police.

1e. The permissible scope of a consent search is defined by the terms (either explicit or implicit) of the consent. Lane could have limited the search to the passenger compartment only, or to the car but not the containers within it. Because he did not place any limits on his consent, however, the police are permitted to search anywhere and anything in the vehicle where the items sought (presumably documentary) might be found. That would include his briefcase.

Where a motorist is asked for permission to search his car for narcotics and the permission is granted, the scope of the search may extend to anywhere in the vehicle where narcotics may be hidden. See *Florida v. Jimeno*, 500 U.S. 248 (1991):

> The standard for measuring the scope of a suspect's consent under the Fourth Amendment is that of "objective" reasonableness — what would the typical reasonable person have understood by the exchange between the officer and the suspect? The question before us, then, is whether it is reasonable for an officer to consider a suspect's general consent to a search of his car to include consent to examine a paper bag lying on the floor of the car. We think it is.

500 U.S. at 251 (citations omitted). Rejecting Jimeno's argument that the police should be required to seek specific permission for each container

they want to examine, the Court held that because a reasonable person may be expected to know that narcotics are generally carried in some kind of container, the driver's consent to search for narcotics implicitly included permission to open the bag. See also *United States v. Coffman*, 148 F.3d 952 (8th Cir. 1998) (in response to officer's question whether there were any weapons on premises, suspect invited officers to look around; consent was broad enough to include search under bed, where weapon was found).

Thus, the search of the briefcase and seizure of the bar exams in our example would probably be upheld as a lawful consent search. The seizure and subsequent analysis of the bottle of pills, however, would appear to be beyond the scope of Lane's consent. He had responded positively to a request to search that was prefaced by reference to the bar exam scheme. His agreement seemed (at least implicitly) limited to a search for evidence of that offense and would not carry over to a laboratory examination of the contents of the bottle.

2. What was the scope of Sally White's consent to search? Arguably, because the officer told White that he was looking for narcotics (as opposed to stolen televisions), she could reasonably have expected that the search would be thorough. It is questionable, however, whether the consent could be construed as broad enough to cover the slashing of a tire.

Even if the search exceeded the bounds of the consent given, however, there is another basis for upholding its legality. As discussed in §6.3, an automobile stopped on the road (as well as any container found within) is subject to search if the officer has probable cause to believe that seizable items are present. While conducting a consent search of the trunk, which properly included an examination of the tire's exterior, the trooper developed probable cause to believe that contraband was hidden inside. The automobile exception would thus permit a warrantless search of the tire's interior. See *United States v. Alverez*, 235 F.3d 1086 (8th Cir. 2000) (officers' observations of defendant's automobile during consensual search gave them probable cause to believe that there was contraband inside a spare tire, so police validly slashed the tire to reveal contraband); *United States v. Anderson*, 114 F.3d 1059 (10th Cir. 1997) (consent search allowing officer to "scout around" vehicle authorized police to look under the car, and when the officer saw a trap door in the gas tank, he had probable cause to have the tank compartment searched).

If Sally gave consent to a search while in the confines of the police cruiser, she could argue, of course, that her will had been overborne. So long as she was not in custody and a reasonable person in her situation would have felt free to leave, however, her consent is probably still valid. See *United States v. Thompson*, 106 F.3d 794 (7th Cir. 1997); *United States v. Rivera*, 906 F.2d 319 (7th Cir. 1990).

3. The Court in *Florida v. Bostick*, 501 U.S. 429 (1991), refused to require that police inform passengers during a bus stop that they are free to leave, and held instead that the appropriate inquiry is whether a reasonable person would believe that consent to search was optional under the circumstances. Although Gus was not informed that he could refuse consent, there was no apparent show of force in our example, probably rendering the search lawful.

At least one circuit court has concluded that a passenger in this situation would not feel free to disregard the officer's request unless there was some affirmative notice that the passenger could do so. See *United States v. Guapi*, 144 F.3d 1393 (11th Cir. 1998). The court found it significant that the manner in which the announcement was made by the police appeared designed to convince passengers that they had no choice, and that the officer stood at the front of the cramped bus, blocking the exit. See also *United States v. Washington*, 151 F.3d 1354 (11th Cir. 1998) (reiterating importance of informing passengers of right to refuse). But *U.S. v Drayton*, 536 U.S. 194 (2004), holds that a valid consent can occur even if the passenger is not informed of his right to refuse consent.

§6.8 THE PLAIN VIEW DOCTRINE

The plain view doctrine permits an officer to make a warrantless seizure of incriminating items that she comes upon while otherwise engaged in a lawful arrest, entry, or search. Unlike the other exceptions to the warrant requirement that we have discussed, this doctrine does not permit a search, but only a *seizure* of something already discovered. The authorization for the search (as well as its permissible scope) emanates from the action that the officer is already conducting at the time—such as a search pursuant to a warrant or incident to a lawful arrest. The plain view doctrine is premised on the notion that once the item has been spotted in plain view by the officer, insistence on a warrant authorizing its seizure would be a needless inconvenience that would not significantly serve the privacy interest of the subject because the item has already been discovered. The Supreme Court has indicated a willingness to expand the doctrine to senses other than sight, such as feel and touch. See *Minnesota v. Dickerson*, 508 U.S. 366 (1993) (police may seize contraband detected through the sense of touch during a protective pat-down).

The three requirements for a lawful plain view seizure are that:

1. the officer's **original intrusion is lawful,**
2. the item is **observed while the officer is confining her activities to the permissible scope of that intrusion** (sometimes referred to as a *lawful right of access* to the object itself), and

3. it is **immediately apparent that the item is contraband or evidence of crime**, without the necessity for any further examination or search. (The prior requirement that the discovery of the item in plain view be "inadvertent" has been eliminated by *Horton v. California*, 496 U.S. 128 (1990).)

These limitations ensure that the plain view doctrine does not eviscerate the usual requirements of the Fourth Amendment. Requiring that the original intrusion be lawful ensures that the officer is in the particular place with proper justification. Requiring that she confine her action to the parameters of the original intrusion ensures that the scope is not enlarged. Requiring that it be immediately apparent that the item in question is connected to criminal activity ensures both that the intrusiveness of the search is not increased by a separate examination of the items found in plain view, and that a general license to seize any of the subject's possessions has not been created.

Suppose, by way of example, that a warrant is issued authorizing a search of Peter's home for stolen VCRs of a particular description. The police enter the home and search those areas in which a VCR might be found. While doing so, they come upon a large bale of marijuana. A strict reading of the Fourth Amendment would require that before the officers may seize the contraband, which was not described in the warrant, they must seek and obtain another warrant specifying the bale. The plain view doctrine recognizes that the delay, inconvenience, and risk that the evidence may be lost by the time the second warrant is secured are generally not justified by the benefit to Peter, given that "the cat is already out of the bag." We certainly cannot require the police to forget what they saw, and the only issue is whether they may seize the item now without a warrant. The plain view doctrine permits such a seizure.

Now suppose instead that police officers are on routine foot patrol when they observe a bale of marijuana through a window in Peter's home. Having seen the contraband in plain view, may they enter the home and seize it? The answer is emphatically no. The plain view doctrine permits seizure of an item while police are engaged in a *lawful intrusion* — which in the case of entry into a private home means that (absent exigent circumstances) a warrant must be obtained. The observation that the police made through the window must be presented in a warrant affidavit to a magistrate who decides whether probable cause has been made out and, if so, what the scope of the search will be. (Remember that the observation made by the police from the street through the window is not itself a search implicating the Fourth Amendment because Peter can have no reasonable expectation of privacy in this situation. See §3.2 of Chapter 3.) The plain view doctrine is triggered only *after* the officers have otherwise lawfully entered the premises; it does not provide justification for the entry.

Now suppose that the officers (having observed the marijuana through the window) secure a warrant authorizing entry into Peter's home and seizure of the bale of marijuana. They enter and, while one officer locates the bale, the other opens the drawers of Peter's rolltop desk and discovers betting slips, which he immediately recognizes as evidence of unlawful gambling. Since these papers have come into the officer's plain view, may they be seized? The answer is no, because when he opened the desk drawers, the officer had impermissibly expanded the scope of the authorized search. The large bale could not be hidden in a desk drawer (except in the unlikely event of some very quick repackaging). The plain view doctrine requires that the discovery occur in the permissible course of the original search and without exceeding its scope. If the betting slips had been found in open view on top of or near the bale of marijuana, they could be lawfully seized.

Finally, suppose that the officers, armed with a warrant to search for and seize the marijuana, come across an unmarked vial of multicolored pills in an open area. If they have a hunch that it may contain a controlled substance, may they seize the vial and bring the pills to the police laboratory for testing? The answer again is no. The incriminating nature of the item in question must be *immediately apparent*. That means that the police must have probable cause to believe, without further inspection or analysis, that the thing that they have encountered is connected to criminal activity. Lifting stereo components to read the serial numbers on the equipment and matching those numbers (by way of a telephone call) with stolen items was deemed beyond the scope of the plain view doctrine, even though the inspection was cursory. *Arizona v. Hicks*, 480 U.S. 321 (1987). The police did not have probable cause to connect the items to a crime based solely on what was already exposed to their view while conducting an otherwise lawful investigation of a shooting.

The plain view doctrine is, in sum, a limited accommodation to the interests of effective law enforcement and not an open license to search and seize any items encountered while on the premises.

What effect the use of body cameras will have on the application of the plain view doctrine remains to be seen, but they certainly provide the potential for documentation of items found, or not found, in plain sight.

Examples

1. Police have a warrant for the arrest of Joseph Barker for the crime of vehicular homicide (a "hit-and-run"). In possession of reliable information that he was at home, they entered his two-room apartment and placed him under arrest. While putting Barker in handcuffs, Officer Keen gazed into the open bedroom and observed items (a scale, razor blade, empty plastic bags, and a jar filled with a white powder) that she immediately recognized as paraphernalia used in the preparation and distribution of narcotics. Keen seized the items. They are subsequently offered

against Barker at his trial on narcotics offenses. Barker objects, arguing that the seizure of items outside his immediate space at the time of arrest was unlawful, and further that the items were not related to the charge of vehicular homicide. Were the items lawfully seized?

2. Assume instead that the officers appeared at Barker's door without a warrant and asked if they could enter to ask him some questions about a traffic accident. He invited them in, and while seated at the kitchen table, Officer Keen observed the drug paraphernalia in the open bedroom. She seizes the items. Same result?

3. Assume instead that the officers, armed with a search warrant, entered the private two-car garage where Barker keeps his car. The warrant authorized a search of the vehicle and the area of the garage immediately surrounding it for evidence of recent impact with the accident victim. The officers inspected the exterior of the automobile, the floor of the garage, and then turned their attention to a workbench located in a separate alcove at the back of the garage. While examining a shelf above the workbench, the officers discovered a plain white envelope that, as they discovered upon opening it, contained a receipt from an auto body shop indicating that significant repair and painting work was done on the front end of Barker's car the day after the hit-and-run occurred. Can the officers lawfully seize this receipt?

4. Drug enforcement agents secured a warrant to search Marcus Pepper's residence for narcotics. They also suspected him of trafficking in unlawful assault rifles, which they believed were on the premises, but did not seek authority from the magistrate to search for or seize them. When executing the warrant, the agents (not unexpectedly) came upon the assault rifles, which they removed. Was the seizure proper under the plain view doctrine?

5. Pursuant to a lawful search warrant for stolen wide-screen televisions, officers proceeded to Suspect's home. While in the den conducting the search, the officers smelled what they recognized to be burning marijuana. They then observed a wooden pipe smoldering in the ashtray. May the officers seize the pipe and its contents?

Explanations

1. Barker is correct that the search permitted incident to his arrest is limited to the area immediately around him while he is being cuffed and cannot encompass the items in the next room. See §6.3. Given the lawful intrusion into his home (remember that the arrest warrant carries the authority to enter the subject's residence, see §5.5), however, items immediately apparent as contraband that are encountered in plain view

while effecting the arrest may be seized. An issue is raised whether the officer, peering in from an adjoining room, had adequate probable cause to believe the items that she saw were related to criminal activity. Given their appearance and the officer's expertise, the "immediately apparent" requirement of the plain view doctrine would appear to be satisfied. The fact that the items seized had no connection to the crime for which Barker was arrested is of no consequence. The plain view doctrine often operates to permit seizure of items unrelated to the reason the officers are on the premises. Nexus to the original investigation is not a prerequisite to a plain view seizure.

2. Yes, the seizure would be permissible under the plain view doctrine. The officers have lawfully entered Barker's apartment by way of his consent (assuming it was voluntary). Once lawfully inside, the doctrine operates to permit seizure of items observed in plain view that are immediately apparent as contraband. The point of the example is that the initial intrusion, which begins the plain view process, can take any of the several warrant or warrantless forms we have discussed; it simply must be lawful.

3. There are two problems here. First, the officers may have exceeded their authority under the search warrant at the point at which they discovered the envelope because the workbench was not adjacent to the automobile (the area specified in the warrant). If so, seizure of the envelope would be unlawful because their intrusion into that part of the garage was not authorized. Second, even if the warrant could be read to authorize a search of the workbench and shelves, the officers opened an envelope that was not immediately apparent as evidence or contraband. As in *Arizona v. Hicks*, 480 U.S. 321 (1987), the police lacked probable cause to connect the envelope to criminal activity based *solely on what was already exposed to their view*. Probable cause to support a plain view seizure has been defined as "more than hunch, guesswork, and cop-on-the-beat intuition, but less than proof beyond a reasonable doubt or a near certainty that the seized item is incriminating. There must be enough facts for a reasonable person to believe that the items in plain view may be contraband or evidence of crime." *United States v. Giannetta*, 909 F.2d 571, 579 (1st Cir. 1990).

Opening the plain envelope is analogous to lifting Hicks's stereo components to read the serial numbers—both are impermissible searches outside the boundaries of the plain view doctrine.

The officers would be allowed to photograph the envelope without that being deemed an unreasonable seizure because taking photographs does not interfere with the possessory interest of the defendant. See *United States v. Mancari*, 463 F.3d 590 (7th Cir. 2006). Photographing information on an envelope exposed to plain view is no more intrusive than recording the serial numbers of a stereo, which was permitted in *Hicks*.

4. Until recently, inadvertency was a requirement for a lawful plain view seizure. As Justice Stewart explained in *Coolidge v. New Hampshire*, 403 U.S. 443 (1971), the rationale of the doctrine is that the police should not be put to the inconvenience of leaving the place of the original search to procure a warrant to seize contraband or evidence that was inadvertently discovered. "But where the discovery is anticipated, where the police know in advance the location of evidence and intend to seize it, the situation is altogether different. The requirement of a warrant to seize imposes no inconvenience whatever, or at least none which is constitutionally recognizable in a legal system that regards warrantless searches as per se unreasonable in the absence of exigent circumstances." 403 U.S. at 470-471. If, in other words, the officers are not surprised by the discovery but rather anticipated it, they should be bound by the warrant requirement.

In our example, because the officers had reason to believe they would find the weapons at Pepper's home, the *Coolidge* logic would require them to seek the magistrate's authorization to seize the guns prior to the search. In *Horton v. California*, 496 U.S. 128 (1990), however, the Court dispensed with the requirement that the plain view discovery be inadvertent. Officers had probable cause to believe that stolen jewelry and weapons would be found at the Horton's home, but the search warrant specified only the jewelry. Horton challenged the seizure of the weapons during execution of the warrant on the grounds that, because their discovery was not inadvertent, the plain view doctrine did not apply. Reasoning that the inadvertence requirement added no significant privacy protection beyond the other requirements for a plain view seizure (lawful initial intrusion, limited scope of search, items immediately apparent as incriminating) and further that it required unworkable judicial inquiries into the subjective state of mind of the officers, the Court abandoned it. Some states continue to require inadvertence under their own constitutions. See, e.g., *Commonwealth v. Balicki*, 762 N.E.2d 290 (Mass. 2002); *State v. Padilla*, 728 A.2d 279 (N.J. Super. Ct. App. Div. 1999); *People v. Manganaro*, 561 N.Y.S.2d 379 (Sup. Ct. 1990). Also see *State v. Nieves*, 160 N.H. 245 (2010) (abolishes inadvertency requirement under the state constitution, but only for drugs, weapons, and other items dangerous in themselves).

After *Horton*, the fact that the agents in our example anticipated finding the guns does not preclude seizure under the plain view doctrine. Officers may seize whatever contraband or evidence of crime that they discover in the course of a lawful search, provided that it is immediately apparent as such, and provided that the officers have not exceeded the permissible bounds of the original search.

With the abandonment of the inadvertence requirement, the problem of pretext emerges more dramatically. Aware that he may make a warrantless seizure of items immediately apparent as incriminating, so long as he has made lawful entry, what is to prevent an officer from gaining such access on a pretext (by, for example, asking Tenant if he could enter the apartment to ask questions relating to a neighbor's complaints about loud noise), but for the real purpose of seeking incriminating items? The problem of pretext is the subject of our next section.

What would be the outcome if a suspect voluntarily opened his door to somebody he believed was not the police? In *United States v. Gori*, 230 F.3d 44 (2d Cir. 2000), officers gained access to the defendant's apartment when he voluntarily opened the door for a food delivery person, whom the officers had accompanied. The court upheld the seizure and removal of the occupants after a "plain view" of them from the hallway, provided that there was reasonable suspicion of criminal activity. Judge Sotomayor disagreed with what she described as an "unprecedented step" undercutting the sanctity of the home. See also *Hadley v. Williams*, 368 F.3d 747 (7th Cir. 2004) (reasoning that since few people would refuse to open the door to the police, the effect of *Gori* would be to undermine the principle that a warrant is required for a home arrest. See *Payton v. New York*, 445 U.S. 573 (1980); §5.6 of Chapter 5, supra).

5. The officers are lawfully present on the premises, but they are conducting a search for large-screen televisions. The warrant itself would not authorize a search or seizure of other items. The sight of the wooden pipe does not broaden the range of the search because it is not immediately apparent as an item related to crime. The smell of marijuana, however, would probably provide the officers with authority to seize the pipe and its contents, as it is now immediately apparent as contraband. See *Minnesota v. Dickerson*, 508 U.S. 366 (1993) (expanding plain view to other senses, such as plain touch). It is interesting to note the prediction of one court: "Because of their common doctrinal base, the plain view and plain feel doctrines will in all likelihood come to be seen, probably within a decade, as nothing more than instances or variations of an omnibus Plain Sense Doctrine or Plain Perception Doctrine, which will embrace plain view and plain feel and, by a logically compelling growth process, plain hearing, plain smell, and plain taste." *State v. Jones*, 653 A.2d 1040, 1044 (Md. Ct. Spec. App. 1995).

Keep in mind that the senses of smell or hearing can also provide probable cause to search. See, e.g., *United States v. Vasquez-Castillo*, 258 F.3d 1207 (10th Cir. 2001) (inspector had probable cause to search secret compartment in truck driver's trailer where officer detected odor of raw marijuana upon entering trailer for safety inspection); *United States v. Staula*, 80 F.3d 596 (1st Cir. 1996) (warrantless search of truck was valid because smell of burned marijuana provided probable cause); *United States v. Arvizu*, 32 Fed. Appx. 873 (9th Cir. 2002) (border patrol agent had probable cause to search bags because smell of marijuana emanated from them); *United States v. Jackson*, 588 F.2d 1046 (5th Cir. 1979) (conversations overheard from adjoining motel room provided probable cause).

§6.9 THE PROBLEM OF PRETEXT

As we have seen, numerous exceptions to the requirement for a search warrant have been carved out in an effort to accommodate the interest of effective and efficient law enforcement. As with any set of rules, the potential for abuse exists. Suppose, for example, that narcotics squad detectives Spanking and Clean have a hunch that Dirty Dan is engaged in the distribution of crack cocaine. They would like to search his car but lack sufficient probable cause to do so. The enterprising detectives follow Dan as he drives through the city's streets, and as soon as he commits a traffic infraction (like going 32 mph in a 30 mph zone), they pull him over. Because they have authority to arrest for that offense (an authority rarely invoked, of course), Spanking and Clean take Dan into custody. They exercise their prerogative to subject Dan and the interior of his vehicle to a warrantless search incident to the arrest (see §6.3), and they find (as they hoped) crack cocaine. Or suppose the detectives follow Dan until he parks his car in a towaway zone, and as soon as he leaves it, they have it towed back to the station and searched pursuant to the routine inventory procedures for impounded automobiles (see § 4.5).

Although outwardly the conduct of the detectives in both cases is lawful and "by the book," does the fact that the police actually used the traffic or parking offense as a *pretext* to search for narcotics invalidate their action? *Whren v. United States*, 517 U.S. 806 (1996), says no. Defendants conceded that there was probable cause to stop their car for several traffic offenses, but sought to suppress the cocaine found as a result on the ground that the stop was pretextual. Given that the use of automobiles is so heavily and minutely regulated that total compliance with traffic and safety rules is nearly impossible, defendants argued that a police officer almost always will be able to catch a motorist in a technical violation. This, it was asserted, creates the irresistible temptation to use traffic stops as a means of investigating other offenses as to which no probable cause or even reasonable suspicion exists. (This becomes even more of a concern in light of *Atwater v. City of Lago Vista*, 532 U.S. 318 (2001), discussed in §6.3, permitting arrest and search incident even for a nonjailable offense.) To avoid this danger, defendants argued in *Whren* that the Fourth Amendment test for traffic stops should not be merely whether probable cause existed to justify the stop, but rather whether a police officer, acting reasonably, would have made the stop for the reason given. A unanimous Supreme Court rejected this proposition and held that ulterior motives do not invalidate police conduct that is otherwise justified on the basis of probable cause. The Court reaffirmed this position in *Arkansas v. Sullivan*, 532 U.S. 769 (2001). (It should be noted that the search of the interior of the car is now governed by *Arizona v. Gant*, discussed in §6.3, supra).

Whren did leave open the possibility that in the administrative or inventory search contexts, where probable cause is absent, a pretext inquiry might be appropriate, as had been suggested by previous decisions. *Florida v. Wells*, 495 U.S. 1 (1990), invalidated the opening of a locked suitcase during an inventory search of an automobile because there was no standardized policy regulating the opening of containers; the Court feared that such wide latitude would permit the police to use the inventory as a ruse to search for evidence. In contrast, *Colorado v. Bertine*, 479 U.S. 367 (1987), upheld a similar search where the police *did* follow standardized caretaking procedures (although allowing for some discretion regarding the disposition of inventoried vehicles) and there was no evidence that they acted in bad faith for the sole purpose of searching defendant's van for evidence.

In addressing an alternative argument made by defendants in *Whren*, that their car was stopped because they were black,[10] the Court indicated that this issue of selective enforcement must be addressed under the Equal Protection Clause, not the Fourth Amendment. But *United States v. Armstrong*, 517 U.S. 456 (1996), made clear how difficult it would be to establish a selective prosecution defense: The claimant must demonstrate that the prosecutorial policy *both* had a discriminatory effect (i.e., similarly situated individuals of a different race were not prosecuted) *and* was motivated by a discriminatory purpose.

Examples

1. The County Sheriff's Department was anxious to stem the transport of drugs into town from the airport. They decided to set up what appeared to be a drunk-driver checkpoint on the exit road from the airport. Jones was stopped at the checkpoint in his rented car and Lucy, a trained drug-detecting beagle, was brought over to sniff. Lucy's high-pitched bay indicated the presence of narcotics, and a search of the car confirmed her expert opinion. Jones was charged with possession of cocaine, and he sought to suppress the evidence before trial. At the hearing, defense counsel established that the checkpoint was staffed by narcotics detectives, not traffic officers, and that there was no Breathalyzer at the scene. Moreover, the checkpoint was funded from the department's drug interdiction budget. Conceding that the checkpoint met the outward requirements for a sobriety checkpoint (see §4.5), defense counsel nonetheless argues that the entire operation was pretextual, and the fruits of the search should be excluded from evidence. What result?

---

10. Much attention has been given recently to the problem of "racial profiling," the targeting of certain minorities and ethnic groups. A study of stops along the New Jersey Turnpike indicated that while only 13 percent of speeders were black, 35-45 percent of those stopped for speeding were black. Similarly, along Interstate 95 in Maryland, blacks represented only 17 percent of motorists but 73 percent of the persons stopped by police. See *USA Today*, June 3, 1999, p.14a. Several states have enacted laws authorizing the collection of such data. See *The Nation*, October 11, 1999, at 16.

2. The St. Petersburg police set up a drug interdiction operation in which they would stop cars that were in any way in violation of the motor vehicle code (such as an unilluminated license plate). Upon being stopped, the motorist would be approached by narcotics detectives, who would identify themselves and request consent to search the vehicle for narcotics. If the motorist refused, the vehicle would be detained while Austin (a trained drug-detecting terrier) was summoned to sniff the vehicle. His signal that drugs were present would result in a thorough search of the vehicle by the detectives. Is this operation constitutional?

Explanations

1. *Whren v. United States*, 517 U.S. 806 (1996), upheld a pretextual stop, reasoning that since it was based on probable cause, there was at least some assurance that police discretion was (and in similar cases would be) constrained. In our example, however, the stop was justified solely upon an administrative rationale, which turned out to be a ruse. *Whren; Florida v. Wells*, 495 U.S. 1 (1990); and *Colorado v. Bertine*, 479 U.S. 367 (1987), suggest that such pretextual administrative searches violate the Fourth Amendment. The Sixth Circuit reached that conclusion in *United States v. Huguenin*, 154 F.3d 547 (6th Cir. 1998). On the topic of drug interdiction programs, see also *City of Indianapolis v. Edmond*, 531 U.S. 32 (2001), discussed in § 4.5.

2. The fact that the police have probable cause to stop the cars for motor vehicle violations seems to satisfy *Whren v. United States*, 517 U.S. 806 (1996), notwithstanding the real purpose behind the stops. Moreover, there is no requirement that police inform drivers that they are free to refuse consent to search (see §6.7), thus rendering the searches of compliant motorists lawful. For those drivers who do refuse consent, the use of the terrier Austin to detect drugs would not be considered a search because no expectation of privacy would be violated. See *United States v. Place*, 462 U.S. 696 (1983) (discussed in §3.2). *Pennsylvania v. Mimms*, 434 U.S. 106 (1977), and *Maryland v. Wilson*, 519 U.S. 408 (1997) (discussed in §4.4), permit police to order the driver and passengers out of the vehicle pursuant to a lawful stop. It would appear, therefore, that the only possible constitutional problem with the procedure is if the cars of those drivers who refused consent are detained for an unreasonable period—that is, beyond the time necessary to perform a routine computer check on the vehicle (as discussed in §4.3). See *United States v. Holloman*, 113 F.3d 192 (11th Cir. 1997).

   Illinois v. Caballes, 543 U.S. 405 (2005) permits a dog sniff of the exterior of a car that has been legitimately stopped, provided that it does not prolong the stop.

CHAPTER 7

The Exclusionary Rule: Rationale, Operation, and Limitations

The centerpiece of the constitutional criminal procedure framework is the exclusionary rule. Virtually unique to American jurisprudence, the rule requires the suppression of evidence obtained in violation of the defendant's constitutional rights. This remedy has been applied not only to violations of the Fourth Amendment, but to evidence obtained in contravention of the Fifth, Sixth, and Fourteenth Amendments as well. In this chapter, we will explore the rationale of the exclusionary rule, its operation (including the fruit-of-the-poisonous-tree doctrine), and the limitations that have been placed upon it over the years.

§7.1 THE RATIONALE OF THE EXCLUSIONARY RULE

What purpose is served, one might ask, by keeping from the fact finder at trial evidence that is relevant to the question of the defendant's guilt, but that was obtained through unlawful means? And are the benefits gained by suppression sufficient to justify the cost, which in some cases is the freeing of a guilty party? These questions have generated a vigorous debate in the years since *Mapp v. Ohio* (see Chapter 1), which applied the exclusionary remedy to state (as well as federal) prosecutions. The following imaginary panel discussion provides a glimpse of the controversy.

Law Professor Moderator (*well prepared, erudite, and, of course, scrupulously neutral*): We are here today to discuss the relative merits of the exclusionary remedy, which was mandated for federal trials in 1914 [*Weeks v. United States*, 232 U.S. 383 (1914)] and imposed upon the states by *Mapp v. Ohio* in 1961. The *Mapp* Court told us that the exclusionary remedy was constitutionally required to ensure police compliance with the commands of the Fourth Amendment. The theory was that unlawful searches and seizures would be discouraged (if not eliminated) when the law enforcement community realized they could not use the evidence so obtained when the case went to court. In addition to deterrence, the Court suggested that the "imperative of judicial integrity" required that courts not soil their hands with tainted evidence. Let's start then with the stated purposes for the remedy. Was *Mapp* correct in its assessment that the exclusionary rule would deter police from acting unlawfully?

Police Chief (*tough, streetwise, and not a big fan of lawyers*): The Supreme Court, with all due respect, was all wet. Take a typical case. Two officers on the beat in a large city see a guy they know in their gut is dirty (that is, in possession of drugs). They approach him and shake him down, and sure enough, there's the crack cocaine. Now because there was no probable cause or reasonable suspicion, the search and arrest are technically unlawful, which means that as this guy's case winds slowly through the system, at some point some judge may order the coke excluded and throw the charges out. Maybe that happens months later at trial, or maybe it happens years later on appeal after trial and conviction, or maybe if the guy pleads or his lawyer misses the issue, it never happens. The point is, the cop on the street isn't thinking ahead to the risk of suppression. It's not in their mind. He or she just sees somebody who needs to be shaken down and taken off the street.

Prosecutor (*committed public servant, models herself on Jimmy Stewart in Mr. Smith Goes to Washington*): I'd have to agree with the Chief that the *Mapp* remedy doesn't work to deter violations, but I think it could work under the right circumstances. The problem is really an institutional one. Take the example used by the Chief. Who suffers when the cocaine is excluded from evidence? Obviously the public, since a bad guy is back on the street. But among the actors in the criminal justice system, it's the prosecutor—not the offending police officer—who is most directly hurt by the suppression. Winning convictions is the coin of the realm for us, and here's a case that's lost before trial even begins. We might grumble something to the officers about how they screwed up, but we have no real power over them, and certainly no way to punish them. Police departments and district attorneys' offices are on the same side of the fight, but they're not the same institution (just watch *Law and Order* on TV!). Unless and until the departments police themselves by disciplining their own officers for violating the rights of citizens, the deterrence function of the exclusionary rule will never be realized because the cop on the street just isn't hit where it hurts—job security and promotion.

That having been said, let me add a couple of my own gripes about *Mapp*. First, there's no language in the Fourth Amendment about excluding evidence. The suppression rule was devised by judges, and if it isn't working or the costs of its operation are too high, it can and should be erased by judges. So even though I personally wouldn't want to prosecute a case with tainted evidence, the drafters of the Bill of Rights didn't tell me that I can't. The *Mapp* Court overstepped its authority, big time, when it tried to micromanage the prosecution of crime.

Second, there is no proportionality to the *Mapp* sanction. Whether the police commit an egregious violation or a minor indiscretion, whether we're dealing with a terrorist or a shoplifter, the remedy is always the same—the evidence is thrown out. Oh, and by the way, experienced police can always get around suppression anyway by "testilying"—don't you think they know what they have to say to make a search stick? I don't think we should be encouraging police perjury.

Public Defender (*overworked, underpaid, unappreciated, but wouldn't switch places with anyone*): I couldn't agree more with my worthy opponent about the need for internal enforcement of constitutional standards in our police departments, but that ain't about to happen. The exclusionary rule is all that stands between the citizen and the overzealous cop. The Supreme Court adopted the sanction only after it correctly (and unavoidably) concluded that all other remedies had failed miserably, and after many of the states had already imposed their own rules of exclusion in utter frustration at police lawlessness. We all know that both criminal and civil actions against the police for constitutional violations are doomed to failure in front of jurors more concerned about crime and violence than police misconduct. The police are their protectors, and the jury isn't about to convict or award damages against the cops for just "doing their job."

So we're really left with the exclusionary remedy as the only real method of discouraging, if not completely deterring, violations of the Constitution. We all hope that, over time, enforcement of the suppression remedy will produce police departments committed to compliance with the Fourth Amendment, and maybe then we can think about abandoning it. Let's remember that before *Mapp*, scant attention was paid to the requirements of the Fourth Amendment. Now, at least, all police departments provide their officers with training about probable cause, the permissible bounds of a "stop and frisk" or a search incident to an arrest, and all the rest. This is no time to retreat to the days before 1961, when freedom from unreasonable search and seizure was an unfulfilled promise. And just because the *Mapp* rule isn't operating perfectly doesn't mean that we should scrap it.

Average Urban Citizen (*impatient with lawyer jargon and convinced that violent crime is out of control*): You're never going to convince me that it makes any sense at all to let criminals off just because the police made a mistake. The cops finally get the goods on some dirtbag, and the courts throw out the evidence because they didn't dot the *i*'s and cross the *t*'s. I'd do some "testilying" myself if I were in their position. No wonder nobody respects the system anymore! Talk about judicial integrity! Letting murderers and rapists off on technicalities is making us the laughingstock of the world. And of course, the judges and lawyers go home to the 'burbs at 5 P.M., leaving the rest of us to deal with the lowlifes they set free that day.

Public Defender: I think you're missing the essential point of the *Mapp* rule. It's not because we want to do the criminals a favor that we let them off. (And, by the way, it's really only a small percentage of defendants who are actually released as a result of suppression. There's usually other evidence and witnesses available, and so it's mostly just in simple narcotics possession cases where suppression means dismissal.) The premise of *Mapp*, and I firmly believe it, is that the exclusionary rule is protecting all of us, innocent as well as guilty. What makes a police officer pause before searching me or you on some wild hunch, or because he just doesn't like your face or nose ring or attitude? It's the knowledge that if something is found, it can't be used at trial. Now you might say that the innocent don't need protecting because the officer won't find anything anyway. But we all cherish our little bit of privacy in this country. We don't want law enforcement personnel stopping and searching us willy-nilly, on the street or in our cars. The only way to prevent that is to take away the goodies when the police *do* find them. Unfortunately, that means letting criminals walk sometimes. Keep in mind that tossing the evidence is an entirely avoidable result—if the officers had simply followed the Fourth Amendment in the first place, we wouldn't be talking about the exclusionary rule, would we?

Moderator: I should point out that the *Mapp* rule has been significantly modified since its inception, and those modifications have really curtailed its scope. For example, the exclusionary sanction can be enforced only by someone with standing to raise it, which has come to mean that the victim must have had a close connection to the place searched in order to challenge the police action.[1] A so-called "good faith" exception has been carved out, which avoids the exclusionary sanction in situations where the police act in reasonable reliance on a warrant issued by a magistrate, even if it turns out that the warrant wasn't valid.[2] And the remedy has been limited to criminal trials and direct appeals; it's not

1. See §7.3.1.
2. See §7.3.3.

available in habeas proceedings, at the grand jury, or in civil actions.[3] In other words, the Supreme Court has not been unmindful of the need to adjust the rule constantly to accommodate the interests of law enforcement and public safety.

Police Chief: Unfortunately Rome is burning while the Justices are tinkering, Professor. It's time to get rid of *Mapp*, and I think the Court will do just that. It's just a matter of time.

Moderator: Well, I'll leave prediction to those of you with the tea leaves, but the Court is certainly moving in that direction. Anyway, the debate over the suppression sanction won't be resolved here today. The problem is, as always, balancing the public interest in prosecuting crime against the equally important public interest in maintaining a free society that respects individual rights. We've run out of time, so I'll thank you all for your insights.

As we discuss the operation of the exclusionary rule and the limitations that have been placed upon it, do not lose sight of the sharp policy debate that underlies the controversy concerning the rule. Be assured that the Supreme Court never does.

§7.2 THE DERIVATIVE EVIDENCE (FRUIT-OF-THE-POISONOUS-TREE) DOCTRINE

The exclusionary remedy applies not only to evidence obtained as a direct result of a constitutional violation, but also to evidence indirectly derived from the violation. In a manner not unlike "but-for" causation in tort law, courts trace the chain of events from the initial violation to both its primary and secondary products. If police conduct an unlawful search of Jones, the ledger book that they seize from him indicating his involvement in narcotics transactions is rendered inadmissible against Jones at trial. Beyond that, evidence that is derived from the book is tainted as "fruit of the poisonous tree" and also subject to suppression. If, therefore, the police use the information found in the ledger to obtain warrants to search the homes of the buyers listed, evidence obtained from those searches is not admissible against Jones (discussion of the critical issue of who has standing to raise the illegality follows in § 7.3).

Like the doctrine of proximate cause in tort, there are limits on how far courts will trace the chain of a Fourth Amendment illegality. As we shall see, if the taint becomes too attenuated, or there is an independent source

---

3. See §7.3.2.

for the evidence, or the evidence would have been inevitably discovered anyway, exclusion does not follow.

The genesis of the derivative evidence doctrine is *Wong Sun v. United States*, 371 U.S. 471 (1963). James Toy was arrested on suspicion of narcotics trafficking, and he made a statement to police implicating Johnny Yee. The police then proceeded to arrest and search Yee. After they discovered narcotics in his bedroom, Yee made a statement implicating Wong Sun. Wong Sun was then arrested, released on his own recognizance, and several days later made a statement concerning the narcotics transactions. The arrest of Toy was held unlawful because it was not based on probable cause. The question before the Court was how far the taint of that illegality should travel down the road of subsequent events. Were the statements and evidence obtained from Yee and Wong Sun inadmissible against Toy because they could all be traced back to his unlawful arrest?

To make this determination, the Court adopted the following analysis: Where the secondary evidence was discovered by exploitation of the initial illegality, it must be suppressed; however, where it is obtained by means sufficiently removed from the initial illegality, it is admissible. The statement made by Toy was excluded from evidence because it was the direct product of his unlawful arrest, having occurred immediately thereafter. The statement of Yee, as well as the narcotics found in his home, were also suppressed because the federal agents got to them solely and directly by using the information illegally obtained from Toy. Wong Sun's statement, however, was admissible against Toy because, although it was the "fruit of the poisonous tree," its connection to the initial illegality was attenuated—Wong Sun had been released on his own recognizance and had voluntarily returned days later to make the statement. The taint of Toy's unlawful arrest had dissipated, the Court concluded, with the passage of time and the intervention of Wong Sun's own free will.

The Court elaborated on the concept of attenuation in *United States v. Ceccolini*, 435 U.S. 268 (1978). An unlawful discovery of betting slips in an envelope on a flower shop cash register led police months later to a witness, who testified against the shop owner at his trial. The issue before the Court was whether that testimony should be suppressed as the fruit of the poisonous tree. The Court held that a live witness willing to testify requires "a closer, more direct link between the illegality and that kind of testimony" in order to justify suppression than is required for physical evidence. The rationale for the distinction is that the witness's exercise of free will in deciding to testify is a significant intervening act that breaks the chain of causation from the initial illegality. The Court also rejected any application of the derivative evidence doctrine that would "permanently disable" a cooperative witness from testifying. "Witnesses are not like guns or documents which remain hidden from view until one turns over a sofa or opens a filing cabinet. Witnesses can, and often do, come forward and offer evidence entirely of their own volition. And, evaluated properly, the degree of free will necessary to dissipate the taint will very likely be found more often in the case of live-witness testimony than other kinds of evidence." 435 U.S. at 276-277.

Mindful of the deterrence rationale underlying the exclusionary rule, as well as the societal costs of banning relevant evidence from the trial, courts weigh a number of factors in assessing whether the poison of a constitutional violation has been purged:

1) **The time period between the illegality and the acquisition of the secondary evidence**—The longer the period, the more likely that attenuation will be found. In *Ceccolini*, where four months elapsed between the initial illegality and the interview of the live witness, the Court concluded that the taint had dissipated.

2) **The occurrence of intervening events**—The more links in the chain between the illegality and the secondary evidence, the more attenuated the connection. Events representing an individual's free choice, such as Wong Sun's decision to make a statement or a suspect's consent to a search, are likely to be viewed as breaking the connection. Similarly, the giving of *Miranda* warnings is viewed as an intervening event in the analysis.

3) **The flagrancy of the initial illegality**—The more deliberate and flagrant the constitutional violation, the more reason there is to suppress all evidence that can be traced back to the illegality. Conversely, where the violation is unintentional and minor, the necessity for deterrence of future misconduct is less compelling. In *Ceccolini*, where the offending officer inadvertently (albeit illegally) discovered evidence of gambling while conversing with a friend in the flower shop, the Court observed: "[There is] not the slightest evidence to suggest that [Officer] Biro entered the shop or picked up the envelope with the intent of finding tangible evidence bearing on an illicit gambling operation. Application of the exclusionary rule in this situation could not have the slightest deterrent effect on the behavior of an officer such as Biro." 435 U.S. at 279-280.

Thus as the Fourth Circuit has put it, "a direct, unbroken chain of causation is necessary, but not sufficient to render derivative evidence inadmissible." *United States v. Najjar*, 300 F.3d 466, 477 (4th Cir. 2002).

Hudson v. Michigan, 547 U.S. 586 (2006), involving the "knock-and-announce rule" (see §5.3 in Chapter 5), added a new wrinkle to the analysis. Attenuation can occur not only when the causal connection is remote, but also when suppression would not serve the interest protected by the constitutional guarantee violated. Because the seizure of evidence has nothing to do with the concerns underlying the knock-and-announce rule (primarily the protection of human life because unannounced entry may provoke violence), the exclusionary sanction would not be applied. As discussed in Chapter 1, *Hudson v. Michigan* (especially its "substantial social costs" argument) puts the future of the exclusionary remedy itself in doubt.

Utah v. Strieff, 136 S. Ct. 2056 (2016), further expanded the attenuation loophole. An opinion by Justice Thomas validated a search incident to an arrest, even though it was preceded by an unlawful stop (without reasonable suspicion), on the grounds that the officer learned during the stop of a valid arrest warrant for Strieff. The majority concluded the original illegality was attenuated because the police misconduct was at most negligent, not flagrant, and not part of a systematic or recurrent policy.

In addition to the concept of *attenuation*, there are two other important limitations on the operation of the derivative evidence doctrine. If the prosecution can establish that the secondary evidence was obtained from an *independent source*, and not solely by exploiting the original illegality, the evidence will not be suppressed. In this situation, it can be said that the fruit does not derive from the poisonous tree. If police learn of the whereabouts of narcotics from the ledger book unlawfully seized from Jones, but they can demonstrate that they also had independent knowledge of these locations from an informant, suppression of the narcotics is not required.

Murray v. United States, 487 U.S. 533 (1988), illustrates this point. Police illegally entered a warehouse without a warrant and observed bales that they believed to be marijuana. Without disturbing the bales, they left and sought a warrant to search. In their affidavit in support of the warrant, the police relied solely on information they would later contend they had prior to the illegal entry (and, indeed, the officers neglected to mention the previous foray in their affidavit). The warrant was issued and executed, and the bales were "rediscovered." The Court ruled that the evidence would be admissible at trial if the warrant affidavit was in fact based on sources independent of the illegal entry (to be determined on remand). The Court set aside the concerns expressed by Justice Marshall in his dissent that this approach would encourage police to circumvent the warrant process and, further, that the independent source exception is too vulnerable to manipulation by police because they alone know what information was secured independently and what was discovered through the illegality.

Another limitation on the reach of the derivative evidence doctrine is the *inevitable discovery* exception. Even if the evidence in question is found to have been the fruit of the poisonous tree—evidence that can be traced directly back to the initial illegality and for which there is no independent source—suppression can nonetheless be avoided if the prosecution establishes that the evidence would have ultimately been discovered anyway by lawful means.

In Nix v. Williams, 467 U.S. 431 (1984), the initial illegality was the violation of the suspect's Sixth Amendment rights—the officers deliberately elicited an incriminating statement from him in the absence of his counsel. See §10.1 in Chapter 10. The detective's "Christian burial speech" prompted Williams to divulge information that led to the homicide victim's body. Evidence concerning the body was later introduced at trial, and Williams was convicted. Despite the straight line of causation from the constitutional violation to the secondary evidence, the Court held the evidence admissible because the body would have been discovered shortly anyway by a search party of volunteers operating in the area. Casting aside objections that "inevitable discovery" will often be a matter of speculation, the Court indicated that there must be a basis in fact, readily verifiable, for the conclusion that discovery would have occurred. The search party provided that basis in Nix. Had the search not been suspended when the body was found, it would have been discovered "within a short period of time" in the same condition (the freezing temperature would have prevented tissue deterioration). It must be emphasized that in order to fit within this exception, it is not sufficient to show the evidence *could have* been discovered—the government must demonstrate that the evidence *would have* inevitably been discovered even absent the illegality.

These limitations on the derivative evidence doctrine reflect continuing concern about the costs of the exclusionary rule. The deterrence rationale does not, it is argued, require suppression of evidence that police obtained, or would have obtained, without the unlawful action. Such "overkill" would unfairly deprive the prosecution of probative evidence without achieving the corresponding benefit of educating the police. Offending law enforcement officers should not be placed in a *better* position as a result of an illegality (and must therefore be deprived of the fruits of their violation); but they should not be deprived of evidence that they actually secured through an independent source, or would have inevitably secured, notwithstanding the illegality. So says Nix v. Williams, supra.

In sum, the suppression remedy is triggered only where 1) the connection between the secondary evidence and the original violation is close and unattenuated, and 2) there is no independent lawful means that led, or would have led, police to the evidence.

Figure 7-1 illustrates the operation of the derivative evidence doctrine.

Examples

1. Which of the following situations justify suppression under the derivative evidence doctrine? How should each be analyzed?
   a. Police make a warrantless entry into *A*'s apartment and place her under arrest. Days after being taken into custody (and after receiving *Miranda* warnings), A volunteers an incriminating statement, which the prosecution proposes to use at trial.

203

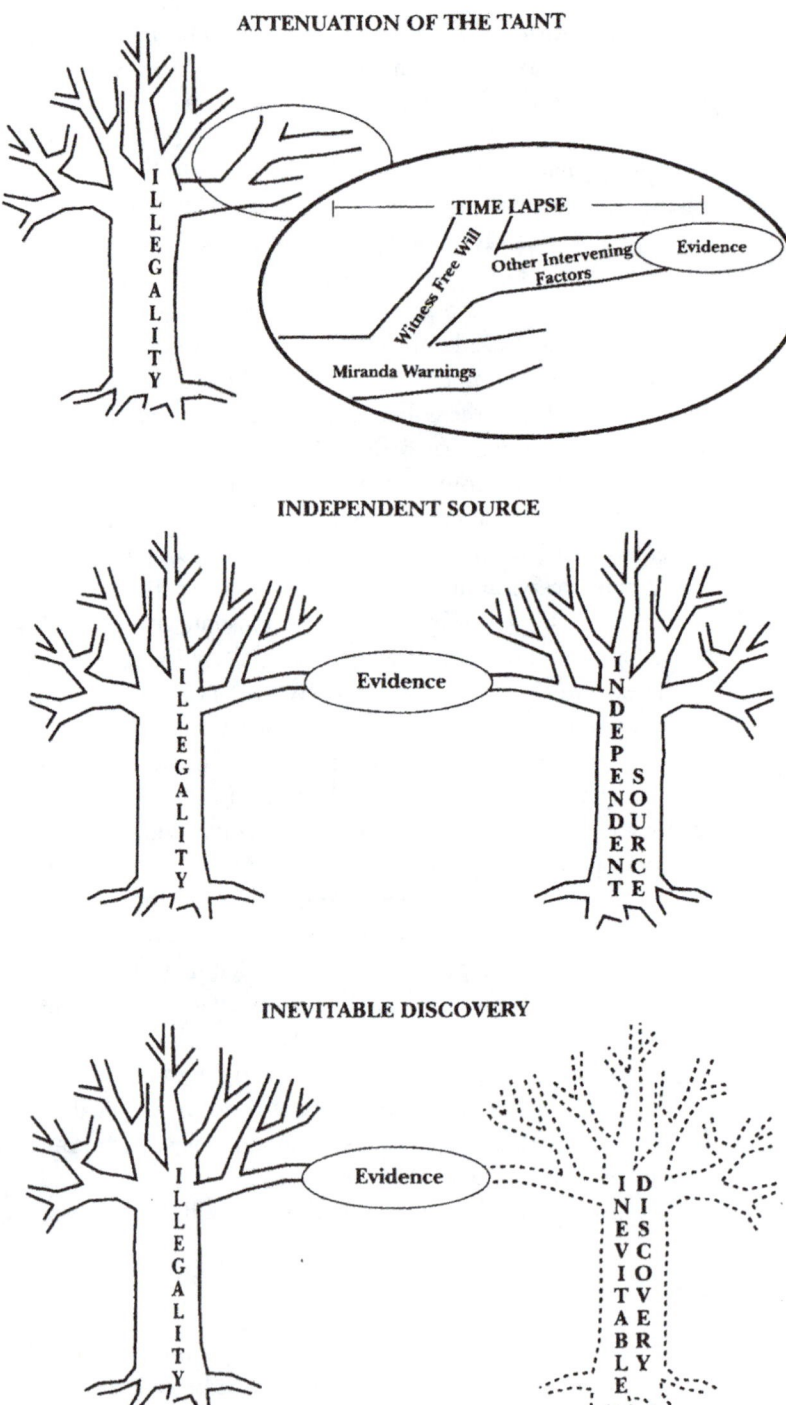

Figure 7-1. Derivative Evidence Doctrine—Exceptions.

    b. Police make a warrantless entry into B's apartment and seize a diamond tiara, which they suspect has been stolen. They take the tiara to a jewelry store that had previously reported a theft, and the proprietor recognizes it as the one taken from his establishment. The proprietor also selects B's photograph from an array that the police show him and is prepared to identify B in court as the person he had observed suspiciously casing his store the day before the burglary.

    c. Police lawfully arrest C, and then coerce a confession from her that she has been operating an illegal gambling business from her pharmacy. The officers rely on her confession in their affidavit in support of a warrant to search C's store. The warrant is issued, the search conducted, and evidence of gambling operations is seized.

    d. Police forcibly (and without a warrant or probable cause) enter D's RV trailer, which is parked unoccupied in her driveway. They conduct an intensive search and, in a hidden compartment behind a cabinet, locate dozens of packets containing heroin. Days later, police apprehend D and, when confronted with the narcotics by her interrogators, she confesses to possession with intent to distribute.

    e. Police illegally stop Jones on the street, lacking reasonable suspicion. After running his ID through the data base, they learn there is an outstanding arrest warrant for traffic violations, at which point they place him under arrest and find incriminating evidence during the search incident.

2. Based on a tip from a neighborhood resident, Los Angeles police officer Rodriguez suspected that a blue van parked at the same downtown location each evening after midnight was involved in the smuggling of illegal aliens. Rodriguez and his partner approached the van and ordered the occupants out. He then looked inside and observed several sheets of paper hanging from the sun visor. Reaching in, the officer removed the papers and noted that they contained a long list of names and numbers. Rodriguez asked the van's occupants what the numbers next to the names meant, and one of the men (later identified as Juan Colon) responded that he had just been transported into the United States from Mexico and the number next to his name represented the amount of money he had paid the driver. The officers then placed the driver, Hector Ortiz, under arrest for illegal transportation of aliens. The prosecution proposes to use Colon's statement made at the scene of the arrest, as well as his live testimony against Ortiz at trial. Will this evidence be admissible?

3. Working undercover, narcotics squad detective Roland Rambo purchased a large quantity of crack cocaine from Lance Spear at his home on Elm Street. The detective reported this information to his supervisor,

Sergeant Marsha Brady, who immediately proceeded to the courthouse to seek warrants to arrest Spear and to search his home. In the meantime, Rambo and several of his colleagues returned to Spear's home, where they were to wait for Brady and the warrants. When the sergeant failed to appear after one hour, the officers got impatient and decided to act on their own. With guns drawn, they knocked on Spear's door and told him he had no choice but to let them in. Spear relented, and the officers entered. They discovered a large cache of cocaine and weapons in plain view in the hallway.

At that point, Sergeant Brady finally appeared with the arrest and search warrants. She arrested Spear, searched the home, and "rediscovered" the items previously found by Rambo. Spear has moved to suppress the evidence on the grounds that it was the fruit of a coerced consent and illegal entry. What result?

4. State police officers, armed with a valid warrant to arrest Peter Swope for the crime of defrauding the state welfare agency of $10,000, stopped Swope in his car on the throughway. He was taken into custody, and his automobile was locked and left on the shoulder of the road. Later that day, the troopers returned and searched Swope's car. They located a plastic trash bag on the passenger seat, which they brought back to the station and opened to find a large quantity of marijuana. Although the welfare fraud charges have been dropped, the prosecution intends to use the marijuana against Swope at his upcoming trial for possession with intent to distribute an unlawful substance. Swope's counsel has filed a motion to suppress and has persuaded the court that because there was no probable cause to believe that seizable items were present in the car, the search was unlawful. Is there any way the prosecution can nonetheless avoid suppression of the marijuana? What if state police regulations require that vehicles of persons taken into custody on the open road be impounded and subjected to an inventory inspection?

5. Wilma is driving a rental car accompanied by her husband, Fred. The car is lawfully stopped for speeding. On request, the officer is shown the rental agreement, which is in Wilma's name, as well as her license. The officer issues Wilma a warning, but when she appears unusually nervous, he asks if she has any narcotics in the car. She says no, but upon the officer's request, she gives him the keys to the trunk, which he opens to find a garment bag that has a tag labeled "Fred" on it. The officer feels the bag, removes a large manila envelope, and asks Fred if he can open it. Although Fred hesitates, the officer threatens to get a drug-sniffing dog, and Fred finally relents (muttering that he doesn't really have a choice) to the opening of the envelope, which contains cocaine. What are the chances of suppression at trial?

Explanations

1. The point here is that the derivative evidence doctrine is potentially applicable in any situation where there has been an initial illegality followed by a chain of events leading to incriminating evidence. The illegality can take the form of a violation of any of the constitutional commands discussed throughout this book—the Fourth, Fifth, or Sixth Amendment.[4] It may be an unlawful search or arrest, a coerced confession, or the deliberate elicitation of incriminating statements in the absence of counsel. The secondary evidence can take the form of physical evidence, a confession, testimony of a live witness, or an eyewitness identification.

   For any illegality identified in a given fact situation, the analytical task is to trace its ripple effects. With regard to each item of evidence that is causally connected to the illegality, it must be determined 1) whether the chain has become too long or otherwise attenuated so that it can be said that the taint has dissipated, 2) whether the police secured the evidence through an independent source, and 3) whether the police would have secured the evidence inevitably through another means. If the answer to each of these questions is no, then the derivative evidence doctrine applies, and the evidence will be suppressed as the fruit of the poisonous tree. (An additional inquiry must often be made into the question of who has standing to raise the issue of illegality. See §7.3.1.)

   In each of the fact situations presented in example 1, there are indirect products that flow from the unlawful police action. In example 1a, the suspect's confession can be traced back to the unlawful entry and arrest. Thus even if the confession was voluntary and not subject to challenge on due process grounds (see Chapter 8), it appears to be the fruit of a Fourth Amendment violation. Certain factors, however, point toward a conclusion that the connection is too attenuated to support application of the exclusionary rule. First, several days passed between the arrest and the confession. Therefore, it could be said that the original taint has dissipated. What this means in reference to the deterrence goal of the exclusionary rule is that the offending officers are less likely to be "educated" by suppression of a confession remote in time from the unlawful arrest. Compare *Brown v. Illinois*, 422 U.S. 590 (1975) (suppressing confession that occurred within two hours of defendant's unlawful arrest). Second, A volunteered the confession, and this free choice on her part may break the chain of causation. See *Wong Sun*, supra. A third factor to be weighed is the flagrancy of the initial violation: Did the police merely misjudge a situation that they reasonably believed was an emergency that justified

---

4. Violations of the *Miranda* requirements are treated somewhat differently, and the fruits of such violations are not subject to suppression under the same standards as fruits of an illegal search or coerced confession. See §9.3.3 in Chapter 9.

immediate entry into A's apartment, or did they deliberately disregard the commands of the Fourth Amendment?

Finally, where (as in example 1a) the secondary evidence is a confession, we consider whether the suspect received proper *Miranda* warnings prior to the statement. *Brown v. Illinois*, supra, rejected the conclusion that such warnings are *per se* sufficient to purge the taint of a prior illegal arrest:

> If *Miranda* warnings, by themselves, were held to attenuate the taint of an unconstitutional arrest, regardless of how wanton and purposeful the Fourth Amendment violation, the effect of the exclusionary rule would be substantially diluted. Illegal arrests would be encouraged by the knowledge that evidence derived there from could well be made admissible at trial by the simple expedient of giving *Miranda* warnings. Any incentive to avoid Fourth Amendment violations would be eviscerated by making the warnings, in effect, a "cure-all."

422 U.S. at 602. Nonetheless, provision of *Miranda* warnings to A is a factor weighing against application of the derivative evidence doctrine.

In *New York v. Harris*, 495 U.S. 14 (1990), dealing with a confession following an unlawful arrest, the Court emphasized the need to weigh the costs of exclusion against the deterrent purpose served. Police, armed with probable cause but without an arrest warrant (as required by *Payton v. New York*; see §5.6 in Chapter 5), arrested the suspect in his home. Harris made incriminating statements, both at home and later at the station house. The Court refused to apply the derivative evidence doctrine to the station house statement, reasoning that the purpose of the *Payton* warrant requirement, protection of the privacy of the home, was fully accomplished by suppressing the statement made in the home. "Because the officers had probable cause to arrest Harris for a crime, Harris was not unlawfully in custody when he was removed to the station house, given *Miranda* warnings and allowed to talk." 495 U.S. at 18. The Court distinguished *Brown v. Illinois*, supra, where the police lacked probable cause to arrest, and thus suppression of all subsequent confessions was deemed justified.

Turning to example 1b, the unlawful search yielded the tiara, which would be excluded as the direct product of the illegality. The officers further exploited that illegality to obtain an identification of B from the proprietor. Thus, even if the identification process was not unnecessarily suggestive and violative of the suspect's rights (see §11.1 in Chapter 11), it could be challenged as evidence derived from the initial unlawful search. Because the selection of B's photograph followed closely in time from the seizure of the tiara, which was used by the police to obtain the identification from the proprietor, that identification may very well be suppressed as fruit of the poisonous tree. The proposed in-court identification, however, may be admissible because it is much further removed in time from the initial illegality and may have been based on an independent source—the proprietor's observation of the person casing the store prior to the burglary. See *United States v. Crews*, 445 U.S. 463 (1980) (in-court identification admissible despite the fact that prior photographic and lineup identifications were suppressed because of their closer proximity to defendant's unlawful arrest).

It should be remembered that whenever the derivative evidence in question is the testimony of a live witness, as in example 1b, suppression requires a closer link to the initial illegality than is the case with physical evidence. See *United States v. Ceccolini*, 435 U.S. 268 (1978).

In example 1c, the initial illegality is coercion of the confession, which must be excluded from evidence. See Chapter 8. Because information from that tainted confession was used to secure the search warrant, the items seized during the search are subject to suppression under the derivative evidence doctrine. Even if the search and seizure met constitutional standards, they may be poisoned because of their genesis in the violation of the suspect's right against compelled self-incrimination. The deterrence rationale supports exclusion here—unless the police are deprived of *all* fruits of a coercive interrogation, they will not be sufficiently discouraged from conducting another in the future. The items seized in C's store, therefore, should be excluded from evidence. See *Commonwealth v. White*, 374 Mass. 132, 371 N.E.2d 777 (1977), *aff'd by an equally divided court*, 439 U.S. 280 (1978) (suppressed evidence seized pursuant to search warrant because affidavit in support of warrant was based on information obtained during unlawful interrogation of defendant). See also *United States v. Woerner*, 709 F.3d 527 (5th Cir. 2013) (defendant's unlawfully obtained custodial statements should not have been used to secure a warrant; but the good faith exception applied to prevent suppression).

In example 1d, the police clearly exploited the illegal search by confronting D with the evidence seized, and thereby obtained her confession. Thus, even though the confession may have been secured without coercion, it is subject to suppression under the derivative evidence doctrine. This close connection between the illegality and the confession argues in favor of suppression: In order to deter future unlawful searches, the police must be deprived of all the evidence that they gained from it, directly and indirectly. Arguing against suppression is the fact that several days separate the search from the confession, and that D's confession may be an intervening act of free will. The provision of *Miranda* warnings (if they had been given) would also weigh against exclusion of the confession.

In example 1e, based on *Utah v. Strieff*, 136 S. Ct. 2056 (2016), the initial taint of the illegal stop would be attenuated as long as there was no indication the stop was part of a systemic pattern of abuse.

2. While the officers might have had reasonable suspicion to stop and briefly detain the occupants of the vehicle (see §4.4 in Chapter 4), their intrusion into the vehicle required either 1) reasonable fear for their safety (see §4.4); or 2) probable cause either to arrest and conduct a search incident to that arrest (see §6.3 in Chapter 6), or to search the vehicle (see §6.4). All such justification would seem to be lacking here. The intrusion into the van and removal of the papers thus becomes the initial illegality, the ripples of which can clearly be traced to the statement made by Colon implicating the defendant. Given the short time frame between the search and the on-the-scene statement, as well as the actual use of the unlawfully seized list to obtain the statement, it is unlikely that a court would find that the taint had become attenuated, and the statement would be inadmissible.

On the separate question of the admissibility of subsequent in-court testimony from Colon, there is obviously a looser temporal connection. Moreover, as *Ceccolini* teaches, live testimony is less likely than physical evidence to be suppressed as the fruit of the poisonous tree. In our example, however, the witness was questioned immediately following the illegal search, the officer's question was prompted by the very fruits of the search, and the witness himself was discovered only as a result of the search. This contrasts sharply with the situation in *Ceccolini*, where the officer's unlawful discovery of the betting slips was far removed from the questioning of the witness months later, the slips were not used during the questioning, and the witness was known to the investigators before the illegal search occurred. Further, unlike *Ceccolini*, it is unlikely that Colon would have come forward as a witness on his own initiative to inform police of his illegal alien status; he spoke in the pressure of the moment as the officer read the papers removed from the van. Compare *Satchell v. Cardwell*, 653 F.2d 408, 409 n.7 (9th Cir. 1981) (court concluded that a brutally beaten rape victim would probably have come forward to testify even if she had not been discovered as a result of an unlawful entry, and thus her testimony was admissible); *Jefferson v. Fountain*, 382 F.3d 1286 (11th Cir. 2004) ("There is not simply a probability, but a virtual certainty, that if the officers had not stopped Jefferson that night, they inevitably would have discovered all the evidence that resulted from that stop. The efforts to locate Jefferson so that, among other things, [the victim] could hear him speak, were already underway and inevitably would have resulted in [her] identifying his voice as that of the rapist. Subtract the stop from the factual picture in this case and the most that would have changed is the timing of [her] identification of Jefferson; it would have been delayed, which would have changed nothing of substance. Under these circumstances the inevitable discovery exception to the exclusionary rule applies, and any suppression motion should have been denied.").

There was no likelihood in our example that the witness would have been inevitably discovered without the occurrence of the unlawful search. The in-court testimony would probably be suppressed under the derivative evidence doctrine. See *United States v. Ramirez-Sandoval*, 872 F.2d 1392 (9th Cir. 1989) (suppressing both the on-the-scene statement and live testimony under similar circumstances). See also *United States v. Vasques De Reyes*, 149 F.3d 192 (3d Cir. 1998) (alien's putative husband's statement and alien's confession, acquired as result of an illegal stop, were not admissible under inevitable discovery exception, where it was speculative whether INS or police procedures would have led to discovery of the sham marriage).

3. Rambo and his colleagues discovered the contraband as a direct result of their forced unlawful entry into Spear's residence, thus rendering the evidence presumptively inadmissible. The prosecution might avoid suppression, however, through the independent source exception. Sergeant Brady, without knowledge of Rambo's actions, secured the warrants with information separate from and untainted by Rambo's entry, and she seized the evidence pursuant to those valid warrants. As *Murray v. United States*, 487 U.S. 533 (1988) teaches, evidence that is initially discovered through unlawful means, but is later acquired through genuinely independent and lawful means, may be admissible in evidence. On facts similar to our example, the Fourth Circuit so concluded:

> The warrant authorizing a search of Curtis' residence was issued solely upon information known to the officers before the illegal entry. And the record clearly demonstrates that a search warrant would have been sought regardless of the entry because detective McCracken had already departed to obtain a warrant prior to the entry and had no knowledge of the actions of the other officers. Thus, the search pursuant to the warrant was independent of the entry, and the district court did not err in refusing to suppress the evidence seized pursuant to it.

United States v. Curtis, 931 F.2d 1011, 1014 (4th Cir. 1991). See also *United States v. Najjar*, 300 F.3d 466, 479 (4th Cir. 2002) ("Even if the original illegal search in some slight way was a but-for cause of the later searches, [officer's] two-year investigation and the intervening circumstances were sufficient to break the causal link between any primary illegality and later obtained evidence."); *United States v. Runyan*, 290 F.3d 223 (5th Cir. 2002) (searches conducted pursuant to warrant were an independent source of evidence initially obtained in illegal search of computer disks); *United States v. Souza*, 223 F.3d 1197 (10th Cir. 2000) (high probability that the evidence would have been discovered pursuant to a search warrant that officers were seeking); *United States v. Pena*, 924 F. Supp. 1239, 1257 (D. Mass. 1996) ("Despite the fact that the wrapper and cocaine were discovered during the initial illegal searches, they were 'rediscovered' during the lawful search pursuant to the warrant.").

United States v. Markling, 7 F.3d 1309 (7th Cir. 1993) involved a variation on the situation in this example. Information found as a result of an unlawful search of the defendant's briefcase was included in an affidavit to obtain a warrant to search the defendant's hotel room. Unlike *Murray*, the warrant application in *Markling* was partially based on what was seen during the illegal search. The Seventh Circuit, however, found that the independent source doctrine still applied, and the warrant was valid. The test that the court used involved two questions: 1) Did the illegally obtained evidence affect the magistrate's decision? 2) Was the officer's decision to seek a warrant prompted by the illegal search? With regard to the first question, the court found that the application, minus the illegally obtained evidence, still showed sufficient probable cause of illegal activity. With regard to the second question, the court remanded to determine whether the officer would have sought a warrant even if he had not conducted the illegal search.

4. Even if the search of Swope's car was unlawful because it was not contemporaneous with the arrest and there was no probable cause to search, so that the fruits of the illegality are presumptively inadmissible, the prosecution may use the evidence nonetheless if it can demonstrate that the police would have inevitably discovered it anyway in the normal course of their work. See *Nix v. Williams*, 467 U.S. 431 (1984). Because Swope was arrested, his automobile was subject to impoundment and inventory under police regulations. So long as such procedures are not a pretext for a search for evidence of crime (see §§4.5 and 6.9), the inventory would be lawful. The marijuana would thus have been discovered by routine procedures even if the police had not conducted their unlawful search on the highway. In similar situations where an illegality resulted in the discovery of evidence that would have been found in any event pursuant to a lawful inventory, courts have applied the inevitable discovery exception and admitted the evidence. See, e.g., *United States v. Rhind*, 289 F.3d 690 (11th Cir. 2002); *United States v. Kirk*, 111 F.3d 390 (5th Cir. 1997); and *United States v. Mendez*, 139 F. Supp. 2d 273 (D. Conn. 2001). See also *United States v. Kennedy*, 61 F.3d 494 (6th Cir. 1995) (evidence discovered by airport police in defendant's suitcase during allegedly unlawful search was subject to inevitable discovery exception to the exclusionary rule, as police would have simply returned the suitcase to the airline if they could not obtain a search warrant, and the airline would have opened the suitcase to determine identification of the owner).

Although the Court warned in *Nix v. Williams* that inevitable discovery cannot rest on mere speculation as to what might have been, some courts seem to be doing just that. See, e.g., *United States v. Christy*, 810 F. Supp. 2d

1219 (D.N.M. 2011) (notwithstanding unlawful search when deputies peered into defendant's residence through a crack in the blinds, the child pornography would have inevitably been discovered when the FBI investigator would have secured a search warrant); *United States v. Garreau*, 735 F. Supp. 2d 1155 (D.S.D. 2010) (handgun would have been inevitably discovered as part of an inventory search following defendant's unlawful arrest); *United States v. Hammons*, 152 F.3d 1025 (8th Cir. 1998) (cocaine inside envelope found during search of defendant's garment bag was admissible, despite officer misconduct in opening envelope after obtaining defendant's involuntary consent, given that officer would have summoned a drug-canine unit if defendant had not consented to search, as he informed defendant he would do, and the dog would have alerted to the presence of drugs); *United States v. Lamas*, 930 F.2d 1099 (5th Cir. 1991) (agents would have inevitably discovered contraband, even if they had not done so by way of defendant's involuntary consent, because they had probable cause to search and one of the officers testified that he was about to seek a warrant when defendant made that unnecessary by agreeing to the search); *United States v. Ivey*, 915 F.2d 380 (8th Cir. 1990) (records were properly admitted into evidence, despite the fact that they were seized during an unlawful search of the defendant's purse, because the government had an alternative line of investigation; that is, the police had suspicions and leads that would inevitably have led them to the lawful discovery of the evidence). But compare *United States v. Stokes*, 733 F.3d 438 (2d Cir. 2013) (government failed to establish that the firearms would have been inevitably discovered after the warrantless entry into defendant's motel room because there were too many contingencies regarding prediction of the actions of third parties); *United States v. Reilly*, 224 F.3d 986 (9th Cir. 2000) (agents' obtaining consent to a search from defendant after he had requested counsel, in violation of his constitutional rights, would not be excused under the inevitable discovery doctrine based merely on the assertion that the FBI, through routine procedures, would have gotten a search warrant and searched room had he withheld consent).

Sometimes the inevitability is hard to dispute. In *United States v. Oakley*, 731 F. Supp. 1363 (D. Ind. 1990), the court held that even if the digital rectal cavity probe of the prisoner was unlawful, the balloons containing narcotics that were found were nonetheless admissible because they would have been inevitably discovered as a result of the prisoner's normal excretory process. "Although physically and mentally capable humans learn at an early age to postpone the call of nature at most times, this control mechanism merely delays the inevitable release of our body's metabolic by-products. If Oakley was to survive, it was inevitable that he pass the balloons through his system. Once eliminated from Oakley's system, the balloons were destined for discovery by prison authorities." 731 F. Supp. at 1372-1373.

The inevitable discovery exception significantly curtails, and has the potential to emasculate, the operation of the exclusionary rule and its derivative evidence component. Mindful of this, one circuit has required as part of the analysis consideration of the following question: "Does the application of the inevitable discovery exception [in this case] either provide an incentive for police misconduct or significantly weaken [F]ourth [A]mendment protection?" *United States v. Silvestri*, 787 F.2d 736, 744 (1st Cir. 1986). Following this mandate, the district court refused to apply the inevitable discovery exception where the defendant's gun had been found as a direct result of his coerced admissions, but would have been discovered anyway when the police searched the area of the arrest: "Application of the inevitable discovery doctrine here would encourage law enforcement officers to believe they can avoid the burden of a prolonged area search by physically abusing a suspect, without significant risk of forfeiting the admissibility of any physical evidence. Thus, this is the type of case in which the exclusionary rule has a substantial potential deterrent effect which would be significantly weakened if the inevitable discovery doctrine were applied." *United States v. Rullo*, 748 F. Supp. 36, 44 (D. Mass. 1990). See also *United States v. Holmes*, 183 F. Supp. 2d 108 (D. Me. 2002); and *United States v. Felix*, 134 F. Supp. 2d 162 (D. Mass. 2001) (inevitable discovery doctrine did not apply). *Silvestri* has apparently not been adopted elsewhere. See *United States v. Alexander*, 540 F.3d 494, 503 (6th Cir. 2008).

Concerned about the potential overuse of the inevitable discovery doctrine, some courts have suggested that it be applied only when there is a high level of confidence that each of the contingencies required for the discovery of the disputed evidence would in fact have occurred. *United States v. Heath*, 455 F.3d 52, 55 (2d Cir. 2006) (defendant, arguably prematurely arrested, could have been validly arrested moments later, supporting the application of the inevitable discovery doctrine). Other courts have emphasized that the government must prove that the information that made discovery inevitable was possessed by the police at the time of the misconduct, and that the police were actively pursuing a lawful alternative line of investigation to seize the evidence prior to the time of the misconduct. *State v. Flippo*, 212 W. Va. 560 (2002) (photographs unlawfully seized from defendant's rented cabin during a warrantless search were not admissible, during a murder trial, under the inevitable discovery exception to the exclusionary rule, where, after defendant's implied consent to search the cabin was revoked, police did not initiate procedures to obtain a search warrant before the photographs were seized).

It should be noted that the application of the inevitable discovery exception in cases such as *Oakley*, supra, where the issue is the admissibility of a direct fruit of an illegal search, as opposed to the indirect derivative result (the balloons were obtained directly from the rectal search), raises a serious question about the continued viability of the exclusionary rule.

5. Since Wilma is driving and the car is rented in her name, she clearly has authority to consent to the search of the trunk. This permission extends to any closed containers in the car. See *Florida v. Jimeno*, 500 U.S. 248 (1991), discussed in §6.7 in Chapter 6. The complication arises here because the garment bag is labeled with Fred's name. Does Wilma have apparent authority to consent to the opening of Fred's bag? A reasonable officer under the *Illinois v. Rodriguez* standard (see §6.7) would probably not conclude that she does. And Fred's consent under threat of the dreaded sniffer-dog may very well be deemed coerced under totality-of-the-circumstances analysis.

   Assuming that the consents are invalid, what about the possibility of applying the inevitable discovery doctrine to justify admission of the cocaine? Would the evidence have ultimately been discovered by lawful means? The Eighth Circuit answered yes in *United States v. Hammons*, 152 F.3d 1025 (8th Cir. 1998), concluding that the officer would have called upon a drug-detection dog, which would have sniffed out the contents of the envelope. Application of the inevitable discovery exception required not only a showing that there was a reasonable probability that the evidence would have been discovered by lawful means, but also that the government was indeed pursuing a substantial, alternative line of investigation at the time of the police misconduct. (*Hammons* notes that the circuits are split on this issue, some requiring only the first prong.) The officer's assertion that he would call a drug-sniffing dog was deemed sufficient showing that he had initiated an alternative plan. But compare *United States v. Allen*, 159 F.3d 832 (4th Cir. 1998) (even though drug-detection dogs *could have* alerted officers to the presence of cocaine in a bus passenger's duffel bag, there was insufficient evidence they *would have* under the circumstances because officer testified she had never used a dog inside a bus).

§7.3 LIMITATIONS ON THE EXCLUSIONARY RULE

The tension between the goal of effective law enforcement (apprehending and convicting bad guys) and the protection of individual rights and privacy has played itself out over past decades in judicial expansion or contraction of the exclusionary rule. The suppression remedy reached its high-water mark in the Warren Court era, and the years since have witnessed a slow but steady recession. Thus, although the Supreme Court has chosen to maintain the rule excluding unlawfully obtained evidence at trial, it has chipped away at it by imposing a number of substantial limitations on its scope, coverage, and operation.

§7.3.1 Standing

One major restriction on the operation of the exclusionary rule is the doctrine of standing. Only those who are actual victims of the alleged violation have "standing" to challenge it. In its most basic form, the doctrine prevents *A* from complaining about an infringement of *B*'s rights. If, for example, *B*'s home is subjected to an unlawful search and items are seized that implicate *A* in criminal activity, *A* is not permitted to seek exclusion of that evidence at his trial based on the Fourth Amendment violation. Although the search certainly has consequences for *A*, he lacks standing to seek suppression because his rights were not directly violated when the police entered *B*'s home. Only if the evidence were offered against *B* would the exclusionary remedy be available, and then only to *B*.[5] As the Court has put it, "a person who is aggrieved by an illegal search and seizure only through the introduction of damaging evidence secured by a search of a third person's premises or property has not had any of his Fourth Amendment rights infringed." *Rakas v. Illinois*, 439 U.S. 128, 134 (1978).

The definition of a victim who has standing to challenge a violation was expanded and then sharply narrowed over the past decades. While initially tied to property law concepts, *Jones v. United States*, 362 U.S. 257 (1960), conferred standing on anyone "legitimately on the premises" where the search occurs, even if not owners or lessees of the property. (Jones was a friend staying at the apartment searched.) *Jones* also established a rule providing automatic standing to any defendant charged with a possessory offense. Recognizing the dilemma faced by such defendants—in order to establish standing to challenge the search, the accused would have had to admit that the contraband was his, thus incriminating himself—the Court conferred standing categorically and without regard to the particular circumstances of each case.

Neither prong of *Jones* survives today. The automatic standing doctrine was overturned in *United States v. Salvucci*, 448 U.S. 83 (1980).[6] And the

---

5. The concept is also reflected in the requirement of Fed. R. Crim. P. 41(e) that a party moving to suppress evidence must be a "person aggrieved."

6. Some states have retained their own automatic standing rules under the state constitution. See, e.g., *Commonwealth v. Amendola*, 406 Mass. 592 (1990). Massachusetts has also indicated a willingness to recognize "target standing" (rejected by the Supreme Court in *Rakas v. Illinois*, discussed immediately below) where the police engage in egregious conduct violating the rights of a third party in an effort to obtain evidence against the defendant. In such case, the defendant may assert the third-party's claim. See *Commonwealth v. Santiago*, 470 Mass. 574 (2015). "Unconstitutional searches of small fish intentionally undertaken in order to catch big ones may have to be discouraged by allowing the big fish, when caught, to rely on the violation of the rights of the small fish, as to whose prosecution the police are relatively indifferent." 470 Mass. at 578.

"legitimately on the premises" standard has been replaced by an expectation of privacy analysis first adopted in *Katz v. United States*, 389 U.S. 347 (1967) (see §3.2 in Chapter 3).

In *Rakas v. Illinois*, 439 U.S. 128 (1978), passengers in a car stopped by the police sought to suppress a rifle and shells found in the glove compartment and under the front seat. They argued they had standing to challenge the search of the car (which they did not own) and the seizure of the incriminating items (which they did not claim were theirs) because they were "legitimately on the premises." Concluding that the *Jones* standard was too broad, the Court abandoned it and held that the standing requirement "is more properly subsumed under substantive Fourth Amendment doctrine." The question of standing thus becomes merged with the question of whether the challenged action infringed an interest protected by the amendment, which translates into whether *this particular defendant's reasonable expectation of privacy was intruded upon.*

Applying this analysis, the Court concluded that the search of the car did not violate the rights of the passengers, who asserted neither a property interest in the place searched nor in the items seized, and thus they had no expectation of privacy. The Court emphasized that the places searched — the glove compartment and under the seat — were areas in which mere passengers (in contrast with the car's owner) would not normally have a legitimate expectation of privacy. In a concurrence, Justice Powell indicated that the passenger might gain standing if the stop was illegal. The passenger could then utilize the fruit-of-the-poisoned-tree doctrine to challenge the search of the vehicle. This approach was upheld in *Brendlin v. California*, 551 U.S. 249 (2007).

While the *Rakas* Court purported to agree with *Jones* that property interests should not control standing analysis, property concepts focusing on the defendant's relationship to the place searched do indeed appear to dominate contemporary standing analysis. In *Rawlings v. Kentucky*, 448 U.S. 98 (1980), the defendant challenged a search of his female companion's purse, in which he had hidden drugs. Despite Rawlings's admission of ownership of the drugs on the scene and during the suppression proceedings, the Court ruled that he lacked standing to challenge the search. While observing that Rawlings's claim of ownership was a factor to be considered, the Court held that because he had no reasonable expectation of privacy *in the place searched* (the purse), his rights were not implicated. The Court emphasized the following facts relating to the defendant's interest in the purse: 1) Rawlings had known his companion for only a few days at the time of the "sudden bailment"; 2) he had never sought nor received access to the purse before; 3) he had no right to exclude others from access to the purse, and indeed, on the very morning of the search, another friend of his companion's had rummaged through the purse for a hairbrush; 4) the "precipitous nature" of Rawlings's placing the drugs in the purse indicated that he failed to take "normal precautions to maintain his privacy"; and 5) Rawlings admitted he had no subjective expectation that the purse would be free from governmental intrusion.

Reference to property concepts also led the Court to a unanimous decision in *Byrd v. United States*, 138 S. Ct. 1518 (2018), holding that as a general rule, someone in lawful possession and control of a rental car has a reasonable expectation of privacy in it even if the rental agreement does not list them as an authorized driver. Having been entrusted the vehicle by the renter, Byrd was lawfully the driver and sole occupant, with the attendant right to exclude others from it.

Standing to enforce Fourth Amendment protections appears limited to persons who either own or have some other close connection to the place searched, or in the case of a vehicle, possession and control. The group includes the defendant in *Jones*,[7] who, although lacking ownership in the apartment, was nonetheless alone there with his friend's permission at the time of the search, had a key, and kept some of his possessions there. An overnight guest who did not have a key and was never alone in the home was nonetheless held to have standing to challenge his warrantless arrest in *Minnesota v. Olson*, 495 U.S. 91 (1990), the Court reasoning that society recognizes a guest's expectation of privacy in the host's home in such a situation. Where, however, individuals went to an apartment for the sole purpose of packaging cocaine in exchange for some of the product, spent only two hours there, and had never been to the apartment before, the Court refused to confer standing to challenge a search. See *Minnesota v. Carter*, 525 U.S. 83 (1998); see also *United States v. Gray*, 491 F.3d 138 (4th Cir. 2007) (defendant/visitor who was involved in drug dealing in an apartment was a business guest and had no expectation of privacy there). In sum, lacking a possessory interest in or a close connection to the place searched, defendants will not be permitted to pursue their claims of unconstitutional search and seizure.

On a final note, it should be added that while *Rakas* purported to merge the procedural standing question with the substantive Fourth Amendment analysis, it still makes sense conceptually to keep them separate. As Justice Blackmun observed, it is possible for a defendant to demonstrate standing to challenge a search and yet fail to prove the search was unlawful; and conversely for a defendant to show that an illegality occurred but fail to establish that he has standing to challenge it. See *Rawlings v. Kentucky*, 448 U.S. at 112 (Blackmun, J., concurring). Analytically, the standing issue should be resolved first and independently from the substantive issue of the illegality.

---

7. *Rakas* suggested that *Jones* would come out the same way under its new privacy analysis.

Examples

1. In which of the following situations does the defendant have standing to challenge the police action?

   a. Acting on an unsupported hunch that he was involved in gambling activities, officers arrested Clyde as he left his downtown office. A search of his briefcase turned up documents linking his friend, Bonnie, to a major bookmaking ring, and the prosecution now proposes to use the evidence against Bonnie at trial.

   b. Harry Homicidal hid a hatchet (which he had used on his latest victim) in a garage owned and used by his landlord. Police investigating the murder conducted a warrantless search of the garage and found the weapon. May Harry challenge the search if the hatchet is offered into evidence at his murder trial?

   c. Narcotics detectives had Dealer under surveillance as she rented a room at the Fleabag Hotel and entered it with a key. One hour later, they observed Buyer knock and enter. The detectives waited five minutes and then stormed the hotel room, interrupting a narcotics transaction. Does either Dealer or Buyer have standing to challenge the seizure of narcotics and cash when offered in evidence against them at trial? Would it help either's argument if they admitted that the items seized belonged to them?

   d. Bill was a passenger in the rear of a sedan owned by Ted (who was seated in the front) and driven by Cynthia. Believing there was something suspicious about the car, state police officers stopped it, ordered the occupants out, and subjected the car to an intensive search. They discovered several opaque plastic bags containing marijuana on the rear seat, Cynthia's purse containing drug paraphernalia in the locked glove compartment, and a large quantity of hashish in the trunk. Bill, Ted, and Cynthia are charged with drug offenses, and the prosecution proposes to use the items seized against each of them. Which of them, if any, has standing to object on Fourth Amendment grounds?

   e. Bill rented a Honda from Ace Car Rental, which under the contract was to be returned by January 20. On January 24, Bill was stopped for speeding. Officer Jones asked for and was given the rental agreement, from which he learned that the car was overdue. Jones impounded the Honda and pursuant to departmental policy conducted a full inventory search, uncovering a gun in the glove compartment and narcotics in the trunk. Does Bill have standing to challenge the search?

Derivative Evidence Meets the Standing Doctrine

2. Having heard rumors to the effect that John was involved in the unlawful distribution of bootleg compact disks, police officers made a warrantless entry into his apartment and found him in the kitchen. When the

officers threatened to arrest him, John stated that he had nothing to do with such activities but that his friend Paul was involved. Because this information confirmed other reliable sources and thus established probable cause, a warrant was issued to search Paul's apartment. Inside, the police discovered contraband CDs and documents connecting John to the illegal scheme.

a. The evidence seized is offered against Paul at trial. Does he have standing under the Fourth Amendment to object?

b. The evidence seized is offered against John at trial. Does he have standing under the Fourth Amendment to object?

Standing in the Electronic Age

3. Jackie Accountant worked for All-American Defense Products, overseeing the preparation of sealed bids for contracts with the Pentagon. Unbeknownst to her employer, Jackie was disclosing (by way of a computer link) pricing information to a competitor, Military Hardware, Inc. The disclosed information helped Military Hardware underbid All-American. Jackie charged a tidy fee for this service. The FBI got wind of this illegal scheme and, without bothering to seek a warrant, entered and searched the offices of Military Hardware. The agents seized several computer disks, which contained files evidencing Jackie's communications. May Jackie challenge the admission of these files into evidence against her?

Explanations

1a. The Fourth Amendment confers personal rights that may not be vicariously asserted. While Clyde may challenge his unlawful arrest and search, Bonnie has no standing to do so. No matter how egregious the violation, the exclusionary sanction is unavailable to Bonnie in these circumstances. Although she is a victim of the police action in the sense that the fruits of the arrest are being used against her, her right to be free of unreasonable search or seizure has not been invaded by a search of another's briefcase. See *Rawlings v. Kentucky*, 448 U.S. 98 (1980).

1b. In order for us to determine whether Harry's own rights have been violated, *Rakas v. Illinois*, 439 U.S. 128 (1978), requires us to determine whether his expectation of privacy was infringed upon when the officers entered and searched the garage. This in turn requires us to explore whether (by way of his lease or otherwise) Harry had a possessory interest in, use of, or control over the garage. If not, he will likely be deemed to have no reasonable expectation of privacy in the place searched and thus lack standing to raise objections under the Fourth Amendment.

The standing doctrine prevents Harry from complaining about a search of someone else's garage, even when the fruits of that search are used against Harry, not the garage owner. Note that the landlord, who obviously does have standing to challenge the search, has no way to do so through the suppression remedy because the hatchet is not being used against him. (The landlord may be able to pursue a civil action for the violation.)

1c. Unlike the first two examples, the individuals here were actually on the premises (and legitimately so) at the time of the search. While that would have met the test for standing set by *Jones v. United States*, 362 U.S. 257 (1960), it is no longer sufficient. Rather, to invoke the exclusionary remedy, each party must demonstrate that his reasonable expectation of privacy was violated by the police action. See *Rakas v. Illinois*, supra.

Dealer, who rented, had a key to the room and spent an hour in it, was in possession and control, and thus had a reasonable expectation of privacy there. That would establish her standing to challenge the search. Buyer, on the other hand, had a more tenuous connection to the place searched. She neither had a possessory interest in it nor spent more than a few minutes there at any given time. Although Buyer may seek to analogize her situation to the invited guests in *Jones v. United States*, 362 U.S. 257 (1960), and *Minnesota v. Olson*, 495 U.S. 91 (1990), both of whom had standing to challenge searches of their host's dwellings, her relationship to the hotel room appears more analogous to the passengers in *Rakas*, who lacked standing. Compare *Rose v. United States*, 629 A.2d 526 (D.C. 1993), where the defendant was arrested without a warrant while within the home of his aunt and uncle. The arresting officer was aware that the defendant had a key to the apartment. The court focused on three factors in determining that the defendant had standing to challenge the warrantless arrest: the defendant's close kinship with the owners of the apartment, his regular visits (several times a week), and his possession of a key. These factors added up to essentially the same expectations of privacy that an overnight guest might have. Compare *Morton v. United States*, 734 A.2d 178 (D.C. Ct. App. 1999) (defendant had a protectable privacy interest in house that police entered to seize him, even though he did not live there and was not an overnight guest, where owner had known defendant for years and said that defendant was a frequent visitor and was "like family") with *United States v. Gray*, 491 F.3d 138 (4th Cir 2007) (D2 had no standing to contest the physical evidence seized from D1's residence, as their relationship was a business, not a social, one—dealing drugs—and thus D2 had no reasonable expectation of privacy).

It should be noted that casual visitors with no reasonable expectation of privacy in the place searched have been granted standing where they can demonstrate such an expectation regarding the items seized, particularly where they have a property interest therein. See, e.g., *DePugh v. Penning*, 888 F. Supp. 959 (N.D. Iowa 1995) (defendant left his items with friend and business associate for safekeeping).

Another problem for Buyer in our example is the purpose of her presence at the Fleabag. *Minnesota v. Carter*, 525 U.S. 83 (1998), suggested that a person in a protected area such as a home may nonetheless not have a reasonable expectation of privacy if there for purely commercial purposes, such as the purchase of narcotics. See also *United States v. Silva*, 247 F.3d 1051 (9th Cir. 2001) (defendants did not have reasonable expectation of privacy in shed because of their purely commercial activity of manufacturing drugs inside); *United States v. Macias-Treviso*, 42 F. Supp. 2d 1206, 1212 (D.N.M. 1999) (even though defendant had a key and his brother's permission to use the garage, where he worked on cars and stored his tools for almost a year, the commercial nature of defendant's activities and lack of any residential connection meant that he lacked standing to challenge the search).

Although property used for commercial purposes is treated differently for Fourth Amendment purposes than residential property, *Minnesota v. Carter* notes that there are some circumstances in which a worker can claim protection over his own workplace, citing *O'Connor v. Ortega*, 480 U.S. 709 (1987), discussed in §§3.2 and 4.5. See, e.g., *United States v. Evaschuck*, 65 F. Supp. 2d 1360 (M.D. Fla. 1999) (defendant had standing to challenge search of offices that his company rented because he was owner and operator of the company, the only person who used those offices, and the only person who had the keys); *United States v. Anderson*, 154 F.3d 1225 (10th Cir. 1998) (defendant had standing to challenge search of vacant room in his office building where he took steps to protect his privacy there). What if a visitor to the searched premises has a *dual* purpose, both social and commercial, for his presence? Since Justice Kennedy's decisive fifth vote in *Minnesota v. Carter* was expressly based on his view that social guests generally have a legitimate expectation of privacy and hence protection against unreasonable searches in their host's home, it may be argued that the dual-purpose visitor has standing to challenge a search.

Keep in mind that the automatic standing rule of *Jones*, which would have conferred standing on Buyer to raise a Fourth Amendment challenge for any possessory offense, has been abandoned. See *United States v. Salvucci*, 448 U.S. 83 (1980). Moreover, *Rawlings v. Kentucky*, supra, raises substantial doubt as to whether an admission by Buyer that the narcotics and cash were hers would establish standing for her—such admission did not accomplish that result for Rawlings because of his lack of possessory interest in the place searched, his companion's purse.

1d. Ted, as the owner of the vehicle (who was also present during the search), would have standing to challenge the search because his possessory interest creates a reasonable expectation of privacy in all areas of the car. See *Rakas v. Illinois*, supra. He could thus object to the entry into the car and the subsequent seizure of the plastic bags, the purse, and the hashish in the trunk. Note that some decisions would deny him standing to challenge the opening of the purse or the plastic bags, which belonged to the other occupants and in which he had no reasonable expectation of privacy. See, e.g., *United States v. Hephner*, 260 F. Supp. 2d 763 (N.D. Iowa 2003); *United States v. Kelly*, 46 F. Supp. 2d 624 (E.D. Tex. 1999); *United States v. Maling*, 746 F. Supp. 223 (D. Mass. 1990).

As a mere passenger, Bill will not be able to establish a privacy interest in the trunk of the vehicle or the glove compartment, and thus he will not be able to challenge the use of the items seized there against him at trial. *United States v. Hephner*, supra. Bill probably will be able to demonstrate a legitimate privacy expectation in the rear seat area, where he had been sitting, and thus could challenge the seizure and opening of the trash bags. See *United States v. Salazar*, 805 F.2d 1394 (9th Cir. 1986) (defendant, although a mere passenger in a car, had standing to challenge search of a closed container placed out of sight on the floor near where he had been seated). But compare *United States v. Symonevich*, 688 F.3d 12 (1st Cir. 2012) (passenger lacked standing to challenge search of vehicle even though duration of the trip was six hours).

United States v. Paulino, 850 F.2d 93 (2d Cir. 1988) denied standing to a passenger in back seat, who had been seen by officer placing something on the floor, to challenge the search and seizure of counterfeit money that he had hidden underneath the floor mat. The court reasoned that, while the defendant had clearly evidenced his desire to keep the item private and, further, admitted ownership of the money, other *Rawlings* factors militated against conferring standing on him: 1) he had known the owner-driver for only a week; 2) as a passenger, he had no right to exclude others from the vehicle; and 3) he had secreted the money quickly, only moments before the police discovered it. 850 F.2d at 97. Compare *United States v. Barber*, 777 F.3d 1303 (11th Cir. 2015) (passenger had standing to challenge search of his bag placed at his feet); *United States v. Edwards*, 242 F.3d 928 (10th Cir. 2001) (defendant had standing to challenge search of his personal luggage contained within trunk of rental vehicle, even though he did not have standing to challenge search of rental car and its trunk because he was not the renter of the vehicle and not an authorized driver under the rental agreement).

Cynthia, as the car's driver, falls somewhere in between Ted and Bill. While lacking the ownership interest that Ted had, she did have control over the vehicle as well as possession of the ignition key, which probably gave her access to both the glove compartment and the trunk. She can probably challenge the seizure of items in those areas as well as the rear seat. See *United States v. Maling*, supra. Compare *United States v. Kopp*, 45 F.3d

1450 (10th Cir. 1995) (driver of pickup truck did not have standing to contest a search of attached trailer rented by a passenger who kept sole possession of the only key). She may lack standing to challenge the opening of the plastic bags located next to Bill in the rear, an area in which she might be deemed to lack a legitimate privacy interest. If Cynthia has no key or other access to the glove compartment, then *Rawlings* suggests that because she has no control over the place searched, she lacks standing to challenge the search.

What if the opaque bags were in Bill's duffle bag? Would the owner and driver of the car have an expectation of privacy in a duffle bag owned and held by a passenger sitting in the back seat? *Rakas* suggests that the answer is no: If a passenger lacks a privacy expectation in the glove compartment, the driver probably lacks such expectation in a passenger's bag. See *United States v. McCray*, 230 F. Supp. 2d 89 (D. Me. 2002) (driver lacked standing to challenge the seizure of cocaine from a coat that a passenger was wearing).

Wyoming v. Houghton, 526 U.S. 295 (1999) (discussed in §6.4 in Chapter 6), allows a police officer with probable cause to search a vehicle to search the belongings of any passenger as well. One might argue that if probable cause now opens all containers in the car to search, then the driver or owner should have standing to contest search of any container.

In a similar vein, Justice Powell suggested in his concurring opinion in *Rakas* that the passengers there might have had standing had they challenged the *stop* of the car and the order to get out, as opposed to the search and seizure that followed. The fruits of the stop could then be challenged under the derivative evidence doctrine (see §7.2). In our example, Bill could thus argue that he had a reasonable expectation of freedom from an arbitrary stop and therefore had standing to challenge the officer's initial action. This position was upheld in *Brendlin v. California*, 551 U.S. 249 (2007). See also *Arizona v. Johnson*, 129 S. Ct. 781 (2009).

An important factor is whether Bill stayed in the vehicle after it was pulled over. In *United States v. Jones*, 562 F.3d 768 (6th Cir. 2009), a passenger who jumped out of the car after it was pulled over was not seized under the *Brendlin* standard, and therefore did not have standing to challenge the search because he did not submit to a show of police authority. Compare *United States v. Al Nasser*, 555 F.3d 722 (9th Cir. 2009) (driver of a car who was compelled to slow down because of traffic congestion caused by a police stop of a preceding car was not seized and did not have standing to challenge the stop and search because the agents did not intend for defendant to stop and did not shout at him to stop).

As examples 1a through 1d illustrate, standing doctrine operates to separate the victims of a search into those privileged to challenge it, by virtue of their connection to the place searched or items seized, and those not so privileged. It has been suggested that this division encourages the police to engage in unlawful activity with the knowledge that the evidence seized, while inadmissible as to some, may nonetheless be used against others. See *Rakas v. Illinois*, 439 U.S. at 168-169 (White, Brennan, Marshall, and Stevens, JJ., dissenting). This is precisely what occurred in *United States v. Payner*, 447 U.S. 727 (1980). In order to obtain confidential information on bank customers, Internal Revenue Service (IRS) agents entered the hotel room of a visiting bank official, removed his briefcase, and photocopied documents inside. Based on evidence so obtained, Payner was charged with income tax violations. Despite the finding that Payner was a victim of a deliberate IRS policy exploiting the Fourth Amendment standing limitation—agents were counseled that they could violate the constitutional rights of one individual in order to secure admissible evidence against another—the Supreme Court held that he lacked standing to challenge the search of the bank official's briefcase.

1e. The Ninth and Eleventh Circuits have held that a driver of an overdue rental vehicle does have a legitimate expectation of privacy (and thus standing) in the car, where he could have renewed the agreement by simply telephoning the rental company and where the company had not taken any affirmative steps to repossess the car. See *United States v. Henderson*, 241 F.3d 638 (9th Cir. 2000); *United States v. Cooper*, 133 F.3d 1394 (11th Cir. 1998). *Byrd v. United States*, 138 S. Ct. 1518 (2018), establishes that as a general rule, someone in lawful possession and control of a rental car has a reasonable expectation of privacy in it even if the rental agreement does not list them as an authorized driver. Having been entrusted the vehicle by the renter, Byrd was lawfully the driver and sole occupant, with the attendant right to exclude others from it.

Derivative Evidence Meets the Standing Doctrine

2a. Paul clearly has standing to complain about the search of his apartment. If, however, the warrant was (as it appears to have been) lawful, Paul lacks a substantive claim of illegality. Moreover, Paul does not have standing to raise any illegality experienced earlier by John.

2b. It may appear at first glance that John lacks standing because he is objecting to evidence obtained in a search of Paul's apartment. The information that led the police to Paul, however, was derived from the initial unlawful entry into John's own apartment. Since the evidence offered against John is the fruit of an illegality directed at him and his apartment, he does have standing to pursue a Fourth Amendment challenge. The situation is similar to that of defendant Toy, who successfully challenged the use of heroin seized from defendant Yee in *Wong Sun v. United States*, 371

U.S. 471 (1963). The police were led to Yee only through declarations made by Toy during his unlawful arrest, and thus the evidence could not be used against Toy.

The derivative evidence doctrine thus expands the realm of standing for defendants who can trace actions directed against others to initial illegalities directed against themselves. A defendant who has standing to challenge the initial illegality also has standing to challenge the use of evidence derived from that illegality.

The prosecution might argue in response in our example that the other reliable sources concerning Paul's activities established (or would inevitably have established) probable cause for the search of Paul's apartment, and thus the independent source or inevitable discovery exceptions to the derivative evidence doctrine should apply. These issues would have to be resolved based on the particular factual circumstances.

Standing in the Electronic Age

3. Jackie can contest this search and seizure only if it infringed on her own personal Fourth Amendment rights—that is, only if her privacy interest was violated. Because the search occurred in a location in which she had no possessory interest and over which she had no control, it would appear that Jackie is in the same situation as Bonnie in example 1a—attempting to rely vicariously on the violation of someone else's Fourth Amendment rights. Even if Jackie can establish a property interest in the information on the computer tape, such interest in the item seized does not necessarily confer standing in the absence of a close connection to the place searched. See *Rawlings v. Kentucky*, supra (although Rawlings admitted ownership of the drugs seized, his lack of possessory interest in the purse from which they were taken defeated his claim of standing).

In the case upon which this example is based, *United States v. Horowitz*, 806 F.2d 1222 (4th Cir. 1986), defense counsel argued creatively that the search challenged was not really that of Military Hardware's office, but rather of the intangible space where images and sounds are recorded in a computer memory disk, and that the computer images seized constituted the defendant's electronic file cabinet. 806 F.2d at 1224-1225. Applying the traditional analysis, however, the court ruled that Horowitz lacked standing because the search occurred in the offices of a third party, the tapes seized were taken from that third party's files, and whatever interest that Horowitz had in the information contained on the disks was lost when he sold it to a third party. Moreover, Horowitz failed to establish that he had any control over the computer tapes:

> The defendant lacked any ability to exclude others from the tapes; on the contrary, his own access was controlled by EMI. The defendant had no keys

> to either EMI's building or EMI's computer room. His only access to the RER file was by an electronic hookup through the use of a password. But employees of EMI could bar his access simply by removing the tapes from the computer or by changing the password. The defendant could not effectively exclude anyone from access to the tapes since any of several EMI employees knowing the password could give it to others and any employee with a key to the computer room could remove the tapes.

Id. at 1226. Because the defendant lacked standing to challenge the search and seizure, the court did not reach the question of its conformity with Fourth Amendment requirements. See also *Guest v. Leis*, 255 F.3d 325 (6th Cir. 2001) (the only individual with a privacy interest in unlicensed software would be the person possessing the software, i.e., the computer's owner or system operator, and not users of the electronic bulletin board system, so that the latter did not have standing to assert that the officers exceeded the scope of a search warrant directed at obscenity; users lacked a legitimate expectation of privacy in materials intended for publication or public posting, and lost such expectation in e-mail that had already reached its recipient; users did not have standing to challenge seizure of the computers as physical objects). For more on computer searches, see Chapter 12.

§7.3.2 Limitation to Criminal Trial Versus Other Proceedings

A criminal trial is only one of several types of judicial proceedings in which evidence obtained during a search might be offered against a party. Does the exclusionary remedy apply in other criminal contexts, such as grand jury or habeas corpus proceedings? Does it apply in proceedings of a civil nature, such as deportation or tax penalty cases? A series of Supreme Court cases have consistently answered no to these questions and limited the rule to the criminal trial context.

United States v. Calandra, 414 U.S. 338 (1974), involved a witness called before a grand jury who refused to answer questions based on evidence that had been obtained from him during an unlawful search. Expressing concern that utilization of the exclusionary remedy would seriously impede the operation of the grand jury in its investigative function, the Court held that the rule could not be applied in those proceedings. Premised on the notion that the exclusionary rule is a judicially created remedy rather than a constitutional right, the Court utilized a cost-benefit analysis now typical in cases curtailing operation of the rule. It weighed what it viewed as the minimal deterrent effect of suppression in grand jury proceedings against the cost of keeping relevant information from the grand jury. So long as law enforcement officials know that illegally obtained evidence cannot be used at the ultimate trial, the Court reasoned, there is little incentive to violate constitutional requirements merely for the purpose of securing evidence for the grand jury: "A prosecutor would be unlikely to request an indictment where a conviction could not be obtained." 414 U.S. at 351.

The exclusionary remedy has also been held inapplicable in habeas corpus proceedings. The habeas corpus device permits a state prisoner to challenge his conviction in federal court on the grounds that his constitutional rights were violated during the state trial. *Stone v. Powell*, 428 U.S. 465 (1976), removed Fourth Amendment violations from those that can be raised, so long as the petitioner had a full and fair opportunity to assert the violation during the state proceedings. The deterrent effect of the rule will be achieved (if at all), the Court reasoned, by having the suppression remedy available at trial and on direct appellate review; the incremental deterrence that might result from its availability in habeas proceedings is remote and speculative. "The view that the deterrence of Fourth Amendment violations would be furthered rests on the dubious assumption that law enforcement authorities would fear that federal habeas review might reveal flaws in a search or seizure that went undetected at trial and on appeal." 428 U.S. at 493. Police officers do not, the Court suggested, think this far in advance in the conduct of their daily work. The costs of applying the rule, on the other hand, are the deflection of the truth-finding process, diversion from the central question of guilt or innocence, and the exclusion of relevant evidence. In reaching the opposite conclusion regarding *Miranda* violations (see Chapter 9), which can be raised in habeas corpus proceedings, the Court emphasized the potential for distortion of the truth-finding process. *Withrow v. Williams*, 507 U.S. 680 (1993).

The same balancing analysis has led the Court to hold the exclusionary rule unavailable in civil actions brought by the IRS to collect taxes, *United States v. Janis*, 428 U.S. 433 (1976); in deportation hearings, *INS v. Lopez-Mendoza*, 468 U.S. 1032 (1984); and in parole revocation hearings, *Pennsylvania Board of Probation and Parole v. Scott*, 524 U.S. 357 (1998). In each case, the majority and dissent disagree on the costs and benefits of applying the exclusionary rule, particularly around the matter of deterrence. In his decision for the Court, Justice Thomas in *Scott* concluded that the social costs of allowing convicted criminals who violate their parole to remain at large outweigh whatever marginal deterrence that the rule may create for the officer on the street (beyond enforcement of the exclusionary rule in the criminal trial). The dissenters (in an opinion by Justice Souter) saw a significant potential for deterrence if the rule is applied at the revocation hearing because police are often aware of the parole status of the subject of their search and thus would be quite concerned with the admissibility of evidence in those proceedings, which may very well end up being the only action taken against the subject.

The same disagreement about the costs versus benefits of applying the exclusionary remedy underlie the opposing views in *Hudson v. Michigan*, 126 S. Ct. 2159 (2006), refusing to suppress evidence seized during a search conducted in violation of the "knock-and-announce" mandate. The majority bemoaned the social costs of excluding probative evidence from trial, especially freeing the guilty, while the four dissenters complained that the Court was destroying "the strongest legal incentive to comply with the Constitution's" commands. The majority's emphasis on alternative remedies—civil actions and disciplinary proceedings against offending officers—may well spell the eventual demise of the suppression remedy despite Justice Kennedy's concurrence, asserting "the continued operation of the exclusionary rule, as settled and defined by our precedents, is not in doubt."

In refusing to apply the exclusionary rule in these situations, the Court has cast aside the argument that, even in the absence of demonstrable evidence of deterrence, the suppression remedy nonetheless serves the noble purpose of preserving judicial integrity and preventing the courts from acting as partners with law enforcement officials in the violation of constitutional rights.

Examples

1. Detectives investigating a gambling ring had long heard rumors that insurance executive Maxwell Coffee was the main brain at the center of the operation. Lacking sufficient cause to obtain a warrant, but impatient to crack the ring, the detectives broke into Coffee's insurance agency at night and thoroughly searched his office. They discovered records of extensive illegal gambling activities, as well as $120,000 in cash.

   Because they were seized during an illegal search, the district attorney who subsequently prosecuted Coffee agreed not to offer the documents or cash into evidence at his trial. Coffee was, however, convicted on the basis of other evidence and testimony from former colleagues in crime. A sentencing hearing has been scheduled. The district attorney, desiring to bring before the judge all information relating to Coffee's deep involvement in the gambling ring, would like to offer into evidence the illegally obtained items. Will they be admissible during the sentencing proceedings?

2. Assistant principal Highman of Newton Public High School smelled pot coming from the boys' restroom. Upon entering, he discovers 15 boys and proceeds to search each of them, finding marijuana in Brandon's pocket. Assume that this search was in violation of the Fourth Amendment because there was not sufficient justification. Brandon seeks to suppress the marijuana from the school discipline hearing. What is his likelihood of success?

Explanations

1. The courts have generally allowed excluded evidence to be utilized for purposes of sentencing except where there is evidence of deliberate misconduct by the police. See *United States v. McIver*, 186 F.3d 1119 (9th Cir. 1999) (63 marijuana plants found in defendant's basement could be considered as relevant conduct under sentencing guidelines, notwithstanding the fact that the plants were suppressed at trial due to the illegal warrantless entry of defendant's house); *United States v. Tauil-Hernandez*, 88 F.3d 576 (8th Cir. 1996) (in calculating drug quantity for purposes of sentencing defendant for conspiracy to distribute cocaine, trial court could consider 500 grams of cocaine suppressed prior to defendant's guilty plea as illegally seized); *United States v. Ryan*, 236 F.3d 1268 (10th Cir. 2001) (narcotics seized in violation of motorist's Fourth Amendment rights were properly considered at sentencing in arriving at proper offense level for motorist's other, unrelated narcotics offenses, where no evidence that officers had purposefully violated motorist's rights to enhance his sentence); *United States v. Mattarolo*, 209 F.3d 1153 (9th Cir. 2000) (use for sentencing purposes of evidence and testimony related to prior searches of a drug defendant's property was permissible, even though such evidence was ruled inadmissible at trial, where prior searches revealed evidence that defendant was running a "chop shop" and methamphetamine lab on his property).

   In light of *Pennsylvania Board of Probation and Parole v. Scott*, 524 U.S. 357 (1998), refusing to apply the exclusionary rule to parole revocation hearings, and *United States v. Armstrong*, 187 F.3d 392 (4th Cir. 1999), extending *Scott* to federal supervised release revocation proceedings, it is unlikely that the sanction will be applied during sentencing hearings.

2. Utilizing the balancing approach, many courts have found that the interests at stake in school disciplinary hearings are substantially different than those at a criminal trial. In *Thompson v. Carthage School District*, 87 F.3d 979 (8th Cir. 1996), for example, the court refused to apply the exclusionary rule: "To the extent the exclusionary rule prevents the disciplining of students who disrupt education or endanger other students, it frustrates the critical governmental function of educating and protecting children." See also *Scanlon v. Las Cruces Public Schools*, 172 P.3d 185 (N.M. App. 2007) ("[w]hile a child's interest in continuing his education at the school where he is currently enrolled is significant, it is unrelated to the liberty interest at stake in a criminal trial."). Compare *Juan C. v. Cortines*, 647 N.Y.S.2d 491 (N.Y. App. Div. 1996), *rev'd*, 679 N.E.2d 1061 (N.Y. 1997) (the court held that the exclusionary rule applied because "if security aides are to be deterred from engaging in unlawful conduct with respect to the Fourth Amendment rights of students, they must understand that their methods of enforcing school safety rules are subject to scrutiny," but reversed on other grounds).

§7.3.3 The Good Faith Exception

As we have seen, the primary justification for the exclusionary rule is deterrence of constitutional violations. This purpose is most readily achieved when the violation is knowing and deliberate, because in that situation, the offending officer could have conformed his conduct to legal mandates and, presumably, will do so in the future rather than again risk the loss of relevant evidence. Where, however, the officer has made an honest mistake and was not even aware that he was violating the Fourth Amendment, the deterrent effect of suppressing the evidence is much harder to identify. Should the rule apply in such situations?

United States v. Leon, 468 U.S. 897 (1984), a decision representing a major constraint on the scope of the exclusionary remedy, held (at least in cases involving search warrants) that the exclusionary rule should not apply when the officers acted in "good faith." Expressing the Court's frustration with the rule (which it characterized as a judicially created remedy and not a constitutional mandate),[8] Justice White wrote:

> We have frequently questioned whether the exclusionary rule can have any deterrent effect when the offending officers acted in the objectively reasonable belief that their conduct did not violate the Fourth Amendment. No empirical researcher, proponent or opponent of the rule, has yet been able to establish with any assurance whether the rule has a deterrent effect. But even assuming that the rule effectively deters some police misconduct and provides incentives for the law enforcement profession as a whole to conduct itself in accord with the Fourth Amendment, it cannot be expected, and should not be applied, to deter objectively reasonable law enforcement activity.

468 U.S. at 918-919.

Recognizing that police officers are not lawyers and must often make quick judgments under considerable pressure, the Court held that probative evidence should not be excluded when the officers make reasonable mistakes regarding the legality of warrants.

Leon involved a warrant subsequently found to have been issued without an adequate showing of probable cause (the affidavit in support was based primarily on the word of a confidential informant of unproven reliability), and defendants sought suppression of the evidence seized. Finding that the warrant appeared to be valid on its face, the police officers were deemed

---

8. In their dissent, Justices Brennan and Marshall sharply disagreed: "Because seizures are executed principally to secure evidence, and because such evidence generally has utility in our legal system only in the context of a trial supervised by a judge, it is apparent that the admission of illegally obtained evidence implicates the same constitutional concerns as the initial seizure of that evidence. Indeed, by admitting unlawfully seized evidence, the judiciary becomes a part of what is in fact a single governmental action prohibited by the terms of the Amendment." 468 U.S. at 933.

to have reasonably relied upon it in their execution of the search. In such a situation, the Court concluded, the minimal possibility of deterrence of violations in the future is outweighed by the substantial costs of suppressing the evidence; namely, interference with the truth-finding function of the trial and the freeing of guilty parties.

Even if a reviewing court disagrees with the issuing magistrate's conclusion that probable cause existed, it may no longer exclude the evidence seized if the police officers reliance on the warrant was reasonable. The exclusionary remedy, the Court reminded, is directed against police officers, not judges and magistrates who are neutral judicial officers with no stake in the outcome of particular criminal prosecutions. Because the threat of exclusion cannot be expected to significantly deter judges and magistrates from constitutional infractions, it makes no sense to exclude evidence because of their mistakes. Suppression remains appropriate, of course, where the police officer's reliance upon the warrant was unreasonable (as explained below).

This good faith exception was broadened to cover the case of a warrant that erroneously described the items to be seized. See *Massachusetts v. Sheppard*, 468 U.S. 981 (1984). Officers conducting a homicide investigation applied for a warrant to search Sheppard's residence for evidence connecting him to the murder of his girlfriend. Because it was a Sunday, the only standard application form that the officers could locate was for a narcotics search. In their affidavit, they described the items sought as the murder weapon and the rope used to bind the victim. The judge promised to modify the narcotics search form so as to authorize the seizure of these items properly, but he failed to do so, and the warrant listed narcotics as the target of the search.

The warrant was executed and evidence of the homicide was discovered, but the Massachusetts courts suppressed it because the warrant failed to describe correctly the items sought and seized. Concluding however that the officers had acted in reasonable reliance upon the judge's assurance, the Supreme Court reversed: "We refuse to rule that an officer is required to disbelieve a judge who has just advised him, by word and by action, that the warrant he possesses authorizes him to conduct the search he has requested." 468 U.S. at 989-990. (Other decisions involving the interaction of the particularity requirement and the good faith exception are discussed in §5.2.3 in Chapter 5.)

But when officers executed a warrant that utterly failed to describe the things to be seized, but instead left the space for description blank, they forfeited the protection of the good faith defense. Such a warrant, the Court ruled in *Groh v. Ramirez*, 540 U.S. 551 (2004), was so facially invalid that reliance on it could not be regarded as reasonable. Compare *Messerschmidt v. Millender*, 132 S. Ct. 1235 (2012) (it was not entirely unreasonable for officers, in executing a warranted search, to believe that they had probable cause, as authorized by warrant, to search for any and all firearms and firearm-related materials, and not just the shotgun used in the underlying assault; see also §5.2.3).

The good faith exception does *not* apply (and thus the exclusionary remedy remains available) in the following cases:

1. Where the police misled (either deliberately or in reckless disregard of the truth) the magistrate in their application for the warrant (see § 5.2.2)
2. Where the warrant was so obviously invalid (either because probable cause is lacking or it fails to particularize the place to be searched or the things to be seized) that no officer could reasonably rely on it
3. Where the magistrate abandoned his neutral and detached posture

Thus as a consequence of *Leon* and *Sheppard*, a new level has been added to Fourth Amendment analysis in cases involving search warrants. Where it is determined that the warrant was defective because probable cause was lacking (see §4.1 in Chapter 4) or the particularity requirement was not complied with (see §5.2.3 in Chapter 5), it is now necessary to assess the "good faith" issue: Despite the defect(s), were the searching officers acting reasonably in relying upon the warrant? Was their mistake, in other words, a reasonable one (measured against the benchmark of what *Leon* refers to as the "reasonably well-trained officer")? If the answer is yes, then the exclusionary remedy may not be invoked.

Although *Leon* created a good faith exception in the context of searches conducted pursuant to a warrant,[9] the rationale of the decision could arguably support a more general exception to the exclusionary rule that applies to warrantless searches as well. Indeed, Justice Brennan described the decision in global terms as "the Court's victory over the Fourth Amendment," the culmination of a "gradual but determined strangulation of the exclusionary rule." 468 U.S. at 929 (Brennan and Marshall, dissenting).

The Court has in fact subsequently applied the good faith exception in a warrantless search context. In *Illinois v. Krull*, 480 U.S. 340 (1987), the officer conducted a warrantless search pursuant to a statute that was later declared unconstitutional. The Court ruled:

> The approach used in *Leon* is equally applicable in the present case. The application of the exclusionary rule to suppress evidence obtained by an officer acting in objectively reasonable reliance on a statute would have as little deterrent

---

9. In his dissent, Justice Stevens found it particularly ironic that the exception was carved out for warrant searches: "The notion that a police officer's reliance on a magistrate's warrant is automatically appropriate is one the Framers of the Fourth Amendment would have vehemently rejected. The precise problem that the Amendment was intended to address was the unreasonable issuance of warrants. The fact that colonial officers had magisterial authorization for their conduct when they engaged in general searches surely did not make their conduct 'reasonable.' The Court's view that it is consistent with our Constitution to adopt a rule that it is presumptively reasonable to rely on a defective warrant is the product of constitutional amnesia." 468 U.S. at 970-971.

> effect on the officer's actions as would the exclusion of evidence when an officer acts in objectively reasonable reliance on a warrant. Unless a statute is declared unconstitutional, an officer cannot be expected to question the judgment of the legislature that passed the law.

480 U.S. at 349-350.

A further expansion of the good faith exception occurred in *Arizona v. Evans*, 514 U.S. 1 (1995). During a routine traffic stop, the patrol car's computer erroneously (through a court employee's clerical error) indicated an outstanding arrest warrant for the driver, who was placed under arrest and searched. The defendant moved to suppress the marijuana that was found. The Court found no basis to believe that suppression would have a significant effect on court employees who were not engaged in law enforcement and thus refused to apply the rule.

Arizona v. Evans noted that the deterrence rationale was directed toward police personnel, not court employees. *Herring v. United States*, 129 S. Ct. 695 (2009), in turn emphasized that the police conduct must be deliberate to invoke that rationale. The police acted pursuant to information from another police department that there was an outstanding warrant. It turns out the warrant had been recalled and the erroneous information was negligently provided. The Court refused to suppress the drugs and gun that were found as a result of the arrest, since the conduct of the police wasn't deliberate and thus exclusion would have little deterrent effect.

This reasoning was followed yet again in *Davis v. North Carolina*, 131 S. Ct 2419 (2011). Police followed the dictates of *New York v. Belton* in searching the defendant's car incident to his arrest, but *Arizona v. Gant* (see §6.3 in Chapter 6) later modified those rules while his case was on appeal, and the search was unlawful under the new analysis. Since the police conduct was not deliberate, reckless, or grossly negligent, there would be no exclusion. Justice Alito, writing for the majority, observed: "It is one thing for the criminal to go free because the constable has blundered. It is quite another to set the criminal free because the constable has scrupulously adhered to governing law."

In the same vein, *Illinois v. Rodriguez*, 497 U.S. 177 (1990), held that the proper test for determining the validity of a warrantless search premised on third-party consent is not simply whether that party had *actual* authority over the premises, but rather whether there was *apparent* authority—that is, whether the facts known to the officer would justify a person of reasonable caution in the belief that the consenting party had authority over the premises. (See §6.7.) If the mistake by the police officer was reasonable, the exclusionary remedy will not apply.

By focusing exclusively on the goal of deterring individual police officers as opposed to others involved in the criminal justice system, the Court has thus significantly narrowed the exclusionary rule's reach and insulated many violations from judicial review. Several states have refused to read a good faith exception into their own constitutions. See *State v. Martin*, 761 A.2d 516, 520 (N.H. 2000) ("The Framers did not intend the safeguards of the warrant requirement to be circumvented merely by allowing law enforcement officials to act reasonably under the circumstances."); *State v. Prior*, 617 N.W.2d 260, 268 (Iowa 2000) ("Regardless of the good faith of police in relying upon a search warrant approved and issued by a judicial officer, the exclusionary rule remains the best way to protect the integrity of the judicial process and an individual's right under our state constitution to be free from government conduct ultimately determined to be unlawful."); *State v. Balduc*, 514 N.W.2d 607, 611 (Minn. Ct. App. 1994); *Boatright v. State*, 393 S.E.2d 707, 708 (Ga. Ct. App. 1997); *Commonwealth v. Upton*, 394 Mass. 363, 476 N.E.2d 548 (1985); *State v. Novembrino*, 105 N.J. 95 (1987); and *Commonwealth v. Edmunds*, 526 Pa. 374, 586 A.2d 889 (1991).

Examples

1. Officer Jumpthegun has been investigating a string of credit card burglaries. While at a local supermarket, she overhears another shopper say to his companion that "my neighbor Ralph Rabbit has been spending money like it's going out of style." Jumpthegun concludes that Rabbit must be the burglar she is seeking, and she applies for a warrant to search Rabbit's home, setting forth the conversation that she heard in the supermarket as her probable cause showing. Magistrate Rubberstamp hurriedly reviews the application and issues the warrant, which, when executed by Jumpthegun, turns up evidence connecting Rabbit to the burglaries. On the defendant's motion to suppress on the grounds that the warrant was defective, the prosecution concedes (as it must) that probable cause to search was lacking but contends nonetheless that Jumpthegun acted in good faith, and thus the *Leon* exception should apply. What result?

2. Officer Nixon was summoned to the home of Chamber Whittaker, who had received three anonymous typewritten letters setting out threats to bomb his house and car. Whittaker informed the officer that the letters appeared to have been written on the old Underwood typewriter that he had given his former wife, Janet, before they split up (unamicably) one month before. Nixon's investigation developed probable cause to believe that Janet Whittaker had in fact sent the letters. He also learned that Janet had no permanent residence but had been staying for short periods of time with various relatives and friends. Having a hunch that she might be at the home of her father, Fred Findley, Nixon set out the information known to him, as well as his hunch, in an application for a warrant to search Findley's residence for the Underwood typewriter.

The warrant was issued, and Nixon conducted the search. The officer's hunch bore fruit — Janet was living at her father's home, and the typewriter was found and seized. An FBI expert is prepared to testify at trial that the letters sent to Chamber were typed on the Underwood. Janet's attorney has moved to suppress the typewriter, but the prosecution is relying on the good faith exception. What result?

3. Based on an adequate showing of probable cause to believe that large amounts of cocaine would be found at the home of Dennis Demon, 100 Main Street, Magistrate Careless issued a search warrant. Although Demon's address was set out in the police officer's affidavit requesting the warrant, the magistrate neglected to fill in the address to be searched in the space provided on the form warrant that she issued. The police officers conducted the search and seized 600 grams of cocaine. Defendant Demon challenges the use of the evidence at trial on the grounds that the warrant was facially defective in that it did not indicate the place to be searched. What result? Would it make a difference if the officers executing the warrant were not the same officers who had conducted the investigation and filed the application?

4. While on routine cruiser patrol, Trooper Thomas's attention was drawn to a late-model Lincoln luxury sedan being driven by a very young driver. His suspicions aroused, Thomas radioed in the license plate of the vehicle. When he did so, however, he transposed two digits of the plate number and reported it incorrectly as RT-234 (the actual number was RT-324). The dispatcher ran a check on RT-234 and reported back to Thomas that the plate had been issued to a 1995 Chevy Impala. Erroneously concluding that the vehicle he had under observation had been stolen, the trooper pulled it over. When he approached the driver, Thomas observed drug paraphernalia and a large quantity of marijuana on the seat next to the driver. The trooper placed the driver under arrest and seized the contraband. The prosecution relies on the good faith exception to avoid suppression. What result?

5. On March 10, 2014, Jones was lawfully arrested for distribution of narcotics. As part of the search incident to the arrest the police seized an iPhone. The police then went through the phone log and discovered many known drug users in the log. At the trial in the summer of 2014, Jones filed a motion to suppress this evidence and the prosecution relied on the good faith exception to avoid suppression. What result?

Explanations

1. Despite the name it has been given, the "good faith" exception applies only where the police officer's reliance on the warrant was *objectively* reasonable. The subjective good intentions of the officer are not relevant to the inquiry. Because no reasonably well-trained police officer could rely on the warrant issued by Magistrate Rubberstamp (given the clear absence of adequate probable cause), the *Leon* exception would not apply here.

   Needless to say, most cases will fall in a more gray area than example 1. Although Justice White asserted in *Leon* that the good faith exception should not be difficult to apply in practice because it turns on objective reasonableness, lawyers and law students are all too aware of the wide room for disagreement that such a concept imparts.

   Given the flexible probable cause standard established by *Illinois v. Gates* (discussed in §4.1 in Chapter 4), together with the elastic good faith exception to the operation of the exclusionary sanction, the issue that must be resolved in such cases is: Should a reasonably well-trained police officer have recognized that there was not a fair probability that contraband or other evidence of a crime would be found at the place to be searched? Put another way, evidence seized pursuant to a warrant will be suppressed if 1) probable cause was lacking under the totality-of-the-circumstances/fair probability standard of *Gates*, and 2) a reasonably well-trained officer would have recognized this deficiency.

   Another issue could be raised if Magistrate Rubberstamp did not bother to read the affidavit before issuing the warrant. This would bring into question whether Rubberstamp was the "neutral and detached" magistrate required by the Fourth Amendment. See §5.2.1 in Chapter 5. *Leon* indicated that the good faith exception does not apply if the magistrate abdicated his impartial role. Although the example used in *Leon* for a lack of neutrality cited *Lo-Ji Sales v. New York*, 442 U.S. 319, 327 (1979) (see §5.2.1), in which the magistrate actually participated in the execution of the warrant, a credible argument could be made that Magistrate Rubberstamp abdicated his responsibility. However, the Court's emphasis in *Arizona v. Evans*, 514 U.S. 1 (1995) (discussed above), on deterrence of police officers, as opposed to other officials such as magistrates, might signal a willingness to reconsider and perhaps remove this limitation on the good faith exception.

2. Probable cause to search Findley's home (that is, facts and circumstances that would lead a reasonable person to conclude that items related to the bomb threats would be found there) was clearly lacking because Nixon disclosed to the magistrate no solid information to connect Janet or the typewriter to that location. The only question to be resolved, therefore,

is whether Officer Nixon reasonably relied upon the warrant when he conducted the search. *Leon* made clear that an officer cannot manifest objective good faith if the warrant that he is relying upon was "so lacking in indicia of probable cause as to render official belief in its existence entirely unreasonable." 468 U.S. at 923. A reasonably well-trained officer would have recognized that this affidavit, which failed to link the place to be searched concretely with the items sought, was in that category and that consequently, the warrant was not properly issued. The good faith exception thus should not apply here.

As the Ninth Circuit Court of Appeals explained in a case involving similar facts (where the affidavit offered "no hint as to why the police wanted to search this residence") and holding the good faith exception inapplicable: "*Leon* creates an exception to the exclusionary rule when officers have acted in reasonable reliance on the ruling of a judge or magistrate. The point is that officers who present a colorable showing of probable cause to a judicial officer ought to be able to rely on that officer's ruling in executing the warrant. When the officers have not presented a colorable showing, and the warrant and affidavit on their face preclude reasonable reliance, the reasoning of *Leon* does not apply." *United States v. Hove*, 848 F.2d 137, 140 (9th Cir. 1988). Compare *United States v. Bynum*, 293 F.3d 192, 195 (4th Cir. 2002) (even if there was lack of probable cause to support search warrant, good faith exception applied because affidavit was not so lacking in indicia of probable cause to render belief in its existence entirely unreasonable); *United States v. Glinton*, 154 F.3d 1245, 1257 (11th Cir. 1998) (search warrant affidavit submitted to the magistrate was not a "bare-bones" statement of nothing more than conclusory allegations, thus the good faith exception was applicable).

The wide room for disagreement concerning what a reasonably well-trained police officer should know about probable cause to search is illustrated by *United States v. Savoca*, 761 F.2d 292 (6th Cir. 1985). The affidavit in support of the warrant merely recited that two persons who had just been arrested for a bank robbery, which occurred 2,000 miles away, had been seen recently in the motel room to be searched. Conceding that probable cause to search that particular location was lacking, a majority of the Court of Appeals nonetheless concluded that a reasonably well-trained officer could have relied properly on the warrant:

> [T]he defect in the affidavit was that it only tenuously connected the place to be searched with two persons for whom arrest warrants were outstanding. It failed to describe the relationship of the persons to the premises and it did not state how recently the bank robberies had occurred. On these facts, our *Hatcher* decision [emphasizing the well-established legal principle that probable cause to arrest will not necessarily establish probable cause to search] is controlling on the question of probable cause. Whether a reasonably well-trained

officer could believe that this affidavit stated probable cause for the search thus depends in part on whether such an officer would be aware of *Hatcher* and related decisions and the principle for which those cases stand. We conclude that a reasonably well-trained officer would be aware of the principle which *Hatcher* amplifies [sic]; we also conclude, however, that such an officer could conclude that *Hatcher* and related decisions are distinguishable and that the warrant was not, therefore, invalid.

761 F.2d at 297.

Dissenting Circuit Judge Jones, on the other hand, viewed the affidavit as so lacking in indicia of probable cause as to render official belief in its existence entirely unreasonable: "[T]he general principle requiring a nexus between the evidence sought and the place to be searched, in addition to the mere presence of a suspect, is sufficiently clear that a reasonably well-trained police officer should have known that the mere presence of Savoca at the hotel room could not constitute probable cause for a search warrant of the hotel room." 761 F.2d at 302. See also *United States v. Laughton*, 409 F.3d 744 (6th Cir. 2005) (holding that an affidavit that did not indicate that the informant had made multiple drug purchases, that the informant had purchased narcotics from the suspect, and where the residence was or when observations of drug purchases were made, was so lacking in indicia of probable cause that no reasonable officer could have believed it to be reliable); *United States v. Watkins*, 179 F.3d 489, 497-500 (6th Cir. 1999) (collecting cases applying the good faith exception where probable cause was lacking because of an insufficient nexus between defendant and the place searched).

Some courts seem willing to factor in information possessed by the officer that is not contained in the affidavit for the warrant. See, e.g., *United States v. Frazier*, 423 F.3d 526, 537 (6th Cir. 2005) ("A reasonably well-trained officer could infer that a drug dealer who kept drugs in his former home would also keep drugs in his current home. Indeed, Agent Steward averred, based on his training and experience, that drug dealers usually continue their trade after moving to a new residence, and that people who sell drugs often keep drugs and guns in their homes.").

A factor weighed by courts in determining the reasonableness of an officer's conduct is the time pressure under which he operated. In *United States v. Ramos*, 923 F.2d 1346, 1355 n.18 (9th Cir. 1991), the court observed that the officers who had obtained the warrant had generated a nine-page affidavit in a matter of hours after the arrest of several perpetrators: "Under the circumstances it is not entirely inscrutable that the affidavit failed to include some information which officers observed and which may have bolstered a finding of probable cause." See also *United States v. Capozzi*, 91 F. Supp. 2d 423, 434 (D. Mass. 2000) (officers were acting under significant time pressure in obtaining a warrant to search a motel room renewed by the week).

In *United States v. Weber*, 923 F.2d 1338, 1346 (9th Cir. 1991), in contrast, because the government planned the undercover delivery that provided the occasion for the search, it had complete control over its timing. "Under these circumstances, there was no need for the hurried judgment upon which law enforcement decisions must often be based. Although we do not question the subjective good faith of the government, it acted unreasonably in preparing the affidavit it presented." See also *United States v. Zimmerman*, 277 F.3d 426 (3d Cir. 2002) (no good faith exception exists where an officer was not operating under any time pressure, and minimal further investigation would have caused the officer to question the reliability of statements made by the defendant's mother).

3. The warrant in our example fails to indicate the address to be searched, and thus unquestionably violates the Fourth Amendment mandate that the place to be searched be described particularly. The prosecution can avoid suppression only if it can establish that the officers acted in objectively reasonable reliance on it. Suppression is required, on the other hand, if the warrant was so facially deficient in failing to particularize the target premises that the executing officers could not reasonably presume it to be valid.

The courts have tended to view errors such as the one here as more clerical than substantive, and in the absence of evidence that the police officers acted in bad faith (by, for example, deceiving the magistrate, or with knowledge that the warrant was defective, or in reckless disregard for the requirements of the Fourth Amendment), the *Leon* exception has been applied. See *Massachusetts v. Sheppard*, 468 U.S. 981 (1984) (discussed above; failure of warrant to correctly describe items sought because of the magistrate's clerical error); *Maryland v. Garrison*, 480 U.S. 79 (1987) (discussed in §5.2.3 in Chapter 5; the warrant incorrectly authorized a search of the entire floor, where probable cause existed for only one of the two separate apartments); *United States v. Kelley*, 140 F.3d 596 (5th Cir. 1998) (unsigned and undated warrant was due to magistrate's error); *United States v. Smith*, 63 F.3d 766 (8th Cir. 1995) (the fact that the magistrate judge did not sign a jurat on the affidavit supporting search warrants did not render reliance on the affidavit unreasonable, as the exclusionary rule was designed to apply to illegal conduct of police officers, not clerical mistakes by judges); *United States v. Lora-Solano*, 330 F.3d 1288 (10th Cir. 2003) (anticipatory search warrant's single-digit error as to street address did not render warrant invalid on particularity grounds, given the informant's identification of the correct premises, so good faith exception to exclusionary rule applied); *United States v. Albert*, 195 F. Supp. 2d 267 (D. Mass. 2002) (agents who conducted the search relied on the warrant in good faith where omission of any reference to the list of items to be searched was a clerical error).

The decision in each of these cases reasoned that exclusion of the evidence would not significantly deter future violations because the officers had reasonably relied on facially sufficient warrants issued by magistrates. While deliberate police dishonesty or gross negligence can (and of course should) be discouraged, the theory goes, objective reasonable reliance cannot (and should not) be deterred. As for errors made by a magistrate, the suppression remedy is not (as *Leon* emphasized) directed at those players in the criminal justice process.

Would it make a difference if the officers executing the warrant in example 3 were not the same officers who had conducted the investigation and filed the application? In assessing whether reliance on a search warrant was objectively reasonable under the circumstances, courts take into account the knowledge that the searching officer possessed at the time. *Massachusetts v. Sheppard* emphasized that Detective O'Malley, who conducted the search, was also the officer who had filed the affidavit requesting the warrant and therefore knew what items were listed in the affidavit presented to the judge, and he had "good reason to believe that the warrant authorized the seizure of those items." 468 U.S. at 989 n.6. "Whether an officer who is less familiar with the warrant application or who has unalleviated concerns about the proper scope of the search would be justified in failing to notice a defect like the one in the warrant in this case is an issue we need not decide. We hold only that it was not unreasonable for the police in this case to rely on the judge's assurances that the warrant authorized the search they had requested." *Id.*

Similarly in *United States v. Curry*, 911 F.2d 72 (8th Cir. 1990), the court found it significant that the search was conducted by the same officer who had prepared the application for the warrant. 911 F.2d at 78. Although the warrant itself omitted the address, the officer was aware that Curry's correct address was stated in the affidavit, and his reliance upon the warrant was deemed reasonable despite its facial deficiency. See also *United States v. Thomas*, 263 F.3d 805 (8th Cir. 2001) (good faith exception justified denial of defendant's motion to suppress, as the fact that the same officer who filed the application for the warrant executed it, eliminating the chance that the wrong location would be searched); *United States v. Gordon*, 901 F.2d 48, 50 (5th Cir. 1990) (officer who conducted the search had initially provided the information for the supporting affidavit and thus knew correct location of defendant's residence).

Furthermore, in an opinion by Judge Sonia Sotomayor, the Second Circuit used the good faith exception to uphold a search even after it was found that probable cause was lacking. A reasonable police officer could rely on the warrant, the court concluded, and there was no showing that the police officer used a false statement. *United States v. Falso*, 544 F.3d 110 (2d Cir. 2008).

Consequently, the good faith exception might not apply in example 3 if the officer conducting the search had not been the same officer who had filed the earlier application for the warrant. The searching officer would then have been faced with a warrant that did not specify any address, and he would not have known that the address had been provided to the magistrate in the supporting affidavit. An officer under those circumstances would not be acting in reasonable reliance upon the facially defective warrant.

4. A good part of the rationale expressed in *Leon* and *Sheppard* is limited to situations involving warrants—the major premise being that police officers, as nonlawyers, should be able to rely on the judgment of trained magistrates as to the proper circumstances for a search and should not be penalized for the errors of a magistrate. Moreover, an officer's objective reasonableness is easier to measure against the benchmark of a warrant and supporting documentation than it is where the officer simply acts on his own. For these reasons, several circuit courts had refused to extend the good faith exception to warrantless searches. See, e.g., *United States v. Ramirez-Rivera*, 800 F.3d 1 (1st Cir. 2015); *United States v. Scales*, 903 F.2d 765 (10th Cir. 1990); *United States v. Winsor*, 846 F.2d 1569 (9th Cir. 1988). Nonetheless, the Supreme Court has extended the good faith exception to at least some warrantless police conduct. See *Illinois v. Krull*, 480 U.S. 340 (1987) and *Arizona v. Evans*, 514 U.S. 1 (1995), discussed above.

The issue remains whether the exception should apply in the case of a police mistake. In the case upon which example 4 is loosely based, *United States v. De Leon-Reyna*, 930 F.2d 396 (5th Cir. 1991), the court sitting *en banc* held the exception applicable to a stop made in good faith reliance on information that was inaccurate because of an error by the police officer in reporting the subject's license number. Despite the negligence, the officer was deemed to have acted reasonably when he stopped the vehicle that he believed to have been stolen. Under this view, the suppression remedy is unavailable for *any* police error, whether in reliance on a warrant or otherwise, where the officer maintains a good faith and objectively reasonable belief that he has an adequate foundation to act. This rationale was upheld in *Herring v. United States*, 129 S. Ct. 695 (2009), where the Court refused to suppress on the ground that the police misinformation was a result of negligence as opposed to willful conduct.

The same result would follow if the mistake in our example had originated with a clerk rather than the police officer. *Arizona v. Evans*, supra, teaches that because the deterrence behind the exclusionary rule is directed only at law enforcement personnel, there would be no basis for suppression so long as the officer reasonably relied upon the clerk's erroneous report. See also *United States v. Santa*, 180 F.3d 20 (2d Cir. 1999) (arresting officers' reliance on a statewide computer database record erroneously showing existence of an outstanding arrest warrant for defendant was objectively reasonable). At least one circuit court has extended the good faith exception to a reasonable mistake attributed to a police dispatcher. See *United States v. Shareef*, 100 F.3d 1491 (10th Cir. 1996).

5. Because the search occurred prior to the decision in *Riley v. California*, 134 S. Ct. 999 (2014), the good faith exception to the exclusionary rule applies to this case. In *Davis v. United States*, 131 S. Ct. 2419 (2011), the Court considered the retroactive effect of a decision by the Supreme Court subsequent to the officer's actions. As deterrence is the main objective of the exclusionary rule, where the officer believes he was acting lawfully under existing precedent, there is no reason to apply the exclusionary rule. See also *United States v. Clark*, 29 F. Supp. 3d 1131 (E.D. Tenn. 2014) (good faith exception applied to officer's warrantless search of data on defendant's cell phone, which was seized following his arrest; although Supreme Court subsequently ruled that search incident to arrest exception to Fourth Amendment's warrant requirement did not apply to cell phones, officer was objectively reasonable in believing that he did not need a warrant to search the phone, given the state of the law when the search was conducted).

§7.3.4 The Impeachment Exception

We have seen (in §7.3.2) that the Court has confined the exclusionary sanction to criminal proceedings. Within that context, the Court has further limited its scope: Evidence unlawfully obtained is admissible when used solely to impeach the defendant's testimony at trial. As with its counterpart in the *Miranda* doctrine (see §9.3.2 in Chapter 9), the impeachment exception is premised on a cost-benefit analysis that holds that whatever marginal deterrence is achieved by excluding the evidence for impeachment (as well as substantive) purposes is outweighed by the cost of permitting a defendant to perjure himself without effective challenge from the prosecution.

United States v. Havens, 446 U.S. 620 (1980), illustrates the operation and rationale of the exception. Havens was subjected to a search, and a T-shirt was seized that linked him to cocaine carried by his traveling companion. Prior to trial, the court held the search unlawful and ruled that the T-shirt could not be used in evidence. After the government presented its case, Havens took the stand in his own defense, and on cross-examination, denied having any connection to the incriminating T-shirt. At that point, the prosecution was permitted to introduce the shirt for the limited purpose of challenging Havens's credibility. "It is essential to the proper functioning of the adversary system," the Court held, "that when a defendant takes the stand, the government be permitted proper and effective cross-examination in an attempt to elicit the truth." 446 U.S. at 626-627.

Thus, while the prosecution cannot use illegally obtained evidence during its case-in-chief, if the defendant chooses to testify, he may be confronted with the evidence for purposes of impeachment. Concerned that extension of this opening would too significantly undercut the deterrent function of the exclusionary rule, the Court has limited the impeachment exception to testimony by the defendant—it does not allow use of unlawfully obtained items to impeach *other* defense witnesses. See *James v. Illinois*, 493 U.S. 307 (1990). In a rare instance in which the cost-benefit balancing approach resulted in a decision in favor of the exclusion of relevant evidence, Justice Brennan reasoned for a closely divided Court that the costs of extending the impeachment exception to defense witnesses would be greater than those involved in impeachment of the defendant himself, and the benefits would be less. Among the costs are the risks of discouraging defendants from calling witnesses (knowing that this might bring in otherwise inadmissible evidence) and of encouraging police misconduct by making unlawfully seized evidence more valuable to the prosecution. The main benefit achieved—enhancement of the truth-seeking function of the trial—is less compelling in the case of the defense witness than that of the defendant himself because the former is far more likely to be deterred from perjury by the mere threat of a perjury prosecution.

Illustrating the elasticity of the cost-benefit analysis, four dissenters reached the opposite conclusion in *James v. Illinois*. Justice Kennedy reasoned that the cost to the truth-seeking function of excluding relevant impeaching evidence is greater in the case of the defense witness than that of the defendant, whom the jurors are less likely in any event to credit as an impartial witness. Moreover, he asserted it was unrealistic to believe that police officers would be encouraged to violate a defendant's constitutional rights by the knowledge that evidence obtained (although otherwise inadmissible) could be used to impeach a defense witness—the officer's decision to conduct an illegal search does not turn on such a "precise calculation of the possibilities of rebuttal at some future trial." 493 U.S. at 318.

§7.3.5 Harmless Error

Not all errors committed during trial proceedings, even if of constitutional dimension, automatically require a reversal of the conviction. Rather, if it appears that a conviction would have resulted in *any event* because of the overwhelming weight of the prosecution's case, the verdict will not be overturned. See *Chapman v. California*, 386 U.S. 18 (1967). The burden is on the prosecution to establish beyond a reasonable doubt that "the error complained of did not contribute to the verdict obtained"—that the error was "harmless." Reflecting its continuing concern about the costs of the exclusionary rule (particularly the freeing of apparently guilty defendants), the

Court in *Arizona v. Fulminante*, 499 U.S. 279 (1991), broke with precedent and extended the harmless error doctrine to the admission at trial of a coerced confession. If the reviewing court determines that the jury would have convicted the defendant even in the absence of the coerced statement, then the conviction will be affirmed. In making this determination, courts are directed to consider the following factors: whether the conviction depended on the jurors believing the confession, whether the jury's evaluation of an additional uncoerced confession relied on its relation to the coerced confession, and whether the admission of the coerced confession led to the admission of other evidence.

The *Fulminante* dissenters would have adhered to the "consistent line of authority that has recognized as a basic tenet of our criminal justice system the prohibition against using a defendant's coerced confession against him at his criminal trial." 499 U.S. at 295. In addition to the risk that coerced confessions may be untrustworthy, they argued: "More importantly, however, the use of coerced confessions, whether true or false, is forbidden because the methods used to extract them offend an underlying principle in the enforcement of our criminal law: that ours is an accusatorial and not an inquisitorial system—a system in which the State must establish guilt by evidence independently and freely secured and may not by coercion prove its charge against an accused out of his own mouth." 499 U.S. at 293 (White, Marshall, Blackmun, and Stevens, JJ., dissenting).

PART II

Interrogation and Confessions

The Voluntariness Standard

What are the rights of an individual who is being questioned by the police about suspected criminal activity? This issue, like that of search and seizure, requires the delicate balancing of conflicting goals. On the one hand is the compelling interest in obtaining information about crime, which may be available only from the suspect himself. On the other hand is the concern in a democratic society for protecting the individual from governmental coercion and overreaching. Unlike the inquisitorial criminal justice systems of continental Europe, which place primary reliance on incriminatory statements elicited from the suspect, the American accusatorial process reflects a longstanding aversion to convictions obtained solely through the accused's own mouth and a preference for evidence "independently secured through skillful investigation." *Watts v. Indiana*, 338 U.S. 49, 54 (1949) (Frankfurter, J.).

The Supreme Court has, over time, approached the interrogation dilemma from a variety of constitutional perspectives. The Fifth and Sixth Amendment approaches will be discussed in the chapters that follow. Our focus here is on the first cut that the Court took at the problem, which focused on the "voluntariness" of the statement obtained from the suspect.

Invoking the fundamental fairness concept of the Fourteenth Amendment Due Process Clause, the Court ruled in 1936 that a statement obtained by police that was not the product of voluntary choice by the suspect could not be admitted at trial. See *Brown v. Mississippi*, 297 U.S. 278 (1936) (suspects were physically beaten until they confessed). The two concerns prompting exclusion of coerced confessions are their unreliability and revulsion against the methods used to extract them. *Rogers v. Richmond*, 365 U.S. 534, 540 (1961) (Rogers confessed to murder after his interrogator went through the pretense of summoning his ill wife to the police station for questioning). The second concern became the predominant one, so that the critical issue is "whether the police behavior was such as to overbear [the suspect's] will to resist and bring about confessions not freely self determined—a question to be answered with complete disregard of whether or not [the suspect] in fact spoke the truth." *Rogers v. Richmond*, 365 U.S. at 543.

How is it to be determined whether the accused's will was overborne at the time that he confessed? The Court has adopted a totality-of-the-circumstances analysis that weighs numerous considerations. One set of factors focuses on the suspect's peculiar characteristics and vulnerabilities, such as age, level of education, mental stability, state of sobriety, and familiarity with the criminal justice process. The other factors concern the manner in which the police conducted the interrogation, such as the length of the suspect's detention, the duration and intensity of the questioning, the use of trickery, deception, threats, or promises of leniency, the deprivation of access to family, friends, or nourishment, whether the police advised the suspect of her rights (see Chapter 9), and whether she was subjected to any physical or psychological mistreatment.

While the use of physical force to extract a confession would clearly violate the voluntariness standard, most cases fall in the more murky area requiring close attention to the particular characteristics of the accused and the details of the interrogation. The more vulnerable the suspect, the more likely that a confession obtained by police will be suppressed. Thus, for example, a seriously wounded suspect who was questioned in the hospital intensive care unit while in considerable pain and barely conscious was held to have made an involuntary (and thus inadmissible) confession, even though the police did not engage in any "gross abuses" during the interrogation. See *Mincey v. Arizona*, 437 U.S. 385 (1978).

The importance of the police-conduct side of the equation was highlighted in *Colorado v. Connelly*, 479 U.S. 157 (1986). Connelly had initiated contact with the police when he told an officer on the street that he had killed someone and wanted to talk about it; he later confessed to an unsolved murder that had been committed months earlier. Connelly later moved to suppress the confession on the grounds that it was involuntary. A psychiatrist testified that Connelly suffered from command auditory hallucinations, a mental disorder that rendered him unable to resist instructions that he "hears" in his head, and that Connelly had been commanded by the "voice of God" to confess to the murder. Deeming this confession involuntary and not the product of free choice, the state courts ruled it inadmissible. The Supreme Court reversed, ruling (per Chief Justice Rehnquist) that admission of the confession did not violate due process because it was not the product of overreaching by the police.

"Coercive police activity," the Court held, "is a necessary predicate to a finding that a confession is not voluntary within the meaning of the Due

Process Clause of the Fourteenth Amendment." 479 U.S. at 166. While the susceptible mental condition of the subject is a factor to be weighed in the balance, suppression is appropriate only where it can be demonstrated that the police exploited that condition by means of coercion, and that the confession resulted from that exploitation.

Challenging a confession under the voluntariness standard therefore requires a showing that

- the police subjected the suspect to **coercive conduct**; and
- the conduct was sufficient to **overcome the will** of the suspect (given her particular vulnerabilities and the conditions of the interrogation), thus inducing an involuntary statement.

The second requirement incorporates the totality-of-the-circumstances analysis discussed above. As the examples below illustrate, this standard by its very nature is subjective and *ad hoc*, providing police with little concrete guidance as to what conduct is constitutionally acceptable during interrogation. Indeed the "voluntariness rubric has been variously condemned as 'useless,' 'perplexing,' and 'legal double-talk.'" *Miller v. Fenton*, 474 U.S. 104, 116 n.4 (1985) (O'Connor, J.). Because it is so fact-specific, application of the standard to questioning invariably conducted incommunicado frequently leaves courts with credibility contests between the suspect's and the interrogator's versions of the events leading up to the challenged confession. "Such disputes," Justice Black observed, "are an inescapable consequence of secret inquisitorial practices." *Ashcraft v. Tennessee*, 322 U.S. 143, 152 (1944). And *Connelly* brings into the picture an additional level of uncertainty (explored in the examples that follow): What constitutes coercive activity for purposes of the due process standard?

Despite these shortcomings and its partial eclipse by the *Miranda* (Fifth Amendment) and *Massiah* (Sixth Amendment) doctrines (discussed in Chapters 9 and 10, respectively), the voluntariness standard remains an important part of the constitutional analysis of interrogation and confessions. It provides an alternative method of challenging confessions where *Miranda* is not applicable (because the suspect is not in "custody" or subjected to "interrogation"). In *Arizona v. Fulminante*, 499 U.S. 279 (1991), for example, defendant challenged a confession he made to a fellow inmate who, unbeknownst to him, was cooperating with the government to obtain evidence against him. The confession was obtained by playing on his fear of other inmates, and then promising him protection from them. Because there was no interrogation (see §9.2.2 of Chapter 9), *Miranda* was not an available avenue of challenge. Fulminante was nonetheless able to successfully attack the confession as involuntary (in this case, the Court held that involuntary confession would be tested by the harmless error standard but in this case the confession was not a harmless error, see §7.3.5 of Chapter 7). And even where *Miranda* applies and has been complied with, a statement shown to have been involuntary must be suppressed under the Due Process Clause.

Although Congress in 1968 purported to overrule *Miranda* and replace it with the voluntariness test, see 18 U.S.C. §3501, the Court has ruled that Congress has no power to supersede *Miranda* legislatively as it is a constitutional mandate. *Dickerson v. United States*, 530 U.S. 428 (2000). For more, see Chapter 9.

Examples

The Voluntariness Calculus

1. The police arrested Carey Corn on suspicion of homicide and transported him to the police station. He is a 30-year-old high school dropout of below-normal intelligence, and he has an extensive criminal record. Corn suffers from diabetes, requiring him to take medication twice daily and to eat at regular intervals. He arrived at the police station at 9:00 P.M. and was interrogated in a small room for four hours by Officer Maple, during which time Corn refused to respond to questions. He was taken to a cell in which a plank fastened to the wall served as a bed. Corn was not able to sleep. At 7:00 A.M., he was taken again to the interrogation room where he waited alone for two hours before Officer Maple appeared and resumed questioning. At 11:30 A.M. he confessed orally to involvement in the homicide. During the entire time at the police station, Corn received coffee and water but neither requested nor was offered food or medication. Could Corn prevent this statement from being admitted as evidence at trial under the due process voluntariness standard?

Promises, Promises

2. Assume the same facts as example 1. In addition, while conducting the interrogation, the officer tells Corn: "Look, I'm your only friend now. I can make the difference between you doing hard time and getting off easy. But I need your cooperation if you want me to make the right things happen for you. You've got to admit what you did, and then I'll help you." Corn makes an incriminating statement. What effect should the officer's comments have on the voluntariness analysis?

Threats

3. Assume the same facts as example 1. In addition, while conducting the interrogation the officer tells Corn: "This looks like first-degree murder from where I sit. You're looking at the lethal injection, Carey. You can admit you did the crime and save your skin, or go the silence route and die an agonizing death on the table." Corn makes an incriminating statement. What effect should the officer's comments have on the voluntariness analysis?

What if the police threaten to arrest Corn's father, who they think may have known in advance about his son's plans to commit murder?

Deception and Trickery

4. Assume the same facts as example 1, except that during the interrogation, the officer falsely tells Corn that his close friend and alleged accomplice, McCoy, has "given him up" and implicated him in the crime. Corn then makes an incriminating statement. What effect should the officer's comments have on the voluntariness analysis?

Drug-Induced Confession

5. A homicide suspect in custody attempted to hang herself while in her cell. She was rescued and taken to a hospital, where she was injected with a powerful tranquilizer. Officers later appeared in the hospital room and questioned her concerning the crime. Unbeknownst to the officers, the tranquilizer in her system had the properties of a truth serum, and she soon confessed. In support of her motion to suppress the statement as violative of her rights under the Due Process Clause, she has presented medical testimony indicating that an individual under the influence of that drug would not be capable of withholding information or resisting questioning. Should her motion be allowed?

Juvenile Confessions

6. Johnny, age 14, was visited at his home by two armed police officers investigating the murder of a gang member. Johnny had been a member of a rival gang since he was 11 and has had numerous run-ins with the police. Johnny's father was present at the start of the interrogation but left after about ten minutes. The police read Johnny the *Miranda* warnings, and then told him (falsely) that a fellow gang member had fingered him and that if he did not want "to take the rap alone he'd best start talking." After about an hour, Johnny made a statement implicating himself in the murder. What effect should Johnny's age have on the voluntariness of the confession?

Explanations

The Voluntariness Calculus

1. This example (as does example 5) illustrates the substantial impact of *Colorado v. Connelly*, 479 U.S. 157 (1986). Prior to *Connelly*, suppression simply required a showing that under the totality-of-the-circumstances analysis, Corn did not speak of his own free will. Corn would point to his limited education and intelligence and his medical condition, along with the deprivation of sleep, food, and medication during interrogation, to

show that he was vulnerable and his will had been overborne. The prosecution would respond by noting that he is a mature adult who had had considerable experience dealing with the police and was thus not likely intimidated by them. The court would make a finding as to whether the confession was involuntary.

After *Connelly*, that analysis is not reached unless Corn can demonstrate that the police resorted to "coercive" action. As one court put it, *Connelly* renders the personal characteristics of the defendant "constitutionally irrelevant absent proof of coercion brought to bear on the defendant by the State." *Henderson v. Norris*, 118 F.3d 1283, 1288 (8th Cir. 1997). See also *United States v. Boskic*, 545 F.3d 69, 78 (1st Cir. 2008) ("after *Connelly*, only confessions procured by coercive official tactics should be excluded as involuntary"). Thus, several courts have discounted mental disorders of the suspect, even where they rendered him highly vulnerable to suggestion, in the absence of evidence of physical or psychological coercion. See *Dassey v. Dittmann*, 877 F.3d 297 (7th Cir. 2017) (no showing that police interrogators exploited defendant's acknowledged low IQ level); *United States v. Cristobal*, 293 F.3d 134, 141 (4th Cir. 2002) (no showing that police exploited defendant's weakened mental condition); *United States v. Santos*, 131 F.3d 16, 19 (1st Cir. 1997). Compare *United States v. Preston*, 751 F.3d 1008, 1019 (9th Cir. 2014) (under the totality of the circumstances, intellectually disabled defendant's confession was involuntary, without labeling the questioning inherently coercive or not).

Some courts have weighed the suspect's mental instability in determining whether the police interrogation amounted to coercion, holding that the police action must be evaluated in light of the defendant's condition where the police are aware of that condition. Thus, a tactic deemed noncoercive when used against a suspect of normal intelligence may amount to coercive action when the suspect has mental shortcomings. See, e.g., *State v. Carrillo*, 750 P.2d 883 (Ariz. 1988) ("Of course, what is police 'overreaching' must depend in part on what the police know about the defendant. Certainly, the police cannot be allowed to handle a suspect having Carrillo's obvious impediments with the same methods that might legitimately be employed on a suspect of greater intellect and sophistication."). See also *Hill v. Anderson*, 300 F.3d 679, 683 (6th Cir. 2002) (petitioner's mental retardation raised serious questions regarding voluntariness of confession).

To suppress his statement, Corn must establish that it was extracted from him by means of coercion and was not the product of voluntary choice. Specifically, he must 1) make a showing that the police subjected him to coercive conduct; and 2) demonstrate that the conduct operated on him (given his particular characteristics and the conditions of the interrogation) to produce an involuntary statement.

What conduct is deemed coercive? Some courts have taken a rather narrow view. In *McCall v. Dutton*, 863 F.2d 454 (6th Cir. 1988), the court found no coercive activity, despite the fact that the interrogation was conducted by five officers who surrounded McCall with their guns drawn while he lay handcuffed on the ground and was semiconscious as a result of gunshot wounds. There was "no evidence that the officers used these weapons in any way to force a confession out of the petitioner." 863 F.2d at 458. This reading of *Connelly* seems to set an unduly high threshold for the type of police conduct that amounts to coercion, and conflicts with *Miranda*'s presumption (reaffirmed in *Dickerson v. United States*, 530 U.S. 428 (2000)) that custodial interrogation is inherently coercive.

Corn would argue in our example that the deprivation of food, sleep, and medication, coupled with the duration of the two interrogations, constituted coercive activity. It is unclear that these circumstances would satisfy the *Connelly* threshold. See *United States v. Redditt*, 87 Fed. Appx. 440 (2003) (no coercion even after defendant was held in a questioning room for nine hours without a meal).

If the court were to find the police conduct here coercive, we would turn to the question of whether the action played upon Corn's particular characteristics to induce a statement not the product of his free choice. Under *Connelly*, such causal nexus is a prerequisite to a finding of involuntariness. In *Ortiz v. Uribe*, 671 F.3d 863 (9th Cir. 2011), for example, while finding the possibility of coercion in the detective's empathetic and maternal manner of questioning during a polygraph exam, the court concluded nonetheless that this did not render the 18-year-old's confession involuntary because it did not rise to the level of psychological manipulation.

In sum, Corn would have considerable difficulty challenging the statement here under the contemporary voluntariness standard.

Promises, Promises

2. *Bram v. United States*, 168 U.S. 532, 542-543 (1897), established long ago that a confession may not be "extracted by any sort of threats or violence, nor obtained by any direct or implied promises, however slight." Modern decisions, however, have not been as exacting in weighing the importance of promises in the voluntariness calculus, and there is no longer a *per se* proscription. Such promise alone does not render a confession coerced. See *United States v. Stokes*, 631 F.3d 802, 808 (6th Cir. 2011). *Colorado v. Connelly* adds the threshold question as to whether the promises of leniency amounted to coercive activity, now a prerequisite to suppression under the Due Process Clause. Compare *State v. Madsen*, 813 N.W.2d 714, 724-726 (Iowa 2012) (applying instead a *per se* rule, eliminating the "need for the court to attempt to read the mind of defendant to

determine if his confession, in fact, was induced by or made in reliance upon the promise of leniency").

Thus, while courts have sometimes found that manipulation of a suspect through promises of leniency rendered a statement involuntary, see *Sharp v. Rohling*, 793 F.3d 1216 (3d Cir. 2015) (detective promised petitioner she would not go to jail if she admitted to participating in the crime), confessions have frequently been admitted despite the fact that they were made after such promises. See, e.g., *United States v. Flemmi*, 225 F.3d 78 (1st Cir. 2000) (although defendant was assured that he would be held harmless from prosecution, because there were no threats of retaliation or of violence and no evidence of consciously misleading conduct on the part of the FBI agents defendant's statements were voluntary). Where the suspect speaks in the hope of leniency, and not in response to a promise of it, the statement will be held voluntary. See, e.g., *Rachlin v. United States*, 723 F.2d 1373 (8th Cir. 1983).

Where, however, the confession occurs in response to a direct promise of leniency, a close review of the record is required to determine whether it was involuntary. See *United States v. Lall*, 607 F.3d 1277 (11th Cir. 2010) (detective's assurance of non-prosecution). This is especially the case where the promise is accompanied by misrepresentation of the evidence against defendant or threat of an increased charge. See, e.g., *United States v. Lopez*, 437 F.3d 1059 (10th Cir. 2006). Compare *United States v. Jacques*, 744 F.3d 804 (1st Cir. 2014) (repeated threats of a harsher sentence did not overbear defendant's will). Mere representations to the suspect that cooperation is the best course of action do not render a confession involuntary. See *United States v. Coleman*, 208 F.3d 786, 791 (9th Cir. 2000); *United States v. Shears*, 762 F.2d 397 (4th Cir. 1985).

Treating the officer's statement in example 2 as a promise of leniency, the court would engage in a fact-specific inquiry as to whether, in view of all the circumstances (including the suspect's particular vulnerabilities), the promise constituted coercion which induced him to make an involuntary confession.

Threats

3. Threats to pursue a more serious criminal charge can certainly constitute coercion in the context of an interrogation. Like promises, however, they do not automatically render the statement involuntary. As one court put it: "No single criterion controls whether an accused's confession is voluntary: whether a confession was obtained by coercion is determined only after careful evaluation of the totality of the surrounding circumstances." *Green v. Scully*, 850 F.2d 894, 901 (2d Cir. 1988) (detective made reference to the electric chair).

Threats to arrest a suspect's family member have been held not to invalidate a confession if the police have probable cause regarding the family member. See *United States v. Ortiz*, 943 F. Supp. 2d 447, 456 (S.D.N.Y. 2013) (& cases collected).

If it is determined that the threats in our example constituted coercive conduct within the meaning of *Colorado v. Connelly*, the court must proceed with a totality-of-the-circumstances analysis to determine whether Corn's confession was in fact induced by the threats. See, e.g., *United States v. Johnson*, 351 F.3d 254, 260-261 (6th Cir. 2003) (police told suspect that unless he confessed to drug possession, they would arrest his sister); *State v. Garner*, 294 N.W.2d 725 (Minn. 1980) (police told suspect that unless he gave them a truthful statement, he would be charged with additional crimes).

Advising the suspect of the statutory penalties for his crimes is not considered coercive conduct. *United States v. Orso*, 266 F.3d 1030, 1039 (9th Cir. 2001); *United States v. Gallardo-Marquez*, 253 F.3d 1121, 1123 (8th Cir. 2001).

Deception and Trickery

4. Again, the fact that the police engaged in deception during the interrogation does not automatically invalidate the confession on grounds of involuntariness. In *Frazier v. Cupp*, 394 U.S. 731 (1969), although it was determined the police had falsely told the suspect his accomplice had already confessed, that action was held to be an insufficient reason to suppress the confession as involuntary given the totality of the circumstances, including the short duration of the questioning and the fact that Frazier was a mature adult of normal intelligence. Similarly, where the interrogating officer leaned toward the suspect (who had just denied knowing that a package delivered to her house contained narcotics), hit his fist on the table, and accused her of lying, and then falsely told her that her accomplice had already implicated her (when in fact the accomplice had not even been questioned), the Court concluded nonetheless that the statement she made was voluntary. See *United States v. Lux*, 905 F.2d 1379 (10th Cir. 1990).

Misrepresenting evidence or charges against the defendant is not automatically considered coercion. See, e.g., *United States v. Orso*, 266 F.3d 1030, 1039 (9th Cir. 2001) ("While reprehensible, the use of deception, however, does not constitute coercive conduct.").

Miller v. Fenton, 796 F.2d 598 (3d Cir. 1986), *rev'd on other grounds*, 474 U.S. 104 (1985), involved an interrogation in which the detective falsely told the murder suspect that the victim was still alive and could identify her attacker, and that bloodstains had been found at the suspect's home. Throughout the interrogation, the officer portrayed himself as sympathetic to Miller's plight and said that he did not consider him a criminal deserving of punishment, but rather a sick person in need of medical help. Eventually, Miller confessed. Despite the deception and the obvious psychological ploys, the Third Circuit Court of Appeals concluded that the confession was voluntary: "[I]n our view, the manipulative tactics used here did not produce psychological pressure strong enough to overbear the will of a mature, experienced man, who was suffering from no mental or physical illness and was interrogated for less than an hour at a police station close to his home." 796 F.2d at 613. The complexity and fact-specific nature of the totality-of-the-circumstances calculus is reflected in the court's elaboration:

> Detective Boyce's method of interrogation might have overborne the will of another detainee, for example, a young, inexperienced person of lower intelligence than Miller, or a person suffering from a painful physical ailment. It might have overcome the will of Miller himself if the interrogation has been longer or if Miller had been refused food, sleep, or contact with a person he wished to see. Moreover, if Miller had made remarks that indicated that he truly believed that the state would treat him leniently because he was not responsible for what he had done or that he believed that he would receive psychiatric help rather than punishment, we might not find the confession voluntary. We hold simply that, under the totality of the circumstances of this case, the confession was voluntarily given.

796 F.2d at 613. In contrast, the confession was suppressed in *United States v. LeBrun*, 306 F.3d 545, 555-556 (8th Cir. 2002), involving an interrogation in which agents lied about the evidence against the defendant, told him that if he did not confess he would be subject to charges in a distant state, and said that if he confessed to a "spontaneous" act, he could not be prosecuted. The agents also played on the defendant's concerns about his health and his pregnant wife. The court found the confession involuntary despite the facts that the defendant was in his mid-fifties, a military veteran, gainfully employed as a manager in a real estate office, and had a college education and one year of law school. This decision was later reversed in *United States v. LeBrun*, 363 F.3d 715 (8th Cir. 2004).

Thus, in example 4, the court would consider the deception, along with Corn's personal characteristics and the atmosphere of the interrogation in assessing whether his statement was voluntary. The open-ended nature of the totality-of-the-circumstances standard permits courts considerable leeway in assessing the importance of deception. Moreover, whether the deception here will be treated as coercive police activity for purposes of the critical *Connelly* threshold showing remains to be seen.

Drug-Induced Confession

5. *Townsend v. Sain*, 372 U.S. 293 (1963), held a confession induced by a "truth serum" drug to be involuntary and therefore inadmissible. This

was the case even though it did not appear from the record that the police knew the suspect was under the influence of the drug when they questioned him. After *Colorado v. Connelly*, however, it would appear necessary in order to suppress the confession to establish that the police knew of and exploited the suspect's helpless condition. Indeed, Chief Justice Rehnquist portrayed *Townsend* in his *Connelly* opinion as a case of "police wrongdoing" in which the officers *did* know about the drug and its effects. (The dissenters disagreed with this revisionist reading of *Townsend*.)

Being under the influence of drugs or alcohol thus does not automatically render a statement involuntary. In *Elliot v.Williams*, 248 F.3d 1205 (10th Cir. 2001), the court refused to find the defendant's confession involuntary, even though he was under the influence of heroin, because there was no coercive police activity. Nor do symptoms of withdrawal equate with involuntariness. See *United States v. Coleman*, 208 F.3d 786 (9th Cir. 2000). Courts have ruled that being under the influence of painkillers in a hospital or of alcohol during the interrogation does not render a statement involuntary. See *United States v. Cristobal*, 293 F.3d 134 (4th Cir. 2002); *Hubbard v. Haley*, 317 F.3d 1245 (11th Cir. 2003).

The constitutional due process guarantee does not protect a defendant from his own compulsions or internally applied pressures that are not the product of police action. Rather, police must exploit the situation before the confession will be suppressed. Evidence that the police directed the use of the drug for the purpose of inducing a statement would clearly constitute coercion.

Juvenile Confessions

6. The Supreme Court has emphasized the need to exercise "special caution" when assessing the voluntariness of a juvenile confession, particularly when there is prolonged or repeated questioning or when the interrogation occurs in the absence of a parent or lawyer. *In re Gault*, 387 U.S. 1, 45 (1967). See also *Fare v. Michael C.*, 442 U.S. 707 (1979); *Hardaway v.Young*, 302 F.3d 757, 762 (7th Cir. 2002). (The Court has recently held that juvenile status should be weighed in the "custody" determination for *Miranda*. See *J.D.B. v. North Carolina*, 131 S. Ct (2011); also see §9.2.1.) Nonetheless, the totality-of-the-circumstances test still controls, focusing on the juvenile's age, experience, education, background, intelligence, conditions of the interrogation, and the presence or absence of a "friendly adult." See, e.g., *Gachot v. Stadler*, 298 F.3d 414 (5th Cir. 2002).

Our example is similar to *Hardaway v.Young*, supra, in which a 14-year-old's confession was deemed voluntary despite the fact that there was no friendly adult present (the defendant's parents chose not to come to the station with him). The court noted that the defendant was not intimidated, abused, or physically coerced in any way, had extensive prior history with the criminal justice system, and appeared to understand his rights when they were read to him.

In our example, Johnny was read his rights, had a parent present for some of the time, had experience with the criminal justice system, and was interrogated in the friendly setting of his home. The likelihood is high that his confession will be deemed voluntary.

We will discuss juvenile confessions again with regard to the *Miranda* protections in Chapter 9.

It should be noted that some states have adopted an "interested adult" rule requiring a showing that the juvenile was provided an opportunity to consult with a parent or other interested adult before a confession may be admitted. See, e.g., *Commonwealth v. A Juvenile*, 389 Mass. 128 (1983); *Commonwealth v. Alfonso*, A. 438 Mass. 372 (2003).

CHAPTER 9

The *Miranda* Approach

§9.1 THE *MIRANDA* DECISION

Given the amorphous and ad hoc nature of the voluntariness standard (as discussed in the previous chapter), it is not surprising that the Court sought a more precise and efficient method of treating the problems of police interrogation. Premised on the recognition that lengthy incommunicado interrogation creates an atmosphere ripe for coercion, it used its supervisory powers over the federal courts to impose an automatic rule of exclusion for statements extracted from defendants who had not been brought before a judicial officer "without unnecessary delay" after arrest.[1]

In devising an approach that would apply to state prosecutions as well as federal, the Supreme Court turned to the Sixth Amendment right-to-counsel provision.[2] The opportunity arose in the case of Danny Escobedo, a suspect in a murder investigation who was interrogated at the police station despite repeated requests to consult with his attorney, who was present at the station and attempting to see his client. Escobedo made inculpatory statements (after police staged a confrontation with his accomplice, whom they said had already implicated him), which were admitted at trial. On review, the Court reversed, concluding that the statement had been obtained in violation of Escobedo's Sixth Amendment right to counsel. *Escobedo v. Illinois*, 378

---

1. This approach was known as the McNabb-Mallory rule, after the two cases that created it, *McNabb v. United States*, 318 U.S. 332 (1943), and *Mallory v. United States*, 354 U.S. 449 (1957).
2. The Sixth Amendment had already been applied to the States in *Gideon v. Wainwright*, 372 U.S. 335 (1963).

U.S. 478 (1964). A suspect who has become the focus of an accusatory interrogation is entitled, the Court held, to the "guiding hand of counsel" during that process. "[N]o system of criminal justice can, or should, survive if it comes to depend for its continued effectiveness on the citizens' abdication through unawareness of their constitutional rights." 378 U.S. at 490. Applicability of the decision was, however, explicitly limited to situations where an investigation had already focused on the suspect, and where he requests counsel prior to interrogation. *Escobedo* would thus not serve as the elusive all-purpose alternative to the voluntariness analysis.[3]

Miranda v. Arizona, 384 U.S. 436 (1966), decided two years later, was thought to fit that bill. Concluding (in a watershed opinion by Chief Justice Earl Warren) that "the very fact of custodial interrogation exacts a heavy toll on individual liberty and trades on the weaknesses of individuals," 384 U.S. at 455,[4] the Court adopted a comprehensive scheme designed to limit the abuses of incommunicado interrogation and minimize its inherent coercion. Relying on the Fifth Amendment privilege against compelled self-incrimination,[5] *Miranda* mandated the now-familiar warnings prior to interrogation of a suspect held in custody. Two advise the suspect of his right to remain silent and of the implications of not remaining silent—that anything he says can be used against him in court. The other two inform of the right to have an attorney present during questioning and to have one appointed at state expense if he cannot afford to retain one.

If the suspect exercises his right to silence, interrogation must immediately cease; if he requests an attorney, interrogation must cease until one is present. The suspect, in short, has the right to cut off questioning at any time. If the police do obtain a statement, *Miranda* requires (as a condition of its admissibility at trial) that the prosecutor meet a "heavy burden" to demonstrate that the defendant "knowingly and intelligently waived his privilege against self-incrimination and his right to retained or appointed counsel." 384 U.S. at 475.

The conclusion that a suspect has a right to consult with counsel prior to and during questioning represented the Court's resolution of what Justice Robert Jackson had described as a "real dilemma in a free society"; namely, that to question a suspect without counsel is a "real peril to individual

---

3. The Sixth Amendment approach is still applicable to interrogation occurring after initiation of formal criminal proceedings. See Chapter 10.

4. The Court examined various police interrogation manuals that had been submitted together with the briefs and which the Court described as a "valuable source of information about present police practices." 384 U.S. at 448. They described questionable tactics designed to obtain confessions from unwilling suspects, including deception, trickery, promises, and threats.

5. The Fifth Amendment had already been applied to the States in *Malloy v. Hogan*, 378 U.S. 1 (1964).

freedom," but to bring a lawyer into the process is a "real peril to the solution of crime."[6]

The *Miranda* dissenters (Justices Clark, Harlan, Stewart, and White) predicted that the presence of counsel would indeed prevent police from gaining useful information from a suspect. They sharply criticized what they saw as a "constitutional straitjacket" motivated by a "deep-seated distrust of all confessions." The dissenters believed that the extent to which abuses were occurring in the interrogation process had been vastly exaggerated, and they argued that continued reliance on the voluntariness standard could remedy proven instances of coercion. For them, the cost of excluding reliable and uncoerced statements was simply too great a price for society to bear.

One court would later describe the innovation of the 1966 decision as follows:

> The rigidity of the *Miranda* rules and the way in which they are to be applied was conceived of and continues to be recognized as the decision's greatest strength. The decision's rigidity has afforded police clear guidance on the acceptable manner of questioning an accused. It has allowed courts to avoid the intractable factual determinations that the former totality of the circumstances approach often entailed. When a law enforcement officer asks a question of an accused and the accused, without the benefit of *Miranda*'s safeguards, answers, the totality of the circumstances is irrelevant. The accused's answer is simply inadmissible as part of the prosecution's case in chief.

Mayfield v. State, 293 Ark. 216, 220, 736 S.W.2d 12, 13-14 (1987).

Perhaps the most accurate prediction made by the dissenters was that *Miranda* would ultimately fail to provide the bright-line approach intended by the Court. Indeed, it has generated considerable litigation over the definition of the key elements of "custody," "interrogation," and "waiver," as will be discussed below.

Shortly after the decision was rendered, Congress purported to "overrule" *Miranda* in the Crime Control Act of 1968, 18 U.S.C. §3501, which imposes the voluntariness standard as the exclusive method of weighing admissibility of confessions in federal prosecutions. Ignored for decades, the Fourth Circuit Court of Appeals "rediscovered" §3501 in *United States v. Dickerson*, 166 F.3d 667 (4th Cir. 1999). Drawing upon Supreme Court decisions characterizing *Miranda* as merely remedial, but not constitutionally mandated (see, e.g., *Oregon v. Elstad* and *Michigan v. Tucker*, discussed in §9.3.3), the Fourth Circuit upheld §3501, thus displacing *Miranda*.

---

6. *Watts v. Indiana*, 338 U.S. 49, 58 (1949). Justice Jackson pondered: "If the ultimate quest in a criminal trial is the truth and if the circumstances indicate no violence or threats of it, should society be deprived of the suspect's help in solving a crime merely because he was confined and questioned when uncounseled?" 338 U.S. at 58.

But despite predictions to the contrary, the Court declined the invitation to overrule the controversial 1966 decision. Writing for the 7-to-2 majority in *Dickerson v. United States*, 530 U.S. 428 (2000), Chief Justice Rehnquist reaffirmed *Miranda* and its constitutional basis. The Court noted the advantage of "concrete constitutional guidelines" for law enforcement and the courts to follow, and recognized that *Miranda* has become "embedded in routine police practice to the point where the warnings have become part of the national culture." Treating it as a rule of constitutional dimension, Congress had no power to overrule *Miranda* in §3501. Yet the Court declined to overrule any of its prior decisions which, as discussed below, limited the reach of *Miranda* on the theory that it was not of constitutional import.

Ambivalence about *Miranda* persists. *Chavez v. Martinez*, 538 U.S. 760 (2003), took a narrow view of the doctrine when it held there is no *Miranda* violation unless the government seeks to introduce the statement at a criminal trial. Police sergeant Chavez's failure to read *Miranda* warnings to Martinez before questioning him did not violate his constitutional rights because, absent use of his statement in evidence, he was not "compelled to be a witness against himself in a criminal case."

---

§9.2 THE COMPONENTS OF *MIRANDA*

Miranda required the warnings and other protective measures whenever there is "*questioning* initiated by law enforcement officers after a person has been taken into *custody* or otherwise deprived of his freedom of action in any significant way." 384 U.S. at 443 (emphasis added). Any statement obtained during such questioning is admissible at trial only after a demonstration that the warnings were given and that the suspect subsequently waived his rights. It was left for later decisions to elucidate these concepts.

§9.2.1 Custody

Miranda sought through the prescribed warnings to neutralize an atmosphere viewed by the Court as inherently hostile and intimidating. While in custody, the suspect is "cut off from the outside world" and in an environment that is "police dominated." "An individual swept from familiar surroundings into police custody, surrounded by antagonistic forces and subjected to the techniques of persuasion described above, cannot be otherwise than under compulsion to speak." 384 U.S. at 460.

It is only in the context of *custodial* interrogation that the *Miranda* protections are triggered. How do we define "custody"? Is a person stopped by officers in an airport terminal "in custody" when they ask him to identify himself and answer a few questions? Is a person questioned by agents in his own living room "in custody" and thus entitled to the warnings?

The ultimate inquiry is whether there has been either a formal arrest or "restraint on freedom of movement of the degree associated with a formal arrest." *New York v. Quarles*, 467 U.S. 649, 655 (1984). This determination is based on the atmosphere of the interrogation, to determine if it has the inherently compelling pressures that the *Miranda* decision sought to neutralize. The venue in which the interrogation occurs is not determinative, and one need not be in a police station to be "in custody." The suspect in *Orozco v. Texas*, 394 U.S. 324 (1969), was deemed in custody when interrogated (concerning a gun used in a recent murder) by four officers in his own bedroom at 4:00 A.M. Emphasizing that the officers testified at pretrial proceedings that Orozco would not have been free to leave had he made the attempt, the Court determined there was a "potentiality for compulsion" equivalent to a station house interrogation. But compare *Beckwith v. United States*, 425 U.S. 341 (1976), concluding that the pressures associated with a police-dominated station house interrogation were absent when Internal Revenue Service (IRS) agents questioned the suspect in his residence.

The fact that the questioning occurs in a police station does not, however, automatically make it custodial. In *Oregon v. Mathiason*, 429 U.S. 492 (1977), a parolee reported to the police station at the telephone request of an officer. He was told that he was not under arrest, but then he was asked questions concerning a burglary. Mathiason confessed to the crime and was then released pending review of his case. The Court held that *Miranda* warnings were not required because he had come to the station voluntarily, was informed that he was not under arrest, and had not been restricted in his freedom to depart.

Even where the police accompany the subject to the station, questioning may be deemed noncustodial if he goes along voluntarily and is informed that he is not under arrest. The suspect in *California v. Beheler*, 463 U.S. 1121 (1983), having made an incriminating statement to police regarding a robbery-murder, agreed to go with them to the police station for further questioning. He was informed that he was not under arrest. After brief questioning at the station, during which he made additional incriminating statements, Beheler was allowed to leave. The Court concluded that there had not been custodial interrogation because there was neither a formal arrest nor restraint on the suspect's freedom equivalent to arrest. The lack of *Miranda* warnings thus did not preclude use of the statements at trial.

In *Howes v. Fields*, 132 S. Ct. 1181 (2012), the Court ruled that a prisoner who was moved to a secure conference room within the prison for questioning about criminal activity outside the prison was not in custody. Even though his freedom of movement was restricted, the Court emphasized the importance of the environment in determining whether the inherently coercive pressures at issue in *Miranda* were present. Considerable weight was given to the fact that the prisoner was not removed to an unfamiliar or uncomfortable setting.

Where there is no formal arrest, the determinative question is whether a reasonable person (given the totality of circumstances) would have felt at liberty to terminate the interrogation and leave. *Thompson v. Keohane*, 516 U.S. 99, 112 (1995). Only if the answer is no is it necessary to neutralize the pressures of the interrogation by way of the *Miranda* warnings. However, as the Court indicated in *Howes*, curtailed freedom of movement is only the first step in the analysis. It is important to also evaluate the environmental factors to determine if they created an inherently coercive atmosphere.

Atmospheric considerations are paramount in roadside stop scenarios. Warnings are not required in routine encounters between motorists and police, even though there is some restraint on the motorist's freedom, because a traffic stop is usually brief and in public, and the driver reasonably expects that he will be allowed to continue on his way. The atmosphere is substantially less "police dominated" than a station house interrogation. See *Berkemer v. McCarthy*, 468 U.S. 420 (1984) (roadside questioning of driver stopped on highway because he had been observed weaving between lanes did not require warnings). *Pennsylvania v. Bruder*, 488 U.S. 9 (1988), similarly held that roadside sobriety tests are not custodial in nature.

Berkemer, *Bruder*, and the later case of *Stansbury v. California*, 511 U.S. 318 (1994) all emphasize that the *actual* intention of the officer to detain the suspect and take him into custody is irrelevant to the "custody" issue unless the intention is communicated to the suspect. The standard is an objective one based on *the suspect's* perceptions, and the determinative question is how a reasonable person in his position would have understood the situation. Among the factors that courts look to in applying the reasonable person test are the location of the interrogation (familiar or unfamiliar to the suspect?), the duration, and the persons present (just law enforcement personnel?). *J.D.B. v. North Carolina*, 131 S. Ct. 2394 (2011), included the juvenile's age as an objective factor to be taken into consideration for the custody determination, provided that the age was known to the officer or would have been objectively apparent to a reasonable officer at the time.

Despite the effort in *Miranda* to devise a categorical approach, the determination of custody remains a fact-specific and *ad hoc* inquiry, as illustrated by the following examples.

Examples

1. As you will recall from the scenario set out in Chapter 1, police arrested Michael Chestnut, transported him to the police station, and interrogated him there concerning his involvement in narcotics trafficking. Would such an interrogation require *Miranda* warnings?

2. Assume instead that the police briefly chased Chestnut and, upon overtaking him, asked what he was doing. He responded: "I ain't taking this drug rap myself. I'm just the little guy." Could this statement be introduced against Chestnut at trial in light of the absence of *Miranda* warnings? Does it matter whether the officers intended to take him into custody at the time they asked the question?

3. Now assume that upon overtaking Chestnut, police read him the *Miranda* warnings and then asked what he was doing. He responded: "I ain't taking this drug rap myself. I'm just the little guy." Does the reading of the warnings automatically make the situation custodial?

4. Now assume that the police chased Chestnut with their weapons drawn, and when they caught up to him, they pointed their guns at him and yelled at him to freeze and put his hands up. After the officers frisked him, they reholstered their guns and asked what he was doing. He responded: "I ain't taking this drug rap myself. I'm just the little guy." Could this statement be introduced against Chestnut at trial in light of the absence of *Miranda* warnings?

5. Assume instead that Chestnut made a break for it and the police were unable to catch him. Later that day, he decided to find out why the police were after him and went to the police station. After introducing himself and explaining the reason for his appearance, he was taken to an interrogation room and questioned by two detectives. Chestnut ultimately made an incriminating statement and was then placed under arrest. Could this statement be introduced against Chestnut at trial in light of the absence of *Miranda* warnings?

6. Assume instead that the police appeared at Chestnut's apartment and requested entry. He allowed them in, and they questioned him regarding his involvement in narcotics dealing. Could any statement obtained be introduced against Chestnut at trial in light of the absence of *Miranda* warnings? What factors would the court look to?

7. Assume that Chestnut was being held in jail while awaiting trial. The police, who thus far had been unable to get him to make an incriminating statement, decided to place an undercover agent in his cell. The two men engaged in conversation, and the agent asked his cellmate: "So, what do you do for spending money?" Chestnut responded by bragging about his role as a kingpin in a narcotics ring. Could this statement be used against Chestnut at trial in light of the absence of *Miranda* warnings?

8. Police are called to a home to remove a loaded handgun from behind a woman's dresser. The woman says that the handgun does not belong to her or her boyfriend, Peter Parole. Peter, a parolee, was scheduled to meet with his parole officer the next day but was instructed by him

to report to the police station for questioning instead. Parole appeared at the station house and was taken to an interview room; he was not given *Miranda* warnings. Parole twice denied ownership of the gun; but when the police chief asked if he would deny ownership if his fingerprints were found on the weapon (which in fact they were not), Parole admitted the gun was his, in violation of the terms of his parole. He was then asked to give a written statement, and he agreed. The police chief advised Parole of his *Miranda* rights, and he drafted a brief statement admitting his guilt. Could this written statement be used against Parole at trial despite the fact that the *Miranda* warnings were given only after questioning had begun?

9. Police were called by paramedics to the scene of an apparent shooting. They found the victim in the bedroom and a 16-year-old boy standing outside the room. In response to the officers' question as to what happened, the youth stated that the victim had fallen and hit his head. After one of the officers discovered a spent bullet next to the victim, the boy and his mother were taken to the patrol car and seated inside. The boy was confronted with the bullet and asked again what had happened. He changed his story and stated that he had accidentally shot the victim. When the youth was charged with homicide, he sought to suppress both statements on the grounds that they were obtained without *Miranda* warnings. What result?

10. Investigating a report of sexual assault, two agents went to the home of the suspect, a 13-year-old Navajo boy with a "borderline IQ" and other cognitive deficiencies. The agents requested permission from the youth's parents to enter the home and interview him; they were invited in and sat down with the boy and his parents in their living room. The agents tried to interrogate him, but he refused to speak. Eventually he began to respond, but when approached on the subject of the assault, he cried and was again silent. At that point, the boy's parents left the boy alone in the room with the agents, and he subsequently confessed. Should the youth be considered "in custody" for purposes of *Miranda*?

Explanations

1. This is clearly the type of situation envisioned by *Miranda*: the suspect is deprived of his freedom and finds himself in a police-dominated environment. Chestnut is clearly in custody. The *Miranda* warnings are required here, and a statement obtained without the warnings would be excluded at trial.

2. Unlike the situation in example 1, Chestnut is neither under formal arrest nor being held in the police station, the threatening environments

that the *Miranda* Court concluded were inherently coercive. General on-the-scene questioning as to facts surrounding a crime is not regarded as custodial in nature. 384 U.S. at 477. Custody attaches only where the subject reasonably believes that his freedom to depart has been curtailed by the police.

Chestnut would argue that when he was chased and stopped, the degree of constraint on his liberty was more than that associated with routine on-the-scene questioning and that he reasonably believed himself in custody, thus entitling him to warnings prior to questioning. It is unlikely, however, that a court would treat him as having been in custody. Routine roadside stops of motorists (see *Berkemer v. McCarthy*, supra; *Pennsylvania v. Bruder*, supra; *United States v. Trueber*, 278 F.3d 79, 92 (1st Cir. 2001)) and Terry stops and frisks (see *United States v. Swanson*, 341 F.3d 524 (6th Cir. 2003)) are generally treated as noncustodial for purposes of *Miranda*.

You will recall that a subject chased by police is not considered "seized" for purposes of the Fourth Amendment unless and until there is an actual application of force upon him or he submits to police authority. See *Michigan v. Chesternut*, 486 U.S. 567 (1988), and *California v. Hodari D.*, 499 U.S. 621 (1991), discussed in §4.3 of Chapter 4. The Court applies a similar reasonable person standard to determine both the seizure question within the Fourth Amendment context and the custody question within the *Miranda* doctrine.

If the brief public stop grows into something of longer duration or the police escalate the restraint on Chestnut (such as drawing their guns or placing him in a cruiser), he will likely be considered in custody and therefore entitled to the *Miranda* protections. See example 3.

In applying the objective reasonable person standard, the unstated intention of the officers to detain Chestnut (assuming that they subsequently admitted to it) is irrelevant. The determinative issue is whether a reasonable person in Chestnut's position, knowing what he knew then, would have believed himself in custody.

3. If the police provide *Miranda* warnings when they do not have to (because the setting is not custodial), do they then have to abide by the other mandates of that decision (including the requirement for a valid waiver)? Do the warnings themselves, in other words, create a custodial environment? Courts have generally answered no. See, e.g., *United States v. Burnette*, 535 F. Supp. 2d 772, 784 (E.D. Tex. 2007) ("The fact that *Miranda* warnings are given is not per se evidence that a person is in custody. Warnings provided in a noncustodial setting do not convert that setting into a custodial one for *Miranda* purposes. Such a rule would create the interpretation that *Miranda* warnings — intended to preserve an essential liberty — are instead a restraint on the suspect."); *United States v. Gordon*,

638 F. Supp. 1120, 1133 (W.D. La. 1986), *aff'd*, 812 F.2d 965 (5th Cir. 1987). "To suggest that the mere administration of the *Miranda* warnings converts a legally non-custodial situation into custody is to completely strip from *Miranda* its original intention which was to protect a citizen from the coercive effects of police custody."

4. This encounter has probably become custodial. In *United States v. Jones*, 846 F.2d 358, 361 (6th Cir. 1988), the suspect was deemed in custody for *Miranda* purposes when three police officers in three separate cars with lights flashing surrounded Jones's car, blocking him from leaving the scene. Similarly, the suspect in *United States v. Vega*, 72 F.3d 507, 511 (7th Cir. 1995), stopped in a shopping center parking lot by a police officer and an FBI agent with guns drawn and asked to accompany them into a cruiser for questioning, was considered in custody when he received a cell phone call and was told by the officer to hang up the phone. See also *Combs v. Coyle*, 205 F.3d 269 (6th Cir. 2000) (warnings were required where the officer pointed a weapon at the suspect and ordered him to drop his gun, and 10 to 15 minutes passed from that time until the officer asked the suspect what happened). But compare *Coomer v. Yukins*, 533 F.3d 477 (6th Cir. 2008) (defendant not in custody even though police arrived at late hour, police cars blocked her vehicle on her driveway, up to 11 officers came to her building, because defendant voluntarily allowed police in, confession lasted only 30 minutes, taking the form primarily of a narrative and prompted by little police questioning, officers told defendant several times that she was not under arrest and that police would leave if asked, and defendant moved freely around her apartment and offered officers refreshments); *Cruz v. Miller*, 255 F.3d 77, 86 (2d Cir. 2001) (suspect, who was stopped at a train station by two officers with guns drawn, told to put his hands up, frisked, and ordered to wait while an eyewitness was summoned, was not considered in custody and thus *Miranda* warnings were not required because the questioning was brief and occurred in public, and the suspect was not handcuffed).

In order for Chestnut to have his statement suppressed, he would have to show that the encounter had escalated into the type of police-dominated coercive environment that would lead a reasonable person to believe that his freedom was curtailed to a degree associated with formal arrest.

5. If the interrogation here is deemed custodial, the absence of *Miranda* warnings would preclude use of the statement at trial. The fact that the questioning occurs in a police station is not itself sufficient to establish custody. Rather, the determinative inquiry is whether a reasonable person in Chestnut's position would have believed himself in custody or deprived of his freedom in a significant way. Factors weighed in the analysis are whether the suspect was informed that he was free to leave,

possessed unrestrained freedom of movement during questioning, and initiated contact with authorities or voluntarily acquiesced to official requests to respond to questions; whether police used strong-arm tactics or deceptive strategies during questioning; whether the atmosphere of the questioning was police-dominated; and whether the suspect was arrested at the end of the questioning. See *United States v. Galceran*, 301 F.3d 927, 929 (8th Cir. 2002). Other factors include the kind of language used to summon the individual to the place of interrogation, the extent to which he is confronted with culpable evidence, and the duration of the questioning. See *United States v. Hayden*, 260 F.3d 1062, 1066 (9th Cir. 2001). Because Chestnut had come voluntarily to the station and was not told he was under arrest, the court would most likely conclude he could not reasonably have believed himself to be in custody. Although Chestnut (unlike the suspects in *Mathiason* and *Beheler*, supra) was placed under arrest immediately upon making the incriminating statement, that fact would not seem determinative since the relevant inquiry is the suspect's objective state of mind *at the time of the questioning.*

Even where the subject voluntarily accompanies police to the station house and is told he is not under arrest and will be free to leave at the end of the interview, "custody" may sometimes be found. See, e.g., *United States v. Colonna*, 511 F.3d 431 (4th Cir. 2007) (suspect — whose home was raided by 24 FBI agents (whose access was restricted to certain areas of the home) and who was instructed to accompany an agent for questioning — was in custody despite being told that he was not under arrest); *United States v. Hanson*, 237 F.3d 961 (8th Cir. 2001) (suspect misled as to the reason police wanted to talk to him and threatened with prosecution in an intimidating atmosphere); and *United States v. Kim*, 292 F.3d 969, 974 (9th Cir. 2002) (store owner questioned by police during and after execution of search warrant at store was "in custody," even though she had initially come to the store voluntarily because she communicated poorly in English, entered the store to check on her son rather than to speak to police, was told by officers to shut up and not to speak to her son in Korean, was seated for questioning away from her son and husband, was subjected to interrogation for 30 minutes before the interpreter arrived and another 20 minutes with the interpreter, and likely believed that she was a suspect). But see *United States v. LeBrun* 363 F.3d 715 (8th Cir. 2004) (en banc) (even though the subject was confronted with threats of criminal charges and "incontrovertible" evidence of guilt, custody was not found because the defendant was not physically restrained and understood that he was free to terminate the interview and leave, he retained his cell phone during the interview, he was driven home at the end of the interview, and he was an educated, sophisticated individual with past experience in dealing with investigators).

6. Questioning in one's own home can constitute custodial interrogation when there is the potential for compulsion equivalent to a station house interrogation. Where, for example, an interrogation was conducted in the suspect's bedroom by four officers at 4:00 A.M., the Court concluded that it was custodial. See *Orozco v. Texas*, 394 U.S. 324 (1969). Compare *Beckwith v. United States*, 425 U.S. 341 (1976) (questioning in home deemed noncustodial).

   The determinative question is whether a reasonable person in the suspect's position would have felt his freedom significantly constrained by the police action. Courts look at the broad range of factors enumerated in explanation 5. See, e.g., *United States v. Badmus*, 325 F.3d 133 (2d Cir. 2003) (defendant not in custody even though asked to stay seated in the living room and not allowed to move freely though the apartment while six armed officers searched it); *United States v. Axsom*, 289 F.3d 496 (8th Cir. 2002) (defendant not in custody even though nine officers were searching his residence where he was interrogated in the comfort and familiarity of his home while seated in an easy chair smoking his pipe).

7. Even though it is clear that Chestnut was in a custodial environment at the time that he responded to the question, the Supreme Court concluded in a similar situation that the *Miranda* protections did not apply. In *Illinois v. Perkins*, 496 U.S. 292 (1990), the Court turned to the original rationale for these protections; namely, the need to neutralize the coercive aspects of interrogation in a police-dominated environment. When an incarcerated inmate speaks freely to a fellow inmate, *Perkins* concludes, this unique environment does not exist. "*Miranda* was not meant to protect suspects from boasting about their criminal activities in front of persons whom they believe to be their cellmates. [Perkins] viewed the cellmate-agent as an equal and showed no hint of being intimidated by the atmosphere of the jail." 496 U.S. at 298. The Court distinguished *Mathis v. United States*, 391 U.S. 1 (1968), holding inadmissible statements obtained from a prison inmate questioned by IRS agents in the absence of the warnings, on the grounds that Mathis was acutely aware that he was speaking to a government agent and thus likely felt the coercive pressure inherent in that situation. But compare *Howes v. Fields* 132 S. Ct. 1181 (2012) (prisoner questioned in a secure conference room was not in custody because, among other factors, it was "most important" that he was told he was free to leave).

8. The Court in *Missouri v. Seibert*, 542 U.S. 600 (2004), suppressed a confession after police deliberately withheld the warnings until they had obtained a confession, after which they finally administered them and got a second confession that did comply with *Miranda*. The plurality in *Seibert* established a multi-factor test to determine whether *Miranda* warnings delivered midstream are effective enough to accomplish their

objectives. The factors the court is to consider are (1) "the completeness and detail of the questions and answers in the first round of interrogation," (2) "the overlapping content of the two statements," (3) "the timing and setting of the first and the second statements," (4) "the continuity of police personnel," and (5) "the degree to which the interrogator's questions treated the second round as continuous with the first." 542 U.S. at 611.

In his concurrence, which provided the fifth vote, Justice Kennedy suggested that the multi-factor test "cut too broadly" and that the second statement should be suppressed only when it was part of a deliberate two-step strategy designed to undercut the effectiveness of *Miranda* warnings. Kennedy would allow for the admission of even these statements if curative measures (e.g., break in time, explanation that first statement would be inadmissible) were implemented.

It is likely in this example that the court would suppress Parole's confession based on the decision in *Seibert*. The police chief ceased questioning Parole only when he confessed to possession of the handgun. Parole was given *Miranda* warnings only after he agreed to give a written statement, and it is likely that Parole would feel that the cat was already out of the bag and that it would be futile not to comply with a written confession. This example is loosely based on the situation in *United States v. Ollie*, 442 F.3d 1135 (8th Cir. 2006), where the court suppressed the second confession.

Relying on Justice Kennedy's concurrence in *Seibert*, the Eighth Circuit held that the second confession would be suppressed only when *Miranda* warnings were withheld as part of an interrogation technique used in a calculated way to undermine the effectiveness and strength of *Miranda* warnings. The prosecution must prove, by a preponderance of the evidence, that the officer's failure to provide warnings at the outset of questioning was not part of a deliberate attempt to circumvent *Miranda*. *Ollie*, 442 F.3d 1135 at 1142-1143. The court should consider any objective evidence or available expressions of subjective intent suggesting that the officer acted deliberately to undermine and obscure the warning's meaning and effect. *United States v. Williams*, 435 F.3d 1148 (9th Cir. 2006). Compare *United States v. Gonzalez-Lauzan*, 437 F.3d 1128 (11th Cir. 2006) (holding that *Miranda* warnings were sufficient despite being administered "midstream" because, during the first step in the process, the suspect had been repeatedly told that he should just listen and that he was not being asked any questions) with *Hairston v. United States*, 905 A.2d 765 (D.C. 2006) (admitting the initial statement as voluntarily given, even if in violation of *Miranda*, because there was nothing that indicated the police officer in the "just listen" phase said anything to the suspect to pressure him into making an incriminating statement).

9. The initial inquiry as to what happened constituted general on-the-scene questioning. The officers had just arrived and were not certain at that point whether a crime had been committed. Their inquiry did not focus on the boy as a suspect, and there was no custodial atmosphere surrounding the conversation. The questioning in the patrol car was an entirely different situation. By then, the police had reason to believe that a crime had been committed and, further, that the boy had lied in his initial response to them. Moreover, the questioning occurred inside a police vehicle. The defendant will argue that a reasonable person in these circumstances would believe his freedom constrained in a significant way. While this position seems compelling, not all courts would agree. In *United States v. Salman*, 286 F. Supp. 3d 1325 (M.D. Fla. 2018), for example, defendant was questioned by an FBI agent while in the backseat of a patrol car, but was found not to be in custody because she could exit the car with her son and did so at least once, and the questioning lasted only 20 minutes. Compare *United States v. Garreau*, 735 F. Supp. 2d 1155, 1167 (D.S.D. 2010) (defendant was in custody when kept in the backseat of a locked patrol car in handcuffs).

10. In the case upon which this example is based, the trial court suppressed the boy's statements as having been taken in violation of *Miranda*, but the Tenth Circuit reversed. See *United States v. Erving L.*, 147 F.3d 1240 (10th Cir. 1998). Because the interrogation took place in the boy's home, the agents did not make a show of force, and the boy was told that he was not under arrest and would not be arrested no matter what he told them, the court concluded that a reasonable juvenile in his position would not believe that his liberty was constrained to the degree associated with formal arrest. The court emphasized that the standard is an objective one, so that neither the mental nor the emotional condition of the subject, nor the fact that he was in a guilty state of mind, is relevant to the inquiry unless the officers were aware of the particular traits and exploited them. The Circuit Court was willing to look at the case from the vantage point of a reasonable juvenile. Although the juvenile's "actual mindset" does not enter into the analysis (see *Yarborough v. Alvarado*, 541 U.S. 652 (2004)), the Court has recently emphasized that the suspect's age affects the custody determination so long as the age was known to the officer or would have been objectively apparent to a reasonable officer at the time. *J.D.B. v. North Carolina*, 131 S. Ct. 2394 (2011).

§9.2.2 Interrogation

The *Miranda* protections are triggered by "interrogation" of a subject (who, as we have already seen, must be in "custody"). This component was defined by the Court as "questioning initiated by law enforcement officers." Statements volunteered with no such questioning are not covered. The police are not, for instance, required to interrupt a person who is about to blurt out a confession and inform him of his right to silence and an attorney. Moreover, *Miranda* has been read to permit police to conduct limited follow-up questioning to clarify a volunteered statement. The question "*Who* did you kill?" would probably be permitted in response to the volunteered statement "I killed him." See *United States v. Gonzales*, 121 F.3d 928, 940 (5th Cir. 1997); *United States v. Jennings*, 40 Fed. Appx. 1, 2 (6th Cir. 2001).

Rhode Island v. Innis, 446 U.S. 291 (1980), expanded the concept of interrogation to include police conduct that, while not formal questioning, is its functional equivalent. The broader definition includes "any words or actions on the part of the police (other than those normally attendant to arrest and custody) that the police should know are reasonably likely to elicit an incriminating response from the suspect." 446 U.S. at 301. Despite the breadth of this definition, the Court has been narrow in its application. In *Innis*, no interrogation was found where two officers transporting the suspect (who had requested counsel) to the police station in a cruiser engaged in a conversation about the missing shotgun, believed to have been used by Innis in a recent robbery-murder. Referring to a nearby school for handicapped children, one officer expressed his concern that "God forbid one of them might find a weapon with shells and they might hurt themselves." Innis interrupted the officers and offered to show them where the gun was located, which he proceeded to do. Concluding that the police had engaged in a subtle yet effective form of interrogation by psychological ploy, the Rhode Island Supreme Court held that his statement should not have been admitted at trial and reversed Innis's conviction. *State v. Innis*, 120 R.I. 641 (1978). The U.S. Supreme Court disagreed, concluding that the officers could not reasonably have expected their conversation to elicit an incriminating statement. The Court found nothing in the record to suggest that they were aware that Innis was peculiarly susceptible to an appeal to conscience concerning the safety of handicapped children or that the officers' remarks were designed to elicit a response. 446 U.S. at 302.

"Interrogation" encompasses conduct deliberately designed to evoke a confession, as well as conduct that the officers should reasonably have foreseen would elicit such a response. In assessing foreseeability, courts are directed to focus on both the particular susceptibilities of the suspect and the knowledge the officers had of these at the time. The police are not accountable when their conduct unforeseeably results in a confession.

Arizona v. Mauro, 481 U.S. 520 (1987), brought to prominence another factor alluded to in *Innis*—the perception of the suspect that he is being subjected to psychological pressures. Police permitted Mauro and his wife (at her request) to talk together in the police station where he was being held. Both were suspects in the murder of their child. The conversation occurred in the presence of an officer and a tape recorder, and resulted in incriminating statements that Mauro sought to suppress. He argued that he had been subjected to the functional equivalent of interrogation and thus was entitled to the *Miranda* protections. Rejecting this contention, the Court focused both on the perception of the suspect and the conduct of the police. With regard to the former, the Court doubted that a suspect allowed to speak with his spouse would feel he was being coerced to incriminate himself. 481 U.S. at 528. As for the police conduct, Mauro had not been subjected to compelling influences or psychological ploys and the Court found the permission to talk to his wife reasonable under the circumstances.[7]

Similarly, where an agent posing as a fellow prisoner was placed in the suspect's cell in order to elicit an incriminating statement and the ploy worked, *Miranda* protections did not apply because the suspect did not perceive that he was being questioned and thus did not feel the coercive pressures that trigger the protections. See *Illinois v. Perkins*, 496 U.S. 292 (1990). Writing for the Court, Justice Kennedy explained:

> The essential ingredients of a "police-dominated atmosphere" and compulsion are not present when an incarcerated person speaks freely to someone that he believes to be a fellow inmate. Coercion is determined from the perspective of the suspect. [When] a suspect considers himself in the company of cellmates and not officers, the coercive atmosphere is lacking.
>
> It is the premise of *Miranda* that the danger of coercion results from the intersection of custody and interrogation. We reject the argument that *Miranda* warnings are required whenever a suspect is in custody in a technical sense and converses with someone who happens to be a government agent. [When] the suspect has no reason to think that the listeners have official power over him, it should not be assumed that his words are motivated by the reaction he expects from listeners.

496 U.S. at 296.

Thus, while *Miranda* originally sought to standardize the constitutional approach to police questioning by resort to a uniform set of prophylactic measures, case law defining custody and interrogation represent a return to a more fact-specific focus on compulsion and police conduct reminiscent of the voluntariness standard.

One additional point should be made regarding the interrogation component of *Miranda*. Routine background questions regarding the suspect's name, address, and related matters are not considered within the *Miranda* protections because they are not investigatory, do not involve psychological intimidation, and are not likely to elicit an incriminating response. See *Pennsylvania v. Muniz*, 496 U.S. 582 (1990) (warnings are not required prior

---

7. The dissenters, convinced that the police had set up a confrontation designed to elicit an incriminating statement, concluded that the *Miranda* protections should apply.

to routine booking questions, which are asked for administrative reasons as part of the arrest process). Similarly, responses to the "carefully scripted instructions" that typically accompany field sobriety tests (like reciting the alphabet) are outside *Miranda. Id.* [8] One of the sobriety questions, "Do you know what the date was of your sixth birthday?" was held by *Muniz* to trigger *Miranda* because it is incriminating in the *content* of the answer (Muniz could not identify the date) and not just the slurred delivery. 496 U.S. at 599. The Court has held in the context of a street encounter that compelling the subject to identify himself does not trigger the Fifth Amendment because "it presented no reasonable danger of incrimination." *Hiibel v. Sixth Judicial District Court of Nevada*, 542 U.S. 177 (2004).

Examples

1. Assume that Chestnut was arrested and transported to the station house. Without being administered any warnings, he blurted out: "I ain't taking this rap myself. I'm just the little guy in the operation." Could this statement be introduced against him at trial? What if the arresting officer responded "What operation are you talking about?" and Chestnut then spilled the beans. Could that statement be used?

2. Assume instead that after Chestnut was arrested and transported to the station house, the police sat him in a small room and showed him a videotape of Jane Oak implicating Chestnut in a major narcotics ring. Detective Elm said to Chestnut at the end of the viewing: "It sure looks like you're being played for a patsy to take the whole rap for the gang." Chestnut then stated: "I ain't taking this rap myself. I'm just the little guy in the operation." Could this statement be introduced against Chestnut at trial in the absence of *Miranda* warnings?

3. Assume instead that Chestnut was arrested at his girlfriend's apartment. Before being removed, he insisted that Stella was not involved in any of his activities and pleaded with the police to leave her alone. As he was being transported to the police station in a cruiser, the two officers accompanying him expressed concern that Stella would have to be brought in for questioning and perhaps kept in custody. Chestnut interrupted and made incriminating statements absolving her of any

---

8. The Court was divided between those who regarded the process as interrogation but created an exception for it, and those who treated the responses to such questions as nontestimonial and therefore not within the constitutional privilege against compelled self-incrimination. This latter group concluded that the incriminating slurred speech of the suspect in response to sobriety test questions was analogous to the disclosure of the physical characteristics of voice or handwriting, which had been held as not protected by the Fifth Amendment because it constituted physical evidence and not content-based testimony.

wrongdoing. Are these statements admissible in evidence against him in the absence of *Miranda* warnings?

4. Assume instead that the police entered Chestnut's empty apartment with a lawful search warrant and found cocaine. He subsequently returned home and was placed under arrest. Chestnut was then seated at the kitchen table while the officers brought in the cocaine and placed it on the table in front of him. Upon seeing this, Chestnut stated "Okay, the stuff is mine." Was Chestnut "interrogated"?

5. Hemlock was involved in a fight with Maple in which Maple was stabbed and later died. Hemlock was arrested but not advised of his rights. The police transported him to the hospital for injuries that he received in the fight. While being treated in the emergency ward, Hemlock was asked several questions by Nurse (in the presence of the arresting officers). Nurse asked how he had been injured, and he responded that Maple had hit him. Nurse then asked if he had stabbed Maple, and he replied that he had. Nurse inquired as to what type of knife he used, and he described it. The police officer then asked Hemlock for further details of the fight and he provided them. Was Hemlock subjected to "interrogation"?

6. Following a car chase, police apprehended Drake, who was suspected of having just robbed the Northern Bank of $10,000. The police asked him to identify himself, and he answered falsely that his name was Smathers. Later, at the police station, Drake gave the officers his real name. The prosecution seeks to use the fact that Drake initially provided a false name as consciousness-of-guilt evidence at trial. Defendant argues that because he had not been advised of his *Miranda* rights before being asked to identify himself, his response must be suppressed. How should the court rule?

7. Responding to a radio call, officers arrived on the scene of a domestic dispute and found Husband on the sidewalk yelling up to Wife, who was at the window of a third-floor apartment. One officer asked Husband: "What's going on here? You're making a lot of noise." Husband replied: "She's my wife and I can do anything I want to her." Wife then came down to the street, looking like she had been beaten. She accused Husband of assaulting her, and the police arrested him. Wife was transported to the police station in another cruiser. At the station (before *Miranda* warnings were read), as he was led from the front desk toward a back room, Husband passed Wife seated on a bench. Upon encountering her, he stated: "They can't do anything to me because I'm your legal husband. When I get out tomorrow, I'll finish what I started."

   Can either of Husband's statements be used against him at trial?

Explanations

1. Chestnut's first statement would be admissible against him. Although he was clearly in custody, there was no questioning initiated by the police. The admissibility of the subsequent confession in response to the officer's question is a closer issue. Because the suspect himself initiated the conversation, some clarification or follow-up is permitted, and the officer's question may fall within this permissible area. If, however, the officer had probed further or initiated questioning in new areas, warnings would be required.

2. Even though there has been no direct questioning by the police, their conduct might be deemed the functional equivalent of interrogation, thus triggering the *Miranda* protections. Chestnut would have to establish that the showing of the videotape and the subsequent comment by the officer was either deliberately designed to elicit an incriminating response or that such response was the reasonably foreseeable result. See *Rhode Island v. Innis*, 446 U.S. 291 (1980). In addition, *Arizona v. Mauro*, 481 U.S. 520 (1987) would seem to require Chestnut to show that he had been subjected to psychological pressures or felt coerced into talking.

   In the absence of an (unlikely) admission from the police that they had engaged in a deliberate ploy, Chestnut would ask the court to infer such intent or, in the alternative, to conclude that officers should reasonably have foreseen the result. It would be helpful to his argument if he could demonstrate that the police were aware of his peculiar susceptibility to the showing of the tape because of his relationship to Oak. If, for example, they knew of bad blood between Chestnut and Oak, or of another relationship between the two that would cause Chestnut to feel betrayed upon viewing the taped accusation, that would be an important factor in determining whether the officers should have anticipated an incriminating response. This type of knowledge, found missing in *Innis*, may result in a determination that Chestnut had been subjected to the functional equivalent of interrogation.

   The showing of the tape and the officer's statement directed at Chestnut seems more clearly the functional equivalent of questioning than either the conversation between the officers in *Innis* or the facilitation of a meeting between spouses in *Mauro*. Justice Stevens, dissenting in *Mauro*, characterized the decision to place the two suspects in the same room as a powerful psychological ploy. 481 U.S. at 531.

   Where police have set up a confrontation between the suspect and an alleged accomplice and either inform the suspect that the accomplice has already implicated him or instructed the accomplice to do so, that action has been regarded as interrogation under the *Innis-Mauro* standard. See *Nelson v. Fulcomer*, 911 F.2d 928 (3d Cir. 1990). Where, however, the encounter does not appear to have been deliberately staged, there may be no finding of interrogation. See *United States v. Hernandez-Mendoza*, 600 F.3d 971, 977 (8th Cir. 2010) (police officer's "act of leaving the appellants alone in his vehicle, with a recording device activated, was not the functional equivalent of express questioning. [The officer] may have expected that the two men would talk to each other if left alone, but an expectation of voluntary statements does not amount to deliberate elicitation of an incriminating response.").

Something more than merely bringing the persons together is required for the action to be regarded as the functional equivalent of interrogation. The something more in example 2 is the detective's statement directed at Chestnut immediately after the showing of the video. That would likely be deemed tantamount to interrogation, thus triggering the *Miranda* protections. See *United States v. Martin*, 238 F. Supp. 2d 714, 718-720 (D. Md. 2003) (detective's statement that he needed the defendant's cooperation to investigate a suspicious trash bag taken from his car and that DEA was involved and the case would be prosecuted in federal court was functional equivalent of interrogation). Compare *United States v. Allen*, 247 F.3d 741, 764-766 (8th Cir. 2001) (where detectives simply told suspect he had been identified by three eyewitnesses, that did not constitute interrogation because it was routine to inform suspects of status of investigations and was not likely to elicit incriminating response); *United States v. Conley*, 156 F.3d 78, 82-83 (1st Cir. 1998) (officer's mere description of the evidence is generally not interrogation). A "benign, informative comment" will not run afoul of *Miranda*. *United States v. Orr*, 636 F.3d 944, 954 (8th Cir. 2011) (officer responded to defendant's question about the validity of the arrest warrant).

3. Does the fact that the police were aware of Chestnut's particular concern regarding his girlfriend compel the conclusion that they subjected him to interrogation by conversing as they did? At least one court has indicated that the desire to keep family and friends out of a criminal investigation does not create the peculiar susceptibility envisioned in *Innis*. See *United States v. Thierman*, 678 F.2d 1331 (9th Cir. 1982). The officers did not ask Thierman any questions, but they discussed in his presence their intention to involve his family in the investigation, a prospect that Thierman had previously sought to avoid. At that point, he interrupted and said he would like to make a statement, which he later did. Rejecting the argument that the police had interrogated him by playing on this concern, the court ruled that the vulnerability required by *Innis* must be something more than commonly held concerns to protect family and friends. It must be shown, for example, that the police knew Chestnut was unusually susceptible to such psychological pressures.

The fact-specific focus of the interrogation issue in such cases is reminiscent of the due process voluntariness standard (see Chapter 8).

In *United States v. Calisto*, 838 F.2d 711, 717-718 (3d Cir. 1988), the officer, having just discovered cocaine in the daughter's bedroom, stated in front of her father that "we'll have to get an arrest warrant for [her]." This caused the father to respond: "Don't lock my daughter up. She has nothing to do with that stuff. That's mine. I'm the one you want." The court held that the officer's statement did not constitute interrogation: "[The officer's] remark was not directed to Calisto, was the kind of remark that an officer would normally make in carrying out his duties under the circumstances that confronted him, and was not made in a provocative manner. Moreover, it was a single isolated remark made in the presence of a suspect who showed no signs of being emotionally upset or overwrought. Finally, even if it could be said that reasonable officers might have expected a protest of some kind from Calisto on hearing of his daughter's possible arrest, we do not think it was reasonable to expect an inculpatory response from Calisto."

Dissenting in *Thierman*, supra, Judge Wallace concluded that the police capitalized on their knowledge of the suspect's concern and deliberately elicited the incriminating statement. Quoting from *Innis*, he emphasized that "where a police practice is designed to elicit an incriminating response from the accused, it is unlikely that the practice will not also be one which the police should have known was reasonably likely to have that effect." 678 F.2d at 1339. The contrast between the dissent's focus on the intent of the police and the majority's focus on the vulnerability of the suspect reflects a basic (and yet unresolved) ambiguity in the *Innis* analysis.

4. Did the police action here amount to asking Chestnut: Is this cocaine yours? Translated into *Innis* terms, did the police deliberately display the cocaine as a ploy to prompt a confession, or should they have at least reasonably foreseen that result? Clearly in custody and surrounded by the officers, it is certainly conceivable that Chestnut would feel himself subjected to pressure to make a statement. It is equally conceivable that the police recognized this and took advantage of it. On similar facts, a Massachusetts court ruled that the display of incriminating evidence constituted interrogation. See *Commonwealth v. Rubio*, 540 N.E.2d 189 (Mass. App. Ct. 1989). Several federal courts have concluded that, under certain circumstances, showing evidence to the suspect may be the functional equivalent of interrogation. See *United States v. Stroman*, 420 Fed. Appx. 100, 103 (2d Cir. 2011). This is especially likely where the police "tighten the noose" by revealing one incriminating fact after another — e.g., you meet the description of the perpetrator, the victim is on the way to identify you, the officers found your gun at the scene. *State v. Wright*, 133 A.3d 656, 667-668 (N.J. Super. Ct. App. Div. 2016).

The highly fact-contextual nature of the inquiry is illustrated by the opposite conclusion in *United States v. Genao*, 281 F.3d 305 (1st Cir. 2002), where a detective showed 57 glassine packets of heroin and other drug paraphernalia just seized in his apartment to Genao and said, "We've got a problem here." Genao replied: "Everything's mine. I don't want my wife to get in trouble." The First Circuit viewed the comment as simply an effort to get the suspect's attention, and not the functional equivalent of interrogation. See also *People v. Rowen*, 314 N.W.2d 526 (Mich. Ct. App. 1981) (officers' action in showing a suspected car thief a dent puller, a device frequently used to steal cars, which had been found in his car, was held not to be interrogation because it was not reasonably likely to elicit an incriminating response under the circumstances).

5. In *Arizona v. Mauro*, supra, the police officer's presence during the suspect's conversation with his wife was not held to be interrogation because there was no evidence that the police instigated it or used the wife for the purpose of eliciting incriminating statements. Nor did the officer participate in that discussion. In example 5, the officers sat back and listened to the questioning by the nurse without advising the suspect of his right to remain silent. They awaited the outcome and then asked their own question. On these facts, the New Mexico Supreme Court found that the conduct constituted interrogation. See *State v. Ybarra*, 111 N.M. 234, 804 P.2d 1053 (1990). The court concluded that the atmosphere in the emergency room, given the police presence, was more coercive than that inherent in custody itself, and that the police had taken advantage of that compulsion to obtain incriminating statements. A dissenting judge observed that the officers brought Ybarra to the hospital for treatment and not to elicit statements.

Involvement of third parties in the interrogation process has raised difficult questions. In *Endress v. Dugger*, 880 F.2d 1244 (11th Cir. 1989), the defendant was visited in his jail cell by a detective who was a friend. The detective initiated the visit on his own to inquire about Endress's well-being and was not under the direction of officers connected with the homicide investigation. Although the detective asked no questions regarding the crime, Endress made incriminating statements about it. The detective advised him to say nothing more but reported the statements to his supervisor. Endress sought to suppress the statements as the product of unlawful interrogation. Because the meeting was not initiated by the investigating officer and the only purpose of the meeting was personal, the court concluded that the investigating officers (who were apparently aware of the detective's upcoming visit) should not have known that the visit was reasonably likely to elicit an incriminating response.

A similar result was reached in *Cook v. State*, 270 Ga. 820, 514 S.E.2d 657 (1999), where defendant (being held in the sheriff's custody) confessed to murders after a visit from his father, an FBI agent, who urged him to cooperate. Because the father was not connected to the investigative team and was not acting at the instigation of the police, Cook's motion to suppress for failure to provide *Miranda* warnings was denied. See also *Whitehead v. Cowan*, 263 F.3d 708 (7th Cir. 2001) (incriminating statements made after being persuaded by acquaintance were not product of functional equivalent of interrogation).

6. Drake's response will be suppressed only if it was the result of custodial interrogation. Because he was clearly in custody, the pivotal issue turns on whether he was interrogated. Unlike the previous examples, the police clearly directed a question at the suspect. *Innis* instructs, however, that words and actions normally attendant to arrest and custody fall outside the definition of interrogation. 446 U.S. at 301. Taking basic personal information from the suspect, such as name, age, and date of birth, does not constitute interrogation but is merely incident to the booking process. See *Pennsylvania v. Muniz*, 496 U.S. 582 (1990).

   The twist in example 6 is that while such routine questions generally do not result in incriminating statements, the suspect's response here (a false name) did provide evidence that could be used to prove his guilt. *Innis* teaches, nonetheless, that the police cannot be held accountable for the unforeseeable results of their words or actions. 446 U.S. at 301. Because the question concerning identity was routine and not investigatory, the absence of warnings should not prevent the admission of Drake's response. See *United States v. Foster*, 227 F.3d 1096 (9th Cir. 2000) ("limited biographical questions are permitted even after a person invokes his or her *Miranda* rights").

   Where it appears that the officer was using the routine background questions to elicit incriminating evidence, courts have held the *Miranda* protections applicable. Thus where a Coast Guard officer asked several persons taken off a foreign ship suspected of carrying narcotics for their identity and citizenship, the court concluded that warnings should have been provided:

   > [Q]uestions about citizenship, asked on the high seas, of a person present on a foreign vessel with drugs aboard would (in our view) seem "reasonably likely to elicit an incriminating response." When, or whether, the United States can prosecute a person found on such a ship is not immediately obvious; and the possibility that prosecution will turn upon citizenship is great enough (and should be well enough known to those in the drug enforcement world) that Coast Guard officers ought to know that answers to such questions may incriminate. In this particular case, the likelihood of an incriminating response was rather evident.

   United States v. Doe, 878 F.2d 1546, 1551-1552 (1st Cir. 1989). See also *United States v. Virgen-Moreno*, 265 F.3d 276, 293-294 (5th Cir. 2001) (police asked series of questions regarding defendant's addresses that went beyond routine booking questions and were designed to link him to drug conspiracy); *United States v. Tudoran*, 476 F. Supp. 2d 205 (N.D.N.Y. 2007) (though warnings were not required when border patrol agents initially questioned defendant about his status, when they began to suspect him of wrongdoing, subsequent questioning constituted interrogation because likely to lead to incriminating information)..

Statements taken from John Hinckley shortly after his arrest for the attempted assassination of President Ronald Reagan were suppressed because, although taken during a background interview, they were found to be the result of questions that had a clear investigatory purpose and were asked without the *Miranda* safeguards. See *United States v. Hinckley*, 672 F.2d 115, 123 (D.C. Cir. 1982). The interview, which took 25 minutes and covered a wide range of biographical data (including his psychiatric treatment) as well as recent activities, "bore none of the indicia of a clerical operation." Moreover, the officers, knowing that Hinckley would likely raise an insanity defense, were aware of his peculiar susceptibilities and thus should have known that their interview was likely to result in incriminating evidence.

Skeptics have suggested that the distinction between questions that are clerical and those that are investigative is illusive and unworkable. Justice Marshall predicted that the distinction would necessitate "difficult, time-consuming litigation over whether particular questions asked during booking are routine, whether they are necessary to secure biographical information, whether that information is itself necessary for record-keeping purposes, and whether the questions are—despite their routine nature—designed to elicit testimony." *Pennsylvania v. Muniz*, 496 U.S. 582, 610 (1990) (Marshall, J., concurring in part and dissenting in part). Chief Judge Winter also expressed "serious doubts about defining interrogation according to the tenuous distinction between administrative and investigatory questioning." *United States v. Taylor*, supra, 799 F.2d at 130 n.1 (Winter, C.J., dissenting). "Because," he observed, "such 'routine' information may provide the critical link between the suspect and the crime, it is a substantial dilution of the principles established in *Miranda*." *Id.* Moreover, Judge Winters detected investigatory purpose in the routine questions directed at Taylor because they were asked at the scene of the arrest, not the station house, and because the officers already had information from an accomplice that made the suspect's nickname "Snake" not just a mere administrative matter, but rather a direct connection to the crime being investigated.

In *State v. Walters*, 891 A.2d 1003 (Conn. App. 2006), a victim of an assault was brought over to a cruiser minutes after the altercation to identify the defendant. Upon her positive identification, the defendant said, "I didn't do anything, I only asked her for directions and she freaked out." In seeking to suppress his statement, he argued that bringing the victim to the cruiser was equivalent to an interrogation. The court held that the identification was merely part of routine police procedure, and the officer could not have foreseen that it would cause the defendant to respond.

It is interesting to note that the administrative/investigatory distinction that plays so critical a role in Fourth Amendment jurisprudence (see §4.5 in Chapter 4) has now been incorporated into *Miranda* analysis as well.

7. Was either statement the product of custodial interrogation? The first statement in response to the officer's general on-the-scene question was clearly not. Husband was not in custody at that time and could not have reasonably believed that his freedom was being restrained. The police did not draw their guns or overwhelm him with their presence. *Miranda* permits such general nonaccusatorial questioning of citizens as part of the fact-finding process.

The more difficult issue relates to the second statement made by Husband in the police station. Husband will contend that the police deliberately provoked it by confronting him with the alleged victim of his assault, conduct that they should reasonably have foreseen would accomplish that result. If Husband can establish that the encounter was arranged by the police, he may succeed in this contention. If, however, it appears that the encounter was not planned and that the action in leading Husband past the bench where Wife was seated was a routine part of the processing of arrestees and normally attendant to arrest and custody, then there was no functional equivalent of interrogation. See *People v. Reyes*, 506 N.Y.S.2d 541 (Sup. Ct. 1986).

Whether the encounter between victim and offender was an intentionally coercive tactic or not was deemed the determinative issue in *Spann v. United States*, 551 A.2d 1347 (D.C. 1988). Spann was apprehended at the scene of a purse snatching and was being held by an officer within a few feet of the victim, who was asked by another officer whether the suspect was the man who had taken her purse. She responded, "That's the one." Upon hearing the woman's statement, Spann admitted that he took her purse because she owed him money. The court rejected Spann's effort to suppress his admission on the theory that the questioning of the victim within his earshot was the functional equivalent of interrogation. Rather, the court concluded that the challenged question and answer were "merely part of a dialogue between the officer and the victim to which appellant's response was neither invited nor expected," not a deliberate ploy to encourage a statement. 551 A.2d at 1349. The police were reacting to a confused arrest scene, and it was the victim herself who had moved within earshot of the suspect. Moreover, the court found that Spann had no obvious peculiar susceptibilities to pressure (such as alcohol or drug intoxication or mental disability) that were known to the officers. Thus from both perspectives of the *Innis* analysis — the officer's intent and the suspect's perceptions — there had been no interrogation.

§9.2.3 The Substance and Adequacy of the Warnings

Miranda mandates that specific warnings be given prior to any police interrogation of a person held in custody. Two warnings advise the suspect of his right to remain silent and of the implications of not doing so — that anything he says can and will be used against him in court. Two other warnings advise of the right to have an attorney present during questioning and to have one appointed at government expense if the suspect cannot afford to retain his own. The four warnings were deemed essential to counteract the compelling pressures inherent in the process of in-custody interrogation and thus to meaningfully protect the privilege against self-incrimination and the right to counsel.

Many police departments provide their officers with "*Miranda* cards" from which they can read the warnings now so familiar to viewers of television crime shows. But in the heat of the moment during an arrest, police may deviate from the routine language. Or the officers may respond to questions from the suspect in which they elaborate on and explain the warnings. How strictly must the police adhere to the *exact language* of the warnings as they are set out in *Miranda?* The *Miranda* Court in 1966 indicated some flexibility when it explained it was not establishing a "constitutional straitjacket" and suggested that there might be "potential alternatives" or "fully effective equivalents" to its chosen prophylactic measures. There were suggestions that the warnings did not have to be intoned in precisely the manner set out, so that the warning concerning appointment of counsel at state expense could be dispensed with if the suspect was known to have an attorney. Nevertheless, the Court observed that the "expedient of giving a warning is too simple and the rights involved too important to engage in ex post facto inquiries into financial ability," and thus urged that the warning be given in all cases. 384 U.S. at 468.

More generally, the Court admonished that "no amount of circumstantial evidence that the person may have been aware of [his rights to remain silent and to have the assistance of counsel during interrogation] will stand in [the] stead [of the warnings]." 384 U.S. at 472. "We will not pause to inquire in individual cases whether the defendant was aware of his rights without a warning being given. Assessments of the knowledge the defendant possessed, based on information as to his age, education, intelligence, or prior contact with authorities, can never be more than speculation; a warning is a clearcut fact." 384 U.S. at 468.

Years later the Court addressed the issue of deviation from the original warnings in *California v. Prysock*, 453 U.S. 355 (1981), where the state appellate court had reversed the juvenile defendant's murder conviction because the police officer did not explicitly advise him that he was entitled to the services of a free lawyer prior to questioning, and made some additional comments that arguably could have been interpreted as meaning that such a lawyer would not be available until the defendant appeared in court. The Supreme Court reinstated the conviction, emphasizing that "no talismanic incantation" of precise language is necessary to satisfy *Miranda*. Rather, what is required is that police reasonably convey to the suspect his rights to remain silent and to counsel, which the Court found was done in *Prysock*.

If, however, the reference to the right to counsel is linked to some future point in time *after* the interrogation, the *Miranda* dictates are not satisfied. In *Duckworth v. Eagan*, 492 U.S. 195 (1989), the local police, faced with the pragmatic reality that they were not able to immediately provide a lawyer to advise suspects taken into custody at all times of the day and night, modified the warnings in a form that stated:

> Before we ask you any questions, you must understand your rights. You have the right to remain silent. Anything you say can be used against you in court. You have the right to talk to a lawyer for advice before we ask you any questions, and to have him with you during questioning. You have this right to the advice and presence of a lawyer even if you cannot afford to hire one. *We have no way of giving you a lawyer, but one will be appointed for you, if you wish, if and when you go to court.* If you wish to answer questions now without a lawyer present, you have the right to stop answering at any time. You also have the right to stop answering at any time until you've talked to a lawyer.

492 U.S. at 198 (emphasis added).

Eagan, a murder suspect, was read this form and later argued (in an attempt to suppress his statement) that the warnings were inadequate because the "if and when you go to court" language violated the proscription in *Prysock* against linking the appointment of counsel to a future point in time after interrogation. The Court (in a 5-to-4 decision) disagreed, concluding that the warnings did in fact convey the substance of the rights required by *Miranda*. The suspect was informed of his right to talk to a lawyer for advice before any questioning, and of his right to stop the questioning at any time until he talked to a lawyer. *Miranda* does not mandate that each police station have a station house lawyer present at all times to advise suspects; it requires simply that the suspect be advised of his right to counsel and that he cannot be questioned unless and until he validly waives that right.

Sometimes police conduct prior to the administration of *Miranda* warnings can undercut the efficacy of those warnings. In *Missouri v. Seibert*, 542 U.S. 600 (2004), the Court confronted a "question-first" tactic (used by many departments around the country) in which police deliberately withheld the warnings until they had obtained a confession, after which they finally administered them and got a second confession that did comply with *Miranda*. Writing for the plurality, Justice Souter concluded that the second statement must be suppressed: "When *Miranda* warnings are inserted in the midst of coordinated and continuing interrogation, they are likely to mislead and deprive a defendant of knowledge essential to his ability to understand the nature of his rights and the consequences of abandoning them." 542 U.S. at 613-614. Having already confessed, the suspect felt he had no real choice but to repeat his statement; the warnings came too late to counteract this.

In sum, considerable flexibility is permitted in the administration of the warnings so long as the fundamental points of the *Miranda* protections are conveyed.

Examples

1. A suspect in custody at the police station was given a written form to read that advised her of her right to remain silent and further stated: "You have the right to talk privately to a lawyer before, during, and after questioning and to have a lawyer present with you during questioning. However, you must make your own arrangements to obtain a lawyer and this will be at no expense to the Government. If you cannot afford to pay for a lawyer, one *may* be appointed to represent you." (Emphasis added.) Suspect, having made an incriminating statement during interrogation, now seeks to suppress it on the grounds that she was not adequately informed of her absolute right to appointed counsel. Should her confession be admitted?

2. A suspect in custody at the police station was given a written form to read that advised him of his right to remain silent and further stated: "You have the right to talk with an attorney, either retained by you or appointed by the court, before giving a statement, and to have your attorney present when answering any questions." Suspect, having made an incriminating statement during interrogation, now seeks to suppress it on the grounds that he was not explicitly informed of his right to appointed counsel at state expense if he were indigent. Should his confession be admitted?

3. A suspect in custody at the police station was given complete and adequate *Miranda* warnings. She stated that she could not afford an attorney and asked the officer how and when one could be appointed for her. The officer replied that she could get a lawyer appointed when she went to court. Suspect, having made an incriminating statement during interrogation, now seeks to suppress it on the grounds that she was not adequately informed of her right to counsel. Should her confession be admitted?

4. The defendant contends that the warnings that he was given at the police station prior to questioning were inadequate because he was advised that "anything you say *can* be used against you in court" instead of "anything you say *can and will* be used against you in court." He argues that he did not understand the consequences of making a statement. Should his statement obtained during questioning be admitted?

Explanations

1. While talismanic incantation of the precise language of the original *Miranda* warnings is not required, the suspect must be informed of the basic rights in a manner meaningful to the unlearned layperson. *Miranda* dictated that the suspect be warned prior to any questioning that he has the right to the presence of an attorney, and that if he cannot afford an attorney, one will be appointed for him prior to any questioning if he so desires. 384 U.S. at 479. The use of the word *may* in this example was equivocal and open to misinterpretation — it could have conveyed the impression that the appointment of counsel at state expense was discretionary. This is particularly the case here because of the previous statement that "you must make your own arrangements to obtain a lawyer and this will be at no expense to the Government." The suspect's statement should not be admitted because of the inadequacy of the warnings. See *United States v. Connell*, 869 F.2d 1349 (9th Cir. 1989).

2. *Miranda* requires that the suspect be warned that he has "the right to the presence of an attorney, and that *if he cannot afford an attorney one will be appointed for him* prior to any questioning if he so desires." 384 U.S. at 479 (emphasis added). Although the suspect was informed of his right to a court-appointed attorney, he was not told that this lawyer would be free of charge if he was unable to afford private counsel. This omission goes to the core of the protection of right to counsel for all suspects, including indigents. To be adequate, a warning must convey to the accused that if he is indigent, he has the same right to counsel as a person who can afford to retain a lawyer. The suspect's statement should not be admitted because of the inadequacy of the warnings. See *United States v. San Juan-Cruz*, 314 F.3d 384 (9th Cir. 2002) (conflicting warnings failed to convey clearly the suspect's right to have an attorney appointed at government expense).

   Some courts have held that the omission of the specific language regarding indigency does not require suppression of the statement where the suspect was not in fact indigent and could afford his own attorney anyway. See *Chambers v. Lockhart*, 872 F.2d 274 (8th Cir. 1989). The Eighth Circuit Court of Appeals, however, in urging that the full warnings be given to all future suspects, cautioned the police (as did the *Miranda* Court) not to rely on their estimate of a suspect's financial resources in deciding which warnings to provide.

3. The defendant here would appear to have a more compelling argument than either Prysock or Eagan that her right to appointed counsel had been conditioned on the future event of appearing in court. She specifically told the officer that she needed appointed counsel free of charge, and was told in response to her request that this could not be arranged until she went to court. Thus, while the Court permitted the "if and when you go to court" language in *Duckworth*, the context of that advice in example 3 was much more likely to leave the impression with the suspect that she was not entitled to a free lawyer prior to and during questioning. As one state court ruled in a similar case, "rights of which the suspect was informed were, in the next breath, denied him when he was told he would only have a lawyer 'if he went to court.'" *Alabama v. O'Guinn*, 462 So. 2d 1052 (Ala. Ct. App. 1985). Where police inform the suspect that he has a right to an attorney "prior to any questioning," but say nothing about the lawyer's presence *during* interrogation, an essential element of *Miranda* has been omitted. See *Bridgers v. Texas*, 532 U.S. 1034 (2001) (statement of Justices Breyer, Stevens, and Souter respecting denial of certiorari); *Roberts v. State*, 874 So. 2d 1225 (Fla. Dist. Ct. App. 2004) (*Miranda* warnings informing a defendant that an attorney can be present before questioning were inadequate because they did not inform the defendant that he had a right to have counsel present during interrogation).

   In *State v. Strain*, 779 P.2d 221 (Utah 1989), the suspect was warned that "if you cannot afford an attorney, you have the right to have an attorney appointed for you by the court *at a later date*." (Emphasis added.) The court rejected the contention that this was constitutionally inadequate, observing that he was also advised of his right to remain silent and that he had the right to the presence of counsel prior to and during questioning: "[The] immediate right to counsel which defendant envisions is not within the scope of the *Miranda* decision. Once the accused requests court-appointed counsel, it is treated as a wish to remain silent, and the police cannot proceed to interrogate him until such counsel has been obtained or until defendant initiates the interview." 779 P.2d at 224. It should be pointed out that the suspect's inquiry about an attorney might be regarded as an exercise of his right to counsel. If this were the case, interrogation would have to cease. See § 9.2.5.

4. *Miranda* emphasized that the warning of the right to remain silent must be accompanied by the explanation that anything said can and will be used against the individual in court because it is necessary to make him

aware not only of the privilege, but also of the consequences of forgoing it. 384 U.S. at 469. Further, this warning may make the suspect more acutely aware that he is faced with a phase of the adversary system—that he is not in the presence of persons acting in his interest. *Id.*

The language used in example 4 probably sufficed to reasonably convey the substance of the right to remain silent and the implications of not doing so. Indeed, when the *Miranda* Court summarized its holding, it used the very language challenged here. See 384 U.S. at 444 (the person must be warned that he has a right to remain silent and that any statement he does make "may be used against him"). The statement should thus be admissible at trial. See *Ex parte Siebert*, 555 So. 2d 780 (Ala. 1989). See also *Knighton v. State*, 254 Ga. App. 845, 563 S.E.2d 917 (Ct. App. Ga. 2002) (detective's warning that defendant was better off if he "shut up" until he could talk to an attorney adequately informed him of right to silence). But compare *Hart v. Attorney General of Florida*, 323 F.3d 884, 894 (11th Cir. 2003) (telling suspect that "honesty wouldn't hurt him" contradicted the warning that anything he said could be used against him in court); *Commonwealth v. Seng*, 436 Mass. 537, 766 N.E.2d 492 (2002) (warnings in defendant's native Khmer language were deficient where they failed to advise him of right to remain silent, but implied the opposite by warning of the need to be truthful).

§9.2.4 Waiver of *Miranda* Rights

While *Miranda* sought to eliminate the *ad hoc* approach of the due process voluntariness analysis and substitute bright-line standards, that goal has not been fully achieved. One reason is that the doctrine of waiver has evolved into its own totality-of-the-circumstances approach. A second reason is that the due process challenge to an involuntary confession survives *Miranda* as an independent avenue of attack. See Chapter 8. "The question of the voluntariness of a waiver of *Miranda* rights is separate and differs from the determination of the voluntariness of a confession. Once it is clear that a defendant has made a knowing and voluntary waiver of his or her *Miranda* rights, the issue then becomes whether the confession itself was voluntary." *Smith v. Duckworth*, 856 F.2d 909, 911 (7th Cir. 1988) (citations omitted). A confession may be suppressed because, although the suspect freely signed a *Miranda* waiver form, he was subsequently coerced into confessing.

Turning to the waiver question, *Miranda* held that if a statement is obtained from a suspect during custodial interrogation (following provision of the warnings), the statement may be admitted at trial only if the prosecution demonstrates that the suspect "knowingly, intelligently, and voluntarily" waived his privilege against self-incrimination and right to counsel.[9] There is strong indication in *Miranda* that the Court, seeking to avoid the ambiguities of the past, envisioned that such waivers would be explicit. Thus, it observed that "an express statement that the individual is willing to make a statement and does not want an attorney followed closely by a statement could constitute a waiver," but that a valid waiver will not be presumed "simply from the silence of the accused after warnings are given or simply from the fact that a confession was obtained." 384 U.S. at 475.

Subsequent decisions have been more open to implied waivers. *North Carolina v. Butler*, 441 U.S. 369 (1979), held that a waiver may be found even in the absence of an explicit statement if the suspect's words and actions implicitly constitute a decision to forgo his rights. While mere silence in the face of the warnings is not sufficient, the "defendant's silence, coupled with an understanding of his rights and a course of conduct indicating waiver" may suffice. 441 U.S. at 373. Butler was administered the warnings and responded that he understood his rights. He refused to sign the written waiver form, but he agreed to talk about the robbery being investigated and proceeded to admit participation in it. When his statement was offered against him at trial, Butler claimed that in the absence of an explicit waiver, the statement could not be used. The Supreme Court disagreed, rejecting a requirement that waivers be explicit and instead holding that a valid waiver could be inferred from appropriate conduct of the suspect. In determining whether a suspect has implicitly waived his *Miranda* rights, the Court (in a manner reminiscent of the due process voluntariness standard) directed trial judges to look at the particular facts and circumstances surrounding the case, including the background, experience, and conduct of the accused. 441 U.S. at 374.[10]

Whether express or implied, a waiver must be shown to have been "knowing, intelligent, and voluntary" in order to be valid. The first two components are treated together by the courts and focus on whether the waiver was made with an awareness of the rights being abandoned and the consequences of doing so. The third component requires a determination of whether the waiver "was the product of a free and deliberate choice rather than intimidation, coercion, or deception." *Moran v. Burbine*, 475 U.S. 412, 421 (1986).

With regard to the requirement that the waiver be knowing and intelligent, it must be shown that (1) the suspect understood that he had the right

---

9. The *Miranda* decision characterizes this as a "heavy burden" for the prosecution to meet. The Court has since defined it as proof by a preponderance of the evidence. See *Colorado v. Connelly*, 479 U.S. 157 (1987). Some states in interpreting their own laws have established a heavier burden. New Hampshire and Massachusetts, for example, interprets the state constitution to require that waiver be proven beyond a reasonable doubt. *State v. Chrisicos*, 148 N.H. 546, 813 A.2d 513 (2002); *Commonwealth v. Hoyt*, 461 Mass. 143 (2011). One state has read *Dickerson v. United States*, 530 U.S. 428 (2002), to impose a uniform federal standard preventing states from applying a higher standard. See *State v. Tuttle*, 650 N.W.2d 20, 26 (S.D. 2002).

10. The dissenters would have imposed a prophylactic rule requiring the police to obtain an express waiver, and they criticized the doctrine of implying waivers from conduct that is often of uncertain meaning. 441 U.S. at 379.

not to talk to the police or to talk only with counsel present; and (2) that he appreciated the consequences of forgoing these rights and speaking to the police. The Court at one point insisted that the prosecution may not rely on any presumption that the warnings were understood by the suspect, but rather must affirmatively demonstrate such understanding by showing, for example, that he answered affirmatively when asked by the officer whether he understood the rights just read to him. *Tague v. Louisiana*, 444 U.S. 469 (1980). More recently, the Court has been willing to find such understanding in the absence of evidence to the contrary. Thus, in *Berghuis v. Thompkins*, 130 S. Ct. 2250 (2010) (discussed in §9.2.5), the Court concluded that the suspect (who refused to sign a waiver) had understood his rights from the facts that he received a written copy of them, could read and understand English, and was given sufficient time to read them. When he uttered a one-word response after three hours of silence, "he knew what he gave up." 130 S. Ct. at 2262.

The Court has taken a narrow view in recent years of the information that must be disclosed to the suspect prior to a knowing and intelligent waiver. In *Moran v. Burbine*, supra, the fact that the police failed to inform the suspect that an attorney retained by a relative to represent him was trying to see him at the police station was held not to undercut the validity of his written waiver. The police had assured the attorney that the suspect would not be questioned until the next day, but then they proceeded to interrogate him. While the First Circuit Court of Appeals had reversed Burbine's conviction, reasoning that he had been deprived of the information necessary for a knowing and intelligent waiver, the Supreme Court disagreed: "Events occurring outside of the presence of the suspect and entirely unknown to him surely can have no bearing on the capacity to comprehend and knowingly relinquish a constitutional right." 475 U.S. at 421. The Court added:

> No doubt the additional information [that an attorney was seeking to meet with him] would have been useful to respondent; perhaps even it might have affected his decision to confess. But we have never read the Constitution to require that the police supply a suspect with a flow of information to help him calibrate his self-interest in deciding whether to speak or stand by his rights. Once it is determined that a suspect's decision not to rely on his rights was uncoerced, that he at all times knew he could stand mute and request a lawyer, and that he was aware of the state's intention to use his statements to secure a conviction, the analysis is complete and the waiver is valid as a matter of law.

Id.[11] *Moran* did leave open the possibility that "on facts more egregious than those presented here police deception might rise to the level of a due process violation." 475 U.S. at 432.

---

11. Justice Stevens, writing for the dissenters, criticized the Court's "what the suspect doesn't know can't hurt him approach," 475 U.S. at 453 n.38, and concluded that the failure to inform Burbine of the call from his attorney rendered the subsequent waiver invalid. Id. at 450.

Other decisions similarly indicate that the suspect need only have a minimal understanding of his *Miranda* rights and the consequences of relinquishing them. The suspect in *Connecticut v. Barrett*, 479 U.S. 523 (1987), indicated after receiving the warnings that he would not make a written statement but would talk about the sexual assault being investigated. He later confessed orally. Barrett challenged its admission into evidence on the grounds that his inconsistent conduct demonstrated that he did not understand the implications of speaking to the police, and thus his waiver was not knowing and intelligent. The Supreme Court held otherwise, ruling that the police could properly take the opportunity opened by his ambiguous actions to obtain an oral confession: "[The] fact that some might find Barrett's decision illogical is irrelevant, for we have never embraced the theory that a defendant's ignorance of the full consequences of his decisions vitiates their voluntariness." 479 U.S. at 530.

Colorado v. Spring, 479 U.S. 564 (1987), established that a suspect need not even be aware in advance of all the possible subjects of the interrogation in order to make a valid *Miranda* waiver. Arrested by federal agents in Missouri on a firearms charge, Spring signed a written waiver form after being advised of his rights. The focus of the interrogation ultimately changed, however, to an unsolved homicide in Colorado, to which Spring then confessed. Rejecting his assertion that he could not have knowingly waived his right to remain silent when he was unaware that he would be questioned about the unrelated crime, the Court reaffirmed that a valid waiver does not require the subject be informed of all information that would be useful in making his decision or that might affect his decision to confess. The information withheld by the police, the Court observed, might go to the "wisdom" of the waiver but not to its "essentially voluntary and knowing nature." 479 U.S. at 577.

Turning to the separate requirement that the waiver be voluntary, *Colorado v. Connelly*, 479 U.S. 157 (1987), equated this with the due process standard discussed in Chapter 8. "The sole concern of the Fifth Amendment, on which *Miranda* was based, is governmental coercion. Indeed, the Fifth Amendment privilege is not concerned with moral and psychological pressures to confess emanating from sources other than official coercion. The voluntariness of a waiver of this privilege has always depended on the absence of police overreaching, not on 'free choice' in any broader sense of the word." 479 U.S. at 170. Thus, to invalidate a waiver as involuntary, it must be demonstrated that the waiver resulted from police coercion that overcame the suspect's will. If the accused was subjected to compulsion such as intimidation or threats, then the impact of those tactics will be examined in light of the totality of the circumstances surrounding the interrogation (including the suspect's age, mental state, experience, and intelligence) to determine the voluntariness of the waiver. See *Fare v. Michael*

C., 442 U.S. 707 (1979). Absent evidence of objectionable police methods, Connelly signals that the waiver will be found voluntary regardless of the defendant's peculiar vulnerabilities or internal compulsions to talk (such as Connelly's psychosis in which the "voice of God" told him to confess). The *Miranda* Court stated that "any evidence that the accused was threatened, tricked, or cajoled into a waiver will of course show that the defendant did not voluntarily waive his privilege." 384 U.S. at 476. In recent years, however, such deceptive activity by the police has been significantly discounted and is treated by the courts as only one factor among the totality of circumstances determining validity of a waiver. This development parallels the treatment of deception for purposes of the due process voluntariness standard, as discussed in Chapter 8.

Examples

1. Suzanne Suspect was arrested near the scene of a robbery and was transported to the police station. She was advised of her *Miranda* rights and signed a "Waiver Form" indicating that she understood her rights to remain silent and to counsel but chose to waive those rights and submit to interrogation. After two hours of questioning, Suspect admitted participation in the robbery. What must the prosecution show when it offers that statement into evidence at trial?

2. Assume instead that Suspect was advised of her rights, stated that she understood them, but then refused to sign the Waiver Form. The detective on the case then said to Suspect: "You don't have to sign the form, but we would like you to answer some questions for us." The detective proceeded to interrogate Suspect about the robbery, and she made several incriminating responses. How does the analysis of the admissibility of these statements differ from the confession in example 1?

3. Assume instead that after Suspect was advised of her *Miranda* rights, she stated that she would answer questions about the crime but would not give or sign a written statement because, in her words, "I know that could be used against me." She then proceeded to make several incriminating statements during questioning. How does the analysis of the admissibility of these statements differ from the confession in example 2?

4. Now assume that when Suspect arrived at the police station, she appeared to be very disoriented, fatigued, and obviously under the disorienting influence of narcotics. She was advised of her rights and nodded affirmatively when asked whether she understood them. The detective then

said to Suspect: "The sooner you come clean with us, the quicker we can get you help." The detective proceeded to question Suspect about the robbery, reminding her several times in a forceful manner that it would be easier on her if she confessed. Suspect finally agreed to answer questions and eventually admitted committing the crime. How does the analysis of the admissibility of this statement differ from the confession in example 3?

5. Daniel Bernard, a 22-year-old with a fourth-grade education and no prior experience with the police, confessed to a robbery-murder during questioning at the station house. He had been advised of his rights after being arrested, and signed a *Miranda* waiver form prior to interrogation. His attorney, who has filed a motion to suppress the confession, has learned that Bernard is of subnormal intelligence and (according to defense psychiatrists) could not have understood the terminology of the warnings. The police, however, did not engage in any coercive conduct either before or during the interrogation. Is the confession admissible at trial?

6. Suppose instead that Bernard is a 15-year-old of normal intelligence. Assuming again that there is no police coercion, would his waiver be valid?

7. Ned Nave was arrested for embezzlement, taken to the police station, and advised of his *Miranda* rights. He responded that he wished his attorney, Walter Willow, was there to advise him, but he was out of town for the week. Nave said that in light of Willow's unavailability, he might as well talk, and during the subsequent questioning, he made several incriminating statements. Unbeknownst to Nave, Attorney Willow in fact had already arrived back in town, heard about Nave's arrest, and tried unsuccessfully to meet with him prior to his questioning. The police had steadfastly refused to let Willow see his client and had failed to advise Nave of his lawyer's presence. Are his statements admissible at trial?

8. Rodney Ring was arrested for aggravated rape, taken to the police station, and advised of his *Miranda* rights. Before waiting for a response from Ring, the detective told him that he had already been positively identified by the victim from a photograph. Ring asked how long it would take to get a lawyer for him, and the detective told him it could take "quite some while, like a day or so." Ring replied: "Well, I guess I'm on my own, and there's no sense clamming up." He signed a waiver form and, after ten minutes of questioning, confessed. It turns out that the detective lied about the victim's having identified Ring, and also about the availability of counsel. Is his statement admissible in court?

Explanations

1. There are two basic issues that must be resolved concerning the admissibility of the confession: (1) Did Suspect make a legally effective waiver of her *Miranda* rights? (2) Was Suspect's confession voluntary or the result of police coercion? The second issue is controlled by the due process standard discussed in Chapter 8 and is distinct from the *Miranda* waiver issue. A suspect may, for example, make a valid waiver (knowing, intelligent, and voluntary) of *Miranda* and submit to questioning, but then be intimidated by the police into making a confession. That statement could be challenged under the due process standard, even though the waiver was lawfully obtained.

   Regarding the first issue, *Miranda* held that "an express statement that the individual is willing to make a statement and does not want an attorney followed closely by a statement could constitute a waiver." 384 U.S. at 474. The validity of Suspect's written waiver depends on whether it was knowing, intelligent, and voluntary. The prosecution bears the burden of establishing this by a preponderance of the evidence. The waiver will be considered knowing and intelligent so long as it appears that Suspect generally understood the warnings and rights described (which she acknowledged at the time she did) and that she appreciated the consequences of undergoing interrogation — that the prosecution would use her statements against her in court. The waiver will be considered voluntary so long as it was not the product of police coercion or pressure.

2. Unlike example 1, Suspect did not make an explicit waiver (either written or oral) here. The statement may nonetheless be admitted if the prosecution can establish (1) that Suspect's conduct constitutes an *implied* waiver; and (2) that the waiver was knowing, intelligent, and voluntary.

   Although *Miranda* held that a valid waiver will not be presumed simply from the silence of the accused after warnings or from the fact that a confession was eventually obtained, 384 U.S. at 474, silence, together with conduct by the accused indicating that he understands his rights and wishes to relinquish them, may constitute a valid implied waiver. *North Carolina v. Butler*, 441 U.S. 369 (1979). Courts must look at the particular facts and circumstances surrounding the questioning, including the suspect's age, education, background, and prior experience with the police, to determine if he intended to forgo his rights. Like Butler (in *North Carolina v. Butler*) and Barrett (in *Connecticut v. Barrett*), Suspect's conduct in refusing to sign a waiver but then responding to questions appears inconsistent and ambiguous (it would no doubt be described by the dissenters in *Butler* as of "uncertain meaning"). The Court held in both cases, however, that a waiver may be inferred from the facts that the accused was advised of his rights, indicated he understood them, and then proceeded to answer questions. This is particularly so where the accused is a mature adult of reasonable intelligence and has had prior experience with the criminal justice system.

Although Suspect's conduct seems hardly the product of rational deliberation and indeed may reflect a lack of understanding that her responses could be used against her by the prosecution, it probably makes the grade under the prevailing narrow definition of "knowing and intelligent." She stated that she understood her rights and submitted to questioning. Moreover, the detective's prompting here falls far short of coercion undercutting the voluntary nature of the waiver. See *Colorado v. Connelly*, 479 U.S. 157 (1987). As the Court held in *Moran v. Burbine*, 474 U.S. 412 (1986), "Once it is determined that a suspect's decision not to rely on his rights was uncoerced, that he at all times knew he could stand mute and request a lawyer, and that he was aware of the state's intention to use his statements to secure a conviction, the analysis is complete and the waiver is valid as a matter of law." 475 U.S. at 422-423.

Even in the face of evidence that the Somali pirates in custody were unfamiliar with the American legal system, were illiterate, and spoke no English, the warnings (translated to them) were deemed sufficiently understood so that their waiver was knowing and intelligent. *United States v. Dire*, 680 F.3d 446 (4th Cir. 2012).

As noted above, *Berghuis v. Thompkins* (2010) evidences a Court that is more willing to imply "knowing and intelligent" waivers from ambiguous circumstances. By way of example, the Second Circuit concluded that the intervening decision in *Berghuis* required reconsideration of its earlier decision finding defendant's refusal to sign a waiver form sufficient to invoke his *Miranda* rights. *United States v. Plugh*, 648 F.3d 118 (2d Cir. 2011).

3. There is a much clearer indication here than in the previous example that the accused misunderstood the warnings and the consequences of submitting to interrogation. Unlike example 2 or *Connecticut v. Barrett*, 479 U.S. 523 (1987), Suspect explicitly disclosed her misunderstanding (that only written statements could be used against her and not oral responses) to the police and they failed to correct it. She thus has a more persuasive argument that her waiver was not knowing and intelligent.

4. Suspect, in agreeing to answer questions, has made an explicit oral waiver. The validity of that waiver must be analyzed in light of the pressures placed on Suspect by the detective's remarks, as well as Suspect's apparent vulnerability. In other words, it must be determined whether the waiver was voluntary under a totality-of-the-circumstances analysis: Did the police conduct themselves in such a manner as to overcome the will of the accused, given her unique personal characteristics? See *Fare v. Michael C.*, 442 U.S. 707 (1979). For a waiver to be voluntary, it must be the product

of a free and deliberate choice rather than intimidation, coercion, or deception. *Moran v. Burbine*, 475 U.S. at 421. The detective's encouragements may very well have worn down Suspect's resistance to being questioned, particularly given her apparently impaired state of mind. *Colorado v. Connelly* teaches, however, that a waiver is involuntary only if the police used coercive tactics to overcome the accused's will. The detective's conduct here probably does not rise to the level required by *Connelly*.

It is possible, nonetheless, that a court would conclude that Suspect's waiver was not knowing and intelligent because her impaired mental state (exhaustion and the effect of narcotics) precluded her from understanding the warnings and the consequences of answering questions. Unlike the voluntariness requirement, coercive tactics are not a prerequisite to such a finding under the separate "knowing and intelligent standard." See, e.g., *United States v. Trejo-Islas*, 248 F. Supp. 2d 1072 (D. Utah 2002) (waiver was invalid where the defendant did not understand his rights or the waiver form he signed because of his head injuries and sleep deprivation).

5. Because the waiver was not the product of police coercion, it cannot be considered involuntary. The requirement that a waiver be knowing and intelligent is, however, a distinct prerequisite to validity and is not dependent upon a finding that the police engaged in coercive conduct. See *United States v. Cristobal*, 293 F.3d 134, 142 (4th Cir. 2002); *United States v. Crews*, 171 F. Supp. 2d 93 (D. Conn. 2001) (and citations). Even under the minimal standard set by the Supreme Court—that the suspect be mentally aware that he may remain silent and request a lawyer and, further, that the prosecution will use his statements against him in court—Bernard could probably not make a knowing and intelligent waiver on his own (assuming, of course, that the court accepts the conclusion of the defense experts). See *United States v. Betters*, 229 F. Supp. 2d 1103 (D. Or. 2002) (waiver was not knowing and intelligent where a defendant with severe mental deficiencies was not able to understand concept of waiver and was highly intoxicated).

The extent to which mental defect may foreclose a knowing and intelligent waiver depends upon the nature of the defect and the other factors peculiar to the situation. In *United States v. Gaddy*, 894 F.2d 1307 (11th Cir. 1990), where there was no contention that the *Miranda* waiver was involuntary, there remained serious questions as to whether it was knowing and intelligent. Factors weighing against the validity of the waiver were the suspect's addiction to drugs and mental illness. Weighing in favor of the waiver were his above-average intelligence, his previous experience with the law (he was "no novice to law enforcement procedures"), and the fact that he did not exhibit scattered thinking or panicky behavior. The court concluded that the waiver was knowing and intelligent.

A moderately retarded and functionally illiterate individual was similarly held to have made a voluntary, knowing, and intelligent waiver of his *Miranda* rights in *Dunkins v. Thigpen*, 854 F.2d 394 (11th Cir. 1988). Under the *Connelly* standard, as we have seen, mental retardation by itself does not render a waiver involuntary without the element of police coercion. Mental retardation is just one of the factors to consider in the determination of whether the waiver was knowing and intelligent. The court concluded that a person functioning as Dunkins in the high mild range of retardation could understand his rights and intelligently waive them. See also *United States v. Rosario-Diaz*, 202 F.3d 54, 69 (1st Cir. 2000) (suspect with low I.Q. and no prior involvement with criminal justice system who was interviewed for over six hours made valid waiver).

In *Smith v. Zant*, 887 F.2d 1407 (11th Cir. 1989), the court came to the opposite conclusion when it held that a mentally retarded suspect had not knowingly and intelligently waived his *Miranda* rights. The court-appointed psychiatrist who examined Smith testified that a person functioning at his level of intelligence would have difficulty understanding his rights and the consequences of relinquishing them unless those rights were slowly and carefully explained to him, which they were not. See also *Brown v. Crosby*, 249 F. Supp. 2d 1285 (S.D. Fla. 2003) (a 15-year-old with mild developmental disability and an I.Q. below third-grade level could not understand rights); *People v. Braggs*, 209 Ill. 2d 492 (2003) (a mentally disabled suspect did not knowingly and intelligently waive rights); *State v. Blackstock*, 19 S.W.3d 200 (Tenn. 2000) (mentally disabled 24-year-old who could not read or write, did not know the shape of a triangle, thought the American flag had only three stars, and could not count numbers in sequence past ten).

Summarizing the case law, one court observed that the government is required "to clear only a relatively low bar in proving an intelligent waiver. Generally, the courts will hold that a defendant's waiver is knowing if he understands that he can refuse to talk to the people asking him questions or stop the questioning once it begins; that the people asking him questions are not his friends but are police or law enforcement personal who are trying to show he is guilty of a crime; that he can ask for and get a lawyer who will help him; and that he does not have to pay for that lawyer." *Collins v. Gaetz*, 612 F.3d 574, 575 (7th Cir. 2010).

6. If Bernard were a 15-year-old of normal intelligence, the concern would be whether he had the maturity to appreciate the nature of his rights and the implications of waiving them. Courts weigh the presence of a parent or other helpful adult as an important factor when determining the validity of a waiver by a juvenile. See, e.g., *Commonwealth v. Pacheco*, 87 Mass. App. 1172 (Mass. App. Ct. 2015) (officers interfered in with juvenile's opportunity to consult with his guardian); *State v. Burrell*, 697

N.W.2d 579 (Minn. 2005) (where 16-year-old defendant repeatedly asked for his mother before and after he was given his *Miranda* warning, court held that his waiver was not knowing and intelligent); *State v. Presha*, 163 N.J. 304, 748 A.2d 1108 (2000); *State v. Jimenez*, 799 P.2d 785 (Ariz. 1990). Some states, in their desire to establish at least some bright lines, have adopted per se rules requiring that the consequences of the waiver be explained to the juvenile by a parent or other "interested adult" in order for the waiver to be valid. See *Commonwealth v. Alfonso A.*, 438 Mass. 372, 380 (2003) (determination that a juvenile over 14 years old has made a valid waiver requires a showing either that he consulted with an adult or that he possesses a high degree of intelligence, experience, knowledge, or sophistication); *State v. Presha*, supra (juvenile under age 14 cannot make a valid waiver without an adult participating).

7. *Moran v. Burbine*, 475 U.S. 412 (1986), held that neither the refusal of the police to allow an attorney to see her new client, nor the failure to inform the suspect of the lawyer's request, invalidated a subsequent waiver because events occurring outside the presence of the suspect and entirely unknown to him "surely can have no bearing on the capacity to comprehend and knowingly relinquish a constitutional right." 475 U.S. at 421. Our example, however, is distinguishable in several material respects. The suspect explicitly stated to the police his desire to have the assistance of counsel before deciding on a waiver, and the police (at least passively) misled him by failing to disclose that his attorney was available and indeed present. This may therefore be considered the case left open in *Moran*, where "on facts more egregious than those presented here police deception might rise to the level of a due process violation." 475 U.S. at 432. It is difficult to categorize Nave's waiver as knowing and intelligent when he made explicit his desire to confer with counsel. Moreover, as we will see in the next section, a suspect's equivocal request for counsel should cut off further questioning beyond clarification of that request. Some state courts have held that withholding information on the presence or availability of a lawyer retained on behalf of a suspect will render the waiver invalid. See, e.g., *Commonwealth v. McNulty*, 458 Mass 305 (2010); *Commonwealth v. Mavredakis*, 430 Mass. 848, 725 N.E.2d 169 (2000); *State v. Roache*, 148 N.H. 45, 803 A.2d 572 (2002); *State v. Reed*, 627 A.2d 630 (N.J. 1993).

8. This example raises the troublesome issue of the effect of police deception and trickery on the validity of a *Miranda* waiver. As is the case with the due process voluntariness standard (see Chapter 8), trickery weighs in as one factor (but not an automatically determinative one) in the totality-of-the-circumstances analysis. Where the issue in the confession context is whether the trickery produced an involuntary confession, the issue in the *Miranda* context is whether it produced an invalid waiver. As

one court put it, "even if some police tricks may be objectionable as a matter of ethics, they are not relevant to the constitutional validity of a waiver unless they interfere with the defendant's ability to understand the nature of his rights and the consequences of abandoning them." *United States v. Farley*, 607 F.3d 1294, 1300 (11th Cir. 2010).

There are two different types of deception here. The detective's lie about the positive identification will probably not invalidate the waiver. In *United States v. Velasquez*, 885 F.2d 1076, 1086 (3d Cir. 1989), the suspect's waiver was deemed valid even though the officer had lied when he told her that a companion had given a statement implicating Velasquez and planned to testify against her. While this misinformation greatly inflated the state's evidence against Velasquez and was at least a partial cause of her waiver, the court did not find that her will had been overcome. 885 F.2d at 1089. The Third Circuit emphasized that the suspect, who had worked as a journalist, was a mature adult with a college degree and thus possessed a full awareness both of the nature of her rights and the consequences of abandoning them. Moreover, she had asked to speak with the police officer prior to her waiver, "thus indicating that it was likely that she wanted to discuss the investigation and less likely that the statement was a spontaneous reaction to [the officer's] falsehood." 885 F.2d at 1089. Finally, she was in custody for only two hours and was not subjected to any threats, promises, or ill treatment.

A similar conclusion was reached in *Shedelbower v. Estelle*, 885 F.2d 570 (9th Cir. 1989), where despite the fact that the police falsely told the accused that he had been identified by the rape victim, his waiver was held to have been knowing, intelligent, and voluntary. Shedelbower had already made incriminating statements before the deception and had said that he was anxious to speak to someone about his involvement in the events to get it off his chest. Therefore, "the false statement by the police was clearly an unimportant element in the mind of Shedelbower when he said that he had to tell someone what had happened.... [I]t is indeed doubtful that the officer's statement to Shedelbower that he had been identified played any role in motivating him to want to talk to them then or later to confess." 885 F.2d at 574. See also *Foster v. Commonwealth*, 380 S.E.2d 12 (Va. 1989) (suspect who was falsely told that his fingerprints were found on the weapon had already indicated his intention to talk and thus validly waived his rights).

In our problem, however, the waiver seems quite clearly the product of the police deception. The officer's false indication of the strength of the case against Ring gave him a feeling of hopelessness, which he expressed immediately before signing the waiver. Unlike *Velasquez* and *Shedelbower*, Ring gave no indication prior to the deception that he wanted to speak about the crime, nor had he already made any incriminating statements. His waiver, therefore, may be held invalid.

Ring will likely have more success with the argument focusing on the officer's misleading statement about the availability of counsel. Unlike deception about the evidence against the suspect, deception that goes to the substance of the *Miranda* rights themselves almost certainly will invalidate a waiver. See, e.g., *Soffar v. Johnson*, 237 F.3d 411, 458 (5th Cir. 2000) (officer's response to question from suspect as to how he could get a court-appointed lawyer, that it could take "as little as a day or as long as a month," was designed to mislead suspect into abandoning request for counsel and thus invalidated the waiver); *Hart v. Attorney General of Florida*, 323 F.3d 884, 894-895 (11th Cir. 2003) (telling suspect that "honesty wouldn't hurt him" and that having a lawyer present would be a disadvantage misled him and invalidated the waiver); *Hopkins v. Cockrell*, 325 F.3d 579 (5th Cir. 2003) (officer misled suspect by telling him, despite the warnings, that their conversation was confidential); *Jackson v. Litscher*, 194 F. Supp. 2d 849 (E.D. Wis. 2002) (false statement that counsel could not be obtained until the defendant was charged rendered the waiver invalid). But compare *Mueller v. Angelone*, 181 F.3d 557, 575 (4th Cir. 1999) (officer's negative and misleading response to suspect's query "Do you think I need an attorney here?" did not invalidate waiver since suspect was a 42-year-old with extensive experience in such matters).

§9.2.5 Waiver After Invocation of the Right to Silence or to Counsel

The flip side of waiver is invocation—one *exercises* rather than relinquishes his rights. *Miranda* mandated that "if the individual indicates in any manner, at any time prior to or during questioning, that he wishes to remain silent, the interrogation must cease." 384 U.S. at 473-474. The Court envisioned that no questioning could properly be conducted after that point because any statement obtained would likely be the product of compulsion, subtle or otherwise. 384 U.S. at 474. Invocation of the right to silence, therefore, would prevent any further interrogation of that suspect.

Invocation of the right to silence, however, must be unambiguous. For example, remaining silent for nearly three hours of questioning was not considered sufficient to invoke the right when the suspect finally responded to a question. *Berghuis v. Thompkins*, 130 S. Ct. 2250 (2010).

Moreover, even when invoked, this right to terminate questioning is not absolute. *Michigan v. Mosley*, 423 U.S. 96 (1975), rejected the concept of a permanent termination and held instead that interrogation may resume so long as the right to cut off questioning is "scrupulously honored." Mosley, under arrest for robbery, was Mirandized and declined to be questioned. Two hours later, another officer gave him a fresh set of warnings, and Mosley agreed to talk about an unrelated murder. Rejecting his challenge to the admission of the incriminating statement made during this interrogation, the Court held that his right to cut off questioning had been scrupulously honored because the police had immediately ceased questioning when he exercised his right to remain silent and had resumed questioning about a different crime only after the passage of significant time and with the provision of fresh warnings.

Thus, if the prosecution seeks to introduce a statement obtained from a suspect who had initially invoked his right to remain silent, it must be demonstrated (1) that his right to silence, once invoked, had been scrupulously honored; and (2) that a knowing, intelligent, and voluntary waiver subsequently occurred (see §9.2.4). Where it is shown that the police failed to cease interrogation immediately, or engaged in repeated efforts to get the suspect to change his mind, his resulting statement will be inadmissible.

Somewhat different consequences flow from invocation of the right to counsel. *Miranda* held that if (upon being administered the warnings) the suspect indicates that he wants the assistance of counsel, then interrogation must cease until an attorney is present. This prohibition against the resumption of questioning until counsel arrives is premised on the view that invocation of the right to counsel shows that the suspect is unwilling to decide on his own whether to submit to interrogation. Subsequent decisions have, again, modified this firm rule.

Edwards v. Arizona, 451 U.S. 477 (1981), permits police to resume interrogation, even in the absence of counsel, if the suspect himself initiates further communication with the police. The questioning of Edwards (who had initially waived his rights) was terminated when he asserted his right to counsel. He was taken to a jail cell where, the following morning, two other detectives sought to talk to him, but he refused. A guard then told Edwards that he had to talk with the detectives and took him to meet them. The detectives informed Edwards of his rights and then played a taped statement of an alleged accomplice who implicated him in the crime. He then indicated a willingness to talk and later made an incriminating statement. Concluding that the playing of the tape constituted the functional equivalent of questioning under *Rhode Island v. Innis* (see §9.2.2), the Court ruled that his statement was inadmissible. When a suspect invokes his right to counsel, a valid waiver cannot be established merely by showing that he received additional warnings and then responded to further police-initiated custodial interrogation. Rather, the Court held, additional safeguards are necessary to protect the right to counsel. Specifically, the suspect may not be questioned further until counsel has been made available to him or the accused *himself* "initiates further communication, exchanges, or conversations with the police." 451 U.S. at 484. Because Edwards's second meeting with the police had occurred at their insistence, his statement could not be used against him at trial.

Thus, if the prosecution seeks to introduce a statement from a suspect who had initially invoked his right to counsel, it must be demonstrated

(1) that counsel was made available to him; or (2) the suspect himself initiated the further communication; and (3) that a knowing, intelligent, and voluntary waiver subsequently occurred.

What constitutes invocation of the right to counsel? "I'd like to speak to a lawyer before answering questions" would clearly suffice. But suspects are often more ambiguous in their language.

Smith v. Illinois, 469 U.S. 91 (1984), where the suspect responded "Uh, yeah. I'd like to do that" when advised of the right to counsel but later equivocated, seemed to set a liberal tone erring on the side of treating such statements as invocations and cautioned against using the suspect's subsequently expressed doubts to undercut his initial request for counsel. (See example 5 below.) Davis v. United States, 512 U.S. 452 (1994), however, changed direction when the Court held that questioning must cease only in the face of an unambiguous request for counsel, and further that police are not obligated (although it is "good police practice") to clarify ambiguous requests but may press on with their interrogation. The defendant's statement "Maybe I should talk to a lawyer" was not deemed a request for counsel.

A defendant's invocation of his Sixth Amendment right to counsel during a court appearance does not constitute an invocation for purposes of *Miranda* when he is subsequently questioned about a different crime. In McNeil v.Wisconsin, 501 U.S. 171 (1991) (discussed in §10.3 in Chapter 10), the Court reasoned that the exercise of the right to representation under the Sixth Amendment is offense-specific and distinct from the prophylactic right provided under *Miranda* to have counsel present during custodial interrogation. In order to effectively invoke one's rights, the invocation must occur either during interrogation or immediately preceding it: *Miranda* rights cannot be invoked in an anticipatory manner, as at a preliminary hearing. 501 U.S. at 182 n.3. See also United States v. Grimes, 142 F.3d 1342 (11th Cir. 1998) (claim-of-rights form signed by a defendant when arrested on state bad check charges could not anticipatorily invoke the defendant's Fifth Amendment right to remain silent with regard to subsequent interrogation on federal explosives charges).

The Court has insisted on a request for an attorney in order to cut off questioning. A request by a juvenile to see his probation officer was not the equivalent: "It is [the] pivotal role of legal counsel [in the administration of justice] that justifies the per se rule established in *Miranda* and that distinguishes the request for counsel from the request for a probation officer, a clergyman, or a close friend." Fare v. Michael C., 442 U.S. 707, 722 (1979).

What constitutes initiation of further communications by the suspect?
"I've changed my mind and want to talk about the crime now without a lawyer" would clearly suffice. But again statements by persons in police custody are often more muddled. In Oregon v. Bradshaw, 462 U.S. 1039 (1983),

the defendant asserted his right to counsel, but shortly afterwards, while being transferred to jail, he inquired of an officer: "Well, what is going to happen to me now?" The officer responded: "You do not have to talk to me. You have requested an attorney and I don't want you talking to me unless you so desire because anything you say — because — since you have requested an attorney, you know, it has to be your free will." 462 U.S. at 1042. Bradshaw replied that he understood. The two then conversed about where Bradshaw would be taken and what he would be charged with, and the officer then suggested that he take a lie detector test, which he agreed to. The next day, following new warnings, Bradshaw took the test and subsequently made incriminating statements.

Reversing the state appellate court, which had suppressed the statements, the Supreme Court concluded that the *Miranda/Edwards* doctrine had not been violated. A four-Justice plurality, noting that questions relating to routine incidents of the custodial relationship (such as request for water or access to a telephone) would generally not constitute "initiation," nevertheless found that Bradshaw's question to the jailer "evinced a willingness and desire for generalized discussion about the investigation," thus permitting interrogation to resume. 462 U.S. at 1045. (The plurality then addressed the separate waiver issue and found it to be knowing, intelligent, and voluntary.) The four dissenting Justices were "baffled," viewing Bradshaw's inquiry as designed simply to find out where the police were going to take him and not an invitation to discuss the subject matter of the criminal investigation. 462 U.S. at 1055.

It should be noted that the constraint against further interrogation once a suspect invokes his right to counsel applies even if the second interrogation would concern an offense unrelated to the subject of the initial arrest. In *Arizona v. Roberson*, 486 U.S. 675 (1988), the defendant was arrested for burglary and exercised his right to counsel after receiving the warnings, thus foreclosing interrogation. Three days later, while still in custody, he was again Mirandized and questioned by a different officer about a different burglary. This officer was not aware that the defendant had previously invoked his right to counsel. An incriminating statement was obtained. The state argued that the *Edwards* rule cutting off interrogation should not apply regarding a different crime. The Supreme Court, emphasizing the importance of maintaining clear and unequivocal guidelines to law enforcement officers, disagreed: "[W]hether a contemplated reinterrogation concerns the same or a different offense, or whether the same or different law enforcement authorities are involved in the second investigation, the same need to determine whether the suspect has requested counsel exists. The police department's failure to honor that request cannot be justified by the lack of diligence of a particular officer." 486 U.S. at 687.

Maryland v. Shatzer, 130 S. Ct. 1213 (2010), added an important gloss: The *Edwards* rule barring further interrogation expires if there has been a break in custody lasting more than two weeks, on the presumption that whatever coercive influences may have existed have dissipated by then. The prisoner's return to the general population was deemed such a break. But see *Grant v. Warden, Maine State Prison*, 616 F.3d 72, 76 (1st Cir. 2010) (where police seek to renew interrogation after the suspect's invocation of the right to remain silent, not the right to counsel, *Shatzer* is inapplicable).

What does the *Edwards* rule mean when it mandates that a suspect who has invoked his right to counsel may not be interrogated until counsel has been *made available* to him? The Court has held that merely providing the opportunity to consult with counsel outside the interrogation room is not sufficient. Rather, the accused is entitled to have his attorney present with him during questioning. See *Minnick v. Mississippi*, 498 U.S. 146 (1990). Minnick, in custody on suspicion of murder, terminated interrogation by requesting a lawyer. He later consulted with an appointed attorney two or three times. The police subsequently told Minnick that he would now have to talk to them, and they reinitiated interrogation. Refusing to suppress the resulting confession, the Mississippi Supreme Court read *Edwards* as satisfied by permitting consultation with an attorney. In reversing, the U.S. Supreme Court observed that the purpose of the "clear and unequivocal guidelines" of *Edwards* was to protect the suspect's right to have counsel present at the interrogation; mere consultation with counsel is not enough to remove the pressures inherent in custody. "[T]he need for counsel to protect the Fifth Amendment privilege comprehends not merely a right to consult with counsel prior to questioning, but also to have counsel present during any questioning if the defendant so desires." 498 U.S. at 154 (citation omitted). Police-initiated reinterrogation cannot take place until counsel is "present" in that sense.

Examples

1. Sylvia Suspect was arrested, taken to the police station, and booked for selling narcotics. She was advised of her *Miranda* rights by Detective Oak and responded, "I don't have anything to say." No questioning was attempted, and she was placed in a small holding cell. One hour later, Oak approached her, read her rights again, and stated, "Have you had enough time in there yet?" Suspect replied that she was "tired of rotting in this cell" and would talk. During questioning, she admitted her participation in the narcotics ring. Is her statement admissible in court?

2. Assume instead that after Sylvia Suspect was advised of her *Miranda* rights by Detective Oak she responded, "I won't say anything until I talk to my lawyer." No questioning was attempted, and she was placed in a holding cell. One hour later, Oak approached her, read her rights again, and

asked, "Are you ready to talk now?" Suspect submitted to interrogation and made an incriminating statement. Is her statement admissible in court? Would it make any difference if Suspect had sent word through her guard that she wanted to see Detective Oak?

3. Assume instead that after Sylvia Suspect was advised of her *Miranda* rights by Detective Oak, she orally agreed to waive those rights. After several minutes of interrogation, Suspect interrupted and said, "When will you let me go home? I really need to talk to someone about this before I answer your questions." The detective responded, "Why don't we get this over with? It'll be easier on you if you just tell me what happened out there." The detective continued questioning and elicited an incriminating statement from Suspect a short time later. Is Suspect's statement admissible in court?

4. Lyle Loser was taken into custody on suspicion of rape and read his *Miranda* rights. At first he agreed to answer questions, but after ten minutes, he stated, "You know, I'd better talk to my lawyer before I say anything more." As the two interrogators were gathering up their papers to leave, Officer Mutt said to Officer Jeff, "Let's go see the victim. I heard she picked Loser's photo out of the array." Upon hearing this, Loser said, "I've changed my mind, guys. I don't need to talk to anyone. Let me tell you what happened and let's work something out." Loser proceeded to respond to questions and confessed. Is his statement admissible at trial?

5. Steven Smith was arrested and taken to the interrogation room of the police station by two detectives. The following conversation occurred:

Q. Steve, I want to talk with you in reference to the armed robbery that took place at McDonald's restaurant on the morning of the nineteenth. Are you familiar with this?

A. Yeah. My cousin Greg was.

Q. Okay. But before I do that I must advise you of your rights. Okay? You have a right to remain silent. You do not have to talk to me unless you want to do so. Do you understand that?

A. Uh. I was told to get my lawyer. I was told you guys would railroad me.

Q. Do you understand that as I gave it to you, Steve?

A. Yeah.

Q. If you want to talk to me, I must advise you that whatever you say can and will be used against you in court. Do you understand that?

A. Yeah.

Q. You have a right to consult with a lawyer and to have a lawyer present with you when you're being questioned. Do you understand that?

A. Uh, yeah. I'd like to do that.

Q. Okay. If you want a lawyer and you're unable to pay for one, a lawyer will be appointed to represent you free of cost, do you understand that?

A. Okay.

Q. Do you wish to talk to me at this time without a lawyer being present?

A. Yeah, and no, uh, I don't know what's what, really.

Q. Well. You either have to talk to me this time without a lawyer being present, and if you do agree to talk with me without a lawyer being present, you can stop at any time you want to.

A. All right. I'll talk to you then.

In subsequent questioning, Smith admitted participation in the robbery. Can his admission be offered into evidence against him at trial?

6. Barry Bash was arrested at a train station on probable cause to believe that he was a narcotics dealer and taken to an Amtrak police interrogation room, where he was advised of his *Miranda* rights and agreed to submit to questioning. After a question about the identity of his supplier, however, Barry said he was "pleading the Fifth." At this point, questioning stopped, and he was transported by the arresting officer to the police station. En route in the cruiser, Barry inquired as to where he was being taken. The officer described the procedure that would take place when they arrived at the police station. The officer then asked Barry what he did for a living, and he said that he was studying electronics. The officer observed that "it's a shame you got mixed up in this, because you're young and have a trade and you're going to screw up your whole life." Barry responded, "I'm just doing it to see how much money I can make." The officer then asked: "Where does a kid like you get the drugs to sell?" Barry responded, "Somewhere uptown." Can these incriminating answers be used against Barry at trial?

Explanations

1. If a subject in custody indicates in any manner at any time prior to or during questioning that he wishes to remain silent, the interrogation must cease.[12] Sylvia Suspect's statement "I don't have anything to say" appears to be an exercise of this right to remain silent, and the police complied. Her right to terminate questioning is, however, neither permanent nor irrevocable. *Michigan v. Mosley*, 423 U.S. 96 (1975), teaches that interrogation may resume so long as the right to cut off questioning is scrupulously honored.

   The prosecution would argue that that was the case here because no questioning occurred when Suspect invoked her right to silence and questioning began only after a fresh set of warnings some time later.

---

12. Courts have permitted routine personal information questions even after the suspect has exercised the right to terminate interrogation. See, e.g., *United States v. Thompson*, 866 F.2d 268 (8th Cir. 1989) (officer's question "Where are you from?" did not violate the suspect's already invoked right to silence).

Suspect would argue that, unlike the case in *Mosley*, the resumption of questioning here was for the same crime, by the same officer, and with the passage of less time. Moreover, she would portray the police conduct as an effort to wear down her resistance to further questioning. Some courts have extended *Mosley* to include questioning for the same crime, and the only relevant question is whether Suspect's right to remain silent was scrupulously honored. *Dewey v. State*, 169 P.3d 1149 (Nev. 2007).

The analysis to determine if the right to cut off interrogation was scrupulously honored is fact-specific. Courts consider a variety of factors including (1) the amount of time elapsed between interrogations, (2) the provision of a fresh set of warnings, (3) the subject matter and scope of the second interrogation, and (4) the officer's zealousness in attempting to pursue questioning after the suspect has invoked his rights. Generally, no one factor is determinative, but the provision of fresh warnings is considered the most important and critical. New Jersey has even adopted a per se rule that the failure to administer new warnings will result in a finding that the right to cut off questioning was *not* scrupulously honored. See *New Jersey v. Hartley*, 511 A.2d 80, 88 (1986).

It is useful to look at examples of the *Mosley* analysis in action. In *United States v. Hsu*, 852 F.2d 407 (9th Cir. 1988), the suspect invoked his right to remain silent while being questioned by federal drug agents at the scene of an arrest. He was questioned again 30 minutes later by different agents at a different location after another set of warnings. The court ruled that Hsu's right to cut off questioning was scrupulously honored because fresh warnings had been given, the agents had conducted themselves in a deferential manner and did not harass or pressure him to change his mind, and the location and atmosphere of the second interrogation was different from the first. The court observed that "the change in scenery served as an intervening event to help alleviate any pressure that Hsu may have felt to waive his rights at the [first location]. The fresh warnings, of course, furthered this same end in a powerful way, as did the agents' restraint after Hsu asserted his *Miranda* rights." 852 F.2d at 412. Thus "although the passage of time in this case [only 30 minutes] might ordinarily incline us toward a conclusion that right to cut off questioning was not respected, the clear evidence of scrupulous conduct by the DEA agents and free informed choice by Hsu militates against such a judgment." *Id.*

In contrast, the court in *Charles v. Smith*, 894 F.2d 718 (5th Cir. 1990), found that the police had not scrupulously honored the suspect's refusal to speak when the same police officer asked two questions just a few minutes after invocation of the right to silence. The questions concerned the same crime that the suspect had just refused to discuss, and the officer admitted that he had used "psychology" on the suspect to obtain an admission. The court in *Nelson v. Fulcomer*, 911 F.2d 928 (3d Cir. 1990), reached a similar conclusion that the police had failed to respect the suspect's right to remain silent:

> While the Commonwealth argues that it fulfilled its duty to scrupulously honor Nelson's right to cut off questioning, its confrontation ploy [in which the suspect was confronted with an accomplice who had just confessed, and which was deemed the functional equivalent of interrogation] bears none of the indicia of respect identified in *Mosley*. The Commonwealth failed to contend, let alone to demonstrate, that it waited a significant amount of time after Nelson cut off questioning, that it gave Nelson a fresh set of *Miranda* warnings, that Nelson had invoked his right in connection with an offense other than the rape and murder, or that the officers who engineered the confrontation were different from those to whom Nelson initially refused to talk.

911 F.2d at 939-940. See also *United States v. Ortiz*, 943 F. Supp. 2d 447 (S.D.N.Y. 2013) (police had not scrupulously honored suspect's refusal to speak when the same officer asked: "Do you have anything more you want to talk about?" just minutes after invocation).

Getting back to example 1, despite the provision of fresh warnings, it is likely that the court would conclude that Suspect's right to silence was not properly respected when the same officer resumed questioning only one hour later, concerning the same crime, and after needling Suspect about her time in the small cell. If the court ruled otherwise, we would have to resolve the separate issue of whether Suspect's subsequent waiver was valid (that is, knowing, intelligent, and voluntary; see §9.2.4).

2. Like the right to remain silent, invocation of the right to counsel is not irrevocable. The police may resume interrogation in the absence of counsel if the *accused himself initiates* further communication, exchanges, or conversations with the police. *Edwards v. Arizona*, 451 U.S. 477 (1981). Further *police-initiated* interrogation is forbidden, even if the accused is again advised of his rights and makes a valid waiver. In example 2, it is of determinative significance whether the subsequent interrogation was instigated by the police or Suspect. When the detective, without any prompting from Suspect, asked whether she was ready to talk, the right to counsel was clearly violated and the confession would not be admissible.

In the variation posed where Suspect summoned Detective Oak, it must be determined whether that constituted initiation. We would have to uncover more details regarding Suspect's request and the subsequent conversation. Merely requesting to see the detective, without indicating a willingness to discuss the crime, would not constitute a sufficient green light under *Edwards v. Arizona* to resume interrogation. Suspect may simply have had a question relating to the routine incidents of custody ("Where can I get a drink of water?"). It is significant, however, that Suspect asked to see the officer investigating the case, as opposed to another officer or guard, because that makes it more likely that she desired to discuss the investigation. See *United States v. Velasquez*, 885 F.2d 1076, 1085 (3d Cir. 1989).

Given *Oregon v. Bradshaw*'s broad interpretation of what constitutes a willingness to discuss the crime ("Well, what is going to happen to me now?"), any communication from Suspect that arguably reflects a desire to talk about the investigation could be deemed initiation. If that were the case here, the separate issue of waiver would have to be addressed — that is, having initiated further discussions and thus revoked her exercise of the right to counsel, did Suspect then knowingly, intelligently, and voluntarily waive her right to remain silent and submit to questioning? Again, more details of the interrogation would have to be learned.

3. A suspect undergoing interrogation after waiver of his rights may cut off that interrogation by invoking *in any manner and at any time* his right to silence or to counsel. An accused need not rely on talismanic phrases or magic words to invoke those rights. The issue in example 3 is whether Suspect's ambiguous statement constituted invocation of either of those rights.

Suspect's inquiry "When will you let me go home? I really need to talk to someone about this before I answer your questions." will probably be considered an understandable expression of concern, not an invocation of the right to remain silent. See *United States v. Lux*, 905 F.2d 1379, 1382 (10th Cir. 1990) (suspect's question during interrogation as to how long it would take if she wanted a lawyer and whether she would have to remain in jail while she waited for one was held not to be an invocation of the right to counsel); *Moore v. Dugger*, 856 F.2d 129, 134 (11th Cir. 1988) ("We are not persuaded that this statement evidences a refusal to talk further."). Compare *Commonwealth of Pennsylvania v. Zook*, 553 A.2d 920, 922 (Pa. 1989) (when suspect asked to use the phone to call his mother to see if she could get him an attorney, this was a clear invocation of right to counsel and should have terminated the interrogation). Suspect's indication of a desire to talk to someone may have been an attempt to exercise the right to remain silent or to counsel. Although a request to see a probation officer was not deemed to be an exercise of the right to counsel in *Fare v. Michael C.*, 442 U.S. 707 (1979), Suspect's statement here may very well have been referring to an attorney.

Given the importance of the rights involved, the courts have permitted (and indeed encouraged) the police to seek clarification of such equivocal statements to determine whether they do in fact constitute an exercise of *Miranda* rights. There is, however, no obligation to do so. See *Davis v. United States*, 512 U.S. 452 (1994). "Are you saying you want to consult with an attorney?" would be an appropriate response from the officer. Such questioning is, however, strictly limited to clarifying the ambiguous request and must not coerce or intimidate the suspect into waiving his rights. See *Campaneria v. Reid*, 891 F.2d 1014, 1021 (2d Cir. 1989); *Nash v. Estelle*, 597 F.2d 513, 517-518 (5th Cir. 1979) (en banc). Interrogation concerning the crime must cease, of course, until the accused makes clear that he is not invoking his rights.

A suspect's claim that the police violated his *Miranda* rights by failing to terminate interrogation immediately is not negated by the fact that he answered additional questions. As *Smith v. Illinois*, 469 U.S. 91, 100 (1984), cautioned: "An accused's post-request responses to further interrogation may not be used to cast retrospective doubt on the clarity of the initial request itself." Compare *Bradley v. Meachum*, 918 F.2d 338, 342 (2d Cir. 1990) (when the suspect initially stated that he did not wish to discuss his involvement in the crime but then denied any connection to it and explained his whereabouts at the time of the crime, this conduct did not constitute an invocation of the right to silence but rather evidenced a willingness to discuss his involvement). Any doubts concerning a suspect's desires must be resolved in favor of protecting *Miranda* rights. Cf. *Michigan v. Jackson*, 475 U.S. 625, 633 (1986) (Sixth Amendment right to counsel). But see *Davis v. United States*, 512 U.S. 452, 459 (1994) (in order to cut off questioning, suspect must articulate the desire to have counsel present sufficiently clearly that a reasonable officer under the circumstances would understand the statement to be a request for attorney).

In our example, Detective Oak ignored Suspect's statement that, while equivocal, at least arguably invoked her right to cut off questioning. Rather than seek clarification, Oak tried to persuade Suspect to talk and continued questioning her concerning the crime. It would appear Suspect's rights to remain silent and to counsel were not scrupulously respected, and her subsequent confession should be inadmissible. See *United States v. Pena*, 897 F.2d 1075, 1078 (11th Cir. 1990) (police had not scrupulously honored defendant's right to cut off questioning when they continued to question him rather than clarify his ambiguous statement "I want to [cooperate]. I really want to but I can't. They will kill my parents."). Whether *Davis v. United States*, supra, changes this result remains to be seen.

4. Because Loser made a clear invocation of his right to counsel, all interrogation must cease. The issue raised here is whether the police complied. While formal questioning terminated, the statement by one officer to the other regarding the identification of Loser arguably constitutes the functional equivalent of interrogation (see *Rhode Island v. Innis*, §9.2.2), which is equally violative of the *Edwards* rule. If the statement was one that the police should know was reasonably likely to elicit an incriminating

response from Loser, then interrogation continued improperly, and the confession is inadmissible.

If, however, the statement does not fall within the *Innis* standard, then the police (having discontinued interrogation) were permitted to resume interrogation upon initiation by Loser of further communications. Loser's statement to the officers that he wished to talk about the case would certainly constitute such initiation (it clearly evinced a willingness to discuss the investigation). Assuming, therefore, that Loser is found to have made a knowing, intelligent, and voluntary waiver, his confession would be admissible. Based on similar facts, *Shedelbower v. Estelle*, 885 F.2d 570 (9th Cir. 1989), concluded that the officer's statement did not constitute the functional equivalent of questioning, and thus interrogation had ceased and was properly resumed after the suspect initiated the further communication. The court also concluded that the waiver was valid despite the fact that the officer's statement indicating that the witness had identified the accused was actually false: "[T]he totality of the circumstances compels the conclusion that Shedelbower's taped confession was not the product of that falsehood, and that he was fully aware of the nature and consequences of his actions." 885 F.2d at 574. The court reached a similar conclusion in *Plazinich v. Lynaugh*, 843 F.2d 836 (5th Cir. 1988), where the suspect exercised his right not to submit to questioning but, while being transported to a cell, was told by the officer that his alleged accomplice had just attempted suicide. The suspect then asked to speak to an assistant district attorney and confessed shortly thereafter. Rejecting Plazinich's argument that he had been improperly subjected to the functional equivalent of interrogation after exercising his right to silence, the court held that the officer's statement was merely informational ("food for thought") and not reasonably likely to elicit an incriminating response. 843 F.2d at 840.

5. The threshold issue here is whether Smith effectively invoked his right to counsel, in which case questioning would have to cease and not begin again until either counsel were present or Smith initiated further communication. Upon being advised that he had a right to counsel, Smith said, "Uh, yeah. I'd like to do that." This appears to be a clear and unequivocal assertion of his right, and thus all interrogation should have stopped.

The Illinois Supreme Court in the case upon which this problem is based ruled, however, that Smith's subsequent hedging — "Yeah, and no, uh, I don't really know what's what, really" — undercut and nullified his initial request, and thus held that the police could properly continue their interrogation. The U.S. Supreme Court reversed:

> No authority, and no logic, permits the interrogator to proceed on his own terms and as if the defendant had requested nothing, in the hope that the defendant might be induced to say something casting retrospective doubt

> on his initial statement that he wished to speak through an attorney or not at all. [A]n accused's post-request responses to further interrogation may not be used to cast doubt on the clarity of the initial request itself. Such subsequent statements are relevant only to the distinct question of waiver.

Smith v. Illinois, 469 U.S. 91, 98-99 (1984). Because the suspect had invoked his right to counsel and did not himself initiate the further communication, the confession was not admissible.

With *Davis v. United States*, 512 U.S. 452 (1994), the Court appears to have abandoned its "resolve ambiguities in favor of invocation" approach. Although the facts are distinguishable from *Smith*, in which there was a direct invocation of counsel and a later equivocation, *Davis's* "Maybe I should talk to a lawyer" was at least arguably an invocation, but was not treated as such by the Court.

6. The pivotal issue here is whether by "pleading the Fifth," Barry effectively exercised his right to remain silent. If so, questioning should have ceased and the suspect's right not to speak should have been scrupulously honored. It could be argued that Barry intended to "plead the Fifth" only in response to the specific question directed at him, not to cut off all interrogation. Because his equivocal statement at least arguably invoked his *Miranda* rights, however, further police inquiry should have been limited to clarification of his wishes. Assuming that Barry did invoke his right to silence, the police could resume questioning only if, having scrupulously honored the right by terminating interrogation, the suspect subsequently waived his right in a knowing, intelligent, and voluntary manner. Under the *Michigan v. Mosley* analysis, it would be very difficult to demonstrate such a waiver here. Only a short period of time elapsed between the invocation of the right to silence and the resumed questioning, which involved the same crime. And, most important, the suspect was not afforded a fresh set of warnings, which would have served to alleviate the continued pressures of custody.

The prosecution would argue that the officer in the cruiser was merely engaging in idle chatter (not interrogation) with the accused, who spontaneously incriminated himself. In this scenario, the right to cut off questioning was thus scrupulously honored. Alternatively, it could be argued that Barry himself initiated the conversation with the question as to where he was being taken. While the definition of initiation is quite broad in *Oregon v. Bradshaw*, 462 U.S. 1039 (1983), and the statement there ("Well, what is going to happen to me now?") is similar to Barry's, the latter would seem more clearly related to the routine incidents of the custodial relationship and not an indication of a desire to discuss the crime. Moreover, it was the officer who turned the conversation to the subject of the crime by making a statement reasonably likely to elicit an incriminating response ("it's a shame you got mixed up in this"), and then asked the specific question concerning the source. It is likely, therefore, that Barry's statements would not be admissible in evidence.

§9.3 LIMITATIONS ON THE SCOPE OF THE *MIRANDA* EXCLUSIONARY RULE

From its inception, the *Miranda* doctrine (like the Fourth Amendment exclusionary rule) has been a lightning rod for criticism.[13] The requirement of the warnings has been attacked as an undue interference in the investigative work of law enforcement, and the suppression of noncomplying statements as inconsistent with the search for the truth at trial. In the face of persistent challenge, it is not surprising that the original *Miranda* scheme has been significantly limited by an increasingly conservative Supreme Court in recent years. What is perhaps surprising is that *Miranda* survives at all.

Like the debate surrounding the exclusionary rule (see Chapter 7), the doctrinal controversy over *Miranda* has centered on the question whether its rules are constitutionally required or merely remedies chosen in 1966 to enforce the right against compelled self-incrimination. If *Miranda* is prophylactic and not of constitutional stature, modification or even abolition by the Court or Congress[14] is obviously more easily accomplished.

The *Miranda* Court appeared to suggest that the devices were not a constitutional imperative:

> It is impossible to foresee the potential alternatives for protecting the privilege which might be devised by Congress or the States in the exercise of their creative rule-making capacities. Therefore we cannot say that the Constitution necessarily requires adherence to any particular solution for the inherent compulsions of the interrogation process as it is presently conducted. Our decision in no way creates a constitutional straitjacket which will handicap sound efforts at reform, nor is it intended to have this effect.

384 U.S. at 467.

---

13. The Reagan Justice Department under Attorney General Ed Meese adopted the following policy position: "We accordingly regard a challenge to *Miranda* as essential, not only in overcoming the detrimental impact caused directly by this decision, but also as a critical step in moving to repudiate a discredited criminal jurisprudence. Overturning *Miranda* would, accordingly, be among the most important achievements of this administration—indeed of any administration—in restoring the power of self-government to the people of the United States in the suppression of crime." Office of Legal Policy, U.S. Department of Justice, Report to the Attorney General on the Law of Pre-Trial Interrogation (Feb. 12, 1986).

14. Title II of the Crime Control Act of 1968, 18 U.S.C. 3501, purports to repeal *Miranda* and impose in its place a return to a voluntariness standard for confessions. As discussed below, *Dickerson v. United States*, 530 U.S. 428 (2000), rebuffed the effort.

In the years since *Miranda*, the Court emphasized the right versus remedy distinction as justification for cutting back on the protective scheme. Characterizing the warnings and associated rules as "not themselves rights," but merely "procedural safeguards" designed to reinforce the right against compelled self-incrimination, see *Michigan v. Tucker*, 417 U.S. 433, 443-444 (1974), the Court has significantly limited the scope of *Miranda* in the manner outlined below.

But *Dickerson v. United States*, 530 U.S. 428 (2000), has now apparently resolved the doctrinal debate, holding that the warnings-based approach to determining admissibility of statements obtained during custodial interrogation is constitutionally based and not subject to overruling by Congress. Yet *Dickerson* also puts the Court's stamp of approval on the limitations and exceptions that have been imposed on the *Miranda* scheme.

It should be noted that the Court has declined to limit review of *Miranda* claims in habeas corpus proceedings the way it has Fourth Amendment violations (see §7.3.2 in Chapter 7). In *Withrow v. Williams*, 507 U.S. 680 (1993), the Court, distinguishing *Miranda* violations from those involving search and seizure because the former compromise the truth-seeking function of the trial, permits state prisoners to challenge their convictions on the ground that they rested on statements obtained in violation of *Miranda*.

§9.3.1 Use of the Statement for Impeachment

The *Miranda* decision indicated that statements obtained in violation of the protections could not be used at trial for *any* purpose. But in its first modification of the doctrine, the Burger Court held in *Harris v. New York*, 401 U.S. 222 (1971), that such statements (so long as they are voluntary, as discussed in Chapter 8) could be used to impeach the defendant's testimony at trial. Harris made incriminating statements at the time of his arrest for the sale of heroin, but he had not received complete warnings. While he could prevent the statements from coming into evidence during the prosecution's case-in-chief, the Court held that he could not stop the prosecutor from confronting him with these admissions on cross-examination when he chose to testify. "[The] shield provided by *Miranda* cannot be perverted into a license to use perjury by way of a defense, free from the risk of confrontation with prior inconsistent utterances." 401 U.S. at 226.[15] In such a situation, the judge will instruct the jury (for whatever it is worth!) that they are to consider the prior statement only in weighing the credibility of the defendant's trial testimony, and not for the truth of the matters asserted.

---

15. Statements obtained in violation of the Sixth Amendment right to counsel may similarly be introduced for impeachment purposes. See *Michigan v. Harvey*, 494 U.S. 344 (1990), discussed in §10.4 of Chapter 10.

Four years later, *Oregon v. Hass*, 420 U.S. 714 (1975), extended the impeachment exception to a situation where the suspect, after receiving the warnings, invoked his right to counsel, which the police ignored as they persisted in questioning him. Despite the deliberate nature of the *Miranda* violation, the Court held that the statements obtained (which were found to have been voluntary) could be used to challenge defendant's testimony on the stand.

The Court has refused to extend *Harris v. New York* to situations where the prosecution seeks to use the defendant's *post-warning silence* for purposes of impeachment. In *Doyle v. Ohio*, 426 U.S. 610 (1976), the arrestee remained silent after receiving *Miranda* warnings. When Doyle later testified at his trial on narcotic offenses that he had been framed by a police informant, the prosecution elicited (over objection) on cross-examination that he had not protested his innocence at the time of arrest. Reversing the conviction, the Court held that it would be "fundamentally unfair and a deprivation of due process to allow the arrested person's silence to be used to impeach an explanation subsequently offered at trial." Because the warnings advise the suspect that he has the right to remain silent, the Court recognized that his silence may simply represent an exercise of those rights and thus should carry no penalty.

It must be emphasized that the impeachment exception (like the public safety exception discussed below) does *not* apply to statements obtained that are coerced and involuntary. These remain inadmissible for *all* purposes.

Example

Talia Teller was arrested on suspicion of embezzlement from the bank that she worked for. She was questioned for five hours at the police station, without being advised of her *Miranda* rights, and finally confessed. As defense counsel in her upcoming trial, what would you advise her as to whether she should testify or not? What further information would you seek?

Explanation

Talia's confession, obtained in violation of *Miranda*, may not be admitted in the prosecution's case-in-chief. Under *Harris v. New York*, 401 U.S. 222 (1971), it may be used for purposes of impeachment during cross-examination if Talia chooses to testify. She would have to be advised, therefore, that if she elects to testify and denies the charges, the prosecutor would be allowed to bring to the jury's attention the otherwise inadmissible confession as a prior inconsistent statement. Also, if Talia is convicted, the statements that she made in violation of *Miranda*, so long as they were voluntary, may generally be considered during her sentencing. *United States v. Nichols*, 438 F.3d 437 (4th Cir. 2006).

The impeachment exception does not apply to statements found to have been involuntary under the due process totality-of-the-circumstances standard. Thus, it would be necessary to explore the nature of the five-hour interrogation and the manner in which Talia was treated. See Chapter 8.

§9.3.2 The Public Safety Exception

In a significant limitation on the original scope of *Miranda*, the Supreme Court has created an exception for questioning conducted in "public safety" situations. The incriminating statement at issue in *New York v. Quarles*, 467 U.S. 649 (1984), was obtained when police pursued a rape suspect believed armed with a gun into a supermarket and captured him. Upon frisking Quarles and finding an empty shoulder holster, the officer questioned him about the location of the missing gun. No warnings were given. Quarles responded: "The gun is over there." The officer, following the suspect's direction, retrieved the loaded pistol. Both the statement and gun were excluded at trial on the grounds that they were obtained in violation of *Miranda*.

The Supreme Court reversed, holding that "under the circumstances involved in this case, overriding considerations of public safety justify the officer's failure to provide *Miranda* warnings before he asked questions devoted to locating the abandoned weapon." 467 U.S. at 651. Employing the cost/benefit rationale typical of the decisions cutting back on Warren Court precedent, *Quarles* concluded: "[T]he need for answers to questions in a situation posing a threat to public safety outweighs the need for the prophylactic rule protecting the Fifth Amendment's privilege against self-incrimination." 467 U.S. at 657. The Court was careful to emphasize that the public safety exception (like the impeachment exception; see §9.3.1) does not apply to an involuntary or coerced statement.

Where the officer's questions are *reasonably prompted by a concern for safety*, he may engage in noncoercive questioning without complying with *Miranda's* dictates. Applicability of the exception does not depend upon the actual motivation of the police, but rather on the objective facts of the case. Despite the potential uncertainty with this standard, the Court asserted that it would be easy to apply as "officers can and will distinguish almost instinctively between questions to secure their own safety or the safety of the public and questions designed solely to elicit testimonial evidence from a suspect." 467 U.S. at 658.

In her separate opinion, Justice O'Connor disagreed with the adoption of a public safety exception, suggesting that it "unnecessarily blurs the edges of the clear line heretofore established and makes *Miranda's* requirements more difficult to understand." 467 U.S. at 663. She predicted:

> In some cases, police will benefit because a reviewing court will find that an exigency excused their failure to administer the required warnings. But

in other cases, police will suffer because, though they thought an exigency excused their noncompliance, a reviewing court will view the "objective" circumstances differently and require exclusion of admissions obtained. The end result will be a finespun new doctrine on public safety exigencies incident to custodial interrogation, complete with the hair-splitting distinctions that currently plague our Fourth Amendment jurisprudence.

467 U.S. at 663. Indeed, the New York Court of Appeals had concluded in its *Quarles* decision that the missing gun did not pose an imminent threat to public safety because the suspect had been overpowered by police, no accomplices were thought to be nearby, and the supermarket was empty at 12:30 A.M., when Quarles was apprehended.

Justice O'Connor also observed that *Miranda* never prohibited police from asking questions to protect the public or themselves. It simply required that in the absence of warnings, the answers to those questions could not be used as evidence *at trial*. 467 U.S. at 664.

In a post-*Dickerson* decision, *United States v. Patane*, 542 U.S. 630 (2004) (see §9.3.3), the Court indicated that *Quarles* is still good law.

Examples

1. Drug enforcement agents had probable cause to believe that Dudley was dealing narcotics in lower Manhattan and that the heroin that he was selling from a suitcase was (unbeknownst to him) laced with a deadly chemical. The agents apprehended Dudley, but his suitcase was empty. After placing him under arrest (and without *Miranda* warnings), they asked Dudley where the heroin was. He told them he had hidden it in a nearby alleyway, and they recovered it. Could Dudley's statement and the narcotics be admitted against him at trial? What if agents had asked Dudley (without warnings) where his accomplice was?

2. Newark police responded to reports of a man beating a woman. An investigation on the scene revealed that the man had forced the woman into a black Thunderbird and driven off. The police located the car parked down the block and approached it. As the woman jumped out and ran, the officers asked the man to step out and they frisked him, finding nothing. By that time, a crowd of people had gathered around the car, and the officers became anxious about a potential confrontation. Holding their pistols pointed at the suspect, the officers asked if he had any weapons in the car, and he responded that he had a revolver under the seat. The police reached in and seized the unregistered weapon. Given the absence of *Miranda* warnings, may the suspect's statement and the gun be used against him at trial?

3. Stevens summoned police to her home, advising them that a shooting had occurred. Upon arrival, the police found two wounded persons

lying in the living room. The officers asked where the shooter was, but Stevens was evasive. After explaining that the ambulance crew would not treat the victims until the scene was safe, Stevens admitted that she had shot the persons, believing them to be burglars. In response to a later question, Stevens told the officers that she had left the gun in the bedroom, where they retrieved it. May these responses and the gun be used against Stevens at trial?

4. The NYPD has received a reliable tip that pipe bombs are being constructed in an apartment in Brooklyn, and that there is a plan to use these in the New York subway system. Upon entering the apartment with a search warrant, a scuffle ensues as the occupant grabs a black bag with wires sticking out. This individual is shot and rushed to a nearby hospital. Police proceed to question him immediately in the emergency room, without *Miranda* warnings, about how to disarm the items found in the black bag and about where other pipe bombs have been placed. He makes several incriminating statements, which he later seeks to suppress on grounds of *Miranda* as well as due process involuntariness standards because he was in considerable pain while questioned.

Explanations

1. Although the product of custodial interrogation and obtained in apparent violation of *Miranda*, Dudley's statement may nevertheless be admissible under the public safety exception created by *New York v. Quarles*. Given the deadly nature of the narcotics here, the prosecution would contend that the questioning was reasonably prompted by a concern for public safety — to retrieve the lethal substance before it got into other hands (or veins).

   This example illustrates some of the uncertainties that Justice O'Connor warned of in *Quarles* (and on which the Court has not provided guidance since its decision). Does the public safety exception embrace deadly chemicals as well as weapons? If so, would questioning be permissible regarding any narcotic (even if not laced with a deadly chemical), given the inherently dangerous nature of such substances? How important is the setting of the interrogation when applying *Quarles* (contrast the same confrontation in a sparsely populated rural area as opposed to a crowded urban street corner where the risk of someone discovering the missing item is greater)? Will the officers questioning Dudley (and the courts reviewing their action) realistically be able to distinguish between questions necessary to protect the public safety and those designed to elicit evidence to be used at trial?

   While the contours of the public safety exception are yet to be definitively drawn, some courts have already extended it beyond the missing weapon scenario. In *State v.Vickers*, 159 Ariz. 532, 768 P.2d 1177 (1989), a prisoner on death row became angry with another inmate and set him on fire. Responding to the ensuing alarm, a guard pulled Vickers out of the burning cell and asked what had happened. He replied: "I burned Buster [the other inmate]." Asked whether Buster was dead, Vickers responded: "He should be, he's on fire." The guard proceeded to rescue the other trapped inmates. Both statements were held admissible despite the lack of warnings because the court concluded that the guard's questions were motivated by a desire to devise a rescue plan, not to develop evidence of guilt.

Like the administrative search doctrine in Fourth Amendment jurisprudence (see §4.5 in Chapter 4), *Quarles* is based on the often illusive distinction between action taken to obtain evidence of crime and action taken for noninvestigative public-protection reasons. In *United States v. Carrillo*, 16 F.3d 1046 (9th Cir. 1994), a police officer's inquiry before a search of the arrestee as to whether he had any drugs or hypodermic needles on him fell within the public safety doctrine. The danger of contact with a contaminated needle was deemed an objectively reasonable concern, justifying questioning without *Miranda* warnings.

Is questioning about the whereabouts of an accomplice within the *Quarles* exception? Several decisions have answered affirmatively where, in a volatile situation, police reasonably fear that another perpetrator may be afoot and a danger to the public.

See *United States v. Johnson*, 2003 WL 22715856 (D. Kan. 2003). The admissibility of tangible evidence (the narcotics) seized as a result of the incriminatory statement in this and the following examples raises a "fruit-of-the-poisonous-tree" issue, discussed in the next section of this chapter.

2. Because it appears that the suspect was in custody at the time that the question was asked, the unwarned response must be suppressed unless it falls within the public safety exception. Unlike *Quarles* (where the police captured a suspect believed to be armed and with an empty holster), the police in this example had no reason to believe that the suspect had disposed of a weapon anywhere nearby. The Ninth Circuit Court of Appeals nonetheless held that the public safety exception applied. See *United States v. Brady*, 819 F.2d 884 (9th Cir. 1987). Focusing on the potential danger of the crowd gathering around the police in a rough neighborhood, as well as the possibility that a passerby could seize a weapon in the car, the court concluded that the officers reasonably believed that prompt action was necessary and that the purpose of their question was not to elicit evidence but to secure their own safety and that of the public. Ignoring other available alternatives (such as securing the car until it could be impounded and removed), the court refused to suppress the suspect's response.

Vickers, Carrillo, and *Brady* illustrate the significant potential for expansion of *Quarles*. See also *People v. Gilliard*, 234 Cal. Rptr. 401, 189 Cal. App. 3d

285 (1987) (a man under arrest for public drunkenness was brought to the nearby scene of a shooting and asked by the officer where the gun was; his incriminating response was held admissible under the public safety exception even though there was no hot pursuit of the suspect, nor imminent danger to the officers, nor even any basis for believing the suspect had disposed of a weapon in a place accessible to the public). The exception has even been applied where the questioning occurs within the suspects' own home. See *United States v. Oung*, 490 F. Supp. 2d 21, 33-34 (D. Mass. 2007) (police had information that suspects possessed an arsenal of weapons and an armed co-conspirator could be hiding nearby).

Thus, like the emergency exception to the warrant requirement in the Fourth Amendment context (see §6.2 of Chapter 6), the public safety exception potentially could swallow the *Miranda* protections.

Not all courts have taken such an expansive view. The Fourth Circuit Court of Appeals, while extending the public safety exception to situations where the suspect has invoked his right to counsel, simultaneously emphasized that there must be *specific*, objectively reasonable need to protect the police or public from an *immediate* danger to trigger the exception. *United States v. Mobley*, 40 F.3d 688 (4th Cir. 1994). A generalized suspicion that weapons or narcotics are present is not enough to justify deviation from *Miranda*. 40 F.3d at 693.

In *People v. Roundtree*, 482 N.E.2d 693 (Ill. App. Ct. 1985), a white Cadillac slammed into the rear of a police cruiser parked on the highway. When the officers approached the car, they heard a gunshot and observed two men in the front seat fighting over a gun. The officers disarmed and arrested the men. When a search of the car turned up an aluminum suitcase in the back seat, the officers asked whose suitcase it was. Roundtree admitted that it was his; when it was opened, it was found to contain narcotics. At trial, Roundtree moved to suppress his response because the question had been asked without *Miranda* warnings. The court agreed:

> The State, relying on *Quarles*, argues that the question asked by Trooper Martinez was only meant to secure control of the scene and was not designed to elicit testimonial evidence from defendant. However, the record establishes that all the suspects in the present case were handcuffed and positioned away from the car and its contents when Trooper Martinez asked the question. It is evident that Trooper Martinez had secured control of the scene before he asked the question. Furthermore, the record does not support the inference that either the suitcase or its contents posed a threat to the public safety or that Trooper Martinez perceived such a threat. Thus, the limited *Quarles* exception to *Miranda* is inapplicable under the facts of this case, and defendant's response to Trooper Martinez's question should have been excluded from evidence.

482 N.E.2d at 697-698.

Similarly, a New York state court refused to apply the exception to the questioning of a juvenile in an apartment that was the scene of a shooting. After finding the victim on the bedroom floor, the officer asked the juvenile if he had shot the victim, and he said yes. The officer then escorted him to the living room and questioned him as to the location of the gun; after approximately one hour, he told the officers that he had given it to a friend who lived across the street. Emphasizing that *Quarles* is a narrow exception and that if inquiry as to the location of weapons were permitted in every case, without the police being required to give *Miranda* warnings first, the exception would "overcome the rule," the Appellate Division reversed the trial court's ruling that it applied. See *In the Matter of John C.*, 130 A.D.2d 246, 252, 519 N.Y.S.2d 223, 227 (App. Div. 1987). Noting that the questioning about the gun occurred after the suspect had been removed from the immediacy of the crime scene and the apartment had been secured by 14 police officers, the court concluded that there did not exist "the type of volatile situation calling for immediate action upon which the Supreme Court predicated the narrow public safety exception to the *Miranda* rule." 519 N.Y.S.2d at 228. Further, the court concluded that the officer's motivation in asking the questions was to solve the crime, not to protect the public.

Thus, *the immediacy of the threat to public safety* and the *motivation of the officers* (viewed from an objective perspective) are the important factors weighed by courts in determining the applicability of *Quarles*. And it must be emphasized that the exception is only to the *Miranda* requirements, not the basic due process command that confessions be voluntary in order to be admitted into evidence. See Chapter 8. If it is determined that the questioning of the suspect was coercive, his response would be inadmissible regardless of the public safety exception.

3. Unlike *Quarles*, the incident in this example occurred in a private residence, not a public place. The state court that decided a case on similar facts concluded that the distinction was determinative: "In *Quarles*, the accused entered a public place carrying a gun. Here, we have a man's private residence which is not open to the public at large. Furthermore, there were no other persons around who could have gained access to the gun and the trial court found there was an opportunity to get a search warrant. Therefore the 'public safety' exception to *Miranda* is inapplicable here." *State v. Stevenson*, 784 S.W.2d 143, 145 (Tex. Ct. App. 1990).

This distinction is not universally recognized. In *State v. Jackson*, 756 S.W.2d 620 (Mo. Ct. App. 1988), also involving a shooting at a private residence, the court suggested that *Quarles* was not limited to incidents taking place in a public setting, but applied in any situation where there was a threat to police or public safety.

The Second Circuit, in a decision written by Judge Sotomayor, held that the public safety exception encompasses three principles: (1) *Miranda* warnings need not come before questions that are reasonably prompted by a concern for public safety; (2) pre-*Miranda* questions cannot be investigatory in nature or designed to elicit an incriminating response (although a question prompted by public safety concerns, yet broad enough to elicit information, may fall within the public safety exception); (3) pre-*Miranda* questioning of suspects is not a routine matter and should be used only when the safety of the public is clearly at risk. *United States v. Estrada*, 430 F.3d 606 (2d Cir. 2005). *Estrada* found that the suspect's violent criminal history and an informant's statement that the suspect kept drugs in the apartment could lead to a reasonable belief that there was a gun present, and the statements made pre-*Miranda* that related to the location of a gun were admissible because of the officers' concern for their safety. It is interesting to note that Sotomayor focused on the safety of the police, as opposed to the public, as she applied the public safety exception in a private residence.

4. This scenario is loosely based on *United States v. Khalil*, 214 F.3d 111 (2d Cir. 2000). Given the condition of the suspect (in great pain in the emergency room), a good argument could be made that the statement should be suppressed because his will was overborne. In addition, this was clearly a custodial interrogation in apparent violation of *Miranda*. The latter raises the applicability of the public safety exception in terrorism cases. In October 2010 the U.S. Justice Department sent a memo to the FBI and the Joint Terrorism Task Force emphasizing the need to question promptly and without warnings given the immediacy of the threat in such cases. The memo goes on to state that once the public safety question has been exhausted, *Miranda* warnings should be given before any further interrogation. In exceptional circumstances, however, where the agents conclude that valuable intelligence can be obtained not related to the immediate threat, interrogation may continue without warnings provided that approval is obtained by supervisors.

Following the 2013 Boston Marathon Bombing, the FBI interrogated injured and hospitalized Dzhokhar Tsarnaev for 16 hours over the course of two days without *Miranda* warnings. The court never addressed the applicability of the public safety exception because the government never introduced his statements at trial. Thus the issue of how narrowly focused the public safety exception should be in terrorism cases was not tested.

§9.3.3 Suppression of the Fruits of a Statement Obtained in Violation of *Miranda*

As discussed in §7.2 of Chapter 7, constitutional doctrine generally mandates that the indirect as well as the direct products of unlawful police activity (the fruit of the poisonous tree) are subject to the exclusionary rule. Thus, if the police conduct an unlawful search of Sam's home and find a map that describes the location of buried loot from a burglary, both the map and the evidence the police derive from the map (the loot) will be suppressed under the Fourth Amendment unless one of the exceptions noted in §7.2 applies. Similarly, if the police unlawfully coerce a statement from Sam describing where the loot may be found, both the statement and the loot will be suppressed under the Fifth Amendment. The rationale for the exclusion of derivative evidence is deterrence—in order to ensure compliance with constitutional dictates, the prosecution must be deprived of the use at trial of *all* evidence gained from a violation, both immediate and more remote.

Consistent with the Supreme Court's pre-*Dickerson v. United States*, 530 U.S. 428 (2000), theme that *Miranda* violations are not constitutional in nature (see §9.1), the Court pruned back the application of the poisonous fruit doctrine in *Oregon v. Elstad*, 470 U.S. 298 (1985). While the failure to comply with *Miranda* requires suppression of the unlawfully obtained statement, evidence derived from the statement is not rendered inadmissible.

In *Oregon v. Elstad*, police obtained an oral admission from an 18-year-old burglary suspect while he was in custody at home, without advising him of his rights. One hour later at the station house, Elstad received *Miranda* warnings, indicated that he understood them, and made a detailed statement (which was reduced to writing and signed by him) describing his involvement in the crime. Elstad argued that the second statement, although obtained in compliance with *Miranda*, was the tainted fruit of the first statement, which was not in compliance with *Miranda* and thus should be suppressed. The Oregon Court of Appeals agreed, holding that after Elstad's first admission, the "cat was sufficiently out of the bag to exert a coercive impact on later admissions." 61 Or. App. 673, 678.

The U.S. Supreme Court reversed. Reasoning that the *Miranda* remedy sweeps more broadly than the Fifth Amendment protection against compelled self-incrimination and that *Miranda* represents a "prophylactic rule" and not a constitutional right (a view ultimately abandoned in *Dickerson*), the Court confined suppression to the immediate product of the *Miranda* violation, not its indirect fruits. Thus, while Elstad's unwarned first statement was excluded from evidence, his second statement (even if derived from the first) was admissible.

Elstad emphasized that the consequences are different if the statement is obtained not only in violation of *Miranda*, but also through coercion. Where the police elicit an involuntary statement (see Chapter 8), then *all* fruits, indirect as well as direct, must be suppressed. Because the context of Elstad's first statement had none of the earmarks of coercion, no unconstitutional taint carried to the second statement; and because the second statement was itself in compliance with *Miranda* as well as voluntary, it was admissible against the defendant at trial. 470 U.S. at 316.

But what if the police deliberately fail to provide *Miranda* warnings as part of a "question-first" strategy designed to elicit an incriminating statement from an unknowing suspect, and only then (after a short coffee-and-cigarette break) provide him with the warnings before they obtain a second statement repeating the confession? Faced with this increasingly common interrogation tactic, the Court in a plurality opinion by Justice Souter distinguished *Elstad* and ruled in *Missouri v. Seibert*, 542 U.S. 600 (2004) (previously discussed in §9.2.3), that the second statement must be suppressed. The delayed warnings coming after "the cat is out of the bag" were an affront to *Miranda*'s core purpose of avoiding the risk of a coerced confession. Justice Kennedy's fifth, concurring vote emphasized the deliberate ploy used here and the need for curative measures following an initial *Miranda* violation.

What if the fruit of the *Miranda* violation is physical evidence? In *United States v. Patane*, 542 U.S. 630 (2000), the suspect was arrested for violation of a restraining order and questioned without being given full *Miranda* warnings. He revealed the location of an illegal gun and was charged with a firearms offense. The lower courts suppressed the gun as the fruit of a *Miranda* violation, but the Supreme Court disagreed. Thomas, writing for the plurality, reasoned (in reliance on *Chavez v. Martinez*, discussed in §9.1) that *Miranda* is "not a code of police conduct," but merely protects against use of a self-incriminatory statement at a criminal trial. Non-testimonial physical evidence does not implicate that protection. Dissenters Souter, Breyer, Ginsburg, and Stevens were concerned that allowing use of physical evidence would give police an incentive to violate *Miranda*.

The Court passed on an opportunity to decide whether the *Elstad* rationale applies in the context of a Sixth Amendment violation (see Chapter 10) when it remanded *Fellers v. United States*, 124 U.S. 1019 (2004), involving a motion to suppress a jailhouse statement as the fruit of a prior statement elicited in violation of the right to counsel.

In sum, while a statement obtained in violation of *Miranda*'s dictates is not itself admissible in the prosecution's case, evidence (testimonial as well as tangible) derived from it is admissible, provided that the statement is found to have been voluntary and uncoerced and provided the warnings are found not to have been deliberately withheld.

Example

After extensive investigation into the theft of a priceless Impressionist paint-ing from the City Museum, police concluded that it was an inside job and that Sticky Finger, a security guard at the museum, was involved. Finger was taken into custody and questioned without being advised of his *Miranda* rights. After some time, he admitted that he had unlocked the museum to let his accomplice in to steal the painting, and he told the police where they had hidden it in the museum gift shop stockroom. Detectives immediately went to the location and discovered the painting wrapped in old newspaper. They then sought out the accomplice and obtained a confession implicating Finger. Would the painting be admissible against Finger at trial? What about the accomplice's statement?

Explanation

Because Finger was subjected to custodial interrogation without benefit of the warnings, the statement obtained from him must be suppressed. Under the rationale of *Patane*, exclusion of the painting would not be required even though it was discovered as a result of the *Miranda* violation. The painting would be tainted fruit only if, in addition to that violation, Finger's state-ment had been unconstitutionally coerced. We would need more informa-tion as to how the interrogation was conducted to determine whether that was the case under the due process voluntariness standard. See Chapter 8.

§9.4 SUMMARY — WHAT'S LEFT OF *MIRANDA*?

A statement obtained in violation of the *Miranda* rules (warnings, waiver, right to counsel) may not be admitted against the suspect at trial except in the following situations: The statement was voluntary, and either

1. The interrogation falls within the *Quarles* public safety exception
2. The response is used solely to impeach the defendant's testimony at trial, and not as substantive evidence of guilt during the prosecu-tion's case-in-chief

Where a *Miranda*-violation statement does not fall within either of the above criteria, it cannot itself be used at all at trial. Evidence derived from the statement (either physical or testimonial) will be admissible, though, so long as the statement was not coerced.

10

The Sixth Amendment "Right to Counsel" Approach

---

§10.1 THE *MASSIAH* DOCTRINE

The Sixth Amendment, which guarantees an accused the "assistance of counsel" for his defense, provides another approach to the problem of interrogation and confessions that supplements (and at times overlaps) the two approaches previously discussed—due process voluntariness (Chapter 8) and *Miranda* (Chapter 9).

The role of the Sixth Amendment in this area can be traced to *Massiah v. United States*, 377 U.S. 201 (1964), a drug prosecution in which the defendant's incriminating statements made to his codefendant Colson were admitted into evidence at trial. Unbeknownst to Massiah, Colson was cooperating with the government and had initiated the conversation at the request of federal agents, who recorded it. This occurred after both men had been indicted, retained counsel, pled not guilty, and were released on bail. Massiah challenged his conviction on the ground that his admissions should have been suppressed, and the Supreme Court agreed, holding that once adversary judicial proceedings have commenced against an individual, government efforts to "deliberately elicit" statements from him in the absence of his attorney (whether done openly or surreptitiously) violate the Sixth Amendment. The Court reasoned that the right to the assistance of counsel at trial would be rendered meaningless if the prosecution could obtain incriminating statements from an uncounseled defendant prior to trial.

Although the *Massiah* doctrine appeared to have been displaced by *Miranda* (decided two years later), it reemerged in 1977 with the decision in

Brewer v. Williams, 430 U.S. 387 (1977). Williams, a suspect in a child murder in Des Moines, Iowa, surrendered to police in Davenport following the issuance of a warrant for his arrest. He spoke by telephone to an attorney in Des Moines and was advised not to make any statements to the police until he could consult in person with the attorney upon his return to that city. After being booked, arraigned, and advised of his *Miranda* rights, Williams was transported the 160 miles to Des Moines by police officers who had expressly agreed with Williams's lawyer that he would not be questioned en route. During the trip, a detective, knowing that Williams was a former mental patient and deeply religious, suggested that since he was the only person who knew the location of the missing girl's body, he was obliged to take police to her so that she could get a decent burial. Williams subsequently led police to the body and made incriminating statements.

Despite the admission of the detective that he had used the so-called "Christian burial speech" with the deliberate design of obtaining incriminating evidence, the discovery of the body and the inculpatory statements were admitted at trial. Relying on *Massiah*, the Supreme Court reversed the conviction: Williams had been denied his Sixth Amendment right to assistance of counsel when, after the initiation of judicial proceedings at his arraignment, the police deliberately elicited incriminating statements without affording him the opportunity to consult with his attorney. The evidence was inadmissible.

Unlike the due process standard, the Sixth Amendment does not require a finding of coercion (which was not present in either *Massiah* or *Brewer v. Williams*). Unlike *Miranda*, neither custody nor interrogation is a prerequisite. (Neither Massiah nor Williams was subjected to interrogation in any traditional sense, and Massiah was not in custody at the time he incriminated himself.) What is required for invocation of the *Massiah* doctrine is 1) that the government *deliberately elicited* incriminating statements from the accused in the absence of counsel (or a waiver of counsel), and 2) that this occurred *after the initiation of judicial proceedings*, the point at which the right to counsel is triggered.

§10.2 THE "DELIBERATELY ELICIT" STANDARD

The constitutional wrong committed by the police in both *Massiah* and *Brewer v. Williams* was the pursuit of incriminating information from the suspect after his right to counsel had attached. The fact that no actual questioning occurred in either case was not significant; it was sufficient that the officers had "deliberately elicited" the inculpatory statements. The Court recently reaffirmed this standard in *Fellers v. United States*, 540 U.S. 519 (2004).

Although "deliberate elicitation" seems to bear a close resemblance to the "functional equivalent of interrogation" under *Miranda* (see §9.2.2 in Chapter 9), the Court has not treated the concepts as interchangeable. See *Rhode Island v. Innis*, 446 U.S. 291, 300 n.4 (1980); *Fellers v. United States*, supra, 124 U.S. at 1023. The emphasis in the Sixth Amendment context is on the *deliberate* or *intentional* nature of the officer's effort to gain incriminating evidence, while the test for interrogation under *Miranda* is broader: Whether the police engaged in conduct that they could *reasonably foresee* would elicit an incriminating response from the suspect, even if not designed to achieve that result.

A second and more subtle difference is that "functional equivalent of interrogation" focuses on the susceptibilities and perceptions of the suspect, while the *Massiah* doctrine looks to the state of mind of the officer—did she *intend* to elicit the confession? Both *Rhode Island v. Innis* and *Arizona v. Mauro* (discussed in §9.2.2) refused to find that the police conduct constituted the functional equivalent of interrogation—in *Innis*, because the suspect had not been shown to be particularly vulnerable to the conversation about handicapped children; in *Mauro*, because the suspect could not reasonably have felt coerced by the confrontation with his wife. In contrast, the determinative factor in both *Massiah* and *Williams* appeared to be the deliberate nature of the police effort to secure a confession. In any event, the distinction between interrogation under *Miranda* and deliberate elicitation under *Massiah* has yet to be clearly drawn by the Court.

The *Massiah* doctrine has been extended to "jailhouse snitch" cases. In *United States v. Henry*, 447 U.S. 264 (1980), the FBI arranged to have Nichols, a paid informant, placed as Henry's cellmate. Although the agents instructed Nichols not to question Henry about the crime, he was told to report incriminating statements to them, which he did. The Court suppressed the statements, concluding that the government had intentionally set up a situation likely to induce Henry to make incriminating statements and thus violated his Sixth Amendment right to counsel. Nichols was not a "passive listener" but rather had "stimulated" conversations with the defendant designed to produce incriminating admissions. 447 U.S. at 271. See also *Ayers v. Hudson*, 623 F.3d 301 (6th Cir. 2010) (defendant's right to counsel was violated where a jailhouse informant was permitted to testify to incriminating statements that he had elicited after authorities returned him to cell in proximity to defendant's).

"Where the informant is merely a passive listener, however, the Sixth Amendment is not violated. The jail plant in *Kuhlman v. Wilson*, 477 U.S. 436 (1986), did nothing to stimulate the conversation in which the suspect made incriminating statements, and thus there was no deliberate elicitation. A defendant does not make out a Sixth Amendment violation "simply by showing that an informant, either through prior arrangement or voluntarily, reported his incriminating statements to the police." 477 U.S. at 459. Rather, it must be shown that the police and their informant took some deliberate action beyond merely establishing a "listening post." The "primary concern of the *Massiah* line of decisions is secret interrogation by investigatory techniques that are equivalent to direct police interrogation." *Id.*

Massachusetts goes further than the federal cases in protecting inmates from "informants at large" who troll the prison for any information they can collect. Where the government enters into any agreement offering a benefit in return for incriminating evidence, the informant becomes an agent of the government for purposes of the *Massiah* doctrine. See *Commonwealth v. Murphy*, 448 Mass. 452, 465-468 (2007).

§10.3 AT WHAT POINT DOES THE *MASSIAH* DOCTRINE APPLY? — THE INITIATION OF JUDICIAL PROCEEDINGS

The triggering event for the application of the *Massiah* doctrine is the initiation of adversary judicial criminal proceedings — meaning either indictment, information, arraignment, or preliminary hearing. Only at that point is the suspect an "accused" entitled to assistance of counsel under the Sixth Amendment. See *Kirby v. Illinois*, 406 U.S. 682 (1972). The right can attach even if the prosecutor is not yet aware of the defendant's court appearance. *Rothgery v. Gillespie County*, 128 S. Ct. 2578 (2008).

The government may therefore elicit admissions from a suspect *prior to* initiation of formal proceedings against him without running afoul of *Massiah*. In *Maine v. Moulton*, 474 U.S. 159 (1985), the prosecution obtained incriminating statements from the defendant by recording a meeting between him and a codefendant who was cooperating with the government. The statements related both to the charges that were already pending against Moulton (he had been indicted for receiving stolen property), and to a plan to kill prosecution witnesses expected to testify in the upcoming trial. Concluding that the government had deliberately elicited these statements from Moulton, the Court ordered that the admissions concerning the pending charges be suppressed. "[T]he Sixth Amendment is violated when the State obtains incriminating statements by knowingly circumventing the accused's right to have counsel present in a confrontation between the accused and a state agent." 474 U.S. at 176. Those incriminating remarks concerning crimes *not yet charged* but brought subsequently (the plan to kill a witness), however, were not subject to exclusion. No judicial proceedings had been initiated and thus no right of counsel had yet attached.

The offense-specific nature of Sixth Amendment protection was underscored in *McNeil v. Wisconsin*, 501 U.S. 171 (1991). McNeil was represented by a public defender at a bail hearing on charges of armed robbery. While in jail on that charge, he was questioned by police about an unrelated murder in another town. McNeil executed a *Miranda* waiver and made statements implicating himself in the murder. When he was subsequently charged with the murder, McNeil moved to suppress these admissions, arguing that his invocation of the right to counsel at the bail hearing prevented the police from any subsequent questioning of him in the absence of counsel. The Court disagreed: "The Sixth Amendment right is offense-specific. It cannot be invoked once for all future prosecutions, for it does not attach until a prosecution is commenced, that is, at or after the initiation of adversary judicial proceedings whether by way of formal charge, preliminary hearing, indictment, information, or arraignment." 501 U.S. at 175. Because the murder charges had not yet been brought against McNeil at the time, questioning in the absence of counsel did not violate the *Massiah* doctrine. See also *Scarberry v. State of Iowa*, 430 F.3d 956 (8th Cir. 2005) (questioning suspect about a methamphetamine lab after Sixth Amendment right to counsel had attached for methamphetamine charges in another county was permissible).

Texas v. Cobb, 532 U.S. 162 (2001), adopts a rather narrow definition of "offense" for these purposes. Cobb, indicted for a home burglary and represented by counsel, was questioned by police in the absence of counsel (after a *Miranda* waiver) regarding the murders of the homeowner and her daughter. He sought to suppress his resulting confession to the murders on the ground that it was obtained in violation of his right to counsel, which he argued attached not only to the offense charged, but to factually closely related offenses as well. The Supreme Court disagreed, holding that police may question a suspect about related, but uncharged, offenses without violating the Sixth Amendment.

In a significant extension of federal doctrine, New York law holds that the right to counsel under its own constitution attaches "indelibly" on a charge once defendant is represented, preventing police from eliciting admissions through an informant even years later. See *People v. West*, 81 N.Y.2d 370, 615 N.E.2d 968 (N.Y. 1993).

§10.4 WAIVER AND EXCEPTIONS TO THE *MASSIAH* DOCTRINE

As with any constitutional right, the Sixth Amendment right to counsel may be waived. A statement elicited in the absence of counsel may nonetheless be admissible if the prosecution can demonstrate a voluntary relinquishment of this right. The Court has equated the standard for waiver here with the "knowing, intelligent, and voluntary" standard of the *Miranda* waiver (discussed in §9.2.4). See *Patterson v. Illinois*, 487 U.S. 285 (1988). A showing that the defendant had been advised of, understood, and voluntarily waived his *Miranda* rights (which includes the right to an attorney) suffices to establish a waiver under the Sixth Amendment as well (at least where he has not yet, as in *Patterson*, retained counsel).

The *Miranda* doctrine, as we have seen, protects a suspect who has invoked his right to counsel from being badgered into waiving it. The *Edwards v. Arizona* rule (§9.2.5) terminates interrogation at that point unless the suspect is either provided with counsel or himself initiates further communication. Finding that *Edwards* acts as a sufficient safeguard, the Court has declined to import a similar requirement into the Sixth Amendment. *Montejo v. Louisiana*, 129 S. Ct. 2079 (2009) (overruling *Michigan v. Jackson*, 475 U.S. 625 (1986)), declined to suppress an incriminating letter even though the suspect wrote it while on an excursion with police to locate the murder weapon *after* he had been formally charged in court with the murder, and *before* he had an opportunity to confer with counsel.

As with a statement taken in violation of *Miranda* (§9.3.1), admissions obtained in contravention of *Massiah* may nonetheless be admitted to impeach a defendant's testimony at trial. Donnie Ray Ventris took the stand at his murder trial and blamed his partner for the shooting. The prosecution was permitted to contradict him with the testimony of a jail plant to whom Ventris had admitted the crime, concededly a violation of *Massiah*. *Kansas v. Ventris*, 129 S. Ct. 1841 (2009). Quoting earlier cases involving Fourth and Fifth Amendment violations, the Court reasoned: "It is one thing to say the Government cannot make an affirmative use of evidence unlawfully obtained. It is quite another to say that the defendant can provide himself with a shield against contradiction of his untruths." 129 S. Ct. at 1846. See also *Michigan v. Harvey*, 494 U.S. 344 (1990).

The Court has, however, refused to adopt a Sixth Amendment counterpart to the *Quarles* public safety exception to *Miranda* (see §9.3.2). *Maine v. Moulton* (discussed in §10.3) rejected the argument that the Sixth Amendment violation should be excused because the police had a compelling reason to listen in on the defendant's conversation independent of the gathering of evidence — i.e., to investigate Moulton's plan to kill state witnesses. In an unusual expression of cynicism regarding law enforcement officials, the Court explained: "To allow the admission of evidence obtained from the accused in violation of his Sixth Amendment rights whenever the police assert an alternative, legitimate reason for their surveillance invites abuse by law enforcement personnel in the form of fabricated investigations and risks the evisceration of the Sixth Amendment right recognized in *Massiah*." 474 U.S. at 180. On the other hand, since *Massiah* applies only to already pending charges, the government may elicit and use incriminating statements regarding *future* crimes which, as in *Moulton*, may involve threats to third parties or the public. See, e.g., *United States v. Ford*, 176 F.3d 376 (6th Cir. 1999) (no Sixth Amendment violation where government placed informant in defendant's cell to investigate threats against officials).

The Supreme Court has not directly addressed the "fruits of the poisonous tree" doctrine in the Sixth Amendment context. In *Fellers v. United States*, 540 U.S. 519 (2004), a statement was elicited in violation of the Sixth

Amendment at the suspect's home. He was taken to the county jail, where he was read *Miranda* warnings and made a second statement. The Court remanded to the Eighth Circuit on the question of whether the second statement should be suppressed as the fruit of the Sixth Amendment violation. That court refused to apply the derivative evidence doctrine, holding that suppression of the initial statement was sufficient to serve the goal of preserving the integrity and fairness of the criminal trial. The case was appealed again to the Supreme Court and it denied certiorari.

Examples

1. Arrest warrants were issued for Tommy Tucker and Max Malone on a charge of armed robbery of a gas station. Police, who had been unable to locate either suspect, received a call from Malone in which he offered to turn himself in "if he could get a good deal." Detective Simpson told Malone that they would consider "giving him a break" if he could "get the goods on Tucker." Malone agreed to wear a wire and engage Tucker in a conversation concerning the gas station robbery. Simpson also directed Malone to "get Tucker talking about that First National bank heist last month, because I think he's our man on that job, too."

   Malone met Tucker the next day, wearing a recorder the police fitted him with, and turned the conversation to reminiscing about the gas station robbery. Tucker made several incriminating statements. Malone also got Tucker talking about other crimes he had been involved in, and Tucker boasted about his participation in the First National robbery.

   May the prosecution use these statements against Tucker at trial on the gas station robbery? On the bank robbery? Would it make a difference if Tucker had already been indicted for the gas station robbery at the time the conversation with Malone occurred?

2. Chatty Charlie, who has been an informant on a number of occasions for the Drug Enforcement Administration (DEA), was sharing a cell at City Jail with Loose Lips, who was under indictment for first-degree murder. Lips and Charlie had a conversation in which Lips shared the details of his involvement in the murder. Charlie, seeking to benefit from this information, informed his DEA contact of the conversation and offered to testify about it in court. Would this evidence be admissible against Lips?

3. Police proceeded to the home of Sam Sellers after his indictment for conspiracy to distribute methamphetamine came down. They told him they were there pursuant to the indictment and engaged him in conversation concerning his involvement in drug trafficking. He made several incriminating statements and was then arrested. Later at the station house police advised him of his *Miranda* rights; he signed a waiver form

and repeated his earlier admissions. May the statements made at home and the police station be admitted against him at trial?

Explanations

1. Because Tucker was not subjected to custodial interrogation or coerced against his will into speaking, he is not protected by either *Miranda* or due process voluntariness. The only challenge he could mount to the admission of this evidence would be based on the *Massiah* doctrine, which prohibits the police from deliberately eliciting incriminating statements from an accused in the absence of counsel after the right to counsel has attached. There is little question here that the police used Malone as their agent to gather evidence from Tucker's mouth, as Colson was used against Massiah.

   It is not so clear, however, whether the right to counsel had attached at the time of the conversation. The issuance of an arrest warrant, an early step in the criminal justice process that does not commit the government to going forward with a prosecution, has been generally held not to constitute commencement of federal adversary criminal proceedings for purposes of the *Massiah* doctrine. See, e.g., *Beck v. Bowersox*, 362 F.3d 1095, 1101 (8th Cir. 2004); *Lumley v. City of Dade, Florida*, 327 F.3d 1186 (11th Cir. 2003); *Von Kahl v. United States*, 242 F.3d 783 (8th Cir. 2001); *United States v. Moore*, 122 F.3d 1154 (8th Cir. 1997). Some federal courts reviewing state prosecutions in habeas cases have, however, looked to state law and concluded that the issuance of an arrest warrant under that law constitutes initiation. See, e.g., *Meadows v. Kuhlman*, 812 F.2d 72 (2d Cir. 1987).

   The requirement for "initiation" in the federal process is either 1) a formal charge (an indictment or information) or 2) the defendant's appearance at an arraignment or preliminary hearing. Because such proceedings had not yet begun in example 1, the government was free to gather evidence from Malone in the manner that they did, and his incriminating statements could be used against him at both the gas station robbery and bank robbery trials. See *Henderson v. Quarterman*, 460 F.3d 654, 664 (5th Cir. 2006) (no Sixth Amendment rights attached prior to defendant being charged with the second offense).

   The situation would be different, of course, if Malone had already been indicted for the gas station robbery. That event would have triggered his right to the assistance of counsel on that charge, and the effort to obtain evidence from him in the absence of counsel would violate the proscriptions of the *Massiah* doctrine. Even in that situation, however, the statements implicating him in the bank robbery would be admissible at trial because no judicial proceedings had been commenced for *that* crime, and thus no right to counsel had yet attached. *Texas v. Cobb*, 532 U.S. 162 (2001); *McNeil v. Wisconsin*, 501 U.S. 171 (1991); *Moulton v. Maine*, 474 U.S. 159 (1985); *Scarberry v. State of Iowa*, 430 F.3d 956 (8th Cir. 2005).

2. The *Massiah* doctrine applies only where the government deliberately elicits incriminating statements from the accused, as in *United States v. Henry*, 447 U.S. 264, 276 (1980). It does not prevent the government from accepting information offered by a private individual who obtained it on his own initiative and not as agent for the government. (See the discussion of the analogous private search doctrine in the Fourth Amendment context in §3.1 of Chapter 3.) Unless there is evidence that the DEA encouraged Charlie to elicit these statements, the Sixth Amendment is not implicated. *United States v. Edwards*, 342 F.3d 168, 182 (2d Cir. 2003). The fact that Charlie has worked as an informant on other occasions is not determinative. *United States v. Johnson*, 338 F.3d 918 (8th Cir. 2003). If the evidence is acquired by luck or happenstance and not by design, there is no constitutional violation. See *Moulton v. Maine*, supra.

   In *State v. Bey*, 610 A.2d 403 (N.J. Super. Ct. App. Div. 1992), a death row inmate made incriminating statements during a conversation with a prison guard. The court rejected his Sixth Amendment challenge, holding that the guard did not deliberately elicit the statements, was never instructed to obtain information, and did not make a report to the prosecuting authorities until a later investigation turned up this evidence. Similarly, in *Beaty v. Stewart*, 303 F.3d 975 (9th Cir. 2002), a death row inmate made incriminating statements to a jail psychiatrist after the conclusion of a group counseling session. There was no violation of the Sixth Amendment because the psychiatrist did not elicit the statements deliberately.

   Where the government asks a cellmate to report incriminating statements by anyone, but has not focused the snitch's attention on a particular target, deliberate elicitation has not been found. See *United States v. Lentz*, 419 F. Supp. 2d 794, 816 (E.D. Va. 2005); *United States v. LaBare*, 191 F.3d 60 (1st Cir. 1999); *United States v. Birbal*, 113 F.3d 342 (2d Cir. 1997).

   In our example, Chatty is acting on his own and not under instructions from the government to gather information from Lips. Thus, there is no deliberate elicitation in violation of *Massiah*.

3. Although *Miranda* warnings were not required here because there was no custodial interrogation, the post-indictment conversation raises a Sixth Amendment issue. Because the officers engaged Sellers in a conversation that may be viewed as deliberate elicitation, *Patterson v. Illinois*, 487 U.S. 285 (1988), would seem to require a showing that he validly waived his right to counsel, which in turn would mean he should have been given *Miranda* warnings.

   The further question raised by this example is the effect that a Sixth Amendment violation would have on the second statement obtained at the police station. Would *Oregon v. Elstad*, 470 U.S. 298 (1985) (see §9.3.3), refusing to enforce the derivative evidence doctrine for *Miranda* violations,

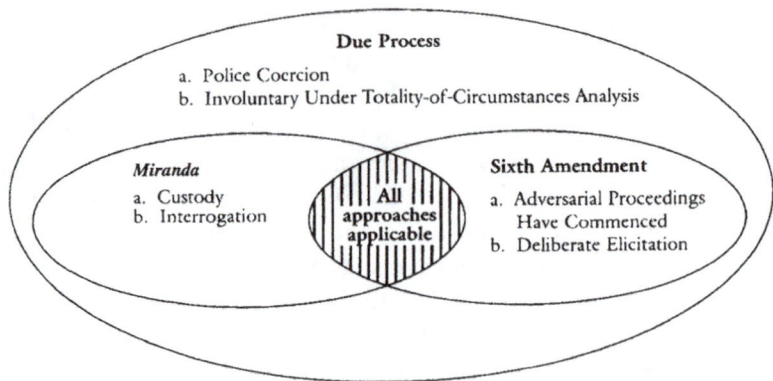

Figure 10-1. Approaches to Interrogation and Confession

also be applicable here? In the circumstances on which this example is based, *Fellers v. United States*, 124 U.S. 1019 (2004), the Court found a Sixth Amendment violation and remanded to the Eighth Circuit to determine whether the rationale of *Elstad* applies to a Sixth Amendment violation. The Circuit Court declined to apply the derivative evidence exclusionary rule, and the Supreme Court denied review.

§10.5 OVERVIEW OF INTERROGATION AND CONFESSIONS

In analyzing any interrogation or confession problem, one must keep in mind the three approaches discussed in this chapter and Chapters 8 and 9. As Figure 10-1 indicates, the due process voluntariness standard applies in *all* contexts, overlapping in coverage with both the *Miranda* and *Massiah* approaches, as well as filling in the gaps where, for whatever reason, the other doctrines do not apply. Neither the Fifth Amendment nor the Sixth Amendment doctrines supplant the due process requirement that the statement be shown to be voluntary and uncoerced as a condition of its admission into evidence. Rather, those doctrines supplement the voluntariness standard.

Thus, if *Miranda* is not applicable because the statement did not result from custodial interrogation (or because the public safety or impeachment exceptions apply), and the Sixth Amendment is not applicable because there was no "deliberate elicitation" after initiation of adversary proceedings, admission of the statement into evidence may nonetheless be challenged on the grounds that it was the product of police coercion (either physical or mental).

Other Investigative Procedures

Other Investigative Procedures — Eyewitness Identification, Bodily Intrusions, Examination of Physical Attributes, Entrapment, and "High-Tech" and Computer Searches

We have discussed in previous chapters two methods by which law enforcement officers seek evidence for use in criminal prosecutions — search and seizure, and interrogation of suspects. In this chapter, we turn to two other categories of investigative procedures — eyewitness identification and the examination of physical attributes of the suspect (including bodily intrusions). As we will see, various constitutional constraints have been applied to such police work. We also take up the problem of entrapment. Last, we will explore some issues unique to electronic surveillance and computer searches.

§11.1 EYEWITNESS IDENTIFICATION

Suppose that the police would like to present Suspect to Victim to determine whether the latter recognizes the former as the perpetrator. May the police require Suspect to participate in a lineup?

While arguably the lineup implicates Fourth Amendment privacy concerns, as well as the Fifth Amendment right not to be compelled to incriminate oneself, it has long been established that neither protection applies to eyewitness identification procedures. The Fourth Amendment is inapplicable because the attributes in question — the suspect's physical appearance — are constantly on public display and thus carry no *reasonable expectation of privacy*.

See § 3.2.[1] The Fifth Amendment is not triggered because it only protects an accused from being compelled to testify against himself or otherwise provide the government with evidence of a testimonial or communicative nature. "Compelling the accused merely to exhibit his person for observation by a prosecution witness prior to trial involves no compulsion of the accused to give evidence having testimonial significance." *United States v. Wade*, 388 U.S. 218 (1967). For the same reasons, neither the Fourth nor Fifth Amendment is implicated when the suspect is required to speak certain words uttered by the perpetrator (for purposes of identifying the voice) (*Wade*, supra) or to provide voice exemplars (*United States v. Dionisio*, 410 U.S. 1 (1973)), or handwriting exemplars (*United States v. Mara*, 410 U.S. 19 (1973)), for purposes of identification.

"Usually the witness must testify about an encounter with a total stranger under circumstances of emergency or emotional stress. The witness' recollection of the stranger can be distorted easily by the circumstances or by later actions of the police." *Manson v. Brathwaite*, 432 U.S. 98, 111 (1977). Concerned about the high risk of mistaken identification because of unreliable or unfairly suggestive procedures the Court has invoked two other constitutional sources to protect the suspect. The right to have counsel present at lineups conducted after the initiation of formal criminal proceedings has been derived from the Sixth Amendment. More generally, all eyewitness identification procedures are subject to review to ensure that they were not so unnecessarily suggestive and conducive to mistaken identification so as to deny the defendant the due process of law guaranteed by the Fifth and Fourteenth Amendments.

The Court has recognized the pretrial lineup as a critically important stage in the prosecution of a case, and thus concluded that the Sixth Amendment requires assistance of counsel there. See *United States v. Wade*, supra. The attorney's presence serves two basic purposes: (1) avoiding intentional or inadvertent prejudice to the suspect at the lineup (as, for example, placing one short, black, bearded suspect in a line of tall, white, clean-shaven men); and (2) ensuring that counsel will be sufficiently familiar (from firsthand observation) with what actually occurred to mount a meaningful confrontation of the witnesses at trial. Unless the accused is afforded the opportunity to have counsel present (or waives that right), evidence of an identification at the lineup is not admissible at trial. The right to counsel has been extended to other live presentations (dubbed "trial-like confrontations") of the accused to witnesses, such as one-on-one show-ups. See *Moore v. Illinois*, 434 U.S. 220

---

1. Unless the suspect consents, it is necessary to have probable cause to hold him in custody at the station house while engaging in the identification procedures. See *Davis v. Mississippi*, 394 U.S. 721 (1969) (fingerprinting). But see *Hayes v. Florida*, 470 U.S. 811 (1985) (suggesting that a brief detention in the field for the purpose of fingerprinting may be permissible on mere reasonable suspicion).

(1977). The right does not, however, apply to photographic arrays shown to witnesses. See *United States v. Ash*, 413 U.S. 300 (1973).

As we have previously seen with regard to the *Massiah* doctrine (see Chapter 10), the Sixth Amendment right to counsel does not attach until commencement of adversary judicial proceedings.[2] Consequently, *Wade* does not require counsel at lineups held prior to indictment or other formal charges against the suspect. See *Kirby v. Illinois*, 406 U.S. 682 (1972). Because many lineups take place earlier in the criminal justice sequence, the right to counsel is of limited practical application.

Of wider importance is the requirement that any identification procedure (whether conducted before or after the initiation of formal charges) conform to due process standards of fundamental fairness. See *Stovall v. Denno*, 388 U.S. 293 (1967). Utilizing a totality-of-the-circumstances approach, a court must determine whether a challenged procedure was (1) *unnecessarily suggestive* and (2) *likely to lead to a mistaken identification*. If so, evidence of the identification is inadmissible at trial.

The first element involves an analysis of both the prejudicial nature of the procedure and the circumstances that necessitated resort to it. In *Stovall*, for example, the handcuffed suspect (a black man) was brought into the stabbing victim's hospital room by white police officers who asked if he was "the man." While conceding that the one-on-one confrontation was indeed suggestive, the Court nevertheless concluded it was not "unnecessarily" so because the police were faced with a situation where they were not sure the victim would survive and thus had to act quickly to obtain the identification from her hospital bed.

The second element of *Stovall* has come into increasing prominence as the Court has described reliability as "the linchpin in determining the admissibility of identification testimony." *Manson v. Brathwaite*, 432 U.S. 98, 114 (1977) (following earlier suggestions to that effect in *Neil v. Biggers*, 409 U.S. 188 (1972)). Identification evidence, even if the result of "unnecessarily suggestive" procedures, is nonetheless admissible if it possesses certain indicia of reliability that reduce the possibility of mistaken identification. Factors to be considered by the courts include (1) the opportunity of the witness to view the perpetrator at the time of the crime; (2) the witness's degree of attention; (3) the accuracy of his prior description of the perpetrator (if any); (4) the level of certainty demonstrated at the confrontation;[3] and (5) the elapsed time between the crime and the confrontation. These

---

2. Some states, applying their own constitutional provisions, require counsel at pre-indictment lineups as well. See *People v. Bustamante*, 177 Cal. Rptr. 576, 634 P.2d 927 (1981); *Blue v. State of Alaska*, 558 P.2d 636 (Alaska 1977).

3. However, many experts in the field of human perception in fact believe that there is no correspondence between a witness's degree of confidence in the identification and its accuracy, and that a witness who is "absolutely certain" is no more likely to be correct. See, e.g., *United States v. Mathis*, 264 F.3d 321, 333-334 (3d Cir. 2001).

factors are to be weighed against the "corrupting effect of the suggestive identification itself." *Manson v. Brathwaite*, supra.

Because an identification procedure must be shown defective on all three grounds — (1) suggestive, (2) unnecessarily so, and (3) unreliable — the Court has rarely found a violation of the due process standard. Even in cases of highly suggestive one-on-one show-ups, such as *Stovall*, the totality-of-the-circumstances approach usually results in a decision admitting the identification. A further limitation was added in *Perry v. New Hampshire*, 132 S. Ct. 716 (2012), when Justice Ginsburg, for an eight-member majority, required as the threshold question for an identification challenged as unnecessarily suggestive that it must have been arranged by law enforcement authorities. Absent law enforcement involvement, there is no constitutional issue.

If a pretrial identification is suppressed because of either a Sixth Amendment or due process violation, the question arises as to whether the witness may nonetheless identify the defendant from the witness stand at trial. Because of the probability that the in-court identification would be influenced by the prior tainted procedure, it too is inadmissible unless the prosecution can establish that it was independently based upon another source, such as the original observations made at the time of the crime. (The premise is similar to the independent source exception to the "fruit of the poisonous tree" doctrine, discussed in § 7.2 of Chapter 7.) The analysis to determine whether the courtroom testimony is free of the taint employs the same reliability factors discussed above — for example, a witness who had a good opportunity to view the perpetrator when the crime occurred and who accurately described the defendant prior to the tainted lineup would likely be permitted to identify him at trial.

Widespread recognition of the fallibility of eyewitness testimony[4] and its role in so many wrongful convictions[5] has led some states to significantly alter their police procedures for securing the identification of a perpetrator. New Jersey led the way with promulgation in 2001 of the Attorney General Guidelines for Preparing and Conducting Photo and Live Lineup Identification Procedures, requiring among other things that the primary investigators should not administer photo or live lineup identification procedures "to ensure that inadvertent verbal cues or body language do not impact on a witness," and in 2011 with the *Henderson* decision[6] requiring

---

4. Recent years have witnessed a proliferation of empirical studies documenting the unreliability of identification testimony. See generally Gary L. Wells, "The Scientific Status of Research on Eyewitness Identification," in *Science in the Law: Social and Behavioral Science Issues*, Faigman, Kaye, Saks & Sanders §8-2.0 (2002).

5. A substantial majority of the DNA-exoneration cases implicate mistaken eyewitness identification as the cause of the wrongful conviction. See Barry Scheck, Peter Neufeld & J. Dwyer, *Actual Innocence* (2000).

6. *State v. Henderson*, 208 N.J. 208 (2011).

more judicial scrutiny of eyewitness evidence and revised jury instructions warning of the risks of such testimony. Courts have become more open to defense testimony from social science experts regarding the limitations of eyewitness evidence.[7]

Examples

1. Victoria was robbed of her wallet at gunpoint while waiting for a bus at 1:00 P.M. The robber, the only other person at the bus stop, had previously engaged Victoria in conversation lasting about ten minutes. Victoria immediately reported the robbery to the police and described the perpetrator as a slim man, about 20 years old, approximately six feet tall, wearing a long tweed coat and a woolen hat. A man of that description was observed in the vicinity shortly after her report and was taken into custody by the police. A search of the suspect turned up a wallet with Victoria's identification inside.

   Victoria was brought to the police station at 3:00 P.M. and shown her wallet. She was told that it was found on the suspect, and the police asked her to observe the man in his cell. Victoria did so and immediately identified him as the robber. The suspect was the only person in the cell and the only individual the police asked Victoria to observe.

   a. Is Victoria's station house identification admissible in evidence?

   b. Assume instead that the suspect had been indicted and arrested pursuant to a warrant prior to Victoria's station house identification of him. How would this change your analysis?

2. Johnson is arrested pursuant to an indictment for armed robbery of Cozy's Convenience Store. The police also suspect him of an unsolved robbery of a nearby gas station.

   a. If the police wish to display an array of photographs, including Johnson's, to customers who were at the convenience store at the time of the crime, must counsel be present?

   b. If the police wish to display Johnson in a lineup to the witnesses of the gas station robbery, must counsel be present?

Explanations

1a. Does this identification pass muster under the due process standard, or was it conducted in so unnecessarily suggestive a manner that there was a substantial likelihood of mistaken identification? *Stovall v. Denno*, 388 U.S. 293 (1967). There is no question that the procedure here was

---

7. See, e.g., *State v. Lawson*, 352 Or. 724, 761 (Or. 2012).

highly suggestive. The victim was shown only one individual—the suspect—and the show-up occurred while the suspect was in a jail cell and after the police had informed the victim that her wallet had been found on the suspect. The message from the police was, in effect, "He's the man, isn't he?" Moreover, unlike *Stovall* (where the elderly stabbing victim appeared to be dying in her hospital bed), in our example, there is no compelling justification for shortcutting the identification process. Although it could be argued that the police were faced with a serious crime and had to determine quickly if the felon was still at large, there appears no necessity for resorting to the jail cell show-up as opposed to a fairer method, such as a lineup.

As *Manson v. Brathwaite* teaches, however, even though the procedures were unnecessarily suggestive, they may still satisfy the due process standard if the identification is shown to have been reliable. Victoria's identification may be admissible if it was based on her lengthy observation of the accused at the time of the crime and not influenced by the promptings and suggestions of the police at the tainted confrontation. The analysis of the reliability question is informed by the following factors: (1) Victoria's opportunity to view the robber at the time of the crime, (2) her degree of attention at that time, (3) the accuracy of her description of the robber prior to the identification, (4) the level of certainty demonstrated at the time of the identification, and (5) the time lapse between the crime and the confrontation.

These factors point to a conclusion that Victoria's identification was reliable. She had a clear view of the perpetrator while standing next to him and conversing in broad daylight for ten minutes. This provided an opportunity to form an accurate mental impression of the robber's appearance. Victoria's degree of attention was high and focused on the person she was speaking to, the only other individual in the immediate area. She was thus able to give a detailed description of the robber to the police.

The accuracy of the description given prior to the identification helps the court determine if the witness had a fixed picture of the perpetrator in mind before the suggestive identification procedure. Here, we would have to know what the suspect actually looked like and compare that to Victoria's detailed description before the jail cell confrontation. Assuming a close fit between the description and the defendant's actual appearance (courts usually discount minor discrepancies), the accuracy of the description bolsters the reliability of the subsequent identification.

While it is recognized that the witness's level of certainty in making a positive identification may reflect the corrupting effect of the suggestive procedures, courts nonetheless weigh a high level of certainty in favor of the reliability of an identification. A prompt, spontaneous "He's definitely the guy!" counts considerably toward a conclusion that the identification was trustworthy. Victoria's immediate identification in our example would thus support a conclusion of reliability.

Finally, the greater the time lapse between the event and the identification, the less reliable the identification is thought to be. In our example, Victoria's identification of the defendant only two hours after the robbery would provide further support for a finding of reliability.

The *Manson* analysis requires the court to weigh the indicia of reliability against the corrupting effects of the suggestive procedures to determine whether there was a substantial likelihood of misidentification. This would likely result in a conclusion that Victoria's station house identification would be admissible. See *Walton v. Lane*, 852 F.2d 268 (7th Cir. 1988).

As with any fact-specific analysis, a change in the circumstances regarding Victoria's encounter might well change the result. If, for example, the crime had occurred in the dark of night and Victoria had only a few fleeting seconds to view the robber, or if Victoria's description did not fit the suspect ultimately identified, the reliability factors might well be outweighed by the suggestive nature of the identification. See, e.g., *Dispensa v. Lynaugh*, 847 F.2d 211 (5th Cir. 1988) (suppressing as unreliable an identification where witness's prior description failed to include several striking features of defendant's appearance). It should be noted that several studies suggest that the reliability of "cross-racial" identifications is particularly problematic. See Science in the Law, supra n.2 at § 8-2.2.2.

1b. The initiation of formal proceedings by way of an indictment triggers the *Wade* rule, which entitles the suspect to the presence of an attorney at a lineup or other physical exhibition. Because the station house confrontation proceeded without the presence of counsel or the suspect's waiver of that right, that out-of-court identification would not be admissible at trial.

There is a separate question as to whether Victoria would nonetheless be permitted to identify the defendant from the witness stand at trial. Admissibility of an in-court identification would depend on an independent source analysis: If we remove the influence of the tainted station house confrontation, is there a sufficiently reliable independent basis for the identification testimony? This analysis is based on the same *Manson v. Brathwaite* reliability factors discussed above. Because Victoria got a good look at the perpetrator and accurately described the suspect before the station house identification, there is a substantial likelihood that an in-court identification would be allowed. The observations at the time of the incident represent an independent source.

Even if Victoria had been shown just one photo of the suspect, her identification might still be upheld if there are exigent circumstances that required the police to proceed that way. This was the situation in

United States v. Shodeinde, 1997 U.S. App. LEXIS 5435 (2d Cir. 1997), in which the Second Circuit upheld a decision by then-District Court Judge Sonia Sotomayor that use of a single photograph to establish an identification was necessary because of exigent circumstances (i.e., the possible flight of the suspect). The court also applied the five factors from *Manson v. Brathwaite* and upheld Sotomayor's decision that would allow the government to elicit an in-court identification at trial, even if the initial identification had been unduly suggestive, because the witness had an independent, reliable basis for recognizing the suspect.

2a. No, Johnson would not be entitled to the presence of counsel. The right to counsel applies at any postindictment identification procedure where the suspect is displayed live. A photo array has not been included in the *Wade* rule. See *United States v. Ash*, 413 U.S. 300 (1973). Some states have interpreted their own constitutions to require the presence of counsel at a photo array. See, e.g., *Commonwealth v. Ferguson*, 475 A.2d 810 (Pa. Super. Ct. 1984).

2b. No, Johnson would not be entitled to the presence of counsel. The Sixth Amendment right to counsel is offense-specific, as we have seen with regard to the *Massiah* doctrine. (See § 10.3 in Chapter 10.) Because no formal proceedings have been initiated against Johnson for the gas station robbery, the *Wade* rule would not apply to this lineup.

§11.2 BODILY INTRUSIONS AND EXAMINATION OF SUSPECT'S PHYSICAL ATTRIBUTES

Certain investigative procedures involve examination of, and sometimes intrusion into, the suspect's body and its functions. We have already discussed drug screening that uses urine and blood tests. See § 4.5 of Chapter 4. Other procedures involve the extraction of blood or analysis of breath for purposes of testing alcohol content. What constitutional protections are implicated with regard to such investigative techniques?

The Sixth Amendment right to counsel is not implicated, the Court has held, because unlike lineups (see § 11.1), "knowledge of the techniques of science and technology is sufficiently available and the variables in techniques few enough that the accused has the opportunity for a meaningful confrontation" even though counsel is not present at the procedure. *United States v. Wade*, supra, 388 U.S. at 227.

If the police conduct is deemed "shocking to the conscience," the Due Process Clause of the Fourteenth Amendment comes into play. In *Rochin v. California*, 342 U.S. 165 (1952), police sought to forcibly remove from the suspect's mouth capsules that he had just swallowed, which they believed contained narcotics. Unable to retrieve them, the officers forcibly took Rochin to a hospital and had doctors pump his stomach with a chemical that brought the capsules up. The Supreme Court reversed his conviction for possession of the unlawful substance, concluding that Rochin's right to due process of law had been violated by the outrageous actions of the police, and thus the capsules should not have been admitted in evidence. Given the egregious nature of the police conduct there, *Rochin* has had limited applicability in subsequent cases as courts have been reluctant to describe police conduct as "shocking to the conscience."

It has long been established that intrusions into the body constitute searches and seizures implicating the Fourth Amendment. See *Schmerber v. California*, 384 U.S. 757 (1966) (involuntary extraction of a sample of motorist's blood to establish whether he was intoxicated was a search and seizure requiring justification). The procedure must be conducted pursuant to a warrant or fit within a recognized exception to the warrant requirement. *Schmerber* upheld the warrantless extraction of blood because (1) the police had probable cause to believe the driver (who had just been involved in an accident) was intoxicated; and (2) the delay necessary to secure a warrant would risk the destruction of the evidence of blood-alcohol content. Given the existence of these two elements of the emergency exception (see § 6.2 in Chapter 6), together with the fact that the procedure was routine, harmless, and performed by medical personnel, the Fourth Amendment was not violated. Since *Schmerber*, minor intrusions into the body have been measured against these standards. See, e.g., *Cupp v. Murphy*, 412 U.S. 291 (1973) (warrantless extraction of scrapings underneath suspect's fingernails held lawful because police had probable cause to believe that he had just strangled his wife, and spots of blood were easily removable by him, making resort to the warrant process impracticable).

Major bodily intrusions, however, are subject to special scrutiny. "Notwithstanding the existence of probable cause, a search for evidence of a crime may be unjustifiable if it endangers the life or health of the suspect." *Winston v. Lee*, 470 U.S. 753, 761 (1985). In that case, the government sought an order (in effect a search warrant) requiring the suspect to undergo surgery to remove a bullet lodged in his chest muscle. There was probable cause to believe the bullet would connect him to a robbery. Concluding that surgical procedures are not *per se* unreasonable, the Court required a case-by-case approach to determine the reasonableness of intrusions beneath the skin. Weighing the intrusiveness and risks of the surgery and anesthesia against the government's need for the bullet (the prosecution had other evidence including an eyewitness identification by the victim), the Court concluded that the proposed procedure would be unreasonable under the Fourth Amendment.

While applying the Fourth Amendment to searches of the body, *Schmerber* held that such procedures do not implicate the Fifth Amendment's protections. This conclusion derives from the testimonial versus physical evidence dichotomy noted above (see § 11.1). The privilege against self-incrimination applies only to compelled communications that relate factual assertions or disclose information. It does not apply where the suspect is merely the source of physical evidence, as in the case of a blood test or Breathalyzer.[8] Nor (as we have seen in § 11.1) is the privilege implicated where the physical characteristics of the suspect's communications are used to identify him (such as requiring him to speak certain words in a lineup or to provide a handwriting or voice exemplar).

Some investigative procedures do not fall neatly on one or the other side of the "testimonial/physical" evidence line. *Pennsylvania v. Muniz*, 496 U.S. 582 (1990) (discussed in § 9.2.2 of Chapter 9) involved field sobriety tests commonly used by police to determine whether a driver is intoxicated. Muniz sought to suppress testimony that his speech was slurred while he performed these tests and later in response to routine booking questions. The Court had little difficulty concluding that this evidence was not "testimonial," but rather was used to reveal the suspect's lack of physical and muscular coordination, and the Fifth Amendment was not implicated. More troublesome was Muniz's answer to the so-called sixth-birthday question: "Do you know what the date was of your sixth birthday?" Muniz argued that his "I don't know" response should have been suppressed because it was testimonial—it was incriminating not just because of its slurred delivery (a physical characteristic) but also because its *content* revealed his disoriented mental state. The Court agreed and ordered the answer suppressed because *Miranda* had not been complied with (no warnings had been administered). Illustrating that the line of demarcation between testimonial and physical evidence is not always bright, four Justices disagreed:

> If the police may require Muniz to use his body in order to demonstrate the level of his physical coordination, there is no reason why they should not be able to require him to speak or write in order to determine his mental coordination. That was all that was sought here. Since it was permissible for the police to extract and examine a sample of Schmerber's blood to determine how much that part of the system had been affected by alcohol, I see no reason why they may not examine the functioning of Muniz's mental processes for the same purpose.

---

8. The refusal to submit to a blood-alcohol test has been similarly held to be outside the protection of the Fifth Amendment, and thus evidence of the refusal is admissible at trial. See *South Dakota v. Neville*, 459 U.S. 553 (1983). Compare *Commonwealth v. McGrail*, 419 Mass. 774, 647 N.E.2d 712 (1995) (reaching opposite conclusion under the state constitution). See also *Com. v. Blais*, 428 Mass. 294 (1998) (a motorist has no right to refuse to perform the field sobriety tests pursuant to a lawful stop).

496 U.S. at 607 (Rehnquist, C.J., concurring in part and dissenting in part, joined by White, Blackmun, and Stevens, JJ.).[9]

What if defendant is compelled by the court to provide a fingerprint to unlock his cell phone? At least one court has ruled that does not violate his right against self-incrimination. See *State v. Diamond*, 890 N.W.2d 143 (Minn. App. 2017).

Finally, the Fourth Amendment's reasonableness clause has been invoked to monitor police actions that do not reach the level of egregiousness of *Rochin v. California*, as where police use excessive force or effectuate an arrest or search in an overly zealous manner. *Tennessee v. Garner*, 471 U.S. 1 (1985), for example, raised questions about the use of deadly force to apprehend an unarmed fleeing suspect. And *Graham v. Connor*, 490 U.S. 386 (1989), a civil action seeking damages for the use of excessive force, subjected such police conduct to reasonableness clause analysis. The test is whether the officer's challenged conduct was objectively reasonable without regard to the officer's subjective motivation. See also *Brosseau v. Haugen*, 543 U.S. 194 (2004). In *Scott v. Harris*, 550 U.S. 372 (2007), the Court specifically held that a high-speed chase that threatens bystanders does not invariably violate the Fourth Amendment. In this case, police rammed a fleeing vehicle from behind.

Examples

1. Dizzy was observed driving erratically by officers on highway patrol. She was pulled over and required to perform several sobriety tests, including balance and coordination tasks, as well as a recitation of the alphabet. Dizzy's unimpressive performance was videotaped and is now offered against her at trial. Would admission of the evidence violate Dizzy's Fifth Amendment right against compelled self-incrimination?

2. What if Dizzy requests a Breathalyzer test, which was available at the station, but instead was required to submit to a blood test drawn by a technician? Can she suppress the results?

3. On November 5, the First Federal Savings Bank was robbed. The bank teller described the perpetrator as a man six feet tall, 175 pounds, with jet black hair, wearing a green nylon jacket, red running shoes, and a blue woolen hat. Suspect was arrested on the other side of town 40 minutes after the robbery, meeting the description perfectly except that he had gray (not black) hair. The arresting officer noted in his report that Suspect's hair was wet and sticky, as if he had just shampooed it.

---

9. In *People v. Bejasa*, 205 Cal. App. 4th 26 (2012), where the defendant was asked as part of the sobriety test to close his eyes and estimate when 30 seconds had passed, the court found this to be testimonial (and thus within the privilege) because it required him to communicate an implied assertion of fact or belief.

A lineup was conducted in which Suspect and five others were displayed to the bank teller. The detective in charge of the case required Suspect (over his objection) to apply black dye to his hair, and he was positively identified. If you were representing him, what constitutional objections would you raise to this procedure?

4. Armed with a valid warrant to search Ann Arbour's apartment, as well as her person, for controlled substances, police conducted an extensive search. Finding nothing, they took Arbour to City Hospital, where, over her objection, she was subjected to a body cavity examination by a staff doctor. Unlawful drugs were removed and turned over to the police. May this evidence be offered against Arbour at trial?

5. While driving home from soccer practice, Sarah Soccermom was stopped by Officer Brute for failing to secure her young children in seat belts. Brute yelled at Sarah, jabbed his finger at her, and accused her of being a neglectful mom. When she was unable to produce her license and registration, explaining that her wallet had just been stolen, Brute placed her under arrest in handcuffs. Fortunately, a friend drove by and took charge of the children. Sarah was taken to the station, booked, and placed in a cell for an hour. Assuming that there is statutory authorization for the arrest on the traffic violation, is the Fourth Amendment implicated by Brute's conduct?

Explanations

1. The Fifth Amendment privilege applies only to evidence of a testimonial nature. A suspect may be compelled to display himself (as in a lineup) or display his coordination (as in a walk-a-straight-line sobriety test) without triggering the privilege. Because the recitation of the alphabet compelled Dizzy to communicate in an incriminatory manner, that question is closer. While the Supreme Court has explicitly left the question open (see *Pennsylvania v. Muniz*, 496 U.S. 582, 603 n.17 (1990), and *Pennsylvania v. Bruder*, 488 U.S. 9, 11 n.3 (1988)), the import of its decisions suggests that the alphabet test is nontestimonial and thus does not implicate the Fifth Amendment. Several lower courts have so held. See *State v. Devlin*, 294 Mont. 215, 980 P.2d 1037 (1999); *Vanhouton v. Commonwealth*, 424 Mass. 327, 676 N.E.2d 460 (1997); *Stange v. Worden*, 756 F. Supp. 508 (D. Kan. 1991). But compare *Alfred v. State*, 622 So. 2d 984 (Fla. 1993) (recitation of the alphabet is a testimonial response within the protection of the self-incrimination clause of the Florida constitution).

2. Where there are alternative methods available to determine the percentage of alcohol in the blood, the *Schmerber* justification for an immediate warrantless bodily intrusion disappears and the insistence upon the

blood test may be unreasonable. See *Nelson v. City of Irvine*, 143 F.3d 1196 (9th Cir. 1998), *cert. denied*, 525 U.S. 981.

3. Requiring a suspect to alter his appearance for purposes of identification arguably violates his right against compelled self-incrimination, but the courts have held otherwise. Reasoning that the Fifth Amendment applies only to testimonial and not physical evidence, it has been held that suspects can be required to dye their hair, see *United States v. Brown*, 920 F.2d 1212 (5th Cir. 1991); shave, see *United States v. Valenzuela*, 722 F.2d 1431 (9th Cir. 1983); wear a wig, see *United States v. Murray*, 523 F.2d 489 (8th Cir. 1975); and wear a false goatee, see *United States v. Hammond*, 419 F.2d 166 (4th Cir. 1969).

4. *Rochin v. California, Schmerber v. California*, and *Winston v. Lee*, supra, all underscore the special protection afforded the body under the Fourth and Fourteenth Amendments. While searches of the type conducted in example 4 are not always unconstitutional, they require substantially more justification than simply a demonstration of probable cause to believe evidence of criminal activity will be found. In *Winston v. Lee*, the surgical procedure contemplated required a demonstration of special need for the evidence, as well as particularized probable cause. But compare *United States v. Husband*, 312 F.3d 247 (7th Cir. 2002) (upholding forced administration of an IV sedative to permit the retrieval of baggies believed to contain crack cocaine from the suspect's mouth); *United States v. Adekunle*, 980 F.2d 985 (5th Cir. 1992) (border search involving stomach X-rays of a drug smuggler suspect and forced ingestion of a laxative not violative of Fourth Amendment because laxatives were found to be given for reasonable medical purposes — defendant was at significant risk of death if the drugs leaked from swallowed balloons; court also noted that the laxatives, unlike the emetic in *Rochin*, did not cause the expulsion from the body of something that would not normally and routinely be expelled; on rehearing, 2 F.3d 559, the court revised its prior decision, reaching the same conclusion, but on the basis that the 100-hour detention was lawful because the custom's officials brought the matter before a magistrate within 48 hours, and the magistrate's order of an X-ray demonstrated an implicit determination that there was reasonable suspicion to warrant continued detention).

In *Rodrigues v. Furtado*, 410 Mass. 878 (1991), police secured a warrant to search the subject's vagina for narcotics, and the procedure was performed by a licensed physician at a designated hospital. Ruling in the civil action, the Supreme Judicial Court took the opportunity to suggest special requirements for such searches:

> It is difficult to imagine a more intrusive, humiliating, and demeaning search than the one conducted inside the plaintiff's body. In cases such as the present one, where the police seek to conduct a search inside the body of an

individual, it may be appropriate to require a higher level of certainty than "mere" probable cause. If less than probable cause is required in cases where the level of intrusion is relatively low [citing *Terry v. Ohio*], it may be appropriate to require a higher level of certainty in cases involving extremely intrusive searches. Additionally, we think it sound policy to require that, in the future, such a warrant be issued only by a person legally trained, i.e., a judge. [W]e shall deem a warrant authorizing the search of a body cavity to be invalid unless issued by the authority of a judge, on a strong showing of particularized need supported by a high degree of probable cause.

410 Mass. at 888.

5. Even when there is probable cause for an arrest or search, the manner in which the police conduct themselves may implicate the reasonableness clause of the Fourth Amendment. See *Tennessee v. Garner*, supra (deadly force may not be used unless it is necessary to prevent the suspect's escape and the officer has probable cause to believe that he poses a significant threat of death or serious physical injury to the officer or others). However, the Court in *Scott v. Harris*, *supra*, raised questions about the viability of the *Garner* test when it indicated that the Fourth Amendment reasonableness standard should be analyzed by the facts of the individual case. But in the case upon which this example is based, the Court concluded that Atwater's arrest was humiliating but no more harmful to her interests than the normal custodial arrest, and found no Fourth Amendment violation. *Atwater v. City of Lago Vista*, 532 U.S. 318 (2001).

§11.3 ENTRAPMENT

Crimes such as drug offenses, prostitution, and bribery involve willing participants, and witnesses are unlikely to come forward to report them. In order to investigate these crimes (as well as terrorism threats; see Chapter 12) the government must resort to unusual means, sometimes even encouraging the commission of the offense itself. Undercover officers engaging prostitutes or purchasing narcotics are examples of this approach. When the government crosses the line between investigating crime and instigating it, however, the entrapment defense comes into play.

There are two sources of law for the entrapment defense. One is a common law defense that has been recognized by the Supreme Court in federal criminal cases (and by some state courts under their own common law). The other, which has not been explicitly adopted by the Court, is premised on the Due Process Clause of the U.S. Constitution. Unlike the exclusionary remedy, which suppresses a particular item of evidence, the entrapment defense acts as a complete bar to the prosecution.

§11.3.1 The Common Law Defense

The entrapment defense can be traced back to *Sorrells v. United States*, 287 U.S. 435, 454 (1932), in which the defendant was indicted for possessing and selling whiskey in violation of the National Prohibition Act. An undercover federal agent, having gained his trust, enticed Sorrells to provide him with liquor. Sorrells had initially resisted, but after several requests, he sold liquor to the agent and was arrested. The Court, concluding that the evidence warranted a finding that the agent had actually instigated an offense that Sorrells had no previous disposition to commit, made the defense of entrapment available to the defendant.

In subsequent cases (see *Sherman v. United States*, 356 U.S. 369 (1958), and *United States v. Russell*, 411 U.S. 423 (1973)), the Court has emphasized that the key question is distinguishing between "the trap for the unwary innocent and the trap for the unwary criminal." The thrust of the defense is a focus on the defendant's predisposition to commit the crime, and it is made out only where a law enforcement agent procures commission of a crime by an individual not otherwise predisposed to commit it. This subjective approach contrasts with an alternative that looks not at the propensities of the particular defendant but rather the conduct of the government: Where law enforcement officers act in a manner likely to instigate a criminal offense, the defense would apply. This objective approach, originally proposed by Justice Roberts in his concurring opinion in *Sorrells*, has never commanded a majority of the Court but is followed by several states and the American Law Institute (ALI) Model Penal Code.

In raising the entrapment defense, the defendant has the initial burden of showing government inducement. The burden then shifts to the government to show that the defendant was ready and willing — predisposed — to commit the offense. Entrapment is generally a jury question, although on occasion, judges have found entrapment to be a matter of law.

In a refinement of the defense, the Court in *Jacobson v. United States*, 503 U.S. 540 (1992), ruled that the government must not only prove predisposition, but also demonstrate that the predisposition was not itself the product of government action. Jacobson claimed that his prosecution for receiving child pornography through the mail should be barred because the crime resulted from a 2 1/2-year campaign of correspondence by the government acting through fictitious organizations and a bogus pen pal. The Court agreed: "Where the Government has induced an individual to break the law and the defense of entrapment is at issue, the prosecution must prove beyond reasonable doubt that the defendant was disposed to commit the criminal act *prior to first being approached by Government agents*" (emphasis added).

Because this entrapment defense is based on common law and not constitutional grounds, the states are not compelled to recognize it.

§11.3.2 Due Process

United States v. Russell, 411 U.S. 423, 431 (1973), while acknowledging that the entrapment defense is not based on the Constitution, nonetheless left open the possibility that "we may some day be presented with a situation in which the conduct of law enforcement agents is so outrageous that due process principles would absolutely bar the government from invoking judicial processes to obtain a conviction." The Court confronted the issue again in *Hampton v. United States*, 425 U.S. 484 (1976), where the defendant, convicted of distributing heroin, claimed that the narcotics he sold to undercover agents had been supplied by a government informant and thus he should be acquitted as a matter of law regardless of his predisposition to commit the crime. The Supreme Court disagreed. Writing for the plurality, Justice Rehnquist held that predisposition precluded any defense of entrapment. Five Justices, however, kept alive the notion that under appropriate circumstances, government conduct amounting to a violation of due process might bar a prosecution even where predisposition had been shown.

Although the Supreme Court has yet to allow a due process defense in any case before it, some circuit court rulings have done so when the government conduct has been found to be outrageous. In *United States v. Twigg*, 588 F.2d 373 (3d Cir. 1978), a government informant proposed to the defendant that a laboratory to manufacture speed be set up and then supplied the equipment, raw materials, and site to accomplish that purpose. The informant maintained exclusive control over the manufacturing process because he was the only one who had the expertise to manufacture the drug. The court held that the government involvement reached a demonstrable level of outrageousness and thus the prosecution was barred.[10] Similarly, *United States v. Lard*, 734 F.2d 1290 (8th Cir. 1984), overturned a conviction based on entrapment as a matter of law, finding the agents' "over-involvement in conceiving and contriving the crimes here approached being so outrageous that due process principles should bar the government from invoking judicial processes to obtain a conviction."

Examples

1. FBI agents posed as employees of a fictitious Sheik Abdul, Mideastern oil billionaire, and spread the word that the sheik was interested in building a convention center complex in South Philadelphia and was willing to "grease palms" to avoid problems with city permits and building inspections. The scheme was designed to nab public officials

---

10. Other circuit courts have reached the opposite result. See *United States v. Santana*, 6 F.3d 1, 34 (1st Cir. 1993); *United States v. Milam*, 817 F.2d 1113, 1115 n.2 (4th Cir. 1987); *United States v. Beverly*, 723 F.2d 11, 12 (3d Cir. 1983).

inclined toward taking bribes. Several private meetings were arranged between the agents and a member of the city council, who, according to information provided by a well-connected source, was open to bribery. At the meetings, held in the penthouse suite at a posh downtown hotel, the councilor was wined and dined while the agents described the convention center project, repeatedly emphasizing the sheik's insistence on "avoiding the usual red tape." The councilor remained silent until the third such meeting, at which he was asked, "So, can you help push this project along?" He assured the agents that the city council would approve the project quickly and that the building inspectors "ain't gonna monkey with your project because they're gonna get the word to lay off." The agents asked, "What's this going to cost the sheik?" and the councilor responded, "Just thirty-K, a special one-day sale!" The $30,000 was paid, and the councilor stated, "Gentlemen, you just bought yourself some true friendship." The entire transaction was videotaped.

The city councilor has been indicted by federal authorities for bribery. What are his chances of successfully raising the defenses of entrapment and violation of due process?

2. DEA agent Sam Stud, posing as an importer of illegal drugs, makes contact with Sarah Susceptible, an owner of several airplanes. Sarah is suspected of working for a Colombian drug organization. Sam proposes that she allow him to use her planes for purposes of drug smuggling. She initially refuses despite the offer of substantial money. Undaunted, Sam sends Sarah various gifts and gradually develops a romantic relationship with her. Ultimately, Sarah allows her planes to be used for drug smuggling. The government has uncovered other evidence indicating Sarah was indeed a drug smuggler, making it difficult for her to use the common-law entrapment defense because the government could readily demonstrate that she was predisposed to commit the offense. Could Sarah claim that Sam's sexual advances constituted outrageous conduct violating due process?

3. The Diablos are a tough motorcycle gang that have been infiltrated by an FBI informant known to them as The Ferret. He has gained their trust and become treasurer of the gang. At the weekly meeting, The Ferret announces that the rent for the gang headquarters is in arrears and they face eviction unless they agree to "run security" for a cocaine trafficking ring in the area, work that pays quite well. Big Al (who, although he has no criminal record, says he's "already done one of these cocaine things") and several other members agree, and are later arrested in connection with the transportation of the cocaine. Can they raise an entrapment defense?

Explanations

1. To make out an entrapment defense, the councilor must show both that the crime was instigated by the government and that he was not predisposed to accepting bribes. Entrapment occurs only when the criminal conduct is the product of government activity, and the defendant would not otherwise have engaged in the prohibited act. Where government agents merely afford opportunities for the commission of the offense, prosecution is not barred. In other words, the councilor must show that he was the victim of a trap for the unwary innocent. See *Sorrells v. United States*, 287 U.S. 435, 454 (1932); *Sherman v. United States*, 356 U.S. 369 (1958); *United States v. Russell*, 411 U.S. 423 (1973).

   The initial burden is on the defendant to prove that his act was induced by the government. More would need to be known about the nature of the conversations at the various meetings, but it appears at least arguable that there is sufficient evidence of inducement to submit the issue to the jury.

   As in most entrapment cases, the crux of the matter is predisposition, an issue on which the prosecution bears the burden of proof. *Jacobson v. United States*, 503 U.S. 540 (1992), mandates that in order to defeat an entrapment defense, the government must not only prove predisposition but must also demonstrate that the predisposition was not itself the product of government action. At issue is the defendant's subjective state of mind. Relevant factors include the defendant's past involvement in similar criminal activity, the reasons law enforcement focused their attentions on him, the nature of the enticements offered, and the extent to which the defendant indicated reluctance and resisted efforts to engage him in criminal activity. Again, more information would be needed to analyze the prospects for an entrapment defense.

   In the case on which this example is loosely based, *United States v. Jannotti*, 673 F.2d 578 (3d Cir. 1982) (the "ABSCAM" case), the trial judge granted the defendants' motions for acquittal following convictions by the jury, concluding there was entrapment as a matter of law because the large size of the bribes created too great a temptation even for an innocent suspect. The Court of Appeals reversed and ordered the jury's verdict reinstated. The Third Circuit observed: "Even if the dollar amount offered were relevant to disprove predisposition, a question which we do not decide, we find nothing in the record to support the district court's conclusion that in today's inflationary times, city councilmen would view sums of $30,000 as so large or generous as to overcome an official's natural reluctance to accept a bribe." 673 F.2d at 599.

   Regarding the due process defense, defendants must demonstrate that the extent of government overreaching was so outrageous as to amount to a constitutional deprivation. In the view of five Justices in

Hampton v. United States, 425 U.S. 484, 495 (1976) (two concurring with and three dissenting from the plurality's opinion), this defense is available even to predisposed defendants. Given the rare successful invocation of this defense, the defendants will very likely fail, as they did in Jannotti. Police involvement in the crime would have to reach what Justice Powell described as a demonstrable level of outrageousness before it could bar conviction. Unlike United States v. Twigg, 588 F.2d 373 (3d Cir. 1978), where prosecution was barred because the government initiated and actively participated in the establishment of a laboratory to produce an unlawful drug, the government in our example merely created a fictional set of circumstances providing an opportunity for defendant to be bribed. See also United States v. Mosley, 965 F.2d 906, 909-910 (10th Cir. 1992) (no outrageous government conduct where defendant approached agent for purpose of buying marijuana, and agent sold cocaine to defendant at allegedly low price); United States v. Payne, 962 F.2d 1228, 1231-1232 (6th Cir. 1992) (no outrageous government conduct where undercover agent posed as drug dealer trying to launder money, even though defendants were unknown when undercover operation commenced and government provided money to be laundered); United States v. Tobias, 662 F.2d 381, 386-387 (5th Cir. 1981) (no outrageous government conduct where DEA provided formula and some chemicals for manufacture of PCP, but chemicals were not difficult to obtain and DEA provided no financial aid for defendants' operation).

Predisposed defendants appear to be more successful in raising the due process defense in state court proceedings. In People v. Isaacson, 378 N.E.2d 78 (N.Y. 1978), the court dismissed the case based on a violation of due process where the police engaged in misconduct and trickery to secure a drug sale by defendant. Isaacson introduces four factors to be considered when determining due process violations: (1) whether the police manufactured a crime that otherwise would not have occurred or merely involved themselves in an ongoing criminal activity; (2) whether the police engaged in criminal or improper conduct repugnant to a sense of justice; (3) whether the defendant's reluctance to commit the crime was overcome by appeals to humanitarian instincts such as sympathy or past friendship, by temptation of exorbitant gain, or by persistent solicitation in the face of unwillingness; and (4) whether the record reveals simply a desire to obtain a conviction, and not to prevent further crime or protect the populace. 378 N.E.2d at 83.

State v. Hohensee, 650 S.W.2d 268 (Mo. Ct. App. 1982), reversed a conviction based on a violation of due process where a predisposed defendant acted as a lookout during a burglary sponsored and operated by the police. See also State v. Glosson, 462 So. 2d 1082, 1085 (Fla. 1985) (finding violation of due process where informant was paid contingent fee conditioned on cooperation and testimony in criminal prosecutions against defendants); Commonwealth v. Mathews, 500 A.2d 853, 857 (Pa. Super. Ct. 1985) (finding violation of due process where police assisted in bringing material from out of town to manufacture methamphetamine, supplied money to purchase food and other supplies for defendants, supplied a manual with a formula to manufacture the drug, and supplied a chemist to instruct defendants on detailed steps through the formula); Metcalf v. State, 614 So. 2d 548 (Fla. Dist. Ct. App. 1993) (finding that a reverse sting operation for manufacture of crack cocaine constituted a violation of state due process).

In contrast, Mondello v. State, 843 P.2d 1152, 1160 (Wyo. 1992), rejected the due process defense where defendant, planning to buy only one ounce of cocaine for his personal use, was tricked by the government into buying two for the purpose of reselling the second. The court emphasized that Mondello had sought out the government informant to purchase cocaine; he was not solicited. In Rivera v. State, 846 P.2d 1, 3 (Wyo. 1993), the court denied the due process defense even though the undercover officer not only fronted a portion of the purchase price defendant paid for marijuana, but also offered the marijuana for lower than the going rate. And State v. Pleasant, 684 P.2d 761, 762-763 (Wash. Ct. App. 1984) (though recognizing the enforcement techniques as personally abhorrent, nonetheless rejected the due process defense where the officer and informant instigated the crime by posing as a construction company reviewing the defendant's application for employment and, after indicating that he might be hired, asked if he could procure marijuana for them).

2. In seeking dismissal of the indictment, Sarah must establish that the government engaged in outrageous behavior in connection with the criminal act and that due process considerations bar prosecution. United States v. Cuervelo, 949 F.2d 559 (2d Cir. 1991), addressing the question in the context of a sexual relationship, suggested that the defendant must show that the government "consciously set out to use sex as a weapon in its investigatory arsenal," that the sexual relationship was initiated by the agent or allowed to continue to exist to achieve the government objective, and that the sexual activity occurred during the same period and was intertwined with the criminal activity. See also State v. Lively, 130 Wash. 2d 1, 921 P.2d 1035 (1996) (reversing conviction where a police informant developed an intimate relationship with the defendant and after persistent prompting, got the defendant to arrange a drug transaction). But compare United States v. Nolan-Cooper, 155 F.3d 221 (3d Cir. 1998) (no outrageous conduct even though an undercover government agent developed a romantic relationship with defendant and had one occasion of sexual intercourse with her, because the major part of investigation was unrelated to the relationship).

From the facts in our example, it appears that Sarah would have at least a chance of making out the due process defense.

3. Big Al must show that the crime was instigated by the government, and that he was not predisposed to commit it. The inducement here played on the members' loyalty to the gang and desire to preserve the headquarters. In the case upon which this example is based, the First Circuit ruled that this tactic was not improperly coercive. *United States v. LaFreniere*, 236 F.3d 41 (1st Cir. 2001). Further, the court found Big Al, despite his lack of prior record, was predisposed to commit the crime — he showed no reluctance to agree, and he readily admitted to prior involvement in cocaine transportation.

§11.4 "HIGH-TECH" SEARCHES

The courts have long struggled with issues concerning the application of the Fourth Amendment, adopted in 1791, to new technologies such as thermal imaging and cell-site locators. See § 3.2 of Chapter 3. This section briefly focuses on two such areas, electronic surveillance and searches of computers.

§11.4.1 Electronic Surveillance and Wiretapping

While *Katz v. United States*, 389 U.S. 347 (1967) (see § 3.2), subjected electronic eavesdropping to the Fourth Amendment, Congress has taken the lead in articulating the specific constraints imposed. Title III of the Omnibus Crime Control and Safe Streets Act of 1968, 18 U.S.C. § 2510 *et seq.*, as amended, requires law enforcement agents to procure a court order authorizing interception of any wire or electronic communication (this includes landline phones, cell phones, cordless phones, and e-mail). Application for an order requires detailed information about the communications to be intercepted, the criminal offenses suspected, and the efforts made to obtain the information by other means. If issued, the order must describe with particularity the persons whose communications are to be intercepted and the nature of the communications, specify the duration of the authorization, and require that the interception be conducted in such a way as to minimize the overhearing of conversations not relevant to the investigation. Title III provides for suppression of communications unlawfully intercepted.

We will have more to say about electronic surveillance in Chapter 12 in the context of investigations into suspected terrorist activity.

§11.4.2 Searches of Computers

Given the centrality of computers and information technology in our modern society, law enforcement agents investigating crime increasingly seek a glimpse into the suspect's cyberspace. What constraints apply here?

We know that the Fourth Amendment generally requires a search warrant issued on probable cause and describing with particularity the place to be searched and the items to be seized. (See Chapter 5.) But what does this mean when the search is of a computer's hard drive and files? How specific does the warrant have to be in describing the items to be seized from the computer? Does the plain view doctrine permit investigators to seize files relating to crimes other than those described in the warrant if they come across them in their search? Are deleted files entitled to any protection under the Fourth Amendment, or are they regarded as discarded trash outside the purview of the Amendment?

In executing a search warrant for a computer, what reasonableness requirements apply? How long may police hold the computer? Who has standing to challenge a computer search? What is the scope of a consensual search regarding a computer? How does the good faith exception (see § 7.3.3.) apply here? Answers to these questions have only begun to emerge from the case law.

Consider the following scenario. Federal agents engaged in an investigation of child pornography are monitoring an Internet chat room. They view a number of images depicting children engaged in sexual activities and discover from the Internet service provider that the computer from which the images were sent is owned by Sal Sleaze at an address in Brooklyn, New York.[11] The agents submit this information on an affidavit for a search warrant, which the magistrate issues. The warrant authorizes a search of Sleaze's computer hardware, software, disks, and disk drives for any visual depictions of minors engaging in sexually explicit conduct.

Pursuant to the warrant, the agents enter Sleaze's apartment and seize his computer, together with dozens of disks. Using a specialized utilities program that has an "undelete" function, the agents are able to recover hundreds of previously deleted images of child pornography, including the photos that the agents had originally viewed on the Internet.

What issues are raised when the prosecution offers these images into evidence at the trial of Sleaze for possession of child pornography?

---

11. There is no reasonable expectation of privacy in materials intended for public posting on the Internet, or in one's Internet address. See *Guest v. Leis*, 255 F.3d 325, 333, 335-336 (6th Cir. 2001); *United States v. Suing*, 712 F.3d 1209 (8th Cir. 2013) (defendant had no expectation of privacy in his subscriber information, including his IP address and name from third-party service providers). But see *State v. Reid*, 945 A.2d 26 (N.J. 2008) (search and seizure provisions of the New Jersey constitution protect an individual's privacy interest in the subscriber information that he provides to an Internet service provider).

Assuming that the agents' information established probable cause to search, the defense would focus on the particularity requirement. In the case upon which this scenario is based, *United States v. Upham*, 168 F.3d 532 (1st Cir. 1999), the defendant's argument that the authorization to search all computer hardware, software, disks, and disk drives was overly broad was rejected by the court, which concluded that it was the narrowest definable search reasonably likely to turn up the pornographic images sought. The court concluded that "sufficient chance of finding some needles in the computer haystack was established by the probable-cause showing in the warrant application," and that a "search of a computer and co-located disks is not inherently more intrusive that the physical search of an entire house for a weapon or drugs." 168 F.3d at 535.

Computer searches raise unique problems with regard to a particularity requirement. Unlike physical objects that can be identified in the warrant and readily discovered by the executing officers, digital files can be manipulated in ways that hide their true content. See *United States v. Evers*, 669 F.3d 645, (6th Cir 2012). And given the enormous storage capabilities of modern computers (like the cell phones in *Riley v. California*, 134 S. Ct. 2473 (2014), see § 6.3) they provide a tempting opportunity for exploratory rummaging, a principal evil that the Framers sought to avoid.

One court has ruled that where the computer files are labeled with sufficient specificity and there is a good likelihood the evidence enumerated in the warrant will be found within those files, the search must be so confined, and extension beyond would violate the Fourth Amendment. See *United States v. Carey*, 172 F.3d 1268 (10th Cir. 1999). Where the files are not clearly labeled, the officer may open them as part of the search for items specified in the warrant. In the process, if he or she comes upon matters immediately apparent as evidence of other crimes, extension of the search may be justified by the plain view doctrine. See § 6.8 and *Guest v. Leis*, supra, 255 F.3d at 334-335; *Commonwealth v. Hinds*, 437 Mass. 54, 768 N.E.2d 1067 (2002) (officer was not required to disregard files listed in plain view in a computer's directory, where titles such as 2BOYS.JPG and KIDSEX1 created probable cause to believe contents contained pornography). But compare *United States v. Carey*, 172 F.3d 1268, 1272-1274 (10th Cir. 1999) (seizure of child pornography from defendant's computer hard drive was not authorized by the plain view doctrine because the officer was lawfully searching document files for evidence of drug dealing, but unlawfully expanded the search by opening JPEG photo image files). Courts have recognized that files may be intentionally mislabeled and have permitted some expansion of searches to accommodate that possibility. See, e.g., *United States v. Gray*, 78 F. Supp. 2d 524, 527 n.5 (E.D. Va. 1999).

In *United States v. Stabile*, 633 F.3d 219, 240 (3rd Cir. 2011), the court acknowledged that the exact confines of the plain view doctrine as it relates to computers vary from "case to case in a common sense, fact intensive manner." "There are three requirements for valid seizure of evidence in plain view. First the officer must not have violated the Fourth Amendment in anyway at the place from which the evidence could be plainly viewed. Second, the incriminating character of the evidence must be immediately apparent. Third, the officer must have lawful right of access to the object itself." (See also § 6.8).

What if the defendant had several computers in his home or office, some of which had no connection to the alleged crime? And what about the files that had been deliberately deleted, which the investigator is now able to recover and *undelete*? While rejecting the government's analogy of deleted files to abandoned trash that lacks a reasonable expectation of privacy (*California v. Greenwood*, 486 U.S. 35 (1988), discussed in § 3.2), the First Circuit nonetheless upheld the search of deleted files as within the purview of the warrant and no different than a detective pasting together scraps of a torn-up ransom note when the warrant authorizes seizure of the note. *United States v. Upham*, supra, 168 F.3d at 535.

Where a warrant authorized a search for the instrumentalities of the crime of computer harassment, seizure of images of child pornography on the defendant's computer was held justified by the plain view doctrine, as the warrant impliedly authorized the officers to open each file and view its contents, at least cursorily, and the contraband nature of the pornographic images was immediately apparent. *United States v. Williams*, 592 F.3d 511 (4th Cir. 2010). See also *United States v. Giberson*, 527 F.3d 882 (9th Cir. 2008) (search for fake I.D. photographs allowed an agent to search all images and photographs on the computer, and child pornography discovered was admissible under the plain view doctrine): "While officers ought to exercise caution when executing the search of a computer, just as they ought to when sifting through documents that may contain personal information, the potential intermingling of materials does not justify an exception or heightened procedural protections for computers beyond the Fourth Amendment's reasonableness requirement."

Another court has observed:

> There is no way to be sure exactly what an electronic file contains without somehow examining its contents—either by opening it and looking, using specialized forensic software, keyword searching, or some other such technique. But electronic files are generally found on media that also contain thousands or millions of other files among which the sought-after data may be stored or concealed. By necessity, government efforts to locate particular files will require examining a great many other files to exclude the possibility that the sought-after data are concealed there.
>
> Once a file is examined, however, the government may claim (as it did in this case) that its contents are in plain view and, if incriminating, the government can keep it. Authorization to search *some* computer files, therefore, automatically becomes authorization to search all files in the same subdirectory, and all

files in an enveloping directory, a neighboring hard drive, a nearby computer, or a nearby storage media. Where computers are not near each other, but are connected electronically, the original search might justify examining files in computers many miles away, on a theory that incriminating electronic data could have been shuttled and concealed there.

United States v. Comprehensive Drug Testing Inc. 621 F.3d 1162, 1176 (9th Cir. 2010).

In our hypothetical scenario, therefore, the scope of the search of Sleaze's computer for pornography is dependent on the extent to which the contents of the files are readily apparent from their titles. If the agents cannot reasonably ascertain from the labels what is contained inside, they may be permitted to scan through the files and seize matters relating to other crimes that they come across inadvertently.

Because of their complexity, courts have allowed as much time as reasonably necessary to conduct thorough searches of computers, and durations of weeks or months (during which the computer is held) have been upheld. See, e.g, *United States v. Triumph Capital Group, Inc.*, 211 F.R.D. 31, 66 (D. Conn. 2002); *United States v. Gorrell*, 360 F. Supp. 2d 48 (D.D.C. 2004) (a ten-month delay in recovering data from computers and camera was consistent with a warrant that did not limit the amount of time in which the government was required to complete its off-site forensic analysis). In addition, because of the significant burdens associated with on-site review, the creation of mirror images (forensic identical copies of hard drives) for offsite review has generally been allowed. However, extended retention of every file for future investigation has been held to be unreasonable under the Fourth Amendment. See *United States v. Ganias*, 775 F.3d 125, 135-138 (2nd Cir 2015).

Keep in mind that where the subject is using a computer provided by his employer, he may not have a sufficient personal interest in it to possess standing to challenge a search. See *United States v. Triumph Capital Group, Inc.*, supra, 211 F.R.D. 54, and § 7.3.1.

Does consensual search (see § 6.7 of Chapter 6) of a residence include examination of the data on computers found there? The scope of such searches is limited to what a reasonable police officer would understand from the conversation with the consenter. Oftentimes, the officer states the objective for the search when seeking consent. If, for example, he asks for permission to search for an intruder, search of a computer would clearly be beyond the permissible scope. See *United States v. Turner*, 169 F.3d 84 (1st Cir. 1999); *United States v. Carey*, 172 F.3d 1268, 1274 (10th Cir. 1999). See also *United States v. Sells*, 2005 WL 6236467 (N.D. Ill. 2005) (government exceeded scope of consent to a computer search of a defendant who was initially arrested for stalking, when authorities, while searching for a "creative writing" file, saw reference to an "offshore" file, which they opened without a warrant and discovered evidence of tax evasion).

Third-party consent applies to computer searches as elsewhere—a third party may consent to search if he shares common authority over or mutual use of the computer. In *United States v. Andrus*, 483 F.3d 711 (10th Cir. 2007), *decision clarified on denial of rehearing*, 499 F.3d 1162, the court held that the defendant's father had apparent authority to consent to search of the defendant's computer where, although the computer was in the defendant's bedroom in his father's home rather than in a common area, the father had unlimited access to the bedroom, the agents knew that the father owned the home and paid for its Internet service, the e-mail address associated with the father was used to register on the website that provided access to child pornography, and the computer was in plain view on the desk and appeared available for use by all household members.

United States v. Adjani, 452 F.3d 1140 (9th Cir. 2006), permitted the search and seizure of a third-party's computer that was in the apparent authority of the defendant. A warrant was issued to search for and seize instrumentalities of extortion in Adjuni's residence. During the search, his roommate's computer, which was readily accessible to the defendant, was also seized, and incriminating information implicating her in the crime was found on that computer. The court held that the officers acted reasonably in seizing the third party's computer, as the warrant specifically called for the search of all computers, hard drives, and other computer devices in the defendant's residence. The Ninth Circuit also upheld the scope of the search, which included the seizure of e-mails, concluding they were within the scope of the warrant, which authorized the seizure of "records, documents, and materials."

It has been held that reasonable suspicion is not required for customs officials to search a laptop during a border crossing. See *United States v. Arnold*, 533 F.3d 1003 (9th Cir. 2008).

Perhaps the greatest threat to personal privacy arises from the use of emerging technologies to snoop on us. Thermal imaging, infrared cameras, and gas chromatography can open our homes (and all the activities therein) to the prying eyes of the government. DNA profiling can reveal the most intimate details about us—a strand of hair or a discarded cigarette butt can be a source of information about our medical condition, life expectancy, and family history. And global positioning system (GPS) devices can track our every movement. See *Jones v. United States*, discussed in § 3.2 of Chapter 3.

While such techniques may optimize the ability of police to investigate and solve crimes, they clearly come at the expense of the privacy rights that lie at the core of the Fourth Amendment. Drawing a proper balance here remains a constant challenge for courts in the twenty-first century.

CHAPTER 12

September 11, 2001, and Its Aftermath

---

§12.1 INTRODUCTION

No treatment of constitutional criminal procedure would be complete without recognition of the tremendous impact of what is now referred to simply as "9/11." The terrorist attacks in New York and Washington, D.C. led quickly to the Joint Resolution of September 18, 2001, authorizing the President to use military force against those responsible for the attacks (the Authorization of Military Force, or "AUMF"), and then the "USA PATRIOT Act," modifying longstanding principles in the area of search and seizure. More generally, 9/11 has prompted a profound rethinking of the delicate balance between civil liberties and law enforcement—for some, 9/11 "changed everything." In Chapter 1, we traced the significant expansion of constitutional protections wrought by the Warren Court, and then their gradual curtailment by the Burger, Rehnquist, and Roberts Courts. 9/11 has accelerated this latter process.

Congress passed the USA PATRIOT Act in an atmosphere of tremendous fear and anxiety 45 days after 9/11. The acronym speaks volumes about the national mood: "Uniting and Strengthening America by Providing Appropriate Tools Required to Intercept and Obstruct Terrorism." The Act dramatically expanded the government's powers to investigate certain types of offenses, making it easier to gather intelligence and conduct electronic surveillance (see the discussion of Title III of the Omnibus Crime Control Act in § 11.4.1 of Chapter 11). Other provisions allowed for greater sharing of foreign intelligence information among law enforcement and security agencies.

367

The USA PATRIOT Act built on the Foreign Intelligence Surveillance Act (FISA), enacted in 1978 on the premise that the traditional constraints imposed on law enforcement officers seeking evidence of crime should not apply where the purpose is to protect against foreign threats or terrorism. FISA created a special secret court with authority to issue orders allowing electronic surveillance of foreign agents on a showing less than traditional probable cause (see § 4.1 in Chapter 4). The USA PATRIOT Act lowered the bar further, first by adopting a broad definition of "terrorism," thus expanding the potential targets, and then by permitting surveillance so long as foreign intelligence gathering is a "significant purpose," whereas FISA had required that it be the "*primary* purpose." The Act also extended permissible interception to include e-mail; allows the government to subpoena (without judicial supervision) records from banks, financial institutions, and Internet service providers; dilutes the particularity requirement for warrants (see § 5.2.3 of Chapter 5); and permits "sneak and peek" searches without notification of the subject.

The FISA Amendments Act of 2008 granted immunity from liability for telecommunications companies that cooperated in the surveillance programs. The Amendments also addressed "exigent circumstances" in which important intelligence information was in danger of being lost in the time required to secure a warrant from a FISA court. The Amendments extended the time from three days to seven, during which the government may conduct surveillance of a U.S. citizen without a court order, so long as the Attorney General certifies that there is probable cause to believe that the subject has ties to terrorism. The legislation also provided for electronic surveillance targeting non-U.S. citizens outside the United States without requiring the government to submit individualized applications identifying particular targets and facilities.

Even though the justification for these relaxed standards was that the purpose of the investigation is to protect national security and not to obtain evidence for use in criminal prosecution, the evidence may nonetheless be admitted in ordinary, non-terrorist-related criminal prosecutions (as we saw regarding so-called "administrative" searches in § 6.6 of Chapter 6). See *In re Sealed Case*, 310 F.3d 717 (FISA Court of Review 2002).

In the wake of 9/11, the Bush Administration implemented highly sophisticated surveillance programs to monitor millions of phone calls and financial transactions, without the oversight of the FISA court and beyond any legislative authorization. The Terrorist Surveillance Program (TSP), begun in 2002 by a secret executive order, authorized the National Security Agency (NSA) to conduct warrantless electronic surveillance of international calls and e-mails of thousands of U.S. citizens and others inside the United States. On the face of it, the enterprise directly conflicted with the constraints of FISA as well as the Fourth Amendment.

Soon after the *New York Times* exposed the TSP, numerous lawsuits were filed challenging the program on statutory and constitutional grounds. The Administration's defense of the program was premised upon a number of theories. First, the President claimed that he was authorized to conduct the warrantless surveillance by virtue of his powers as commander-in-chief, especially as expanded by the AUMF. Second, the administration argued that the TSP was consistent with FISA. While Congress indicated that FISA was to be "the exclusive means by which electronic surveillance may be conducted," it also provided exceptions in 50 U.S.C. § 1809(a)(1); the AUMF arguably was the exception here. Finally, it was contended that the TSP did not violate the Fourth Amendment because foreign intelligence collection in a time of national crisis was a "special need" and, therefore, exempt from the Fourth Amendment's warrant requirement. Under the reasonableness analysis, it was argued, the program passed constitutional muster due to the overwhelming governmental interest in protecting the security of the nation.

These positions were rejected in the first federal challenge to the TSP. The plaintiffs in *American Civil Liberties Union v. National Security Agency*, 438 F. Supp. 2d 754 (E.D. Mich. Aug. 17, 2006), were a group of journalists, lawyers, and scholars who regularly communicated overseas by telephone and the Internet in the course of their work. Because much of the plaintiffs' correspondence was with persons in the Middle East, they expressed a "well-founded belief" that they had been subjects of the TSP's warrantless surveillance and alleged that their contacts abroad were reluctant to continue to communicate with them.

The district court ruled for the plaintiffs, holding that the TSP violated their First and Fourth Amendment rights, as well as the separation of powers doctrine, and was not authorized by the AUMF. The court issued an injunction against the TSP, but the Sixth Circuit overturned the decision on the grounds that plaintiffs lacked standing. *American Civil Liberties Union v. National Security Agency*, 493 F.3d 644 (6th Cir. 2007). The Supreme Court would ultimately dismiss a similar challenge to the FISA amendments of 2008 on the same grounds, ruling that the journalists, lawyers, and human rights activists complaining that their overseas communications were vulnerable to monitoring failed to prove they were victims of actual surveillance. *Clapper v. Amnesty International USA*, 133 S. Ct. 1138 (2013).

President Bush's assertions of virtually unlimited executive authority to detain "enemy combatants" incommunicado until the "war on terror" ends were consistently rejected by the Supreme Court. Yasar Hamdi was seized during military operations in Afghanistan in the fall of 2001 while allegedly serving with the Taliban, and he was held in military confinement in Virginia. A challenge to his indefinite detention was heard by the Supreme Court in *Hamdi v. Rumsfeld*, 542 U.S. 507 (2004). The Court balanced the government's wartime interest in detaining combatants against their due process rights and concluded that they must be given a "meaningful opportunity" to contest the factual basis for their confinement before a neutral decision maker. In one of her last opinions for the Court, Sandra Day O'Connor reiterated that "a state of war is not a blank check for the President when it comes to the rights of the Nation's citizens."

Hamdan v. Rumsfeld, 548 U.S. 557 (2006), followed, ruling that the President had overstepped his authority in ordering military tribunals for suspected terrorists at Guantanamo Bay. Congress responded with the Military Commission Act of 2006, specifically authorizing such tribunals to try enemy combatants, but this drew another rebuke in *Boumediene v. Bush*, 128 S. Ct. 2229 (2008), holding that the section of the Act that denied detainees the right to petition the federal court for habeas corpus was unconstitutional.

Nonetheless, robust exercise of executive prerogatives has continued under the Obama Administration, which claims (without any apparent precedent) the authority to use drones to kill anyone, including U.S. citizens, on foreign soil on the mere determination by the Chief Executive that he or she is involved in terrorist activities. Disclosure of the so-called kill list of targets generated little outcry, although the family of its first victims unsuccessfully litigated the legality of the President's power to act as prosecutor, jury, and executioner.

The Supreme Court, no doubt influenced by the events of 9/11, has taken an expansive view of the statute (18 U.S.C.S. § 2339B) making it a criminal offense to provide "material support" to a foreign terrorist organization. *Holder v. Humanitarian Law Project,* 130 S. Ct. 2705 (2010) held that embraced within the prohibition is support even of a benign nature, such as training members of the group on how to use humanitarian and international law to resolve disputes peacefully. Numerous successful prosecutions have followed, usually involving government informants who at times come perilously close to entrapping the defendants. See, e.g., *United States v. Al Kassar*, 660 F.3d 108 (2d Cir. 2011) ("It is uncontested that the government originated the illegal arms deal and induced the defendants' participation with money and political ideology. However, it cannot be said as a matter of law that the defendants lacked a predisposition to conspire to illegally sell arms to known terrorists." 660 F.3d at 119.)

In 2011, President Barack Obama signed a four-year extension of three key provisions of the USA PATRIOT Act, facilitating roving wiretaps, searches of business records (the "library records provision"), and surveillance of "lone wolves" (individuals who are suspected of terrorist-related activities but not directly linked to terrorist groups). But public and congressional support began to erode in 2013 with whistleblower Edward Snowden's revelations of the "Orwellian" nature of the massive data collection programs conducted by the NSA, as well as several previously secret rulings of the FISA court authorizing the programs.

The USA Freedom Act, enacted in June 2015, imposed some limits on bulk collection of telecommunication metadata on U.S. citizens, particularly by the transferring of this task from NSA to private phone companies, with the government having to seek access to specific data more narrowly on a showing of reasonable suspicion that the records are relevant to an international terrorism investigation. The Act made the FISA court somewhat more transparent by requiring publication of summaries of recurring issues, and it created the role of a special advocate who could appear and contest government applications for surveillance in novel cases.

The Act has been characterized as a weak compromise, and the debate between privacy and security continues.

The events of 9/11 have also brought racial and ethnic profiling to the fore in public discussion. Should airport security procedures be permitted to single out passengers of Arabic descent, or Muslims, or people who appear to be? Is this constitutional? Would such profiling even be effective? What about using biometric identification measures, such as digital fingerprinting, on all non-U.S. citizens entering the United States (unless they are from an exempted nation)? How about cross-checking the usual identification information with a number of databases, including credit and criminal records?

The 2016 Presidential campaign of Donald Trump stoked fears about Islamic terrorism, and led to the new President's January 2017 travel ban excluding refugees from Muslim nations, and creating chaos at the nation's airports. Successfully challenged in the lower courts as unlawful religious discrimination, a revised Executive Order was ultimately upheld by the Supreme Court in a 5-4 decision, *Trump v. Hawaii*, 138 S. Ct. 2392 (2018).

The following imaginary roundtable discussion highlights some of the complexities of the post-9/11 world.

Retired Military Veteran Who Heads His American Legion Chapter: One of the smartest moves we ever made was to round up Japanese-Americans on the West Coast after the attack on Pearl Harbor and keep them secure during the remainder of the war with Japan. Since every one of the 19 terrorists on 9/11 was Arab, why can't we do the same thing now to protect ourselves? I'm tired of hearing the liberals whining about this so-called racial profiling. That is why I voted for Donald Trump — he will make America great again.

Law Professor: Surely you are not suggesting that we detain 3 million Arab-American citizens. And how can you applaud the Japanese internment when there was *not one instance* of sabotage or espionage ever attributed to an American of Japanese ancestry? The government's bogus justification for the forced relocation and internment of 110,000 citizens has long since been totally discredited, and the entire tragic episode (together with the Supreme Court's inexcusable *Korematsu* decision upholding it,

323 U.S. 214 (1944)) ranks as one of the darkest chapters in our nation's history. Congress even authorized compensation payments to the surviving victims in the 1990s. I can't think of a better argument *against* profiling than that sorry experience during the 1940s. But now we have a travel ban clearly based on religious criteria, and greenlighted by the Supreme Court. We've obviously learned nothing from our past mistakes.

Newspaper Columnist: Let's not forget that terrorists come in *all* ethnic varieties. Should we have profiled white male military veterans after Timothy McVeigh blew up the federal building in Oklahoma City?

Retired Military Veteran: This liberal hogwash is driving me to drink, which is not a bad idea given the terrorism crisis we're facing. The reality is that many in the Muslim world want to harm us, and *can*, with weapons of mass destruction that can be easily smuggled in. It's bad enough we let murderers and drug dealers off on technicalities when the cops screw up, but we must be able to protect our homeland without interference from the "Bill of Rights" crowd. Didn't some wise man once say that the Constitution is not a suicide pact? We need to give our President all the power he needs to protect us.

Law Professor: It's become cliche now, but if we suspend our civil liberties to fight terrorism, then the terrorists have won without crashing another plane. We can't just become a police state and pretend we're fighting for our democratic way of life, can we? We're a nation of checks and balances, and even the President must act within the Constitution. Although the Trump Presidency has certainly tested our Constitution principles.

FBI Official: I have to agree with the professor here. 9/11 was an abysmal failure of our intelligence agencies. The clues were right there, and we even red-flagged several of the terrorists from the watch lists before they boarded the planes. We just didn't know what to do with the information staring us in the face. Now that we have better coordination of security with the PATRIOT Act and the Department of Homeland Security, we'll have a chance to stop the next attack in its tracks—I hope. Assuming the President reads and takes heed from our intelligence reports.

Law Professor: Let's turn to the PATRIOT Act, the centerpiece of the "war on terror" at home. Does it go too far toward the "Big Brother" government of George Orwell's 1984? And now, so many years after 9/11, and with the revelations by Edward Snowden of the massive collection of out most intimate personal data, isn't it time for us to rethink these extreme measures?

Newspaper Columnist: For me, that question is twofold. Would the PATRIOT Act, had it been in place before 9/11, have allowed us to detect the plot in time? That I'm afraid we'll never know. But we do know, certainly after

Snowden, that our private lives are open to scrutiny merely on some vague suspicion of involvement with foreign powers or terrorism. If we contribute to a foreign charity, we open ourselves to surveillance of our phone calls and e-mail, or even prosecution. That really scares me. The anti-Muslim travel ban and all the hate rhetoric—That's not the America I grew up in.

Retired Military Veteran: With all due respect, that's the whole point. None of us is living in the America we grew up in. That's what the terrorists have done to us.

FBI Official: Look, let's not overdramatize this. The PATRIOT Act is simple self-defense. If the terrorists are tipped off that they're under investigation, they're not about to wait around for us to catch up with them. So we skip the warrant and delay notice of the search. USA PATRIOT also brings electronic surveillance into the twenty-first century, permitting roving wiretaps because cell phones don't stay in one place like the rotary phones of our youth. These terrorists are sophisticated and trained to thwart surveillance by rapidly changing locations and communication devices. Now our agents can counter these techniques. And your supermarket and bank already know everything you've bought this year—why shouldn't our national security people have access to the same information?

Newspaper Columnist: You're assuming that the PATRIOT Act will only be used to combat *terrorists*, but it creates such a broad definition for the term "domestic terrorism" that the line between an ordinary criminal offense and an act of terrorism is hopelessly blurred. What's to stop federal agents from using the Act against a U.S. citizen who's running a methamphetamine lab, on the theory that it's a "deadly chemical production facility"?

Arab-American Representative: Let's not forget about the *real* victims of this so-called PATRIOT Act and the travel ban. I know people who were detained and denied access to a lawyer and the court system because of who they are, not what they've done! Their families couldn't even find out whether they were being held, let alone where! The PATRIOT Act allows indefinite detention based on the Attorney General's sole discretion and without meaningful judicial review. And then the heartless separation of young children from their parents at the southern border! How is this constitutional? How is this American? I haven't even mentioned the torture, the "enhanced interrogations," and the "extraordinary renditions" we now all know about.

Law Professor: Thank you all for your insights. Let me close by observing that the Framers were prophetic enough to write the notion of "reasonableness" into the Fourth Amendment. It's up to us—politicians, judges, the American public—to recalibrate the proper balance between security and liberty in the light of the threat of terrorism. But let's remember what Benjamin Franklin warned so many years ago: Those who are willing to sacrifice liberty for security deserve neither. Let me further point out that President Obama, a former law professor, has denounced harsh interrogation techniques, saying we "must reject the false choice between our security and our ideals"; yet he presumed to have the authority to order drone killings, even of American citizens, despite their highly questionable legality and morality, to say nothing of their use as a recruiting tool for the next generation of terrorists. The drone killings continue of course with the present Administration.

And so it goes—the conversation will continue.

---

§12.2 TERRORISM AND THE FOURTH AMENDMENT

The administrative search rationale (see § 4.5 of Chapter 4) provides hints for determining how the Fourth Amendment will apply to the "war on terror." The Supreme Court addressed this issue many years ago in *United States v. United States Dist. Court for E. Dist. of Mich., S. Div.*, 407 U.S. 297 (1972). Wiretaps were authorized by the Attorney General against U.S. citizens suspected of planning to bomb government property. A unanimous Court, balancing the government interest in national security against the intrusion into individuals' privacy, held that electronic surveillance in domestic security matters requires *prior judicial approval* through the warrant process. But in *City of Indianapolis v. Edmond*, 531 U.S. 32 (2000), in which the Court forbade traffic checkpoints for interdiction of illegal narcotics, it noted in *dicta* that a suspicionless roadblock would be permissible in order to "to thwart an imminent terrorist attack." Post-9/11, the latter may have become the controlling judicial mindset.

Examples

1. The U.S. Bureau of Customs and Border Patrol became concerned about the Palestinian Rights Conference taking place in Montreal, Canada, after an intelligence report indicated that persons with "terrorist ties" were in attendance. Attendees re-entering the United States at the border crossing in northern Vermont were subjected to fingerprinting, frisking, intense questioning, photographs, and a search of their cars. This process lasted approximately five hours for each subject. Was the Fourth Amendment violated?

2. The New York City police, in the aftermath of terrorist attacks in London and Madrid, implemented a search procedure for the city's subways. Signage advised persons entering the stations that they are subject to

a quick visual inspection of their containers—briefcases, knapsacks, etc.—and manipulation of items if the visual inspection should indicate something suspicious. The process generally lasts only a few seconds, and *everyone* is stopped. Is this consistent with the Fourth Amendment?

Explanations

1. "Routine" border searches, including frisks and inspections of clothing, luggage, wallets, pockets, or shoes, fit neatly into the administrative search rationale and do not require individualized justification. More intrusive procedures, such as strip searches or the one in *United States v. Montoya de Hernandez*, 473 U.S. 531 (1985) (see § 4.3), in which a balloon swallower suspected of smuggling narcotics was detained for over 16 hours and subjected to invasive medical procedures, require individualized suspicion. Note that the Supreme Court in *United States v. Flores-Montano*, 541 U.S. 149 (2004), characterized the dismantling of a gas tank as a routine border search that required no further justification.

   The facts of this example are based on *Tabbaa v. Chertoff*, 509 F.3d 89 (2d Cir. 2007), which upheld the searches of the conference attendees as "routine." The Second Circuit did indicate that the cumulative effect of such "routine" searches could reach the level of intrusion requiring specific cause, but it ruled that that was not the case here. Border searches of laptop computers have also been upheld, even without reasonable suspicion. See *United States v. Arnold*, 533 F.3d 1003 (9th Cir. 2008); and *U.S. v. Cotterman* 637 F.3d 1068 (9th Cir. 2011) (upholding a search of a laptop that began at the border and ended two days later in a forensic laboratory 170 miles away).

2. Given the potential for destruction of life and property in the tunnels underneath the city, the governmental interest here is weighty. On the other side of the balance, the intrusion on individuals is small because people are warned and can opt not to enter the subway, the process takes only a few seconds, and there is no discretion left to the police because everybody is stopped. This type of search was upheld in *MacWade v. Kelly*, 460 F.3d 260 (2d Cir. 2006). Similarly, the First Circuit refused to suppress the fruits of a search of a van parked in an unusual manner at a commuter rail and bus station in Charlestown, Massachusetts, shortly after the Madrid bombings. See *U.S. v. Ramos*, 629 F.3d 60 (1st Cir. 2010).

Checklist and Review Problems

Material in the previous chapters has of necessity been presented in a segmented fashion to permit the reader to explore the discrete issues involved in constitutional criminal procedure. Actual encounters between police and the citizen often raise a whole series of issues and may implicate more than one constitutional provision. It is the purpose of this section to "pull it all together" and demonstrate the interrelations between matters discussed in the text. We begin with a checklist, which is helpful in analyzing complex criminal procedure problems, and then we return to our "Examples and Explanations" format for a final review.

Checklist

Search and Seizure and Arrest

A. Does the Fourth Amendment apply?
   1. Is the conduct governmental (as opposed to private)?
   2. Has a reasonable expectation of privacy been violated or has there been some interference with property? See *Jones* §3.2. [If Yes on both, move ahead.]
B. Was the conduct justified?
   1. Identify the type of intrusion (for example, stop, arrest, frisk).
   2. Identify the level of justification required (for example, probable cause, reasonable suspicion, administrative).
C. Was a warrant required?
   1. For a search, did the conduct fall within an established exception to the warrant requirement? See E, below. If not, a warrant is required.

2. For an arrest, did the arrest occur in a home or in a public place? If the former, a warrant is required.
D. If a warrant was required, were the prerequisites for a valid warrant complied with?
    1. Was it issued by a neutral and detached magistrate?
    2. Was there probable cause supported by oath or affirmation?
    3. Did the warrant particularly describe the place to be searched and items to be seized?
E. If a warrant was not required, were the prerequisites for warrantless search and seizure complied with?
    1. Emergency exception
        a. Exigency
        b. Probable cause
    2. Search incident to arrest
        a. Lawful arrest (probable cause)
        b. Limited to reachable space
        c. Automobiles
    3. Automobile exception
        a. Mobile vehicle
        b. Probable cause
    4. Stop and frisk
        a. Reasonable suspicion to believe criminal activity is afoot
        b. Reasonable suspicion to believe subject is armed and dangerous
    5. Administrative and inventory searches
        a. Non-criminal purpose
        b. Limits on police discretion
    6. Consent
        a. Voluntary
        b. If third-party, proper authority (actual or apparent)?
        c. Was the target of the search present?
    7. Plain view doctrine
        a. Lawful intrusion
        b. Item immediately apparent as contraband or evidence
F. If a constitutional violation occurred, does the exclusionary rule apply?
    1. Does the subject have standing?
    2. Is the proceeding a criminal trial or other proceeding in which the rule applies?
    3. Did the officers act in reasonable reliance upon a warrant (or otherwise act in good faith)?
    4. Is the evidence offered solely for impeachment?
G. Does the derivative evidence doctrine apply?
    1. Is the item the fruit of the poisonous tree (but-for causation)?
    2. If so, does one of the exceptions apply?
        a. Did the taint become attenuated?
        b. Was there an independent source?
        c. Would the item have been discovered inevitably?

Interrogation and Confessions

A. Was the confession obtained in violation of the Due Process Clause?
   1. Was the confession involuntary under totality-of-the-circumstances analysis?
   2. Was the confession the product of coercive police conduct?
B. Was the confession obtained in violation of the *Miranda* doctrine?
   1. Was it obtained during custodial interrogation?
      a. Custody
      b. Interrogation (or its functional equivalent) [If Yes on both, go ahead.]
   2. Were adequate warnings provided?
   3. Was there a valid waiver?
      a. Knowing and intelligent
      b. Voluntary
   4. Did the suspect invoke the right to silence or to counsel?
      a. If right to silence, was the right scrupulously honored?
      b. If right to counsel, did the suspect initiate further communication?
   5. Does either of the exceptions apply?
      a. Public safety
      b. Impeachment
   6. Does the derivative evidence doctrine apply?
C. Was the confession obtained in violation of the Sixth Amendment *Massiah* doctrine?
   1. Deliberate elicitation
   2. Following the initiation of adversary criminal proceedings
   3. Waiver

Examples

Search & Seizure

1. Sarge's Sporting Goods, concerned about shoplifting, has hired security guards to patrol the store and installed video cameras in areas not open to public view, including the three small dressing rooms in which customers try on clothes. Signs in the store advise customers: "Shoplifters are prosecuted to the full extent of the law."

   While monitoring the video, security guard Karp observed a male customer enter a dressing room, shut the curtain, and begin pouring a white powder into a rolled dollar bill. Karp immediately telephoned the state police headquarters and reported her observations. Trooper Trout advised her: "It sounds like coke. You keep watching him until we can get there. Don't let him go!" Karp continued to monitor the dressing room area and saw the customer sniffing the white powder.

   When the state police arrived moments later, the customer was just leaving the dressing room. Trooper Trout grabbed the customer and proceeded to search his pockets, finding a vial of white powder (later determined to be cocaine). Trout took his closed backpack and informed him that he was under arrest. The suspect (later identified as Drew) was then taken to police headquarters and booked. Trout opened Drew's backpack and found a notebook that contained a list of names, addresses, and dates of delivery.

Trout reviewed the list and recognized the name of Kevin Crack, who had been previously identified by a reliable informant as running a narcotics ring in the area. Including all this information in a sworn affidavit, the trooper applied for and was issued a warrant to search Crack's home "for any and all items related to narcotics trafficking."

State police officers executed the warrant four days after it was issued and discovered large amounts of cocaine, as well as scales and packaging materials used to distribute the substance. They also seized several weapons found in a closet in the basement. As the officers were leaving Crack's home, he pulled up in his Jeep, but when he saw the police, he gunned the vehicle in reverse and attempted to flee. The officers gave chase and pulled him over. Upon approaching the vehicle, they smelled marijuana, and Crack was placed under arrest. The officers searched the Jeep and found marijuana in the glove compartment.

At the upcoming trial of Drew and Crack for conspiracy to distribute narcotics, the prosecution proposes to use all the items seized, as well as the testimony of the security guard against the defendants. Based on your Fourth Amendment analysis, what evidence is admissible against each defendant?

Interrogation and Confessions

2. Junior, a 17-year-old high school dropout, is a suspect in a series of burglaries in the Oak Square area. Uniformed officers Mutt and Jeff proceeded to his home, where they found him alone. The officers stated that they wanted to ask him some questions, and Junior responded that his parents were not at home and he did not want to talk to the officers until they returned. The officers asked if they could wait inside, and Junior agreed.

While the three were seated in the living room, Mutt said to Jeff: "Somebody is going to do some jail time for these break-ins, and I'd hate to see this poor kid take the fall." Junior's face dropped, and he began to sweat profusely. He agonized for several moments with a pained expression on his face, and then blurted out: "I guess I've got no choice. Let me tell you about these break-ins." Junior proceeded to implicate himself in the burglary ring.

Will Junior's statement be admissible against him at trial?

3. Assume the same facts as in example 2, except that immediately after Junior's face dropped and he began sweating, Officer Mutt advised him of his *Miranda* rights. Junior responded that he wanted to talk to his parents before he said anything. Officer Jeff stated: "Look, kid, we don't have to involve your folks in this mess. Just tell us about these break-ins and we'll see to it that you get off as easily as possible."

Junior then made the confession set out in example 2. Will it be admissible against him at trial?

The Whole Nine Yards

4. Nell Nigel parked her Saab Turbo in front of the bank and left her infant, Charlie, in the backseat while she quickly ran in to cash a check. When she returned, the car was gone. She frantically asked a teenager standing nearby if he had seen who had driven away in the car, and the boy responded that "an old guy in red suspenders was hanging around the car, but I didn't see if he got in." Nell telephoned the police and reported the boy's statement. Officers arrived on the scene but were unable to determine the whereabouts of the Saab and infant.

Six hours later, an anonymous caller told the desk sergeant at police headquarters that an old man sitting on a park bench near Duck Pond had just "ripped off a neat car but found a surprise inside." Officers proceeded immediately to the pond and found an elderly man on the bench. As they approached him, the officers noticed that he was wearing red suspenders. While his partner pointed his revolver at the man, Officer Booth asked him to identify himself and he responded that he was Sam Soap. "Okay, Soap, you better tell us where the baby is before you get into some real trouble," yelled Officer Booth. Soap responded, "How was I supposed to know the brat was in the car when I took it?" Booth asked, "Where's the baby now?" Soap answered that the infant was at his apartment on Elm Street, but that he didn't know if he was still alive.

The officers grabbed Soap and sped in their cruiser to the apartment. When Soap refused to open the door for them, the officers broke it down. Inside they found Charlie, who was very cranky but otherwise O.K. The officers took the baby and Soap to the police station, where Soap was advised of his *Miranda* rights and Charlie was reunited with his relieved mother. Officer Booth learned that two other patrol officers had just been sent to Soap's apartment in response to a neighbor's call that an infant had been crying loudly all day.

Soap was taken into an interrogation room by Officer Booth and asked if he was ready to talk. Soap responded that he wanted a lawyer. Booth stated, "That's your business, but it's going to really slow things down." Soap was taken to a cell. An hour later, Soap asked the guard if they had found an attorney for him yet. The guard summoned Booth, and when he arrived at Soap's cell, the suspect stated, "How much longer is it going to take to get me a lawyer?" Booth responded: "Why don't we just talk this thing through now?" Appearing dejected and distraught, Soap said, "Yeah, all right," and proceeded to confess to the theft of the Saab and the taking of the infant. Based on his statement, the officers located the car on the outskirts of town; Soap's fingerprints were found on the steering wheel.

Which of the following would be admissible against Soap at trial: His statement at Duck Pond? His statement in the jail cell? The discovery of Charlie in Soap's apartment? The discovery of the Saab and Soap's fingerprints on the steering wheel?

Explanations

Search & Seizure

1. The threshold question with regard to Drew is whether the Fourth Amendment is applicable at all. This depends on whether there is both a) governmental action (see §3.1) and b) violation of his reasonable expectation of privacy (see §3.2).

   In the case of the initial encounter with Drew, it was a *private* security guard who made the observations on the video monitor. Private security personnel are generally not regarded as governmental actors for purposes of the Fourth Amendment. The state police, however, soon entered the picture. Trooper Trout advised (indeed ordered) the security guard to continue monitoring Drew and to hold him until the police arrived. Given this governmental involvement, the requirement for public action is met.

   The Fourth Amendment applies to the monitoring of the dressing room only if it constitutes a "search." Did Drew have a "reasonable expectation of privacy" when he closed the curtain of the dressing room? Although there were signs warning customers of the strict enforcement of shoplifting laws, a court could certainly rule that society recognizes a legitimate expectation of privacy in a closed dressing room.

   If so, what does the Amendment require in this context? The crux of the protection against unreasonable search and seizure is the requirement for justification before a search is conducted. Given the nature of the circumstances, the exigency exception would probably apply to excuse the absence of a warrant. See §6.2. The observations occurring before the conduct became "governmental" might provide adequate justification for the monitoring that followed after the conversation with the trooper.

If there was not sufficient justification for the continued monitoring, however, that search would be in violation of the Fourth Amendment, and the observations of the guard would be subject to suppression. That which followed would be analyzed under the derivative evidence doctrine. See §7.2. It would have to be determined if the notebook found in Drew's backpack was sufficiently attenuated from the illegal monitoring so that the taint had dissipated. With regard to the search of Crack's home, we would have to determine whether the evidence seized was obtained from an independent source (the reliable informant) or would have inevitably been discovered in the usual course of events (as a result of the informant's tip). (For each subsequent unlawful action that occurs in our example, the derivative evidence "ripple effect" consequences must be similarly explored.)

Assuming that Karp's initial observations provided sufficient justification for the continued monitoring, the additional observations of Drew using the cocaine would constitute probable cause for arrest. See §4.1. A lawful arrest in a public place may be effected without a warrant if the officers have probable cause to believe the subject has committed or is committing a crime. See §5.5. The search of Drew's pockets (yielding the vial of cocaine) was within the proper scope of a search incident to an arrest. Note that although the search preceded announcement of the formal arrest, the existence of probable cause prior to the search probably makes it lawful. See *Rawlings v. Kentucky*, 448 U.S. 98 (1980). The opening of Drew's backpack at the police station, however, could not be justified as a search incident because it was not contemporaneous with the arrest. See §6.3.

The warrantless search of the backpack might be justified as an inventory search if it was conducted pursuant to established procedures. See §6.6. A suspicionless inspection of this kind is permitted because its purpose is administrative and not the collection of evidence. Assuming that there was no procedure for an inventory search, a search of this container would require a warrant.

This takes us to the warrant to search Crack's home. Drew could argue that the events (in the dressing room) leading up to the application for the warrant violated his Fourth Amendment rights, and that because information obtained was used to secure the warrant, it is tainted, and the items seized pursuant to the warrant could not be used in evidence against him. (Crack, of course, would have no standing to complain about these actions against Drew and thus could not challenge the warrant on those grounds. See §7.3.1.) The derivative evidence question is complicated by the fact that in obtaining the warrant the police also relied on information from an independent source, the informant. If this other information was itself sufficient to constitute probable cause, then the warrant would be valid and the evidence seized could be used at trial.

In any event, the warrant could be lawfully issued only if the affidavit established probable cause to believe seizable items would be found at Crack's home. See §§4.1 and 5.2. This requires us to analyze the reliability of the informant's tip that Crack was involved in a narcotics ring. Was there sufficient information set out from which the magistrate could reasonably conclude that (1) the informant was credible and (2) his conclusions had a solid basis in fact? On the first point, we would need to know the informant's track record, and on the second point, we would need to know on what his conclusions were based. In the absence of specific details, probable cause might be lacking even under the flexible *Illinois v. Gates* totality-of-the-circumstances standard: whether there is a "fair probability" that contraband or evidence of crime will be found in the place to be searched. The tip would have to be weighed together with the corroborating information developed by the police.

A "staleness" issue is also raised because the warrant was not executed until four days after its issuance. See §4.1. Given that the information known to the police concerns an ongoing narcotics operation, this short delay is likely not to affect the existence of probable cause.

In addition to the probable cause requirement, a warrant must particularly describe the place to be searched and the items to be seized. See §5.2.3. An issue is raised here as to whether "any and all items related to narcotics trafficking" satisfies the latter requirement. The goal of limiting police discretion at the scene of the search appears to be jeopardized by the open-ended nature of this description.

Even if there are problems with the warrant as to probable cause or particularity, the evidence seized may nonetheless be admissible because of the "good faith" exception to the exclusionary rule. We would have to address the issue of whether the officers acted "reasonably" in relying on the warrant. See §7.3.3.

While the seizure of scales and packaging materials together with the narcotics was authorized by the warrant, weapons found in the closet were also seized. The lawfulness of this seizure would depend on the applicability of the plain view doctrine. See §6.8.

Because (1) the items were found while the officers were lawfully on the premises and searching within the proper confines of a search for narcotics, and (2) the items were immediately apparent as either contraband or evidence of crime, they could lawfully be seized.

Finally, the stop of Crack's car as he was fleeing was probably justified by reasonable suspicion, given all the information known to the officers at the time. See §§4.2-4.4. The detection of the odor of marijuana likely provided probable cause both to arrest him and to search his Jeep for items related to narcotics activity under the automobile exception. See §6.4. Because the search was limited to the interior of the vehicle, it could also be justified under the search incident to an arrest exception, as the officers could reasonably conclude that evidence related to the arrest might be found in the vehicle. See §6.3.

Interrogation and Confessions

2. In answering this question, we must keep in mind the three overlapping constitutional approaches to interrogation and confessions: due process voluntariness, *Miranda*, and *Massiah*.

First, a statement that is the product of coercive police action and not the voluntary choice of the suspect is inadmissible for all purposes under the Due Process Clause of the Fifth and Fourteenth Amendments. See Chapter 8. The officers' conduct with regard to Junior was arguably coercive, but probably not sufficiently so to satisfy the threshold requirement of *Colorado v. Connelly*. If coercion is found, we would have to determine whether it overcame Junior's free will sufficiently to compel his statement. We would apply the totality-of-the-circumstances approach, weighing Junior's vulnerabilities (lack of education, tender age) and the circumstances of the interrogation (absence of parents, confrontation with two police officers).

Second, if Junior was subjected to custodial interrogation, he was entitled to the *Miranda* protections. Because he received no warnings, the statement would be inadmissible (except to impeach his testimony if he took the stand; see §9.3.2). See Chapter 9.

Was Junior in "custody"? Even though he was not under arrest or in the police station, he may nonetheless be deemed in custody if a reasonable person in his situation would have believed himself not free to leave, considering the atmosphere of the encounter. Because the incident took place in his home, however, this setting might not be the type of incommunicado atmosphere that *Miranda* had in mind. See §9.2.1. Next question: Was Junior subjected to "interrogation"? Even though there was no formal questioning, if the conduct of the officers was the functional equivalent of interrogation, then *Miranda* is triggered. See §9.2.2. The inquiry is whether the words or actions of the police were such that they should have reasonably foreseen the likelihood of eliciting an incriminating response. Here we must take into account the limitations and susceptibilities of Junior that were known to the officers at the time.

Third, the *Massiah* doctrine renders statements inadmissible when they are deliberately elicited from the suspect in the absence of counsel, provided that the Sixth Amendment right to counsel has kicked in. Because this occurs only when adversary judicial proceedings have been initiated, Junior could not invoke *Massiah*. See Chapter 10. If this encounter had occurred subsequent to a grand jury indictment or to an arraignment following arrest, then the actions of the police would be scrutinized to determine whether the police had intentionally elicited his statement.

3. Assuming that Junior was subjected to custodial interrogation (the direct question asked here clearly constitutes interrogation), the issue becomes one of waiver. We begin the analysis, however, with the question of whether Junior invoked either his right to silence or to counsel when he responded that he wanted to talk to his parents before saying anything to the police. The Court has held that such a request has to be unambiguous, although Junior's age may enter determination of this issue. See §9.2.5. If this amounted to an exercise of the right to silence, then interrogation should have been terminated, and resumed only after Junior's rights had been scrupulously honored. If it was a request for counsel, then interrogation should have been terminated until either Junior was provided counsel or he initiated further conversation himself.

Junior's confession could be admitted only after the prosecution established that he made a knowing, intelligent, and voluntary waiver. See §9.2.4. This showing would be problematic because of Junior's age and lack of education. Moreover, the officer's inducement ("we'll see to it that you get off as easily as possible") may undercut the voluntariness of the waiver and may even constitute sufficient coercion to implicate due process concerns. See Chapter 8.

The Whole Nine Yards

4. We must identify the possible violations of constitutional rights and then trace the ripple effects of each through the exclusionary rule.

Beginning with the initial encounter at Duck Pond, did a seizure occur that triggers the Fourth Amendment and thus requires justification? While not all street encounters constitute seizures, Soap arguably was subjected to one when the officers asked him to identify himself at gunpoint. The test for seizure is whether a reasonable person under the circumstances would have believed himself free to leave. See §4.3. If this confrontation amounted to a "stop," it had to be justified by reasonable suspicion that Soap was involved in criminal activity. While this requires a particularized and reliable basis in fact, the statement of the teenager at the crime scene, together with the anonymous call, probably suffice to justify the brief detention. See §4.2. If not, however, the stop was unlawful and the statement made by Soap would be inadmissible as a direct result.

The confrontation with Soap in which the officer pointed his revolver at him arguably constituted a detention equivalent to a full arrest. See §4.3. If so, probable cause would be required. See §4.1. Although *Illinois v. Gates* has established a flexible standard, on the facts here, it is unlikely that probable cause to arrest existed.

How far would the taint of the unlawful stop (or arrest) extend? Arguably, the discovery of the baby should be suppressed because it was achieved by exploiting Soap's statement directing the officers to his apartment. See §7.2. On the other hand, the entry into the apartment was somewhat removed from the initial stop (separated by time and by Soap's statement), so it could be said that the taint had dissipated. Moreover, there is an argument that the infant would have inevitably been discovered by the officers sent in response to the neighbor's call.

If the encounter at Duck Pond amounted to custodial interrogation, then Soap's statement (and to a limited extent, the fruits of that statement; see §9.3.3) would be subject to suppression on *Miranda* grounds. There was "interrogation" when Officer Booth directed at Soap two questions that did not constitute routine on-the-scene fact-gathering. See §9.2.2. Moreover, the simultaneous pointing of the gun at the suspect may have put him in "custody." See §9.2.1. In the absence of the warnings, his statement would presumptively be inadmissible. But it is arguable that the public safety exception should apply because of the compelling need to find the missing infant as quickly as possible. See §9.3.1. When the officers sped off in the cruiser with Soap, he was clearly under arrest, a situation requiring probable cause. See §4.1. Given all the information known to them at that time (including Soap's incriminatory statement), that standard was probably met. It would also appear that the police had probable cause to search his home for the missing boy. Entry into a home (without consent) generally requires a warrant, but this scenario is an excellent candidate for application of the emergency exception. See §6.2. The discovery of Charlie thus does not appear to have been the result of an unlawful search. But note that it may have been the *indirect result* of an earlier illegality (that is, the stop) and thus subject to suppression under the derivative evidence doctrine.

At the station house, Soap clearly invoked his right to counsel following *Miranda* warnings. The question thus becomes whether the subsequent questioning in the jail cell was proper. Once the right to counsel is invoked, the suspect may not be interrogated until counsel is provided or the suspect himself initiates further communication. See §9.2.5. Did Soap initiate further communication when he inquired as to the appointment of counsel? Although the Court has adopted a broad definition of "initiation" (including Bradshaw's "What is going to happen to me now?"), Soap's inquiry here underscored his desire to have the advice of counsel and should not be interpreted as license to resume questioning. His confession should therefore be suppressed (although it may be introduced for impeachment if he takes the stand; see §9.3.2).

The discovery of the Saab resulted from the information provided in the confession, raising the issue as to whether it must be suppressed together with the fingerprint evidence. Even if his statement is found to be in violation of *Miranda*, the indirect fruits of that statement are not necessarily inadmissible. See §9.3.3. The situation would be different if it were determined that Soap's jail cell confession was the involuntary product of police coercion. It is arguable that Officer Booth's treatment of the elderly suspect constituted coercive conduct that played upon his vulnerable condition, in which case his confession (and its fruits) would be inadmissible for all purposes. See Chapter 8. A finding of a due process violation in these circumstances, however, is unlikely.

If there were indications that the Saab would have been discovered anyway (for example, it was abandoned in an illegal parking space), the inevitable discovery exception to the derivative evidence doctrine might apply. Assuming that the Saab is not deemed the fruit of the poisonous tree, the search of the Saab and the discovery of the fingerprints would likely be lawful because the officers had information constituting probable cause to search the vehicle. The automobile exception to the warrant requirement would thus apply. See §6.4.

Table of Cases

1975 Chevrolet v. Texas, 117
$109,179 in U.S. Currency, United States v., 40
$124,570 in U.S. Currency, United States v., 111, 112

Abdul-Saboor, United States v., 161
Abie State Bank v. Weaver, 6
Adams v. Williams, 65, 72, 92, 93
Adekunle, United States v., 353
Adjani, United States v., 366
A.G. Edwards, Inc. v. Secretary of State, 41
Agapito, United States v., 37
Aguilar v. Texas, 48, 49, 50, 55, 57, 58, 59, 60
A Juvenile, Commonwealth v., 260
Alabama v. O'Guinn, 290
Alabama v. White, 72, 73, 93
Albert, United States v., 240
Alexander, United States v. (540 F.3d 494), 214
Alexander, United States v. (761 F.2d 1294), 126
Alfonso A., Commonwealth v., 260, 301
Alfred v. State, 352
Al Kassar, United States v., 370
Allen, United States v., 215, 280
Almeida-Sanchez v. United States, 105
Al Nasser, United States v., 224
Alverez, United States v., 145, 169, 183
Amendola, Commonwealth v., 216
American Civil Liberties Union v. National Sec. Agency (438 F. Supp. 2d 754), 369
American Civil Liberties Union v. National Sec. Agency (493 F.3d 644), 369
Amuny, United States v., 63, 64
Anderson, Commonwealth v., 114
Anderson, United States v. (114 F.3d 1059), 183
Anderson, United States v. (154 F.3d 1225), 152, 222
Andresen v. Maryland, 69, 131
Andrus, United States v., 366
Aquino, United States v., 152
Arenal, United States v., 125
Arias, United States v., 153
Arizona v. Evans, 234, 237, 242
Arizona v. Fulminante, 245, 251

Arizona v. Gant, 157, 160, 162, 163, 167, 191, 234
Arizona v. Hicks, 40, 186, 188
Arizona v. Johnson, 79, 224
Arizona v. Mauro, 275, 279, 282, 331
Arizona v. Roberson, 306
Arizona v. United States, 76, 78, 79, 97
Arkansas v. Sanders, 170
Arkansas v. Sullivan, 50, 191
Armstrong, United States v. (187 F.3d 392), 230
Armstrong, United States v. (517 U.S. 456), 192
Arnold, United States v., 366, 375
Arvizu, United States v., 66, 72, 190
Ash, United States v., 343, 348
Ashcraft v. Tennessee, 251
Atchley, State v., 50
Atwater v. City of Lago Vista, 156, 157, 191, 354
Axsom, United States v., 272
Ayers v. Hudson, 331

Bacon, Commonwealth v., 90
Badmus, United States v., 272
Bailey v. Newland, 147
Balduc, State v., 235
Balicki, Commonwealth v., 189
Banks, United States v., 136
Barber, United States v., 223
Barone, United States v., 124
Basinski, United States v., 180
Bates, United States v., 136
B.C. v. Plumas Unified Sch. Dist., 40
Beale, United States v., 40
Beaty v. Stewart, 337
Beck v. Bowersox, 336
Beckwith v. United States, 265, 272
Bedford, United States v., 130
Beene, United States v., 34
Bejasa, People v., 351
Beltran, United States v., 153
Bennett, United States v., 162
Berghuis v. Thompkins, 293, 298, 303
Berkemer v. McCarthy, 266, 269

Berry, United States v., 87
Berryman, United States v., 85, 86
Betters, United States v., 299
Beverly, United States v., 356
Bey, State v., 337
Birbal, United States v., 337
Birchfield v. North Dakota, 158, 176
Bishop, People v., 181
Bishop, United States v., 60
Biswell, United States v., 105, 171
Bivens v. Six Unknown Named Agents of the
    Fed. Bureau of Narcotics, 4
Black, United States v., 49, 99
Blackstock, State v., 300
Blair, People v., 41
Blais, Commonwealth v., 350
Blood, Commonwealth v., 26
Blue v. State of Alaska, 343
Board of Educ. v. Earls, 105, 118
Boatright, State v., 235
Bond v. United States, 28
Bonner, United States v., 66
Booker, United States v., 21
Borges, Commonwealth v., 98
Boskic, United States v., 254
Boumediene v. Bush, 370
Boyd, State v., 179
Bradley v. Meachum, 313
Brady, United States v., 322
Braggs, People v., 300
Bram v. United States, 255
Brendlin v. California, 217, 224
Brewer v. Williams, 330
Bridgers v. Texas, 290
Brigham City, Utah v. Stuart, 105, 146
Brignoni-Ponce, United States v., 3, 105
Brock, United States v., 40
Brosseau v. Haugen, 351
Brower v. County of Inyo, 87
Brown v. Crosby, 300
Brown v. Illinois, 207, 208
Brown v. Mississippi, 249
Brown v. Texas, 65, 88, 97
Brown, United States v. (920 F.2d 1212), 353
Brown, United States v. (961 F.2d 1039), 182
Brown, United States v. (984 F.2d 1074), 131
Bryson, State v., 95
Bumpers, United States v., 63
Bumper v. North Carolina, 174
Burdeau v. McDowell, 17
Burnette, United States v., 269

Burns v. Commonwealth, 115
Burrell, State v., 300
Burrows v. Superior Court, 26, 41
Bustamante, People v., 343
Bynum, United States v., 238
Byrd v. United States, 218, 225

Calandra, United States v., 227
Caldwell, United States v., 162
California v. Acevedo, 12, 144, 165, 168, 169
California v. Beheler, 265, 271
California v. Carney, 166
California v. Ciraolo, 28, 35, 38
California v. Greenwood, 23, 25, 39, 364
California v. Hodari D., 74, 88, 269
California v. Prysock, 287
Calisto, United States v., 281
Camara v. Municipal Court, 103, 104, 111,
    113, 115, 137, 170
Campaneria v. Reid, 313
Capozzi, United States v., 239
Cardenas-Alvarez, State v., 7
Carey, United States v., 363, 365
Carpenter v. United States, 23, 25, 30, 44
Carrillo, State v., 254, 322
Carrillo, United States v., 322
Carroll v. United States, 165
Carter, United States v., 169
Ceballos, United States v., 99, 100
Ceccolini, United States v., 200, 201,
    209, 210
Chacon, United States v., 77
Chadwick, United States v., 155, 160, 170
Chambers v. Lockhart, 289
Chambers v. Maroney, 165
Chandler v. Miller, 106
Chang, United States v., 180
Channing, People v., 37
Chapman, United States v., 163
Chapman v. California, 244
Charles v. Smith, 310
Charnes v. DiGiacomo, 41
Chavez v. Martinez, 264, 327
Chimel v. California, 12, 154, 155, 157,
    160, 162
Choate, United States v., 41
Chrisicos, State v., 292
Christy, United States v., 212
Cintron, United States v., 20
Claeys, People v., 36
Clapper v. Amnesty Int'l USA, 369

Clark, United States v. (29 F. Supp. 3d 1131), 243
Clark, United States v. (31 F.3d 831), 126
Clayton v. State, 90
Cleaveland, United States v., 43
Coffman, United States v., 183
Cohen, United States v., 31
Colbert, United States v., 164
Coleman, United States v., 256, 259
Coleman v. United States, 136
Collins v. Gaetz, 300
Collins v. Virginia, 166
Colonade Catering Corps. v. United States, 171
Colondres, Commonwealth v., 137
Colonna, United States v., 271
Colorado v. Bertine, 104, 105, 116, 117, 172, 192, 193
Colorado v. Connelly, 250, 251, 253-255, 257-259, 292, 294, 298, 299, 300, 383
Colorado v. Pollock, 28
Colorado v. Spring, 294
Colyer, United States v., 30
Combs v. Coyle, 270
Commonwealth v. *See name of opposing party*
Comprehensive Drug Testing Inc., United States v., 365
Conley, United States v., 280
Connally v. Georgia, 123
Connecticut v. Barrett, 294, 297, 298
Connell, United States v., 289
Conrad v. State, 36
Cook, United States v., 125
Cooke, State v., 7
Cook v. State, 282
Coolidge v. New Hampshire, 35, 122, 134, 189
Coomer v. Yukins, 270
Cooper, United States v., 225
Cooper v. State, 181
Copeland, United States v., 60
Cortez, United States v., 55, 72, 93
Cote, Commonwealth v., 24
Cotterman, United States v., 375
Couture, Commonwealth v., 67
Covert v. State, 114
Crane, State v., 26
Crews, United States v., 209, 299
Cristobal, United States v., 254, 259, 299
Crowley, United States v., 21
Crozier, United States v., 126
Cruz v. Miller, 270

Cuervelo, United States v., 360
Cupp v. Murphy, 26, 349
Curd v. City Court of Judsonia, Ark., 154
Curry, United States v., 241
Curtis, United States v., 211

Dassey v. Dittmann, 254
Davis v. Mississippi, 26, 342
Davis v. North Carolina, 5, 234
Davis v. State, 181
Davis v. United States (131 S. Ct. 2419), 243
Davis v. United States (512 U.S. 452), 305, 312-313, 315
Davis, United States v. (170 F. Supp. 2d 1234), 147
Davis, United States v. (313 F.3d 1300), 147
Davis, United States v. (326 F.3d 361), 24
Davis, United States v. (458 F.2d 819), 65
Davis, United States v. (482 F.2d 893), 112
Dawdy, United States v., 64
Debooy, State v., 114
Defore, People v., 4
Dejohn, Commonwealth v., 41
Delaware v. Prouse, 75, 79, 89, 113
De Leon-Reyna, United States v., 242
Delgado, INS v., 88
DeLuna, United States v., 122, 126
DePugh v. Penning, 222
Devlin, State v., 352
Dewey v. State, 310
Diamond, State v., 351
Diaz-Castaneda, United States v., 42
DiCesare, United States v., 133
Dickerson, United States v. (166 F.3d 667), 263
Dickerson v. United States (530 U.S. 428), 252, 255, 264, 292, 316, 317, 320, 326
Dionisio, United States v., 26, 342
Dire, United States v., 298
Dispensa v. Lynaugh, 347
District Attorney's Office v. Osborne, 120
District of Columbia v. Wesby, 47, 66
Doe, United States v., 283
Domitrovich, United States v., 36
Donovan v. Dewey, 105, 171
Dow Chem. Co. v. United States, 29, 38
Doyle v. Ohio, 318
Draper v. United States, 48, 49, 55-57, 61
Drayton, United States v., 75, 175, 184
Duarte, State v., 114
Duckworth v. Eagan, 287, 290, 291

Dunaway v. New York, 76
Duncan v. Louisiana, 3
Dunkins v. Thigpen, 300
Dunn, United States v., 27, 29, 34, 36, 37

Earls, State v., 7
Edmond v. Goldsmith, 104
Edmunds, Commonwealth v., 235
Edwards, United States v., 154, 169, 223, 337
Edwards v. Arizona, 304, 306, 307, 311,
    313, 334
Elliott v. State, 56
Elliott, United States v. (50 F.3d 180), 182
Elliott, United States v. (893 F.2d 220), 60
Ellis, State v., 181
Endress v. Dugger, 282
Erving L., United States v., 274
Erwin, United States v., 178
Escobedo v. Illinois, 261-262
Estep v. Dallas Cnty., 96
Estrada, United States v., 325
Evans, Commonwealth v., 89
Evaschuck, United States v., 222
Evers, United States v., 363
Ex parte. *See name of party*

Falso, United States v., 241
Farag v. United States, 99
Fare v. Michael C., 259, 294, 298, 305, 312
Farley, United States v., 302
Fay v. Noia, 3
Feffer, United States v., 18, 43
Felix, United States v., 214
Fellers v. United States, 327, 330, 331,
    334, 338
Ferguson, Commonwealth v., 348
Ferguson v. City of Charleston, 108, 120
Fernandez v. California, 175
Fields, United States v., 36, 86
Fisher, United States v., 63
Flemmi, United States v., 256
Flippo, State v., 214
Florence v. Board of Chosen Freeholders of
    Cnty. of Burlington, 105
Florence v. Burlington, 156
Flores, United States v., 118
Flores-Montano, United States v., 106, 375
Florida v. Bostick, 74, 89, 173, 174, 184
Florida v. Harris, 47, 68
Florida v. Jardines, 30, 40
Florida v. Jimeno, 182, 215

Florida v. J.L., 73, 93, 97
Florida v. Riley, 28, 31, 35
Florida v. Rodriquez, 87
Florida v. Royer, 76, 85, 95, 97
Florida v. Wells, 117, 192, 193
Florida v. White, 13
Ford, United States v. (176 F.3d 376), 334
Ford, United States v. (184 F.3d 566), 125
Forrester, United States v., 42
Foster, United States v., 283
Foster v. Commonwealth, 302
Franklin, United States v., 64, 92
Franks v. Delaware, 123, 132
Frazier, United States v., 239
Frazier v. Cupp, 175, 257
Freitas, United States v., 62
French, United States v., 34

Gachot v. Stadler, 259
Gaddy, United States v., 299
Galceran, United States v., 271
Gallardo-Marquez, United States v., 257
Galvan-Muro, United States v., 75
Ganias, United States v., 365
Garcia-Garcia, United States v., 77
Garner, State v., 257
Garreau, United States v., 213, 274
Gates v. State, 35
Gault, In re, 259
Genao, United States v., 282
Gentry, United States v., 64
Georgia v. Randolph, 175, 182
Gevedon, United States v., 179
Giannetta, United States v., 188
Giberson, United States v., 364
Gideon v. Wainwright, 3, 261
Gilliard, People v., 322
Glass, United States v., 87
Glinton, United States v., 238
Glosson, State v., 359
Glover v. Eastern Neb. Cmty. Office of
    Retardation, 116
Goldstein, United States v., 21
Golson, United States v., 70
Gomes, Commonwealth v., 90
Gonsalves, Commonwealth v., 79
Gonzales, United States v., 86, 96, 275
Gonzalez-Lauzan, United States v., 273
Goodrich, United States v., 94
Gordon, United States v., 241, 269
Gori, United States v., 100, 190

Gorman, United States v., 140
Gorrell, United States v., 365
Graham, United States v., 133
Graham v. Connor, 351
Grant v. Warden, Maine State Prison, 307
Grant, United States v., 85
Grant, United States v. (108 F. Supp. 2d 1172), 69
Grant, United States v. (696 F.3d 780), 85
Gray, United States v. (78 F. Supp. 2d 524), 363
Gray, United States v. (491 F.3d 138), 218
Green, United States v. (324 F.3d 375), 163
Green, United States v. (670 F.2d 1148), 65
Greene, United States v., 69
Greenleaf v. Cote, 119
Green v. Scully, 256
Griffin, State v., 94
Griffin v. Wisconsin, 107, 172
Grimes, United States v., 22, 305
Groh v. Ramirez, 127, 232
Grubb, United States v., 41
Grubbs, United States v., 70, 137
Guapi, United States v., 184
Guest v. Leis, 227, 362, 363
Guidry, United States v., 131
Guillen-Cazares, United States v., 94
Guite v. Write, 153
Gundlach v. Janing, 18
Gustafson v. Florida, 156
Gutierrez-Hermosillo, United States v., 181

Hadfield, United States v., 133
Hadley v. Williams, 100, 190
Hairston v. United States, 273
Hale v. Fish, 60
Hall, United States v., 39
Hamdan v. Rumsfeld, 370
Hamdi v. Rumsfeld, 369
Hamie, United States v., 134
Hammond, United States v., 76, 353
Hammons, United States v., 213, 215
Hampton v. United States, 356, 359
Hanson, United States v., 87, 271
Hardaway v. Young, 259
Hardeman, United States v., 162
Hardnett, United States v., 99
Harris, United States v., 49, 56, 62
Harris v. New York, 317, 318
Hart v. Attorney Gen. of Fla., 291, 303
Hart v. State, 50
Hartwell, United States v., 113

Harvey, United States v., 96
Hatley, United States v., 169
Havens, United States v., 243
Hayden, United States v., 271
Hayes v. Florida, 342
Heath, United States v., 214
Henderson v. Norris, 254
Henderson v. Quarterman, 336
Henderson, State v., 344
Henderson, United States v., 225
Hendricks, State v., 124
Henry, United States v., 331, 337
Hensley, United States v., 86, 95, 102
Hephner, United States v., 223
Herb v. Pitcairn, 6
Hernandez, United States v. (214 F. Supp. 2d 1344), 147
Hernandez, United States v. (219 F. Supp. 2d 556), 94, 98
Hernandez-Lopez, United States v., 94
Hernandez-Mendoza, United States v., 280
Herring v. United States, 5, 234, 242
Hessling, United States v., 37
Hiibel v. Sixth Judicial Dist. Court of Nev., 78, 89, 97, 277
Hill v. Anderson, 254
Hinckley, United States v., 284
Hinds, Commonwealth v., 363
Hinton, United States v., 41
Ho, United States v., 159
Hoffa v. United States, 24, 42
Hohensee, State v., 359
Holder v. Humanitarian Law Project, 370
Holloman, United States v., 193
Holloway, United States v., 64
Holmes, United States v., 214
Hood, United States v., 99
Hopkins v. Cockrell, 303
Horowitz, United States v., 226
Horton v. California, 185, 189
Houle, Commonwealth v., 89
Hove, United States v., 238
Howard, United States v., 151, 169
Howes v. Fields, 265, 266, 272
Hoyt, Commonwealth v., 292
Hsu, United States v., 310
Hubbard v. Haley, 259
Hudson v. Michigan, 5, 136, 201, 229
Hudson v. Palmer, 31
Hudson, United States v., 161-162
Huguenin, United States v., 193

Hunley, United States v., 60
Hunt, State v., 43
Hurtado, United States v., 86
Husband, United States v., 353

Illinois v. Caballes, 29, 40, 79, 193
Illinois v. Gates, 47, 49, 50, 56, 57, 58, 59, 62, 66, 72, 130, 237
Illinois v. Krull, 233, 242
Illinois v. Lafayette, 105, 116, 172
Illinois v. Lidster, 108, 115
Illinois v. McArthur, 80, 147
Illinois v. Perkins, 272, 276
Illinois v. Rodriguez, 175, 179, 215, 234
Illinois v. Wardlow, 63, 74, 92, 96
Indianapolis, City of, v. Edmond, 104, 108, 115, 193, 374
Innis, State v., 275
In re. See name of party
INS v. See name of opposing party
Isaacson, People v., 359
Ivey, United States v., 213

Jackson v. Litscher, 303
Jackson, State v., 324
Jackson, United States v., 37, 190
Jacobs, United States v., 103
Jacobsen, United States v., 19, 22, 29, 42
Jacobson v. United States, 355, 358
Jacques, United States v., 256
James v. Illinois, 244
Janis, United States v., 228
Jannotti, United States v., 358-359
Jason, State v., 90
J.D.B. v. North Carolina, 86, 259, 266, 274
Jefferson v. Fountain, 210
Jefferson v. United States, 68
Jennings, United States v., 275
Jimenez, State v., 301
John C., In the Matter of, 324
Johnson v. LaRabida Children's Hospital, 20
Johnson, Commonwealth v., 29, 94
Johnson v. United States (333 U.S. 10), 122
Johnson, United States v. (12 F.3d 760), 153
Johnson, United States v. (338 F.3d 918), 337
Johnson, United States v. (351 F.3d 254), 257
Johnson, United States v. (364 F.3d 1185), 93
Johnson, United States v. (656 F.3d 375), 182
Johnson, United States v. (2003 WL 22715856), 322
Johnston, Commonwealth v., 29, 94

Jones, State v., 119, 190
Jones v. United States (362 U.S. 257), 62, 216, 217, 218, 221, 222, 366
Jones, United States v. (132 S. Ct. 945), 23, 25, 29, 30, 34, 43, 44
Jones, United States v. (562 F.3d 768), 224
Jones, United States v. (619 F.2d 494), 64
Jones, United States v. (759 F.2d 635), 99
Jones, United States v. (846 F.2d 358), 270
Juan C. v. Cortines, 230
Julio, People v., 160

Kansas v. Ventris, 334
Kant, State v., 56
Karo, United States v., 29
Kaspar v. City of Hobbs, 179
Katz v. United States, 23, 24, 30, 42, 143, 217, 361
Kaupp v. Texas, 76, 174
Kaylor, United States v., 140
Keith M., People v., 179
Kelley, United States v., 240
Kelly, United States v. (46 F. Supp. 2d 624), 223
Kelly, United States v. (128 F. Supp. 2d 1021), 40
Kelsey v. County of Schoharie, 119
Kennedy, United States v., 212
Kentucky v. King, 147, 152
Kerr, United States v., 101
Khalil, United States v., 325
Khoury, United States v., 118
Kim, United States v., 179, 271
Kimball, United States v., 94
Kincade, United States v., 120
Kirby v. Illinois, 332, 343
Kirk, United States v., 212
Kitzmiller v. State, 38
Knighton v. State, 291
Knights, United States v., 13, 107, 120
Knotts, United States v., 29, 44
Knowles v. Iowa, 157
Koenig, United States v., 43
Kopp, United States v., 223
Kordosky, United States v., 117
Korematsu v. United States, 371
Kuhlman v. Wilson, 331
Kyllo v. United States, 12, 30, 31, 37, 38

LaBare, United States v., 337
LaFreniere, United States v., 361
Lall, United States v., 256

LaLonde v. County of Riverside, 138
Lamas, United States v., 213
Lard, United States v., 356
Laughton, United States v., 239
Laws, United States v., 61, 62
Lawson, State v., 345
Le, United States v., 117
LeBrun, United States v. (306 F.3d 545), 258
LeBrun, United States v. (363 F.3d 715),
    258, 271
Leckelt v. Board of Comm'rs of Hosp. Dist.
    No. 1, 116
LeCroy v. Hanlon, 6
Lee, United States v., 98
Lenoir, United States v., 65
Lentz, United States v., 337
Leon, United States v., 123, 126, 132, 231,
    233, 235, 237, 238, 240-242
Leonard, United States v., 41
Leone, Commonwealth v., 20
Lewin, Commonwealth v., 124
Lewis, United States v., 76
Lindsey v. Detroit Entertainment, LLC, 20
Lingenfelter, United States v., 30
Lively, State v., 360
Lo-Ji Sales v. New York, 123, 237
Long, United States v., 39
Longoria, United States v., 24
Lopez, United States v., 256
Lopez-Mendoza, INS v., 228
Lora-Solano, United States v., 240
Los Angeles, City of, v. Patel, 13, 171
Lucas, United States v., 161
Lumley v. City of Dade, Fla., 336
Lux, United States v., 257, 312
Lyons, United States v., 40

Machuca-Barrera, United States v., 95
Macias-Treviso, United States v., 222
MacWade v. Kelly, 375
Maddox, State v., 62
Madiedo, United States v., 69
Madsen, State v., 255
Maine v. Moulton, 332, 334
Malachi, United States v., 95
Maling, United States v., 223-224
Mallory v. United States, 261
Malloy v. Hogan, 262
Mancari, United States v., 188
Manganaro, People v., 189
Manners v. Cannella, 64

Manson v. Brathwaite, 342-344, 346-348
Mapp v. Ohio, 3-5, 7-8, 195-199
Mara, United States v., 26, 342
Marganet v. State, 180
Markling, United States v., 212
Marlar, United States v., 37
Marron v. United States, 125
Marshall v. Barlow's Inc., 105, 137, 171
Marshall v. Teske, 64
Martin, State v., 235
Martin, United States v., 280
Martinez-Fuerte, United States v., 105
Martinez-Gonzalez, United States v., 64
Martinez v. Nygaard, 88
Martin v. Hunter's Lessee, 6
Martwick, State v., 36
Maryland v. Buie, 80, 158, 164
Maryland v. Dyson, 165
Maryland v. Garrison, 126, 132, 240
Maryland v. King, 109
Maryland v. Pringle, 47, 135
Maryland v. Shatzer, 307
Maryland v. Wilson, 79, 103, 193
Mason, People v., 43
Massachusetts v. Sheppard, 126, 132, 232,
    240-241
Massachusetts v. Upton, 59
Massey, United States v., 176
Massiah v. United States, 251, 329-334,
    336-338, 343, 348
Mathews, Commonwealth v., 360
Mathis v. United States (291 U.S. 1), 272
Mathis, United States v. (264 F.3d 321), 343
Matlock, United States v., 175, 179
Mattarolo, United States v., 230
Mavredakis, Commonwealth v., 301
Mayfield v. State, 263
Mayo, United States v., 162
May v. State, 181
McAlpine, United States v., 181
McCall v. Dutton, 255
McCarty, United States v., 112
McClease, Commonwealth v., 90
McCray, United States v., 224
McCray v. Illinois, 124
McGrail, Commonwealth v., 350
McIver, United States v., 29, 230
McKeever, United States v., 36
McLevain, United States v., 134
McNabb v. United States, 261
McNeil v. Wisconsin, 305, 332-333, 336

McNulty, Commonwealth v., 301
Meadows v. Kuhlman, 336
Melilli, Commonwealth v., 44
Mendenhall, United States v., 74, 84, 85, 86,
    87, 88, 97, 173
Mendez, United States v., 163, 212
Messerschmidt v. Millender, 127, 232
Metcalf v. State, 360
Michigan Dep't of State Police v. Sitz, 105, 113
Michigan v. Chesternut, 75, 87, 269
Michigan v. Clifford, 105, 146
Michigan v. Harvey, 317, 334
Michigan v. Jackson, 313, 334
Michigan v. Long, 6, 79
Michigan v. Mosley, 303, 309, 315
Michigan v. Summers, 135
Michigan v. Tucker, 263, 317
Michigan v. Tyler, 105, 146
Mikel, United States v., 151
Milam, United States v., 356
Miller, United States v., 24, 25, 41
Miller v. Fenton, 251, 257
Mincey v. Arizona, 12, 146, 250
Minnesota v. Carter, 218, 222
Minnesota v. Dickerson, 80, 92, 184, 190
Minnesota v. Olson, 139, 140, 145, 218, 221
Minnick v. Mississippi, 307
Miranda v. Arizona, 3, 5, 201, 203, 207, 208,
    209, 228, 243, 251, 252, 253, 255,
    259, 260, 261-309, 310, 314, 315,
    316-328, 329-338, 350
Missouri v. McNealy, 148
Missouri v. Seibert, 272, 287, 327
Mitchell, United States v., 162, 163
Mobley, United States v., 323
Monclavo-Cruz, United States v., 154, 160
Mondello v. State, 360
Montejo v. Louisiana, 334
Montoya de Hernandez, United States v.,
    77, 375
Moore v. Dugger, 312
Moore v. Illinois, 342
Moore, United States v. (122 F.3d 1154), 336
Moore, United States v. (329 F.3d 399), 98
Moran v. Burbine, 292, 293, 298, 299, 301
Morgan, United States v., 86
Morris, State v., 26
Morton v. United States, 221
Moses, Commonwealth v., 98
Mosley, United States v., 359
Moulton v. Maine, 336, 337

Muehler v. Mena, 75
Mueller v. Angelone, 303
Munoz-Guerra, United States v., 152
Murphy, Commonwealth v., 332
Murray v. United States, 202, 211, 212, 353

Najjar, United States v., 201, 211
Namen v. Alaska, 131
Nance, State v., 35
Nash v. Estelle, 313
National Treasury Emps. Union v. Von Raab,
    106, 115, 172
Navarette v. California, 73
Neff, United States v., 95
Neil v. Biggers, 343
Nelson v. City of Irvine, 353
Nelson v. Fulcomer, 279, 310
New Jersey v. Hartley, 310
New Jersey v. TLO, 18, 31, 106, 118, 172
Newton, United States v., 18
New York v. Belton, 155-157, 162, 163, 234
New York v. Burger, 105, 108, 109, 171
New York v. Harris, 208
New York v. Quarles, 265, 319-321, 322, 323,
    324, 328, 334
N.G. v. Connecticut, 119
Nichols, United States v., 318
Nieves, State v., 189
Nix v. Williams, 203, 212
Nolan-Cooper, United States v., 360
Noonan, Commonwealth v., 181
Nordby, United States v., 48
North Carolina v. Butler, 292, 297
Novembrino, State v., 235
Nunley, United States v., 101

Oakley, United States v., 213, 214
O'Connor v. Ortega, 18, 31, 107, 172, 222
Ohio v. Robinette, 173, 174
Olguin-Rivera, United States v., 162
Oliver v. United States, 27, 36
Ollie, United States v., 273
Olson, United States v., 62
Oregon v. Bradshaw, 305, 312, 315
Oregon v. Elstad, 263, 326, 327, 337
Oregon v. Hass, 318
Oregon v. Mathiason, 265, 271
Orozco v. Texas, 265, 272
Orozco, United States v., 68
Orr, United States v., 280
Orso, United States v., 257

Table of Cases

Ortega-Santana, United States v., 86
Ortiz v. Uribe, 255
Ortiz, United States v. (422 U.S. 891),
    105, 114
Ortiz, United States v. (943 F. Supp. 2d 447),
    257, 311
Oung, United States v., 323
Ousley, Commonwealth v., 39
Outler, United States v., 122
Overton v. Ohio, 54

Pace, United States v., 124
Pacheco, Commonwealth v., 300
Padilla, State v., 189
Page, United States v., 178
Panetti, Commonwealth v., 37
Parcels of Land, United States v., 133
Patane, United States v., 320, 327, 328
Patterson v. Illinois, 333, 337
Paulino, United States v., 223
Payne, United States v., 169, 359
Payner, United States v., 225
Payton v. New York, 138, 140, 190, 208
Pelayo-Landero, United States v., 125
Pena, United States v., 211, 313
Pena-Saiz, United States v., 178
Pene-Rodriguez, United States v., 69
Pennington, United States v., 36, 37
Pennsylvania Bd. of Probation & Parole v. Scott,
    228, 230
Pennsylvania v. Bruder, 266, 269, 352
Pennsylvania v. Dunlap, 67
Pennsylvania v. Mimms, 79, 103, 193
Pennsylvania v. Muniz, 276, 277, 283, 284,
    350, 352
Pennsylvania v. Zook, 312
People v. See name of opposing party
Perez, United States v., 180
Perez v. Simmons, 141
Perkins, United States v., 65, 70
Perrotta, United States v., 134
Perry, Commonwealth v., 88
Perry v. New Hampshire, 344
Pervaz, United States v., 43
Pinto, Commonwealth v., 50
Place, United States v., 29, 30, 40, 80, 193
Plazinich v. Lynaugh, 314
Pleasant, State v., 360
Pleasant v. Lovell, 18
Plugh, United States v., 298
Powell, Commonwealth v., 88

Prandy-Binnett, United States v., 66
Presha, State v., 301
Preston, United States v., 254
Prince v. United States, 68
Prior, State v., 235

Rabbia, United States v., 99
Rabinowitz, United States v., 12
Rachlin v. United States, 256
Rainwater v. State, 181
Rakas v. Illinois, 216, 217-218, 220, 221, 223,
    224, 225
Ramirez, Commonwealth v., 124
Ramirez, United States v., 136, 140
Ramirez-Chilel, United States v., 178
Ramirez- Rivera, United States v., 242
Ramirez-Sandoval, United States v., 211
Ramos, United States v., 75, 114, 239, 375
Ramos-Oseguera, United States v., 163
Rawlings v. Kentucky, 154, 159, 160, 217,
    218, 220, 222, 223, 226
Redditt, United States v., 255
Redmon, United States v., 27, 39
Reed, State v., 301
Reeves, United States v. (210 F.3d 1041), 133
Reeves v. Churchich, 34
Reid, State v., 362
Reid v. Georgia, 87, 96
Reilly, United States v., 213
Reinholz, United States v., 178
Replogle, United States v., 178
Reyes, People v., 285
Rhind, United States v., 212
Rhode Island v. Innis, 275, 279, 280, 281,
    283, 286, 304, 313, 331
Rhodes, State v., 39
Richardson v. Quitman County, Georgia, 61
Richardson v. State, 44
Richards v. Wisconsin, 136
Rickus, United States v., 94
Riley, United States v., 131
Riley v. California, 25, 155, 243, 363
Rister, People v., 114
Rivera, United States v., 183
Rivera v. State, 360
Roache, State v., 301
Roberts v. State, 290
Robinson v. California, 3
Robinson, United States v., 99, 155, 156,
    157, 160
Rochin v. California, 2, 348, 349, 351, 353

Rodrigues v. Furtado, 353
Rodriguez v. United States, 29, 79
Rodriguez, Commonwealth v., 115
Rodriguez, State v., 119
Rodriguez, United States v., 180
Rodriguez-Escalera, United States v., 86
Rogers v. Richmond, 249, 250
Rollins, People v., 58
Romanski v. Detroit Entertainment, LLC, 20
Romero, United States v., 153
Rook v. State, 39
Rosario-Diaz, United States v., 300
Rose v. United States, 221
Ross, United States v., 165, 166, 168
Rothgery v. Gillespie Cnty., 332
Roundtree, People v., 323
Rowen, People v., 282
Rowland, United States v., 70
Rubio, Commonwealth v., 281
Rullo, United States v., 214
Rumney, United States v., 133
Runyan, United States v., 22, 211
Russell, United States v., 355, 356, 358
Rutkowski, Commonwealth v., 131
Rutkowski, United States v., 133, 134
Ryan, United States v., 230

Safford Unified Sch. Dist. No. 1 v. Redding, 18, 107, 119
Salazar, United States v., 223
Salgado, United States v., 40
Salman, United States v., 274
Salvucci, United States v., 216, 222
Sampson v. California, 176
Samson v. California, 107
San Juan-Cruz, United States v., 289
Santa, United States v., 147, 151, 153, 242
Santa Maria, United States v., 37
Santana, United States v. (6 F.3d 1), 356
Santana, United States v. (427 U.S. 38), 138, 150
Santiago, Commonwealth v., 216
Santos, United States v., 95, 254
Sarantopoulos v. State, 36
Satchell v. Cardwell, 210
Saurini, People v., 35
Savoca, United States v., 238, 239
Savva, State v., 170
Scales, United States v., 242
Scanlon v. Las Cruces Pub. Schs., 230
Scarberry v. State of Iowa, 333, 336

Schmerber v. California, 26, 148, 349, 350, 352, 353
Schmitt, State v., 124
Schneckloth v. Bustamonte, 173, 174, 178
Schofner, State v., 21
Schwarz, State v., 181
Scott, United States v., 39
Scott v. Harris, 351, 354
Scroger, United States v., 152
Sealed Case, In re (153 F.3d 759), 161
Sealed Case, In re (310 F.3d 717), 368
See v. City of Seattle, 170
See, United States v., 101
Segura v. United States, 147
Sells, United States v., 365
Seng, Commonwealth v., 291
Shabazz, United States v., 182
Shadwick v. City of Tampa, 122, 123
Shahid, United States v., 20
Shakir, United States v., 162
Shareef, United States v., 243
Sharpe, United States v., 77, 97, 98
Sharp v. Rohling, 256
Sharrar v. Felsing, 164
Shears, United States v., 256
Shedelbower v. Estelle, 302, 314
Shelton, United States v. (181 F. Supp. 2d 649), 180
Shelton v. United States (929 A.2d 420), 67
Sherman v. United States, 358
Shodeinde, United States v., 348
Sibron v. New York, 63, 91, 159
Siebert, Ex parte, 291
Silva, United States v., 222
Silvestri, United States v., 214
Sims v. Stanton, 138
Singer, Commonwealth v., 124
Singleton v. Board of Educ., 118
Skinner, United States v., 44
Skinner v. Railway Labor Execs. Ass'n, 18, 26, 106, 112, 115, 116, 120, 172
Smith v. Duckworth, 291
Smith v. Illinois, 305, 313, 315
Smith v. Maryland, 24, 41, 42, 43, 44
Smith v. Ohio, 159
Smith v. Taylor, 119
Smith v. Zant, 300
Smith, United States v., 240
Snipe, United States v., 146
Soffar v. Johnson, 303
Sokolow, United States v., 72, 73

Solomon, United States v., 58
Sonntag, United States v., 154
Sorrells v. United States, 355, 358
South Dakota v. Neville, 350
South Dakota v. Opperman, 105, 116
Souza, United States v., 21, 211
Spang, State v., 7
Spann v. United States, 285
Speights, United States v., 119
Spinelli v. United States, 47-49, 55, 56,
    57, 59, 60
Stabile, United States v., 363
Stanford v. Texas, 126
Stange v. Worden, 352
Stansbury v. California, 266
Stapleton v. Superior Court, 18
State of New Mexico v. Anaya, 95
State v. *See name of opposing party*
State v. Wright, 281
Staula, United States v., 190
Steagald v. United States, 138, 139-141
Steele v. United States (267 U.S. 498), 125
Steele, United States v. (147 F.3d 1316), 122
Steiger, United States v., 22
Stevenson, State v., 324
Stokes, United States v. (631 F.3d 802), 255
Stokes, United States v. (733 F.3d 438), 213
Stoner v. California, 175
Stone v. Powell, 228
Stovall v. Denno, 343-346
Strain, State v., 290
Strand, United States v., 131
Stroman, United States v., 281
Strother, United States v., 62
Stubbs, United States v., 132
Suing, United States v., 362
Swanson, United States v., 269
Swepston, United States v., 34
Sykes, Commonwealth v., 88
Symonevich, United States v., 223

Tabbaa v. Chertoff, 375
Taborda, United States v., 35, 38
Tague v. Louisiana, 293
Talley, United States v., 61
Tapia, Commonwealth v., 56
Tauil-Hernandez, United States v., 230
Taylor, United States v., 284
Tejada, United States v., 162
Tennessee v. Garner, 351, 354

Terry v. Ohio, 54, 65, 67, 71, 72, 73, 74, 76,
    77, 78, 79, 80, 90, 91, 92, 93, 94, 95,
    97, 98, 99, 100, 269, 354
Texas v. Brown, 29
Texas v. Cobb, 333, 336
Thacker v. City of Columbus, 151
Theodore v. Delaware Valley Sch. Dist., 105
Thierman, United States v., 280, 281
Thomas, Commonwealth v. (646 N.E.2d
    428), 89
Thomas, United States v. (263 F.3d
    805), 241
Thomas, United States v. (757 F.2d 1359), 30
Thompson v. Carthage Sch. Dist., 230
Thompson, Commonwealth v. (985 A.2d
    928), 67
Thompson v. Keohane, 266
Thompson v. Louisiana, 146, 176
Thompson, United States v. (106 F.3d
    794), 183
Thompson, United States v. (866 F.2d
    268), 309
Thornton v. United States, 156-157
Tobias v. United States, 359
Tompkins, United States v., 178
Torres, United States v., 117
Townsend v. Sain, 258, 259
Trejo-Islas, United States v., 299
Triumph Capital Grp., Inc., United States
    v., 365
Trueber, United States v., 269
Trullo, United States v., 100
Trump v. Hawaii, 371
Tucker, United States v., 180
Tudoran, United States v., 284
Turner, United States v., 365
Turner v. Driver, 96
Tuttle, State v., 292
Twigg, United States v., 356, 359

United States Dist. Court for E. Dist. of Mich.,
    S. Div., United States v., 374
United States v. *See name of opposing party*
United States v. Whitaker, 40
Upham, United States v., 363, 364
Upton, Commonwealth v. (390 Mass. 562), 59
Upton, Commonwealth v. (394 Mass. 363),
    59, 235
Urban, United States v., 69
Utah v. Strieff, 158, 202, 209

Valdez v. McPheters, 138
Valentine, United States v., 55, 65
Valenzuela, United States v., 353
Vale v. Louisiana, 151
Van Damme, United States v., 36
Vanhouton v. Commonwealth, 352
Van Leeuwen, United States v., 80
Vanness, United States v., 61
Vasey, United States v., 163
Vasques De Reyes, United States v., 211
Vasquez-Castillo, United States v., 190
Vega, United States v., 270
Vega-Rodriguez v. Puerto Rico Tel. Co., 21
Velasquez, United States v., 302, 312
Vernonia Sch. Dist. 47J v. Acton, 104, 118
Vickers, State v., 322
Viegas, United States v., 69
Virgen-Moreno, United States v., 283
Virginia v. Moore, 156, 157
Von Bulow, State v., 22
Von Kahl v. United States, 336

Wade, State v., 156, 160
Wade, United States v., 342, 343, 347, 348
Waldon, United States v., 90
Walter, People v., 179
Walters, State v., 284
Walter v. United States, 19
Walther, United States v., 18, 19, 43
Walton v. Lane, 347
Wanless, United States v., 117
Ward, State v., 49
Warden v. Hayden, 144, 145, 150
Warren, Commonwealth v., 63
Washington v. Boland, 26
Washington, United States v. (151 F.3d
    1354), 184
Washington, United States v. (782 F.2d
    807), 125
Watkins, United States v., 239
Watson, United States v. (273 F.3d 599), 138
Watson, United States v. (423 U.S. 411), 138,
    150, 173
Watts v. Indiana, 249, 263
Weber, United States v., 240
Weeks v. United States, 3, 196

Weinbender, United States v., 134
Welch, United States v., 180
Welsh v. Wisconsin, 145
West, People v., 333
Whaley, United States v., 35
White, Commonwealth v. (374 Mass.
    132), 209
White, Commonwealth v. (469 Mass.
    96), 156
White, United States v. (81 F.3d 775), 76
White, United States v. (401 U.S. 745), 24, 42
White, United States v. (655 F.2d 1302), 66
White, United States v. (890 F.2d
    1413), 86, 93
Whited, United States v., 70
Whitehead v. Cowan, 283
Whiteley v. Warden, 102, 123
Whren v. United States, 50, 157, 191,
    192, 193
Williams, State v., 60
Williams, United States v. (435 F.3d
    1148), 273
Williams, United States v. (592 F.3d 511), 364
Williams, United States v. (827 F. Supp.
    641), 169
Wilson v. Arkansas, 136
Wilson v. Layne, 136
Wilson, United States v., 86
Winsor, United States v., 150, 242
Winston v. Lee, 26, 349, 353
Winters, United States v., 40
Withrow v. Williams, 228, 317
Woerner, United States v., 209
Wolf v. Colorado, 3
Wong Sun v. United States, 45, 63, 64, 200,
    207, 225
Wyoming v. Houghton, 135, 166, 224

Yarborough v. Alvarado, 274
Ybarra, State v., 282
Ybarra v. Illinois, 135
York v. Wahkiakum Sch. Dist. No. 200, 104

Zelinski, People v., 20
Zimmerman, United States v., 240
Zurcher v. Stanford Daily, 126

Index

Adequacy of *Miranda* warnings, 286-291
Administrative searches, 103-120
  antihijacking screening program, 113
  balancing analysis, 107f
  basic test of, 111
  contraband discovered during, 113
  criminal searches *vs.*, 104-108
  DNA evidence obtained during, 109
  evenhandedness in, 104, 112-113, 116
  evidence inadvertently discovered
     during, 112
  Fourth Amendment, 111-112
  notice, 112
  reasonableness, relaxed standards
     of, 109
  suspicionless searches, 107
  warrantless searches, 173-174
Aguilar/Spinelli test, 48, 49-50, 58-60
AIDS virus testing, 116
Airport encounters, 85
Airport screening, 111-112
Anonymous tips
  probable cause, 57-59, 62
  stops, 72, 93
Anticipatory warrants, 70
Arrest
  probable cause, 46-47, 55. *See also*
     Probable cause
  search incident to, 154-164
  stop and frisk justification, 78f
Arrest warrants. *See* Warrants
Assumption of risk analysis,
    reasonable
  expectation of privacy, 24-26, 41-43
Attorneys. *See* Right to counsel
Automobiles
  delayed-search option, 168
  justification for searches of, 167f
  overdue rental fees for, 225
  owners *vs.* passengers, 222-224
  roving patrol stops, 114
  search of, 164-170
  sobriety. *See* Drunk driving
  sobriety testing, 113
  stops of, 75, 79, 113-115
  warrantless searches, 164-170

Banks, reasonable expectation of privacy, 41
Bill of Rights, 2-3
Blackmun, Harry, 218, 245, 351
Blood-alcohol level, 148, 349, 350
Bodily intrusions, 348-354
Brennan, William J., Jr., 6, 31, 73, 80, 108,
    225, 231, 233, 244
Breyer, Stephen, 54, 290, 327
Burger, Warren, 4-5, 6, 54, 317, 367
Bush, George W., 25, 368, 369

Camara balancing test, 113, 115
Cell phones. *See also* High-tech searches
  expectations of privacy on, 25
  warrant required for search and seizure,
    155-156, 362
Checkpoints
  auto safety, 114
  border, 94, 105
  drug interdiction, 115, 374
  sobriety, 94, 105, 110, 113, 192
  suspicionless, 108, 115
Children. *See* Juveniles
Clark, Tom, 4, 263
Combined DNA Index System (CODIS), 109
Common law defense against entrapment, 355
Computer searches, 362-366
  exclusionary rule, 226-227
  Fourth Amendment, 362-365
  in homes, 366
  reasonable expectation of privacy, 42
  warrants, 362-366
Confessions, 249-260
  admission at trial, 249-250
  challenging, 251-252
  derivative evidence doctrine, 208
  drug-induced, 258-259
  juvenile, 259-260
  Miranda rule. *See* Interrogation and
    Miranda rule
  police conduct, 250-251
  right to counsel approach. *See Massiah*
    doctrine
  Sixth Amendment approach, 338f
  voluntariness standard. *See* Voluntariness
    standard

Consent to searches, 172-184
Container doctrine, 155, 166
Contraband, seizure of, 79-80
Counsel, right to. *See Massiah* doctrine; Right to counsel
Criminal procedure, overview, 1-8
Cruel and unusual punishment, prohibition against, 3
Curtilage, 26, 27f, 27n, 34-40
Custody and *Miranda* rule, 264-274
    defined, 265
    formal arrest requirement, 265
    in-home questioning, 271-272, 274
    intent irrelevant, 266
    multi-factor test, 272-273
    objective standard, 266
    on-the-scene questioning, 268-269, 274
    police station questioning, 265-266, 270-271
    reasonable person standard, 266, 270, 272

Derivative evidence doctrine, 199-215
    application of, 199-203, 207-209
    attenuation, 200-202
    confessions, 208
    costs of, 203
    factors for assessing, 201
    figure showing, 204f
    independent source, 202
    inevitable discovery, 202
    rationale for limitations, 202-203
Digital data, 155-156, 361, 363. *See also* High-tech searches
DNA Act, 111
DNA evidence, 109
DNA profiling, 110, 120, 366
Dogs, drug-sniffing. *See* Drug-sniffing dogs
Drones, U.S. use on foreign soil, 370
Drug courier profile, 73
Drug screening and testing
    candidates for public office, 106
    employee, 106
    suspicionless, 115
Drug-sniffing dogs
    probable cause, 68
    reasonable expectation of privacy, 40
    stops, 77, 79
Drunk driving
    breath test and, 158
    field sobriety tests, 276-277, 350
    sobriety checkpoints, 94, 113

Due process
    bodily intrusions, 348-349
    entrapment, 356, 358-361
    eyewitness identification, 342, 344
    identification procedures, 343-344, 346
    incorporation of, 2-3
    police conduct, 348
    standards of fundamental fairness, 343-344

Effects, detention of, 80
Eighth Amendment, incorporation of, 3
Electronic surveillance. *See* High-tech searches
E-mail. *See also* Computer searches; High-tech searches
    court order authorizing interception of, 361
    reasonable expectation of privacy, 42, 227
Emergency exception to warrant requirement, 144-153, 349
Entrapment, 354-361
    common law defense, 355
    crimes instigated by government, 361
    defense requirements, 358-361
    due process, 356, 358-361
    key questions in, 355
Escobedo, Danny, 261-262
Exclusionary rule, 195-245
    casual visitors, 221
    commercial property *vs.* residential property, 222
    computer searches, 226-227
    criticism of, 4-5
    derivative evidence. *See* Derivative evidence doctrine
    errors, 240-242
    evolution of, 7-8
    forfeitures, 232
    "fruit of the poisonous tree." *See* Derivative evidence doctrine
    good faith exception, 5, 231-236
        limits, 237-238
    grand jury proceedings, 227
    habeas corpus proceedings, 227-228
    harmless error, 244-245
    historical background, 2-4
    impeachment exception, 243-244, 317-319
    independent source exception, 211
    inevitable discovery, 214-215
    "knock and announce" rule, 5
    limitations on, 215-218, 316-328
    live witness testimony, 209
    Miranda rule, 208, 316-328

noncriminal proceedings, 227-229
officer conduct, 239-240
police officer knowledge of probable cause, 238-240
rationale, 195-199
sentencing, 229-230
standing, 216-218, 219-223
unlawful entry, 225
unlawful police activity, 225
vehicle intrusion, 210
warrantless searches, 242-243
Exigent circumstances exception to warrant requirement, 144-153, 368
Expectation of privacy. *See* Reasonable expectation of privacy
Eyewitness identification, 341-348
appearance altering, 353
due process, 342, 345
Fifth Amendment, 341-342
Fourth Amendment, 341
indicia of reliability, 343-344
lineups, 341-342
one-on-one show-ups, 342
photographic arrays, 343
right to counsel issue, 342-343, 348
standards of fundamental fairness, 343
time lapses, 346
totality-of-circumstances approach to, 344
at trial, 344
trial-like confrontations, 342
Wade rule, 347

Federalism, 2-7
Field sobriety tests, 350
Fifth Amendment
bodily intrusions, 350
eyewitness identification, 341-342
identification procedures, 350, 353
Miranda rule. *See Miranda* rule
rights of suspect, 262-263
Financial records, reasonable expectation of privacy, 41
First Amendment rights
search warrants, 126
FISA Amendments Act of 2008, 368
FISA (Foreign Intelligence Surveillance Act of 1978), 368, 371
Flight
probable cause, 63-64
unprovoked, 63, 74

Foreign Intelligence Surveillance Act of 1978 (FISA), 368, 371
Fourteenth Amendment
due process. *See* Due process
incorporation of Bill of Rights, 2-3
Fourth Amendment
administrative searches, 111-113
applicability of, 14, 17-44
bodily intrusions, 348-349, 352-353
computer searches, 362-366
criminal *vs.* administrative searches, 104-108
exclusionary rule. *See* Exclusionary rule
eyewitness identification, 341
governmental action requirement. *See* Governmental action requirement
high-tech searches, 361
historical background, 11
interpretation of, 12-13
justification, 45-46, 46f
no-knock entry and destruction of property, 136
overview, 11-14
pen registers, 41-43
probable cause. *See* Probable cause
purpose of, 11
reasonable expectation of privacy. *See* Reasonable expectation of privacy
reasonableness clause, 351
"reasonableness" interpretation, 12-13
reasonable suspicion. *See* Reasonable suspicion
school officials conducting searches, 118
search and seizure. *See* Search and seizure
seizure under, 85
state action requirement. *See* Governmental action requirement
stop and frisk standard, 70-74
stops, 74-74
student expectation of privacy, 118
terrorism, 374
Terrorist Surveillance Program (TSP), 368
triggering stops, 77
waiver of rights under, 172-176, 178-179
"warrant preference" interpretation, 12
warrant requirements, 125-128
warrants, 12, 123-124, 125-128. *See also* Warrants
Franks remedy, 124
Frisking. *See* Stop and frisk
Fruit of the poisonous tree. *See* Derivative evidence doctrine

Index

Gang members, searching for firearms, 127
Garbage, reasonable expectation of
     privacy, 39
Ginsburg, Ruth Bader, 75, 147, 176, 327, 344
Good faith exception, 231-235
Governmental action requirement, 15-23
  agent of state, 18
  meter readers, 21
  private searches, transformation into
     governmental searches, 17-19,
     21-23
  security guards, 20
  utilities, 21, 42-43
GPS tracking device, 7, 23, 30, 366

Habeas corpus proceedings
  exclusionary rule, 227-228
  Miranda claims, limited review of, 317
  state law and, 336
  suspected terrorists, detention of, 370
  Warren Court, 3
Hacking, computer, 20, 22
Hamdi, Yasar, 369-370
Harlan, John Marshall, II, 4, 30, 71, 91,
    165, 263
High speed chase, 351
High-tech searches, 361-366
  cell phones, 155-156, 361, 363
  computer searches. *See* Computer searches
  digital data, 155-156, 361, 363
  electronic surveillance, 361
  Fourth Amendment, 361
  new technologies, 361
  telecommunications surveillance
     programs, 369
  thermal imaging, 30, 36, 361, 366
  third-party consent, 366
  warrants, 155-156, 362-365
  wiretapping, 361
Homes
  arrest in, 164
  computer searches in, 366
  probable cause not sufficient to
     search, 151
  protective sweep, 80
  questioning in, as custody, 271-272, 274
  reasonable expectation of privacy, 27f, 39
  restriction on access to, 80
  seizures within, 99-100
  warrantless search of, 145-147
Hot pursuit, 150-151

Identification procedures
  due process, 343, 345-346
  eyewitness. *See* Eyewitness identification
  Fifth Amendment, 350, 353
  stops, 78
Immigration status, questioning on, 75-79,
    97, 105n15
Incorporation of Bill of Rights, 2-3
Independent and adequate state grounds, 6
Indigents, right to counsel, 289
Informants, probable cause issues, 58-61
Interrogation, confession during. *See*
    Confessions
Interrogation and *Miranda* rule, 274-286
  defined, 274-275
  deliberate action designed to elicit
     confession, 280-281, 285
  field sobriety tests, 276-277
  functional equivalent, 279-280
  psychological pressure, 275-276
  routine questioning, 276, 282-284
  third-party involvement, 282
Inventory searches, 172

Justification
  administrative searches. *See* Administrative
    searches
  balancing test, 45-46
  probable cause. *See* Probable cause
  reasonable suspicion. *See* Reasonable
    suspicion
  standards, 46f
  stops. *See* Stops
Juveniles
  confessions, 259-260
  "custody" determination, 266
  detention and strip searches, 119

Kennedy, Anthony, 5, 87, 109, 222, 229, 244,
    273, 276, 327
"Knock and announce" rule, 5, 136

Lineups, 341-343
Lockers, reasonable expectation of privacy,
    39-40

Mapp rule, 197-199
Marshall, Thurgood, 73, 160, 173, 202, 225,
    231, 233, 245, 284
Massiah doctrine, 329-338
  application of, 332-333, 337

cellmates, 337
"deliberately elicit" standard, 330-332
government elicitation of incriminating
    statements, 337-338
"jailhouse snitch" cases, 331
officer's state of mind, 331
voluntariness standard, 251
waiver, 333-335
Media "ride-alongs," 136
Mendenhall test, 86-87
Meter readers, private searches by, 21
Minors. *See* Juveniles
Miranda rule, 261-328
    admissibility of statements, 326
    challenges to, 264
    components, 264-316
    current state of, 328
    custody. *See* Custody and *Miranda* rule
    exclusionary rule, 208, 316-328
    impeachment exception, 317-318
    interrogation. *See* Interrogation and
        Miranda rule
    Miranda cards, 286
    other perpetrators, 322
    perjury, use of, 317
    physical evidence, 327
    police conduct prior to warnings, 287-288
    post-warning silence used for
        impeachment, 318
    potential for expansion of public safety
        exception, 322-324
    public safety exception, 319-325
    "question-first" strategy, 327
    reasonable person test, 266
    suppression of fruits of statements, 326-328
    violations and physical evidence, 327
    waiver of rights. *See* Waiver of *Miranda* rights
    warnings, adequacy of, 286-291
Motorists. *See* Automobiles

National Prohibition Act of 1919, 355
National Security Agency (NSA)
    metadata collection by, 26, 371
    warrantless electronic surveillance, 368-369
New federalism, 6
Noncriminal searches. *See* Administrative
    searches

Obama, Barack, 370, 374
Occupational Safety and Health Act of
    1970, 171

O'Connor, Sandra Day, 54, 157, 251, 319,
    320, 370
Omnibus Crime Control and Safe Streets Act of
    1968, 361
Open fields, 27f, 36-37
Overflight cases, reasonable expectation of
    privacy, 28

Particularity requirement for warrants,
    125-128
PATRIOT Act of 2001, 26, 367-368, 370,
    372-373
Pen registers, 41-43
Personal privacy, emerging technologies, 366
Pervasively regulated industries, 171-172
Photographic arrays, 343
Physical setting, reasonable expectation of
    privacy, 26-31
Plain view doctrine
    limits to, 187-190
    particularity requirement, 125-128
    requirements, 184-187
    warrants, 125-128, 133-135
Poisonous fruit. *See* Derivative evidence
    doctrine
Police. *See also* Arrest; Search and seizure
    police station questioning. *See* Custody and
        Miranda rule
    probable cause, 353-354
        exclusionary rule and, 238-240
        expertise, 66
    voluntariness standard and, 250-251
Posner, Richard, 104
Pretext problem, 191-193
Prisoners, questioning in secure conference
    room, 265, 272
Privacy, reasonable expectation of. *See*
    Reasonable expectation of privacy
Private searches, transformation
    into governmental searches,
    17-19, 21-23
Probable cause, 46-70
    adequacy of, 48
    Aguilar/Spinelli test, 48, 49, 58-60
    anonymous tips, 58, 61
    arrest, 46-47, 55
    assessing, 60
    credibility of informants, 48
    defined, 46-47
    establishing, 62-63
    evaluating, 48

Probable cause (*cont.*)
   exchanging small objects for currency,
      66-67
   exclusionary rule, police officer knowledge
      of probable cause, 238-241
   flight from law officer, 63
   high crime areas, 65
   homes, not sufficient to search, 151
   Illinois v. Gates standard, 62
   informants, 58-61
   knowledge, 48
   nature of, 47
   noncriminal procedures, 104
   particular point in time, 68
   police conduct, 354
   police expertise, 66
   reasonableness, 55
   reasonable suspicion compared, 72-74
   specific facts, 66-67
   standards of justification, 45-46
   stops, 50
   supporting facts, 55-57
   totality-of-circumstances approach to, 49
   two-pronged test, 48-49, 56-57
   warrantless searches and seizures, 154-158
   warrants, 59-60, 123-125
   weaknesses, 58-60
Profiling
   DNA profiling, 120
   drug courier, 73
   racial and ethnic, 371
Public exposure analysis, reasonable
   expectation of privacy, 24-26
Public safety exception, 319-325

Quarles public safety exception, 319-325

Reasonable expectation of privacy, 22-44
   assumption of risk analysis, 24-26, 41-43
   banks, 41
   computer searches, 42
   curtilage, 26, 27f, 34-40
   drug-sniffing dogs, 40
   e-mail, 42
   enhancement devices, 26-31, 35, 38
   financial records, 41
   homes, 27f, 39
   lockers, 39-40
   open fields, 27f, 36-38
   overflight cases, 28
   physical setting, 26-31

   public exposure analysis, 24-26
   subjective expectation, 37
   tracking devices, 23-24, 29, 30, 366
   trash bags, 39
   vantage point, 26-31, 35, 37-39
   what constitutes search, 22-23
"Reasonableness" interpretation of Fourth
   Amendment, 12-13
Reasonable person standard
   Miranda rule, 266, 270, 272
   search and seizure, 74-75, 77, 84-88
Reasonable suspicion, 70-74
   defined, 71
   investigative detention, 97-101
   officer experience, 96
   probable cause compared, 72-74
   stop and frisk standard, 70-74, 90-97
   stops, 89-90
Regulatory searches. *See* Administrative searches
Rehnquist, William, 6, 85, 139, 157, 250, 259,
   264, 351, 356, 367
Residences. *See* Homes
Right to counsel
   eyewitness identification, 342-343, 348
   incorporation of, 3
   indigents, 289
   invocation of, 305, 311-315
   Massiah doctrine. *See Massiah* doctrine
   waiver of *Miranda* rights after invocation of,
      303-316
Right to Financial Privacy Act of 1978, 41
Right to remain silent, 318
Roberts, John, 155, 355, 367

Scalia, Antonin, 5, 12, 23, 30, 87, 109, 157
School officials conducting searches, 118
Search and seizure, 367
   administrative searches. *See* Administrative
      searches
   after September 11, 2001, 367
   aggressive encounters, 89
   airport encounters, 85-87
   airport screening, 111-112
   arrest, search incident to, 154-164
   borders, 375
   defined, 84-85
   detention, 88
   DNA profiling, 120
   exclusionary rule. *See* Exclusionary rule
   failure to notify suspect of freedom to
      leave, 86

governmental action requirement. *See*
Governmental action requirement
government interests, 374
high-tech searches. *See* High-tech searches
inventory searches, 172
juvenile detention and strip searches, 119
officer vigilance during, 117
pen registers, 41-44
plain view doctrine. *See* Plain view doctrine
prerequisite for lawful inventory, 117
pretext problem, 191-193
primary goals, 108
probable cause, 46-47. *See also* Probable cause
probationers and parolees, 120
reasonable expectation of privacy. *See*
Reasonable expectation of privacy
reasonable person test, 75, 85-88
restraining effect, 87
state action requirement. *See* Governmental
action requirement
suspicionless inventory, 116
suspicionless searching of students, 118
time factor, 68-69
totality-of-circumstances approach
to, 93, 96
warrantless. *See* Warrantless searches and
seizures
Search incident to arrest, 154-165
Search warrants
administrative, 137
anticipatory, 137
components, 122, 139-141
computers, 362-366
exceptions. *See* Warrantless searches and
seizures
execution of, 136-137
First Amendment rights, 126
knock-and-announce rule, 136
neutral and detached magistrate, 122-123
no-knock entry, 136
requirements, 138-139
seizure of contraband, 79-80
staleness problem, 47
third-party residences, 138-139
Security guards, private searches by, 20
Seizure. *See* Search and seizure
Self-incrimination. *See* Miranda rule
September 11, 2001, search and seizure after,
367-375
Show-ups, 342, 344
Silent, right to remain, 318

Sixth Amendment
confessions and interrogations, 336, 338f
"deliberately elicit" standard, 330-332
government elicitation of incriminating
statements, 337
incorporation of, 3
informants, 331-332
Massiah doctrine. *See Massiah* doctrine
right to counsel. *See* Right to counsel
Snowden, Edward, 26, 370, 372
Sobriety. *See* Drunk driving
Sotomayor, Sonia, 23, 25, 43, 100, 119, 169,
171, 190, 241, 325, 348
Souter, David, 29, 54, 75, 157, 175, 228, 288,
290, 327
Staleness issues, 47, 68
Standing, 216-218, 220-222
State action requirement. *See* Governmental
action requirement
Stevens, John Paul, 6, 13, 30, 54, 73, 75, 144,
157, 225, 233, 245, 279, 290, 293,
327, 351
Stewart, Potter, 85, 189, 263
Stop and frisk
anonymous tips, 93
crime investigation, 95
evasive action, 92
forcible, 92-93
Fourth Amendment, 70-74
gradation of intrusion, 101
hunch not adequate for, 95
informants, 92-93
investigative detentions, 170
justification, 78f
reasonable suspicion, 70-74, 90-97
scope of search, 91-92
standard for, 70-74
Stops, 74-103
arrest, 97-101
of automobiles, 75, 78, 108, 113-114
checkpoints, 108. *See also* Checkpoints
conversion to detention, 76
crime investigation, 95
defined, 74-78
degree of intrusion, 77
duration, 76
evidence discovered during, 109
factual context, 85
Fourth Amendment and triggering, 77
gradations of justification, 77
location, 94

Index

Stops (cont.)
  Mendenhall test, 86-88
  motorists, 76
  objective analysis, 94
  past crimes, investigation of, 108
  reasonable suspicion, 89-90
  sobriety. *See* Drunk driving
  suspicionless, 108
  Terry stops. *See* Terry stops
Strip searches, 156n3
Students, search of, 118-119

Target standing, 216
Telecommunications metadata, bulk collection
  of, 26, 371
Terrorist Surveillance Program (TSP)
  constitutionality, 369-370
  racial and ethnic profiling, 371
  warrantless surveillance under, 368-369
Terry stops
  automobiles, 77
  evaluating legality of, 97-101
  requirements, 79-80
  seizures within home, 99-101
Thermal imaging, 30, 36, 361, 366
Tips, anonymous
  probable cause, 58, 61-62
  stops, 93
Totality-of-circumstances approach
  eyewitness identification, 344
  juvenile confessions, 259
  probable cause, 49
  search and seizure, 93, 96
  voluntariness, 251, 253
  warrantless search and seizure, 148
Tracking devices, reasonable expectation of
  privacy, 7, 23-24, 29, 30, 366
Trash bags, reasonable expectation of
  privacy, 39

USA Freedom Act, 371
USA PATRIOT Act of 2001, 26, 367-368, 370,
  372-373
Utilities, private searches by, 21, 42-43

ntage point, reasonable expectation of
  privacy, 26-31, 35, 38-39
le stops. *See* Automobiles
riness standard, 249-260
ions at trial, 249-250
us and ad hoc nature of
ndard, 261

challenging confessions, 251
coercive conduct, 254
coercive threats, 256-257
deception and trickery, 257-258
direct or implied promises, 255-256
drug-induced confessions, 258-259
Massiah doctrine, 251
mental condition of the subject,
  250-251, 254
Miranda rule, 251-252
misrepresenting evidence or charges, 257
police conduct, 250-251
representations of cooperation as best
  action, 256
totality-of-circumstances approach to,
  251, 253
Waiver of *Miranda* rights, 291-316
  deception and trickery, 301-302
  express waiver, 292, 297
  implied waiver, 292, 297
  initiation of further communications by
    suspect, 305-307
  invocation of right to counsel, 304-305,
    311-314
  invocation of right to silence, 309-315
  "knowing, intelligent, and voluntary,"
    289-293, 297-300
  minors, 300-301
Waiver of rights
  Massiah doctrine, 251, 333-335
  Miranda rights. *See* Waiver of *Miranda* rights
  warrantless searches, 172-176
"War on terror," 367-369
Warrantless searches and seizures
  absent occupant, objection by, 176
  administrative searches, 171-172
  arrest in home, 164-165
  authority to give consent to search, 175-176
  automobile search exception, 164-170
  categorical rules, 155-157
  cell phones and, 155, 361, 363
  children, 181
  consent, 172-184
  container doctrine, 155, 166
  custodial arrest process, 161
  delayed-search option for vehicles, 168
  emergency exception, 144-153, 349
  exceptions to warrant requirement, 143-148
  exclusionary rule, 242-243
  exigent circumstances exception,
    144-153, 368
  facts of encounter, 160

Index

homes, 145-147
hot pursuit, 150-151
inventory searches, 172
lacking compelling justification, 147
landlords, 182
pervasively regulated industries, 171-172
plain view doctrine, 184-186
    limits, 187-190
pretext problem, 191-193
probable cause, 154-158
    not sufficient to search home, 151
purpose of exception, 159
scope of search, 176, 182-183
search incident to arrest, 154-163
Terrorist Surveillance Program (TSP),
    368-369
third-party consents, 180-181
totality-of-circumstances approach to,
    147-148
vehicle searches, 164-170
waiver of rights, 172-176, 178-180
"Warrant preference" interpretation of Fourth
    Amendment, 12
Warrants, 121-141
    anticipatory warrants, 70
    challenges to, 123-124, 132-133
    computer searches, 362-366

contraband or other evidence of crime, 127
defined, 121
detention of subject during, 135-137
effective law enforcement, 121
emergency exception, 349
false statements, 124
Franks remedy, 123-124
frisking persons found during search
    under, 135
good faith exception, 123, 126-127,
    233-235
major bodily intrusions, 349
media "ride-alongs," 135
notice to subject, 127
particularity requirement, 125-128
plain view doctrine, 125-128, 133-135
probable cause issues, 59-60, 123-125
requirements, 130-132, 140-141
searches of records under, 131
search warrants. *See* Search warrants
staleness, 47
suppressing evidence found under, 123-125
time lapse, 130
Warren, Earl, 3, 4, 215, 262, 319, 367
White, Byron, 57, 85, 225, 231, 237, 245,
    263, 351
Wiretapping. *See* High-tech searches